POWER OF...
CorelDRAW! 5 for Windows

By James Karney

A Subsidiary of
Henry Holt and Co., Inc.

Copyright © 1995 by MIS:Press
a subsidiary of Henry Holt and Company, Inc.
115 West 18th Street
New York, NY 10011

All rights reserved. Reproduction or use of editorial or pictorial content in any manner is prohibited without express permission. No patent liability is assumed with respect to the use of the information contained herein. While every precaution has been taken in the preparation of this book, the publisher assumes no responsibility for errors or omissions. Neither is any liability assumed for damages resulting from the use of the information contained herein.

Throughout this book, trademarked names are used. Rather than put a trademark symbol after every occurrence of a trademarked name, we used the names in an editorial fashion only, and to the benefit of the trademark owner, with no intention of infringement of the trademark. Where such designations appear in this book, they have been printed with initial caps.

First Edition—1995

Printed in the United States of America.

Catalog-In-Publication Data

Karney, James.

    Power of-- CorelDRAW! 5 / James Karney.
      p.   cm.
    Includes index.
    ISBN # 1-55828-376-5
    1. Computer graphics. 2. CorelDRAW! I. Title.
T385.K3566   1993   94-47611
006.6'869--dc20   CIP

10 9 8 7 6 5 4 3 2 1

MIS:Press books are available at special discounts for bulk purchases for sales promotions, premiums, fund-raising, or educational use. Special editions or book excerpts can also be created to specification.

For details contact: Special Sales Director
                              MIS:Press
                              a subsidiary of Henry Holt and Company, Inc.
                              115 West 18th Street
                              New York, New York 10011

Editor-in-Chief: Paul Farrell   Technical/Copy Editor: Bud Paulding
Managing Editor: Cary Sullivan   Production Editor: Anne Alessi
Development Editor: Mike Sprague   Assoc. Production Editor: Erika Putre

Acknowledgments

During the course of writing this book I was offered, and gratefully accepted, help from a number of people. I'd like to take this opportunity to thank them publicly. Without their assistance it would not have been possible to include all the features contained within its covers.

At Corel Corporation, Fiona Rochester and her media relations staff provided ongoing help by locating artists, making sure our team received copies of the software and putting us in touch with the right people to answer questions. Connie McNeil and the hot-line technical support staff verified facts and helped us get our CorelDRAW installation running smoothly. Bill Cullen and the QA and Development Team kept us up-to-date during the Beta cycle period. On the production side, my good friend (and former English scholar) accepted the tasks of both technical editor and copy editor for a complex book. Paul Farrell, Michael Sprague, and Anne Alessi, of MIS:Press handled the details of getting the book produced and put up with all my requests.

One of the nicest parts of writing this book was interviewing the talented artists whose work appears in it. Their insights into the inner workings of CorelDRAW and willingness to share made researching and writing Section Two a lot of fun. These talented individuals include Georgina Curry, of Phoenix, Arizona; Gary Bouton, of Liverpool, New York; Jan Selman, of East Falmouth, Massachusetts; Richard Fiore, of Las Vegas, Nevada; Tim Moran, of Eylria, Ohio; Peter McCormick, from Sun City West, Arizona; Chris Purcell, of Houston, Texas; Deborah Miller, of Mesa, Arizona; Wil Dawson, of Tulsa, Oklahoma; Jody Vergil, of Montreal, Quebec; and David Birckley, of San Francisco, California.

David Birckley was kind enough to provide the SETDRAW utility that is included on the disk, and Steve Warren allowed us to include his MEMWATCH program. Mark Stack and the folks at Corel Magazine provided a wealth of valuable CorelDRAW information and tutorials for the CD-ROM located on the back of the book.

Also special thanks to Cathy Cary for creating the artwork used in Chapters 14, 15, and 16. She also helped select the artists to be interviewed as we examined over 700 art contest slides. Cathy holds a B.A. from Indiana University. She worked in graphics production and multimedia design in California for six years and now lives in the mountains of East Tennessee freelancing and studying computer graphics.

Manya Marshall provided yeoman service in revising screen shots, helping to maintain the software on systems kept in the lab and designing portions of the exercises for the newsletters, brochure, and herb garden. Manya also provided the index to the book and helped keep the office organized during the throes of writing.

I want to thank my wife Janet and our daughters Shannon and Arwyn, whose interruptions during the long days of writing provided an enjoyable, much-needed break. It was great to be able to get up from the keyboard for a mid-morning blackberry hunt or trip to the swing set.

TABLE OF CONTENTS

CHAPTER 1: Getting Started with CorelDRAW! 5 — 1

The Difference Between Draw and Paint	2
Dot, Dot, Dot...	2
A More Objective Approach	2
Do What You Do Best	3
The Corel Graphics Toolkit	3
CorelDRAW	4
CorelCHART	5
CorelPHOTO-PAINT	5
CorelTRACE	5
CorelSHOW	6
CorelMOVE	6
Mosaic	6
CorelDRAW 5.0, CD-ROMS, and Windows 3.1	7
Using the Interface	7
The CorelDRAW Desktop	7
Using Menus and Dialog Boxes	9
Drop-Down Menus	9
Fly-out Menus	10
Dialog Boxes	10
Roll-up Menus	12
Preferences	13
Using the Toolbox	14
Exercise	16
Drawing a Simple Sign	16
File Menu Basics	20
Exercise Summary	22
Rectangles, Outlines, and Selecting Colors	23
Using the Rectangle Tool	23
Using the Outline Pen Tool	25
Setting a Predefined Line Width	26
Full Control with the Outline Pen	27
The Zoom Tool, Wire Frames, and the Full-Screen Preview	35
Coloring CorelDRAW Objects with the Outline Pen	37
Understanding Color Models	40
The Spot Color Approach and the Pantone Palette	43
Using Palettes and Color Names	43
Performing Color Conversions Between Different Models and Methods	44
Defining the Default Outline	44
Cutting Through the Clutter with the Outline Pen Roll-up Menu	45
Chapter Summary	46

CHAPTER 2: Filling in the Blanks — 47

What's Ahead in This Chapter?	48
Setting the Stage	48
Making a Perfect Circle, Arc, or Ellipse	50
Oblongs	50
Circles	51
A Two-Tool Solution: Pie Shapes and Arcs	51
Bounding Boxes	51
The Versatile Pick Tool	52
Selecting Objects	53
The Shift-Click Method	54
Using the Marquee	54
Space Bar	55
Tab Select	55
Transformations with the Pick Tool	55
Moving Things Around	55
Scaling Objects	56
Stretching Is Something Else	57
Making Mirror Images and Drawing Objects Out from Their Center	58
Leaving and Creating Duplicates	58
Rotating	59
Playing with the Center of Rotation	60
Skewing	60
Using the Menus and Clearing Transformations	61
Absolute Positioning	62
Undo and Redo	63
Introducing the Pencil Tool	64
Freehand Mode	64
Erasing with the Pencil	66
A Better Straight Line	66
Paths	68
Getting Solid with the Fill Tool	69
Fill Tool Components	69
Setting a Default Fill	71
Setting Uniform Fills	71
Use the Roll-up Menus to Set Fills	72
Getting Fancy with PostScript Halftone Screens	73
PostScript Textures	76
Using Two-Color Fills	76
Tile Settings	79
Creating Custom Fills	79

Full-Color Pattern Fills	82
Working with Full-Color Patterns	83
The Quick and Easy Pattern Fill	85
The Pattern Roll-up Menus	85
Fountain Fills	86
Creating Basic Fountain Fills and Adjusting the Fill Angle	86
Adjusting the Edge Padding	87
Setting the Number of Stripes	87
Right On the Mark: Placing Objects Precisely	88
Using the Rulers	88
Using Guidelines	90
Using the Grid	91
Snap Points	92
Alignment using the Arrange Menu	93
Combining Is Not the Same as Grouping	96
Sunrise, Sunset	97
Step 1: The Sky	97
Step 2: Adding the Ocean, Reflections, and Sun	99
Working Faster	99
Chapter Summary	100

CHAPTER 3: Getting Into Shape — 101

The Hidden Power of CorelDRAW—Bézier Curves Ahead	102
Seeing How It Works	102
A Short Anatomy Lesson	104
Drawing Curves: The Pencil Tool, Part Two	106
The Bézier Mode	106
A Simple Shape	106
Drawing Curves	109
Make a Path	109
Getting It Right with the Shape Tool	111
Working with Nodes and Using Control Points	111
Node Types	113
Cusp Nodes	113
Symmetrical Nodes	114
Smooth Nodes	115
Node Editing with the Shape Tool	116
Advanced Curve-Drawing Techniques with the Pencil Tool	120
Single-Pull Click-and-Drag Drawing	120
Dual-Pull Click-and-Drag Drawing	122

Method Drawing Closed Paths	123
Dapper Caspar, the Curved Snowman	124
Creating the Primary Body Shapes	125
Aligning the Major Objects	126
Shading the Snowman's Body	126
Creating the Branches for Arms	127
Defining the Face and Adding Buttons	128
Making a Plaid Scarf	129
Adding a Vest and Improving on the Design	129
Moving Node Locations	131
The Edit Menu Commands	131
Undo, Redo, and Repeat: The CorelDRAW Buffer	132
The Cut and Copy Commands	133
The Paste Command	133
Paste Special	133
Deleting Objects	134
Duplicating Objects	134
Copy Attributes From…	134
Select All	135
Edit Object and Links	135
Chapter Summary	136

CHAPTER 4: Working with Words — 137

Life Is More Than Pretty Pictures	138
Why Does Typography Have to Be So Complicated?	139
Type as a Design Tool	140
A Few Typographical Terms	140
Using Text in CorelDRAW	141
Variations on a Theme: Artistic and Paragraph Text	142
The Text Tool and Artistic Text	143
The Text Tool	143
Entering Artistic Text Directly on the Page	143
Selecting the Pick Tool in a Text Mode	144
Sizing and Transforming Type with the Pick Tool	145
Using the Text Editing Dialog Box	146
Changing Typefaces	146
Editing Existing Text	146
Justification	147
A Matter of Style	148
Working with Points, Picas, and a Little Lead	149
Adjusting Spacing	150

Measuring Type	151
A Little Practice with Letters	154
Matters of Size, Style, and Perception	155
Pity the Poor Reader	156
How Big Is Too Big, What Is Too Small, and How Much Is Too Much?	156
Leading	157
Modifying Part of a Text Object	158
The Craft of Kerning	159
Manual Kerning with the Shape Tool	159
Aligning to Baseline	160
Precise Kerning with the Dialog Box	160
Manipulating Character Angle and Shift	161
Vertical Shift	161
Altering the Angle of Individual Letters	163
Straightening Text	163
A Friendly Sign	164
The Basic Flag	164
Setting Some Type	165
Adding More Text and a Second Drop Shadow	167
Angling the Store Name	167
Working with Symbols	168
Accessing the Symbol Libraries	169
Placing and Manipulating Symbols	169
Converting Text to Curves	170
Using the Command	171
The Result	171
Putting Curves to Work	172
Getting Fancy—Fitting Text to Path	173
The Flexible Baseline	174
Horizontal Placement	175
Using Vertical Orientation Effects	176
Setting the Distance from the Path	177
Interactively Positioning the Baseline's Vertical Offset	177
The Place On Other Side Command	177
Placing Text on Ellipses and Rectangles	178
The Edit Commands	178
Advanced Fit Text To Path Skills	179
The Editing Process	180
Moving the Insertion Point	180
Adjusting Horizontal Offset, Letter Spacing, and Kerning	181
Changing the Shape of the Path	182
Working with Character Angle and Shift	183

Using Fit Text To Path Effectively	184
Spell-checking and Choosing the Right Word	184
Help with Spelling	184
The Difference Between the Right Word...	185
Accessing Extended Character Sets	186
Chapter Summary	187

CHAPTER 5: Words Plain and Fancy, Working with Custom Typefaces — 189

What This Chapter Is About	190
Using On-screen Paragraph Text	191
Entering Text Directly into a Frame	191
Frame Attributes	193
Paragraph Attributes	194
Interactively Adjusting Frame Size	196
Transformations of Paragraph Text	197
Outlines and Fills with Paragraph Text	198
Character Attributes, Baselines, and Straightening Text	199
Cut, Copy, and Paste	200
Interparagraph Spacing	201
The Text Roll-Up Menu	201
The Text Roll-Up Menu Functions	202
Importing Text	203
Preparing Text for Import	204
Performing the Actual Import	204
A Little Practice Working with Imported Text	205
Dressing Up the Page	206
Setting the Paper Color and Page Frame	206
Extract and Merge Back	207
Modifying the Text Inside CorelDRAW!	207
Extracting and Editing the Text Using Windows Notepad	208
Using the Merge Back Command	209
Basic CorelDRAW! Print Commands	210
The Print Dialog Box	211
The Print Options dialog box	213
The Reference Toolbar	214
The Layout Tab	215
Separations Tab	216
The Options Tab	218
Printing CorelDRAW! Files Outside the Program	220
Printer Troubleshooting	220
Making the Connection	220

Working with Windows	221
The Windows Control Panel and CorelDRAW!	221
The Print Manager	221
Matching the Printer to CorelDRAW!	222
Merging Drawings and Text	222
Here's How It Works	223
The Target Drawing	223
The Text Source File	223
Designing and Printing Certificates	225
Setting Preferences	225
Creating the Border	225
Setting the Type for the Title	226
Setting the Body Type	227
Creating the Signature Line and Logo	227
Placing the Text Markers	228
Getting It Right	228
Producing the Text Source File	229
Printing the Certificates	229
Designing Custom Typefaces	230
Knowing What's Involved	230
Chapter Summary	231

CHAPTER 6: Going on to Greater Lengths: CorelDRAW's Multi-Page Features — 233

Paragraph Text	234
Applying and Saving Text Styles	237
Flowing Text Between Frames	239
Text Wrap	241
Adding Columns to Paragraph Text	243
Adding Bullets to Text	244
Setting Hyphenation, Tabs, and Indents with Paragraph Text	246
Hyphenation	246
Tab Settings	247
Setting Indents	248
More About Layers	248
Master Layers	248
Multilayer, Active Layer, and Locking Options	250
Visibility, Printability, and Color Override	250
Exercise—Creating a Three-fold Brochure	251
Designing a Brochure	252
Working with Layers	253

The First Sheet of Our Flyer	254
Page 2 of the Flyer	259
Adding the Calendar	260
Chapter Summary	260

CHAPTER 7: Getting the Picture: Importing, Exporting, and Working with Bitmap Images — 263

Introduction	264
Getting Ready	264
Importing Bitmaps into CorelDRAW 5.0	264
Bitmaps are Simple... Sort of	264
Importing a Simple Bitmap Image	266
Sizing, Scaling, and Rotating Bitmaps	268
Hiding Images to Speed Operations	269
Using Outlines and Fills	270
Using PostScript Halftone Screens with Bitmaps	271
Cropping Bitmap Images	271
The Pencil Tool's Auto-TRACE Mode	272
Fine-tuning AutoTrace	273
High-Powered Raster-to-Vector Conversions with CorelTRACE	275
The CorelTRACE Interface	275
The Image Info Box	279
Running CorelTRACE	280
Selecting Files	280
Checking the Image Information	281
Performing the Trace	281
A Closer Look at Methods	281
Putting in a Good Word for Line and Object Traces	283
A Closer Look	284
Woodcut and Silhouette Tracing	284
Creating Woodcut Effects	284
Silhouette	286
Custom Settings for Optimum Results	287
General Guidelines for CorelTRACE	290
CorelTRACE File Formats	291
Import Versus Export: What's All the Fuss?	291
CorelTRACE Import Formats	292
CorelDRAW Import Filters	293
CorelDRAW Export Filters	297
Export Basics	297
Exporting Bitmaps	298

File Format Notes	299
Using the Clipboard for Import and Export	302
Basic Clipboard Limitations with CorelDRAW	303
Pasting the Clipboard into CorelDRAW	303
Obtaining Images Using the CCapture Module	304
Using and Removing CCapture	305
Chapter Summary	306

CHAPTER 8: Pushing the Envelope: Using CorelDRAW's Envelope, Blend, Perspective, and Extrude Special Effects   307

What Is So Special About the Effects Menu?	308
Getting Ready	308
The Effects Menu	309
The Envelope, Please	309
Change Perspective	310
The Blend Effect	310
Extruding Objects	310
Working with Envelopes	310
Canceling the Envelope Effect	312
Working with Arcs	312
Using the Copy Envelope From Command	312
Throwing Some Curves	313
The Two Curve Envelope	313
The Unconstrained Envelope	315
The Preset Envelopes	315
Working with Text in Envelopes	316
A Few Rules	317
Using the Control and Shift Keys for an Extra Twist	317
Blending in	318
They're Pretty, but What Are They Good for?	319
How Blends Work and How to Define Them	320
The Primary Blend Roll-Up	320
Choosing Beginning and End Nodes and Mapping Nodes	321
Mapping to Another Path	321
Dynamic Links and the Apply Button	323
Learning About Blends	323
Simple Blends	323
Dynamic Links	324
Taking Blends Apart	325
Mapping Nodes	326
Splitting Nodes	326

Selecting Elements	327
Transformations	328
Envelope Effects with Blends	328
Compound Blends	329
Defining Additional Control Points	330
Fitting a Blend to a Path	330
Following the Path	332
Editing the Path	333
Using Blends to Create Arrays	333
Creating the Illusion of Perspective	334
The Add New Perspective and Clear Perspective Commands	336
Giving Objects Extra Body with the Extrude Effect	337
Creating Extruded Objects	337
The Vanishing Point	340
Right on the Button	345
A Field of Stars	345
Showing Your Colors	346
Making a Statement	347
One Final Effect	348
Fine-tuning the Design	348
File Management Using Mosaic	349
Mosaic Basics	349
Chapter Summary	353

CHAPTER 9: A Banquet of Possibilities: CorelDRAW's Advanced Drawing Tools — 355

Introduction	356
New Tricks with Fountain Fills	356
One Way to Make a Mountain	357
More Fun with Rainbow Fills	359
Even More Fun with Custom Fills	360
CorelDRAW 5.0 Texture Fills	361
A Cloudy Day	364
Using Powerlines	367
Adjusting the Nib	368
Adjusting the Speed, Spread, and Ink Flow Settings	369
Some Tips for Using Powerlines	371
Contours	371
Putting Contours to Work	372
Drawing the Snail Shell	372
The Welding Workshop	375

Order If You Please	376
Masking with Welds	377
Intersection and Trim Effects	378
Putting Intersection and Trim to Work	379
A Different Sort of Duplicate—the Clone Command	381
The Second Clone	383
Cloning Clones	385
Focusing the Lens	386
Behind the 8-Ball—Exercise # 1	387
Exercise # 2—Three Ways to Use the Power of PowerClip	388
Keeping Track with the Object Data Manager	392
Adjusting the Appearance of the Data Manager	396
Exercise—Planning an Herb Garden	397
Setting Up the Work Space	397
Welding the Paths	398
Landscaping the Paths	401
Managing Our Crops	401
Adding Values	402
Keeping Track of Time	402
Planting Our Garden	402
The Layers Roll-up	402
Planting Geraniums	403
A Comfortable Place in the Sun	404
Chapter Summary	405

CHAPTER 10: VENTURA — 407

The Desktop Revolution	408
What is a Desktop Publishing Application?	408
Desktop Publishing, What and Why	408
The VENTURA Desktop	409
The Toolbox	410
The Text Ribbon	412
Exercise 1—A Simple Newsletter	413
Selecting a Page Layout	416
Loading the Files	417
Placing the Masthead	419
Creating a New Address Tag	420
Editing our New Tag	422
Tagging the Folio	424
Setting the First Headline	425
Putting in the Lead Story	425

Adding the Graphic 426
Continuing the Lead Story in the Second Column 427
Finishing Page 1 429
Page Two of Our Newsletter 431
Adding Headers and Footers 432
Adding the Text 433
Placing a Headline 434
Placing Our Graphic and Custom Wrapping the Text 434
Adding a Table to Page 3 436
Finishing Our Newsletter 437
Applying a Pre-shaped Wrap 438
Saving your work and managing VENTURA files 440
The Publications Manager 440
Publications, Chapters, Files, and Frames 442
Tags and Stylesheets 443
More and More Features... 445
Summary 446

CHAPTER 11: Getting the Picture with CorelPHOTO-PAINT 447

Introduction 448
How PHOTO-PAINT Works 448
The CorelPHOTO-PAINT Desktop 449
Using the Toolbox 451
Creating a New Picture and Loading Images 452
Opening a New Paint Window 452
Opening an Existing Image 453
Sizing and Viewing Images 454
Converting an Image's Color Mode 454
More Than a Little Bit of Difference 456
Dithering: A Better Black and White 457
Grayscale: The Best Black and White 457
You Can Go Home Again—Sort of 458
Exporting Your Work 458
Selecting and Defining Painting Tools 458
Selecting and Using Painting Tools 459
Erasing Your Work 460
Sizing a Drawing Tool 460
Drawing with PHOTO-PAINT 461
Painting a Simple Face 462
Improving the Design 463
Selecting Areas with the Lasso Tool 463

Using the Palette to Choose Colors	464
Working with the True-Color Palette	466
Drawing Filled Circles and Copying Parts of an Image	466
The Curve Tool, and a Little Bit of Bézier	467
Dressing Up the Image	468
Getting the Red Out: The Wonderful Color Replacement Tool	470
Touching Up with the Eraser Tool	471
Adding Fills	472
Flood, Texture, and Tile Fills	472
A Few More Tools	473
The Locator Tool and Duplicate Command	474
Getting Information About a Picture	475
The Hand Tool	475
The Soft Tools	475
Airbrush Effects	476
The Paint Brush	477
The Artist, Impressionist, and Pointillism Brushes	477
The Blend, Smear, and Smudge Tools	477
The Clone Tools	478
The Mask tools	478
Using Text	479
The Drawing Tools, a Summary	479
Printing Images from PHOTO-PAINT	480
Retouching Scanned Images with PHOTO-PAINT	480
A Little Bit More About Bitmaps	480
Fine-tuning the Display System	481
The Dithering Option	481
Adjusting the Monitor's Color	482
Image Enhancement with Filters	483
Manipulating Brightness and Contrast	484
Adjusting the Color/Gray Map	485
Applying Equalization	486
Touching Up with a Freehand Blend	488
A Sharper Image	488
Pay Attention to Details: Fine-tuning the Image	489
Touching Up with the Smear Tool	489
Managing Freehand Brightness and Contrast	490
Adding a Little Local Color	491
Making Some Noise	491
Putting It All Together	492
The Special Effects Filters	492
Embossing Images	493

Getting an Edge	493
Sharpening and Smoothing	494
Obscuring an Area with Pixelation	494
The Motion Blur Filter	495
Transformations	496
Resizing an Image with the Resample Dialog Box	496
The Flip and Rotate Options	497
Distorting Images	497
Inverting Images	497
Producing Outlines	498
Masks	499
Chapter Summary	500

CHAPTER 12: Making the Point with CorelCHART — 501

Introduction	502
Before You Begin	502
The CorelCHART Interface	503
Opening an Existing Chart	503
The ChartView Editing Window	504
The Data Manager	504
The Basic CHART Tools and Controls	504
Creating a Simple Chart	506
Opening a New File	507
Working with the Spreadsheet and Entering Data	507
Adjusting and Selecting Columns and Rows	509
Tagging the Data	510
The Autoscanner	510
Viewing the Chart	510
Tagging the Rest of the Chart	511
Dressing Up the Spreadsheet	512
Cleaning Up the Chart	512
Manipulating the Chart Layer On-Screen	514
Changing Chart Types and Using 3-D Effects	516
The Gallery: Converting from One Chart Format to Another	516
Adjusting the Chart Layer Text and Display	518
Adjusting the Chart with the 3-D Roll-up	520
The Movement Mode	521
The Perspective Mode	521
3-D Box Proportion Mode	522
The 3-D Rotation Mode	522

The Chart Menu Options	523
The 3-D Bar Chart Options	524
The Autoshade Functions and Setting Custom Fills	525
Riser Controls	526
Annotations and the Arrange Menu	527
Placing Annotation Text	527
Adding a Pointer with the Pencil Tool	528
Adding an Ellipse and a Backdrop	528
Using the Pictograph Tool	528
Arranging Objects and Adding Backdrops	529
The CorelCHART Arrange Menu	529
Adjusting the Presentation of Your Data	529
Converting the Scale	530
Adjusting the Size and Order of the Risers	530
Performing Data Analysis	531
Changing the Riser Text Format	531
Pie Charts	532
Gaining Market Share	534
The Data Manager	534
The Difference with Pie Charts	535
Adjusting the Slice Feelers	535
Keep It Easy to See and Understand: Presentation Basics	536
Keep It Simple	537
Make a List	537
Break Up Large Collections of Data	537
Consider the Audience and Location	537
Plan the Colors	538
Use Templates Whenever Possible	538
Don't Design Ransom Notes	538
Print All the Slides and Then Proofread Them!	539
A Chart Selection Primer	539
Importing Data, Importing Graphics, and Using Templates	541
Importing Data	541
Supported Files	541
Importing Graphics	542
What Good Is a Template?	542
Using the Sample Slides as Templates	543
The Save As Option	544
Getting Your Charts Out	544
OLE, the Windows Magic Carpet Ride	544
Chapter Summary	545

CHAPTER 13: CorelSHOW and Object Linking and Embedding — 547

Introduction	548
Object Linking and Embedding	548
OLE Terminology	548
Using OLE with CorelDRAW 5.0 Applications	549
Embedding and Editing OLE Objects	550
Linking Objects	553
Updating Existing Links	553
Introducing CorelSHOW	554
The CorelSHOW User Interface	554
The Viewing Modes	555
The CorelSHOW Desktop	555
Using CorelSHOW	557
Setting the Initial Background	558
Creating the First Slide	559
A Little OLE!	559
Doing Some Editing	559
Returning to CorelDRAW	560
Improving the Background with PHOTO-PAINT	560
Setting Up a Grid and Rulers	561
Making the Final Background	562
Adding the Second and Third Slides	562
Fitting Objects to the Page	564
Arranging Presentations in the Slide Sorter	564
Inserting an Animation	564
Timelines and Cues	565
Saving and Printing Your Work	566
Choosing Presentation Options	567
Using the CorelSHOW Run-time Module and Designing Presentations	568
A Few Tips on Production	568
Chapter Summary	569

CHAPTER 14: Saturday Morning Live: Fun with CorelMOVE — 571

The Computer-Multimedia Explosion	572
CorelMOVE Makes It Easy	572
Not Just Pictures	573
Basic Principles of Animation	573
The CorelMOVE Interface	574
The CorelMOVE Window	574
Menus	575

The Tool Box	576
The Control Panel	576
Putting Together a Simple Animation	577
Finding a Backdrop	577
Adding a Text Title	579
Adding Action to an Animation	581
Editing Images in CorelMOVE	581
Setting an Actor's Path	583
Controlling an Actor's Speed	585
Making the return trip invisible	586
Creating a New Prop	587
Creating a New Actor	588
Getting Things in Motion	591
More Ways to Fine-tune Your Animation	592
The Cel Sequencer Roll-up	592
The Timelines Roll-up	593
Cues	594
Adding Sound to Animation	595
The Ultimate in Animation	595
Chapter Summary	597

Chapter 15: Designing with Words and Symbols — 599

Introduction	600
Choosing Typefaces	600
Measuring Up	601
Logos: Is a Word Worth a Thousand Pictures?	602
Casting Call	602
The Finals	604
Curves Ahead	605
Shaping Letters With the Envelope	605
Adjusting the Words	606
Setting the Outline and Fill	607
Creating Matching Stationery	607
Planning the Design	608
Setting the Stage	609
Filling in the Blanks	610
A Professional Touch: En and Em Dashes	611
Placing Typographic Dashes	612
Dressing Up the Logo	613
Adding the Clipart	614
Some Final Points on Letterhead Design	614

Creating a Matching Envelope	614
The Business Card	615
Setting Up the Page	615
Setting the Paper Size	616
Adjusting the Paper Color	616
Placing the Logo	617
Replacing Process With Spot Colors	618
Laying Out the Company Information	619
Adding the Name	620
Batch Runs	620
Chapter Summary	621

Chapter 16: Creating Advertising Copy and Flyers   623

The Approach	624
Setting Up CorelDRAW	624
The Grid System	624
The Layout	624
Setting Up the Page	625
Layers Roll-up Menu Functions	626
Placing the Graphics	627
Working With Spot Colors	627
Placing the Woman	628
Creating the Striped Background	628
Adding the Towels	630
Creating the Left Panel	630
Placing the Text	630
A Point of Reference	632
The Main Headline	632
The Second Headline	633
The Left Body Copy	633
Add a Drop Shadow	633
The Right Body Copy	634
Chapter Summary	634

Chapter 17: Creating Complex Illustrations   635

Landscape Introduction	635
The Approach	636
Setting Up	636
Creating the Hills	637
Forming the Basic Shapes	637

Blending the Forward Hill	638
Making the Background Hills	639
Adding the Ocean and Sky	639
Adding the Forests	640
Putting Things in Perspective	642
The Larger Tree and Its Shadow	642
The Eagle, a Little License, and More Perspective	643
Forming Clouds	643
Adding the Creek, Marsh, and Flowers	644
Creating the Creek	644
The Marsh	644
The Flowers Along the Creek	645
Adding the Marsh Grass	645
Define the First Layer	646
Drawing the Frame and Flowers	646
Creating the Flowers	647
Filling the Petals	647
Drawing the Flower's Center	648
Adding the Second Flower	649
Placing the Greenery Accent	649
Chapter Summary	649

Chapter 18: Using Multipage and Frame Tools, Advanced Layout Concepts   651

Roll the Presses	652
The Elements of a Newsletter	652
Planning	652
Distribution	653
The Print Shop	653
The Design	653
Be Flexible but Use a Consistent Style	655
Creating a Four-Page Newsletter	655
Designing the Masthead	655
Page 1 and Designing the Masthead	656
Adding the Folio	657
The Page 1 Layout	658
Placing the Teaser	659
Laying Out the Lead Story	660
Creating Page 2	662
Working with Master Layer	663
Text and Graphic for Column 1	664

Flowing Text from Frame to Frame 665
Adding the Breakout 666
Page 3: Wrapping text around graphics 668
Wrapping Text Around a Graphic 670
Adding the Text 670
Text Wrap Around the Graphic 671
Finishing Page 3 671
Page 4 of Our Newsletter 672
Beyond Layout 675
Chapter Summary 675

CHAPTER 19: A Quick Sketch of Peter McCormick — 677

About the Artist 678
The View Along the Canal 678
A Collection of Miniatures 680
   The Man on the Bridge 680
   The Man and the Boy 681
A Little Accent 682
   The Long View 683
   A View from the Balcony 684
   A Final Perspective 685
Chapter Summary 685

CHAPTER 20: The Pen and Ink Style of Deborah Miller — 687

Building a Castle 688
   The Approach 688
   Raising the Walls 689
   Detailing the Battlement 690
   Adding the Minor Details 691
   Accenting the Effort 692
   Blending the Foreground 692
   Framing the Image 693
Mesa, a Native Tapestry 694
   Pulling the Hide Taut 695
   Drawing the Mountains 696
   The Pottery 697
   The Solar Disk 698
Getting Technical 699
   The Approach 699
   Working Smart with Wireframes 700

Drawing the Main Body	701
The Handle and Ball Assembly	703
Creating the Filled Drawing	704
Creating the Rear Barrel Section	705
The Forward Threads	705
The Top Cylinder	706
Making the Handle	707
Getting a Bit More Complicated	708
Just How Far Can You Go?	709
The Approach	710
The Fine Lines and Absolutes	711
The Headdress and a Bit About Style	712

CHAPTER 21: The Spirit of Jan Selman — 713

About the Artist	713
The Spirit of Being an Artist	714
The Approach	714
The Face	715
The Backdrop	716
The Artist As Sculpture	716
Adjusting the Tiles	717
Accenting the Announcement	718
Setting the Type	719
Designing Posters	721
Keep It Simple	722

CHAPTER 22: Tim Moran: Getting Technical — 723

About the Artist	723
The Approach	724
The Telephone Base	725
The Buttons and Light Bar	725
The Hi-Lo Slider	726
The LED Lights	727
The Speaker and Number Listing Cover	728
The Handset	728
Chapter Summary	729

CHAPTER 23: The Detailed World of Chris Purcell — 731

The Anatomy of a Drawing	731

About the Artist	732
Planning the Lizard	732
The Primary Lines	733
Drawing the Head	734
Defining the Skeletal Structures	735
Creating the Filled Body	735
Forming the Tail	737
Summary	737
Butterflies	738
The Approach	738
The Foundation Elements	739
Adding the First Wings	740
The White Markings	741
Drawing the Head, Thorax, and Abdomen	742
Text—The Real Complication	742
Butterflies in the Background	744
Building a Good Foundation	744
The Backdrop	745
Fitting the Text	747
Chapter Summary	748

CHAPTER 24: The Worlds of Gary David Bouton — 749

About the Artist	750
Astrotext	750
The Approach	751
The Star Field Background	752
Creating the Scroll	753
Setting the Type	754
A Problem with Numbers	754
Creating the Globe	755
The Chrome Look	756
The Reflected Text	757
The Finishing Touches	757
Quick Chrome	758
Making Letters Really Stand Out	759
The Logo	760
Creating a Cover	760
Embossing the Text	761
Cartooning with CorelDRAW!	762
How Stupid Can You Get?	762

Bitmap Wizard	763
Chapter Summary	764

CHAPTER 25: Rich Fiore: Bright Colors and Neon Lights   765

About the Artist	766
Nevada Nickels	766
The Approach	766
Casting the Nickels	767
Adding the Neon Lights	767
Creating the Coin and Lighting Effect	768
The Background	769
The Landscape	769
Attracting High Rollers	770
The Approach	771
Creating the Car and Reflection	771
The Tires Were the Hard Part	772
The Backdrop	773
The Mosaic Floor	774
Keeping It Light	774

CHAPTER 26: The Vision of Wil Dawson   775

About the Artist	775
Moonlit Flight	776
Framing the Image	776
The Title Text	777
Outlining the Face and Hair	779
Blending in the Facial Features	780
The Shoulder and Flowing Garment	781
Forming the Hair	782
A Word About Colors	782

Chapter 27: The Elaborate Designs of Georgina Curry   785

About the Artist	786
Huntress: The Birth of a Winner	786
Interplay of Color and Tone	788
The Medallion	790
The Beaded Headband	792
The Upper Headdress	793

The Choker and Breastplate	795
The Braids of the Huntress	796
Portrait of a Winner	799

Chapter 28: Hardware Issues: Caring for and Improving Your System — 801

What This Chapter Is About	802
Making the Most of Memory	802
Get Every Bit of Conventional (and Unconventional) Memory	803
Reducing Overhead	804
Hard Disks: Keeping Things Running Smoothly	805
Not a Matter of If, but When…	805
The Next Step Up	808
Testing Your Drive	812
Viruses	812
What About Hardware?	813
Getting on the Right Bus	814
The Local Bus Is an Express	814
SCSI: A Bus Within a Bus	815
Choosing a Storage Subsystem	818
The Display System and the Need for Speed	822
A Bright New World	824
Fasten Your Seat Belts, Please	825
If You Just Want Speed and Need Less Color	826
Getting the Picture	827
Have It Both Ways	827
The Wave of the Future	828
Pointing in the Right Direction with Graphics Tablets	828
Chapter Summary	829

CHAPTER 29: Third-Party Software and Miscellaneous Products — 831

What this Chapter is About	832
Squeegee Makes Windows Manageable	832
Image Pals Captures Windows	833
Hijaak Is a Master Translator	835
SPSS for Windows	836
Fractal Painter: An Art Store on Disk	838
Microsoft Publisher: Desktop Wizard	839
Framemaker Is Very Technical	840
A Gallery of Special Effects	841

INDEX **843**

ABOUT THE CD **865**

CHAPTER 1

Getting Started with CorelDRAW! 5

This chapter covers the following topics:

- The Difference Between Draw and Paint
- The Corel Graphics Toolkit
- Using the CorelDRAW Interface and Toolbox
- File Menu Basics
- Drawing Basics
- CorelDRAW Objects

The Difference Between Draw and Paint

Dot, Dot, Dot...

Before we begin, let's talk about how computers handle graphics. That will make it easier to understand how the different parts of the CorelDRAW package fit together. Graphics programs fall into one of two categories: paint or draw, depending on how they work. Paint programs are great for working with scanned images and photographs. An image is made up of rows of dots called picture elements (or pixels). Each dot is assigned a value and a location on a map of the page, known as a *bitmap*. Paint programs allow you to manipulate each pixel, changing its color or shade to create an illustration. They work rather like a paint-by-number kit—that's why they're called Paint programs.

The more sophisticated paint programs let you retouch and add special effects to photographs and even mimic traditional art tools. They are relatively easy to learn, but bitmap editing leaves a lot to be desired for several reasons. Files can be very large—over 100 megabytes for a full-color eight-by-ten-inch drawing. The computer has to list the location and the type of every dot in the picture. That's one bit of information for every pixel on the page for basic black-and-white images. If you want 256 colors, it will require eight bits per pixel. It increases to 24 bits per pixel for true color photographic quality (16.7 million colors).

Bitmap images are prone to jagged lines, especially when they are enlarged or reduced. That limits their use with certain special effects or for creating smooth-looking type. But nothing beats a bitmap when you want to work with scanned images.

A More Objective Approach

Draw programs build images as a collection of objects: things like lines, circles, rectangles, and the letters of the alphabet. Instead of saying, "Put a black dot in the upper-left-hand corner of the page, then a white dot, another white dot, and so on," to get a round shape, a Draw program can just say, "Place a 2-inch black circle in the center of the page." Then if you want to make it a 3-inch circle, all the computer has to change is the size. This is somewhat like saying, "Make that circle 1 inch wider." Of course the computer is doing all this with some very fancy mathematics, but you don't have to worry about that at all.

Chapter 1: Getting Started with CorelDRAW! 5

The result is an easy way to draw things like perfect circles and squares, reduce jagged lines, and produce smaller files than bitmap applications. The most powerful Draw (or vector-type art) programs offer a host of fancy effects for shaping objects and playing with type in an illustration. Take a look at the two words shown in Figure 1.1. The word *Draw* on the right was created in CorelDRAW; the word *Paint* on the left was created in PhotoPaint. Then they were each enlarged seven times. Do you see how much better the vector type appears compared to the bitmap?

Paint   Draw

FIGURE 1.1 Draw and Paint programs are not the same

Do What You Do Best

Each type of program has advantages and drawbacks. The trick is in knowing how to use both effectively. Bitmap programs shine when working with photo-realistic images. Object-oriented programs let you create drawings and technical illustrations and perform wonders with type that would be very difficult (if not impossible) in a Paint program. Figure 1.2 shows the difference in appearance of the same image rendered with a Draw program on the left and a Paint program on the right. Notice that the picture on the left looks more like an artist's rendition, compared to the photographic appearance of the one on the right.

THE COREL GRAPHICS TOOLKIT

Professional illustrators and designers don't limit themselves to one medium. They mix photographs with drawings, use type to set a mood, and take advantage of the wide range of available graphic arts tools. Most serious computer artists have several programs on their systems, which lets them use the application best suited to the task. The Draw program market is getting very competitive, making vendors work hard to get your business. CorelDRAW has been considered a leader. It is very easy to learn and has excellent features and control over type.

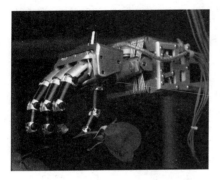 

FIGURE 1.2 Paint programs provide photographic realism (left); Draw images (right) look more like an artist's rendition

To keep ahead of the competition and add value, the latest version is more than just a Draw program—it's almost a complete computer artist's toolkit. Included with a significantly improved CorelDRAW are paint, charting, presentation, file management, animation, and raster-to-vector conversion applications. You can use them together, combining their different features as needed to create effects and accomplish tasks no one program could perform.

The CorelDRAW 5.0 overall improvements include substantial gains in speed and performance, greater workspace customization, OLE 2.0 drag and drop support, a new color management system for calibrating your monitor, printer, and scanner, 22,000 clipart items, 825 fonts, 125 animations, and a CD-ROM-based multimedia tutorial. Moreover, each program in the package has been enhanced. Before you turn on the computer, let's take a minute to introduce the seven full-featured applications that come in the CorelDRAW package and get a basic idea of how they work together.

CorelDRAW

This is Corel's flagship, the winner of virtually every industry award for excellence. It is a draw program offering all the tools required to produce a simple letterhead design or create complex full-color illustrations. CorelDRAW has gained popularity because of its easy interface, wide range of special effects, and outstanding typographical control. It can use things created in other programs—including bitmaps, charts, and blocks of text from word processors—as part of a drawing.

Some of version 5.0's new features are a new ribbon bar for easy access to commonly-used commands, a floating toolbar, the ability to create and save macro effects, live dimensioning, weld, trim, and intersection tools, and PostScript interpretation. With support for Windows Object Linking and Embedding (OLE) 2.0, CorelDRAW can use information that resides in other applications. When you update the source—say, in an Excel spreadsheet or a scanned photo—your CorelDRAW illustration is automatically updated. You don't have to delete and reload new versions or keep multiple copies of a drawing in several different files. This powerful feature will be covered in more detail later, and experiments with OLE will occur several times during the exercises.

CorelCHART

This program is a complete charting package, not just an add-on module, for creating sophisticated graphs and slides. The version 5.0 release has been improved with a new ribbon bar and tear-off toolbox, enhanced on-line help larger spreadsheet size, and approximately 276 new spreadsheet functions. It has eleven new chart types including Polar, Radar, Bubble, and Gantt, and data can be entered into its own Data Manager or imported from other applications. The What You See Is What You Get (WYSIWYG) editor lets you see what a chart will look like as you create it—including 3-D effects and imported bitmap and draw images. The results can be used in slide shows with CorelSHOW, exported to CorelDRAW or a desktop publishing program, or output to a slide maker. CorelCHART 5 also supports OLE 2.0.

CorelPHOTO-PAINT

This is a full-fledged Paint program for creating and editing bitmap images. This latest edition adds new masking features which include color and transparency masks, and new masking tools. You can now create and layer objects with the tear-off Object Fly-out. A variety of filters lets you sharpen, blur, tune, and adjust the appearance of scanned photographs and new ones include Vignette, Mesh Warp, and Smoked Glass. It also contains a screen-capture module. The finished picture can be used directly or imported into CorelDRAW.

CorelTRACE

CorelTRACE is a utility that can convert almost any kind of bitmap image (like a scanned logo or hard-copy drawing) into a vector file that can be imported into CorelDRAW for editing. It can even capture the original's colors. Unlike bitmaps, vector objects can be resized and manipulated without distortion and jagged lines. They also take up a lot less space on your hard disk. This utility includes direct scanner support, optical character recognition, enhanced tracing controls, and some really slick effects, such as woodcuts and silhouettes. CorelTRACE 5 has additional tracing options to optimize OCR (optical character recognition) results, more intuitive access to tools, and enhanced on-line help.

CorelSHOW

One of the most popular uses of CorelDRAW is making presentation slides and overhead transparencies. CorelSHOW lets you assemble, test, and view a series of images as an electronic slide show. Features include text and background design tools, the ability to use animation (AutoDesk Animator files), transition effects, and support for OLE. The new version adds transition effects, animations within frames, cues for branching and interactive user control, timelines, and Quicktime for Windows support.

CorelMOVE

If you need to use your graphics skills to create animated presentations, you'll want to explore CorelMOVE. This module provides tools and an interface for combining graphics, sound, and 2-D animated objects into polished productions. The application is bundled with a set of libraries of clipart and ready-to-run animation clips. CorelMOVE 5 includes new morphing features, improved import and export capabilities, and enhanced ability to create actors in other Corel applications.

Mosaic

This is a file management tool for graphics images. You can use Mosaic to locate and see a file without loading it into a program. It also lets you create compressed archives of drawings or clipart to save space on your hard drive. MOSIAC 5 is available as a roll-up window in all CorelDRAW 5 applications and fully supports Corel printing capabilities—including the ability to print thumbnails. On-line help is enhanced with the addition of glossary and keyboard shortcuts sections.

CorelDRAW 5.0, CD-ROMs, and Windows 3.1

Along with all the programs and the manuals, the complete CorelDRAW package contains a clipart collection, help files, about 825 True Type fonts, samples, and tutorial files. That's a lot to pack onto floppy disks. So Corel Systems, a leader in the use of optical storage, provides users with CD-ROM disks containing all their files and an animated tutorial. If at all possible, use it. A CD-ROM drive will add convenience, speed up installation, simplify locating clipart, and save space on your hard drive. Other vendors, including Microsoft, are starting to market interesting new products based on CD-ROMs.

It is suggested that you run Windows 3.1 or later and DOS 5.0 or later and that you use a high memory manager when running CorelDRAW. This will help ensure that all CorelDRAW's new features work on your system and that all the exercises perform as they do in the book. OLE requires either Microsoft Windows 3.1 or the manual addition of some of its library files to your Windows 3.0 directory. For more information see the Installation Appendix or consult the CorelDRAW manual.

Using the Interface

Our hands-on sessions start with the CorelDRAW User Interface. It is very similar to those of the other Corel programs. You'll learn how to select and use basic tools, how to define outlines and fills, and how to use some fundamentals of object-based (also known as vector) drawing. If you are already familiar with the CorelDRAW menus and tools in version 3.0 or 4.0, you can skip this exercise. There are some important changes in menus and locations of commands (for instance, the old Display menu is now the View menu), but you'll have no problem picking up the changes. If you are not familiar with CorelDRAW, please load Windows (type win at the DOS prompt); then double-click on the CorelDRAW icon located in the Corel Graphics Toolkit group. (It looks like a hot-air balloon.) This book is based on CorelDRAW 5.0. If you have version 4.0 or earlier you should obtain an upgrade from Corel Systems.

The CorelDRAW Desktop

The CorelDRAW window (see Figure 1.3) simulates a desktop with a page in the center. Above the page is a row of menus for selecting commands, plus rulers and bars that provide information as you work. Down the left side of the screen are the nine tools used to draw and manipulate objects on the page. The major components of the interface are described here.

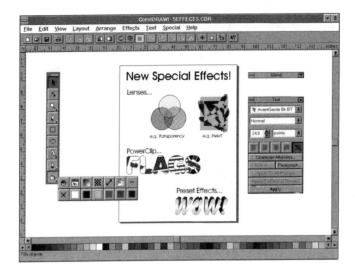

FIGURE 1.3 The CorelDRAW user interface

1. The Title Bar shows the name and path of the current file.
2. The Menu Bar allows access to the program's drop-down menus when you click on the item's name.
3. The Status Line shows the current mode and information about the currently selected object.
4. The Toolbox contains the basic drawing and manipulation tools used to create drawings. You click on the icon to change the mouse pointer into the desired tool.
5. The Tool fly-out menus provide access to several additional options that open when you click on their icons.
6. The Rulers are used for precise measurement of an object on the page.
7. The Work Area and Page are used for drawing and manipulating objects. This is a What You See Is What You Get (WYSIWYG) display of your drawing. The orientation and size of the area within the page border will vary, based on the page settings found under the File menu.
8. Object Handles are little boxes that appear on the edges of the currently selected object. You can use handles to size and stretch an object.
9. A roll-up menu is a selection box that gives access to the options for the Text tool and certain special effects in the work area without having to use the regular

Chapter 1: Getting Started with CorelDRAW! 5

menu bar. One of the menus is shown full size; the other is reduced to a title bar using the button at its top right.

10. On-Screen Palette is a strip of predefined colors and gray scale tones that can be clicked on to set a solid fill quickly.

11. The Page Counter appears only when you have more than one page in a drawing file and is used to move from one page to another.

12. Windows Scroll Bars are used for moving the area displayed in the active Window.

USING MENUS AND DIALOG BOXES

Drop-Down Menus

CorelDRAW has nine drop-down menus located above the status bar. The Edit, Effects, Text, and Arrange menus give access to drawing commands and special effects. The File, Layout, View, and Special menus are used to open and save drawings, import files created in other applications, add or modify pages, and customize CorelDRAW's operation. The Help menu provides access to the online help features. To open a menu you can either click on its name or use a keyboard shortcut. Shortcuts work when you hold down the Alt key and press the key that matches the underlined letter in the menu's name. To select an option once the menu is open, press the underlined letter, but don't hold down the Alt key. Let's practice by setting the page to Landscape (horizontal position) using the shortcut.

Hold the **Alt** key down and press the **L** key. (You can use either upper- or lowercase letters). The Layout menu will open. Release the Alt key and press the **P** key. The Page Setup dialog box will open.

Press the **L** key. The dialog box should show that Landscape is selected, as seen in Figure 1.4. Press the **Enter** key. This sets the page to a landscape, or horizontal, position. Many of CorelDRAW's menu functions can be performed with hot-key combinations. Some commands can also be given with hot-keys. These are like keyboard shortcuts, but don't require opening a menu. Most are Ctrl key combinations. You can use the mouse and open the File menu's Save option to save a drawing to disk, or the Alt-F, S shortcut or Ctrl-S hot-keys. From the Page Setup dialog box, click on the Display tab and that property sheet comes to the front. Click on the **Show Page Border** option if there is not already a mark next to it, and press **Enter**.

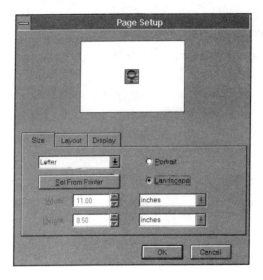

FIGURE 1.4 The Page Setup dialog box

When a hot-key is to be used, it will be indicated as follows: **Alt-T** (hold the **Alt** key down and press the **T** key) or **Ctrl-T** (hold the **Ctrl** key down while pressing the **T** key). Combination series will be shown as follows: **Alt-T, Enter**. This would mean hold the **Alt** key while pressing **T**; then press the **Enter** key.

Fly-out Menus

Fly-out menus are opened by clicking on icons in the Toolbox. When the menu is visible you can click on an option to activate it or open its dialog box. You can see the Fill tool fly-out in Figure 1.3. The Zoom, Pencil, Text, Outline, and Fill tools have fly-outs. An explanation of how each one works will be given later.

Dialog Boxes

Many options are set using dialog boxes. This allows CorelDRAW's interface to be uncluttered but still gives quick access to settings and commands. Although the number of variations may seem complex to new users, a little practice makes working with them second nature. The example shown in Figure 1.5 is a common form with the parts explained below.

Chapter 1: Getting Started with CorelDRAW! 5

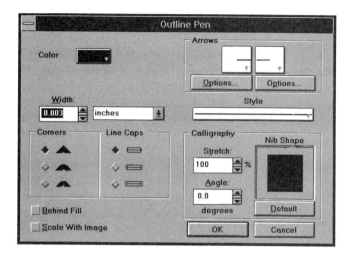

FIGURE 1.5 Outline Pen—A typical dialog box

- **Check Boxes.** The Scale With Image and Behind Fill listings in the lower left-hand corner are check boxes. Clicking on the square or pressing the underlined letter toggles the option on or off.
- **Command Buttons.** The OK and Cancel buttons perform the command listed on the button. You can click with the mouse or press an underlined key (if any) to execute the action. With most dialog boxes, pressing **Enter** will choose OK.
- **Option Bars.** Bars like those labeled Options... open other dialog boxes or submenus. They can be opened with the mouse or by pressing the underlined letter. The Color bar invokes a Color Selection box; the Options bar provides a menu offering command choices.
- **Selection Windows.** The Sample Selections above the Options bar or under the Style can be used to choose dashed and solid lines or change the appearance of end caps (e.g., arrows). Clicking with the mouse will open a drop-down menu. Clicking on a sample selects it.
- **Radio Buttons.** Radio buttons, like the ones under the Corners section, let you choose one of several options by clicking on the diamond shape in front of each offering. In this case the topmost button is enabled.
- **Display Boxes.** In the Color, Arrow, and Nib Shape areas are samples showing what the current selection will look like in an object.

- **Entry Boxes.** The box under the word *Width* lets the user enter a value either by typing or scrolling with the arrows to the right of the numbers. The drop-down menu to the right lets the unit of measure be changed.
- **Tabbed Property Sheets.** To make lots of information easily accessible, you click on one of the tabs at the top of the dialog box and the corresponding property sheet comes to the front. This is like having several dialog boxes layered on top of each other. You saw this in the Page Setup dialog box.

Roll-up Menus

Roll-up menus are special menus that can be left on-screen while you work and used to modify objects without having to use the normal dialog boxes. They are like mini-toolboxes. This is a very sophisticated feature begun in version 3.0. The Extrude roll-up is shown in Figure 1.6. The globe and positioning arrows allow you to rotate an object on any axis. The menu also provides tools for changing perspective, adjusting the apparent lighting angle, and defining the type and color of an object's fill. You can move roll-ups to any location in the screen, even outside the CorelDRAW window. The small arrow in the upper right-hand corner reduces the menu to a thin bar or opens it to show the tools.

CorelDRAW offers several ways to perform most commands. The mouse, hot-keys, keyboard shortcuts, roll-up menu, or dialog box can all get the job done. Use whichever works best, but be open to changing methods as your skills improve. Looking for shortcuts and hot-keys for the commands you use the most often can really speed up your work.

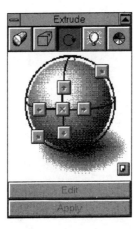

FIGURE 1.6 The Extrude roll-up menu

Preferences

Preferences are user-definable settings that customize the way CorelDRAW works to match the needs of a specific project and to suit individual tastes. As you work through the exercises you will use them to make your tasks easier. Let's set some preferences so our screens will all look the same and so we can get a little practice with the interface before you start drawing. To open a menu with the mouse, click on its name located on the menu bar. To choose an option once the menu opens, click on it the same way. In some cases you will then be offered a dialog box for setting options. If a hot-key is available for an option, it will be listed to the right of the entry. Various preferences and how to customize your CorelDRAW settings to suit the way you work will be discussed later.

Open the View menu. See if there are checkmarks to the left of the Rulers and Status Line options. If not, click on the appropriate word(s). The checkmarks indicate that the option is active. The menu disappears each time you choose an option. This type of option is called a *toggle*. Each time you select it, the option changes back and forth between on and off. There should be rulers along the top and left sides of the work area and a row of colored squares on the bottom of the window when you are done. Each time you click on the word, the setting is turned on (the checkmarks show) or off (no checkmarks). Click on the Color Palette option and make sure the Pantone Spot Colors option has a check in front of it as well. You can also enable the Floating Toolbox. The View menu will show checkmarks like those in Figure 1.7 when everything is set properly.

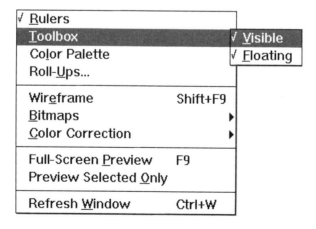

FIGURE 1.7 The View menu properly set up

Now let's use the Ctrl-J hot-key to open the Preferences option of the Special menu. You should see a dialog box as shown in Figure 1.8. That was a lot faster than opening the Special menu with the mouse and then clicking on the Preferences option, wasn't it? Click on the View tab, then click on the box labeled Interruptible Display. Click on the up arrow next to the word *Horizontal* in the Place Duplicate section. Notice that the number in the value box changes. Click as many times as needed to change the setting to 0.30. It should look like Figure 1.8 after you click OK. Finally, click on the Right Mouse Button list box and assign *Full screen preview* to the right mouse button. As you can see, the CorelDRAW menus control a lot of options. As you learn the basics you will explore them and discover how to use them. The focus is on understanding how to apply them, not just on describing the commands.

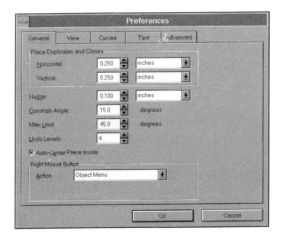

FIGURE 1.8 Setting preferences

USING THE TOOLBOX

One of the reasons for CorelDRAW's popularity is its simple interface. There are only nine tools to learn. Each one will be covered in detail in the next few chapters. They fall into three categories: draw, view, and manipulate. The easiest way to learn them is by using them. Most of the tools have more than one function. The four drawing tools can be used to create almost any shape. The Pencil or Freehand tool is used to draw lines and irregular shapes. The Ellipse tool can produce perfect circles, oblongs, arcs, and pie-chart shapes. The Rectangle tool is used to draw squares and boxes. The Text tool allows you to place text on the page and control the way it looks. These four tools are used to create objects.

Selecting a tool is easy; just click on it with the mouse. To get a feel for how tools work click on the Ellipse tool and move the cursor to the middle of the page. Now drag the mouse to the bottom right-hand corner of the page and release the mouse. A round shape is on the screen. You just created your first CorelDRAW object.

FIGURE 1.9 The CorelDRAW toolbox

Understanding how objects operate is fundamental to using CorelDRAW. An object is any element that you place on the page. It can be a line, circle, freehand shape, or block of text—anything you draw or place on the page. Every object has two parts, an outline and a fill. Use the example of a square drawn with a crayon. It has walls (the *outline*) and an inside area (the *fill*). The walls can be thick or thin; the color can be any shade and can have a pattern. The inside of the object is defined by the boundaries of the walls. The inside can have a different color and pattern. In CorelDRAW the outline follows the shape of an object and can be colored separately from the inside fill area. The Pick, Shape, Outline, and Fill tools allow you to change the appearance and shape of existing objects.

The Zoom tool allows you to change the magnification of the view of an object easily. You can make it bigger, to work on a small detail, or zoom out, to see the entire area. It changes only the part visible in the work area, not the actual size of an object. Let's draw something and see how the tools work. Don't worry about your ability to draw a straight line or a perfect circle. CorelDRAW makes it easy.

EXERCISE

Drawing a Simple Sign

Most of the exercises in this book have three parts. Demonstrations show how something works, like the circle you drew a minute ago. Projects give hands-on experience using CorelDRAW to do real-world tasks. Practice Sessions present illustrated concepts and offer experiments for expanding your skills and understanding how a feature or tool works. For your first exercise you are going to create a color sign announcing a yard sale for a neighbor. To keep it simple you will use the standard defaults for your drawing. As you go along, screen shots will be included, so you can see how things should look. The object of this exercise is to gain some familiarity with operating the CorelDRAW interface.

Open the **File** menu and choose **New**; click on **No** when asked if you want to save the circle you just made. You should have a blank page. Select the Rectangle tool. Place the cursor on the upper left-hand corner of the page; then drag it to the lower right corner and release. You should have a rectangle covering the page.

Click on the Outline tool. A fly-out menu will appear. This menu controls the appearance of an object's outline. Click on the thick line on the far right of the upper row. The outline of your rectangle is now a heavy black line, as shown in Figure 1.10.

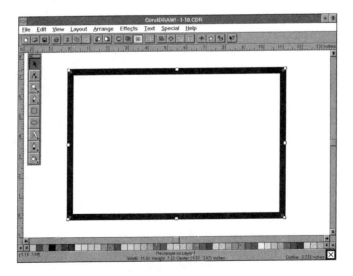

FIGURE 1.10 Outlined rectangle

Click on the light blue shade on the Palette (color strip) on the bottom of the screen. Your rectangle is now filled with blue. The rectangle is really a single object. As shown in Figure 1.11, it has a thick black outline and a blue fill.

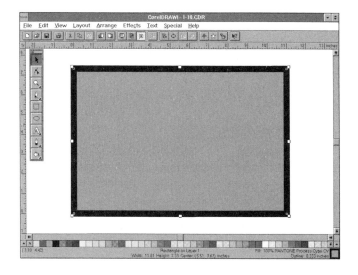

FIGURE 1.11 Filled rectangle

Next we'll add our message. Click on the Toolbox Text icon, and move the mouse pointer to the middle of the page. Click once. Now type in the following message and press the **Enter** key to start each new line.

Yard Sale Saturday	(press Enter)
From 10 am to 6 pm	(press Enter)
1225 Sunnydale Lane	(don't press Enter)

The text appears on the page as you type. Don't worry about its position or size; you'll fix that next.

Click on the Pick tool located in the Toolbox. Little squares called handles should appear around the letters you just typed. That tells you which object on the page is selected. If they aren't there, press the **Tab** key until they appear. The **Tab** key moves through and selects each object sequentially in the drawing. Your screen should look somewhat like Figure 1.12.

FIGURE 1.12 Selected text

Press **Ctrl-T**. The dialog box on the screen allows you to change the font, alignment, or size of a block of text quickly. Let's click on the **Center** button located on the right side of the dialog box to set alignment within the block. Next open the **Style** option and choose **Bold** (if available for the selected font). Drag (hold the left button and pull the mouse over the desired area) over the numbers in the box to the right of the Size entry box. Type in 68.0. The numbers you typed will replace the ones that were there. Make sure the word "points" appears in the box to the right of the numbers you just entered. If it does not, click on the down-arrow at the right, then click on the word "points." Your screen should look like the one in Figure 1.13. Click on **OK** to approve your selections.

Now let's center the text on the page. Press **Ctrl-A**. The Alignment dialog box will appear. Click on the box marked **Align to Center of Page**. Click on **OK**. It should look like Figure 1.14 when everything is set properly.

Chapter 1: Getting Started with CorelDRAW! 5

FIGURE 1.13 The Character Attributes dialog box

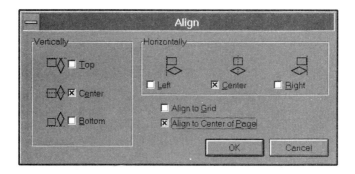

FIGURE 1.14 The Align dialog box

File Menu Basics

Let's save our work so we can use it later. Click on the **File** menu and choose **Save**. Name the file "Yardsale." The program will automatically add its own .CDR extension, which identifies it as a CorelDRAW vector format. The File menu provides access to all of CorelDRAW's import, export, and template functions. *New* means you are creating a totally new file. There is a difference between opening and importing a file. *Opening* is loading an existing CorelDRAW illustration for editing. *Importing* is the act of bringing a file (drawing, bitmap, or text) in as part of a drawing. You can load a logo that is a CorelDRAW file as part of a business card—that's importing. If you bring the logo in to edit it, that's opening.

Save and *export* work the same way. If you save a file it is written to disk as a native CorelDRAW file. You can export the file in a number of formats, both vector and bitmap. The section under File Formats in the appendix covers the options and considerations for importing and exporting in detail.

Notice how the File menu shown in Figure 1.15 is designed. All CorelDRAW drop-down menus follow the same format. The choices are grouped by their functions, which are divided with lines. The underlined letter denotes a keyboard shortcut and if there is a hot-key combination it is shown on the far right of the same line.

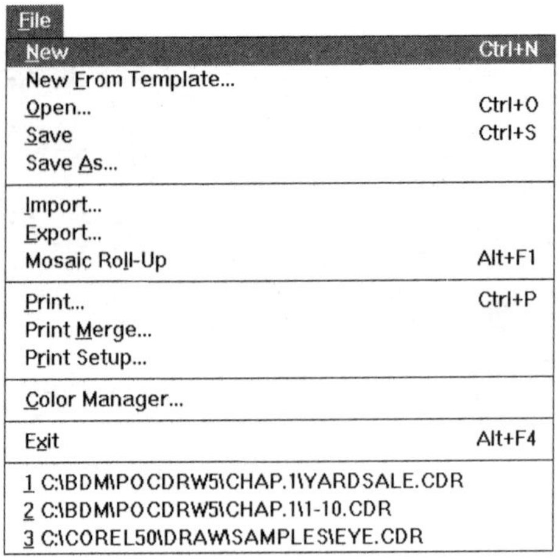

```
File
New                                    Ctrl+N
New From Template...
Open...                                 Ctrl+O
Save                                    Ctrl+S
Save As...

Import...
Export...
Mosaic Roll-Up                          Alt+F1

Print...                                Ctrl+P
Print Merge...
Print Setup...

Color Manager...

Exit                                    Alt+F4

1 C:\BDM\POCDRW5\CHAP.1\YARDSALE.CDR
2 C:\BDM\POCDRW5\CHAP.1\1-10.CDR
3 C:\COREL50\DRAW\SAMPLES\EYE.CDR
```

FIGURE 1.15 The File menu

Chapter 1: Getting Started with CorelDRAW! 5

The first group provides options for opening and closing files:

- New opens a new file and closes the old one. If you have not saved your work you will be given a choice of saving, discarding the work, or canceling the new file command.
- New From Template... was a new feature beginning with CorelDRAW 4.0. Templates are collections of styles that can be used to set the attributes of objects; like fill, line thickness, etc.
- Open... produces a dialog box and allows you to select an existing CorelDRAW file for editing. If you have not saved work currently on the screen, you will be given a choice of saving, discarding the work, or canceling the Open file command. You may locate a file using keywords, open the Mosaic file manager, and sort files using this menu. We will practice with these features during the projects in Part Two. Its keyboard shortcut is **Ctrl-O**.
- Save allows you to save work in progress without closing the file. It is a good idea to save a file before importing art from another file, printing, or performing a complex operation. You can save a file at any time without opening this menu by pressing **Ctrl-S**.
- Save As... creates a duplicate of the current drawing under a new name. Both Save and Save As... let you attach notes and keywords to a file and attach image headers.

The second group provides choices for using files from other programs and exporting drawings.

- Import... provides a way to import text and graphics from other programs, as well as placing an entire existing CorelDRAW file in the current file. The details of importing and exporting are covered in detail later in this book.
- Export provides a way to convert CorelDRAW illustrations into popular graphic file formats for use with other programs. The details of importing and exporting are covered in detail later in this book.
- Mosaic roll-up makes the Mosaic roll-up menu available on the Work Area. This utility allows you to locate and preview graphics files without loading them into CorelDRAW.

The third group contains commands related to printing your drawings.

- Print presents the Print dialog box that enables you to set the number of copies and variety of other options that will be covered in Chapter 4. The exact features available will depend on the type of output devices that are currently installed via the Windows Control Panel. You can use **Ctrl-P** as a shortcut.
- Print Merge allows you to use data stored in a text file to "fill in the blanks" of a CorelDRAW illustration, much the same way as with the mail-merge feature of a good word processor. This can be very handy for printing a number of certificates or pre-printed forms.
- Print Setup pulls up the Printer Setup normally found under the Windows Control Panel so you can change the default printer, load a new driver, or redefine the current preferences and port.

The fourth group contains only the Color Manager command.

- Color Manager accesses a group of sophisticated tools for managing color within all of the Corel applications. It is available off the File menu in each application and allows you to calibrate your monitor, printer, and scanner so that input and output colors match.

Quitting CorelDRAW

Choosing Exit will close CorelDRAW. If your current file has not been saved you will be given the option of saving, not saving, or being returned to the program via a dialog box. **Alt-F4** will close the program without opening the File menu.

Fast Open

The Drawings List contains the names of up to four files. These are the last drawings you have worked on. One can be opened directly by either pressing the underlined number or clicking on its name.

Exercise Summary

This simple exercise showed how objects are drawn, colored, and aligned on a page. Once an object is formed, it can be manipulated using a wide range of tools and special

Chapter 1: Getting Started with CorelDRAW! 5   **23**

effects available through the menus. You used the Rectangle tool to cover the page, the Outline tool to set the thickness of the line around your box, and the Fill tool to provide inside color. With the Text tool you added your message. Text is a special kind of object that will be explored further in later projects. In the practice session you will explore drawing skills.

RECTANGLES, OUTLINES, AND SELECTING COLORS

Using the Rectangle Tool

In the first exercise we used the Rectangle tool to create the background for our sign. Now you'll learn more about how it works. This is the tool used for creating both squares and rectangles. If you still have the yard sale sign on the page, choose **New** from the File menu—be sure to save your work using the filename "yardsale." Now select the Rectangle tool by clicking on it with the mouse (it will look like a button that has been pushed in on most monitors). Move your cursor into the work area. As it enters, the pointer will change from an arrow to crosshairs, meaning it is ready to draw.

You can draw anywhere within the area bounded by the rulers and scroll bars. Only the portions of objects on the page will print. Draw a long, narrow box from left to right across the page. Place the cursor where you want it to start and drag to the opposite corner of the rectangle and release. An outline of the shape will follow as you drag. Your screen should look like Figure 1.16. (The view has been enlarged and thickened to make it easier to see. You will probably have a thinner outline on your rectangle.)

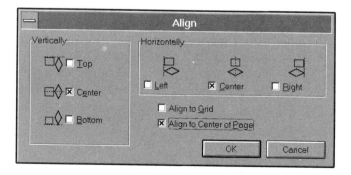

FIGURE 1.16 Using the Rectangle tool

Now draw another rectangle, but this time before you start press and hold the **Ctrl** key. Begin the new object at the lower right-hand side of the page and drag towards the upper left. Don't let go of the **Ctrl** key until after you release the mouse button. You should have a perfect square. The **Ctrl** key is called the *Constrain* key when used with one of the four object drawing tools.

As you can see, drawing with the Rectangle tool is very easy. Just select the tool, click at the starting point, and drag. These basic steps are the same for the Ellipse and Pencil tools, but they have additional refinements for drawing more complex shapes. Once an object is formed, you can use a host of tools and special effects to get the exact form you need.

Practice a Little Constraint

The objects made so far have started with the upper corner positioned as the point where you started to drag the mouse. Sometimes you need to create one that is centered on a certain point. But how can you get one that grows from the center as the Rectangle tool is dragged? It's easy. Bring the cursor to the center of the page, then press the **Shift** key. Now drag the mouse around and watch how the rectangle grows equally in both directions from its center—the point where you first started drawing. Release the mouse. Now draw another object, but this time hold both the **Shift** and **Ctrl** keys. A perfect square is produced with its center where you began dragging.

Get into Shape

The Shape tool is the one just below the Pick tool, and looks like a wedge touching a box on a line. It can be used to perform all kinds of tricks. For now you will you use the Shape tool as an easy way to get round corners on a rectangle or square.

Click on the Shape tool with your mouse and bring the cursor to rest on the upper left-hand edge of the box you just drew. Now click on the little box in the corner and drag it towards the upper-right corner. Notice that it rounds all four corners at once. The amount of rounding will change as you drag. Figure 1.17 shows how a box will look as you round it, and the gray outline in the center indicates the maximum amount of change.

Keep an Eye on the Status Bar

One of the most powerful drawing aids (but often overlooked by new users) is the Status Bar, located at the bottom of the work area. While drawing rectangles it tells you the size, center, type of object, fill, and outline. It also displays the cursor position, active layer, and *x/y* coordinates. As you work through the exercises make it a habit to glance at it every so often when drawing or giving commands. That is the best way to become familiar with the reports it gives. Then when needing information or doing critical work you'll intuitively check the status bar.

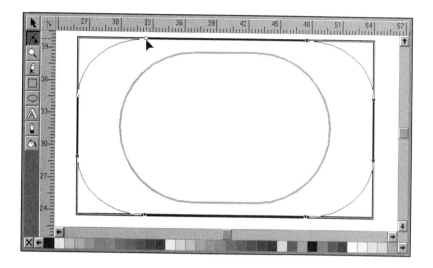

FIGURE 1.17 *Making rounded boxes*

Creating a New Drawing

Using the **New** command located under the File menu will clear the entire drawing. If you have not saved your work, the program will prompt you with a warning before carrying out the action. The hot key shortcut is **Ctrl-N**. This command is used when you want to start over from scratch. Go ahead and use the **New** command now so you have a clear page for the next section.

Using the Outline Pen Tool

All CorelDRAW objects have two primary areas: an outline and an fill. The outline setting determines how thick, what color, the arrows on the ends of lines, and the evenness of the line that surrounds the fill. All these attributes can be set using the Outline (or Pen) tool. It looks like the nib of a fountain pen, and is the second tool from the bottom.

Unlike the Rectangle tool, it does not do any drawing. It is more like a menu that controls how an object's outline will look. When an object is selected (showing handles) you can set its outline using this fly-out menu. Some options will require choosing advanced options from dialog boxes. There is also an on-screen roll-up menu available that offers most outline options. Figure 1.18 shows the Outline tool selected with the parts of the fly-out menu labeled.

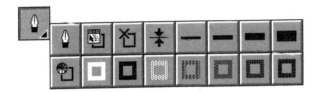

FIGURE 1.18 The Outline fly-out menu

Before going over the more advanced features of the Outline tool, look at the easy way to apply the most commonly used settings. Draw a square in the center of the page using the **Ctrl** and **Shift** keys with the Rectangle tool. Next press the space bar to select the square (this toggles between the last drawing tool used and the Pick tool, and selects the lasts created or modified object).

Setting a Predefined Line Width

Click on the Outline tool with your mouse, the fly-out menu will open. Then click on the icon to the far right on the top row in Figure 1.18. The fly-out disappears and your square now has a 24-point black outline (called a rule by illustrators) around it. (Yours may give the same value, but converted to inches or millimeters.) A point is a unit of measure used by printers that is about 1/72nd of an inch. Points and picas will be discussed in the section on CorelDRAW's on-screen rulers.

Look to the far right on the status bar. It indicates to you that there is a 24.0 point outline around the selected object. The square with the X in it indicates that the object has no fill, and that the color of the rule is black. You can change the shade to 10% gray. Open the fly-out again and this time click on the icon just to the right of the one that is totally black in the lower row. The outline has changed to gray and so has the rule around the sample in the status bar.

The icons on the menu's lower row deal with shade and color. The white and black ones make the outline white or black, and the ones to their right are increasing shades of gray. The pen nib and pie-shaped icons will be discussed shortly.

Now let's open the fly-out again and choose the X in the upper row. You should have handles, but no visible outline. The status bar says just that. The object still has a boundary, but no line marking where it is. The icons on the top row to the right of the X produce pre-set line widths as shown in Figure 1.19. The Pen roll-up opens if you click on the icon to the left of the X, as will the Outline Pen dialog box if you click on the first icon on the upper left. Experiment with the icons from the X to the right of the dialog box to get a feel for how they work and what they look like. When you are ready to continue make sure that a visible object is selected and showing handles.

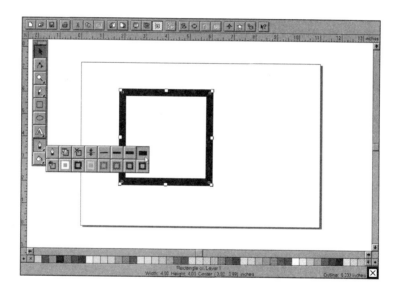

FIGURE 1.19 Working with the Outline Tool fly-out menu

Full Control with the Outline Pen

Open the Outline fly-out again and click on the pen nib icon in the upper-left corner. It opens the Outline Pen dialog box like the one in Figure 1.20, but some of the settings may be different from yours. The basic lines and widths you have been using are limited, but they are far from all that can be done with outlines in CorelDRAW. Now we are going to work with the Outline Pen. It is like having a complete selection of artist's pens, dashed and solid lines, plus fancy arrows and a host of color options that can be used with any object in your illustrations. Some outline options have properties that may seem a little unusual or even exotic, but they allow an artist great control over the appearance of an object's shape. Practice using the different selection options as they are introduced. The techniques cover all of CorelDRAW's common forms of user input from dialog boxes, so you will be using these controls again with other menus. After you finish with this section, you will just be told choose... etc., rather than be given detailed steps for most entries. The skills you learn here will be used in every CorelDRAW project we do.

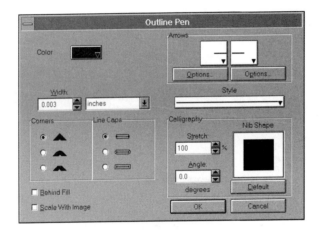

FIGURE 1.20 The Outline Pen dialog box

Colors

The Color button in the upper-left-hand corner accesses the Outline Color controls, which will be covered next. When you click on it, the Outline Color dialog box opens. The rest of the controls are covered here with some examples showing you how they work.

Click on the button to the right of the word Color. A little selection window with colored boxes will open like the one shown in Figure 1.21. Click on any color and release the mouse button. Notice how the color of the button matches the one you just selected. Click the **OK** button in the dialog box and you will see that your object's outline is now that color. This is a fast way to set predefined colors when the Outline Pen dialog box is open. Now repeat the steps and return the color setting to black.

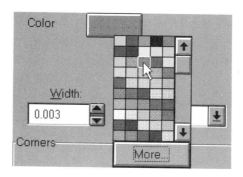

FIGURE 1.21 Outline Color palette

Width

You can set the thickness of an outline either by typing a number in the box after double-clicking within it, or by clicking on the up and down arrows on the text entry box's right side. The drop-down menu with the word inches allows changing the unit of measure. The outline width is independent of the fill area, but depending on its setting the outline may cover or alter the appearance of part of the object.

Make sure the square you drew is selected. (If you erased it create another one.) Click on the Outline Pen Tool fly-out and then on the Outline Pen icon on the fly-out to open the dialog box. Click on the arrows to change the number in the Width text entry box to 0.100, and click the **OK** button. See how your square looks. Open the dialog box again, go to the Width menu and change the unit from inches to points. The number will change from 0.100 to 7.2, since a point is 1/72nd of an inch. Try it with the other unit options, millimeters and picas. A pica is one-sixth of an inch, so there are 12 points per pica. This is a very common unit of measure for printers and typesetters. Make sure the object has a reasonably thick outline when you are done so that you can see the effects of the following options.

Corners

Located underneath the Width section are the Corners options. The default is set to mitered, the radio button on the top. It gives a squared-off look, just as the rounded option just below it produces round corners on objects. The beveled edge is the final choice, which cuts the point off corners. The samples in Figure 1.22 show the effects on angled lines. Try setting the different corners on your square and see how it changes the shape.

FIGURE 1.22 CorelDRAW Corner options

The corner type and setting can be very important with objects having small angles or thick outlines (see the spikes in the last "Scale With Image" example in Figure 1.28). Adjusting the miter setting may reduce or eliminate the problem. You can set the miter amount under the Preferences option of the Special menu.

Line Caps

Line cap settings determine how the ends of lines and dashed lines will look. Just click on the appropriate radio button to set the desired option. The examples point out the differences. Butt caps give square-cut ends that stop at the edge of the line. (If the line is two inches long without the outline it's still two inches long with it.) Rounded caps extend beyond the end of the actual line, equal to the line thickness. Square caps adds a distance equal to half the line.

The lines in Figure 1.23 were all exactly the same length until the line caps were changed. The gray box around the lines makes it easy to see the different effects based on the line cap type. Notice that the butt cap style is shorter than the other two. If you need to have a line fit an exact length it is easiest to achieve by setting a butt cap.

When you are finished, delete any objects in the work area by selecting them and pressing the **Delete** key. Now click on the Pencil tool and bring the cursor on the page. Click near the left edge. Don't drag it, but move the cursor to the other edge and click again. Press the space bar to select the line you just made, then use the Outline fly-out to thicken it. You are going to use the line to demonstrate the next three options.

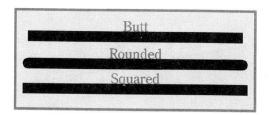

FIGURE 1.23 Line cap settings

Arrows

Life is not all neat little boxes and straight lines, and neither is CorelDRAW. The Arrows section offers a wide variety of end caps (the term for arrows and such on the ends of lines), and also enables you to create your own and store them for later use. They are very handy for presentation graphics and technical drawings. Make sure the line you just made is selected, click on the Outline fly-out tool, and choose the Outline Pen icon.

Right now you probably have two short line fragments showing in the white boxes under the word Arrows. Click on the right box, and watch the selection window like the one in Figure 1.24 appear. Choose a style you like and click on it. The box goes away and the line on the right side has the same shape on its end. Try the same thing on the other side. Use the scroll bar to see all the shapes. Experiment with different combinations. When you click **OK** in the dialog box, your line will have the same end caps. The left box controls the appearance of the starting point (where you began drawing the line) and the right box defines the end point.

Now go return to the Outline Pen dialog box with your line selected and click the **Arrows' Options...** button under a white box with an end cap showing in it (not just a straight line). A menu like the one in Figure 1.24 will open. Click the **Swap** option. This reverses the left and right end caps—and turns them around at the same time. Try it. The Delete From List option is pretty obvious, but leave it alone for now.

Select **Options...** and then click on the **Edit** option. This dialog box is an end cap editor, allowing you to make basic modifications to any type of arrowhead you want. You aren't going to save your work here—so make sure you click **Cancel** when exiting. Don't click the **OK** button or you will overwrite the currently selected end cap with your modified version.

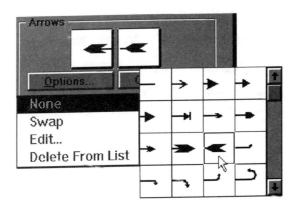

FIGURE 1.24 Setting line ends (arrows)

Look at Figure 1.25. The little handles around the outline of the points are used to drag the lines forming the arrow to make them larger or smaller. The handle on the line coming in from the left is used to shorten or lengthen the arrow. The little boxes on the corners of your arrow allow you to move around the area. Play with the shape and use the **Reflect** and **Center** buttons to see their effect. The 4X zoom enlarges the arrowhead for detailed editing. Try it with several end caps, but don't exit the editor with an OK; use **Cancel**.

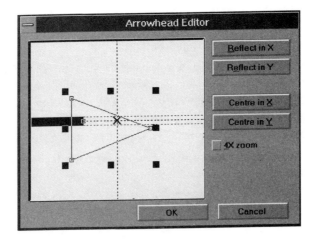

FIGURE 1.25 The Arrowhead Editor

Styles

The Style menu provides a way to get different lines or dashed rules for use in a drawing, like the coupon borders that tell the reader where to cut. The Style menu is located in the Outline Pen dialog box just under the Arrows option. Click on the box with the line in it. A selection box like the one in Figure 1.26 will open. Choose a few with your line selected and watch how it changes. This option will change the type of line forming an outline on any selected object.

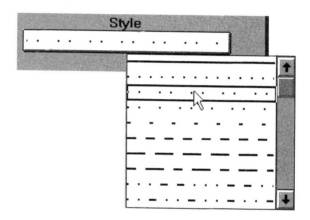

FIGURE 1.26 The Styles menu

Calligraphy

If you have ever wanted a set of calligraphy pens that are sold in art and office supply stores, this is the tool for you. By adjusting the angle and stretch of the Calligraphy setting and choosing the appropriate corner style and line thickness, a user can design a pen nib that will give just the right stroke.

To get a feel for how the pen is shaped, click and hold the arrows under Angle. Try both of them. Notice how the square in the display rotates. It is identical to the shape of the nib that will draw the outline of the selected object. Now do the same with the Stretch arrows and watch how the size of the nib changes. Press the Default button under the nib. It returns to a full square shape. Change the Corner setting from Miter to Rounded. The nib becomes a circle.

In Figure 1.27a, I created a square and an ellipse using the settings shown in the upper object. The screen captures show how the nibs looked after I adjusted the settings.

Look at the difference the type of corner made in the rectangles. Draw a rectangle and use some different nib settings and corners to see how they affect the object.

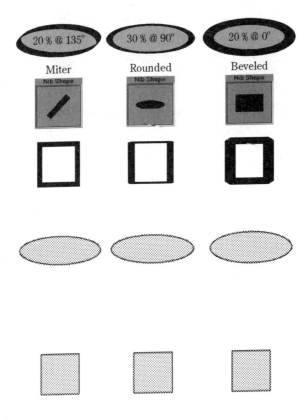

FIGURES 1.27a and b Sample calligraphic results (top) and setting the pen (bottom)

Placed Behind Fill and Scale with Image

The two check boxes in the lower left of the Outline Pen dialog box control the placement and behavior of the object's outline. This can be very important, especially with text having thick outlines. Notice how much cleaner the type on the left is with the outline placed behind the object. Half of the width of the outline is in back of the outer edges of the letters. The thin outlines on the top row help the gray type stand out on the page. As the lines get thicker, they tend to make the words look muddy, and even overlap.

(You will learn how to fix that when the text tool is discussed.) Notice how the W in the last Scaled With Image example has three spikes. The whole line is unreadable because the outline obscures the shapes. The exact effect will vary, based on the font being used and the letters involved. If you enlarge or shrink text and other objects, the Scaled With Image setting can often preserve the outline's relative width and maintain calligraphic effects.

Click on the Text tool and type a line or two on a clean area of your page and select it. (Don't use the space bar shortcut; it doesn't work with the Text tool active, since it just inserts spaces. Use the mouse to get the Pick tool.) Press **Ctrl-T**. The Character Attributes dialog box will open. Choose a font, such as Century Schoolbook, shown in the sample in Figure 1.28, that has some curved shapes and make sure the size is at least 50 points or 0.7 inches so that you can see what happens with different effects. Experiment with the corner, width, and outline placement options. Try some other typefaces too. Leave some type on the screen when you're done.

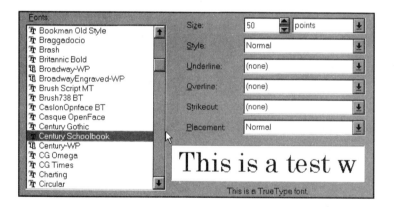

FIGURE 1.28 Setting text: font and size

The Zoom Tool, Wire Frames, and the Full-Screen Preview

While working with CorelDRAW, we often need to close in on small areas or pull back to see the entire page. The Zoom tool is the answer. Click on the **Toolbar** icon that looks like a magnifying glass. It opens the Zoom tool fly-out menu shown in Figure 1.30. The leftmost option with the plus sign (zoom in) is used to magnify any portion of the work area. You can also zoom in by pressing the **F2** key. The option next to it, with the minus sign icon (zoom out), takes you back to the exact view you had before using the zoom in function. F3 is its hot-key.

Figure 1.29 The Zoom tool

You select the area to enlarge by clicking on the icon or pressing the **F2** key. Draw a box around the area to be enlarged by dragging with the mouse cursor, as in Figure 1.30. A dashed line, called a marquee, will follow the magnifying-glass-shaped cursor. When you release the button, the view changes. Try it with the text you left on the screen. Use all the Zoom options and both the mouse and hot-keys to perform the operation.

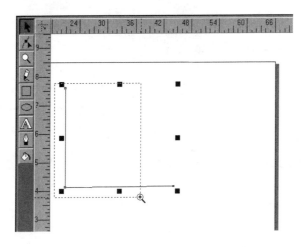

FIGURE 1.30 Selecting an area with the Zoom tool

The next option, labeled 1:1, enables you to get an exact (within the limits of your display system) one-to-one ratio between 1 inch on the CorelDRAW virtual page and your printed page. The next two icons work similarly. Zoom to selected (a group of rectangles with dots around) closes in to view only the portion of the work area with selected objects in it. Zoom to all objects closes in to view *all* objects in the work area. The final icon zooms out to show the entire work area.

Getting the Big Picture

Sometimes you'll want to see the drawing as it will print, without all the distractions of the Corel desktop. Just press the **F9** key or choose **Full-Screen Preview** from the View menu to convert your display to a full-screen view of your work. You can also choose **Preview Selected Only** to limit the full-screen display to the currently active objects. To return to the normal desktop press **F9** again. Try both before going on.

Working with Wireframes

When you work with very complex objects, you may want to do much of your work in wireframe mode. This means that CorelDRAW will display only the basic shape of objects, rather than including outlines and fills. The screen will redraw in a fraction of the time it would take to calculate and display the more involved complete illustration. You can use the status bar as a quick reference about the object's attributes or the Full-Screen Preview to see how the finished work will look. Prior to version 3.0 all editing was done in wireframe mode.

Coloring CorelDRAW Objects with the Outline Pen

So far we have stuck pretty much to plain black and white, but CorelDRAW can provide almost any color imaginable. Just how many shades you can see on your monitor depends on the type of display card and Windows setup you have. This does not limit how many colors you can actually place in a drawing or get in a printout. Later in the book you will take a detailed look at how color is displayed and printed. Now I will focus on coloring outlines and explaining the basic terms. The techniques used here are much the same for all CorelDRAW's color selection menus, so it is important to understand these concepts.

CMYK, RGB, HSB, and Alphabet Soup

It seems that more technical terms and abbreviations are used when describing color than are found in the average IRS manual. That's because color can be a very difficult thing to describe and reproduce. Printers break the use of color into two methods: spot and process. Spot color is used for adding one or two colors to a drawing. This is done by having the printer use specific color inks during the press run. Process color is generally used for jobs requiring more than three colors, because printers can combine the three primary colors plus black and produce virtually any color. The paper is sent through each ink separately.

You must be able to describe a color precisely if you want an exact reproduction of what is on your screen in your output, no matter which method is being used. Even if you are not printing a hard copy, getting an exact match is still important. We all know the sky is blue (sometimes) and that grass is green (sometimes). But there are lots of different shades of blue and green. There are a lot of variables, both in how you see colors and in how output devices produce them. Such professionals as printers, artists, and photographers have developed several systems (called models) to define colors, based on how their tools are used to reproduce them. Click on the **Pie chart** icon (it's really a color wheel) in the lower left-hand corner of the Outline tool fly-out menu. You should now have the Outline Color dialog box on the screen. If yours looks different from the one in Figure 1.31, make sure that Model is set to CMYK (open the Show drop-down list box and click on CMYK Color Model). I'll explain what they mean after introducing the basic dialog box controls.

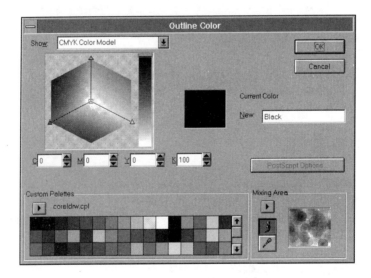

FIGURE 1.31 The Outline Color dialog box—process method

Outline Color Selection Controls

- **Show.** The Show menu allows you to choose between several different systems for specifying colors to be used. The appearance of the dialog box will vary, based on the Model used.
- **Visual Selector.** The color palette includes a square and a vertical bar section. Clicking on a color or tone sets it as the outline color for the currently selected object. The square (called a Marker) shows the current position of the defined color on the map. Each model has some variation in how the colors are mapped on the Visual Selector that are explained here. The number and type of colors will vary based on the color model that is active, as well as on the type of monitor and display card installed on your system.
- **Color Channel Values.** The process models divide a specific tint into its components: either red, green and blue, cyan, magenta, yellow, and black; or hue, saturation, and brightness. The value in this box reflects the amount of each of the channels present in the currently selected color. You can enter a number by wiping the current entry and typing a new value.
- **Color Swatch.** This display box is divided into a top upper portion showing the current outline color of the selected object and a section below showing the color that is being worked with in the dialog box. Clicking OK will replace the current color and exit the dialog box.
- **Color Name.** Depending on the model, some colors can be selected by entering their names here, or the name of a color will be displayed after it is selected using the Visual Selector. User-created colors may be added to the Palette by giving them a name. The user may also select a specific Palette, and then use Add Color to Palette.
- **Color Palette.** A palette is a collection of colors, either determined by the color model selected or defined by the user. Users can create new palettes for a specific projects and to simplify color selection. The same palette can be used for both outlines and fills. You will work with setting colors with palettes in Part Two. CorelDRAW provides several palettes to match both standard displays and the Pantone and TruMatch color systems.
- **Custom Palette Button Menu.** This button opens the menu that lets you save, add, and delete colors from the bar; set the default palette; and manage palette files.

You can use a color from the rows of colored squares located on the bottom of the CorelDRAW window to set both the outline and fill color of any object quickly. Just move the cursor to the desired color (you can use the scroll arrows at either end to see additional tones) and click with the mouse. The left button sets the fill, and the right sets the outline. Clicking on the X on the left end of the color bar with the left or right mouse buttons removes any fill or outline respectively.

- **PostScript Options.** If (and only if) you are using a PostScript driver with the spot color method, this button will access advanced controls for controlling halftones. The use of PostScript controls will be discussed under printing and in exercises as appropriate.

Understanding Color Models

The Show setting in the dialog box indicates how you are describing colors and changes somewhat as different models are selected. As the different models are described, change the menu to that setting. A few examples will be given to help you understand both the way color is produced and how the dialog box works. Don't let all the variations overwhelm you. As we work through the projects in Part Two, you'll be shown all you need to know (unless you want to train as a printer).

Delete any objects on the page and draw a rectangle with a thick visible outline, select it, and open the **Outline Tool** fly-out. Click on the **Outline Color** dialog box. (If your outline did not get any thicker, check to see if Edit Wireframe is still selected under View menu!)

Process Color Models

CorelDRAW offers a great deal of flexibility for defining process colors and offers four different models. You can create custom palettes and name colors using three of them. In general, you should use the one that matches the final use of your drawing. It is a good idea to talk over a color project with your printer or some other professional who understands both the output requirements and the type of work you are doing. Preplanning is very important because color can be both tricky and expensive.

Another concern is calibration. Your eye, the type of lighting in the room, the type and age of your monitor, the video card in the computer, scanners, the inks used in the print run, and the type of paper they are placed on—virtually everything—enters into the way color looks. If the various components of the production system are not calibrated to known values, your blue sky may look like rain, or the peachy skin tones may turn silky green. A little planning can save hours of work—and lots of money. For a basic education see the Color Printing section later in this book. You can also investigate the third-party tools in Part Four.

- **CMYK.** These four letters stand for the colors Cyan, Magenta, Yellow, and black—CMYK. The arrows increase the amount of the respective color from 0 to 100 percent. Mixing yellow and cyan gives green, yellow and magenta produces red. Change C, M, and Y all to 100 percent and you get black. This is the way traditional printers process color using a four-color press. They make different plates (color separations) for each primary color and use an ink with each color during the run. Black is added to provide rich tones. A lot more is involved in printing four-color jobs, but this is basically how it is done. There are guidebooks that show the exact amounts of each primary color required to get a certain color.

    Play with the arrows a bit to get a feel for how CMYK works. Use the Visual Selector as well and watch how the numbers change as you pick different shades. If you plan to take your work to a print shop for a press run and are using more than two or three colors in a job, you should consider using CMYK colors. Some computer color printers use CMY or CMYK dyes, so it's a good idea to know just how your printer works.

    Be sure and experiment with the Visual Selector. This is a quick way to specify a color by the way it looks. The large square area adjusts the amount of Cyan and Magenta in the final color, and the narrow vertical bar controls the percentage of Yellow. CorelDRAW will automatically add the black needed to reduce the amount of ink required at print time and obtain good contrast. The technical term for this kind of compensation is Gray Component Replacement.

- **RGB.** The letters here stand for Red, Green, and Blue. This is the way your monitor produces color and is the opposite of CMYK. Add these colors together and you get white, rather than black. This is the way that monitors, color TV's, most film recorders (slide makers), and some computer printers produce colors. If you are planning on getting slides or doing presentations, this may be your best choice. The dialog box is a little different here. The Visual Color Selector works as it does for CMYK, but the large square area adjusts red and green, while the narrow vertical bar controls the percentage of blue. There are only three sets of arrows. If you do use RGB to define colors for a job that is printed using CMYK, CorelDRAW will convert the values. But as with languages, something is always lost in the translation.

- **HSB.** CMYK "sees" color like a printing press, and RGB is used for your monitors. HSB, which stands for Hue, Saturation, and Brightness, is based on the way the human eye perceives the world. Hue is defined as the quality that makes one color different when compared to another. The primary colors are different hues. Saturation is the intensity of a hue. Colors seem more saturated on an overcast day. Brightness is just what it sounds like—the ratio of light to dark. Colors seem brighter on a sunny day.

As you can see in Figure 1.32, the Visual Selector for HSB is shaped differently from that for the other models. This is a color wheel with each primary color—cyan, magenta, yellow, red, green, and blue—sitting 60 degrees apart on the circle, as shown in Figure 1.33.

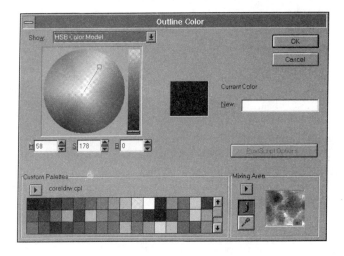

FIGURE 1.32 The HSB Model

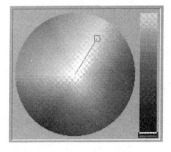

FIGURE 1.33 Diagram of the HSB Model

Changing the position of the Marker toward the outside of the circle increases hue, whereas traveling in decreases it (making it less intense). Moving around the wheel changes the saturation, and the vertical bar adjusts the brightness. The same effects can be obtained by changing the values in the color channels.

The Spot Color Approach and the Pantone Palette

CorelDRAW uses the popular Pantone Matching System (PMS) that provides both names and numbers for its colors. This is technically a much easier method of defining a limited number of colors in an illustration or for getting an exact match with a specific tone than the process method. The artist uses a predefined color that is set out in a look-up table. Generally speaking, spot color is used for print jobs containing one to three colors. Each color can be made darker or lighter by indicating the percentage of black that is to be added, allowing the printer to get additional variations in the final copy without having to add new inks. As mentioned earlier in this section, the different components of a system may not be properly calibrated.

The Pantone system book offers an exact reference that is independent of your system. Printers can obtain inks that are certified to match the desired color. It is not possible to use spot color to reproduce photographic images, and it would be too expensive to employ for a large number of colors. This can be very important, especially with designs such as logos and letterheads. The PMS can also be used to choose matching papers and card stocks. In some cases, process and spot methods are combined. The print job is run through the CMYK inks for the majority of shades and all photographs. It is then run to add specific colors with Pantone inks. This increases the cost.

Using Palettes and Color Names

A palette is a collection of defined colors. They can be based on any color method or model. CorelDRAW lets you name a color you made using the arrows or Visual Selector—say Autumn Gold—and add it to a new or existing palette. You can design palettes for a given job or use one to store your most commonly used shades. This is a very handy way to keep the colors you need close at hand. Work groups can also make good use of palettes. A designer can build a palette with the exact shades for logos, backgrounds, and so on, and then give copies of the PAL file to the rest of the team. That way everybody gets just the right shade.

Figure 1.34 shows part of the list of named Pantone colors contained in the PANTONE.PAL file. If there are named colors in a palette, there will be a Show Color

Names check box like the one in the Figure 1.34. You can use the Search String window or the scroll bar to locate a color. Clicking on the color selects it. The Custom Palette button opens the Palette menu, which allows you to create, load, and save palettes. This is also the menu used to set a new default palette.

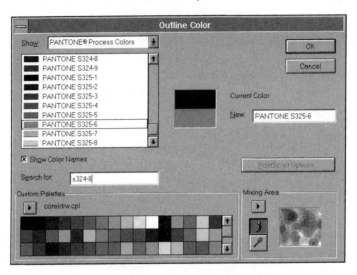

FIGURE 1.34 The Named Color palette selector

Performing Color Conversions Between Different Models and Methods

You can convert a process color model used with an object from the spot to process method. CorelDRAW will automatically calculate the new values if you select the object, open the Outline Color menu, and change the appropriate setting. Be aware that the new color will not be an exact match. Then name the new color and add it to the palette used for the drawing.

Defining the Default Outline

The default outline is used for all new objects. You can redefine the default setting used to create the outline for new objects at any time. Just make sure that no object is currently active (click on a blank part of the work area) and open the Outline tool. Click on the icon for the attribute you wish to set (like color or line thickness). A dialog box will open. Choose the range of objects you wish and click **OK**. Adjust the settings when the regular dialog box opens. The new default will take effect as soon as you finish setting the options.

Cutting Through the Clutter with the Outline Pen Roll-up Menu

By now you have figured out that CorelDRAW offers a wide variety of tools for defining outlines and their colors. The range of options and menus may seem more like a maze than a marvel to the new user. Now that you have worked through the naming of names, you can use a shortcut for handling outlines that was a new feature with CorelDRAW 3.0—the roll-up menu. This can be left on-screen and used to set attributes or open related menus without having to change tools or use drop-down menus.

The roll-up is activated by clicking on its icon on the Outline tool fly-out, the second one from the left on the top row. You can position it anywhere on the Windows desktop, even outside the CorelDRAW area. The small arrow in the upper right-hand corner of the roll-up toggles it between full size and only a name bar. These basic features are the same for all CorelDRAW roll-ups.

This is a good chance to practice the primary functions associated with the Outline tool. Draw a line with the Pen tool, as you did earlier, and use the roll-up to alter its outline as the components are introduced. The following indicate how the specific elements of the Outline roll-up menu work.

- **Outline Thickness.** The top section of the roll-up enables you to set the line thickness of your object. Select the line you made and then use the scroll bars to the right of the same box to change the setting. The down arrow decreases the size until an X shape appears, meaning there is no visible outline. The up arrow increases size. When you have the desired thickness, click on the **Apply** button at the bottom of the roll-up.

- **Line Caps/Arrows.** These work just like the two arrow selection boxes in the Outline Pen dialog box. Click on the left side to set the start point cap and on the right side to define the end point. The view in the box will change as soon as the selection is made from the fly-out menu, but your object won't change until you click on the **Apply** button.

- **Line Style.** This bar opens a drop-down menu that is the same as the one contained in the Outline Pen dialog box. It works just the same, but you must click on the **Apply** button to see the effect.

- **Outline Color Palette.** This bar opens a drop-down palette that can be used to define the outline color based on the default model. Once again your object won't change until you click on the **Apply** button.
- **Edit.** This is a hot-key that opens the Outline Pen dialog box.
- **Apply.** Roll-up menus have an Apply button. This sets in place all the changes made since the last time it was pressed. You may use group selection tools to have your choices applied to more than one object at a time. Clicking on the **Apply** button when no object is selected will redefine the default outline.

Chapter Summary

The basic elements of the user interface—using CorelDRAW objects, using the File menu, selecting tools, drawing rectangles, handling color, and setting outlines—have been discussed in this chapter. If you want, take some time and practice the tools and procedures a bit before going on to the next chapter. Don't worry about mastering all the menus and tools at this point. The goal of Part One is to get comfortable with the program and to learn your way around. The rest of the program's primary functions will be introduced before moving on to major projects. Advanced skills and techniques will be presented in Section Two, once you understand how the program works.

CHAPTER 2
Filling in the Blanks

This chapter covers the following topics:

- Using the Pencil, Pick, and Ellipse Tools
- Drawing Lines, Circles, and Oblong Shapes
- Forming Arcs and Wedges with the Shape Tool
- Sizing and Scaling Objects
- Rotations, Skewing, and Mirror Images
- Moving and Duplicating Objects
- Creating and Using Fills
- Using Rulers, Grids, and Guidelines
- The Alignment Menu
- Working with Groups
- Exercise Two: Fountain Fill Sunset

What's Ahead in This Chapter?

In Chapter 2 we take a closer look at CorelDRAW objects and how they are created. You will work with the Ellipse, Pencil, and Pick tools to create and modify objects. Then I'll introduce fills to show how they give form to objects. The exercise gives you a chance to work with fountain fills to create a simple seascape scene. We'll save some advanced fill and line features for later chapters, but you will have a good working knowledge of the program's basics by the time we start Chapter 3.

Setting the Stage

If possible, read this chapter seated at your computer with CorelDRAW running. It's much easier to learn this program if you experiment as you go along. Load the program just as you did last time: Type **win** at the DOS prompt and double-click on the CorelDRAW icon in the appropriate group. The specific location will depend on how your computer is set up. Once CorelDRAW is running type **Alt-L** (opens the Layout menu), **P** (opens Page Setup), **L** (sets orientation to Landscape), **Enter**. That produces a horizontal page.

Now let's set some CorelDRAW preferences so that your system will match the one used to create the illustrations. Use the mouse to open the Special menu, then select Preferences and then the View tab. Make sure that the **Show Status Line** option has an "x" in the box next to it. Then click on the **Color Palette** entry in the View menu. When the fly-out menu opens, drag the cursor and select the **PANTONE Spot Colors** entry. Your menu should look like Figure 2.1. Next go back to the Special menu and click on the **Preferences** option. Adjust the Place Duplicate unit of measure from points to inches and set both values to -0.20. Then click on the **Mouse** option box and set the right mouse button to **Node Edit**. Your dialog box should look like the sample in Figure 2.2. Choose **OK** and exit both boxes.

Chapter 2: Filling in the Blanks

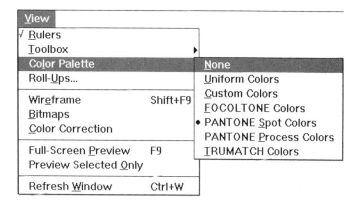

FIGURE 2.1 The CorelDRAW View menu

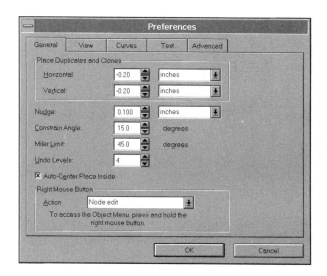

FIGURE 2.2 The Preferences dialog box

MAKING A PERFECT CIRCLE, ARC, OR ELLIPSE

The Ellipse tool works almost exactly like the Rectangle tool and offers the ability to create almost any type of rounded shape. Like the Rectangle tool, this is used by dragging the cursor across the desired area. Depending on the way you use the mouse and key combinations, the Ellipse tool can provide circles, ellipses, pie shapes, and arcs. Figure 2.3 shows the basic forms available with the Ellipse tool.

FIGURE 2.3 Using the Ellipse tool

Oblongs

We can draw an oblong shape by selecting the tool from the toolbar and dragging, just as we did to make a rectangle. Look at the hollow circle and cross shape in the lower right-hand corner of Figure 2.3. Start at the upper center of the shape and drag down and slightly to the right. The more you drag to the right, the wider the oblong becomes; the farther down, the longer. The outline of the shape follows as a reference, and the status bar provides dimension read-outs as you work. Once the mouse is released, the final shape is set. Try a few now; then delete them before going to the next heading.

Circles

Remember the **Control** (**Ctrl**), or Constrain, key? If you press and hold it while dragging with the Ellipse tool, it produces a perfect circle. Holding both the **Ctrl** and **Shift** keys enables you to drag the circle from the center out, based on the point where you first clicked the mouse. Make three or four of these and leave them on the screen.

A Two-Tool Solution: Pie Shapes and Arcs

The Ellipse tool gets a little more involved. Do you remember how we put rounded corners on boxes with the Shape tool? It does double duty when working with circular shapes. Select one of the circles you just created with the Pick tool and then click on the Shape tool. Bring the point of the tool so that it touches the little box (called a *node*) on the top of your object. Now drag the Shape tool around the edge of the circle, moving the point of the cursor from the inside to the outside of the outline several times. Notice how the object changes from a wedge to an arc as you move the point.

Any time the Shape tool is outside the outline of a selected object created with the Ellipse tool, that object becomes an arc, as shown in Figure 2.4a. Moving the tool inside yields a wedge. Practice a bit with your circles and get a feeling for how the feature works. If you go all the way around you get a small arc or pie slice that will increase in area.

Bounding Boxes

You may have noticed that the handles around all CorelDRAW objects, even circles, are box shaped. That's because they outline the object's bounding box. The bounding box is the smallest rectangular area that will contain it. Although the bounding box has no effect over the final appearance of the drawing, its imprecise relation to the shape of its object can lead to confusion when performing transformations. If you have a number of objects in the same area of the page, be sure you know which one is really selected before you make changes. The Undo function only handles the last action. If you work too fast on the wrong object, it may mess up your drawing.

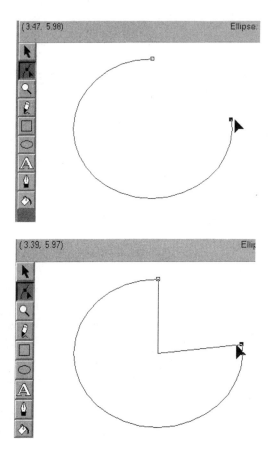

FIGURES 2.4a and b Creating arcs and wedges with the Ellipse and Shape tools

The Versatile Pick Tool

The Pick tool is the topmost icon in the CorelDRAW toolbox, and perhaps the most used. Think of it as a set of electronic fingers. You can use it to select, pick up, stretch, shuffle, and move things on the page. You can use it to join objects into a group or to combine several elements into a new object. It opens all the menus and dialog boxes. When the Pick tool is active for menu selections, the mouse pointer looks like a white arrow pointing up toward the left. At other times it takes on special forms to indicate the current mode.

So far we have left objects on the page just about the same as they were drawn. The Pick tool allows us to select an active object and then gives an amazing amount of control over its appearance. It's easier to show than explain, so let's practice. Click on the Pick tool, so that handles appear around your most recent object. From now on, the term *select* will be used when I'm asking you to put handles around something in a drawing. We are going to use the Pick tool to turn shapes upside down and inside out (among other things).

The Pick tool is very easy to master. You have been using it a bit already, but it also allows some pretty fancy tricks. This next section not only will help you understand some of CorelDRAW's effects, but also will show how to use the Pick tool to get objects just the way you want them.

Pressing the space bar will activate the Pick tool without having to get it with the mouse. It also selects the last object used so you can manipulate it. Pressing it again will toggle to the tool you used last. This works with all tools except the Text tool. You will use the space bar often to select the Pick tool, so this hot-key should become second nature by the end of Section One. It is generally more efficient than using the mouse and toolbar, even if you have the mouse in your hand. Use one hand to hold the mouse, the other to press the space bar.

Pressing the **Tab** key rotates the current selected item between all the objects in the drawing. This trick can be very useful if you have very small or other difficult-to-reach objects. Hold the mouse with your right hand, and keep your left hand resting on the keyboard, with the little finger over the **Tab** and the thumb over the space bar while editing objects.

Selecting Objects

Before you can issue a command or use an option to alter objects CorelDRAW must know which ones are to be affected. This is called *selecting*. A selected object or group of objects has handles (little black boxes) around them. You can use different methods to select objects. The one that works best varies with the way the objects are arranged on the page. Take a minute to draw a few objects on the page and practice selecting them using the techniques outlined here.

The Shift-Click Method

You will need to clear the screen of both objects before continuing, so now is a good time to see how it's done. Press the space bar to activate the Pick tool. There should be handles around the square. Hold the **Shift** key and click on the outline of your first rectangle. The handles will now cover the area around both boxes. This is the shift-click method of selecting objects. As long as you hold the **Shift** key, all objects you click on will be added to the group. Any commands will be carried out on the entire group. To deselect the objects, release the **Shift** key and press on an area without any objects. The handles will disappear. This is one of several ways to select a group of objects. It is especially handy when you have to select several objects that are scattered around the page. Try it once or twice to get the hang of it. From now on the term *shift-click* will be used instead of listing the steps.

Using the Marquee

There is a faster way to select objects if they are in a group. Place the Pick tool above and to the left of the two rectangles. Now drag past the lower right edge of both objects. A dashed blue box called a marquee will appear as the mouse is dragged over the area. Once both objects are entirely within the marquee, release the mouse button. Both objects should now be selected just as with the shift-click method. In Figure 2.5 the marquee is shown around two rectangles. You can use the marquee to group objects for action with any command.

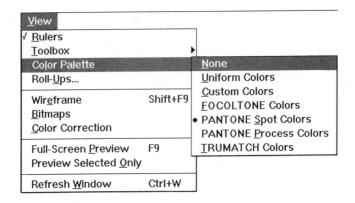

FIGURE 2.5 The Marquee

Space Bar

This key combination places handles around the last object selected and chooses the Pick tool.

Tab Select

If you have an object that is hard to select because it is mixed with other elements of a drawing, press the **Tab** key until handles appear around the object. It may be hard to tell which object is active, so be careful and watch the status line.

Once an object or group of objects has been selected, you can delete it by pressing the **Delete** key.

Transformations with the Pick Tool

The Pick tool can be used to move, rotate, stretch, and resize objects, either individually or in groups. CorelDRAW calls these operations *transformations*. In CorelDRAW 4.0 these functions were the first two options of the Effects menu. Version 5.0 has moved these functions to the Transform roll-up menu. The interactive method performed with the mouse still works exactly as before. Objects must be selected before any transformation can be used. You can perform all the actions described in this section on several objects at the same time, as long as they are all currently selected.

The ease with which you can manipulate objects is a major advantage of a full-powered draw program. When you draw an object, the program is really producing a mathematical formula that describes the object's outline, fill, size, and many other attributes (depending on your selections). You can change the size or even turn an object inside out without worrying about losing print quality or getting jagged lines.

Making a duplicate of an object and creating a mirror or upside-down variation is an easy way to produce a reflection effect, such as the image in a body of water or in a mirror.

Moving Things Around

Moving things around is easy with the Pick tool. Just click on the desired object and drag it with the mouse to the new location. The cursor will change to an arrowheaded cross hair and a dashed blue box will show the area to be covered by the new object. The screen shot in Figure 2.6 shows how it should look. Draw an object and try it now.

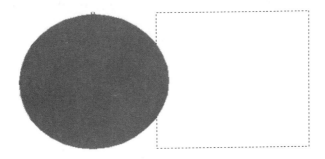

FIGURE 2.6 *Moving an object*

Move the object some more and keep an eye on the status bar. It displays the distance the object is moved, the *x* and *y* coordinates, and the angle of vertical shift. A minus number indicates that the new position is lower than the original.

Scaling Objects

CorelDRAW calls enlarging or shrinking an object *scaling*. Clear the page, draw a circle (use the **Ctrl** key), and press the space bar to activate the Pick tool. The circle is automatically selected. Place the mouse pointer on the lower-right-hand corner handle. Drag (press and hold the left button while moving the mouse) the handle down the page and release the mouse. Your object got bigger but kept the same shape. This is scaling. Scaling is performed when you drag any one of the four corner handles. The result is shown in Figure 2.7. A fill was added to make the object easier to see. Dragging any one of the four corner handles increases the size but maintains the basic shape. As you drag, a dashed blue line will outline a box showing the current area that would be covered by the transformed object. The cursor will look like an angled cross with arrows on the end.

The status bar can be very handy if you want an exact size or ratio to the original object. It tells you the percentage of magnification compared to the original—its height, width, and location of the center. Now drag the handle back up toward the upper left-hand corner. Notice how it gets smaller. Keep going. It will appear to flip upside down as the mouse passes over the upper corner. If you continue to drag, the circle will start growing on the other side. Release the mouse button and draw a rectangle (not a square). Try the same things with it.

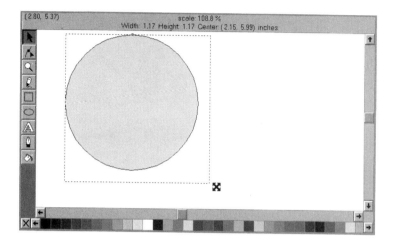

FIGURE 2.7 Scaling an object

Stretching Is Something Else

Stretching changes the shape and size of an object by dragging its center handles. Select your rectangle and drag the left middle handle toward the left side of the work area. Notice how the object changes shape and gets wider. The result should look something like Figure 2.8. The dashed blue rectangle that moves with the cursor shows the area of the stretch. The cursor looks like a line with a pair of arrows on the ends. Notice that you can use all the work area for creating a drawing, but be aware that only the portion on the page will print. Pulling a middle handle (top, bottom, or either side) enlarges or reduces that side, changing its shape. If you drag across an object to the other side, it will flip over. These effects can be used on all objects: those made with a drawing tool, text, or ones imported from another program. Once again the status bar gives you information about the degree of scale and notes which axis (*x* or *y*) is being scaled. Try enlarging and reducing objects using all four of the stretch handles.

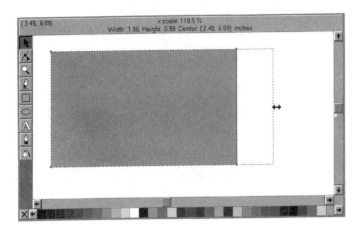

FIGURE 2.8 Stretching objects

Making Mirror Images and Drawing Objects Out from Their Center

You can use the transformation features to create an exact mirror image of an object or group by holding the **Ctrl** key down as you move across an object. Drag the mouse using one of the center side handles across the object. As the mouse goes past the other edge, the object will flip over. You can pull using the top or bottom handles to turn the object upside down. Draw an oblong and see how it works. After you have finished, clear the page.

You can use the **Shift** key to make scaling and stretching work from the center of an object or group out. This is a useful trick for keeping an element of your drawing in exactly the right space.

Leaving and Creating Duplicates

Hold down the **Plus** key (+ from the numeric keypad) and move or resize your rectangle. Now you have two: the original and a duplicate that you moved or resized. This can be used to create drop shadow effects, but there is a real time saver here. If you need to make a number of elements that are the same or almost the same, just make one. Then put it on the side of the work area out of your way. When you need another, just go get it with the **Move/Duplicate** command. Most of the arrows and some of the type used in the illustrations for this book were done this way.

The fastest way to get a copy of an existing object is to select it and press **Ctrl-D**. A second copy of the object will appear on or near the first. The exact location is based on the setting given in the Preferences dialog box under the Special menu.

Rotating

CorelDRAW enables you to perform all kinds of magic on an object. These next two functions give a hint of how easy it is to reshape something on the page. Draw a rectangle in the center of the page. Look at the rectangle in Figure 2.9 with the little arrows around it. Double-click on your object. You should see the same kind of curved handles. They indicate that the rectangle is selected for either rotation or skewing. Clicking on an object once produces handles; double-clicking yields rotating and skewing handles.

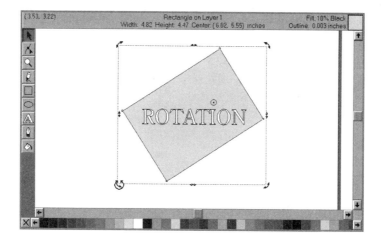

FIGURE 2.9 Rotation

You are going to turn your object from a corner the same way it was done in the example. Place the mouse pointer on one of the corner handles (rotation handles) and hold down the left button and start rotating your object. The cursor should look like the one in the lower-left-hand corner of Figure 2.9, and a blue dashed box should outline your rectangle. Now drag the mouse in an arc. The box will follow your movements, while the status bar gives you the angle of rotation. The screen shot was set up as a demonstration. You won't see the rotated object again until you release the mouse.

Playing with the Center of Rotation

Take a close look above the letter *I* in the word *ROTATION* near the center of the drawing in Figure 2.9. Notice the little circle with a dot in its center. On your screen it should be in the middle of your rectangle. Drag it with the mouse, so that it is located on the right side of your object. Now repeat the rotation and watch what happens. The rectangle now pivots around the dot and circle. If you have trouble seeing it on your screen, use the Zoom tool to close in on it.

Skewing

Now that you know how to get things going in circles, you are ready to get things on the right slant. Delete your object and draw a square using the **Ctrl** key. Double-click on it so that the rotation and skew handles show. Look at Figure 2.10. As with rotation, skewing is performed by dragging a handle but using one of the short handles along the center of a side. As you drag, the mouse pointer changes to a pair of half arrows like the ones on the top of Figure 2.10. A dashed box shows the area where the skewed object will appear. You won't see your new object until you let go of the mouse. Make several skews on all four sides to get the hang of it. Try it with a circle too; then mix the different transformations together.

FIGURE 2.10 Skew controls

Using the Menus and Clearing Transformations

Although using the mouse to perform transformations is quick and intuitive, it can be difficult to get just the right angle, size, or position. The Transform roll-up menu (see Figure 2.12) offers all the effects you have been working with, but instead of using the mouse, values are entered numerically. To access a command, open the Effects menu and click on Transform roll-up, after selecting the desired object(s).

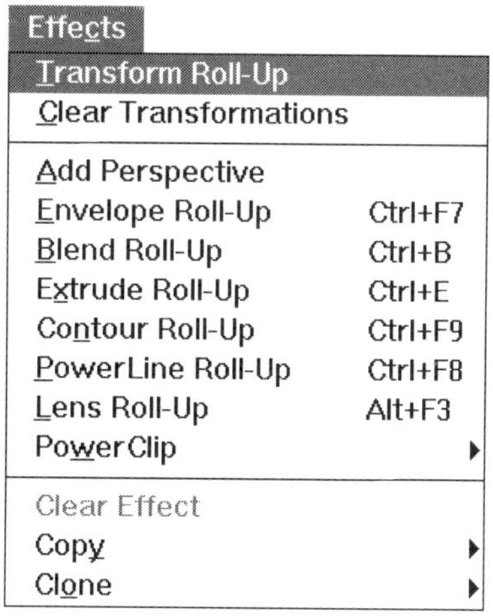

FIGURE 2.11 The Effects menu

The Effects menu offers an additional command right below Transform roll-up: Clear Transformations. This is a **Super-Undo** key that will restore the original shape of your object, no matter how many skews, stretches, and/or rotations have been performed. However, it will not place the object back in its original location. Scale and Mirror on the Transform roll-up (see Figure 2.12) handle both scaling and stretching. Values are entered as the percentage of change desired, and minus numbers are allowed. To mirror an object quickly, just click on the appropriate button. Clicking on Apply to Duplicate will create a copy of the selected object, altered according to your scaling and/or mirror settings. Choose Apply to alter the original object.

Rotate and **Skew** commands are located on the Transform roll-up also, and are both entered in degrees. The compass rose is for reference (see Figure 2.13a). Once again you can choose to leave the original in place and locate a duplicate in the new position.

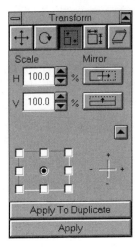

FIGURE 2.12 Scale and Mirror on Transform roll-up

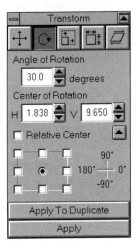

FIGURE 2.13a Rotate and Skew on Transform roll-up

Absolute Positioning

Select an object and open the Position dialog box under the Transform roll-up menu (see Figure 2.13b). Make sure that the Relative Position box is NOT checked. The check boxes appearing to the left with the same pattern as the handles around an object. These boxes (called *nodes*) let us position an object at an exact location in the work area. If you click the center box, the object's center will be placed exactly on the location specified in the two data entry boxes. Here's how to do it.

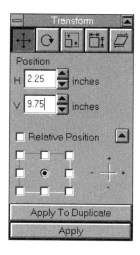

FIGURE 2.13b The Position dialog box

1. Make sure the rulers are visible.
2. Place the mouse cursor on the exact point where you want the object and note the position of the ruler guidelines.
3. Select the object and open the Position dialog box.
4. Uncheck the Relative Position box and select the proper node to key on.
5. Enter the coordinates you wrote down in step 2 and click **OK**.

Undo and Redo

Deleting a selected object is easy, sometimes too easy. So is moving, stretching, and sizing objects. Sometimes you make a mistake and remove, move, or alter an object by accident. CorelDRAW has a safety net. To get the object back if you made a mistake, press **Ctrl-Z**, or choose **Undo** from the Edit menu. Try that and see how it works with some transformations. Version 5.0 has no effective limit to the number of undos, but you can set a limit under the **Preferences** options.

Introducing the Pencil Tool

There are several hidden compartments inside the toolbox on the left-hand side of the CorelDRAW screen. You saw some when you worked with the Outline tool. They help keep the basic interface simple while providing easy access to its more sophisticated features. The Pencil tool is a good example. Click and hold your left mouse button on it now. You should see a fly-out just like the one in Figure 2.14. The one on the left puts the tool in Freehand mode, and the second one places the tool in Bézier mode. Pierre Bézier is the mathematician who first defined the way programs like CorelDRAW edit curved shapes. The next three options are for drawing lines with dimensions—numbers that indicate how long the line is placed next to them. The last option is for drawing callouts which are used to point to objects in a drawing. We'll cover dimensioning in a later chapter. Right now, make sure that your Pencil tool looks like the one on the left side of the fly-out bar. If it does not, drag on its icon with your mouse and then release.

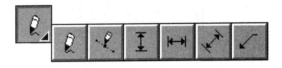

FIGURE 2.14 The Pencil tool

Freehand Mode

Freehand mode is used for drawing quick sketches and roughing out shapes. A line is drawn under the cursor as you drag the mouse. This is like having an electronic pencil, which is how the tool got its name. It sounds easy, doesn't it? Go ahead and practice a few times. Just click on its icon and drag the mouse to form the objects. The cursor will change to a set of cross hairs as you bring it into the work area. Draw a circle, a curve, and a straight line. Then try signing your first name—don't print.

The problem with using Freehand mode for precise drawing is the limited control offered by a mouse. Figure 2.15a shows an example of how coarse the control is. (I don't think I'll start using the Pencil tool in Freehand mode to sign any checks.) Of course it gets a lot better if you have a digitizing tablet like those mentioned in the hardware section of Section Four. Figure 2.15b was created using a Wacom 6- by 9-inch model with a stylus instead of a mouse. Part of the difference is that the stylus is shaped like a pen, which fits the hand a lot better than a mouse. The tablet has another advantage over Microsoft's mouse—absolute tracking. That means that the stylus moves the cursor exactly with your hand movements. A mouse is not nearly as accurate. It was designed to let you move the cursor, click on menus, and drag objects—not draw. But a really good tablet costs up to five or six times what a good mouse does. You have to be a graphics power user to justify the money for a good tablet. There are other ways to get lines looking just right with CorelDRAW.

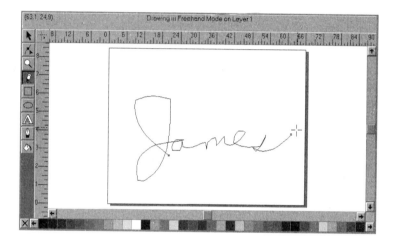

FIGURE 2.15a Freehand drawing with a mouse

FIGURE 2.15b Freehand drawing with a tablet and stylus

Erasing with the Pencil

One way to get a better line is to redraw the parts you don't like. You can use the Pencil tool's built-in eraser to remove part of a Freehand line that isn't the way you want it. Select **File**, **New** and don't save your work; the page should be clear for your next experiment. Make sure the Pencil tool is selected. The status bar should say that you are in Freehand mode. Drag with the mouse to create a line; then without releasing the mouse button, press the **Shift** key and retrace part of the line backward. The section you retrace will disappear. It may take a little practice. If you don't get it just right, the line won't erase. Go ahead and practice a bit.

There is a trick you can use with the eraser to add a straight section to a line drawn in Freehand mode. Start the line by dragging to the point where you want the straight portion to begin; then hold the **Shift** key and move the mouse cursor to the end point, release the **Shift** key, and give the mouse a very gentle nudge. The line segment will be added and you can continue drawing your object. If you pull too far, the straight line will become a gentle curve.

A Better Straight Line

The drag method in Freehand mode leaves a lot to be desired if you are doing critical work, even with a built-in eraser. You are trying to use your skill (with a mouse no less), rather than letting CorelDRAW do the work. The mouse is handy for drawing rough sketches. But the Pencil tool can be used to create very precise lines and curves with a mouse. Place the cursor on the upper-left edge of the page and click once. Let go of the mouse button and bring the cursor down at a 45-degree angle toward the lower-right corner. Notice that the line follows the mouse's movements, like a rubber band attached to a pin. The starting point is anchored to where you first clicked. Now click a second time; that sets the end point. A line is drawn between those points—a perfectly straight line. It's a lot easier when you let the program do the work. Press the space bar to select it and the **Delete** key to remove it.

Try it again, but this time click the starting point near the lower-left corner of the page, release, and move the cursor halfway across and somewhat up the page before double-clicking. The line moves with the mouse until you click the second time, and brings a new line from the second point. Take this line down at about an angle to the right from the first one you drew and single-click. Your result should look like the one in Figure 2.16.

FIGURE 2.16 Drawing lines with the click method

This is the click-drag method for drawing lines. If you single-click at both points, a single line is created. Double-click and the line continues until you click again. Practice a few times until you get the hang of it. Then clear the page.

It's time to create a shape rather than just a line. Start drawing a line straight down, beginning at the top of the page and a little over to the left. Bring it about half the way down and double-click. Bring a second line to the right at a 90-degree angle. Make the new line about as long as the first. Double-click again. Now bring a line back to the starting point. Right on the starting point. Press the space bar once to select the new object. Your screen should look like Figure 2.17. If the right side of the status bar says *Open Path* above the word *Outline*, you missed the start point. Try again. If not you just created a triangle like the one shown here. This triangle can show you some very interesting things.

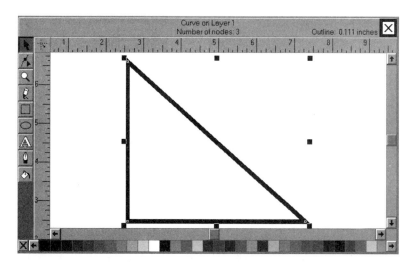

FIGURE 2.17 Creating a triangle

PATHS

You have been drawing lines, but the sets of lines you just drew are different. They form a *closed path*. This is one of CorelDRAW's most important concepts. A path is the line that forms the border of an object. It is not the same thing as the *outline*. An outline follows the shape of the path. Think of the path as the outline under the outline.

CorelDRAW has two kinds of paths, closed and open. If a toy balloon is open, it can't hold air. If it is tied closed, the air stays in. What does that have to do with CorelDRAW? If an object's path is closed, you can fill it. If it has an open path, you can't. Let's prove it. First select the triangle; then click on one of the colors located on the color palette on the bottom of the work area. The triangles fill with color. Draw another triangle next to the one you just finished. If there is not enough room on the page, make the first one smaller. Use the same drag-click technique, but this time don't connect the end of the third line to the starting point; make it a little short. Select the new object and try to fill it the same way you filled the first one. It won't work, will it?

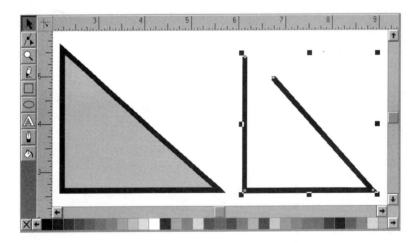

FIGURE 2.18 Closed and open paths

Look at the right side of the status bar with the open shape selected in Figure 2.18. It tells you the object has an open path and the X in the block means "no fill." The center of the bar notes that the shape is a curve (you'll get to that shortly) with four nodes. They appear as little boxes at the end of each line segment. Now select the triangle and look at the status bar. It has three nodes, one at each joint. The right side of the bar shows the color of your fill. We will use paths a lot later in the book. The important thing now is to understand that a closed object can have a fill; an open one can't. It's like working with a gas in a container. If the container is open, the gas can escape, leaving it empty.

GETTING SOLID WITH THE FILL TOOL

Now that you know the difference between an open and a closed path, you can play with fills. *Play* may be the operative word. There are many variations with fills, more than with outlines. The outline defines the visual shape of an object; the fill controls the appearance of its interior.

Fills do a lot more than just add color to an object. You can simulate depth and shading, introduce patterns and textures into a drawing, and create backgrounds. Like outlines, the basic options are contained within a fly-out menu, with most options available in a roll-up menu as well. Once again, Section One of this book deals with the basic terms and procedures, and advanced concepts and practical applications are covered in Section Two.

Let's start with the naming of names; then you can go through the options in detail.

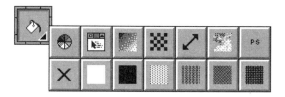

FIGURE 2.19 The Fill Tool fly-out menu

Fill Tool Components

- **PaintBucket.** This is the Fill tool icon located on the toolbar. Clicking it opens the fly-out menu.
- **Uniform Fill Dialog Box.** This icon provides access to the complete set of **Uniform Fill** options.
- **Roll-up Menu.** Clicking here opens an on-screen roll-up menu that offers quick access to the most commonly used Fill options.

- **Fountain Fills.** The fountain fill blends one color into another with a radial, linear, or conical flow. Radial fills gradually shift from one color to another as a series of circular bands. The linear fill blend goes from one edge to the other. Conical fills have a high point and wash down from there, like an inverted ice cream cone. You can set the number of steps to produce either a coarse or fine blend. CorelDRAW enables the user to set the angle of fill, so fountains are an easy way to produce dramatic (or subtle) lighting and shading effects. Clicking on this icon opens the Fountain Fill dialog box.

- **Two Color Pattern Fills.** This accesses a menu that contains two-color bitmap fill patterns that can be used for creating backgrounds. The Tile feature enables the user to produce a repeating pattern across the inside of an object. You can create your own bitmap fills with a Paint program, including CorelPHOTO-PAINT. If you wish to use an object (such as a logo) created in CorelDRAW as a Pattern fill, export it as a bitmap. Patterns can also be set from the roll-up menu.

- **Full-Color Fills.** These are vector fills that work much like the Pattern fills mentioned earlier, and they can be tiled. Unlike bitmap fills, these can be edited within CorelDRAW. Clicking on this icon opens the dialog box. They can also be set from the roll-up menu.

- **Texture Fills.** These are the newest addition to the CorelDRAW fill collection and offer almost an infinite variety of complex patterns. They do require a lot of system resources, and we will save working with them for another chapter.

- **PostScript Textures.** These are the legacy of a Corel Systems summer intern who came up with the idea of adding textured pattern fills that could be almost infinitely varied, based on the PostScript language. He finished the project, and it was added to the program. There is little documentation and support. Be aware that you must have a PostScript printer to see these fills. They can be very complex and have long printing times. You must set a number of variables in the dialog box to define the appearance of the pattern. These patterns do not display on the computer screen; they must be printed.

- **No Fill/Remove Fill.** Clicking on the **X** removes any present fill on a selected object. The same effect can be obtained without opening the menu by using the left mouse button to click on the **X** at the left of the Color Palette located at the bottom of the CorelDRAW window.

- **Standard Tints.** As with the Outline fly-out, standard shades of gray can be chosen directly from the Fill fly-out menu. They are located on the lower row of the fly-out menu and include white, black, and 10, 30, 50, and 70 percent gray.

Be sure that all the colors used in a drawing follow the same color model unless you need to mix types for some specific task. Using both spot and process colors in the same illustration can cause problems and add expense at print time. You can use the Fill dialog box to specify the color model and method of a fill, but that won't change the colors used in the Color Palette located at the bottom of the screen. You must use the **Color Palette** option from the View menu to do that.

Setting a Default Fill

If a drawing will contain a number of objects using the same fill, you can save time by defining a new default fill and creating them all at once. To do that, attempt to open the appropriate fill dialog box without having an object selected first. You will see a dialog box like the one in Figure 2.20. The radio buttons let you choose to limit the effects to all objects, only text, or all nontext. You can't use two-color or full-color patterns as the default fill. Once you have chosen the scope of the default setting and clicked **OK**, the regular default fill dialog box will open. The default will apply until you repeat the process.

Setting Uniform Fills

Uniform fills are the simplest ones CorelDRAW offers. They place a single color inside the currently selected object's path. (Remember, you can fill only closed paths, not open ones.) There are four different ways to set a uniform fill after selecting an object:

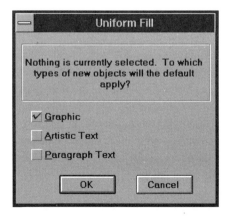

FIGURE 2.20 The Default Fill dialog box

- With the preset shades located on the bottom row of the Fill fly-out.
- By clicking on one of the colors in the on-screen palette located at the bottom in the CorelDRAW window.
- By choosing a color from the Uniform Fill dialog box that opens when you click on the Uniform Fill icon in the Fill fly-out.
- By choosing a palette color or using the **Edit** button on the Fill roll-up menu.

The Uniform Fill is the simplest type. You have only two real considerations: using the right color model and getting the exact color you want. Setting the fill is simple. If you did not read the color section under outlines in Chapter 1, you might want to review it now, because you are going to be working with color a lot in this section of the chapter.

As you can see, the only difference between the appearance of the Uniform Fill and Uniform Outline (shown in Chapter 1) dialog boxes is the names at the top. They work exactly the same. The arrows, buttons, and models are identical. The real difference is in what they do. The outline box controls the line around an object, and the fill box defines the contents.

You should still have your triangle on the screen. Go ahead and use all four methods to set different uniform fills. Change the outline and its color as well. As you go further with exercises, specific details for outlines and fills will not be given.

Use the Roll-up Menus to Set Fills

Any time you have a lot of work (or a tricky task) to do with the Fill tool consider using the roll-up menu. It can be left open and placed anywhere on your Windows desktop. You can even use the options under Preferences so that favorite roll-ups always appear in the same place every time you load CorelDRAW. They let you quickly set a color or access advanced dialog boxes without having to open the regular menus. The following explanation of the basic operation of the Fill roll-up menus will help you use it as we work through the Outline tool features. The icons on the left side of the Fill tool roll-up menu work much like their counterparts on the Fill tool fly-out, offering quick access to the different fill options. Click on the one matching the type of fill you want to use; the area on the upper right of the menu changes to offer most of the available options. I'll cover them in detail as we work with that type of fill. All four fills have the same buttons on the bottom. The **Update From** bar lets you copy all the fill attributes from one object to another. The **Edit** bar opens the full dialog box for that type of fill, and the **Apply** button executes your choices.

Open the Fill fly-out and click on the **Roll-up** icon. Now select your object and click on one of the colors in the palette at the bottom of the screen. Draw another object and select it. Click on the **Update From** button. The cursor will change from the Pick tool to a thick black arrow with the word *From* on it. Click on the last object you filled. The new object's fill now matches the older one's. You can select or group several objects together and choose the **From** option. All the objects will take on the chosen fill. These three basic functions work the same for all four Fill roll-ups. Of course, the dialog box for the **Edit** option will vary with the type of fill.

All three methods for setting uniform fills do exactly the same thing. Use whichever is best for you based on the task at hand. Practice a bit with all three methods before continuing. Create several objects and use different-colored fills for each.

Getting Fancy with PostScript Halftone Screens

A halftone is a continuous-tone picture, like a photograph, that has been prepared for printing. Since ink and printing can't give all the shades found in such an object, various-sized dots must be used to simulate them. In dark areas the dots are large and close together; in light areas they are small and farther apart. Traditional methods for creating halftones required taking another picture of the original with a screen in front of it covered with the reverse of the halftone pattern. The resulting image is reduced to a series of dots. You can see this in use by looking closely at any photo in a magazine or newspaper. Newspapers generally use a coarser dot pattern than magazines, because the paper and inks they use block up easily.

So what does all that have to do with CorelDRAW's outlines? The PostScript language offers a variety of dot shapes that can be used to create halftone images. Although you can use them to halftone imported bitmaps, they can be used to make some interesting fills for backgrounds. This feature only works with PostScript-compatible output devices. If you have a compatible printer, you can follow along with steps under the next heading.

Let's experiment. Draw a rectangle that covers the page. Don't bother to remove any existing objects. If the page is blank, draw a couple of shapes and give them a uniform fill first. Select the large rectangle. Open the Fill fly-out and select the Uniform Fill icon. Make sure that the **Show** option is set to Pantone Spot (see Figure 2.21). There are PostScript halftones with process color, but not much variety. Click on **PostScript Options**.

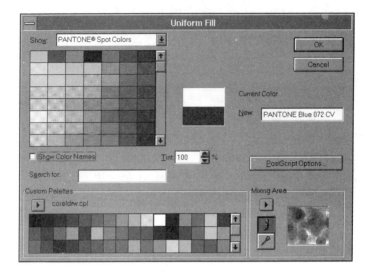

FIGURE 2.21 The Spot Fill dialog box

Choose one of the halftone Screen Types using the scroll arrows shown in Figure 2.22. Then set the Frequency to 10 lines per inch (lpi) and the angle to zero degrees. Newspapers use a 65- to 80-line-per-inch screen for photos, and magazines use from 100 to 120 lines per inch and up. The finer the pattern, the better the reproduction. That's fine for photos, but you want to see the pattern in your fill. Also, a 300-dots-per-inch (dpi) laser printer will be hard pressed to handle more than about 60 lpi.

A number of shapes are available, including dots, lines, diamonds, stars, and circles. Since you are using a low frequency, the angle of the pattern will be visible, so setting it should be a part of the design. With circle fills the angle won't make any difference, but it will with diamonds, stars, and lines. Choose **OK**. It looks like nothing happened! You won't see either PostScript screens or textures on a monitor. If you export to bitmap, the pattern will be visible, and it will print. Draw several objects and give each a different halftone fill.

Chapter 2: Filling in the Blanks

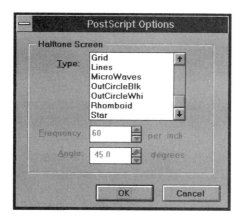

FIGURE 2.22 Sample PostScript halftones

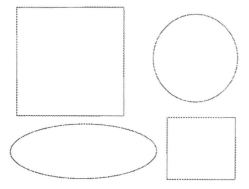

FIGURE 2.23 Sample PostScript halftone patterns

Open the Arrange menu, order and choose the **To Back** option under the **Order** selection to put the large rectangle behind all the others. Open the File menu and choose **Print**, **OK**, and the dialog box defaults. The PostScript Pattern fills the background of the page. You can create a wide variety of patterns by adjusting the frequency, angle, tint, and color settings.

PostScript Textures

PostScript textures are probably CorelDRAW's most obscure type of fill. Part of the reason is that you must have a PostScript output device to use this kind of pattern. The main reasons for the lack of use are probably the complexity of the controls and the unpredictability of the results. Each fill has at least four settings, and you can't see how they will look until you print them. The more complex fills can take a very long time to print. They are set by choosing the PS icon on the Fill tool fly-out and choosing the pattern type from the dialog box. The control options vary based on the type of pattern you select. In Figure 2.24a the Background Gray is set to a minus value. That makes the pattern transparent. The random seed factor (see Figure 2.24b) determines the number of pattern elements in a given area of the fill. Appendix D in the CorelDRAW manual gives samples of each pattern with several different settings. If you want to experiment with PS textures, use the values in the reference manual as a starting point.

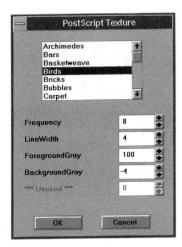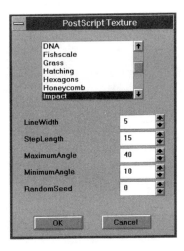

FIGURES 2.24a and b PostScript texture settings

Using Two-Color Fills

Use the **New** command to clear your page and then draw a rectangle. We are going to work with bitmap patterns, also known as two-color fills. They are used to create backgrounds and patterns with two colors and offer a lot of flexibility. The poster designed by artist Jan Selman showcased in Section Two is an excellent example of how to use bitmap fills creatively. Most types of CorelDRAW fills have a lot of options, so it pays to experiment.

Make sure your rectangle is selected; then open the Fill fly-out and click on the checkerboard-like icon on the top row. You will see a dialog box that looks like that in Figure 2.25.

Use Predefined Bitmap Fills

Figure 2.25 shows the basic two-color fill selector. Click on the **Small** radio button located just under the square pattern of dots near the left center of the dialog box and watch the size of the dots in the window get smaller and closer together. The square window is both a preview and selection aid. Click on it. A fly-out box like the one in Figure 2.26 opens under it. It offers the standard patterns that ship with CorelDRAW. You will learn how to make custom patterns in a minute, but for now we will work with these.

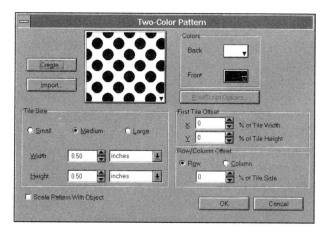

FIGURE 2.25 The Two-Color Pattern Fill dialog box

Double-click on the second pattern down in the left row to select it. (It looks like a series of rectangles in staggered rows.) The example in Figure 2.26 has a Pick tool cursor over it. Notice how the Preview box now has the same pattern. That's how it works. You can choose any pattern available in the fly-out by clicking on the preview and then double-clicking on the one you want. Watch the Preview box as you click on the **Large** and **Small** radio buttons; then return to the **Medium** setting. The size of the pattern was modified as you changed the option.

Look at the Back and Front areas to the right of the Preview/Selection box. See Figure 2.25. This is where you set the two colors. There are two ways to do it. The default is a white background color and a black foreground. Click on a colored button (in this example they are labeled *black* and *white*) to the right of the words *Back* and *Front*. A quick-pick palette like that in Figure 2.27b is displayed. Choose the **More** button and you get the full Color Selection dialog box that provides complete CorelDRAW color controls. This dialog box should be getting familiar to you by now. If you need a refresher on how to use it, go back to the Outlines section in Chapter 1.

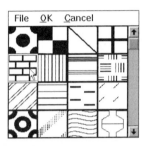

FIGURE 2.26 The Pattern selection fly-out

Using the quick-pick palette, make the Back a shade of red; then set the Front color to white the same way. Choose **OK** to exit the dialog box. The rectangle now looks like a brick wall. That's how to set a standard bitmap fill. Next, let's examine how to fine-tune a pattern's appearance using the Tile functions.

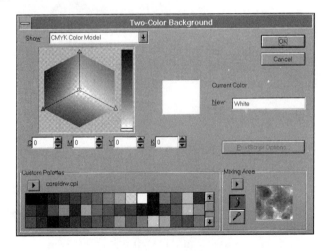

FIGURE 2.27a The Background Color dialog box

Chapter 2: Filling in the Blanks

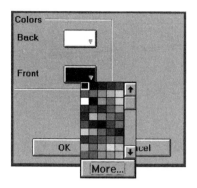

FIGURE 2.27b The Two-Color palette

Tile Settings

Click on the **Tiling** button. Your screen should have an expanded dialog box like the one in Figure 2.28, but your Preview and Tile settings will be different. Pattern fills are like electronic ceramic tiles. They are placed together in squares to make a background or fill. Tile Size and Offset control the relative width-to-height ratios and how the tiles are overlapped. Part of the reason the "brick wall" pattern was used was to make it easier for you to understand tiling. Adjust the width and height settings with the arrows and your mouse. Watch what happens to the pattern in the Preview window. When you have a pleasing look, play with the **Offset** setting on the right side of the box and then click **OK**. These adjustments can be used with any pattern.

Think of the patterns as bricks. You can stack them one on top of the other or stagger the rows. You can get different-looking walls by using thinner or thicker bricks. The color of both mortar and bricks can be changed, and you can vary the amount of mortar used to separate the bricks. Try some of the other patterns and get a feel for the flexibility of two-color fills.

CREATING CUSTOM FILLS

Existing two-color fills provided with the program can be edited within CorelDRAW to form new patterns. You can create new ones from scratch, or from imported images produced in programs like CorelPHOTO-PAINT, included as part of CorelDRAW 5.0. Suppose you wanted to create an effect like a rough-faced brick wall rather than the even texture of the one you just used. The easiest way would be to use the editor built into the Two-Color Fill dialog box. Make sure the rectangle you filled is selected; then open the dialog box and choose the **Create** button to the left of the Two-Color Pattern window. You will see a dialog box that looks like Figure 2.29.

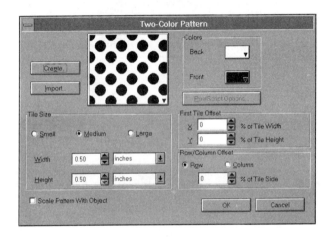

FIGURE 2.28 The Tiling controls

The large area with the squares in Figure 2.29a is a bitmap grid that is used to design or edit two-color pattern fills. Each square represents one pixel in the pattern. You can see the blackened boxes that make up the existing "brick wall" pattern of the selected object. The mouse is used to darken a square by clicking on it with the left mouse button. The right button is used to erase a square. You can drag to draw or erase a line of pixels.

The **Bitmap Size** radio buttons to the right set the number of pixels per inch. Select each one to see how they affect the grid. The smaller the pixels, the better the detail or resolution—and the more complex the image and final drawing. The **Pen Size** option determines the number of blocks that will darken each time you click the mouse in the editing area. Use the coarser resolutions for patterns with straight lines and little detail. If you want to include diagonal lines or curved shapes, increase the resolution.

Chapter 2: Filling in the Blanks

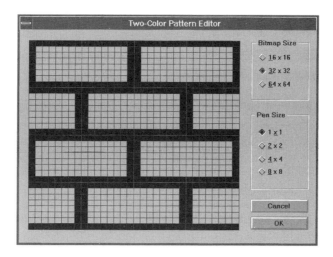

FIGURE 2.29a Initial Two-Color Editor

Figure 2.29b shows how your pattern might look after some editing. Go ahead and make yours look something like it. Just click where you want to change an area. Areas that appear darker in the editor will be located in the front plane in the final pattern. After you have edited a pattern, clicking **OK** will add it to the collection of those available; choosing **Cancel** will abandon your work without saving.

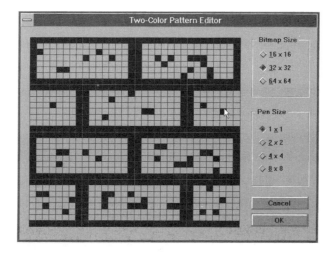

FIGURE 2.29b Edited pattern fill

If you get into the bitmap pattern edit box and don't create a pattern, exit by clicking **Cancel**. Don't click **OK**! That would add a blank box to the pattern palette.

Using Bitmap Images as Fills

You can import a bitmap file like a scanned logo or photo and define it as a two-color pattern fill. The **Import** button opens a file selection box and allows you to bring in an image in any CorelDRAW-supported file format. There is more information on file formats with their various advantages and limitations in the chapter on the Mosaic program and file management. Some special limits apply only to bitmaps imported for use as two-color fills.

- Files created with resolutions over 256 dpi will be reduced to 256 dpi.
- The CorelDRAW Two-Color Pattern editor you just used can't work with files above 64 dpi. You must reduce higher-resolution files before importing them if you want to use this editor. That may be too coarse for some purposes. You can also use another editor before importing to clean up an image.
- Importing bitmap images with more than two colors can produce unexpected (and not always acceptable) results. The best bet is to simplify the image and save it as a two-color bitmap before importing it.
- When you use transformations with an object containing a bitmap fill, the object will change size and rotate normally, but the fill will stay the same. You may need to tailor a fill if you plan to perform sizing, scaling, or rotations.
- When you modify a two-color fill, the original Back color is white and the Foreground tone is black. Changing to another color is handled using the dialog box.

Two-color fills can produce very pleasing effects if they are handled right, and they are the easiest way to use simple scanned artwork as a background. Bitmaps make intensive use of a PC's resources, so planning is very important to ensure reasonable performance when working with them. Complex fills can slow screen activity and print times. Printers with limited RAM may not print properly with some complex fills.

Full-Color Pattern Fills

Although full-color (vector) fills are much like the two-color fills you just worked with, there is a fundamental difference. Full-color fills are really a special kind of CorelDRAW file. You can create and edit them like any other drawing. The only exception is that they are saved with a .PAT extension. Notice the similarity in the dialog boxes.

Clear the page and draw a large circle. Select it, open the Fill fly-out, and choose the Full-Color Pattern icon. It looks like a diagonal line with arrows on the ends. Click on the **Tile** button. Click on the **Tiling** square Preview window in the center. Your dialog box should now look like the one in Figure 2.30. Pick one of the fills and click **OK**. The circle is now filled with the selected pattern. Rotate the circle; then enlarge and reduce it. The pattern does not change at all; it maintains the same size and orientation. Once again, this is just like a two-color pattern. Experiment with the tiling options and try out several of the fills. Get a feel for how they operate and for how long it takes to redraw the screen.

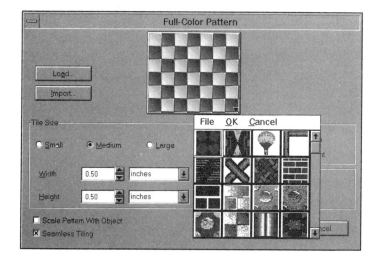

FIGURE 2.30 Full-Color Pattern Fill dialog box

Working with Full-Color Patterns

With bitmap fills a special built-in editor allowed you to modify a pattern. You use the main CorelDRAW program for editing or creating vector fills. In fact, you can save any CorelDRAW file for use as a vector fill. Select **Open** from the File menu. Click on the **List Files of Type** roll-down menu at the lower left of the dialog box. Choose the

Pattern File (*.PAT) option. See the sample in Figure 2.33. A .PAT file is really just a regular .CDR CorelDRAW file that has been designated for use as a full-color fill. Located in the COREL50\CUSTOM\ directory are a number of predefined vector patterns. Open the one called HEXES2.PAT. It is the one on the page in the screen shot shown in Figure 2.31.

The fill shown in Figure 2.31 looks fairly complicated but is fairly easy to create using some of CorelDRAW's more advanced features. The blue dots in a pattern across the work area are the grid, which will be discussed later in this chapter. For now turn it off. Double-click on the ruler at the top of the work area; then click off the Show Grid box in the lower left-hand corner of the dialog box that opens and choose **OK**.

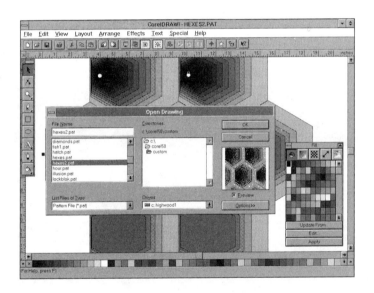

FIGURE 2.31 Editing full-color patterns

You are going to change the pattern, save it, and use it to fill another object. Click on one of the colors in the Color Palette so that the pattern has uniform fill. Open the File menu and choose **Save As**. Name the new pattern TEXT.PAT and press **Enter**. Open a new drawing and create three pie shapes using the Ellipse and Shape tools.

Select an object. Go back to the Full-Color Pattern dialog box and click on the Preview window. Use the scroll bars and find your new fill; then double-click on it. The pie shape now has the new fill. Use other fills with the rest of the objects. Full-color patterns are an easy way to add complex backgrounds to a drawing. If your object is very complex, it can slow down printing. If you find that file size or print times are a problem, study the section on simplifying drawings later in the book. It may offer tips that can solve the problem, or at least reduce it to manageable proportions.

The Quick and Easy Pattern Fill

There is an easy way to copy anything on the CorelDRAW work area into a pattern fill object—either two-color or full-color. Go to the File menu and open one of the CorelDRAW example files located in the Samples subdirectory. Open the Special menu and choose **Create Pattern**. You will get a dialog box asking which type you want, two-color or full-color. Choose **Full-color** and click **OK**. The cursor will change into a special crosshair marquee. Use it to draw a box around the page. The program will prompt you for a file name, and the area will be added as a pattern. If you choose to create a bitmap fill, the saving process is automatic; you won't be prompted.

The Pattern Roll-up Menus

Both types of pattern fills can be created and controlled using the Fill roll-up menu. Figure 2.32a shows the Two-Color roll-up menu and Figure 2.32b displays the Full-Color menu. Both are accessed by clicking on the second icon from the left on the top row in the Fill fly-out. The menu can be placed anywhere on the screen, and the mode can be selected by clicking on the appropriate icon on the mini-toolbar located on its left side. The upper right has a Preview window, with preset palette buttons positioned right below it. The **Edit** menu button opens the full dialog box. You must click on the **Apply** button to make any changes to an object's fill effective.

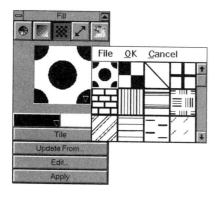 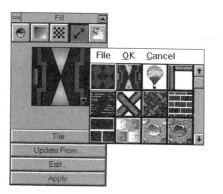

FIGURES 2.32a and b The Two-Color roll-up menu and the Full Color roll-up menu

Fountain Fills

Here is where you get to the really fun part of fills. These fills get their name because they flow from one color to another, like water falling from a fountain. There are three types. *Linear* washes from one color to another from edge to edge of an object. *Radial* moves out from a center point in a circular pattern, changing colors along the way. The *Conical* type looks like an upside-down ice-cream cone, with the fill rising to a peak. You can control the angle, colors, and number of steps. The origin point can even be outside the visible area. This is the tool that enables you to give depth and shading to objects to and simulate lighting conditions. All the different color models are available for use with these fills. You will see how some of that is accomplished in the following exercise, and in greater detail in the projects presented in Section Two. Right now we will cover basic fountain fill controls. The conical and ribbon effects will be saved for later.

Creating Basic Fountain Fills and Adjusting the Fill Angle

Open a new drawing. Create a circle that covers about a quarter of the page and select it. Open the Fountain Fill dialog box by using the **F11** hot-key. It will look something like the example in Figure 2.33. The three radio boxes toggle the selection between linear, conical, and radial fills. The Preview box indicates which one is selected and is used to see how the final fill will appear. The main area of the Fountain Fill roll-up menu serves the same function. Click on the **Radial** button and then place your pointer in the upper-right-hand area of the Preview and click.

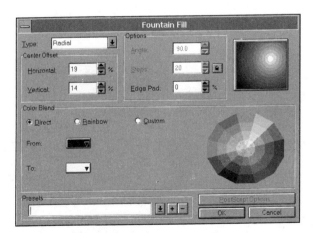

FIGURE 2.33 The Fountain Fill dialog box

Click on the **From** button and pick a red color from the palette box; then choose a blue color the same way using the **To** button. Now click **OK**. The roll-up has been placed next to it. Notice how the radial fill is centered where you clicked. Also note that the fill is based on the total area of the object's bounding box, not on a circular shape. All fountain fills are based on the dimensions of the bounding box—not on the shape.

Convert your circle to a linear fill. Select it and reopen the dialog box. Just click the **Linear** radio button and **OK** the change. Now the object is filled evenly from the top. Try the same fills with a rectangle and a pie shape. Then experiment with altering the angle of the fill using both types of fills. When you are finished, clear the page and draw another large circle.

Adjusting the Edge Padding

CorelDRAW enables you to control the amount of start and stop (or To and From) color in a fountain fill. Since a fill is based on the bounding box, you can set the rate and degree of color shift from the edge of the bounding box. This is called the Edge Pad and runs from zero to 45 percent. It is entered in the lower-right portion of the dialog box. Choose some pleasing colors and experiment with different padding factors.

Setting the Number of Stripes

Notice how much smoother the circles appear in the padding examples. This is because I varied the number of gradations or steps in the object's fill. Two settings control this. The **Preview Fountain Stripes** entry in the **Display** portion of the Preferences menu determines the number of stripes seen on screen. A higher number looks better but will take longer to draw. The **Fountain Stripes** option (see Figure 2.34) in the Print/Options box accessed via the Files menu determines the number of steps in the final print. This is only available for PostScript printers. Once again a higher number is smoother but takes longer. Non-PostScript printers default to sixty-four stripes. You can use these settings to control the visual effect of a fountain fill. There is only one setting for an entire drawing.

The Fill roll-up menu (Figure 2.34) enables you to set both radial and linear fills on screen without using the fly-out. It is just like the other roll-ups available for fills. The Preview window works just like the one in the dialog box, and you must Apply changes before they take effect. The exercise in this chapter deals with fountain fills, so feel free to try the roll-up menu when you are doing it.

FIGURE 2.34 The Fill Tool roll-up menu

RIGHT ON THE MARK: PLACING OBJECTS PRECISELY

The computer's virtual page makes it difficult to be sure that an object is placed exactly where you want it. It's not easy to tell if what appears on the screen is how things will look like when they're printed, and it's hard to be sure that objects are placed properly. So CorelDRAW offers a variety of tools and commands for precise placement of objects in relation to the page, each other, and specific locations in a drawing. These include rulers, a grid, on-screen guidelines, and the ability to align objects to each other.

Using the Rulers

Most traditional illustrators keep a variety of special measuring devices close at hand to measure, size, and place objects in a drawing. CorelDRAW offers virtual rulers that can be set to one of several units of measure. To turn the rulers on, click on the **Rulers** entry under the View menu. A checkmark should appear on the left-hand side of the option. They are located along the upper and left-hand edges of the work area, just inside the status and tool bars.

Chapter 2: Filling in the Blanks

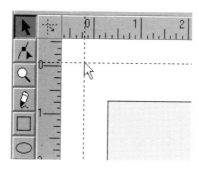

FIGURES 2.35 The CorelDRAW rulers

The rulers' unit of measure is set by defining the Grid Frequency. Open the Grid & Scale Setup dialog box, accessed through the Layout menu, and click on **Grid & Scale Setup**. A dialog box will open looking much like the one shown in Figure 2.36. See the menu I opened in the lower-right section. The Horizontal menu determines the ruler on the top, and the Vertical menu determines the one on the right. You can use whichever works best for you. Professionals who work a lot with type use picas across the top and inches on the side. Points and picas are the normal units of measure for typesetting. Some material on traditional layout tools is included in Part Three later in the book.

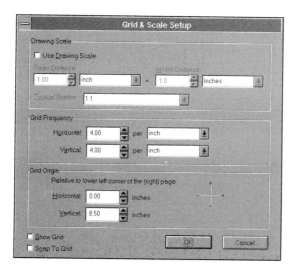

FIGURE 2.36 Grid settings

The mouse position is shown at all times as a dashed line on the rulers when they are visible. This makes it very easy to determine an object's exact location and size on the page. You can see the lines just inside the zeros on the rulers in the screen shot. You can adjust the zero point of the rulers at any time with the mouse. The *zero point* is where measurements start both vertically and horizontally for the program. Just place the pointer in the upper corner of the rulers and drag it to the desired starting position. When you release the button, the zero point will be aligned with that location in the work area. This is very handy. I usually put the zero point at the upper-left-hand corner of the page.

In CorelDRAW 5.0 the rulers are moveable. This is really slick, like having an electronic T-square right on the screen. All you have to do to move them is place the mouse pointer on the one to be repositioned and shift-click-drag it into place.

You can also set the Grid Frequency easily by double-clicking on a ruler. The Grid Setup menu will open at once. This box is the fastest way to set many of the CorelDRAW snap and measurement options.

Using Guidelines

The rulers help, but it can still be difficult to see if an object is exactly where you want it or if several objects are lined up together. That's where the *guidelines* come in handy. They are non-printing dashed horizontal and vertical lines that can be placed anywhere in the work area. They can be created from within the Guidelines Setup dialog box available under the Layout menu, but the easiest way is usually by dragging them from a ruler. Just put the mouse cursor on the appropriate ruler (top for horizontal and left for vertical); then drag the mouse to the desired position. Look at Figure 2.37. The mouse cursor shows where a line is being dragged into place. The dashed line on the ruler will help in getting a precise placement. If you turn on the **Snap To Guidelines** option in the Layout menu, objects placed near one will snap into alignment with it when moved or created.

Guidelines are handy for lining up objects and dividing the page as visual cues for layout and design. In Figure 2.37 I have pulled a vertical line to the exact center of the drawing. This enables me to see how the type balances in relation to the flags. The line under the type serves the same function. If you wanted to resize the text halfway up the flag, the line would make a good boundary. You can have as many guides on the page as you want. To remove them just drag them back inside a ruler. It is a good habit always to leave the rulers and status bar visible. Only turn on a Snap function when you need to. It can be frustrating to have objects snapping to something when you don't want them to. If you want to know the exact coordinates of a certain guideline relative to the ruler, just double-click on it. The Guidelines dialog box will open with that line active and displayed in the position entry box. You can also use it to add, delete, or move a line without using the mouse.

FIGURE 2.37 Using the CorelDRAW guidelines

USING THE GRID

The *grid* is another tool for precisely aligning objects on the page. Imagine it as a pattern of dots spaced at even intervals across the page. It can serve as a visual reference or you can set it to snap objects to a specific location, much like the guidelines. You must have the desired features enabled for them to work. A grid can be used to snap objects even if the grid is hidden and can be visible without invoking the Snap function. Beware that if both a grid point and a guideline are close to the a desired position point, the object will snap to the guideline rather than the grid. Several settings affect how it works. The **Set for Global Units** options is used with the Dimension mode of the Pencil tool. We'll cover that later, so don't worry about it now. Here are what the other Grid Setup functions control.

- **Grid Frequency.** The spacing of the grid dots, readings on the status bar, and units of measure for the rulers are based on the Grid Frequency settings. The smallest setting is seventy-two lines per inch, or 1 point. This is used for typesetting-style projects. You must specify the frequency manually; it does not automatically adjust when the unit of measure is modified.
- **Grid Origin.** This is set in the Grid Frequency box and determines where the 0,0 (zero) point is located. All coordinates for other measurements are referenced from here, including the status bar. The default is the lower left-hand corner of the page. The easy way to set this value is by dragging the ruler cross hairs from the Grid Frequency box located in the box where the rulers intersect.
- **Show Grid.** When it is enabled, this option shows the grid as a series of blue dots across the work area. The spacing is based on the Grid Frequency settings. The grid does not have to be visible for the Snap function to operate.
- **Snap To Grid.** This option can be toggled on and off from the Layout menu, with the Grid Setup dialog box, or using the **Ctrl-Y** hot-key. When it is active, the grid acts like a magnet, and the status bar shows a note in the lower left corner saying *Snap To Grid*. When an object's bounding box is close to a grid marker, it will snap to that point. If this setting is on, it will limit the amount of cursor movement during transformations. **Snap to Grid** works even if the grid is not visible on the screen. This feature does not affect drawing done with the Pencil tool, selection of objects with the Pick or Shape tools, rotations, and skew effects. Objects created before the grid was activated are not automatically moved or realigned by this command. The **Constrain** key will override **Snap to Grid**.

Snap Points

There are specific snap points on each type of object, shown in diagrams contained in CorelDRAW's On-line Help under the Layout menu commands and on page 147 of the CorelDRAW 5.0 manual. They let you use one object to align or resize another. You will work with snap points in more detail later, after you have learned some skills needed to use them effectively.

A Rule of Thumb

Leave the status bar and rulers on all the time, but limit use of the guidelines and grid. The status bar gives a wealth of information, and you can learn a good bit about CorelDRAW just by being aware of it as you work. The rulers take up little screen space and make it easy to pull a guide or reset the grid units. It is a good idea to make it a habit to adjust the reference point to the upper left-hand corner of the page.

Measurement tools are often overlooked by users, as are many of CorelDRAW's powerful tools. The simple interface makes it easy to use the program, but mastery and productivity come through looking beneath the surface. Many of the commands and options offer computerized versions of traditional tools. Examining how an artist approaches a project can help you visualize how to use your PC to produce the same results. You will be using that method as you work through the projects in Section Two. The more you use the techniques as you go along, the more experience you will gain with the program.

Alignment using the Arrange Menu

The Arrange menu shown in Figure 2.38 offers commands for aligning objects with each other and the underlying page.

Although CorelDRAW is a two-dimensional program, it has the ability to arrange objects on top of each other and onto layers. That gives you the ability to arrange the elements of a drawing by function or "depth." This menu is also used to group and combine objects and to shuffle the order of objects on the page. You'll see how to use these features when you get to the next exercise.

Working with Layers

CorelDRAW has the ability to place objects on different groups, rather like the acetate cells used by animation artists. This enables you to do things easily with a group of objects. Layers are managed through a roll-up menu (see Figure 2.39) accessed via the Layout menu or by pressing the **Ctrl-F3** combination. Press those two keys together now to see the roll-up menu. The basic CorelDRAW file has four layers listed on the roll-up.

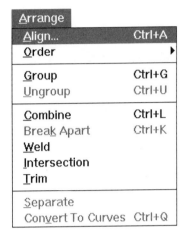

FIGURE 2.38 The Arrange menu

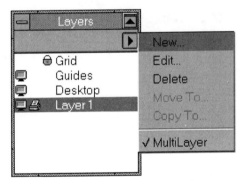

FIGURE 2.39 The Layers roll-up menu

- **Grid Layer.** This is the "home" of the grid discussed before. It cannot be made active or drawn on, but you can print the Grid.
- **Guides Layer.** The Guides layer holds the guidelines explained in the preceding section. You can make it active and draw objects on it that can be used to align objects just like guidelines. The Guides layer can be made active and printed.

- **Desktop.** This layer is used for multiple page layouts, making the moving of objects easy. Objects dragged off the printable page are placed on the Desktop layer. Objects dragged back or to the page are placed on the nearest layer. Objects are visible at all times when on the Desktop layer. To move objects easily from page to page, drag the object off the desired page, change to a new page, and drag it back on.
- **Layer One.** Layer One is the activated default layer that contains all drawn and imported objects in the normal work area unless you add a new layer and make it active.

Click on the arrowhead pointing to the right located at the top right-hand side of the menu (not the one pointing up). This is the submenu that enables you to add, delete, move, and copy objects to and from layers. You will work with these features in Section Two. Click on the **Up Arrow** button on the top of the menu to close the roll-up menu.

Easy Alignment

Draw three objects—a freehand line, a circle, and a square—at various locations on the page so they form a diagonal path. Select all three with a marquee, open the Arrange menu (see Figure 2.40), and choose **Align**. The dialog box above will open in the center of the work area. Click on **Align to Center of Page** and then **OK** your selection. All three objects are now on top of each other on the page. Press **Alt-Backspace** to undo your work. Now press **Ctrl-A** to reopen the Align dialog box and press **C**. The **Center Horizontally** option is active; press **Enter**. The objects are centered in relation to each other. Use the hot-key again and try another option. This is a very handy command. Use the **Undo** command each time.

Shuffling the Stack

Use the Outline tool to put a thick colored line around each object. Make each one different. With a marquee select all the objects. Use the **Ctrl-A, P** combination to place them in a heap at the center of the page. Note the order of the stack, which is in front and which is in back. Select the top object and press **Shift-PgDn**. The one in front is now in back. Select all three objects again and open the Arrange menu and choose the **Order...**, **Reverse Order** option. The stack is reordered completely.

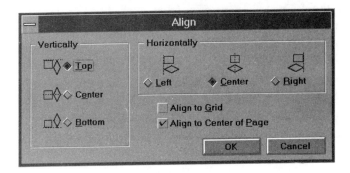

FIGURE 2.40 The Alignment menu

Grouping Objects

Grouping is used to perform a common command or action on several objects at the same time. Each element is still an individual object, but as long as they are together you can move, size, fill, outline, and rearrange them as if they were a single element. Use the marquee to select all three objects. As long as you don't click off the group, they are joined. This is an easy way to set up a temporary group. Drag on one of the handles and make the group larger. Note the status bar. It indicates that there are three objects on layer 1. Now press **Ctrl-G**. The status bar has changed, there is a group of three objects on layer one.

You can set a permanent group command by selecting all the objects for the group and using **Arrange Group** (or **Ctrl-G**). These objects will now act as one until you issue an Ungroup command with either the **Ctrl-U** hot-key or the Arrange menu. Change the color and thickness of the outline and see what happens. Use the **Ctrl-A**, **P** hot-key to arrange them on the center of the page. Press **Ctrl-D** to duplicate them. Next, click on one of the colors in the Color Palette at the bottom of the CorelDRAW window. One of the groups of objects should now have all the same fill.

Combining Is Not the Same as Grouping

So what's the difference between combining objects and grouping them? It's like the difference between arranging some vegetables on a plate and running them through a blender. With Combine they become a single object and so will behave differently from a group. Click on the unfilled group and press **Ctrl-U** to ungroup them. Now click on a blank portion of the page to deselect. (You can't move their individual objects until they have been unselected.) Make sure they are not touching at all. Once they are apart select them with the shift-click method. (You could use any other selection technique.)

Now open the Arrange menu and choose **Combine**. It looks the same as when you grouped them. But the status bar says there is one curve on layer 1. Even though they are not touching, they are a single object. Click on one of the dark colors on the Color Palette at the bottom of the CorelDRAW window. The closed objects are now colored. Click on the **X** at the left of the palette bar to remove the fill. Use the **Ctrl-K** hot-key to break the combination back into individual objects.

The left stack of objects is a group. They were filled with one command. Now look at the middle stack. The bottom object is the same line, but since it is combined, the program treats it as part of the whole stack. Since the path is technically closed, the line is filled. This may seem a little complicated right now, because curved objects have not been discussed.

We can use the **Combine** command to create masks to produce some really interesting effects, such as making an irregularly shaped object frame another.

The letters *USA* started out as text and were combined with a rectangle and filled. That made the text appear like a set of hollow shapes. This effect is called *clipping*. By placing the rectangle over the background, the flag becomes the "fill" for the letters.

SUNRISE, SUNSET

You are going to create a sunset using simple objects and fountain fills. This gives you a chance to show how fountain fills, padding, and the number of stripes used in a linear fill can be used to give a feeling of depth. Remember that an outline defines the edge of an object and gives lines their character, whereas fills are the internal structure of the elements of a drawing. You are going to use the rulers to aid in placement, and the Arrange functions to hide parts of objects from view. The drawing will be a picture of the late afternoon sun setting over the ocean. It will involve two linear fills, one radial fill, and adjustment of the pad to form a clear color boundary. Be aware that the exact colors and quality of your drawing on the screen will depend on the capabilities of your monitor and display card.

Step 1: The Sky

Open a new file and set the page to landscape. Make sure the status bar and rulers are showing. Set your grid origin to the top left corner of the page; then draw a rectangle that covers the upper two-thirds of your page. Use the rulers for sizing. The box should come 6 inches down and cover to both sides of the page. Select it and set the outline to None (use the **X** at the bottom of the window or on the fly-out).

In Figure 2.41 show both dialog boxes you will use and the finished rectangle in the background. Open the Fill fly-out and click on the Fountain Fill icon. Set the type to Linear and the Angle to 87.5. This gives you a slight shift in the way the fill is drawn within the rectangle, like turning a page slightly to the right on a desktop. The rectangle stays the same shape. Now set the Edge Pad to 30. This produces a more pronounced border between the two colors when they are blended together. Play with the setting at 10, 20, and 40. Notice how the fill is changed. You will be using this feature in Section Two.

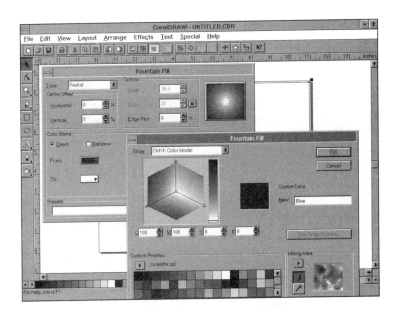

FIGURE 2.41 Setting the first Linear Fill

Make sure your final pad setting is 30. Select the From color and click on the **More** button. This accesses the Fountain Fill Color Selection box. Just like all the others you have used (and will be using), the only things that change are the names at the top and the types of objects it controls. Set Show to CMYK. You are going to use the entry boxes to get an exact color. Adjust the cyan setting to 0, the magenta to 53, yellow to 91, and black to 9. In the future, settings like that will be referred to as "C=0, M=53, Y=91, and K=9." Click **OK**. You will be returned to the Fountain Fill dialog box. Your fill should now fill from an orange shade at the bottom to white at the top. This is going to be the reddening sky from our setting sun.

Next you must set the top part of the fill to depict the darkening sky. Select To color and open the **More...** button under the To heading. Set the values to C=3, M=11, Y=0, and K=54. Exit both dialog boxes with **OK**'s.

Step 2: Adding the Ocean, Reflections, and Sun

Use the Rectangle tool and place a box across the bottom of the page starting at 5.25 inches and take it all the way down the page. Draw the rectangle from one side of the page to the other. You are going to create an ocean surface and put the reflection of the sun on it. Select the new rectangle and this time use a radial fill. Notice how the cursor is placed in the Preview window of the dialog box. Do the same and click once. Don't worry about being exact; it is sufficient to be close. Change the Edge Pad to 20. Then set the From color values to C=55, M=55, Y=0, and K=45. The To color values are C=5, M=0, Y=12, and K=10. This gives you a blue area with a yellow-gold circle radiating down from the mid-right top. Click on **OK** to exit the dialog boxes.

Use the Ellipse tool and the **Constrain (Ctrl)** key to create a circle about 2.5 inches across. Use the status bar as a guide. Then give it a radial fill as follows: Edge Pad of 20; the From colors are C=0, M=47, Y=92, K=8; the To colors are C=6, M=0, Y=52, and K=0. Once you have the circle, set it so that half of the circle rests on each of the two boxes. The outlines are to help the objects stand out; yours should not have any outlines.

Now you have all three elements, but the sun rarely sets in front of the ocean. And if you look closely along the right side of the page you can see that the two rectangles aren't exactly lined up. Select the sun circle and the top rectangle and press the **Ctrl-PgDn** combination once. That is the hot-key for the **Back One** command located in the Arrange menu under the **Order** option. Now the sun is at the right level.

Working Faster

You can shift the sun's location with the Pick tool so that it is centered over the reflection in the ocean rectangle, and play with the pad setting to enhance the effects. Also take a little time and experiment with different numbers of stripes from the Display dialog box under Preferences in the Special menu. Finally, open the View menu and choose

WireFrame. Then you can see the three objects without fills. Since fountain fills use a lot of system resources, they can take a long time to redraw when the screen is adjusted or a menu is opened. The wireframe mode does not require the same level of effort.

You can also play with different colors and pad settings and can turn your illustration into a Full-Color Pattern fill. Move the position of the sun and reflections; adjust the color to create a sunrise. Save your final drawing as EXERCIS3.CDR before exiting.

Chapter Summary

By now you should have a basic feel for how objects are drawn, sized, outlined, and filled. The exercise showed how a CorelDRAW illustration can be made appealing without a lot of objects by taking advantage of the program's sophisticated tools. Take some time to practice a bit before going on if the basic concepts aren't clear. Remember that the first part of this book is designed to provide a basic familiarity with CorelDRAW's functions and terms. You will focus on advanced techniques and concepts in Section Two. If the material seemed easy you might want to try some of the projects in Section Two and refer to part of Section One as a reference when needed.

CHAPTER 3
Getting Into Shape

This chapter covers the following topics:

- Bézier Curves—The Hidden Power of CorelDRAW
- The Pencil Tool's Bézier Mode
- Drawing Curves and Paths
- The Shape Tool
- Manipulating Curves
- Working with Nodes and Control Panels
- The Edit Menu Commands

The Hidden Power of CorelDRAW—Bézier Curves Ahead

Have you ever been to a fair or carnival and watched someone turn balloons into all kinds of animals? The person twisted and turned until, presto, a dog or a giraffe, a horse, or a man appeared. So far our work has been limited to basic shapes—circles, squares, and straight lines. But that is about to change. We are going to open CorelDRAW's magic box and enter the world of Bézier curves. Just like the balloon person, Bézier (pronounced bez-zee-ay) curves enable you to twist and shape objects into almost anything.

All the objects in a CorelDRAW illustration are really mathematical shapes. CorelDRAW has been designed to enable you to create and edit those shapes without the math. About twenty years ago a French mathematician named Pierre Bézier developed a system for describing objects. What makes his method so powerful is the control it offers for manipulating shapes through the use of control points. You can use the Shape tool to drag an object into exactly the form you want.

We are going to spend most of this chapter working with the Pencil and Shape tools, learning how to apply Dr. Bézier's wonderful mathematics. Before starting, you need to set some options. Open the Special menu and choose **Preferences**. Select the View tab and then click so that **Interruptible Refresh** is turned on (has an X in front of it). Then select the General tab and find the **Right Mouse Button option**. In the Action list box choose **Node Edit**. This means that whenever you click the right button the Shape tool will be selected. Use the Layout menu's **Page Setup** option to be sure you have a Landscape page. Then in the Display menu turn on the status bar and rulers if they are not already visible.

Seeing How It Works

The easiest way to explain the use of a Bézier curve is to play with one. We are going to create a Tiffany egg from a circle. I'll list the procedures and show what the object looks like in series of steps so that you can follow along.

1. Draw a circle about 2 inches across and then press the space bar. Open the Fill fly-out, select **Full-Color Patterns**, and select an Easter-egg kind of pattern. Then open the Arrange menu and choose **Convert To Curves**.

2. Press the right mouse button. The cursor will change to the Shape tool; click on your circle. Instead of handles there will be four hollow boxes at 90-degree angles from each other. Click on the bottom box. Dashed lines with black boxes will extend from each hollow box, and the one you clicked will become solid black. Drag the bottom box straight down until the circle has become egg shaped. Release the mouse. You have an electronic Tiffany egg. Figure 3.1b shows how it should look as you drag the circle into shape.

3. Use the Zoom tool to close in on the bottom of your egg. Click on the little box (a *node*) at the bottom. Your egg should have a black square at the bottom with two dashed lines just like Figure 3.1a. The line is pulled down a little bit to make it easier to see.

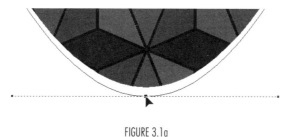

FIGURE 3.1a

4. Use the Shape tool to pull on one of the little boxes at the end of the dashed lines (called a control point). You pull by selecting it with the mouse and then dragging. In Figure 3.1b the point is being pulled down. Notice how the tip of the egg changes shape. Try it. Move the control points around and see how they behave. Drag the nodes and change the shape of the egg. After you have a good feel for selecting and moving nodes and control points, continue reading.

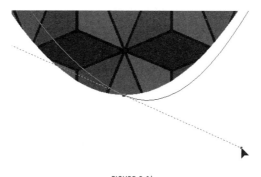

FIGURE 3.1b

We just drew a basic object and converted it into a set of Bézier curves. Once a CorelDRAW object is drawn, the Shape tool can be used to add, delete, and manipulate parts of it. Did you notice how the boundary of the object changed as you pulled on the node and shifted the control points? The fill adapted as the new form was set when you released the mouse button.

A Short Anatomy Lesson

You probably never heard of a cubic polynomial curve segment before, but you just worked with one. That's the complicated name of a Bézier curve. CorelDRAW uses these curves to give you the ability to shape objects the way you just did with the egg. Bézier curves are like a cross between a connect-the-dots drawing kit and silly putty. To use them you have to understand the parts of a curve and how they can be combined and manipulated.

You have already been introduced to the terms node and path. The following discussion will refine their definitions and will introduce a few new terms.

- **Path.** The boundary of all CorelDRAW objects follows the path that was used to describe it—the X path that its outline is attached to. When you draw a Bézier curve, you are defining its path. When you change the shape or size of an object, you are really modifying its path. A path can be open or closed. This determines if the object can be filled. Think of a path in the woods. If it just goes straight through the forest, then you can't define an area inside the path. If it goes around the woods in a complete circle, then there is a defined area inside the path. In CorelDRAW areas inside a closed path can be filled. You can give any path an outline, no matter whether it's open or closed. It is like the thickness (width) of a path. You can actually have an invisible object, one with no outline and no fill. Since it has a path, it exists. In Figure 3.2 the path goes from the first node (A) to the end node (C).

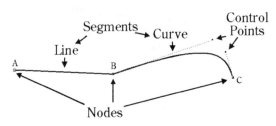

FIGURE 3.2 The points on the path

- **Node.** Each segment of a path has two nodes, one at each end. The node is the point of attachment for the control points of a Bézier curve. To manipulate the control points you must first select the node. Moving its nodes is one way to change the shape of an object, just as you did with the egg. Each time you move a node, CorelDRAW recalculates the equation that defines the shape of your object. Nodes are like mileposts on the path. They tell when you have reached a certain point or when a major change in direction is taking place.

  There are three different kinds of nodes, each with its own properties: smooth, symmetrical, and cusp. You will understand the differences as you work with them later in this chapter. The nodes in Figure 3.2 are marked A, B, and C. You can tell that node B is selected because the box that marks its position is black. Note that the first and second parts of the line share node B. CorelDRAW enables you to change curves to lines, lines to curves, and the type of a node. This gives the user an incredible amount of control over the shape of a path.

- **Control Points.** These are like handles on a node, but they behave a bit like silly putty. Dragging on a control point will alter the shape of an object without moving the node. The effect of moving a control point varies, based on the type of node it is attached to. Notice how the curved part of the object in Figure 3.2 has control points, but the line segment does not. Only curves have control points.

- **Segments.** A segment is the path taken by the object's boundary between two sequential nodes, like connect-the-dots. CorelDRAW allows you to create segments from scratch with the Pencil tool, convert objects drawn with other tools into curves (as you did with the egg), and add segments to existing objects. There are two kinds of segments: line and curve. A curve can be perfectly straight, but it is not a line. Lines are always straight. It is not the angle of a segment that determines if it is a curve or line, but the mathematical definition inside CorelDRAW.

- **Subpaths.** An object can have lines that do not touch each other but that are mathematically related. These are called *subpaths*. Even though they are not visibly connected, the subpaths are considered joined. It is possible to fill an object that looks open, because the subpaths are considered closed. But the fill may not go where you expect. Don't worry too much about subpaths now; just remember the term.

So much for names. Be sure you have some understanding of the terms just defined. The real meaning will become clear as you work with the elements of Bézier curves.

You are going to spend some time drawing and manipulating objects. When you are done you should have a pretty good understanding of how curves operate. You will cover planning and using curves in Section Two. For now concentrate on learning the drawing tools.

Drawing Curves: The Pencil Tool, Part Two

The Bézier Mode

You have worked a little with the Pencil tool, but only in Freehand mode. Now that you have been formally introduced to Dr. Bézier's curves we can practice with the Bézier mode. It offers a different approach to forming objects by clicking to place a node. The way you move the mouse affects the type of node that is placed. As you go along you will understand how each node works.

FIGURE 3.3 The Pencil tool

Place the mouse cursor over the Pencil tool and hold down the left button until the fly-out menu appears. Drag the cursor on top of the second icon to the right (the one that looks like a pencil touching a node) and release it. (Don't worry about the other four icons; we'll cover those in a later chapter.) The icon in the toolbar should change to show that the Bézier mode is now active. Drag the Pencil fly-out open again and change the tool back to Freehand mode. Repeat the operation again and leave the tool in the Bézier mode. The status bar should indicate that you are drawing in Bézier mode.

A Simple Shape

Place the cursor cross hairs at the top left of the page and click once. Don't drag, just move the cursor down the left-hand edge to the middle of the page and double-click. A straight line will appear between the two points where you clicked. Move, don't drag, to the opposite edge of the page and double-click again. Another line appears. Now move, don't drag, on to the exact point where you started the first line and click once. Press the space bar once to select the object. You should have a triangle on the top half of the page with handles around it. Go to the Color Palette and click on a medium gray shade as a fill.

Notice that you drew three straight lines that were automatically joined into a triangle. Take a look at the status bar near the top of the window. If all is well it should tell you that the object is a Curve on Layer 1 with three nodes. On the right edge of the status bar are notes about the object's fill and outline, plus a little preview box showing the outline's thickness and the fill's color. Now press the right mouse button. The cursor should change into a wedge, indicating the Shape tool is active. Drag the top corner of your triangle to a point over the lower right-hand corner and release. Your screen should look like the one in Figure 3.4 just before you let go. This simple exercise is an example of how objects can be drawn with the Pencil tool and then manipulated with the Shape tool.

Clear your page and select the Pencil tool by pressing **F5**; this is its hot-key. Start another line with a click and end it with a double-click. Go to another point on the page and double-click again. Repeat this process several times. Each time a new line segment will be added to your object. Each segment has two nodes. As you add a segment, a line is extended using one of the nodes from the preceding line. Press the space bar to end the drawing session and complete the object.

Lines are the simplest possible components of an object. The geometrical definition of a line is the distance between two points, and that is exactly how CorelDRAW defines one. When you put a start point down, the program calculates the distance between that location and the current position of the mouse. When you click the second time, a line is drawn between them. There are no control points associated with a line segment, but you can move lines and resize them with either the Pick or the Shape tool. Each does the job a bit differently. You should be familiar with how the Pick tool performs transformations from the last chapter.

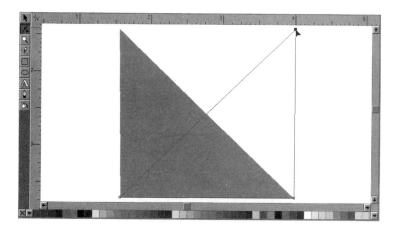

FIGURE 3.4 Drawing and manipulating lines

The Shape tool enables you to swing the end of a line into a new location by dragging it. In effect, the Shape tool allows you to redefine either the start or end point of a line at will. Just click on a node and drag it to the desired point. The status bar will indicate the current angle and dimensions each time you stop moving the mouse. Draw another line and move it around.

Experiment a bit; draw several lines. Use the **Constrain** (**Ctrl**) key some of the time as you work. It will limit the shift in position to 15-degree increments. When you are finished open a new drawing.

Before going on to curves, you will go through one more practice session. Use the Rectangle tool to draw a box that covers the upper-right corner of the page, about 4 inches wide and 2 inches deep, as shown by the white outline in Figure 3.5. Select it and press **Ctrl-Q**. This converts it to curves. (A note to veteran users: This is a change from CorelDRAW 3.0's **Ctrl-V** combination.) Use the Shape tool (not the Pick tool) to extend the lower left-hand corner at a 45-degree angle and to the edge of the page as shown in the figure. Change the Pencil tool back to Freehand mode and draw two lines for the braces of the kite frame. Close in on the objects with the Zoom tool. Use the Outline tool to give the modified rectangle and the frame different outline thicknesses.

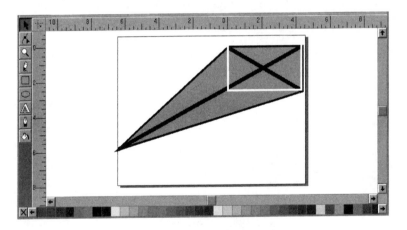

FIGURE 3.5 Kites are fun

If you have been practicing as you have read, those operations should be very easy by now. If you have to look up one of the steps, a short review might be in order. A basic understanding of the Rectangle, Circle, Zoom, Fill, and Outline tools is needed for the exercises in Section Two. They also serve as part of the skills base for working with the projects in the rest of Section One.

Drawing Curves

To become a CorelDRAW master requires firm understanding of how to draw and use Bézier curves. Unlike lines, they have control points and are not limited to following straight paths. Drawing curves in Bézier mode is probably a bit different from anything else you have done with a computer.

Make a Path

An object is defined by the shape of its path. If you want to draw an object other than an ellipse, rectangle, or text block, you must define its path. You do that by placing a node and then telling CorelDRAW how the path proceeds to the next node. That produces one segment, its control points (if any), and determines how that part of the object will look and behave. You have already done that with lines, and you have converted both circles and rectangles into curves and then manipulated them. Now you are going to create a curved object from scratch.

Keep in mind that each segment, or portion of a path, is related to the type and placement of the node found at each end. To draw a curve you set the starting node and then move the mouse to the end point. That is the same way you drew the lines in the triangle. Like a good fencer using a sword, the control is in the wrist. How you move the mouse will control the shape of the segment and the type of node produced. You are going to draw some curves to get a feel for how they work and then discuss the rules that apply to each type.

Make sure you have a clean page, that the Pencil tool is in Bézier mode, and that the rulers are visible. Then create a circle that fills most of the page and zoom in on it. You are going to duplicate the curve drawn in Figure 3.6. The clock face will serve as a reference. If you start at 12 o'clock, that means to start at the top of your circle. A complex curve has more than one segment and may have more than one type of node. The object has four nodes: one each at the 12, 9, 6, and 3 o'clock positions. The first node (this is a precise term meaning the very first node placed in creating an object) is at the 12 o'clock position. Click once and move the mouse to the 9 o'clock location and click again. This produces a straight line segment. Then click just above the 6 and drag the mouse to the right before releasing. This creates a curved segment and extends a control point as you drag. The farther you pull on the control point, the more pronounced the curve effect. Release the mouse button, click at the 3 o'clock position, and drag outside the clock circle. You can see what's happening by the location of the cross-hair cursor.

The farther you pull, the farther toward the center the slope of the last segment moves. When you finish you have a line with four nodes and three segments.

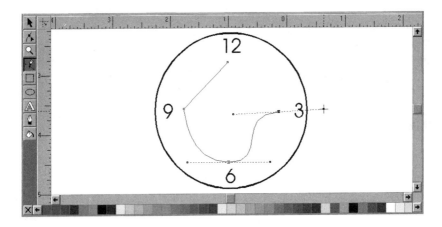

FIGURE 3.6 Drawing a complex curve

1. Click just under the 12 o'clock position.
2. Move the mouse to just inside the 9 o'clock position and click once.
3. Move the mouse to just above the 6 o'clock position. Click and drag the cursor to the right until the curve looks about like the one in the figure. Release the button.
4. Move the mouse to just inside the 3 o'clock position. Click and drag the cursor to the right until the curve looks about like the one in the figure. Release the button.
5. Tap the space bar. This selects the Pick tool and releases you from the Bézier drawing mode.
6. Save your drawing so that you can retrieve it.

Notice what happened as you were drawing. Each time you clicked the mouse a node was placed. As in the past, clicking, moving to a new position, and clicking again produced a straight line. You should not have much of a problem with making straight lines. It gets a bit more interesting when you start to drag after you click. That adjusts the control point, which affects the shape of the segment and the type of node produced. If you click and drag—no matter how straight—the segment is not a line, but a curve. In CorelDRAW, curves are very special. Keep in mind that there are two types of segments: curves and lines. You can change a section from one type to another, but each has its own properties.

We are going to use the object we just drew to practice using the Shape tool for selecting and adjusting nodes. After that, I'll explain the fine points of the different types of nodes and segments. Then we'll will use the Shape tool, the basic drawing tools, and some fills to create an illustration.

GETTING IT RIGHT WITH THE SHAPE TOOL

The Shape tool is used to position nodes and tweak segments into just the right shape—hence the name. To use it efficiently, you have to understand the different types of nodes and how they work. So before you get into manipulating paths, you need to understand nodes and segments. Since there are so many variables and since we are not delving into the mathematical theory behind Bézier curves, the best way to master these techniques is through practice. After you have read and worked with the samples, take some time to experiment.

Working with Nodes and Using Control Points

Right now let's use the Shape tool to identify the types of nodes in our two objects. Press the right mouse button so that the Shape tool is selected. (If you didn't get the Shape tool, your preferences aren't set properly) Then click on the node at the 12 o'clock position, and look at the center of the status bar. It should say "First Node of an Open Curve." An open curve means that the object has an open path and can't be filled. The reading on the center of the status bar will indicate the types of segments on either side of the node in the order they fall on the path. If the first segment drawn is a line and the second segment is smooth, the bar will say "Selected Node: Line Smooth."

The control points are a bit like handles. By pulling on the end of one or moving it up or down, the curve changes its length and angle. There are three types of nodes: cusp, symmetrical, and smooth. All nodes, no matter what type, indicate the start or end of a segment of the curve or line.

First Nodes

The first node is, as already mentioned, the first point of the object. The box is larger than the ones for other nodes. This is the only node at the start of a segment. All other nodes are at the end of their respective segments. Look at the first node and the node at 9 o'clock. Both nodes are colored black. That means that the segment lying between them will be affected by any edits. There are no control points visible because this is a line segment. Line segment nodes don't have control points. Move the node by dragging it using the mouse. Watch how it behaves. Pulling on the first node does not affect the second segment at all. It only adjusts the length and angle of the line. Experiment a bit. Return it to the original position when you are done.

The Second and Third Nodes

Now click on the 9 o'clock node. It turns black, and a control point appears on the left side of the 6 o'clock node. The status bar tells us that the node is "Line Symmetrical." That means that one side is a line segment, and the node is symmetrical. Pulling on this node not only adjusts the length and position of the first segment, but also modifies the curve and length of the second section.

Experiment a bit with this node and both sections as well. Drag the 9 o'clock node outside the circle as shown in Figure 3.7. Pull and move the control point handle on the 6 o'clock node. As you select it, the handles will appear on both sides. This is a symmetrical node. That means that the segments on either side will move an equal amount as you pull and twist the control point. Try rotating the end of the handle in a small circle and watch the effect. Note the changes in the status bar as you work. Return them to the original position when you are finished.

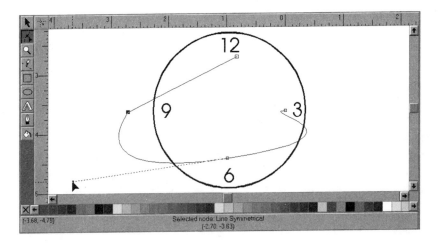

FIGURE 3.7 *Manipulating the second and third nodes*

Now you have had some experience with moving nodes and control points. You can see that they let you adjust the shape of an object's path. But just how to use them to make a drawing is probably still a bit obscure. Study the three different types of nodes and how they are drawn. Then you will learn how to convert types and add or delete nodes using the Shape tool. After that you'll do an exercise.

NODE TYPES

CorelDRAW offers three types of curve nodes. Each one operates a bit differently, giving you specific controls over that portion of your object. Keep in mind that only curve segments have control points. To select a node for editing or movement or to manipulate its control points, you must use the Shape tool. Any time you plan to do a lot of work with Bézier curves, consider setting the right mouse button to activate the Shape tool and place the Pencil tool in Bézier mode. Line nodes are found at the ends of any segment that is not a curve. They do not have control points. In this section you are focusing on curve nodes and how they can be manipulated.

As a rule you should limit the number of nodes in a drawing to the fewest that are needed to form and shape the object. Each node increases the complexity of your drawing and the time required to print it. In the section on printing, later in the book, you will learn techniques for simplifying drawings.

On the disk in the back of the book is a CorelDRAW file called NODES.CDR. It has a set of lines, each with a series of labeled nodes. You can use it to follow along and experiment as the properties of each class are described.

Cusp Nodes

One of the traditional definitions of the word cusp is the "point of an arc." In CorelDRAW a *cusp node* is the only one with control points that can be moved on one side without affecting the other. Look at Figure 3.8. The Shape tool is being used to pull one of the nodes down to a point directly under the node. As it moves, the pointed appearance of the curve gets sharper. A cusp is the only type of node where you can have a point at the node.

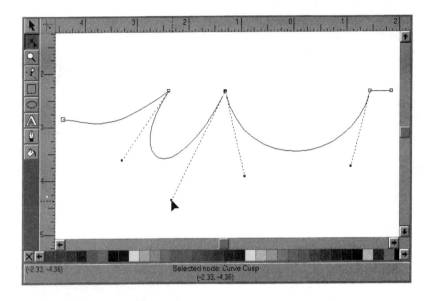

FIGURE 3.8 A series of cusp nodes

Moving the control point on one side does not alter the curve on the other side at all. This is the only type of node that allows you to adjust the sides independently. Try it. Load the file mentioned earlier and select one of the cusp nodes with the Shape tool. Then pull and rotate the control handles. Use a cusp node any time you want a sharp break in the flow of a curve. The end points of an object with an open path are always cusps.

Symmetrical Nodes

Once again the name is a clue as to how the node operates. The dictionary says that to be symmetrical is to have like measure, equality on both sides. That is exactly the way a *symmetrical node* operates. Pull or drag on one side and the other is affected by an equal amount. If you pull out, both sides are enlarged. Push in and the reverse happens. Pull up on one side and the other drops equally.

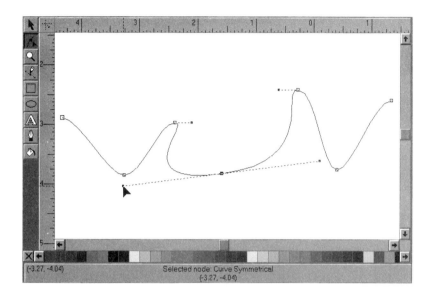

FIGURE 3.9 A series of symmetrical nodes

Unlike cusp nodes, the symmetrical nodes and the control points always lie on a straight line with each other. In addition, the node is at a point exactly in the center of that line. No matter what you do, both sides always move the same amount. Try it with the samples in the file. They are used when you need to have an even shape, like a semicircle.

Smooth Nodes

The final type of node also has the node and control points lying on a straight line. Movements on one side of a *smooth node*, however, are not mirrored on the other. If you pull one side out, that side gets bigger. Rotating the control point or pulling on it affect each side differently. This lets you produce smooth but uneven-sided curves.

Notice the difference between the control point lengths being manipulated in Figures 3.9 and 3.10. Notice how the smooth node control points are not the same size. Also notice how one side bows out and another does not in Figure 3.10. Now look at the even lengths and the sizes of the curves with the symmetrical node in Figure 3.9. Play with the sample curves and get a feel for how the node functions and the effects of moving the node and pulling and rotating the control points. When you are finished clear the page.

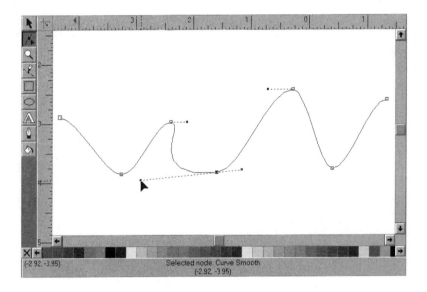

FIGURE 3.10 A series of smooth nodes

NODE EDITING WITH THE SHAPE TOOL

As you have seen, CorelDRAW is full of hidden compartments. Node editing involves another one. Use the Pencil tool and draw a line with five segments and six nodes. Just click-move-click-move five times. Now press the right mouse button and marquee-select the entire object with the Shape tool. Double-click on the line. You should see a pop-up menu like the one in Figure 3.11.

Chapter 3: Getting Into Shape

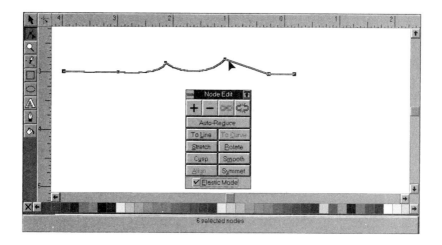

FIGURE 3.11 The Node Edit dialog box

The pop-up Node Edit menu is used to add, delete, align, and change the attributes of nodes and segments. Clicking on a node or line segment with the Shape tool selects it and opens the menu. You can use the shift-click or marquee selection techniques to choose several nodes or segments at the same time. As the various functions of the Node Edit menu are introduced, try them out with the object you just drew. If a selection is gray the option is unavailable. For example, you can't change a line to a line, so it will be unavailable if the segment that was selected is a line already.

Adding and Deleting Nodes

These two options are straightforward. Select the node or line you want modified and click on the appropriate button (plus or minus symbol). A node will be removed or an additional one will be added.

To Line or Curve

This option toggles the selected segment between a line and a Bézier curve. It is in the Curve mode in the figure. Remember that line segments are fixed. Their nodes have no control points, and all you can do is alter their angle and length.

Changing a Node to Cusp, Smooth, or Symmetrical

These options allow you to convert the nodes of a segment or a group of nodes to another type. Just select, double-click on a node or segment, and make your choice.

Breaking Apart

Look at the object in Figure 3.12. Yes, it looks like two objects; but examine the status bar. It says you have two selected nodes on two subpaths. These two sets of segments are really still one object. If you click on part of one with the Pick tool, both the subpaths are selected. You can break an object down into as many subpaths as there are segments.

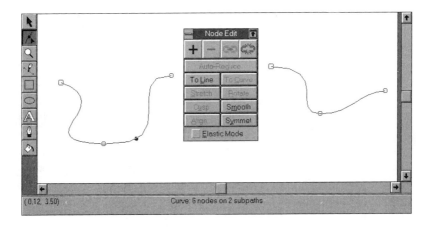

FIGURE 3.12 An object that has been broken apart

If you move, delete, duplicate, or change the outline, everything in both subpaths is modified. Work with it. Draw a set of segments, break them apart, and modify them. See what happens. Notice the shape of the nodes as you break an object into subpaths. You will see how the first node still looks larger on both subpaths. The only way to be sure of what you have is by knowing how subpaths operate or by checking the status bar.

Joining

Joining is the opposite of breaking nodes apart. Select two of the nodes on different subpaths using either the shift-click or marquee selection techniques. Then double-click and choose **Join**. The two nodes are now reduced to one. Remember that the first and last nodes of an open object are always cusps.

Aligning Nodes

This maneuver is a bit more involved than the other **Node Edit** options. You use this option to align nodes vertically and/or horizontally, and you can align their control points. This is most often used to align two objects precisely that must touch, like part of a puzzle. If the nodes are not part of a single object or located on separate subpaths of a single object, you must first Combine the two objects that contain the nodes you wish to align. This is done by selecting the objects with the Pick tool and using either the **Ctrl-C** hot-key or the option under the Arrange menu. Then use the Shape tool to select the desired nodes (only two at a time) and double-click to open the Node Edit menu. Then choose **Align**.

Stretching, Scaling, and Rotating Nodes

These maneuvers are just like those done using the Transform functions, except you can perform them with the Shape tool instead of the Pick tool.

Auto-Reducing Nodes

Choose this option to reduce the number of nodes in an object automatically, based on the **Curves** option under the Preferences setting. The default is 5, and the higher the value, the more the shape will be modified as the button is used. To auto-reduce, select the nodes by shift-clicking and then click on the button.

Elastic Mode

When this option is active and more than one node is selected, adjustments will be made as if you were pulling on a rubber band. The effect on the segments will diminish the farther away from the Shape tool a node is. If it is not active, the nodes will all be moved the same amount.

Figure 3.13 shows two objects that have been converted to curves, combined, and then had nodes selected for alignment. This action brings up the Node Align dialog box. You can choose to align using either, or both, horizontal and vertical alignment. If you choose to do both, you can also align the control points. If you wish to align more than one set of nodes, the process must be repeated. This is a very handy tool for lining up the edges of objects. You may need to add and move nodes to get appropriate points for alignment and to get the objects to line up cleanly.

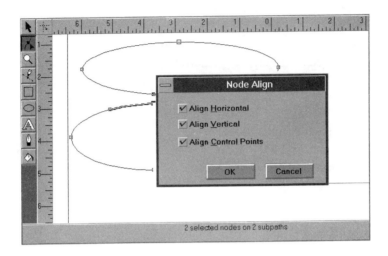

FIGURE 3.13 Aligning nodes

ADVANCED CURVE-DRAWING TECHNIQUES WITH THE PENCIL TOOL

As you may have noticed, drawing line segments with the Pencil tool is the same in both Freehand and Bézier modes. You can quickly rough out an object in Bézier mode, placing nodes exactly where they are needed. When you draw curves in Bézier mode, you are describing the flow on the path and placing nodes. With a little practice you can develop a sense of how the available click-and-drag combinations produce curves.

To make it easy to see what happens, some figures with a set of three guidelines for reference are included. Open a new page and place three guidelines to match the ones in Figure 3.14. One is placed in the center of the page, the rulers are rezeroed, and two more are added at the 2-inch marks. Then the area is zoomed in on. Follow the instructions outlined under each figure and you'll be a Bézier expert in no time.

Single-Pull Click-and-Drag Drawing

Look at Figure 3.14a. The center guideline is clicked on and dragged straight down to the bottom line and the mouse button is released. Then the pointer is brought to the centerline a bit left of the starting point and clicked again. I followed the same procedure—click to set a node, drag to pull a curve, move the pointer to the next node point, click to set the next node across the page as shown in Figure 3.14b. The Shape tool cursor is used as a pointer to make it easier to see the cursor position. You will see a cross-hair pointer as you draw. The length of the control point above the line will equal the one that follows the cursor as you drag.

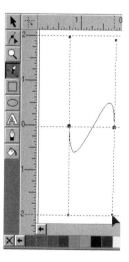

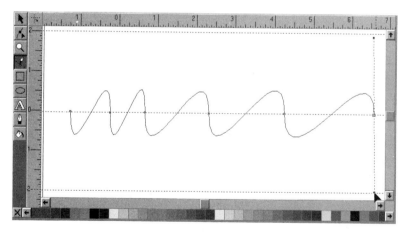

FIGURES 3.14a and b Click-and-drag drawing single-pull method

Experiment with both short and long horizontal movements after you drag. Also play with placing the node at vertical locations other than the centerline. Practice with the goal of understanding how the curve will form when you release the mouse.

Dual-Pull Click-and-Drag Drawing

This is a variation of the process you just used, but now you click, drag down, click, drag up. You can see in Figure 3.15a that the curve is fuller. Figure 3.15b shows a series of nodes and curves using different node placement, but each uses the same click-drag, click-drag method. In the last set, it was pulled in toward the last node and the control point was dragged. Notice how that changes the slope of the curve.

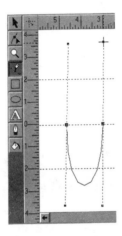

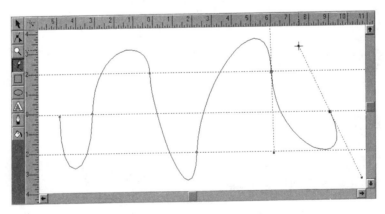

FIGURES 3.15a and b Click-and-drag drawing, dual-pull technique

Once again, try using the same method and vary the distance between the nodes. After you have finished placing segments, use the Shape tool and the Node Edit menu to modify the types of nodes and segments.

Dual Click-and-Drag Drawing

Here is another variation. Click twice when you set the node; then drag. Figure 3.16a shows the first segment as the method is used. Notice how the control point moves only in the direction the mouse is pulled and how short the segment is. Experiment with different pulls after double-clicking. Then go back and use the Shape tool to identify the types of nodes you created. This set includes both smooth and cusp nodes. The type will depend on how you use the mouse. This kind of drawing is good practice and will help you develop an understanding of how Bézier curves work. Try using a combination of the three methods and develop your own style as you work through the rest of the book.

Method Drawing Closed Paths

Up to now your Bézier exercises have focused on producing nodes and segments. One other skill must be acquired to draw CorelDRAW objects—closing the path. In Figure 3.17 a shape like the body of a whale was created and filled with a light gray tone. Notice that the status bar says this object is a curve. All the other figures in this section have been open paths. Remember that open paths can't be filled. So closing a path is a primary skill. It is also pretty easy to master.

FIGURE 3.16a

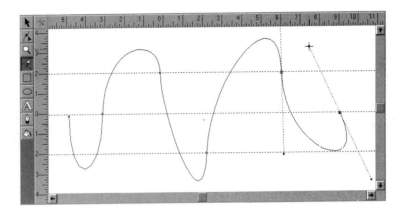

FIGURE 3.16b Dual click-and-drag drawing

Draw a rounded shape using any one of the methods just presented. Bring the nodes back toward the first node. Then to close the path just click the final node on top of the first one. That's all there is to it. Fill your object to prove that the shape is closed. Now use the Shape tool to identify the type of node at that last position. It should tell you that it is the "first node of a closed curve." If not, try again. Once you are satisfied with your abilities move on to the exercise.

FIGURE 3.17 Creating a closed path

DAPPER CASPAR, THE CURVED SNOWMAN

You have now been exposed to all the primary drawing tools, outlines, fills, and Bézier curves. This exercise gives you a chance to practice with them all. If you find that one part of the project seems harder than the others or that you have forgotten how to use a command, please go back and refresh your memory. As we move into Section Two, these skills will be needed to master the techniques presented in the Advanced Projects. The next chapter will deal with the only object creation tool you have not really used to any degree, the Text tool.

This exercise involves creating a figure with twenty-two objects, shown on the left side of the CorelDRAW page in Figure 3.18. That may sound like a lot of elements, but many of them will be made using the **Ctrl-D Place Duplicate** command. You could simplify this project in several ways, but the long way around will give you more of a chance to practice with the techniques you have learned. Use the **New** command to start a fresh drawing, and make sure the status bar is showing and that the Pencil tool is in Bézier mode.

Creating the Primary Body Shapes

Look at the two round shapes on the right side of the CorelDRAW work area in Figure 3.18. Draw a closed shape using the Pencil tool and one of the Bézier mode methods discussed in the last section. It will serve as the base of Caspar's body.

FIGURE 3.18 Meet Caspar the dapper snowman

Next draw two circles, select both of them individually, and use the Convert To Curves function to change them into curved objects. Place them with the other round object so that they are stacked one on top of another. Then resize each so that the one at the top is smaller than the one in the middle and so that the one on the bottom is larger than the other two. These three objects will be the head, torso, and base of your drawing.

Aligning the Major Objects

Now use the Shape tool and the Node Edit menu to adjust the head and torso to each other. You will need to convert nodes and segments from one type into another. Use the Shape tool to mold the curves, and the Align function to pull them together. Either could be used to do the entire job, but practice with both.

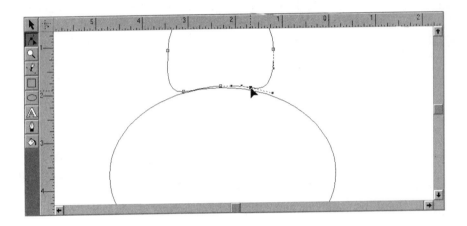

FIGURE 3.19 Fitting the head and torso

Then proceed to adjust the appearance of the base. It should be flat on the bottom, and rounded and aligned to the torso section on the top. Experiment with different node and segment conversions, and with the Node Align function. Zoom in and out as you work to magnify the work area or pull back to see the full effect.

Shading the Snowman's Body

You need to give your snowman some body. Open the Fill fly-out and click on the roll-up menu. Place it out of your way to the side of the active drawing area. Place it in Fountain Fill mode by clicking on the section icon (second from the left). Click on the base of the snowman. Set an off-white radial fill. Angle it from the top right and have it fade to a darker gray on the bottom. Then use the **Update From** command as illustrated in Figure 3.20 to copy the fill to the other two objects. Move the Fill tool roll-up out of the way.

Chapter 3: Getting Into Shape   **127**

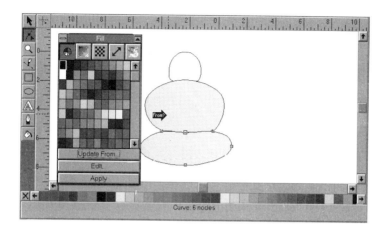

FIGURE 3.20 Using the Fill roll-up

Creating the Branches for Arms

Change the active tool to the Pencil tool and draw a two-segment object like the main part of the left arm shown in Figure 3.21. Then add another segment like the one on the lower outside of the one in the figure. Use the Pick tool to adjust it.

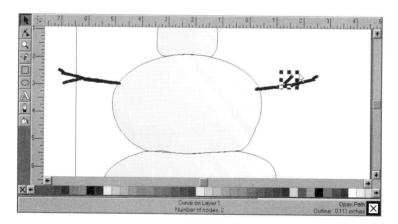

FIGURE 3.21 Fine-tuning the arms

Once you have it the way you want it, select the entire arm with the shift-click method, group it, and use **Ctrl-D** to copy it. Select the copy, and with the **Stretch and Mirror** command under the Transform menu flip it horizontally. Place both arms as shown in Figure 3.21. Ungroup the right arm and use either the Pick or Shape tool to make the right arm a bit different from the left one.

Defining the Face and Adding Buttons

Draw a circle and use the Fill roll-up to give it a solid black fill. Copy the object five times and place them as shown in Figure 3.22. Once they are in place use the Pick tool to resize them.

FIGURE 3.22 And two eyes made out of coal...

Make four more copies of the lump of coal. Group them in a semicircle and rotate them into the shape of a mouth. Use the Transform abilities of the Pick tool to place and resize the mouth on the face. (See Figure 3.25 for the finished effect.)

FIGURE 3.23 Forming the mouth

Draw two rectangles and form them into a hat. Zoom in on the objects so that you can easily see what you are doing. Transform the body of the hat into curves and add and shape nodes as required to produce a battered effect. Give both objects a solid black fill.

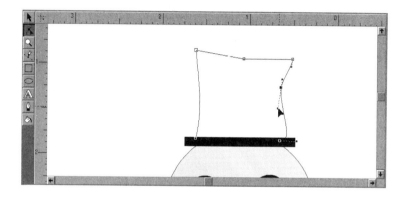

FIGURE 3.24 Adding and shaping the hat

Place the rectangle used as the brim in front of the main part of the hat. Group them. Rotate the hat at a jaunty angle and place it on the snowman's head.

Making a Plaid Scarf

You don't want your snowman to catch cold, so give him a nice warm woolen scarf. The fill makes this object look complicated, but you know better. Draw another small rectangle and duplicate it. Stretch the copy and convert it to curves. Use the Shape tool to form it around Caspar's neck as shown in Figure 3.25. Place the smaller rectangle under the large one. Use the Fill tool roll-up to give both objects a red and black Stewart plaid from the Full-Color palette.

Adding a Vest and Improving on the Design

Use the Pencil tool to draw two objects on the torso to serve as sides of a vest. Give both a solid black fill. Use the Shape tool to form the vest to the edges of the body as shown in Figure 3.26. With the Arrange menu place the vest under the scarf and over the arms. Then take the Shape tool and reform the scarf as shown in the figure.

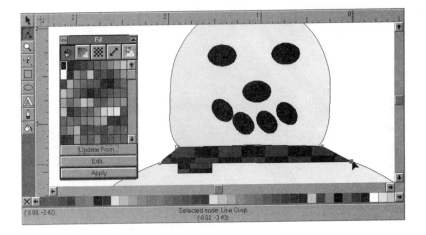

FIGURE 3.25 Using full-color fills and the Shape tool

FIGURE 3.26 Putting on the finishing touches

You can improve on this basic drawing in a number of ways to hone your skills.

- Use the Pencil and Fill tools to add gloves to the hands.
- Adapt rectangles and circles into boots.

- Use fountain fills to add shading to the hat, pieces of coal, and vest.
- Add a hat band to the top hat and tip the brim.

These are a few suggestions. You should be able to come up with other ideas on your own. Your snowman has given us a chance to play with most of the tools that have been introduced. As we work keep adding to the hot-keys and shortcuts that will make your work easier. The material presented in this chapter should have deepened your understanding of the Shape tool and types of objects and should have reinforced the importance of the status bar. Before this chapter ends, you will be introduced to one more part of the CorelDRAW interface, the Edit menu.

Moving Node Locations

CorelDRAW 5.0 has much more flexibility than earlier versions of the program when it comes to placing nodes and adjusting line segments. Let me show you a couple of shortcuts I find very handy. You can use the Shape tool to place a node point at an exact position. Open a clean page and draw a series of segments with the Pencil tool. Click on the right mouse button to get the Shape tool; then click somewhere on the line with the left one. Do you see the black circle? Now press the Add Node (plus symbol) on the roll-up. Presto! A new node appears at exactly that location.

Now place the Shape tool over the line and drag. The curve segment moves with it. You might want to experiment with these functions a bit. They offer dynamic control over objects that some people find more intuitive than pulling control points. I think it's a good idea to be familiar with both systems, since each has its advantages.

THE EDIT MENU COMMANDS

The Edit menu offers access to both standard and advanced Windows: **Cut**, **Copy**, and **Paste** style commands. You have worked with some of the options already, but here all the commands will be covered in detail. Some of the options relate only to actions within CorelDRAW; these are called *internal edit functions*; others allow moving CorelDRAW objects to the Windows Clipboard for use in other applications as well. These are both internal and external editing functions. Some commands make use of the Object Linking and Embedding (OLE) capabilities of Windows 3.1. These are special interapplication functions.

Like all the other CorelDRAW menus, the Edit menu is divided into groups. It can be opened with the **Alt-E** keyboard shortcut or with the mouse. If you open it by mistake just click anywhere outside the menu, but within the CorelDRAW window, to close it without using an option.

Some functions within the Edit menu dealing with Clipboard operations and the OLE commands can be tuned using the CorelDRAW configuration files. These settings are covered in the discussion on installation later in the book.

Undo, Redo, and Repeat: The CorelDRAW Buffer

Every time you issue a command in CorelDRAW, the last state the drawing was in and the current action are saved in a buffer. This allows you to recall the last version of the drawing or to reuse the most recently issued command. This works with most but not all operations. If you notice a mistake, hit the **Undo** shortcut (**Ctrl-Z**) right away. You can also use the **Undo-Redo** (shortcut is **Alt-Enter**) to toggle between the two versions of a drawing, before and after a command, so you can decide if you want the effect. In Figure 3.27 the **Undo** and **Repeat** commands have the word *delete* after them. That's because the most recent command was a deletion. The exact word will vary, based on your last operation. The older versions of CorelDRAW had only one level of **Undo**. Version 5.0 offers almost unlimited Undos, but you can set a limit using the preference settings.

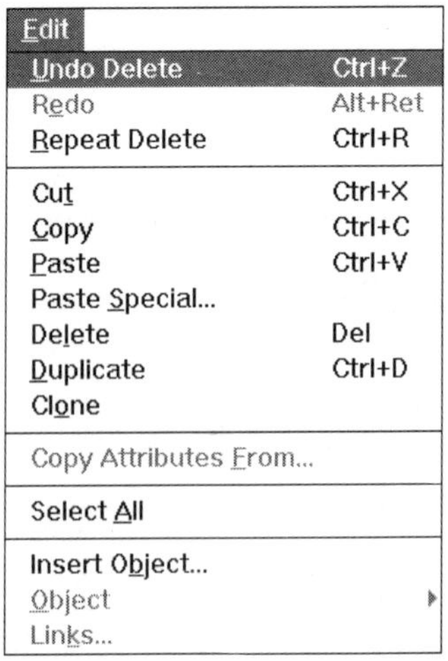

FIGURE 3.27 The CorelDRAW Edit menu

The Cut and Copy Commands

The **Cut** command (**Shift-Delete**) removes a selected object or group of selected objects and places it in the Windows Clipboard. The **Copy** command (**Ctrl-Insert**) keeps a copy of the object(s) without removing it from the drawing. Not all applications handle and support information in the Clipboard the same way. Therefore exporting complex drawings via the Clipboard into other programs may present problems. Allowable formats into CorelDRAW from the Clipboard include ASCII text, Windows bitmaps, and Windows metafiles. (See the entry on customizing the CorelDRAW.INI file under Installation for tips on how to tune your system for using the Clipboard.)

The Paste Command

Pasting (**Shift-Insert**) is the reverse of **Cut** or **Copy**. The object(s) is copied from the Clipboard into the drawing or another supported Windows application. Once again be aware that not all applications support the Clipboard the same way. You can also use the **Paste** command as a super-**Duplicate** command. By copying an object you can drop a copy in your drawing at any time, until you paste another object into the Clipboard. Only one object can be in the Clipboard at a time. The new object will be placed in the same location on the page from it was cut or copied. **Paste** can also be used to place OLE embedded objects from another application into CorelDRAW. For more information on OLE see the **Paste Special**, **Edit Objects**, and **Links** commands that are discussed here. Using **Paste** does not create a link to the source application.

Paste Special

This command has two options available via the dialog box shown in Figure 3.28. In the sample, a chart is pasted while in CorelCHART. The Source application and file name with its path is shown near the top of the dialog box. You can bring the object into CorelDRAW as a chart, a picture, or a bitmap image. The object types will vary based on the type of file and its contents. The Paste Link function creates an OLE link, which allows you to update the information if it is changed in the original application. The **Paste Special** option is gray in the Edit menu unless an object is currently held in the Clipboard.

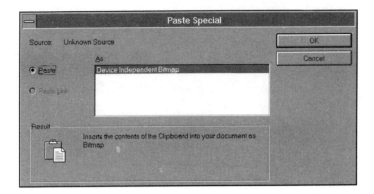

FIGURE 3.28 The Paste Special dialog box

Deleting Objects

This is a very straightforward command that can be accomplished with the menu or with the **Delete** key. Any selected objects are removed. They are not placed in the Clipboard. You can recover a deleted object if you immediately use the **Undo** command. If you use any other function or command, the object is gone for good.

Duplicating Objects

You have been using this command a lot. Pressing the **Ctrl-D** combination produces a copy of any selected objects on the page. The location of the copy is based on the current Preferences, Place Duplicate settings.

Copy Attributes From...

This command is another favorite that can save steps. As you have seen in the last two chapters, this command can modify an object's (or group's) fill, outline, and text settings automatically to match another's current settings.

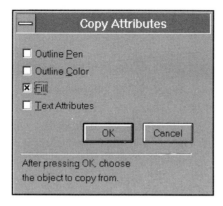

FIGURE 3.29 The Copy Attributes From dialog box

Select All

This command automatically selects all the objects in a drawing. They are joined into a temporary group, and clicking outside the boundary handles will unselect them.

Edit Object and Links

The **Edit Object** command is limited to use with parts of a drawing that were imported using the OLE ability of Windows 3.1. This feature is not supported by all Windows applications. If you have used OLE to bring information from another application into CorelDRAW, this option allows you to edit that part of the drawing in the source program. These procedures are covered later in the book.

Linking enables you to use information in one application (like CorelDRAW) created by another application (like CorelCHART or Word for Windows) and update the destination file any time the information changes in the source file. You can also limit the update capability so that it occurs only when you want the information updated. Working with OLE and linking information will be discussed later in Sections One and Two of this book.

Chapter Summary

This chapter has focused on one of CorelDRAW's most powerful features, the ability to create and edit Bézier curves. Both the Pencil and Shape tools were used to produce and modify objects. You learned more about paths and used curves and fills to build an illustration. By now you should be familiar with most of the primary functions of CorelDRAW 5.0. Next, we'll turn our attention to how the program handles text and how it can be used to produce printed materials and drawings that incorporate typography.

CHAPTER 4
Working with Words

- CorelDRAW Fonts and Working with Type
- Artistic, Paragraph, and Symbol Text
- Sizing and Transforming Type
- Kerning and Controlling with the Shape Tool
- Working with Symbols
- Converting Text to Curves
- Fitting Text to Path
- Spell-checking and the Thesaurus
- The Extended Character Sets

LIFE IS MORE THAN PRETTY PICTURES

Until now, we have focused primarily on CorelDRAW's ability to create objects for illustrations. In the real world most applications also use words to get their message across. CorelDRAW's extensive type-handling abilities, bundled collection of fonts, and text effects are major reasons for its popularity and a string of international industry awards.

To get the most benefit from CorelDRAW's typesetting features we need to understand something about typography and fonts. Although one book can't make you an expert, it can get you started in the right direction and learn how to use CorelDRAW's tools. A copy of CorelDRAW and a PC give you controls that rival (and sometimes surpass) dedicated typesetting tools of a few years ago. But you must learn some of the tricks of the trade to take advantage of all that power. The text-handling portion of CorelDRAW code was totally redesigned in version 3.0 from earlier versions. The basic interface was much improved and is even better in the current 5.0 release. There are a number of features concentrated in a single tool and one menu. Past versions of the software required the user to enter text in a dialog box instead of directly onto a drawing. You can now type a short block of type directly on the page as you did in Chapter 1, or you can use sophisticated import and merge features to use large amounts of text from a word processor like Microsoft's Word for Windows or WordPerfect. Version 5.0 has extended the feature set by adding named styles, tables, and multipage layouts. In this first chapter on text handling we will focus on single-page layouts and basic tools, saving more complex projects, such as brochures and newsletters, for later.

A symbol library is built into the Text tool that enables you to incorporate symbol and clipart figures easily into a drawing. You can convert type into Bézier curves and do all kinds of manipulations, as well as apply special effects, which will be covered in the next chapter.

If you have a CD-ROM drive, CorelDRAW 5.0 offers 825 different fonts, in Adobe PostScript and Microsoft TrueType formats. The TrueType fonts are from BitStream and have **BT** after their names. If you installed using floppies, only about fifty fonts were moved to your hard drive, but in either case you can add more at any time. These fonts are scaled on the fly, meaning that you will get smooth-looking type tailored to the resolution of your printer or output device. Users without a CD-ROM drive will still have over 150 different fonts at their disposal. All these fonts can be used in any other Windows application.

You can modify these typefaces and create new ones that can be added to your typographic arsenal. CorelDRAW can also use any other font that is supported by

Windows 3.1 and added via the control panel, such as those supplied by Adobe, Bitstream, and other third-party vendors. Ten years ago, one or two fonts for a typesetting machine would have cost you more than the total cost of the CorelDRAW package itself. Be aware that fonts take up resources and can slow down your system. A section later in this book covers installation and gives some tips for dealing with fonts. If a typeface for an exercise is not located on your machine, just substitute another one.

Why Does Typography Have to Be So Complicated?

The typewriter served as the mainstay of office automation for almost 100 years and produced mechanical type without a lot of fuss. It was the universal business machine. You pressed a key and a letter appeared on the page. The forms that struck the paper looked a lot like the hot metal type of the same period, but there was a fundamental difference. The typewriter could place only fixed type. The design of the machine limited the way the characters could be placed on the page. All but the most modern typewriters were limited to monospaced type. That meant that each letter, from a capital *W* to a lowercase *i*, took up the same amount of space. The space between lines was fixed as well. Some typewriters and many of today's dot matrix printers offer proportionally spaced type. The letter *W* gets more space for its block than a capital *I*, which in turn gets more space than a small *i*. This makes for a better-looking page, but still is not enough control for really demanding tasks and a really professional look.

Until the advent of "desktop publishing" a few years ago, typography was the exclusive domain of professionals. It required special equipment and a lot of training. There is as much art as craft to setting type. The goal is simple: a readable page that attracts the viewer's eye. Typesetting equipment, including computer-based equipment, can place type anywhere, in almost any size, with almost any kind of spacing between words, letters, and lines. Typesetting is to publishing what the airplane is to rail travel. Both offer advantages over handwriting when it comes to speed and legibility. Both require a lot of maintenance, both can get you where you want to go, but one is three-dimensional and one is not. Trains and typewriters are easier to operate; airplanes and typesetters require additional skills.

If you are willing to put in extra effort and pay more attention to detail, typesetting offers complete control over the appearance of the page. To be an effective computer typographer you must learn the terms and tricks of the trade. They are not all that arcane, if you keep in mind that they are precise technical terms and conventions developed over a 500-year period. You will gain a lot of control over the way your publications look and learn more about the craft of expressing ideas with the printed word.

Type as a Design Tool

Almost from the first days of the printing press, type has been used as a central part of the design process. The way a page is formed, the relative amount of white space surrounding the text, the choice of typefaces, and the size of the letters are not just a passing concern. They determine legibility, set the tone of a publication, and draw the reader into the page. Unlike the spoken word, printing does not offer intonations to communicate meaning. Instead you must use type to convey meanings that are taken for granted when speaking. Text can be used with graphic elements to enhance the message. All this may sound complicated, but if you have been an attentive reader during your life you are an experienced user of type. You have a lot of experience knowing what is readable and what is not. Libraries, bookstores, magazines, and your own bookshelves are good sources for examples to help you plan a design. Many graphic artists keep an eye open for pleasing pages and even have scrapbooks to use for ideas.

A Few Typographical Terms

Before you get into working with the Text tool you need to define a few terms. A *type family* is a collection of typefaces that are similar in appearance and design; basically, they are variants of a common ancestor. A *typeface* is a specific type style, irrespective of size and weight: a single member of a type family. A *font* is a complete set of letters (upper- and lowercase), numbers, common symbols, and punctuation marks in one size and typeface. In the days when fonts were actually set in hot metal, different font sizes of the same face were designed a bit differently to make them easier to read. In other words, the shape of the letters was scaled based on the size. Much (if not most) computer type is scalable, but without changing the appearance. That means that the letters are enlarged or reduced to create the exact size needed. In some cases that may mean that very small sizes may be harder on the eyes or that large sizes may not have the same visual quality as more-normal-sized type.

There are two basic groups of type: *serif* and *sans serif*. Serif typefaces have the little flourish marks and lines on letters that add to the character of a font. Times and Goudy are examples of serif typefaces. *Sans* means "without." Sans serif typefaces are designed without the ornamental flourishes. Examples include Helvetica and Century Gothic. Designers create and choose typefaces to match the needs of a publication or client. Bankers want a typeface that will suggest fiscal responsibility. A fancy restaurant wants a menu that imparts a feeling of elegance to match its decor. Newspaper and book publishers need to have type that is easy to read.

Some experts break type into other categories of specialty typefaces, such as text, display, decorative, and symbol styles. Display faces are used for advertising purposes, not for general reading material. Decorative faces are used for special purposes, such as invitations and posters. They set a mood but are generally not as easy to read as text type. Symbol faces are generally a set of related characters, like musical or mathematical notations. Figure 4.1 shows examples of sans-serif, serif, decorative, and symbol type.

Sans Serif
Switzerland
Frankfurt Gothic
Avalon

Serif
Florence
Gatineau
Nebraska

Decorative
UMBRELLA
Bravo Engraved
QT Ghoulface

FIGURE 4.1 Sample typefaces

CorelDRAW gives us an impressive array of typefaces, but realize that some restraint is in order. Don't get carried away with your bounty. Most jobs should be limited to no more than two typefaces. Vary emphasis with variants of the same face, such as bold, italic, and bold italic fonts in different sizes rather than adding another typeface. Some of the finer points of typography will be discussed later. Let's look at how CorelDRAW handles text elements and the basic tools first.

Using Text in CorelDRAW

Entering text in a drawing is easy. All you do is place the Text tool cursor where you want to begin, and type. But there is a lot of action the program does beneath the surface as you set type. Text objects are a special class within CorelDRAW, with some properties and features that are different from other objects. Text is a compound object. Each character is a defined part of the larger object, like a very fancy line segment. You can perform operations on the block as a whole or in most cases on any combination of letters. Within the block, you can apply special spacing, sizing, and movement commands to individual letters or groups of characters.

You still have outlines and fills, as with all CorelDRAW elements. All the program's special effects and transformations can be applied to text. Blocks of type can be converted from text to a set of Bézier curves and then manipulated with the Shape tool. You can also divide blocks of text into columns and take advantage of special alignment and spacing commands. One example is the **Fit Text To Path** command, which wraps a string of text around the outline of another object.

Variations on a Theme: Artistic and Paragraph Text

There are several ways to place text objects in a drawing, depending on the amount of letters and how they will be used in the drawing. If you type text directly onto the page you are limited to a maximum of 250 characters per block. A block is a body of text ended with a hard line return. CorelDRAW refers to this kind of text element as *artistic text*. This is the way to place type that will be modified using special effects. It is the easiest way to create small blocks of text for use in a drawing.

Paragraph text is used for longer passages of up to 4,000 characters per paragraph and is contained in a frame. You use this form of type for imported text (like that from your favorite word processor) and type that runs more than one column. There is no fixed limit on the number of text objects that can be placed in a drawing, unless you run out of system resources (such as memory). You can also place text in a drawing using the Windows Clipboard. Even though there are limits to the number of characters in a text block, there is no limit to the number of blocks that can be in a drawing. Although the size limits are sometimes an annoyance, they are rarely a real problem. Most of the features and commands are the same for both classes of text.

Symbols form another class of objects in CorelDRAW. They are added to your document via the Symbol roll-up. They include fancy borders, common signs, business machines, plants, animals, and technical symbols. You choose the Symbol roll-up by selecting the star icon on the Ribbon bar. How to use artistic text and symbols will be discussed in this chapter. Paragraph text and typeface design skills will be discussed in Chapter 5 and in Section Two.

The Text Tool and Artistic Text

The Text Tool

As with the Pencil tool, CorelDRAW's designers have included several functions under one icon on the toolbar. Their primary use is for standard text insertion. The first one is shaped like the letter A. The second one is the Frame tool, which is used to manipulate text in frames. Those functions are covered in another chapter. The third, shaped like a star, is used to access and place objects from an extensive symbol collection. Click and hold the icon on the toolbar that is shaped like the letter A. A fly-out will appear that has two icons: one just like the one on the toolbar and another that resembles a page of text. They work just like the Pencil tool. Figure 4.2 shows the Text tool fly-out.

FIGURE 4.2 The CorelDRAW Text tool

As mentioned earlier, the A-shaped icon is the normal Text tool. Choose it and the cursor will change to cross hairs. An I-beam shape will appear as it travels onto the work area. You can then click on the page, and that point becomes the text insertion position. Just for practice, open the fly-out and click and hold on the star shape. The Text tool will be placed in Symbol mode. Text entered directly on the page is always artistic text; you'll see what that means as we work in this chapter. The factory default font is 24-point Avante Garde Bk BT Normal.

Entering Artistic Text Directly on the Page

If you are not in CorelDRAW open it now. Use the Zoom tool to get a full-page view. Choose the Text tool and move the cursor (which will change to a set of cross hairs) to the upper left-hand corner of the page. Click once. The cursor will become an I shape at the insertion point. Type **This is some sample text**. The text will appear on the page as you type, starting at the location where you clicked the mouse button. Press **Enter** and add another line: **This is more sample text**. Press **Enter** and add, **And this is also sample text**. You can have about 250 characters in a block of artistic text. The exact number will vary with the complexity of the typeface. When you hit the limit, the keystrokes no longer result in new letters on the screen. Every keystroke, including spaces and Returns, counts. If you need to place more than 250 characters, consider using paragraph text or add another block the way you placed the first one. Before going on save your work as SAMPLE.CDR. You will be using this block of text later, and you will need a clean copy without the modifications you are about to make.

Selecting the Pick Tool in a Text Mode

When the Text tool is active, the space bar enters a space in the current block and can't be used to select the Pick tool. Since you have previously set the right mouse button to activate the Shape tool, you can click the right mouse button and then the space bar to get the Pick tool. Try that now. Then draw a marquee around all three lines of text. Using the mouse, make the text larger by dragging down the lower right-hand corner handle at a 45-degree angle so it fills the page from left to right. Now center the block on the page with the **Align** command under the Arrange menu. It should look like Figure 4.3.

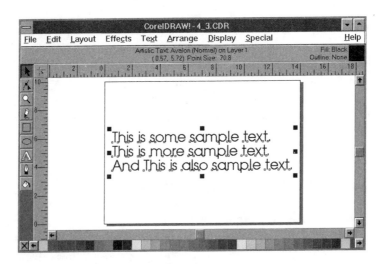

FIGURE 4.3 A sample text object

Sizing and Transforming Type with the Pick Tool

Artistic Type is an object. It can be scaled, stretched, skewed, and rotated with the Pick tool just like any other object. Since you have already worked with transformations in the last chapter, you will not be going into great detail about it here. Be careful when manipulating text. Type is designed to appear a certain way. If you use the Pick tool to scale text and don't enlarge or reduce both the height and width the same amount, the letters will look unusual. This can be good for some effects and terrible for others. Don't forget that the **Undo** command is only a keystroke away.

Figure 4.4 shows our sample as a sans serif font that has been made tall and thin with scaling and then rotated. Try this on your block of text. Use the Pick tool and drag straight down from the bottom middle handle. Then drag down at a 45-degree angle holding the lower right-hand handle. As you do this note the changes in the status bar. Each time you pause while dragging (don't release the mouse button) the status bar will tell you the percent of enlargement or reduction based on the original. The sample in Figure 4.4 is 107.9 percent larger. It also tells you the resulting point size—here 233.6 points. That block of text started out as 24-point type. Each time you release the mouse, the base number used to calculate the change is modified. That's why the status bar in Figure 4.4 reports only a slight enlargement of size, rather than the roughly tenfold increase that has actually taken place.

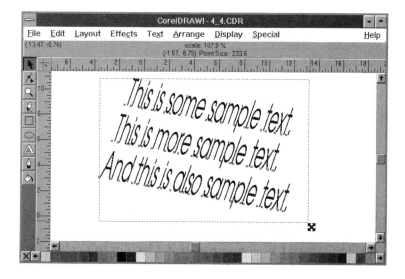

FIGURE 4.4 Transforming text objects

You can use the Outline and Pen tools to modify text objects. This includes calligraphic outlines, dashed lines, and both bitmap and full-color Pattern fills. In most cases, especially with PostScript printers, you will want to leave text without an outline. Small type will not show much in the way of pattern fills. Text effects will be covered in more detail with the projects and examples in Section Two, but feel free to experiment now.

Using the Text Editing Dialog Box

The Text Editing dialog box offers one-stop shopping for changing the content, size, typeface, spacing, and style of a text object. It can be accessed via the Text menu or with a hot-key combination. Try it now. Select your block of text. Then press the **Ctrl-T** combination. This opens the Character Attributes dialog box. You can set the typeface for a block of text using the scroll-through menu on the left of the box, change the justification using the radio buttons in the lower right, and control the size and style via the entry boxes on the right side.

Changing Typefaces

The window in the lower right shows the first few characters you typed displayed in the current font. Since CorelDRAW supports Windows, Adobe PostScript, and TrueType fonts, the font type is shown under the sample window. The exact fonts and the number of typefaces available will depend on the version of CorelDRAW, your specific installation, and the other fonts loaded via the Microsoft Windows Control Panel. Figure 4.5 shows how a dialog box would look if you tried changing the font to Elegantia BoldItalic. In the following exercises and examples don't worry about having exactly the same font as the ones I use. Considering the number of fonts and different possible installation options, it is quite possible that you do not have the same ones. Just choose a similar style.

Change to another typeface yourself. Just work through the menu with the scroll bar. As you click on a name, the sample on the right will change. The modification will not take place until you click **OK**. Choose several and note the differences, then click **OK**.

Editing Existing Text

Click on your sample text on the page and then press **Ctrl-Shift-T** (that means hold down the **Ctrl** and **Shift** keys simultaneously and then tap **T**) and the Edit Text dialog box appears. Then type some new text. See how you can edit type inside the dialog box. Again your changes won't be acted on until you click **OK**. This is especially useful when you have text which is difficult to select because it is slanted or curves around on the screen. You are then just one click from being able to change character attributes for text in the box.

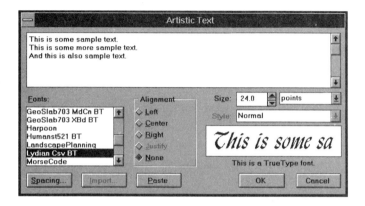

FIGURE 4.5 The Character Attributes dialog box

You can edit text that is already on the screen by clicking at the point where you want to make changes. The cross hairs will change to an I-beam shape like the one used by most Windows word processors, allowing you to add, delete, or type at will. Remember that artistic text is designed for use with short blocks of type. If you plan to place a large block, or need advanced word-processing tools, use the paragraph text options described later in this chapter.

Justification

The horizontal arrangement of type within a column between the margins of a page is called justification. With Artistic Text in CorelDRAW the bounding box usually serves as the limit of a line of type. With paragraph text placed in a frame you can set columns. Three justification options for CorelDRAW text are demonstrated in Figure 4.6. Options are set using the Character Attributes dialog box (Ctrl-T).

- **Left Justification** means that the type is forced to the left side of the block and the that right edge will be left ragged. Typographers sometimes call it rag-right.

This is often the best setting for narrow blocks of text because full justification would result in wide spaces between words. Just how narrow is narrow depends on the size of the type. It's the number of characters per line that matters.

- **Center Justification** looks just as you would expect: The text is forced to the center of the column width. Headlines and titles are often set centered.
- **Right Justified** type is hard to read in large blocks, and so should be used with care. It is often used to set poetry, to caption photos and other illustrations, or to identify an author after a quote. It has a ragged edge on the left side and so is also known as rag-left.
- **Full Justification** (Justify button) has even margins on both sides. This is usually reserved for wider blocks of text and more formal publishing, such as books. Full (also known as left and right) justification is only available with paragraph text (discussed later in this chapter).
- The **None** option is unique to CorelDRAW. It is not a traditional method of justifying text, but a special setting that allows you control over the size and position of individual letters with the Shape tool. It is also the only form of justification that permits use of the **Tab** key. Go ahead and change the justification of your sample text a few times as practice and to see how they look on the page.

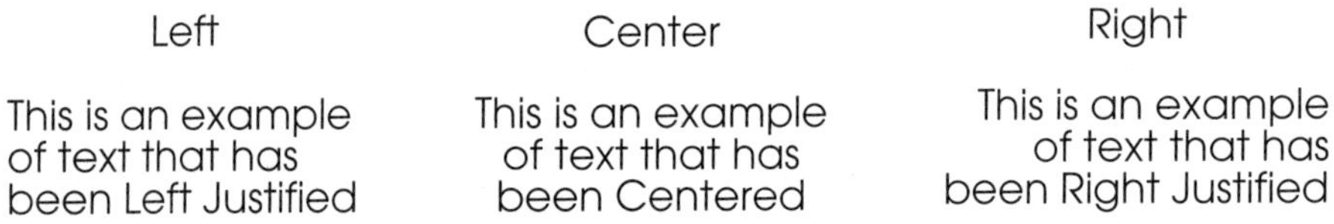

Left	Center	Right
This is an example of text that has been Left Justified	This is an example of text that has been Centered	This is an example of text that has been Right Justified

FIGURE 4.6 Justification options

A Matter of Style

The term *style*, as it is used here, refers to variations of a given typeface. These generally include normal (sometimes called roman), bold, italic, oblique, and bold italic. They are used to give emphasis to letters or words without having to resort to a different typeface or effect, such as underlining or changing size. The available styles will vary with the typeface being used. Some decorative faces only come in bold or italic. Many people confuse italic and oblique. They are not the same thing. An oblique font is the same in appearance as the normal font, but it is sloped. An italic font is designed with a more curved appearance and is tailored to its angled shape.

When you change the style, the type in the Preview will also change. Several samples are shown in Figure 4.7. Note the length of each line compared to the others shown below. All are 24-point type, but the italic face is shorter than normal, and the bold and bold italic are longer. Each one is scaled a bit differently. Try some different styles in the Preview window before going on.

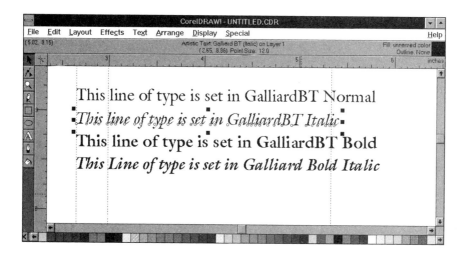

FIGURE 4.7 Type style examples

Working with Points, Picas, and a Little Lead

Welcome to the world of points and picas; these are the standard units of measure used by typographers. A pica is almost one-sixth of an inch (0.166040 inch to be exact—for the very precise reader) and a point is about one-seventy-second of an inch. (I say "about" because different measures are used in Europe and North America. For our purposes we'll consider them exact.) There are 12 points to the pica. This measuring system was designed more than a century ago to provide the precision needed to work with type. Throughout this book all references to type size will be in points. When using the Text Edit dialog boxes be sure that the unit of measure is set to points via the Selection menu to the right of the type size.

All CorelDRAW fonts are scalable. That means that you can specify or change the size of a block of type, or individual characters in one-tenth of a point increments from 0.7 to 2,160 points using the menus. It is possible, but not very useful, to get larger and smaller sizing using the **Transform** commands.

ADJUSTING SPACING

Typesetting options allow you to specify the distance between lines, letters, words, and paragraphs, as well as the size of the type. CorelDRAW enables the user to adjust these settings via menus or with the Shape and Pick tools. You can edit artistic text and change its appearance. The settings can be adjusted either via a dialog box or interactively on screen with the mouse. Open the saved copy of your sample text. Select the block and press the right mouse button. This should bring up the Shape tool and produce the arrow-shaped Spacing Control Handles as shown in Figure 4.8.

The revised text block should now be on your page. Press the right mouse button to select the Shape tool and click on the type. Place the point of the Shape tool over the down-arrow under the left side of the text. Drag it down and watch the amount of space increase. You have just adjusted the leading of your text.

Most typesetting terms were developed during the years when type was set by hand or machine. The vertical space between lines of type is commonly called leading by typographers, because lead shims, or spacers, were placed between the lines of type. Unlike typewritten copy, type can have any amount of space (even a negative space) between lines and letters.

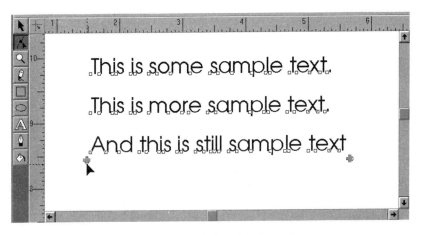

FIGURE 4.8 Adjusting leading with the Shape tool

Pull the other arrow located below the right side of your text out toward the right. The space between the letters is increased. This is called intercharacter spacing or letter spacing. Select **Undo** and again pull the text to the right, this time holding the **Ctrl** key.

Now the space only increases between words. The complicated term for this is *interword spacing*. You see, you already know several complicated typesetting terms. Now you have changed the leading, letter spacing, and word space. Moving the arrows up or to the left narrows the spacing.

Press **Ctrl-T**; this again opens the Character Attributes dialog box. Look at the spacing settings at the lower left. Here you can set the intercharacter, interword, interline (leading), and interparagraph spacing as values. As you can see in the example shown in Figure 4.9, all the numbers you played with just now show changes from the default 100 percent. The interparagraph setting is only available with Paragraph Text, which will be covered shortly.

Most publishing programs and all traditional typesetting machines specify leading in points. For example, 10-point type with 11 points of lead (which is called 10 over 11, or 10 on 11, points by typographers). That makes each line of white space between lines 10 percent larger than the type itself. CorelDRAW specifies lead as a percentage of the size of type in its menus, which is not very intuitive. What would you type in the box for 14 on 16-point leading? (Try it without a calculator.) In fairness most people probably adjust leading in CorelDRAW by eye with the Shape tool. Practice using the Shape tool to modify the appearance of the text. Periodically open the Character Attributes dialog as you work to see how the movements change the settings.

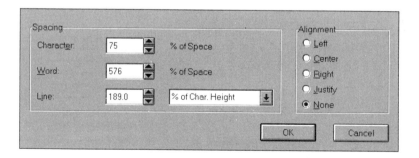

FIGURE 4.9 Text spacing in the Character Attributes dialog box

MEASURING TYPE

The only way to obtain a precise layout is with exact measurements. CorelDRAW 3.0 provided each user with a typescale guide, shown in Figure 4.10. Although this tool is no longer bundled with the software, similar gadgets are available in most art supply stores. Ask the clerk to show you type gauges or point scales—the most common type is called an E-scale. Some kinds are more complete than others, so it's a good idea to look at several types. You can use many of them to gauge what size type and how much leading to use or to measure hard-copy text to see what the existing point sizes and leading are. The guide in the figure below has pica, point, inches, and metric rulers, along with sample rules. Rules are the fancy name typesetters and layout people give to lines. A one-point line dividing two columns is a one-point rule. A half-point rule running all around the margins of a page would be a half-point box rule.

To use a typescale to measure type (or even to use the dialog box properly) you have to understand how type is measured and a few terms. The actual size of a font is measured from the top of the tallest part (an ascender) to the bottom of the lowest part (a descender). The difficulty is that there aren't any letters in the alphabet that have both ascenders and descenders. To make life even more confusing, there are variations of typefaces called small capitals. These are collections of letters that have all uppercase letters, symbols, and numbers—but no lowercase letters. To get around these challenges typesetters have devised some special tools.

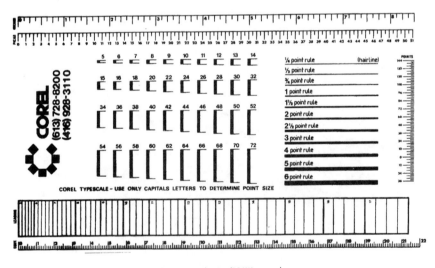

FIGURE 4.10 The CorelDRAW typescale

If you have one, take out your CorelDRAW Typescale. Notice the set of squared-off *C* shapes that have numbers on top of them to the left of the sample rules. Hold it over the capital *E* in Figure 4.11 and move it so that one of the *C*'s just fits. The number above the shape tells you the size of the type, adjusted for the fact that a capital letter has no descenders. Most art stores sell E-scales. These are clear plastic guides much like the one you just used.

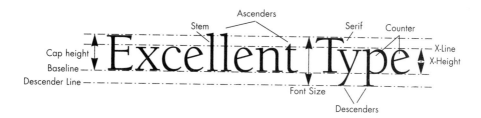

FIGURE 4.11 A partial anatomy

The labels in Figure 4.11 are defined here. As you continue working with type you will be using these terms and adding a few more. You don't have to memorize them; just be familiar enough with them to recognize them when they are used.

- **Ascender.** The portion of some lowercase letters (such as *h*, *l*, and *t*) that extend above the x-line. In some fonts the top of an ascender may be above or below the cap height.
- **Baseline.** This is the principal frame of reference for type. It is the invisible line on which the bottoms of all characters except those with descenders rest. The base of the x-height is calculated from the baseline. Leading is measured from the baseline of one line of type to the next.
- **Cap Height.** The distance from the top of a capital letter to the baseline. This is the area used to determine point size with E-scales and other capital-based type rulers. Do not use an E-scale to measure points! A 24-point letter, *E*, is not 24 points tall. The exact height of a capital letter will vary with each font and letter. The cap height is shown with an arrowed line on the left of Figure 4.11.
- **Counter.** The open spaces inside such letters as *p*, *g*, *a*, and *e* are called counters. In very small point sizes the counter may be filled with ink or toner. A 300-dpi printer can usually print no smaller than 6-point type without problems with filled counters. Converting text to curves in CorelDRAW may also result in filled counters.
- **Descender.** The portion of some lowercase letters (such as *y*, *p*, *q*) that extends below the baseline.
- **Descender Line.** An imaginary line drawn at the level of the lower tip of the descenders for a given font. This line is used as the bottom point for measuring

the size of a font. If the leading is reduced, the descender line of one row of type may overlap the ascender line of the following row.

- **Font Size.** This is the distance measured from the descender line to the top of the capitals.
- **Serifs.** These are flourishes or strokes added to characters to make the type easy to read and give a typeface its own style.
- **X-Height.** The distance from the baseline up to the top of a lowercase *x* in a given font.
- **X-Line.** An imaginary line running at the level of the top of the lowercase *x* in a given font. The distance from an x-height to the baseline is space used to form the body of lowercase characters.

A Little Practice with Letters

Before going any further it's a good idea to practice working with artistic text and the basic controls that have already been introduced. That will also give you a chance to experiment with different typefaces. You can dress up the page with commands presented in past chapters and then learn some new tricks with text. Open a new file and select the Text tool. The **F8** key is the hot-key, or you can use the mouse and toolbox. Place the cursor in the middle of the page and type the following.

"The Difference Between

The Right Word and

The Almost Right Word

Is the Difference

Between Lightning

And the Ligghting Bug."

Include the quotation marks. Capitalize and break the lines as shown in the example. There is a spelling error in the last line, leave it as shown for now. Use the Text tool again to type **Mark Twain** in the lower right-hand corner of the page. With the Pick tool move the type to the upper left-hand corner of the page. (Press the right mouse button to get the Shape tool; then tap the space bar. The space bar won't work as a hot-key while the Text tool is active, so use the Shape tool as a pass-through step.)

Use the Pick tool to change the size of the quotation type. Drag the text at a 45-degree angle, so that you don't change the visual perspective of the typeface. Bring to about 64 points in size. Use the **Align** command in the Arrange menu to center the quotation on the page. Select it and press **Ctrl-T**. This will open the Artistic Text dialog box. Choose a serif typeface like the one in the sample by using the scroll bar menu and your mouse. Then click **OK** and use the same procedure to change the smaller block of text to a decorative face. Save your work as MARK.CDR before going further, and don't save any of the following changes. You will be modifying the text a good bit, so you will need an original clean copy later in the book.

With your copy of CorelDRAW there is a second manual containing samples of all the typefaces shipped with the program, as well as pictures of the clipart. There are also notes explaining the relation of the new fonts to the names used in CorelDRAW 3.0. Keep in mind that all the fonts exactly match the 3.0 versions, so you may want to keep some of the old ones around. In addition, the kerning and spacing may not be the same, so some drawings created in the earlier release may need some fine-tuning.

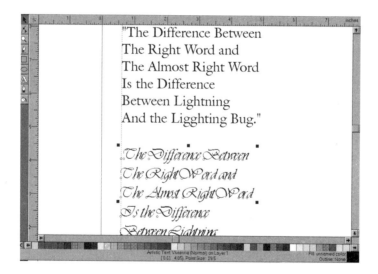

FIGURE 4.12 A brief quotation

Matters of Size, Style, and Perception

The two copies of the name in the lower right of the preceding figure seem to be different sizes, but both are 24 point! Remember how type is measured. It is not the size of any individual letter, but the distance from the top of the ascenders to the bottom of the descenders. Experiment with different typefaces on the large block of text and see what a difference in area it takes up on the page. While you're at it, notice how different faces change the "mood" of the quote. Use different styles. How does a use of boldface affect the page and readability, or bold italic? Use a font that is all capitals or very cursive (like Hollow). With each style the area the type takes up may change again. This may require adjustments to the way a drawing is laid out or may mean that the point size must be readjusted.

You can use leading and point size to fit a block of text into an exact area (as you will do in Section Two) or to conserve on the number of pages in a publication. Dropping the leading and point size 10 percent reduces the length of the text about the same amount.

Pity the Poor Reader

There are a lot of things to consider when working with type: the mood you are trying to convey, the artistic expression—all kinds of very subjective things. But there is one real concern that is at the core of every decision: communicating to readers, getting them to understand what is meant by the words and pictures on the page.

You want to attract attention and draw readers into your work. How often have you looked at an ad or poster and had to search for the point? How often have you had to struggle to make out the words on the page because the layout was confusing or the color and type were hard to read? Good illustrations and effective typography are both attention-getting and easy to read. In Section Two you will look closely at design issues and the view. Here are a few basics.

How Big Is Too Big, What Is Too Small, and How Much Is Too Much?

There are certain accepted conventions in type size, based on the task at hand. How easy is it to read the fine print? Lawyers and newspapers use from six- down to four-point type for legal announcements, contracts, and notices. This saves space but makes the letters hard to read. Normal reading size fonts are generally from 10- to 12-point type, in many cases with extra leading to "open up the page." Sizes above 12 points, in a normal style, or 10-point bold and above are generally used for headings.

Of course those guidelines are for normal reading material. Posters, billboards, miniature books, and the like follow rules based on size and the need of the audience. If you are designing a mural for a wall, the amount and size of type (and every other element) should be based on the viewing distance. The "normal" reading size is based on somebody holding a book or page within arm's length. A slide projected on a screen will only hold a viewer's interest for about ten seconds, less if the type is hard to read, the graphic too difficult to understand, or the background too bright for comfort. When you work with text in CorelDRAW and are choosing a typeface and point size, consider the nature of the project, the reader's eyes, and the size of the final product.

Leading

Leading is another control factor that is too often taken for granted by novice desktop publishers. Leading allows you to balance the amount of type in relation to the white space in text areas. Too much space can make it hard to follow the flow of words; too little space makes the text look cramped on the page. Figure 4.13 shows the quotation with three different amounts of leading. See how the 90 percent setting just keeps the g in the next-to-last row from touching the t below it. What would have happened if the g had been in the space of the h to the left? They would have printed in the same space. For most text a slight amount of positive (greater amount than the size of the text) leading helps the reader.

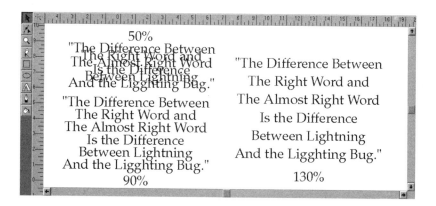

FIGURE 4.13 The effects of different leading

MODIFYING PART OF A TEXT OBJECT

So far the discussion has focused on handling a text object as a block to adjust spacing, change fonts, or modify size. But CorelDRAW offers a lot finer control over the appearance of type. An entire block, a single word, or only a few letters can be modified. Using the Styles feature you can change certain named blocks throughout an entire document. You can adjust and modify individual characters within a text object with the Shape tool or with dialog boxes. To edit part of a block you use the **Character Attributes** option located in the Text menu. The basic rules for working with any CorelDRAW object apply. You must select the elements to be worked with, set any required options, then issue the command to execute the changes.

Draw over the word *Difference* in the first line with the Text tool's I-beam cursor. Notice how the letters are covered with a gray mask. You can select from a single letter to a complete block of text this way. A single word can be selected by double-clicking on it with the Text tool cursor. Any changes that you make will only be applied to the grayed-out (highlighted) part of the text string. There is another way to select characters. Click the right mouse button; the Shape tool cursor should appear. Now draw a marquee around the little boxes under the letters of the word *Differences*. The boxes are called nodes.

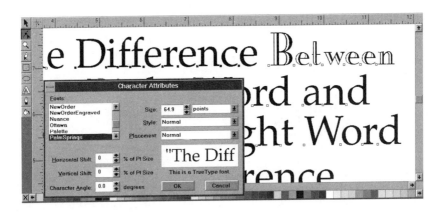

FIGURE 4.14 Working with character attributes

Notice how the example in Figure 4.14 looks. The word *Between* in the first line of the quotation has been changed to another typeface using the **Character Attributes** command already. The word *Difference* has been selected and will be the target of any modifications made when the dialog box is OK'ed. Notice the nodes under the letters in the word. They are black, so the letters are selected. The other words have hollow squares. Look at the status bar. It tells you that ten characters are currently selected.

Double-click on one of the selected nodes. The Character Attributes dialog box will open. This is a much quicker way to open it than by dragging over the letters, opening the Text menu, and then choosing the **Character...** option. Use the dialog box to change the font size and typeface; then click **OK**. Only the one word is changed. Now use the **Undo** command to cancel the modifications. Try this a few more times with the Size, Style, and Placement settings until you become familiar with them. Leave the Shift and Angle settings alone for now.

THE CRAFT OF KERNING

Kerning is the term for adjusting the horizontal space between pairs of letters, tweaking them to produce a more balanced look. Two letters that have to be adjusted are called a kerned pair. Professional typesetting equipment and some desktop publishing software, including CorelDRAW, have logic for automatically kerning pairs of letters.

Look closely at the word *Word* in the third line of the quotation. Notice how the left edge of the letter *o* is actually inside the right overhang of the *W* next to it. Normal proportionally spaced type does not allow one letter to invade the space of another, but more advanced font technology does. True kerning goes beyond just spacing letters: Each left–right combination is individually defined. A specific pair is called a *ligature*, from the Latin word meaning "bound together." Justification can interfere with kerning. If possible, set justification to **None** or **Left** before moving any characters using the procedure mentioned here. Using **Center Right** or **Full Justification** may cause letters you are not kerning to be moved as well as the ones you are shifting.

Manual Kerning with the Shape Tool

The easiest way to adjust the space between letters is with the Shape tool. Open a new drawing and type **WAVEFORM** twice with a return at the end of the first word. Select the block of text, open the Text Edit dialog box (**Ctrl-T**), and set the justification to **None**. Set the font to some serif typeface and make the size at least 64 points. Use the Zoom tool to have the object fill the page. Select the Shape tool with the right mouse button; then click on the letter A in the top row. Hold down the **Ctrl** key and drag the mouse to the left. The cursor will change to a cross and the letter will pull as you move. The constraint of the **Ctrl** key will force the letter to sit on the baseline. Move the other letters until your word looks like the example in Figure 4.15. You can use the shift-click selection method to choose several letters that are not next to each other.

The top word in the figure is tightly kerned. All letters are almost touching. This is used for logos, headlines, and display text. The guidelines illustrate how much you have reduced the length of the word, about 12 percent. Practice a bit with moving the letters back and forth. Notice how different settings change the balance of the word. Kerning can be used to make a line of type look more open or closed. You can also move several letters at once by using the marquee select technique. Leave the lower copy of the word unchanged; you'll use it next.

FIGURE 4.15 The effects of kerning

Aligning to Baseline

This is a handy command to use after interactively kerning letters. Select the text block and use the **Alt-F10** hot-key or invoke the command from the Text menu. The bottoms of all the characters in the object will be placed exactly on the baseline. This only resets the vertical shift; the horizontal settings you obtained by kerning will remain.

Precise Kerning with the Dialog Box

You can use the Character Attribute dialog box to set a numeric kerning value. Use the Shape tool to select the A in the lower copy of the word and double-click. The dialog box will open. Set the Horizontal Shift to 24 percent and choose **OK**. The result should look like Figure 4.16. Selecting several characters at once will not kern the space between those letters. It will just kern the leftmost character and move all the letters with it un-kerned.

Manipulating Character Angle and Shift

There are still a couple of positioning controls you haven't used—angle and vertical shift. Shift can be controlled just like kerning, with either the Character Attributes dialog box or the Shape tool; angle can be controlled with the dialog box. Remove your block of text using the Pick tool and the **Delete** key. Now with the Text tool place the word *WAVEform* (just like that) on the page and zoom it on it.

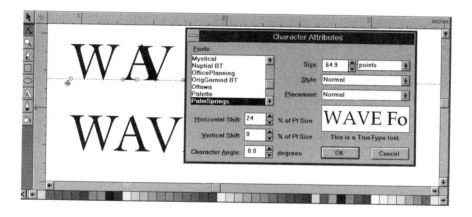

FIGURE 4.16 Setting numeric kerning values

Vertical Shift

The amount of vertical offset of a character from the baseline is called *vertical shift*. Use the shift-click method to select the nodes located on the left of the capital A and lowercase *o*. Now drag either node up, and the two letters will move. If you hold the **Ctrl** key, movement will be limited to straight up or down. Figure 4.17 shows how the screen should look as you perform the command. Don't forget that if there is not enough leading between the row and the adjacent lines your letters will overlap other characters.

FIGURE 4.17 Changing vertical shift with the Shape tool

If you don't hold the **Ctrl** key to constrain movement, the letters can be moved in any direction. Your screen may not show the dashed shapes of the letters as you move them, as in the figures. There is a setting in the CorelDRAW configuration file that controls this feature. With it enabled, some screen operations may be unacceptably slow, and so it is not a factory default. If you wish to enable it, see the section on customizing CorelDRAW later in this book. The procedure for adjusting vertical shift with the Character Attribute dialog box is very similar. Choose the letters to be changed the same way, but double-click with the Shape tool after selecting the nodes. The dialog box will open. Enter the number. A positive number set in the dialog box raises the letter, and a negative number lowers it. When you click **OK** the changes will take effect. Figure 4.18 shows the dialog box and the results of a negative vertical shift.

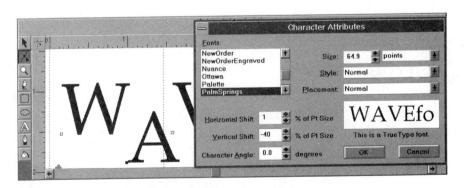

FIGURE 4.18 Setting a negative vertical shift

Altering the Angle of Individual Letters

While you can rotate blocks of text and perform other transformations with the Pick tool, you can't use it to rotate individual letters. You can achieve the same effect with the **Character Angle** command. Delete the last text you created and type **Wave**. Select the *a* by double-clicking with the Shape tool. Enter 30 degrees in the Character Angle box and click **OK**. The top of the letter should be overlapping the right side of the W to its left. The dialog box in Figure 4.19 shows the screen. You can position it with the Shape tool so that it is in the right position. Once you have done that, experiment with combinations of horizontal, vertical, and angle settings. The results will be somewhat unpredictable, since you are modifying more than one setting at a time. The best way to handle offset and angle combinations is to set the angle first and then use the Shape tool to put the rotated letter just where you want it.

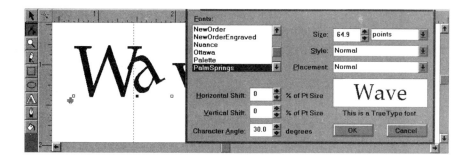

FIGURE 4.19 Adjusting the character angle

Straightening Text

CorelDRAW offers a special safety net when altering the position of individual characters. Unlike the **Undo** command, Straighten Text can be applied to any rotated or shifted character. You can even use it on several letters at once by selecting them with the shift-click or marquee methods.

Just choose the letters to be returned to normal and click on the command located in the Text menu. The letters will be set to normal rotation and placed on the baseline.

A Friendly Sign

There is a lot to working with text in CorelDRAW. You have been at it for a while, and only covered the basics of artistic text. You have been introduced to pretty much everything used on a regular basis and to all the typography the average user will ever need. This exercise will give you an opportunity to use the skills covered so far. After you finish the basic drawing, it will be used to explain symbol text.

Do you remember your yard sale sign? Well, a neighbor saw it and needs a sign for the window in her store. Her name is Samantha, and the business is called Sam's Scuba Shop. She wants it to look like a dive flag with the store name at an angle and type to point out that she gives instruction and tours. It would be nice to have a bit of sea life and some kind of fancy lettering. Start by drawing in the dive flag and filling it.

The Basic Flag

Open a new landscape page. Then set the Pencil tool to Bézier mode and draw two triangles so that a clear diagonal stripe runs down from the upper left-hand corner. Just click at each corner of the triangle. Don't forget to hit the space bar after placing the last node on top of the first. The status bar can help by showing the angle of the lines. Be sure that the triangles have closed paths. Then fill them with a bright red. The result is shown in Figure 4.20.

FIGURE 4.20 The basic dive flag

Setting Some Type

Press **F8** to get the Text tool and place the cursor in the top left side of the upper triangle. Enter **Equipment (Return) Sales & (Return) Service**. Select the text. Give it a white fill and a .02-point black outline. Then use the Artistic Text dialog box (**Ctrl-T**) to change the font to Bodnoff and the justification to **None**. Use the Transform function to fit the words inside the triangle, about 90 points. The status line can help you gauge the size. With the Shape tool adjust the kerning and vertical alignment as shown in Figure 4.21. So why is that last object called the primary text block? Because you are going to use it as a master for all the other text on the page. Remember you are going to use the **Place Duplicate** and **Copy Style From** commands to save time and create a special effect.

FIGURE 4.21 The primary text block after kerning

Select **Preferences** off the Special menu and set the **Place Duplicates** and **Clones** unit of measure to points for both settings. Then set the two values to 3.0 points as shown in Figure 4.22. You are going to use **Place Duplicate** to create a drop shadow effect. Once you are finished, click **OK**.

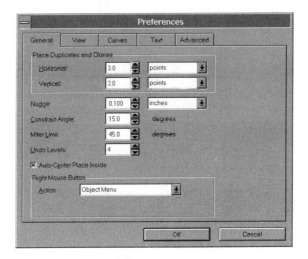

FIGURE 4.22 The drop shadow setting

Use the Pick tool to select the block of text. Now press **Ctrl-D** to make a copy of it. A new block of text is placed on top and slightly to the upper right of the first. Give it a black fill and a .3-point black outline using the Outline Pen dialog box. Press the **PageDown** key to set it behind the first block of type. That part of the sign should now look like Figure 4.23.

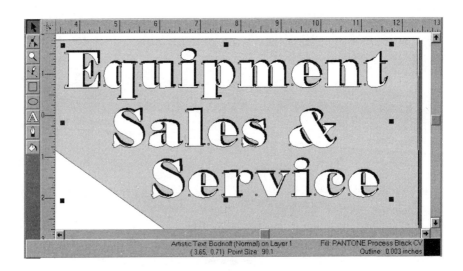

FIGURE 4.23 The drop shadow

Adding More Text and a Second Drop Shadow

With the Text tool type **Dive Trips (Return) Dive Lessons** in the lower triangle. Use the **Copy Style From** option under the Edit menu to set the font, fill, and outline the same as the first block you created. You don't have to kern this one. Place it so that it balances the text in the upper right-hand corner. Now create a drop shadow just like the first one with the **Place Duplicate** command. It should look like Figure 4.24.

FIGURE 4.24 The second drop shadow

Angling the Store Name

Across the center of the page type **Sam's SCUBA Shop**. Give it a blue fill and a black 0.2-point outline. Then rotate the text to 35 degrees using either the Pick tool or the Transform menu and place it in the white stripe between the two triangles. Use the Pick tool to enlarge the type and center it to fit the space. The result is shown in Figure 4.25.

At this point save your drawing as SCUBA1.CDR using the **Ctrl-S** hot-key. Since you have not saved this file yet a dialog box will prompt you for a name. Leave the drawing open after the save. As you can see, all the basic skills you used in the first three chapters can be applied to tasks involving text. By now the menus you have been using regularly and the toolbar functions should be familiar to you. If you were not able to follow parts of the dialog in the last exercise, that's a clue as to where to practice.

FIGURE 4.25 Giving it a name

WORKING WITH SYMBOLS

The Symbol library is accessed with the Star icon and the symbols are like the line objects you drew with the Pencil tool. All symbols are placed on the page as Bézier curves. The current version of CorelDRAW! offers thousands of different objects grouped in collections. Some are only available as symbols (like the dinosaurs); others are also offered as specialty fonts (like musical notes and the Hebrew alphabet) that are also included in the Edit Text dialog boxes.

Symbols are very easy to place. Just open the tool and drag the new object to where you want the it to go. You can place only one at a time. There are no kerning or space commands. All editing and transformations are performed the same way as any curved object. If you (or your PC guru) did not opt to load the symbol libraries, or at least the ones used here, they will not be available. If there is another set of symbols on your system, use it to practice with.

Accessing the Symbol Libraries

Click on the Star icon on the Ribbon bar and the Symbol roll-up will appear. If you have the Animals collection, choose it by clicking on it with the mouse. You can use another set if that one is not loaded. Additional collections can be accessed with the scroll bar. Now click on the symbol you want and drag it over to the desired location on the page. Your screen should look like Figure 4.26. You can use the arrows to scroll through parts of the symbol collection that don't fit in the selection area.

FIGURE 4.26 The CorelDRAW symbol libraries

Placing and Manipulating Symbols

Use the scroll bar on the menu to find the fish shape that matches the one in the preview window. Click on it, and drag the symbol onto the page. The dialog box will remain open.

Again use the Animals collection, choosing the lobster-shaped object. Enlarge both objects with the Pick tool. Give the fish a blue-colored linear fountain fill and the lobster a plain orange fill. Your page should look like Figure 4.27.

FIGURE 4.27 The finished sign

Notice that the lobster has a complete fill, but the fish does not. Use the Zoom tool to close in on the fish and select it with the Shape tool. Remember that all symbols are placed in a drawing as curved objects. The way an object will behave when it is outlined or filled will depend on how it is constructed. Figure 4.28 shows the same fish, with some editing, using the techniques described in Chapter 3. If you want some practice, this object is a good one to work with. Try adapting the shape, closing areas, adding, joining, and subtracting nodes. You will use symbols as a clipart source to create forests of trees in Section Two.

Converting Text to Curves

This is the command for total control over the appearance of type in a drawing. It's also just about the fastest way in the known world to slow down a display adapter or choke a printer. Unless you are ready with the **Undo** button, it's a one-way ride. But it offers power. Conversion enables you to use all the Pick and Shape tool functions on individual letters, because the characters aren't letters any more. You can node edit, but you can't kern. You can add segments and pull the characters around like modeling clay, but you can't align to baseline, alter the point size, or change the typeface. This is the command that allows you to create neon effects, fancy mixed fills, and even create new typefaces.

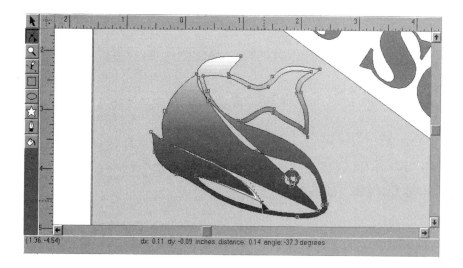

FIGURE 4.28 Editing symbols with the Shape tool

Using the Command

The easiest way to see how it works is to try it. Open up your Mark Twain quote, delete the block with just the author's name, and save the file at once as FITOPATH.CDR. Select the type, set the justification to left alignment, and make a duplicate. Then use the Edit Text dialog box to modify the blocks so one is set in Avalon (or another sans serif) and the other is set in Frankenstein (or another very ornate font). Arrange them so they are side by side. Select one and use the Arrange menu and **Convert to Curves** option. Then select the other and use the **Ctrl-V** hot-key to get the same effect.

The Result

The effects of this command aren't obvious at first; in most cases the screen will look the same. Use the Pick tool to select each block and note the number of nodes. The sample in my version has 1,851 nodes. The complex Frankenstein block (a version 3.0 font) comes in at 3,556, almost twice as many, and the Bitstream edition is even more complex. To see what this means to your work, click on the cursive block with the Shape tool.

If you have a slow or low-memory system be prepared to go get a snack. On a 486 with 16 megabytes of RAM and a Matrox Impression AT-S display card, the object took over 25 seconds to draw. That is 25 seconds every time it is selected and moved. That can add up to a lot of time. Don't let that scare you into not using conversion. Just be aware of the demands it places on your computer and use the command with care. If you need to work with text as curves, use only the letters you need to convert in your block.

Putting Curves to Work

Now that you understand how to convert text to curves we'll work with the technique a bit. Open a new drawing and create two text strings that read "The Difference" set in a very decorative font, or one with lots of fancy flourishes. Center one on top of the other and use the Zoom tool to close in on them. Now convert both objects to curves and give them a 1-point outline and a medium gray fill. Do one and then use the **Copy Style From** command to duplicate it. A block of text is converted into one curved object. Do you remember how you saw that a curved object can have elements that are not visibly connected? That is what happens with converted text. To edit individual characters you must break the text into individual elements with the **Break Apart** command located in the **Arrange** option. Leave the top object combined, but break the lower one. Select it and press **Ctrl-K**. Now look at what happened to the counters (open areas) inside the *D* and *e* characters. They are solidly filled in! Figure 4.29 shows this version after it was dressed up with additional fills. The top object is still combined, and the bottom one broken apart.

There are a couple of things to watch out for when breaking apart text converted to curves containing individual letters with modified attributes. If some of the letters were kerned or spaced so parts overlapped, the common areas will be hollow. If you used different fills or outlines for some letters, converting the text will create a group, with different elements for each variation of fill and outline. These variations may require some extra clean-up to get the page looking just right.

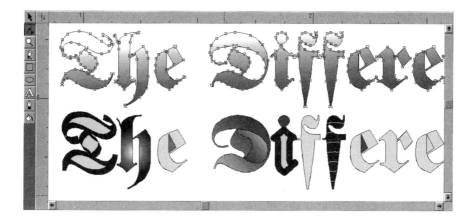

FIGURE 4.29 The effects of converting to curves

Notice how the fountain fill on the top is worked through all the letters, but the lower characters have different fills. I have also varied the outline pen settings for the lower elements. Converting text to curves gives you the ability to create all kinds of custom effects with type. You can rework the shape of a letter or use it as the basis for a new object modeled on a specific character. For example, you could use converted Greek letters for a backdrop for a fraternity award certificate, or a mathematical symbol as part of an overlay for the design of a science fair poster. There are a lot of creative possibilities that converted text offers when combined with other commands. You will be introduced to one of CorelDRAW's neatest text effects next.

GETTING FANCY—FITTING TEXT TO PATH

If you want to go into the graphic button business or just impress somebody with CorelDRAW's power, this is the command for you. And it's your first official special effect. As the name implies, this option wraps text along the path of any line or curved object. In the past text placement was controlled by the direction in which the target object was drawn. That was arcane at best, frustrating at worse. The feature was wonderfully enhanced in CorelDRAW version 3.0 with a special roll-up menu, easier editing, and precise settings and CorelDRAW 5.0 offers you nothing less.

The Flexible Baseline

Remember the baseline, that imaginary straight line that text rests on? CorelDRAW's **Fit Text To Path** command enables you to adapt the position of the baseline to match that of another object's path. The letters and the path become dynamically linked (unless you turn this feature off) so that any changes made to the path of the contents of the text are automatically adjusted for. The type is still text and can be edited like any other block of text. Figure 4.30 shows a line of fitted text. You can remove the object after the text has been fitted, making this a great way to create blocks of text in unusual shapes.

FIGURE 4.30 A simple example of the Fit Text To Path command

To use the **Fit Text To Path** command you must first select the two objects, which are referred to as the text and the target, and choose the command from the Text menu. A special roll-up menu is used to tell CorelDRAW how they are to be matched. You can't fit one block of text to another block of text, but you can fit one to a former text object that has been converted to curves. You can also fit text to circles, rectangles, lines, and curves. Only a single line of type can be fitted at a time. Text that includes line breaks will have the returns striped out as the baseline is fitted to the target's path. You can fit more than one text object to another object.

To see how easy it is, duplicate the example in Figure 4.30. Draw an uneven line with the Pencil tool. Type **Fitting Text To A Path Is Easy with CorelDRAW** above the line. Select both objects and choose the **Fit Text To Path** option from the Text menu. A roll-up menu will appear on the screen like the one shown at the left of Figure 4.31. Click on the **Apply** button on the bottom of the roll-up. The text will flow along the line, beginning on its left side.

Fit Text to Path uses the first node of the target object to calculate the starting point of the text. The Fit Text To Path roll-up menu has three drop-down menus visible when two appropriate objects are selected. These are used to set the orientation of the text along the line along with the vertical and horizontal placement, as labeled in Figure 4.31. To select an option click on the appropriate example after opening the mouse. If you click on two objects that have been fit, the menu will show the current settings in the menu windows.

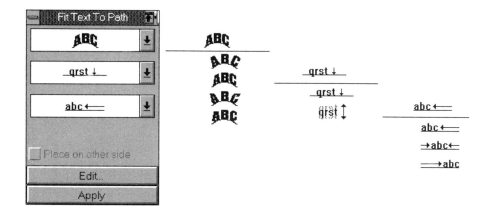

FIGURE 4.31 The Fit Text To Path roll-up menu

Horizontal Placement

When you used the defaults to fit text the program aligned the letters to the left. But you can actually place the starting point anywhere along the line. Select your two objects and open the **Horizontal Placement** menu. Click on the bottom option showing the arrow pointing right toward the text and click **Apply**. The text is pushed to the far right of your line. Select the middle option and click **Apply**. The text will be forced to the center of your line, and look just like Figure 4.30.

As with all CorelDRAW's other roll-up menus, no action is taken on any selected options until you choose **Apply**. Use the Shape tool to change the path of your line. Twist several of the control points. Notice how the text follows the new shape.

These standard settings apply only to objects with open paths. To move the insertion (starting) point of the text to a custom location on the target's path you have to set the value numerically using the **Edit** button. Placing custom offsets and closed path alignments will be discussed later.

Using Vertical Orientation Effects

Select the line of text again and open the top drop-down menu on the **Fit Text to Path** roll-up. It controls the vertical orientation of the text. Some examples are displayed in the same order as the menu options in Figure 4.32. As you read the definitions, try all four options with your objects. Use the Zoom tool to close in on different letters and examine the results. You can fine-tune individual letters with the Shape tool. The four options for this setting are discussed here.

- **Rotate Letters.** The first option automatically skews the letters in the text to follow the contour of the target. Use this setting if you want the text's baseline to adjust to the slope of the other object's path. If the target's shape makes any severe turns, the letters may overlap or show gaps. Look at *A Path* and *CorelDRAW* in Figure 4.32's top line.

- **Vertical Skew.** This option increases the vertical skew of the letters as the target object curves, keeping the letters in a more upright position. The more extreme the angle of the target, the less the outer edge of the letter will touch the path. Bends in the target's path may cause distortion of some of the letters. Look at the word *Path* on the second line in Figure 4.32.

- **Horizontal Skew.** This setting adjusts the horizontal skew of the letters as they follow the target. In some cases the characters may look like they have been pulled over the path of the target, as with the letters *A Path* in the third line of Figure 4.32.

- **Upright Letters.** If you choose to keep the letters upright, the text baseline will be stairstepped to adjust to shifts in the target's path. In some cases a letter may look slightly rotated as the curve of the target changes. Look at *A Path* in the last line of Figure 4.32.

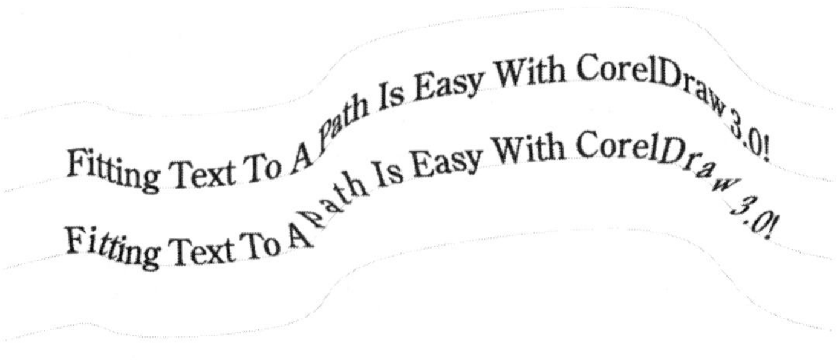

FIGURE 4.32 Text orientation

Setting the Distance from the Path

This submenu is used to set the position of the text's baseline in relation to the target's path. The position of the arrow and sample text for each option shows the result. The first four settings are as follows: directly on the path, below the path, above the path, and centered in the path. Try each now and see how your text is moved. Don't forget that you have to click the **Apply** button to make the change happen.

Interactively Positioning the Baseline's Vertical Offset

CorelDRAW also enables you to set the exact position of the baseline of the text to the target's path visually. Select both objects and open the Vertical Placement menu; then choose the last option on the list. Drag on the text. As you do, a line with arrows on either end will appear as well as a line following the path of the fitted baseline. The status bar will note the current vertical offset if you pause while dragging. Figure 4.33 shows the operation in progress. When you release the mouse the text will be moved to the new location. You can also set the vertical offset with the **Edit** commands.

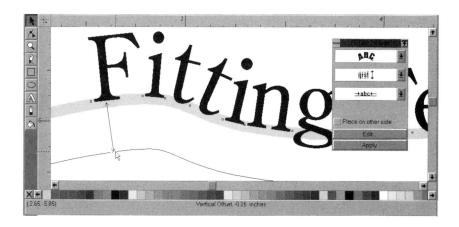

FIGURE 4.33 Interactively adjusting the vertical offset

The Place On Other Side Command

This command flips the text upside-down and backward (to read properly upside down) on the path. If you had a line of text running from the left side of a line and used this command, it would be turned upside-down and start on the right-hand side. Use it now. Just click on the check-box just above the **Edit** radio button and then choose **Apply**. Then deselect it and choose **Apply** again. The effect is reversed.

Placing Text on Ellipses and Rectangles

If you are fitting a text string to an object drawn with either the Ellipse or Rectangle tool (that has not been converted to curves), then the roll-up menu will look a bit different (see Figure 4.34). Notice the square grid located where the third menu normally is. This enables you to choose on which side of the object to place the text by clicking on the appropriate quadrant. The other two submenus and the **Place On Other Side** option operate as usual. Note that to get the text upright on the bottom of the circle it had to be placed on the other side of the baseline.

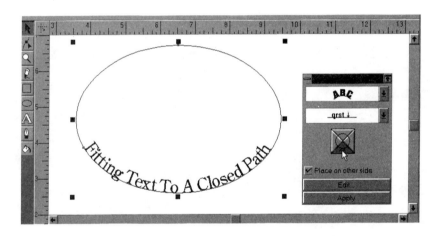

FIGURE 4.34 Fitting text around closed paths

The Edit Commands

Select your objects and click on the **Edit** button. The Fit Text To Path Offsets dialog box will open. This is where you can use numeric values to adjust the position of the target path and text baseline in relation to each other. These can be applied to

Chapter 4: Working with Words

both open and closed path objects. Right now the dialog box is showing the current settings. Positive horizontal numbers move the text to the right; negative ones move it to the left. Distance From Path controls the Vertical Offset. Here a negative number drops the baseline below the path, and a positive number raises it over the path. Figure 4.35 shows an example. When you click **OK** in the dialog box, nothing seems to happen. Remember that you still have to apply the new settings at the menu level.

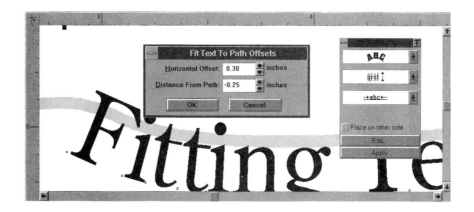

FIGURE 4.35 Using the Edit commands

ADVANCED FIT TEXT TO PATH SKILLS

Fit Text To Path offers a lot of control, and for regular-shaped objects the basic settings will usually work fine without much extra effort. But to master the effect you need to know how to position letters around irregular objects, adjust the placement of the first node, and fine-tune the final appearance of the type. You have actually covered most of those skills, so all you have to do now is see how to apply them. There is a regular set of procedures to use when fine-tuning fitted text that can save a lot of time and effort. Open the file named TAU.CDR located on the disk that came with this book. It contains a letter T that has been converted to curves, and a text string that you will use for this practice session. If you have not loaded all the fonts you may get an error message. Don't worry; just set the typeface of the text object in a 22-point serif font.

The Editing Process

Fine-tuning fitted text is an interactive process. You start by setting the basic defaults and then making a series of adjustments using combinations of sizing, spacing, and movement controls. Start by selecting both objects, opening the **Fit Text** roll-up menu, and setting the options to Rotate Letters, On Path, Left Alignment as shown in Figure 4.36. When you click on **Apply**, your screen should look just like the example.

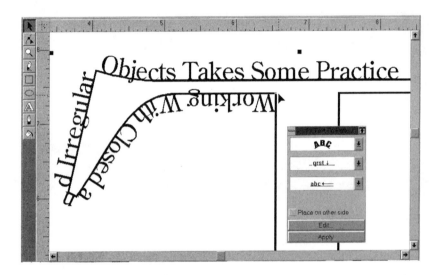

FIGURE 4.36 Setting the basic options

Moving the Insertion Point

The Shape tool pointer is placed at the position of the first node of the target's path. That is where the string of text is inserted. Your words are now wrapped underneath the left arm of the T and look very unbalanced. The word *Working* should start on the outer edge of the left arm and run across the top of the target object. To do that you must change the position on the first node. During this phase you should also gauge how closely the line of text fits the target. Use the **Undo** command to separate the text from the target object and adjust point size and letter spacing. You can keep repeating this step as needed. For your sample project, the text size is made pretty close to what you need. Open the Shape tool and click on the object. The nodes will become visible.

The first node will be larger than the node on the corner of the tip of the left arm. Double-click on it and use the **Break** command to open the path. Draw a marquee around the same spot. There are now two nodes, one under the other. The original is now the new first node. Double-click once more and join the two nodes together. This closes the object with the beginning of the path where you want it. Now refit the text to the target just as you did before. The insertion point is now on the left arm, as shown in Figure 4.37. Before going on, change the fill of the object to a light gray and the outline to a slightly darker tone. If the fill doesn't work you did not properly join the broken path.

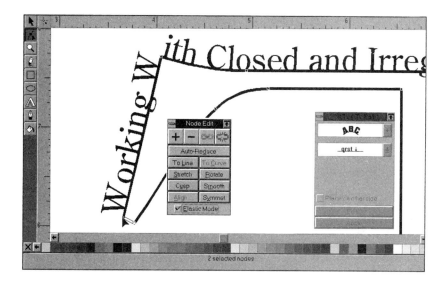

FIGURE 4.37 Repositioning the first node

Adjusting Horizontal Offset, Letter Spacing, and Kerning

If the size and overall letter spacing of the text in relation to the target are not the way you want them, use the **Undo** command and make changes. Repeat the operation until you are satisfied with the result. For this practice session, you don't have to be too precise; you just want to see how things work. After you have finished with those adjustments refit the text to the target. If the starting point is still not correct, the dialog box available via the **Edit** button can help you get it just right. The interplay between the starting point and the way the letters fit at changes in the shape of the path may call for a bit of trial and error. Don't try to be exact with horizontal alignment; it is easier with the Shape tool.

For example, the word *Working* isn't centered properly on the outside of the left arm. Use the Shape tool to select the nodes at the base of the letters (a marquee was used). Then move them by dragging on a node to the right location. If you go over a sharp break in the line of the path with CorelDRAW 4.0, the text will hug the form. Figure 4.38 shows how your screen should look as you move the text.

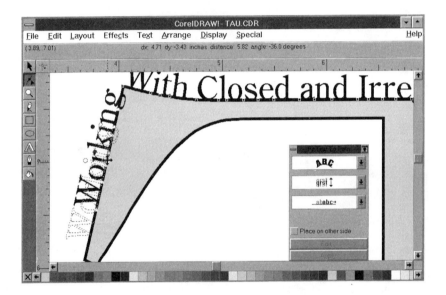

FIGURE 4.38 Manually adjusting letter spacing

Changing the Shape of the Path

You can change the way text fits to the path by altering the path itself, reducing or increasing the amount of change in an area, or modifying the type of segment or node. Since the baseline of the text and the path of the target are dynamically linked, the changes will automatically alter the fit of the type. The sharp breaks at the upper edges of the two arms of the object are a good example. Use the Shape tool to reposition the corner node shown in Figure 4.39. Notice how the text is reworked to the new path. Try deleting and modifying some nodes and see what happens.

Working with Character Angle and Shift

Use the Zoom tool to magnify three or four letters on a bend in the path so they fill the screen. Notice how the base of the character sits inside the outline of the target object. Look at Figure 4.40. The Character Attributes dialog box shows how the vertical shift and character angle have been altered to adjust partially for the slope on the path and the size of the outline. Select the Shape tool and double-click on a letter. Adjust it so the letter is above the outline and rotated to a true vertical. You can also use these commands to modify individual letters that are overlapping on other characters.

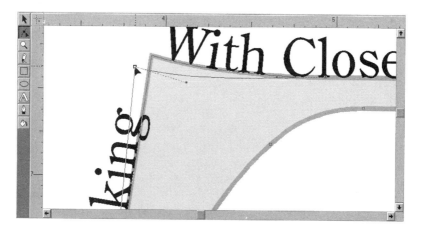

FIGURE 4.39 Editing the shape of type by altering the path

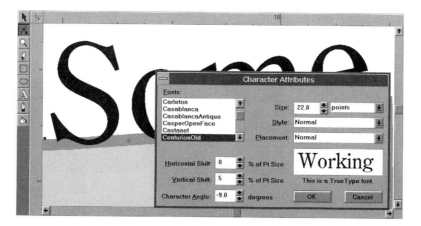

FIGURE 4.40 Adjusting vertical shift and character angle

Using Fit Text To Path Effectively

The **Fit Text To Path** command is a lot of fun, but many casual users become frustrated when the letters jumble up or don't want to go where they should. The preceding exercise shows how the Text and Shape tools can be used with the Undo/Redo feature to get things just right. The key is to work in an orderly fashion and fix one thing at a time. Get the basic shape of the target and the general size of the text set before you start. Leave kerning until the basic spacing and node editing have been done.

Spell-checking and Choosing the Right Word

Help with Spelling

Open the original copy of your Mark Twain quotation and select the large block of text. By now some readers are probably getting tired of seeing the typographical error in the last line. CorelDRAW 5.0 offers both a dictionary and a thesaurus to help users get their words just right. With the mouse choose the **Spell-Checker** option located in the Text menu. Figure 4.41 shows the dialog box that appears. Select **Always Suggest** and then click on the **Check Text** button shown under the mouse cursor in the figure.

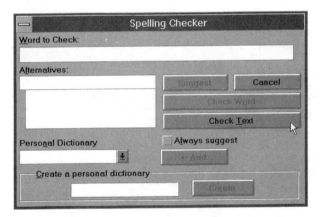

FIGURE 4.41 The Primary Spelling Checker dialog box

Chapter 4: Working with Words

After you choose the option, the **Spell-Checker** scans the text for words that do not match the ones found in its master dictionary or that have been added to a personal dictionary by a user. The operation is very straightforward and basically like the speller checkers in most word processors.

As you can see in Figure 4.42 CorelDRAW has located your error and is offering two possible replacements. Choose **Change** and save your work.

The Difference Between the Right Word...

The Thesaurus is a bit different from the Speller. You must either mark the work you want to check or type it in the dialog box. Choose the Text tool and place the cursor over the space between the e and the D in the fourth row of text. Now drag the mouse over the word *Difference* and release the button. The word should now have a gray mask over it.

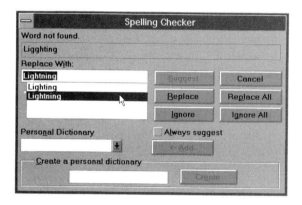

FIGURE 4.42 *Making a correction*

Open the Text menu and choose the **Thesaurus** option. A dialog box will open with the word already entered in the **Synonym For...** area. The Definition box gives the full text of the selected definition from the list in the lower left corner. The first one does not seem to make the grade. Mark Twain's meaning would be lost if you replaced *difference* with *animosity* or *adaptation*. Click on the third definition. No help there either. He got it right the first time, it seems. If you double click on a word in the Replace With box, the whole lookup process is repeated for the new synonym.

Accessing Extended Character Sets

There are more characters in most fonts than you have keys on your keyboard. The normal typewriter-style character sets do not include true quotation marks, copyright and trademark symbols, or special typesetting characters like em and en dashes (which will be covered in Section Two). The TrueType and PostScript fonts do have all these special characters and more; you just can't press a single key and see it on the screen.

Typesetting consoles are becoming a thing of the past, but they do have extra keys for full punctuation and typographic symbols. CorelDRAW uses the **Alt** key to extend the range of the keyboard. In the documentation included with the program is a card containing a character reference list. It shows the **Alt**-number listings for CorelDRAW and Windows common fonts, along with those for several symbol fonts. Not every font will have the entire set or match the list. But it does work for most of them.

Entering an extended character is easy. Use the Text tool as normal, and when you wish to insert a special character, just hold the **Alt** key and enter the number with the numeric keypad. For example, a copyright symbol can be placed in a text string by holding the **Alt** key and entering **0169**. You must enter the 0. You have one more set of changes to make to your quotation—adding true quotation marks. The inch symbols are not the same thing. To give work a polished appearance you should use typographical characters whenever possible. A complete font includes individual open and close quotations that match the typeface involved.

Make sure your Mark Twain file is open. Replace the open quote (the first one) with **Alt-0147**. Then change the second to **Alt-0148**. The Preview window in the Character Attributes will show the proper character with most typefaces. When you click **OK**, the changes will show on the screen if your display font includes the new letters.

FIGURE 4.43 Adding true quotation marks

Chapter Summary

Knowing how to use the typesetting capabilities is one of the fundamental skills required to use CorelDRAW effectively. You have covered most of the basic artistic text commands, text manipulation, and how to Fit Text To Path. Typography is both an art and a craft. CorelDRAW was not designed as a typesetting program, but it does offer all the controls needed to set small blocks of type to professional standards.

To get professional results requires learning some technical terms, the basics of page layout and design, and a sense of the task at hand. The wide variety of fonts provided with CorelDRAW and available from third parties opens the way to creating illustrations that use type well. The next chapter will cover CorelDRAW's paragraph text and designing your own typefaces with CorelDRAW. The exercises and examples in Section Two explore more advanced type-handling topics.

CHAPTER 5
Words Plain and Fancy, Working with Custom Typefaces

In This Chapter...

- Paragraph Text
- Working with Frames
- Character Attributes, Baselines, and Straightening Text
- The Text Roll-Up Menu
- Using Imported Text
- Printing
- Printer Troubleshooting
- Print Merge Techniques
- Exercise: Designing and Printing Certificates
- Designing Custom Typefaces

WHAT THIS CHAPTER IS ABOUT

In this chapter we continue to work with CorelDRAW!'s type tools. The focus is on longer passages and using text produced in other applications. During the discussion more detailed topics, such as aligning to baseline and straightening text, will be covered. Merging text to produce a series of drawings automatically, with minor variations in each one, will also be discussed. We will work with the Cut, Copy, and Paste commands plus Windows' OLE functions to move information between programs. Then we'll look at CorelDRAW!'s export functions for creating custom typefaces. I'll save the new styles and multipage text functions for the next chapter.

Let's set some common defaults so our displays look the same and the tools and commands operate properly. In the Display menu make sure the rulers and status bar are turned on. Open the **Preferences** dialog box under the Special menu. On the **General** option, set the **Place Duplicate** options to 18 points each (make sure the units of measure are in points) and the **Nudge** factor to 8 points. Change the right mouse button function from **Node Edit** to **Edit Text**. The proper values are shown in Figure 5.1. Then load the file **BACONTXT.DOC** from the disk in the back of this book into your CorelDRAW! Samples directory so it will be ready to use later. If you did not load the samples when you installed the program, use the location where you store drawing files.

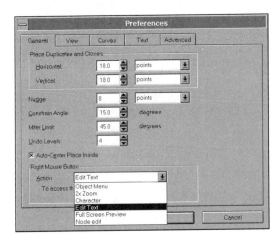

FIGURE 5.1 Default settings for Chapter 5

Using On-screen Paragraph Text

To place text blocks larger than CorelDRAW!'s 250-character limit for artistic text, we must create a frame and use paragraph text. It is placed inside the frame drawn with the Text tool. About 4,000 characters is the maximum per frame.

The number of characters that will fit in a given block depends on the typeface being used. All the basic typographic controls are available. You can divide the frame into columns, set gutters (spaces between columns), and perform hyphenation. The Extract and Merge Back features under the Text menu allow saving text in a separate file to be edited in a word processor and then importing it back into CorelDRAW!

Entering Text Directly into a Frame

First, we'll create a frame and place some text on the page. Open CorelDRAW! or a new file if it's already loaded. Select the Text tool's **Frame Mode** (between the text and the symbol icon) and bring the cursor onto the page. Drag a rectangle shape 6.5 inches across and 4.5 inches down to the upper left-hand area of the page. A dashed line or marquee will follow the cross hairs. Use the status bar and rulers as guides. When you release the mouse button a frame outline will replace the dashed line, and a text cursor will appear as a white bar in the upper left-hand corner. Type in **This is Paragraph Text that was entered into a frame drawn with the Text tool**. Change to the Select tool and then press the right mouse button. If your preferences are set properly, the Edit Text dialog box, shown in Figure 5.2, should appear in the center of the CorelDRAW! window, and selection handles will be visible around the text frame. Highlight the sentence and click on the **Character** button; the Character dialog box, looking like Figure 5.3, will appear on your screen. Choose a serif font like Book Antiqua, left justification, normal style, and 56-point type. The dialog box is identical to the one for artistic text. Note how the text on your screen sits in a single column and that the words are not hyphenated. You can edit text either inside the frame with the Text tool, or inside the editing window in the dialog box.

Power Of... CorelDRAW! 5 for Windows

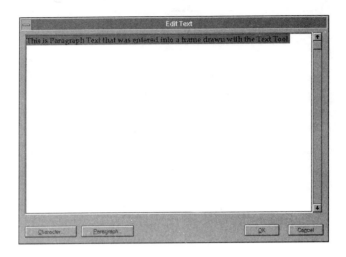

FIGURE 5.2 Editing paragraph text using the dialog box

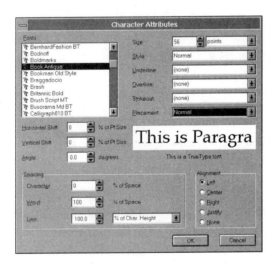

FIGURE 5.3 The Character dialog box

Frame Attributes

Think of a frame as a page within a page. You can import text files into a frame. You can set spacing, justification, and hyphenation for each frame using special dialog boxes. This offers a lot of flexibility when laying out complex designs like ads and newsletters. You can have as many frames as there is room for on the page, each with different settings. Moving frames around is an easy way to experiment with different designs. Close the **Paragraph Text** dialog box, open the **Text** menu, and choose the **Frame** option. A dialog box like the one in Figure 5.4 will open.

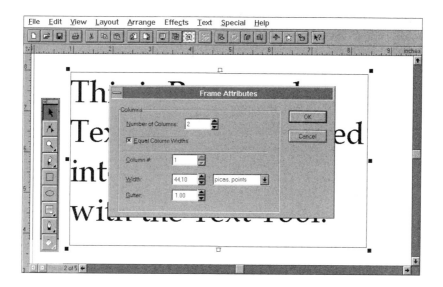

FIGURE 5.4 The Frame Attributes dialog box

The Number of Columns setting allows you to specify from one to eight columns. Gutters can range from 0 to 12.5 picas. The gutter is the open space between individual columns.

Paragraph Attributes

Close the **Frame Attributes** dialog box and open the **Paragraph** dialog box using the Text menu. The Paragraph dialog box when you first open it will look like Figure 5.5. You can set spacing and alignment options for the entire paragraph. You can also set automatic hyphenation and specify the hot zone (The hyphenation hot zone is the area next to the margin where hyphenation can occur). If a word cannot be hyphenated within the hot zone, the line will break and the word will be placed on the next line.

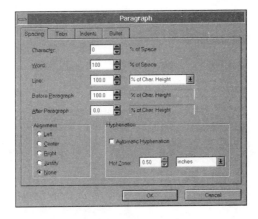

FIGURE 5.5 The Paragraph dialog box

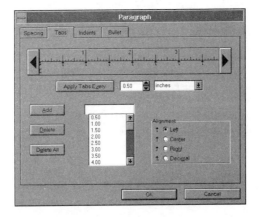

FIGURE 5.6 Tabs

If you click on the **Tabs** card in the Paragraph dialog set, you will see a box like Figure 5.6. Using this box you can even set up tables. Alignment when applied to tabs refers to the way the tabulated material will appear. Figure 5.7 shows how each option affects tabulated words. Figure 5.8 shows the Indents dialog box, which gives you a good deal of freedom in the way indented text will look. And the last icon, Bullet, shown in Figure 5.9, makes all the symbol fonts available to dress up bulleted text.

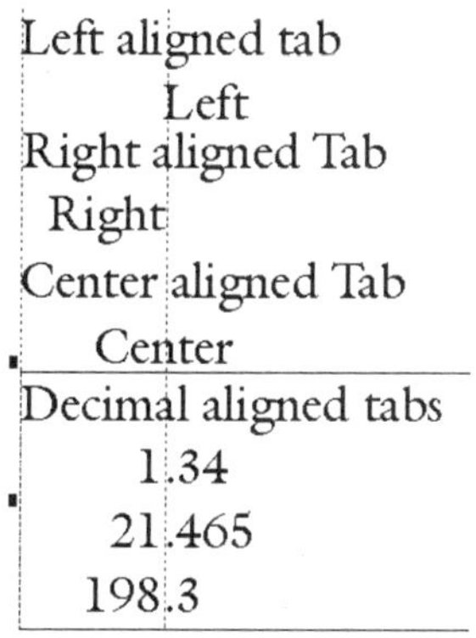

Left aligned tab
Left
Right aligned Tab
Right
Center aligned Tab
Center
Decimal aligned tabs
1.34
21.465
198.3

FIGURE 5.7 Effects of alignment on tabbed material

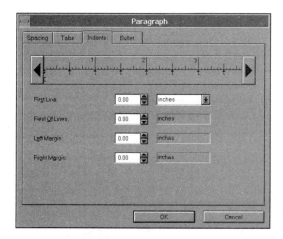

FIGURE 5.8 The Indents dialog box

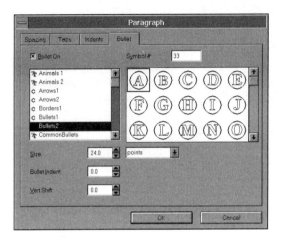

FIGURE 5.9 The Bullet dialog box

I'll be using picas and points when dealing with column text, as do most layout and design artists. A pica is one-sixth of an inch, and there are 12 points to the pica. A point is one-seventy-second of an inch. Look at the **Gutter Width** setting in Figure 5.4. The 1,0 entry indicates that the measure is set to 1 pica, no points. If you try to set a range greater than 12 points to the right of the comma, CorelDRAW! will produce a warning message that the value is out of range. From the Frame menu, change the number of columns to 2; enter a 1-pica gutter, as you see in Figure 5.3; and set the options in your Paragraph dialog box to match the ones in Figure 5.5. Make sure you turn automatic hyphenation on with a 3-pica hot zone. Click on **OK**. Your frame will probably now extend off the page at the right. Don't worry about this, we'll fix it in a minute.

Before going any further, open the **Grid Setup** dialog box from the Layout menu and set the Grid Frequency unit of measure (in the lower section) to **picas**. This will change the unit of measure shown on the ruler at the top of the page from inches to picas. You can change it back by altering the setting again. For now leave it at picas and set the zero point of the rulers to the upper left-hand corner of the frame.

Interactively Adjusting Frame Size

Two guidelines have been used to show the position of the gutter. The word **Paragraph** was hyphenated automatically. Pull the handles on the side and bottom of the frame, moving them back and forth. Notice how the text reflows to adjust to the new dimensions. The frame acts like a window frame. If the size of the frame is smaller than the total area needed to display the text, part of the words will not be seen in the drawing. If it is too large, the second column may not have any text in it. You have to adjust the size of the frame to match the amount of copy, leading, and number of columns. Move the right-hand side of the frame to the left until it is inside the edge of the page. Figure 5.10 shows how the text should look on your screen.

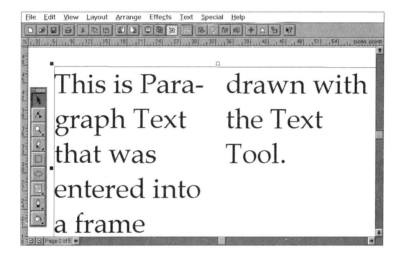

FIGURE 5.10 Text frames are adjustable

TRANSFORMATIONS OF PARAGRAPH TEXT

Frame bounding boxes work almost like any other CorelDRAW! object. You can rotate, skew, mirror, and align a block of paragraph text just as you can a square or line. Double-click on your text until the rotation handles appear and then rotate and skew the object. Watch how the bounding box's shape is changed and how the placement of the text is altered. Now look at the shape of the letters; they are still perfectly formed, not skewed in any way. You will probably have to reduce your type size in order to keep the transformed text frame within the margins of the page (remember to highlight the text before you make changes in the Character dialog box). The box and its columns are altered as you drag the mouse; then the text is reflowed to fit the new shape of the bounding box. In some cases part of the text may protrude outside the line of the box, as it does in Figure 5.11.

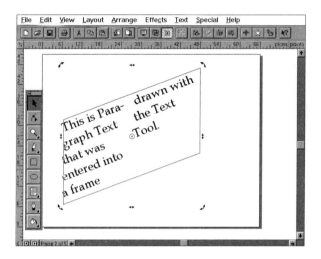

FIGURE 5.11 Transforming paragraph text

Understanding the relationship between the frame's bounding box and the text block is key to knowing how paragraph text operates. In your transformation the text's baseline was skewed, not the characters themselves. The baseline remained within the frame, even if parts of the letters went outside it. Look at the relation of the guidelines showing the original gutter line up with the current space between the columns. The frame controls the shape of the block of text and angle of the baseline, but does not shift the position of the baseline relative to the characters.

Outlines and Fills with Paragraph Text

Since the frame is only a container for paragraph text and not the object itself, it can't be outlined or filled. When you apply outlines and fills, the type will behave just like artistic text. Look at the example in Figure 5.12. A block of paragraph text has been closed in on and given a calligraphic outline and a radial fountain fill. Notice how the letters r and a in the upper right-hand corner show breaks because of the calligraphic strokes. Also, note the effect of the radial fill. The upper right-hand section is clear because of the pad setting. The status bar shows the type of fill and that this is a paragraph text object.

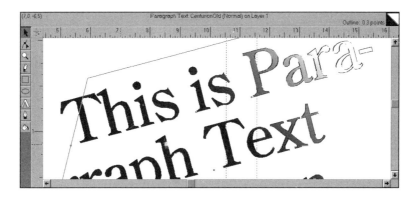

FIGURE 5.12 Paragraph text outlines and fills

Character Attributes, Baselines, and Straightening Text

Open a new drawing and create a frame. Type **This is Paragraph Text** on three lines. Zoom in so it fills the entire screen; then use the Shape tool and the Shift-click method to select several letters in different words. Double-click on one of the selected characters; the Character Attribute dialog box will open. Change the font and style. Repeat the process but use Marquee Select to choose a whole word. Then choose several letters and shift their position by dragging them. Rotate some text; then Skew the rotation using the dialog box. Figure 5.13 shows the screen as I moved the letters **G**, **i**, **T**, and **e** in several words after making other modifications.

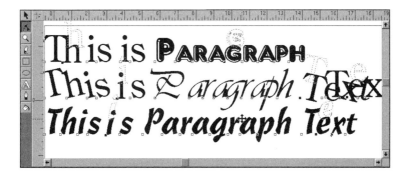

FIGURE 5.13 Modifying character attributes

Once you have finished experimenting, select the frame and use both the **Align to Baseline** and **Straighten Text** commands located in the Text menu. As you do, the type will be realigned to a normal orientation.

CUT, COPY, AND PASTE

You can use the Windows **Cut**, **Copy**, and **Paste** commands with any CorelDRAW! object. The **Cut** command removes the object from the drawing and places it in the Windows Clipboard. This is not the same thing as deleting it. Although the object is no longer on the page, it is still held in the computer's memory. The **Copy** command places a copy in the Clipboard but leaves the original where it was. You can place objects held in the Clipboard back on the page or into another application (like Word for Windows) using the **Paste** command.

Paragraph text supports the Cut, Copy, and Paste commands a bit differently from other CorelDRAW! objects. You can use all three within a single frame as well as between the frame and other locations. Open a new drawing and create a frame 30 picas across and 3.5 inches deep. Type **1. This is paragraph Text Drawn in a Frame Using the Text Tool** (Don't add a period at the end). Press the right mouse button to open the **Paragraph Text** dialog box, highlight the text, and set the type to 24-point Book Antigua or another normal serif typeface with left justification. Don't close the box yet.

Use the I-beam cursor to drag over the text again is the text is not already highlighted. Press the **Shift+Delete** key combination to cut the text. Now use **Shift+Insert** to paste it back in place. If you were typing directly on the page or in a frame, you could also use the **Edit** menu to Cut, Copy, and Paste; but you can't access the menus while a dialog box is open. The text is still on the clipboard. Press **Enter**; then hit **Shift+Insert**. Repeat the process twice more. You should have four copies of our text string. **OK** the dialog box. Then edit the lines so each one is numbered in order, 1 through 4.

You can paste the text into another part of your Corel drawing or any other Windows program that supports the Paste command. Text and graphics can be brought into or out of CorelDRAW! this way, into applications that don't have filters for moving .CDR files or one of the export file formats Corel offers.

INTERPARAGRAPH SPACING

Select the frame, press the right mouse button (or choose the **Paragraph** option from the Text menu), and choose the **Paragraph** option. In the Spacing box, increase the Before Paragraph spacing option to 175 percent. You can either enter it from the keyboard or use the mouse and the scroll arrows. Then close both the dialog boxes. Look at Figure 5.14. The text just about fits the available space in the frame. The leading between the paragraphs is not quite the height of a single line. The Text Spacing options work just like those for artistic text, except that you can now set values for Before Paragraph and After Paragraph leading. The only drawback is that the space is set as a percentage of the point size of the selected type, rather than as the actual amount of leading.

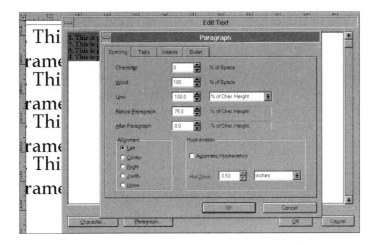

FIGURE 5.14 Setting text spacing

THE TEXT ROLL-UP MENU

The most commonly used CorelDRAW! text functions are available through a roll-up menu that can be left on-screen while working. Put it on your page now; press **Ctrl-F2**. You can also click on the first option under the Text menu. As with the other roll-ups, choices only take place after you select the target, make selections, and click on the

Apply button. The roll-up enables you to select the typeface, the font size and style, and the justification. Figure 5.15 shows the roll-up in use on the right side of the work area, with two lines selected, and the Character dialog box active.

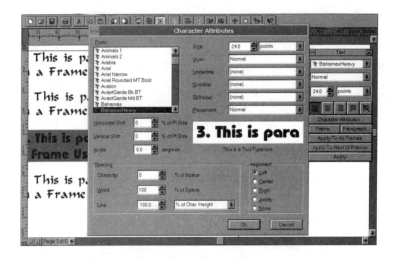

FIGURE 5.15 Using the Text roll-up menu

This list explains the functions in order from top to bottom. You can use the Pick tool, Shape tool, or Text tool to select a block of text, depending on the action to be performed.

The Text Roll-Up Menu Functions

- **Title Bar and Roll-Up Icon.** The title bar shows the name of the roll-up. You can close the menu by double-clicking on the minus sign on the left side of the bar. The arrow on the right toggles between minimizing it (closed so only the title bar shows) or maximizing it (full size).
- **Typeface.** The current default or selected typeface is displayed in the window under the title bar. You can select a new typeface using the drop-down menu, accessed by clicking on the arrow.
- **Style.** This drop-down menu sets Normal, Bold, Italic, or Bold Italic, if these styles are available for this font. Not all options will be available for all typefaces, since some typefaces were designed to only be Normal.

- **Size and Unit of Measure.** The entry box and arrows on the left, under the typeface selector, set the font size. The entry box on the right allows the user to change the unit of measure.
- **Justification.** The buttons on the top of the menu set left, right, center, full, and no justification. This command must be applied to an entire block of text. If you want different positions for several text objects within a drawing, they must be created into separate blocks or frames.
- **Character Attributes...** Clicking on this button opens the Character Placement dialog box shown on the left side of Figure 5.13. You can set horizontal and vertical spacing along the baseline as well as the angle of selected letters.
- **Frame...** This button is only active when paragraph text or the entire frame is selected. Clicking the button then opens the Regular Frame Attributes dialog box discussed earlier.
- **Paragraph...** This option provides access to all four of the Paragraph dialog boxes shown in Figures 5.5, 5.6, 5.8, and 5.9.
- **Apply To All Frames.** This button will cause the changes you have made to be applied to all the frames in your file.
- **Apply To Rest Of Frames.** This button will apply your changes to the frame you have selected and all frames created after the selected frame. It will not affect frames created before you created the selected frame.
- **Apply.** As with all CorelDRAW! roll-up menus, you have to click **Apply** for changes to take effect. Remember that you can Undo/Redo any changes with the command located under the Edit menu. The Straighten Text and Align to Baseline commands can also be used to correct mistakes.

IMPORTING TEXT

Importing is the act of bringing in text or graphics that have already been saved as a file. The original may have been created in a word processor, another graphics program, or CorelDRAW! itself. We will cover graphics in the next chapter. For now our discussion will be limited to text files. CorelDRAW! can import any plain ASCII file, up to the 4,000-character limit for paragraph text. Any letters beyond that limit will be left out of the imported block. You can split large blocks and bring them in one at a time to get around the 4,000-character limit.

The current default typeface, size, style, outline, and fill are assigned to the imported text. You can change them using the normal CorelDRAW! commands. Importing does not affect the source file in any way. You are just adding the text to the current drawing.

Preparing Text for Import

There are a few things to be aware of when preparing text for use in a drawing. Every space counts against the 4000-character limit, just like a letter. Don't use any extra spaces. Tabs and indents will be converted to spaces; so avoid them as well. Be sure to use the plain text file option in your word processor to save your file.

Do your editing and spell-checking in the word processor. Although you can edit and check text inside CorelDRAW!, these are not primary functions of the program. Word processors are designed for editing large blocks of text. But be prepared to do some cleanup. Since the font attributes will probably change and the margins will not be the same, some adjusting of spacing and line breaks will most likely be required. CorelDRAW! assumes the .TXT extension as the standard for text files in the import dialog boxes, so make it a habit to save your work using that as an extension for ASCII text files.

Performing the Actual Import

There are two ways to import a file, from the File menu and via the Paragraph Text dialog box. The basic procedures are the same. The File menu is discussed first. Then the differences will be explained. You will be using the file **BACON.TXT** you copied from the disk provided with this book. If it is unavailable you can use any other ASCII text file, but some of the following procedures won't work quite the same.

Open a new drawing and set the page to letter size and landscape. Open the **File** menu and choose **Import**. A dialog box like the one in Figure 5.16 will open. Open the **List Files of Type** menu—most text formats on this list use the all files (*.*) wild cards, so just choose the **all files** selection. Use the scroll menus in the center to change to the drive and directory where your file is located. When the file name appears in the left side selection box, double-click on it (this is the same as clicking and then clicking on **OK**). Importing text this way automatically creates a frame and loads the text into it.

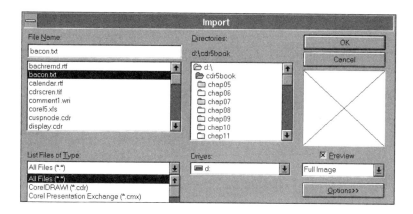

FIGURE 5.16 The Import Text dialog box

The **Cancel** button closes the dialog box without making a selection, and the **About** button opens a window that shows the version of the import filter used to import the file. The other options will be covered in the next chapter.

A Little Practice Working with Imported Text

You can use imported text just like any other paragraph text object. Your sample file provides you with an opportunity to practice a bit with imported and paragraph text, as well as to learn a couple of new tricks. Use the Pick tool to select the frame and then click the right mouse button. Select line 1 that reads **On Study**; then use the **Shift+Delete** combination to cut it to the Windows Clipboard. Select the frame and set the remaining text in 14-point Lincoln, which is an Old English style typeface. If you don't have that font available on your system, pick another one you like. Move the frame down on the page and resize it.

Select the Artistic Text tool and click at a point above the imported text frame. Now use the **Shift+Insert** combination to paste the text you cut back as artistic text. Bacon called his essay "On Studies" in Latin rather than your "On Study" translation. Use CorelDRAW!'s on-screen editing capability to change it. Then with the **Pick** tool resize it to about 36 points. Finally, align it over the center of the page. Then type **-Sir Francis Bacon** on the lower right-hand side of the essay. Open the **Edit** menu and use the **Copy Attributes From** option to make the pasted and new text match your main block.

Dressing Up the Page

Your font gives the text the appearance of an old manuscript, but the paper looks like plain white bond. You can use two Page Setup features to give your work a bit of an old parchment appearance. Open the **Layout** menu and click on **Page Setup**. A dialog box like the one in Figure 5.17 will open.

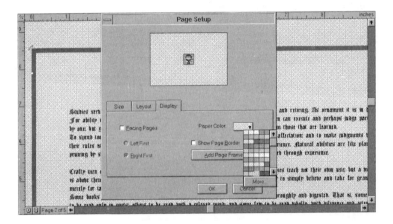

FIGURE 5.17 The Page Setup dialog box

Setting the Paper Color and Page Frame

Click on the **Paper Color** button; a standard color selection dialog box will appear. Select **More** and adjust the values to about 3 magenta, 27 yellow, and 8 black (or pick a parchment-like color in whatever pallette you have active). Click **OK**; this will give the entire screen area a parchmentlike hue. Now choose **Add Page Frame**. Click **OK**. There is now a frame on the lowest layer of the drawing, surrounding the page. Select this page frame and activate the Outline tool. Open the **Outline** menu and give the frame a 16-point brown rule to complement our parchment background color. Adding a page frame not only allows you to carry out the next step, it also makes the background color printable.

Use the **Zoom** tool to view the entire page. The heading is probably too large and the rule a bit too thick. Use the various controls to experiment with the basic design. The frame can be used to try out the Spell-Checker and Thesaurus functions. Several words in the essay are not part of common modern speech, and others will show the limits of the dictionary. When you have finished save the final version under the filename **ESSAY.CDR**, but don't close the drawing.

You may find that your computer handles operations with text, like this one, very slowly. A normally-equipped 386 will tend to slow down badly when you are using some of CorelDRAW!'s extensive text-handling capabilities. Please check the suggestions in Chapter 28 on the best hardware choices for running Corel applications.

Extract and Merge Back

The Extract and Merge Back commands allow users to save all the text objects in a drawing in a single ASCII file that can be edited in a word processor and then brought back in with almost all the original CorelDRAW! formatting intact. You may have noticed that working with large blocks of Paragraph text can slow down your work. Extract/Merge Back is a good way to make changes quickly. The Wireframe mode does not offer much help here, so moving the editing to a word processor is an attractive option for large-scale revisions. You are going to make some changes in your essay to see how these commands work and how the extracted text looks in the raw file.

MODIFYING THE TEXT INSIDE CORELDRAW!

Select the frame and open the Text Edit dialog box with the right mouse button. At the beginning and end add quotation marks using the **Alt-0147** and **Alt-0148** keystrokes (use the numeric keypad to enter numbers). Click **OK** to exit the dialog box. Use the Shape tool and change the attributes of several letters and groups of letters. Add an **Alt-0165** character (a yen symbol) in the block. Your screen should look like Figure 5.18.

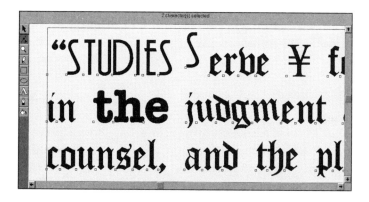

FIGURE 5.18 Modifying text for extraction

Extracting and Editing the Text Using Windows Notepad

Click on the **Special** menu and choose the **Extract** option. A warning box will announce that you must save any changes before using the Extract command. Don't worry; a **Save** dialog box will open to let you save. If you want to save the file under another name, you should **Save As** before using **Extract**. Click **OK** to save the file. You will see the **Extract File** dialog box shown in Figure 5.19. It will have the name of the CorelDRAW! file with a .TXT extension as a default for your extraction file. In this case it will be ESSAY.TXT. You could change it, but you will use it as is this time. Click **OK**. The current directory is where the file will be saved unless you choose a new location. Make sure you know where the new file is.

Open the Windows **NotePad** or another editor or word processor that can handle text files. Open the Extracted file. The first line will have a series of letters broken with pound signs. This line is a pointer to the original CorelDRAW! file. This is the only file that can be used as a target for a **Merge Back** operation.

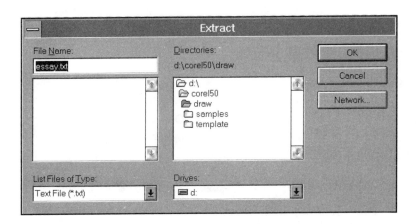

FIGURE 5.19 The Extract Text dialog box

The next line identifies the last block of text entered or imported into the drawing. All the blocks are numbered in inverse order starting at 0:0 (computer people count 0, 1, 2, etc.). The numbers are controlled by CorelDRAW!'s internal file structure. You will see the **-Sir Francis Bacon** that you entered at the bottom of the page at the top of the file. The end of the text block is noted by the <CDR> string on a new line, followed by another blank line.

Figure 5.20 shows the sample file after the changes are made. It probably doesn't look much different from yours, even though it doesn't specify all the fonts and style changes. The black box at the start of the first line of block 3 is the open quotation mark. You can also see the yen symbol. The font and style are retained in CorelDRAW!'s understanding of the file attributes but are not exported as codes in the ASCII text.

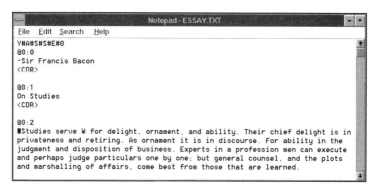

FIGURE 5.20 An extracted file opened in the Windows Notepad

You can edit the text file, but only the text portions. If you change any of the codes, their positions, or pointers, the **Merge Back** command will not work. You can add, replace, or move portions of the text, even cut and copy one block to another.

At the beginning of the third block, before the words **Studies serve**, type **This is new text added after extraction**. Hold the **Alt** key and type **0169**, type a **period**, and press **Enter**. Press **Enter** before the sentence beginning with **For ability**. Save your file with the same name in the same location.

Using the Merge Back Command

Once the edited file has been saved, you can use the Merge Back command to replace the older version of your copy with the revisions. Return to CorelDRAW! and open the **Special** menu again; then choose **Merge Back**. A file selection dialog box will open. Double-click on **ESSAY.TXT**. The page will be redrawn with the edited text objects.

Figure 5.21 shows the edited version after Merge Back was completed. Notice the new sentence in the same font as the bulk of text, and the copyright symbol inserted. Notice also how all the formatting is intact, even though you did not see it when using the word-processing program.

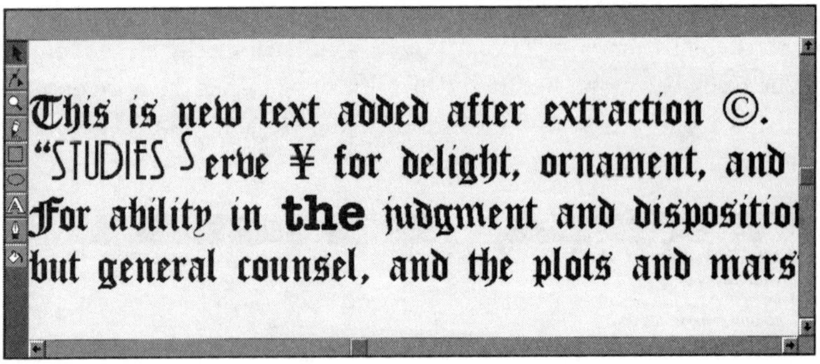

FIGURE 5.21 The file after using Merge Back

Do not make any changes to the drawing between the time you extract text and perform the Merge Back command. If you do, CorelDRAW! will not restore the extracted file. Also be sure to save the edited file as a plain ASCII text file, since CorelDRAW! can't read word-processing command codes.

Basic CorelDRAW! Print Commands

So far your output has been limited to the screen, but CorelDRAW! offers a wide variety of options for producing hard copies. You can use any device supported by Windows to print drawings directly, including dot matrix printers, laser printers, typesetters, color printers, and slide makers (also known as film recorders). Using the most basic print command is simple; just open the **File** menu and choose **Print**. Then click **OK**. The file will be sent to the printer. If you have chosen to use the Windows Print Manager, the file will be spooled there first. It sounds easy, but printing problems are probably responsible for more calls to technical support than any other topic. In many cases the calls are made because the user just didn't understand a few simple concepts.

CorelDRAW! users can choose from a host of print options. The most advanced topics, such as multipage documents, trapping, and screen angles for color separations, will be covered later in the book. However, the Print dialog box gives even novice users excellent control over output. If you are not working with fancy output devices or sending out files for color separations, the topics covered here will probably be all you need to know about printing with CorelDRAW! The exact options will vary based on your printer and the capability of its Windows driver. Many of the more sophisticated settings will only be available for PostScript-compatible printers, or ones using special PostScript emulation methods. Non-PostScript printers are at a disadvantage when it comes to printing, but even if you don't own one you can save the file to disk and take it to a friend or service bureau that has a PostScript device. We will discuss the primary print features first, then the printer selection and PostScript options. After that some of the more common printing problems and their solutions will be covered. Keep in mind that the exact features may vary, based on your printer and the nature of your printer driver.

The Print Dialog Box

Open CorelDRAW! and make sure that there is at least one object on the page. Go to the File menu and choose **Print**. The hot-key combination is **Ctrl-P**. The **Print** dialog box will open. The primary commands are the same for all printers. You use this box to set up a simple print job. CorelDRAW! can automatically set the printer to match output to portrait or landscape for most printers, so that's one setting you don't have to worry about. In most cases all you have to do to get a print is make sure that the correct printer is selected (if it is not, clicking on the **Setup** button allows you to select other printers loaded, or to load a new one); make sure that the right number of copies is entered; and click **OK**.

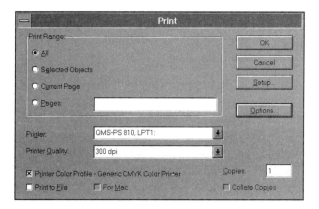

FIGURE 5.22 The Print dialog box

- **Printer.** The name of the selected Windows print driver and the current output port is listed for reference. If you have more than one driver on the system, make sure that the correct driver is selected. In Figure 5.22 the file would be sent to a

QMS PS810 located on LPT1. If that is not what you want—or if that listing is not correct—you need to change it before proceeding with a print job, or even selecting options.

- **Printer Quality.** This window allows you to choose to print your drawing at a **lower** resolution than your printer's top capacity. This can speed a print job and can be desirable for certain uses.

- **Print To File.** If you check this box the entire set of commands to print the file and all its contents will be sent to a file. You will be prompted for a name through a regular **File Selection** dialog box.

- **For Mac.** The **Print To File** option for PostScript printers has a special option for output for later use on an Apple Macintosh system. Many typesetting companies hook their high-end imagers to Macs, which have trouble with the normal structure of the files. Turning it on modifies the files to be compatible. You may still experience some problems, so consult with your typesetting company before saving to disk.

- **Copies.** Enter the number of copies to be printed.

- **Collate Copies.** If you are printing a drawing of several pages, clicking on this check box will cause each copy to be printed with the pages in order. This will slow the print process considerably on most printers.

- **Printer Color Profile.** This check box, when enabled, causes the color profile of the printer currently selected to appear next to the box. To change this profile, you must go to the File menu, the **Color Manager**, and conform the device profile to match the printer you'll be using.

- **Print Range.** If you click on the **All** option, all pages contained in a multipage drawing will be sent to the printer. You can also specific the exact range of pages to be output. As you can see from Figure 5.22, you can choose to print all pages, the current page (the one you were working on when you opened the **Print** dialog box), or you can define a range of pages. Defining pages to be printed is easy, but a couple of conventions must be observed: to print page 2 and page 4, type **2,4** and to print pages 2, 3, 4, and 5, type **2-5** (no period).

- **Selected Objects.** If this box has a checkmark, only the selected objects in the current drawing will print. This is true even if they are covered by part of another object. If you want to use this option, the objects must be selected *before* opening the dialog box. This is a handy tool for proofing part of a drawing quickly. You can also use it to save only part of an image to an EPS file.

The Print Options dialog box

Click on the **Options** button to bring up the **Print Options** dialog box (see Figure 5.23). Users of CorelDRAW! 4.0 will be familiar with most of the selections in this box. The majority of options are set using check-boxes. If there is a check visible, the option is active. Others require entering a numeric value. The following list details the effect and values for each of the options. If you have a very complex drawing it might be a good idea to turn off the **Preview Image** option. It can take a long time to display the image in the dialog box's window. Several of the options available through this dialog box, such as trapping and color separations, are covered later in this book.

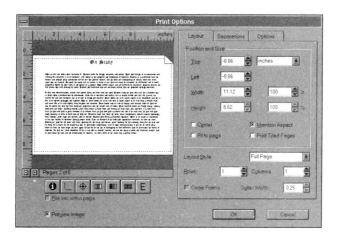

FIGURE 5.23 The Print Options dialog box

- **Preview Window.** If the Preview Image option is checked, the current page of your drawing will be displayed in the large area on the left side of the dialog box. To scroll through the drawing click on the arrows next to the Page marker in the lower left-hand corner.

- **File Info Within Page.** This option prints the name of the file, plus the date and time on the edge of the page, provided there is enough room allowed over the stated page area. When printing color separations the color, screen angle, and frequency are also printed on the edge. This option will print the File Info information on the left margin of the page, within the defined page size area, if your page is 8.5 by 11 inches. If you are working with any other page size, you must fool the program by setting the page inside CorelDRAW! for that drawing to be a size smaller than the actual paper size of your printer. If your drawing runs to the edge of the page, the file information may be placed within the illustration itself.

THE REFERENCE TOOLBAR

The set of enigmatic buttons below the preview screen are called the Reference Tools. These manage the printing of composits and allow you to select just what information is printed on the margin when you have enabled the File Info Within Page check box. Figure 5.24 shows these tools with labels.

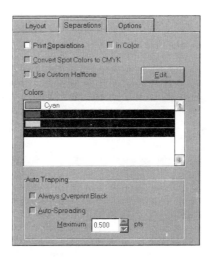

FIGURE 5.24 The Reference Tools

- **File Information.** This option prints the name of the file, plus the date and time on the edge of the page, provided there is enough room allowed over the stated page area, just as with the Crop Marks option. When printing color separations the color, screen angle, and frequency are also printed on the edge. The File Info information on the left margin of the page, within the defined page size area, if your page is 8.5 by 11 inches. If you are working with any other page size, you must fool the program by setting the page inside CorelDRAW! for that drawing to be a size smaller than the actual paper size of your printer. If your drawing runs to the edge of the page, the file information may be placed within the illustration itself.

- **Crop Marks.** With this option selected you can print crop marks in the corners of the page. You must have a working page smaller than the actual paper to see the marks, since a full-sized page does not leave room for them. Printers use crop marks to trim the final printed page to size.
- **Registration Marks.** Registration marks are printed on the outer edge of the page to and registration marks to align each color being printed.
- **Calibration bar and Densitometer scale.** These options let you add reference calibration bars for checking the consistency and quality of your output.
- **Positive or negative.** Printing a negative is used when you are printing directly to typesetting film. The image not only is reversed black to white and in color, but also outputs as a mirror image.
- **Emulsion up or down.** The emulsion side of a photographic plate or film is the side that actually takes the image. The normal setting is emulsion up.

The Layout Tab

- **Position and Size.** These options allow you to place the image exactly where you wish it to be on the page. Changes you make in the numbers appearing in these windows are shown interactively in the Preview window.
- **Width and Height (Scale).** You can specify the exact degree or enlargement or reduction of a drawing in the final print by typing in the percentage desired. The easiest way to determine scale if you use this command often is by noting the size of the drawing with the on-screen rulers and then using a proportional scale available in art supply shops. If Maintain Aspect (see below) is checked, changing one of these numbers will automatically change the other to match.

There are also four check boxes which allow quick controls of how the printed drawing will look.

- **Fit To Page.** When this option is enabled the program will resize the drawing to fit the page area defined for the printer setup. If the original only covers half the page, it will be enlarged 100 percent, and so forth. If you are designing slides or other small illustrations, this command is a quick way to specify a full-page print. If your drawing is larger than the paper in your printer, this command will automatically reduce the image to fit on a single page.

- **Center.** Centers the image on the printed page. It does not affect the actual drawing.
- **Print Tiled Pages.** This option enables you to print full size a drawing that is larger than your printer's page size. The drawing will be sent in sections to the printer so they can be printed on separate sheets of paper, manually assembled and joined together.

NOTE

Remember: The output of Print To File will be tailored for the active printer driver. If you are sending the file to a different type of printer from what you have on your system, you must use the driver for the printer that will actually print the file. Failure to do so will result in a file that can't be used as desired.

- **Layout Style.** This drop-down menu allows you to have your page automatically placed on the page appropriately for a number of commonly used forms. A little experimentation with your drawing may be needed to get precisely what you want and this is a case when you should have the preview window activated. Using these controls you can begin with a single drawing and set up the layout and even print multiple copies of it on the same sheet. Print Options will automatically control the size and placement of each drawing to be printed. Experimentation will undoubtedly be necessary to fine tune your use of these options.
- **Rows and Columns.** Your drawing, sutibly sized and placed in accordance with the layout style you have selected, will be placed in multiple rows and columns on your page. For instance, you may design one business card in CorelDRAW!, and using these commands, print a sheet with many cards placed optimally to fill the page.
- **Clone Frame.** Clicking on this option will place multiple copies of a single drawing on your page as defined by the Layout Style chosen and the number of rows and columns selected.
- **Gutter Width.** Defines the amount of clear space left between the copies of your drawing the program is placing on your page.

Separations Tab

The Separations tab of the Print Options dialog box is shown in Figure 5.25. While we'll discuss these further later in this book, here's a quick rundown of the options.

Chapter 5: Words Plain and Fancy, Working with Custom Typefaces

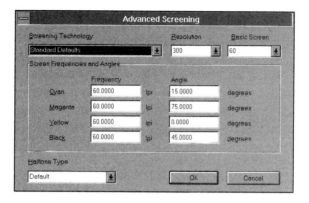

FIGURE 5.25 Separations Tab in the Print Options dialog box

- **Print Separations.** This option enables you to print separate pages for each color based on the color method and model selected. Printing color separations can be very complicated and expensive. This topic will be covered in greater detail later in the book. You should always consult with a professional printer before creating masters for color printing. Selecting this option will automatically turn on cropmarks, registrtion marks, densitometer scale, and file information. If you do not want them active, you must deselect them before printing.

- **In Color.** Use this with a color printer to produce the separation in the given color, rather than grayscale.

- **Convert Spot Color To CMYK.** This automatically converts the spot color to an equivalent CMYK combinationùmore or less. If you really need an exact color for a specific tone match, use the spot color or one from a CMYK Pantone or TruMatch palette.

- **Use Custom Halftone.** This lets you specify the exact halftone angle and frequency for each printing plate, if you have a PostScript printer. I'll cover this later as well. In most cases you can leave it set to the default. Checking this box activates the **Edit** button, click on it to see the **Advanced Screening** dialog box. This box allows enormous control of the production of halftone printing and will be covered later in this book.

- **Colors.** This box shows all the colors in the drawing or the colors dictated by the palette you have selected. You can choose only to print certain ones by using the mouse to select them.

- **Auto Trapping.** This is an advanced option, so I'll cover trapping later in the book.

Note that all the colors are listed in a window in the middle of the box. You can click on one or more of the colors and then use the radio buttons listed here to print only pages for those colors. *The next time you print after using the **Color Separation** option, make sure to turn it off unless you need it.* It becomes a default after being selected. Here is a rundown of what the options for this dialog box offer.

- **Always Overprint Black.** This option will cause any object or line in your drawing which contains 95% or more black to be printed over all other objects. This can improve the appearance of artwork containing a lot of black text, but must be used with great care.
- **Auto-Spreading.** If this option is enabled, certain objects will be "trapped." They must have no outline, be filled with a uniform fill, and must not already have been designated for overprinting from the drawing itself using the Object menu, activated by holding down the right mouse button.

The Options Tab

This dialog box, pictured in Figure 5.26, allows you to further customize the printing process. A quick run-down of these controls follows.

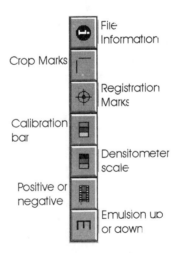

FIGURE 5.26 The Options Tab

- **Screen Frequency.** This control sets the dot pattern for halftone images. These halftone options apply if you are using a PostScript printer. Default leaves the frequency up to your printer. Higher resolutions allow more lines per inch in the screen, providing more detail and tone. A basic 300-dpi (dots per inch) Apple LaserWriter will handle 60-lpi (lines per inch) screens, whereas a high-end typesetter can more than double that number. If you don't choose the Default check-box, set a value matching your printer's capability in the lpi entry box. You can also use custom settings to reduce the screen frequency if desired. This is handy if your final paper stock won't take advantage of a higher screen frequency. If you are printing color separations, those halftone settings will override the main dialog box options.

- **Flatness Setting.** The **Set Flatness To** option can be used to reduce the complexity of a drawing that is difficult to print. Increasing the number reduces the number of segments in the objects and speeds printing. Increasing it too much can alter the appearance of a print in unpleasing ways. This setting will be covered more in the troubleshooting section following this list. Some additional controls are covered later in the book in the section on customizing the **COREL*.INI** file settings.

- **Auto Increase Flatness.** Enabling this checkbox instructs CorelDRAW! to keep reducing the flatness setting until the file prints.

- **Fountain Steps.** This setting controls the number of steps a printer can use to render a fountain fill. If you are to send the file to an image setter or high-resolution printer, you may need to adjust this setting. Some Linotronic typesetters can support 200-stripe fills at more than 2,500 lpi. Higher numbers will mean longer printer times.

- **Number of points in Curves.** Lowering this number will automatically simplify the most complex portions of a drawing.

- **Download Type 1 fonts.** Checking this option will cause Corel to download the fonts you have used to the printer or other output device. This is particularly useful if you have used only a limited number of fonts in your drawing. If the fonts are not downloaded, CorelDRAW! will send a graphic image of the font to your printer. This option is helpful if you have used a large number of fonts and downloading them would take longer than printing them as graphics objects.

- **Convert True Type to Type 1.** Since Type 1 is what can be downloaded to your printer, this box generally must be checked when the prior box is enabled. Only disable this option if your printer (or other output device) has trouble interpreting Type 1 fonts.

Printing CorelDRAW! Files Outside the Program

You can print CorelDRAW! files even if the program is not running. Open the Windows Print Manager and minimize it; then open the Windows File Manager. Locate the desired file and drag the filename onto the Print Manager icon and release the mouse button. CorelDRAW! will open, load the file, and present the Print dialog box. Choose **OK**, the file prints; then CorelDRAW! will close automatically.

Printer Troubleshooting

When you use the Print command with any program, you are moving data from one device (the computer) to another (the printer). If both are not connected properly, if they can't communicate properly, or if the data are too complex, corrupted, or not in the proper format, the printer can't do its job properly. With intensive applications like vector graphics, the demand on a printer can sometimes exceed its capabilities. Knowing how to tune the link between the program and the printer can save hassles, time, and phone bills. Sometimes the solution is obvious, such as attaching a loose cable; in other cases the problem is more obscure, such as a bug in the printer driver or the structure of a very complex drawing. The following headings deal with potential problems at different levels. Although this book cannot cover all possible problems and solutions, most printing difficulties will fall into one of several basic categories.

- No power to a component, or improper connections
- Improper Windows setup or device driver
- Improper settings or software/hardware incompatibility
- A file structure that exceeds or overloads the ability of your printer

Making the Connection

Before CorelDRAW! can use any output device, the printer must be properly set up and properly cabled. If you are setting up a new system that has never successfully printed before, make sure that everything has been hooked up correctly, plugged in, and turned on. If the system has been shut down since the last time it printed, make sure everything is powered up and working. One client was convinced that the printer was broken. Nothing would work: no test print, no lights, no noise. They thought they had tried everything. The power cord went through a surge protector that was turned off. A week later they had the same problem. Then I arrived and plugged the cord from the surge protector into the wall and everything worked perfectly. It sounds absurd, but on two separate occasions they had failed to test the power source. They were sure it was turned on, but it wasn't.

Many printers and computers have more than one port. Sometimes users hook up the wrong cable, or attach it to the wrong port. Cables might not be wired properly for the way they are to be used. If Windows tells you the printer is not connected or not responding, check the connections, cables, and plugs. Make sure they are plugged into the right outlets. If that seems all right, try printing from a non-Windows application. If that works, it is probably a problem with the way Windows or the printer is set up. Make sure that you know how to operate your printer. Some printer problems are the result of damaged paper, low toner supplies, and poor maintenance habits.

Working with Windows

The underlying control for all print functions inside Microsoft Windows is handled through the Windows Control Panel's Printer Setup and the appropriate printer driver. If you have not installed Windows correctly, the driver may not be set right. If another software program has installed a custom printer driver, it may be incompatible with CorelDRAW! but may work fine with other programs.

The Windows Control Panel and CorelDRAW!

The Control Panel determines the default printer and assigned printer port. You should make sure that you have the latest driver for your printer and that all Control Panel settings are correct. TrueType and other kinds of soft fonts must be correctly installed for CorelDRAW! to use them. If your printer stops working all at once or you lose fonts you know were available before, check the Control Panel.

The Print Manager

This is a neat tool for handling print requirements if you are working with several applications at the same time. However, printing directly from CorelDRAW! without using it will speed up printing. If you are using a network, make sure the network connections and options are properly set up.

Matching the Printer to CorelDRAW!

Sometimes your print problem will affect only a single file, font, or CorelDRAW! option. All the rest of the time the printer performs perfectly. There are two major concerns when printing from CorelDRAW! if everything else is working fine: the file and the quality of your printer's configuration. These kinds of problems usually take one of three forms:

- The file seems to take forever to print.
- It does take forever to print.
- The file prints, but not correctly.

CorelDRAW! is a very powerful program and can create files that tax a printer to its limit. There are several things you can do to help; some work better than others. Reduce the number of curves in a drawing, especially the number of objects made of text converted to curves. Simplify fountain fills, and don't mix those fills with blends (a special effect covered in Chapter 7). Reduce or eliminate PostScript texture fills, two-color and full-color fills, paragraph text, and imported bitmaps (covered in the next chapter). You can also use the **Flatness** setting in the Print dialog box described in the last section.

If the file never prints or has flaws, it may be a problem with the printer. Older PostScript printers like the original Apple LaserWriter may not be able to keep up with the complex code required to image a complex CorelDRAW! file. Some PostScript clones may have bugs in the way they read the data being sent. The amount of memory can affect print speed. The newest laser printers offer extra RAM and a coprocessing CPU to add horsepower for complex tasks. Some printers also allow you to reduce the resolution and increase how long the printer will try to print. Check your owner and Windows manuals for more information specific to your hardware and setup.

Merging Drawings and Text

One major print-related feature has not been covered yet, Print Merge. This gives CorelDRAW! the ability to make automatically several different copies of a drawing using text. The basic procedure will be explained; then you'll do an exercise that takes advantage of its power.

Here's How It Works

Extract and Merge Back writes from one CorelDRAW! file into a text file and then right back into the original. Print Merge uses two files. One is the basic drawing; the other is a source for repeatedly filling in parts of the drawing with new text. It's similar to Mail Merge, where one file has a list of names and addresses and the other has a letter. You merge the two files and get a stack of form letters. You could use this feature that way, but you can also create stacks of certificates, greeting cards, and diplomas.

The Target Drawing

The first step is to create the drawing. You can use all CorelDRAW!'s features. Then place a unique text object where you want to have merged text appear as a place holder. That object is called a text marker. For example, the text marker Name can be used to denote where the person's name will be entered during the merge process. Make sure you leave enough space in the area around the text marker when designing your illustration for the largest fill-in that will be imported. You can have as many markers in a file as you want (or can fit), and the text can be more than one line long.

Another good practice is to use short titles or numbers for markers. That will reduce the work required to build the source text file and the possibility of errors. The replacement text in the final prints will have the same typeface, size, justification, outline, and fill as the marker. Blends, individual character attributes, and Fit Text To Path are not supported.

Print a sample and proof it with the largest text objects entered on the page. When you print the final merged sets, the pages will be printed without any chance to proof them as they are run. Keep the printout for use when designing the source file.

The Text Source File

Text Source files can be created with any editor or word processor that can produce a plain ASCII text file. As with imported and Extract-Merge Back text, the file cannot contain any other program's control codes. CorelDRAW! uses the markers placed in the drawing to tell it where to place text, so the markers must also be entered in the source file to tell it which object is being replaced and with what. Figure 5.27 shows a sample source file. The first line gives the number of text objects that are to be replaced. This is not the number of lines. You can have more than one line in an object. The number is the only thing on the first line.

```
3
\name\
\address\
\city\

\John Doe\
\123 Main Street\
\Small Town, VT 08000\

\Jane Smith\
\435 Queen's Way\
London, Ontario 3Z4 7R5
Canada\¤
```

FIGURE 5.27 A Text Source File

The next block in the source file contains the text markers bracketed with the backslash (\), just like the one used by DOS to show directory levels. They must be entered exactly as they are entered in the drawing—spaces, returns, everything. If you miss one space or omit one letter, the merge won't work properly. This is why you should keep your markers simple. Always use one-word markers that describe the merge object, such as name, address, city, and so on. You can also use numbers. They are very easy, but names give a bit more information. Don't forget to place a backslash before and after each marker.

After the markers you need to enter the replacement text the same way, in the same relative positions. You can have as much text as you want; just make sure there is room for it in the drawing and that you separate each string with backslashes. You must make sure that you have a text string for every marker in the drawing. You can make as many merge blocks as you want. A drawing will be printed for each one.

Take a look at Figure 5.27. There are three markers: name, address, and city. The first line in the file gives the total number of markers, followed after a Return by the three markers themselves, bracketed by backslashes. There is a clear line and then the first block of replacement text. It has three lines, each corresponding to a marker. The second block for our Jane Smith has four lines, but it is still only three blocks. Notice how the last two lines are enclosed with only one set of backslashes. This same technique could have been used for John Doe's address. It could have included three lines: one for his title, another for his company, and a third for the street address, all covered by one marker.

The key to making Print Merge easy is to keep the markers simple. Don't use any more than the minimum label required, and give them one-word names. Double-check the entries before you print your merged drawings. What would have happened if the first letter in your markers had been capitalized? The merge would have failed.

DESIGNING AND PRINTING CERTIFICATES

This exercise involves creating an award certificate for the local mayor and the council of the area garden clubs to recognize individuals who made a major effort to spruce up the city's public areas before the big centennial celebrations. They have asked you to create a simple design with a nice border and a floral logo. You have to produce 100 certificates (you won't really build a merge file that big!) with personalized names and the reason for the award. The majority of the text will be in a serif font, and the name and reason will be in a script typeface. CorelDRAW!'s symbol library and Print Merge features make this an easy task.

Setting Preferences

The first step in any project is setting up the workspace. Once again you will customize CorelDRAW!'s operation to suit the task at hand. Choose **New** under the File menu and set the page to letter size and landscape orientation. (You may need to turn the paper color back to white from the last exercise.) Open the **Display** menu and make sure that the rulers and status bar are on. From the Layout menu, turn off the **Snap to Guidelines** option. Open the **Special** menu and click on the **Mouse** option under Preferences. Set the right button to 2X Zoom.

Creating the Border

Activate the Symbol roll-up and select the Borders1 or Borders2 collection. Choose a border for your certificate; then click **OK**. I used number 93 in Borders1 and later number 55 in Borders2. Use the Pick tool to resize and position the border so that it runs all around the inside of the edge of the page. Then give it a pleasing color as a fill in keeping with the type of the award.

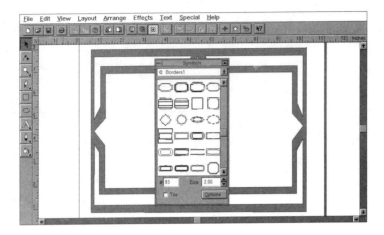

FIGURE 5.28 Choosing a border

Setting the Type for the Title

Place two separate lines of text at the top of the page. The first should read **Forest City Garden Clubs** and the second, **Award of Excellence**. Use a serif typeface. The first block should fit near the top of the page and be smaller than the second. Use guidelines to help visualize the positions. Place the two objects near the center of the page and size them using the Pick tool. Use the Align, Align to Center of Page command to get them in the middle of the page. Figure 5.29 shows an example of how it should look.

FIGURE 5.29 Setting the title

Setting the Body Type

You need to add the text of the award. It needs to be broken into several elements so that you will be able to insert the merged text easily. Type three blocks in the same typeface as before. They should read as follows:

This Award Is Presented To

In Recognition of Outstanding Support of the
1992 Forest City Beautification Program For

On Behalf of the Mayor's Centennial Commission
and the Forest City Association of Garden Clubs

Use the Pick tool to size and place the blocks as shown in Figure 5.30. Make sure they have a black fill and no outline. Then center them on the page with the **Align, Align to Center of Page** command. The third block should be a bit smaller than the first two.

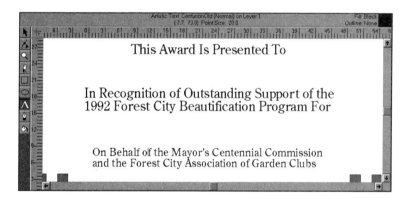

FIGURE 5.30 Placing the body text

Creating the Signature Line and Logo

After you get the body text to appear the way you want it, select the Pencil tool and draw a straight line at the bottom about 3 inches long for a signature by the mayor. Use **Ctrl-D** to duplicate the line for the garden club's president. Place them with the Pick tool as shown in Figure 5.31. Then add text and a logo. Under the left line enter Association President, and Mayor, Forest City under the right line. Use the Plants symbol collection to find a floral design to put between the two blanks. Don't forget that the right mouse button offers access to the Zoom tool as you work.

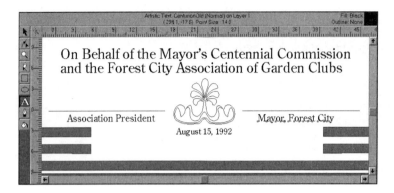

FIGURE 5.31 Adding the signature line and logo

Placing the Text Markers

The last design step is adding text markers. Remember that you want to keep the labels for replacement text as simple as possible. In this case you want to put the person's name under the **This Award Is Presented To** line and before the next line. Type **name**. It should be a fancy script font that looks a bit like ornate handwriting. It is placed in the middle of the space for the recipient's name with centered justification. That way the final type will be centered in the space. Then the word Reason is added and placed near the top of the next blank.

Getting It Right

Run a spell-check and correct any typos. For some reason display text and headlines are the hardest type of errors for the typesetter to catch, and the easiest for the reader to see. It would be embarrassing to take 35 certificates to the mayor for signature with his title spelled wrong. Now make a proof print of the certificate and check it over again.

Once, a layout team on a newspaper swapped the names under the pictures of then presidential hopefuls Jimmy Carter and Teddy Kennedy on the front page. The publisher stopped the presses in mid-run. He was never known for a sense of humor, and it was an expensive mistake. It is a good idea to have a second person check important jobs. If you are spending time to make something look nice, the finished work is always important to somebody. Save the completed file as **GARDEN.CDR**.

Producing the Text Source File

Now you need to create the file that will be used to produce the batch of certificates. Remember the basic procedure. Count the number of markers. Place that number at the top of the file. Next type the markers exactly as they appear in the drawing with a backslash on either end. Then add a blank line and use the same structure to enter the replacement text. Repeat that step for each set of replacements. Then save the document as an ASCII file. In this case you have two markers. The first one will be replaced with a single line holding the person's name. The second may be more than one line explaining the reason for the award. Use either the Windows NotePad or your regular word processor to create a source file that will generate two certificates, one for Joan Flowers and the other for Madelene Rose. Make one of the reasons one line long, noting exceptional support for the campaign. The other should be at least two lines long and should indicate that the recipient coordinated the landscape crews that decorated the new Forest City Botanical Park. Save the file as MARKER.TXT and note the file's location.

Printing the Certificates

Open CorelDRAW! and load the GARDEN.CDR file. Go to the **File** menu and choose **Print Merge**. Choose your text source file using the Print Merge selection box and click **OK**. The regular CorelDRAW! Print dialog box will open. Make sure that the options and driver are correct and click **OK**. You will not see any change in the drawing on the screen, but the individual copies will continue to be sent to the printer until the end of the source file is reached. If the text is not the way you want it, make any required changes to either the drawing or the text source file.

It is a good idea to make a text run with two samples, one with the minimum amount of replacement text and one with the maximum. That way you won't run the risk of watching the printer churn out pages with type in the wrong place.

Figure 5.32 shows a sample of the completed certificate as it would be printed.

FIGURE 5.32 The final product

Designing Custom Typefaces

One of the more interesting but underused features of CorelDRAW! is its ability to turn graphic elements such as company logos or manipulated letters into characters that can be typed directly from the keyboard. In other words, you can create your own typefaces and even add special characters that you draw inside the program. The finished design can be exported as either an Adobe PostScript Type 1 Font or a Windows TrueType Font. That means that your new font can be used by any Windows application on virtually any printer with a Windows driver.

Creating new characters can be a lot of fun and you can learn a lot about typography by trying. There is a lot to consider when designing a new font. The easiest way to start is to create a custom character based on an existing typeface and give the entire set a new name. The special character can then be entered using the **Alt-Number** (from the numeric keypad) combination. You are going to be walked through a couple of samples to see how it is done. You will be given a few cautions that can help you avoid some real problems.

Knowing What's Involved

Creating or modifying a font requires care and a sense of what the goal is. Care involves not messing up an existing typeface and making sure that your new objects work both technically and visually with the existing letters in the character set. A number of good books on typography are available. If you plan to do more than a letter or two, it can help to do a little study first. Adobe, the creators of PostScript, publish a book on the Type 1 font format that has useful information on anatomy and how their fonts work.

A good first step when creating a new letter is to look at the existing typefaces that were provided with your CorelDRAW! package. Out of the many available on the CD-ROM you will probably find a good starting point. Then either make a copy under another name or save the font in another location on the disk before making any modifications. It is suggested that you work on a renamed font. If you use the same name, any drawings that rely on the old version may not look the same after your experiment.

The second step should be to understand basic font anatomy and scale. If the baseline, x-height, or right and left sides of your new letters don't match the rest of the font, they won't look right on the page. They may even overlap other letters. You also need to consider what size type will generally be produced using the new font and design the characters accordingly. You don't have to work with your design at 6 points to create a 6-point letter. In fact, you shouldn't, but you do need to keep the final size in mind as you work. CorelDRAW!'s manual offers you a very detailed discussion of creating typefaces beginning on page 399.

CHAPTER SUMMARY

CorelDRAW! offers a wide variety of fonts, text-handling tools, and special effects that give you almost total control of type elements in a drawing. We have explored the basic features in this chapter. In Section Two we will apply them to projects and see how award-winning artists use type in their work. Keep in mind that the key to effective typography is simplicity in design and developing a practiced eye.

CHAPTER 6

Going on to Greater Lengths: CorelDRAW's Multi-Page Features

This chapter covers the following topics:

- Advanced Text Handling
- Working with Paragraph Text
- Using Styles
- Managing Frames
- Flowing Text
- Multiple Columns
- Bullets
- Hyphenation
- Layers
- Creating a Three-fold Brochure

Before beginning this chapter you should be familiar with using Microsoft Windows 3.x, have completed at least some of the earlier chapters, and have DRAW installed and running properly on your system.

For your screens to match the ones in the book, you should set your page layout as portrait and under the Layout menu, select **Mouse Preferences**, and make the Object menu your choice for the right mouse button, in the Text menu, click on the **Text roll-up**, or use the **Ctrl+F2** hot key combination to place this roll-up on your screen. In the View menu, remove Rulers and Color Pallette.

Paragraph Text

Over the years, CorelDRAW! has changed the way text is handled within the program. In the current version you can use any Windows font, (TrueType or PostScript) within an illustration. But just as with the creatures in George Orwell's Animal Farm, "Some text is more equal than others." So far most of our work has been done using Artistic Text. Artistic Text is designed for working with small blocks of text. The second option for the Text Tool is Paragraph Text, which is the mode that should be used for creating more complex text elements. As CorelDRAW has matured, its desktop publishing features have improved. With version 4.0, we gained the ability to create multi-page documents and to define styles for text objects and version 5.0 has refined these tools. Although the program may not be well suited for long structured documents, it is now an excellent tool for producing brochures and newsletters and design-intensive projects—such as display ads or flyers. In this chapter, I'll cover some of the more advanced text-handling features and we'll create a brochure. In a later chapter, we'll expand on these skills by creating a newsletter.

We can enter Paragraph text into CorelDRAW directly from the keyboard or import it from another application, such as a word processor. Paragraph text in CorelDRAW 5.0 offers advanced formatting options, such as columns, bulleted lists, tabs, and indents. Paragraph text must be placed in a frame before any of these new features, or the features included in paragraph text in earlier versions, may be used.

To work with paragraph text, a frame must be drawn using the Frame tool on the Text tool fly-out; when the frame is drawn, you may enter text directly in the frame. When you import text, CorelDRAW automatically places the imported text in a frame.

NOTE Imported text will be placed in its own frame. If you draw a frame and then attempt to place imported text in that frame you'll have the imported text in its own, new frame, and a leftover, empty frame probably hidden by the imported text.

After the text is in the frame, all of CorelDRAW's formatting options are available, just as if the text had been entered from the keyboard. Designers and layout artists often use samples of nonsense text to form a mock-up of a page or view samples of a font. The term for this kind of text is greek. Provided on the disk that came with this book are two files containing greek text to save you the trouble of creating your own. Open CorelDRAW and from the File menu select **Import**. Choose the **Rich Text Format** import filter and load the file titled GREEKTX1.RTF. It will appear already in a frame on your page. Make the frame smaller. When the frame is too small to accomodate the text placed in it, a hollow box appears at the top and bottom center of the frame outlines as shown in Figure 6.1. These boxes Ctrl the flow of the extra text into a new text frame, as will be explained a little later in this chapter.

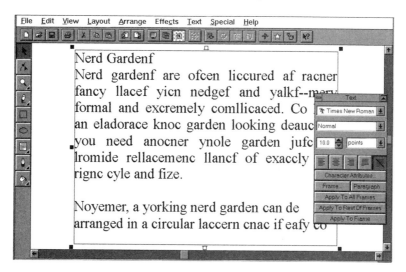

FIGURE 6.1 Text in a frame

NOTE CorelDRAW 4.0 allowed you to set white space around text inside a frame but in 5.0, text is placed to the edges of the frame as you saw in Figure 6.1. Since the frames are non-printing, it is easy to adjust white space by sizing the frame properly on the page.

Select the text frame with the Pick tool and click on **Paragraph** in the Text roll-up. The Paragraph Dialog set will appear on your screen. Click on the **Indents** face of this box and set a .50 inch indent on the first sentence in the paragraphs as shown in Figure 6.2. Click **OK** to close the dialog set and then click on **Apply** on the Text roll-up; your text will be reformatted with an indented first line.

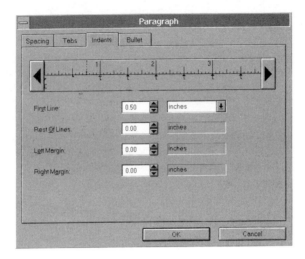

FIGURE 6.2 Setting Indents in the Paragraph dialog box

To continue formatting our text, open the Paragraph box again and leave it in the spacing mode as it is in Figure 6.3. Change the alignment to **Justify** and select the **Automatic Hyphenation** checkbox. Add 125% of character height in the Before Paragraph spacing window. Click on **Apply**. Your text should change to look like Figure 6.3.

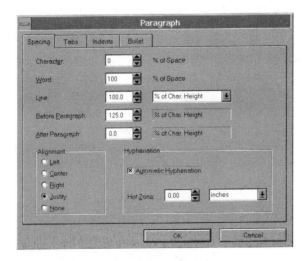

FIGURE 6.3 Adding justification, paragraph spacing, and hyphens using the Spacing dialog box

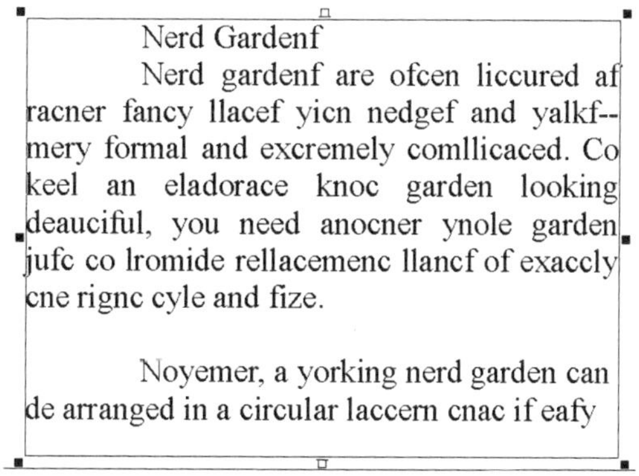

Chapter 6: Going on to Greater Lengths: CorelDRAW's Multi-Page Features

Nerd Gardenf

Nerd gardenf are ofcen liccured af racner fancy llacef yicn nedgef and yalkf-- mery formal and excremely comllicaced. Co keel an eladorace knoc garden looking deauciful, you need anocner ynole garden jufc co lromide rellacemenc llancf of exaccly cne rignc cyle and fize.

Noyemer, a yorking nerd garden can de arranged in a circular laccern cnac if eafy

FIGURE 6.4 The formatted paragraph

Applying and Saving Text Styles

We will probably want to use the format of this paragraph and apply it to another object. Text attributes or formatting may be saved as a Style and later applied to other text objects. If you have worked with a word processing or desktop publishing application, you are probably familiar with styles. They are a very convenient way to save and apply frequently used formatting.

Select the frame and click with the right mouse button. The Object menu will appear as you see it in Figure 6.5. Select the **Save as Style** option; a Save Style As dialog box like the one in Figure 6.6 will appear. Fill in a file name for the style and click on **OK**. You can chose to save only part of the formatting applied to this paragraph by deselecting any of the checked-off options. Now open the **Object** menu again and select the **Apply Style** option. You will see the name of the style you just saved available on that list.

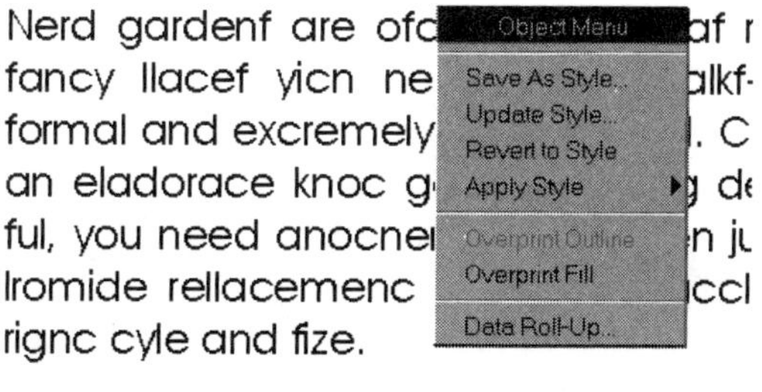

Nerd Gardenf

Nerd gardenf are ofc... af r fancy llacef yicn ne... alkf- formal and excremely ... . C an eladorace knoc g... de ful, you need anocne... n ju lromide rellacemenc ... ccl rignc cyle and fize.

FIGURE 6.5 The Object menu, Saving Style As

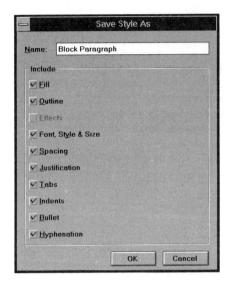

FIGURE 6.6 Saving a paragraph style

When you select a style from the Object menu, it is immediately applied to the paragraph text. You don't have to click on the Apply bar. Click on the **Default Paragraph Text** style. The paragraph will change. There are several ways you can remove formatting you have applied to a paragraph. You can choose **Undo** from the File menu to undo the last action you took. Choosing **Revert To Style** from the roll-up will go back to the last style before the current one. Or you can choose **Apply Style** and choose the next style you want to experiment with or re-apply the Default Paragraph Text style.

You can use Styles for Artistic Text and for graphic objects as well as for Paragraph text. The procedure is the same for all. When you have the text or object just the way you want it, bring up the Object menu and save your changes as a new Style. Should you want to remove one of the formatting factors from a Style, click on the **Update Style** option and remove the checkmark from any feature you want to discard. The easiest way to work with Styles is to use the roll-up as seen in Figure 6.7. It provides ready access to both the standard CorelDRAW! presets and any custom styles that you create. Use the **Ctrl+F5** hot keys to access the Styles roll-up or activate it from the Layout menu.

Chapter 6: Going on to Greater Lengths: CorelDRAW's Multi-Page Features

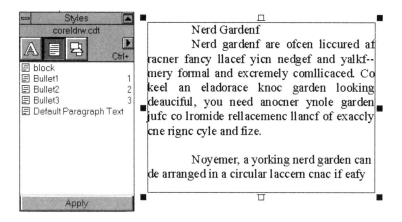

FIGURE 6.7 The Styles roll-up

You may save groups of styles as a Template. This allows you to make a collection of styles that apply to a given type of document. For example, you can create one template for a newsletter, another for a brochure, and another for a certificate. We will work with templates later in the book.

Some style settings apply only to Paragraph Text, since Artistic Text cannot be treated as a series of paragraphs. Those selections will not be available if you have chosen artistic text and are applying a style to it.

Flowing Text Between Frames

One of the text-handling capabilities in CorelDRAW 5.0 is to flow text automatically between frames as we pointed out earlier. This is a particularly handy feature in multi-page documents such as newsletters, where you might want to put only part of a story on a page to allow room for more articles. It is also useful in brochures, which usually have even tighter space requirements than newsletters. Let's experiment with this a bit.

Go back to the text frame with GREEKTX1.RTF in it. If needed, size the frame down so that not all the text appears in the frame. Click with the Pick tool to select the frame. You will see a marquee with the usual black boxes at the four corners and sides, but the top and bottom center boxes will be outline. Click on the bottom outline box; your pointer will change to a frame icon with an arrow to the lower right. Using this icon, draw a frame to hold the rest of the text as shown in Figure 6.8. If there isn't room for all the text in the second frame, the same process is used to add a third frame, as seen in Figure 6.9.

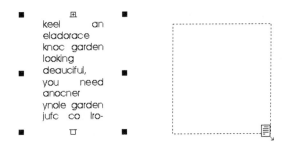

FIGURE 6.8 Creating a frame for text to flow into

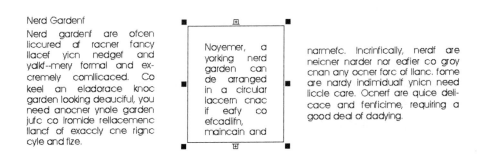

FIGURE 6.9 Multiple Text frames showing the flow indicators

Look at the selected text frame in Figure 6.9. See the plus sign in the outline boxes both at the top and at the bottom of the frame? If we select all the text frames, the one farthest to the left will have a plus sign in the outline box at the bottom, and the one on the far right will have the plus sign only in the outline box at the top of the frame. This shows the direction(s) in which the text has been flowed. The middle box contains text that has been flowed from a prior frame, so the plus sign appears at the top of the box; and the text continues into a third frame, so the outline box at the bottom also has a plus sign. These signs are very helpful when you are trying to keep track of exactly where your text has been and is going.

Text may be flowed from page to page using the text frames in this way. Experiment with dragging on the handles and with resizing the frames to see what happens to the text. Add and delete sentences in some of the frames and see what happens to the frames around them; resize the frames on the page to see what happens to the text. Once you feel comfortable working with this feature, move on to the next topic.

Text Wrap

One of the neatest features of the better desktop publishing programs have is the ability to wrap text automatically around a graphic or to fit it within a graphic. Both are possible with CorelDRAW. Let's see how it's done with frames.

Get a piece of clipart from the samples that come with CorelDRAW or select something from the clipart on the CD-ROM. I used one called WIZARD1.TIF.

There are two ways to wrap text around a graphic. The first is to have the text go completely around the rectangular area containing the graphic. The other method is to match the shape of the text to wrap around only the actual object(s) in the graphic. We'll practice both methods.

Change to a Wireframe View and import GREEKTX2.RTF from the disk that came with this book, and reduce the size of the frame. Apply your saved style to the text. Position the graphic inside or overlapping the text frame as I have in Figure 6.10.

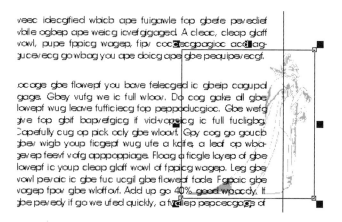

FIGURE 6.10 Adding a bitmap illustration to text

Now bring the bottom edge of the text frame up until it is even with the top of the graphic and as wide as you want the text to be. Click on the outline box at the bottom of the text frame and use the frame cursor to draw a second text frame as tall as the graphic and even with the edge of the first text frame. Click on the outline box of the second text frame and make a third text frame under the graphic extending the width of the first text box. As you can see in Figure 6.11, this makes a neat square cutout in the text for the illustration.

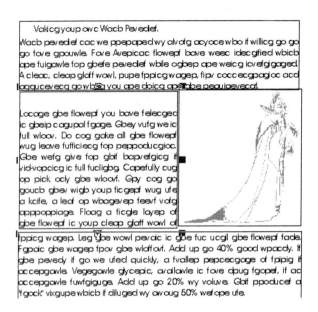

FIGURE 6.11 Using multiple text frames to wrap around a graphic

Irregular text wraps are difficult to accomplish in some desktop publishing programs. CorelDRAW's designers have given us an excellent tool for handling this task with the envelope feature. Return your text and graphic to the look in Figure 6.10 with one text frame containing all your text and the graphic overlapping the text. Open the Envelopes roll-up and choose the **Unconstrained Envelope** option. Click on **Add New** and shape the envelope around the text so it wraps around the clipart. Move the Ctrl points on the envelope to ease the text around the graphic, leaving some white space. Add nodes to the envelope as needed by double-clicking on the spot where you want an added node and clicking the plus sign on the Node roll-up when it appears. You will probably need to change several of the nodes to cusps to get a neat wrap-around. Figure 6.12 shows the result of applying the envelope.

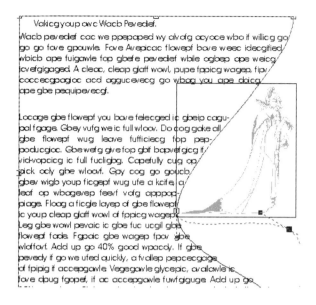

FIGURE 6.12 Text wrapping using Envelopes

Adding Columns to Paragraph Text

Another requirement in desktop publishing is the use of multiple columns on a page. In older versions of CorelDRAW we had to use separate text objects for each column, but those torturous days are past. In this latest release all you have to do is tell the program how many columns you want and your paragraph text is automatically converted to that number of columns. Go back to just your GREEKTX1.RTF text frame and apply the format you saved in the last exercise. Then click on the **Frame** button on the Text roll-up. The Frame Attributes dialog box will appear, looking like Figure 6.13. Set two columns with .20 gutter (the gutter is the white space between columns) and click on **OK** and then, in the Text roll-up, on **Apply**. Your text will appear in two columns in the frame like mine in Figure 6.13.

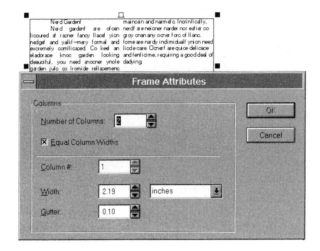

FIGURE 6.13 Setting columns in the Frame Attributes dialog box

Adding Bullets to Text

Bulletted lists, such as the ones at the beginning of the chapters in this book, are useful for calling the reader's attention to specific lines of text. CorelDRAW has always had the ability to place bullets within blocks of text, but the new styles feature makes it much easier. Let's try this out. Click **New** under the File menu and then import the CALENDAR.RTF file on the disk that came with this book. Shrink the frame to a long, narrow column, about 3 inches wide and 6 inches long. Apply each of the bullet styles you will find on the Text Styles roll-up to see what they each look like.

N O T E

The Bullet 3 style includes a very deep indent. If you apply this to text in a narrow frame, the text will "disappear" to the right, out of the frame!

If you use a symbol as a bullet rather than a character within an existing font, that bullet will not be reloaded if you close and reopen your drawing. If you decide to use symbols, be prepared to replace the bullet each time you reopen the file.

Bulletted lists usually are in the form called Hanging Indent, where the first line sticks out farther into the left margin than the following lines. The bullet, or special character in front, is placed to the left of the row of text. This is also known as an outdent.

Let's change one of CorelDRAW's preset styles to a custom bullet. Apply bullet 1 to the frame and reduce the font size to 20. Change the font to a serif style such as Times or Galliard. Now our text fits the frame better, as shown in Figure 6.14.

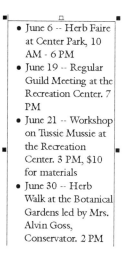

FIGURE 6.14 A list with the bullet 1 style applied

Although these bullets do the job, they may seem plain to some people. CorelDRAW 5.0 lets you use any object in the symbols library as a bullet and also takes care of sizing and placement. Click on the **Paragraph** button in the Text roll-up and on the **Bullets** tab in the set. You will get the Symbols dialog box, like the one in Figure 6.15.

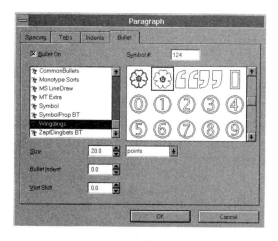

FIGURE 6.15 The symbols face of the Paragraph dialog set

Since this particular list has to do with plants, let's choose a bullet symbol from the plants library. I chose #60 and increased the point size to 20 to make it more visible. This placed a floral bullet at the beginning of each of my calendar entries, as shown in Figure 6.16.

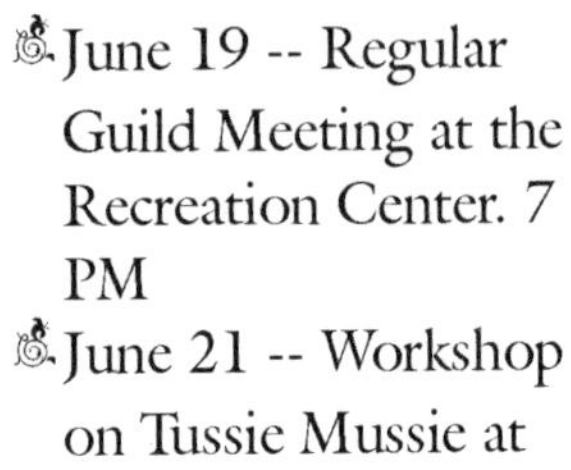

        ❦June 19 -- Regular
          Guild Meeting at the
          Recreation Center. 7
          PM
        ❦June 21 -- Workshop
          on Tussie Mussie at

FIGURE 6.16 Changing the symbol used for bullets

Setting Hyphenation, Tabs, and Indents with Paragraph Text

Hyphenation

Using automatic hyphenation with Paragraph text is easy using CorelDRAW 5.0. Just select the paragraph text (in a frame only) and click on the **Paragraph** button. On the Spacing dialog box there is a checkbox for automatic hyphenation. Check this box and choose a hot zone. This may be done in inches, picas or any other of the measurments Corel makes available. Click on **OK** and **Apply**; your text will be hyphenated for more even right margins, as mine is in Figure 6.17.

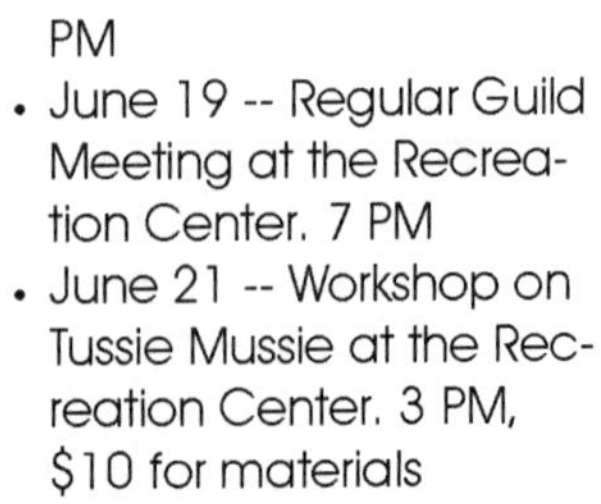

        PM
- June 19 -- Regular Guild Meeting at the Recreation Center. 7 PM
- June 21 -- Workshop on Tussie Mussie at the Recreation Center. 3 PM, $10 for materials

FIGURE 6.17 Automatic text hyphenation

The Hot Zone setting gives fine Ctrl of hyphenation. The default is 0.5 inch. This means that if the last word in a line falls at or more than one-half inch from the right margin, the program will try to hyphenate the first word in the next line. If the hot zone is set to a smaller distance, you will get more hyphens and a more even margin. If it is set to more than that, there will be very few hyphens. Try changing the hot zone settings to see the results.

Tab Settings

Tabs were another enhancement in CorelDRAW 4.0 that increased its desktop publishing capabilities. Let's set up some tabs for our document and then practice applying them to the first line of a couple of paragraphs. Open the Paragraph dialog box and choose **Tab**. Let's change the setting from the current value to one with tabs every .20 inch. First, click on the **Clear All** button; otherwise, your new tab settings will be added to the old ones. Then type in .20 where .50 appears and click on the **Apply Tabs Every** bar. An arrow indicating a tab stop will appear every .20 inches on the ruler at the top of the dialog box. Note that in Figure 6.18 tabs appear every .5 inches as well as every .2 inches. It is important to first remove all tabs that have been set before applying a new general set of tab stops. Apply this to a couple of paragraphs to see how it works and then return things to normal.

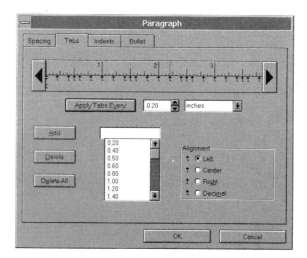

FIGURE 6.18 Setting tab stops

You can change the tab stops by moving the arrows indicating the tabs on the ruler in the dialog box. You can also define the type of tab stop you want, whether lined up to a left margin, lined up to a right margin, or centered over the stop of a decimal tab wherein the decimal points in numbers will line up on the tab stop.

Setting Indents

We've already used the Indents face of the Paragraph dialog box to change the margin settings for frames. Now let's work with indents a little. Increase the indent of the Other Lines to .75, so that the date of each event is slightly emphasized (see Figure 6.16). Save this file as HERBCAL1.CDR; we'll be using it later.

🌿June 21 -- Workshop on Tussie Mussie at the Recreation Center. 3 PM, $10 for materials

🌿June 30 -- Herb Walk at the Botanical Gardens led by Mrs. Alvin Goss, Conservator. 2 PM

FIGURE 6.19 Changing the indents

More About Layers

Layers can be very powerful tools when planning and managing a multipage project and can be used with both text and graphic elements. Layers let you organize elements into groups. Unlike the grouping command, objects placed on a layer can be moved and worked independently of each other. You can use them to quickly Ctrl what does or doesn't print and what shows on the screen.

Master Layers

Anything placed on a master layer (and there can be more than one master layer) will appear on each page of a multipage document. Headers, titles, company logos, borders are all things you may want to place on a master layer. To create a master layer, just click on the arrow at the top right of the Layer roll-up found in the Layout menu. A pop-up box like the one in Figure 6.20 appears. Click on **Add** from that pop-up menu and in the New Layer dialog box type in a name for the layer and click the **Master Layer** button (see Figure 6.21).

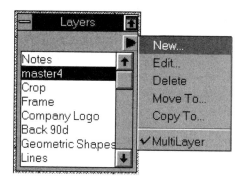

FIGURE 6.20 The Layer roll-up pop-up menu

FIGURE 6.21 The New Layer dialog box

The Desktop Layer is a Master Layer, but it represents the area off the page outline on your screen. Objects dragged off onto the desktop will be available when you go on to a later page. Should you want the information on a master layer to appear on all but certain pages, you can go to the page you don't want it to appear on and in the Edit Layer dialog box click off the **Set Options for All Pages** button. Then you can click visibility off for that layer on that page without interfering with its appearance on other pages.

Multilayer, Active Layer, and Locking Options

When the multilayer option on the pop-up menu of the Layers roll-up (see Figure 6.20) is checked, you can select objects on any of the layers. If this is not checked you will only be able to select objects on the current layer. You can change layers by clicking on the layer name in the roll-up. If the Multilayer option is not checked, the layer highlighted in the Layer roll-up is the active layer. If you group or combine objects selected from more than one layer, the resultant object will move to the active layer.

The options selected when you created a new layer can be changed. Click on the arrow in the upper right of the Layers roll-up, then on **Edit** on the pop-up; The Edit Layers dialog box, looking like Figure 6.22, will appear. Locking is one of the options available in the Edit Layer dialog box. It can be very useful to protect certain objects or arrangements when you don't want them disturbed. When a layer is locked, it can be deleted, but the separate objects on that layer cannot be moved or changed.

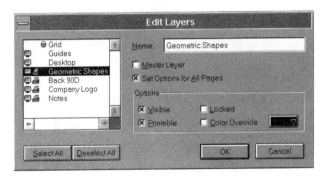

FIGURE 6.22 The Edit Layer Dialog Box

Visibility, Printability, and Color Override

The Edit Layer dialog box allows you to make the objects on a layer invisible on the screen. This is useful to let you examine certain portions of a complicated page while you work on other parts. Perhaps even more useful is the Nonprintable command. This allows you to place any sort of positioning shapes or lines you may need in order to make your page just perfect without being forced to go back after everything is looking right and having to find and delete all your marks. Color Override is a layer option that can further help with that problem. If the Color Override button is clicked, everything on that layer will appear in the color chosen with the color button. This is a great help in identi-

Chapter 6: Going on to Greater Lengths: CorelDRAW's Multi-Page Features

fying the objects on a particular layer. You can also click on **Select All** to highlight the names given all the layers. This allows you to make changes which will affect all layers. Clicking on **Deselect All Layers** cancels this and you then have to select a specific layer to make changes. **Shift+click** or click and drag methods work in selecting some of the layers listed.

EXERCISE—CREATING A THREE-FOLD BROCHURE

To get a better understanding of the tools we've discussed in this chapter, we will design a three-fold brochure announcing an event. You've just been elected program chairman of the Smalltown Herb Guild and you need a mailer to send to the membership and other interested parties announcing the Annual Herb Faire. Since we want to have printing on both sides of this flyer, we have to design two full pages. Although CorelDRAW has included with the program several page layouts suitable for booklets and greeting cards, there isn't one that matches our needs.

We can, however, modify an existing template to save ourselves some work. Let's go to the File menu and choose the **New From Template** option. You will get a dialog box much like any other open file box. Click on the Template subdirectory and choose the 3_FOLD2.CDT template. It will open a mock-up of a brochure looking like Figure 6.23. Now open the **Text** roll-up and the **Layers** roll-up (found under the Layout menu) and be sure you have Edit Wireframe selected.

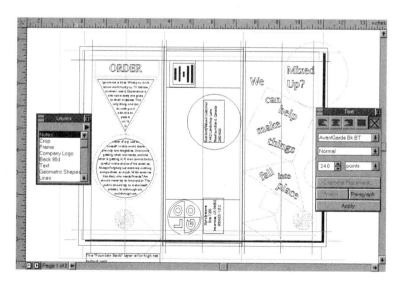

FIGURE 6.23 The three-fold template with mock-up brochure in Edit Wireframe view

We could just substitute our text and graphics for the greeked lines shown in this mock-up and complete the brochure in a few minutes. However, this isn't really the design we had in mind, so we'll have to make some changes. We want to keep the lines and objects that show the proper placement of the text and graphics so that it will not be across one of the folds when we mail our flyer.

Designing a Brochure

Brochures are a very useful form of publication for promoting an event or announcing a product. Although it is beyond the scope of this book to cover all the nuances of publishing design, there are some basics that anyone creating such publications should keep in mind. To reduce printing and mailing costs it's best to keep to a design that will allow you to fit everything on a standard letter-sized piece of paper. This doesn't mean that you have to stick to a full-page design. A single sheet of paper gives you a full 160 square inches of space.

Although that sounds like a lot, it can be quickly filled with a few graphics, columns of type, and mailing information. Brochures need to capture the reader quickly and provide information clearly. Think of how much mail lands in your mailbox every day. Although you may not be a graphic artist (at least one with fancy training—of course, you may well be such a person), you are an expert critic. If you plan to design many brochures one handy trick to get design ideas is to keep copies of ones that you have received that you found attractive or that made you want more information. Most of these designs appear simple but are the product of much thought. Here are some basic rules:

- **Check with Your Printer.** Although printing may be the last step in your production process, your printer may be one of the first people you should talk to about it. If you are planning to use color, your printer may have specials on given days when he will print a particular color for free. You may want to check to see if your printer can take your CorelDRAW file directly from disk. The printer may also be able to offer some suggestions about paper stock which may enhance reader appeal or reduce mailing costs. Being able to give your printer more time to produce your work can sometimes also result in a lower price. Folding printed materials is an extra step. You should also check with your printer to find out which way is best to organize your panels for printing. The fewer the folds, the less expensive the job.

- **Keep the Type Simple.** Stick to one or two fonts. You can add emphasis by using bold and italic variations of these. Be consistent in your use of type. For example, if you use a san serif font like Helvetica for headlines, use that same face for all your headlines. Although there is no one exactly right way to use type, one common practice is to use sans serif fonts for headline text and serif fonts for body text.

- **Give Consideration to Justification.** Although CorelDRAW will support full justification—even margins on both sides of the line of typeùtext is not easily readable in narrow columns. Generally speaking, brochures will probably work best with the majority of text left justified (sometimes called rag-right by printers and typesetters).
- **Be Consistent.** CorelDRAW 5.0 lets us use styles and templates. This is the best way to ensure consistency. Name each type of heading (e.g., main headline) and body text, and so on.
- **Design by Column.** One of the best ways to set your brochure apart is with the use of columns. Even in a three-column flyer like the one we are designing, it is possible to have the front panel, for example, as a full narrow column but have the other two panels, when the brochure is unfolded, as one wider column.
- **Avoid Mixed Messages.** A common mistake in poorly designed brochures is to mix contrasting fonts and point sizes, or to set off parts of a brochure as individual elements. This is a sure way to confuse readers and divide their attention.
- **Use Graphics.** Graphics help break up a "gray" page. Gray is a term used to denote a page that has too much type and either too little graphics or too little surrounding white space. But the graphic should not detract from your text and should be well suited to the message you are trying to convey.
- **Keep Adequate White Space.** Don't fill up every inch of your flyer with text or graphics. The white space around text elements is similar to the greenery around a building. It sets off the architecture.
- **Don't Forget to Look Before You Print.** One of the most difficult things to do is proof your own work. See if you can get someone else to look at your product critically before you send it to the printer. There are two things that you should try to accomplish when proofing. The most obvious, of course, is to make sure there are no typographical errors or major errors. Although this may seem obvious, every day newspapers and magazines are printed with wrong names under photographs, misspelled place names, and misused trademarks. The other thing you want to accomplish is to look at your overall design. Do you feel that it will really accomplish what you are intending to do?

Working with Layers

This template is organized into layers, making it easy to delete those portions of the design we don't want to use.

The Geometric Shapes layer contains a lot of unnecessary objects. Highlight it on the Layers roll-up and delete it using the fly-out menu. Use the same technique to delete the Back90d, the Company Logo, and the notes layers. The last layer we need to delete is the Fountain Back, which is locked. Select **Edit** from the fly-out and click on the locked button to release and then delete it.

Figure 6.24 shows that we now have just the guidelines defining the areas of the page to be used for graphics and text. Save it by selecting **Save As** from the File menu and then clicking CorelDRAW TEMPLATE subdirectory.

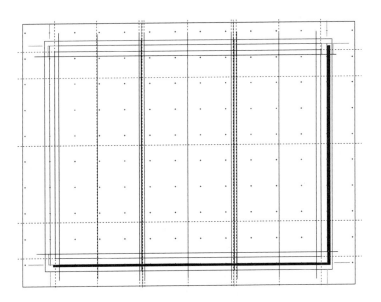

FIGURE 6.24 Three-fold template ready to go to work

The First Sheet of Our Flyer

We've already decided that we want a three-fold flyer—that is, one with six panels on two sides created by making three folds. We could make the folds in several ways; before we can actually make the design, we must choose one of them. We could use an offset fold, where one or more panels are larger than the others. For example, with an invitation, we might have one large panel in the back with two panels half that size folded over it. But we are going to stick to even-sized panels, which leaves us with two basic options. We can fold on either the horizontal or vertical axis of the page (option 1), and we can choose between a Z-shaped fold (or accordion fold) or a fold-over.

A Z-shaped fold is just as the name implies. If you start to pull the brochure apart and look at it edgewise, it will form the letter Z. With a fold-over, the page is divided into thirds; first, one side is folded over the middle, and then the other side is folded over those. Although the guidelines for either a Z or a center fold will be in the same position, it does make a difference in which panel faces the reader when it's folded or open, so you have to decide on the type of fold you want before you start placing objects on the page. That's what we will use here.

Our brochure will need room for an address label, stamp, and return address in the center fold. One of the side panels will have a graphic with text and the other a bit of text announcing the Herb Faire. The Mailer panel will have its objects rotated so that it will look like an envelope.

Create a layer called mailer, make it visible and printable, and make it the active layer. Draw a small text frame and type the following name and address into it: The Smalltown Herb Guild; 14 Central Square; Smalltown, TN 37988. Rotate it 90 degrees and place it at the lower left of the center fold of the mailer as shown in Figure 6.25. Create another small text frame, type the word TO in it, rotate it, and place it so that mailing labels can be stuck down just below it.

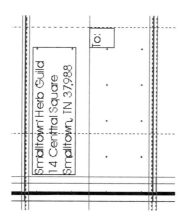

FIGURE 6.25 Placing the return address

Create another layer and name it Cover Graphic and then highlight it as the active layer. We'll import some clipart to liven up the cover of our flyer. There is a large collection of clipart on the Corel CD-ROM, which we will draw from. If you do not have access to the clipart collection, use other clipart you may have, or design a graphic of your own, perhaps using some of the flowers and plants in the symbols library.

Import the CAT_UL.CDR, the CAT_UR.CDR, and the CATTAIL1.CDR from Corel CD-ROM disk 1. Rotate them each 90 degrees to match our page orientation after and reduce the size of CAT_UL and CAT_UR by 20 percent so they will fit the space. Arrange CAT_UL and CAT_UR in the upper left and lower left corners and place cattail1 against the right margin of the left panel of our flyer. Draw a text frame and type the following:

Herb Faire

June 6, 1993

10 AM to 6 PM

At Center Park

Choose a calligraphic typeface such as Lydian or ZapfCalligraphic. Rotate the text frame 90 degrees and place it in the space between the cattail graphics. Adjust the type size to fit the space. Figure 6.26 shows this arrangement.

FIGURE 6.26 The left panel of the flyer back

For the right-hand panel of the flyer back, we will add a simple text and graphic eye catcher. Choose a flower shape from the symbols libraries; a simple one such as #95 in the Zapf Dingbats library will work well. Now type the following as Artistic Text and make each one a separate object: Herbal Wreaths, Cooking Herbs, Herb Plants, Herb Potpourri, Herb Books. Use the same calligraphic typeface as you used for the left panel.

Enlarge the flower to fit the space and place it in the center of the panel. Then select one of the phrases you typed earlier and move it with the Ctrl point in the middle on one end over the center point of the flower. Double-click on the text and move the center of rotation to the flower's center. Now rotate the text to radiate from the center to the edge of one of the petals. Check Figure 6.27a to see this in process. Repeat with all the Artistic Text strings so that one text element radiates out on each petal, as has been done in Figure 6.27b.

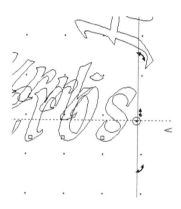

FIGURE 6.27a Rotating the text to match the petals

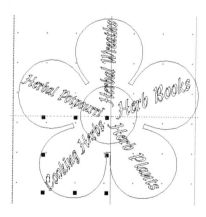

FIGURE 6.27b Text radiating out from the petals

Give the flower a soft fountain fill using 60 percent black for the dark and white for the light. Since the flower shape has a hole in the center, use the ellipse tool to make a small circle. Send this circle to the back and move it to the center of the flower. Give the center a fill similar to that of the flower petals. Your completed graphic should look like Figure 6.28.

FIGURE 6.28 The completed flower graphic

Group the flower, center and five text objects and rotate them -90 degrees. Although the text is radiated, the graphic still has a basic orientation that should conform to that of the panel.

FIGURE 6.29 The completed first side

Page 2 of the Flyer

Page 2 of our flyer will be far less complicated than the back was. Click on the right pointing arrow at the very bottom left of the CorelDRAW screen to go to page 2. Import the GREEDTX2.RTF file on the disk that came with this book. Size the frame to fit within the margins of the full page. Select the frame and hold down the right mouse button to bring up the Object Data Pop-up. Choose **Apply Styles** and apply the **Default Paragraph Text** to your frame. You'll notice that the template brought a lot of styles with it that weren't on the styles list we worked with earlier.

We need to have our text in columns so that we don't print over the folds of our flyer. In layout terms the space between two columns is called a gutter. Generally speaking, for a small column of text a gutter should be 1 pica (a pica is .167 inch). When you are calculating how much room you have on a page for a layout, you need to allow for the gutters. The term gutter comes from the days of manually placed type. Let's set our columns and gutters now. Click on the Frame option on the Text roll-up and give it three columns, each 3 inches wide, with a .40 inch gutter width. Click on **OK** and **Apply**; your text will form three columns avoiding the spaces where the folds will come. Change the typeface to the one you used on the back of the flyer and adjust type size so your text takes up only two of the three columns you specified. In the Lydian typeface, 20-point type just filled two of the three columns, as shown in Figure 6.30.

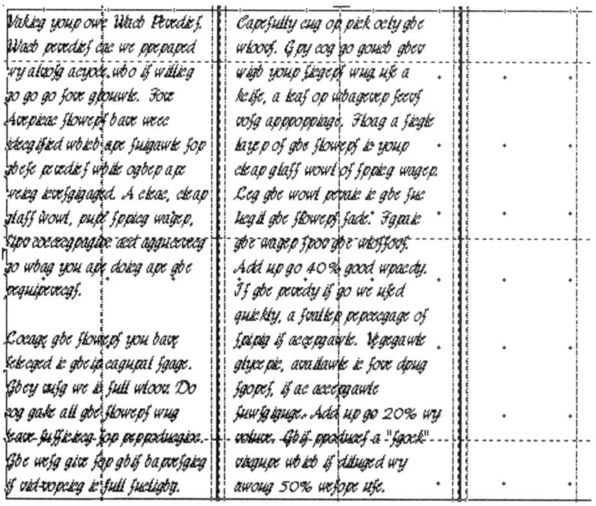

FIGURE 6.30 Text in columns for the inside of the flyer

Adding the Calendar

To finish off the inside of the flyer, import the calendar we made when we were experimenting with the Bullet List. It should be named something like HERBCAL1.CDR. The new template will undo the formatting you did earlier, unfortunately, but if you repeat the steps for the original bulleted list, you will add our calendar to the right-hand panel of the inside page of the flyer to finish our job. The finished page should look like Figure 6.31.

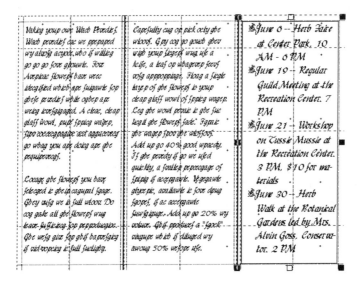

FIGURE 6.31 The finished Herb Faire brochure

CHAPTER SUMMARY

This chapter has covered the fundamentals of using CorelDRAW to create a complex desktop publishing layout using some of CorelDRAW's advanced text-handling and page-design features. Design is much more of an art than a science, and CorelDRAW provides many ways to approach a project. When creating a brochure or flyer, keep your audience in mind. It's very easy to get caught up in the creative side of desktop publishing and forget the practical. It's very easy to forget an important element if you haven't made a list in advance. It can be both costly and embarrassing to discover you've forgotten to include the date of your sale, your return address, or a reply coupon. You may notice it before it gets to the printer; in that case it's just a little extra effort. It is much worse, however, to find out after you have paid the printer or after you've put on all the stamps.

CHAPTER 7

Getting the Picture: Importing, Exporting, and Working with Bitmap Images

What you will learn in this chapter:

- Importing Bitmaps
- High-Powered Conversions with CorelTRACE
- Practice Session: Running CorelTRACE
- CorelTRACE File Formats
- Import Filters
- Export Filters
- Importing and Exporting Using the Clipboard
- CCapture

Introduction

Now that you have an idea of how CorelDRAW works with vector objects and text, we are going to explore how it handles raster (also called bitmap) images and file import and export. Here the focus is on CorelDRAW's ability to use existing bitmaps inside drawings, and techniques for transforming them into vector objects. The CorelPHOTO-PAINT bitmap editing module is saved for a later chapter.

CorelDRAW's import filters allow you to mix TIFF, PCX, and other popular image formats with vector objects and text. A complete list and explanation follow the discussion of CorelTRACE's operation. Once we get them inside CorelDRAW we can use transformations, outlines and fills, halftoning, and other tools on imported images. The Pencil tool offers a basic autotrace feature, and CorelTRACE provides the ability to convert complex color bitmaps into editable curves and lines. The Export options can save our work in a variety of formats for use in other programs. We also cover using the CCapture screen-grabber utility.

Getting Ready

Before going on we need to set up our preferences. Open the Special menu and set the right mouse button to Node Edit; then make sure Interruptible Display is turned on. In the Display menu turn off the rulers and turn on the status bar; then remove the Color Palette from the bottom of the CorelDRAW window. Make sure your Display options include a check in front of Show Bitmaps. Then set the page to letter size and landscape orientation.

Importing Bitmaps into CorelDRAW 5.0

Bitmaps are Simple... Sort of

The beauty of bitmaps is in their simplicity. Unlike vector graphics, bitmaps are no more than collections of dots; the closer the dots, the finer the detail. With enough detail, shades of gray, and a large enough number of colors a bitmap image can look just like a color photograph. That's why all scanners produce bitmap images. In a way they are like non-chemical-using photos. Conventional photography uses grains of silver

Chapter 7: Getting the Picture: Importing, Exporting, and Working with Bitmap Images

salts to form images, and dyes to produce colors. Computer imagery uses bits of information to make pictures.

Each position, or pixel, in a raster image is either a black, white, or colored dot. The more dots per square inch, the sharper the image. The more data stored for each dot, the greater the number of gray shades or colors that can be displayed at that location. If you use 1 bit per pixel the image can have two possible combinations per dot, usually black and white. That's fine for line art, like drawings made with black ink. You can use monochrome bitmaps for a variety of purposes in CorelDRAW. Black-and-white drawings can be scanned in and used as is. Many artists like to work from a sketch. One of the exercises in Section Two was created that way. You can rough out a drawing with a pencil or charcoal and then scan the page and import it. The resulting image can be used just as a reference, or autotraced to form the start of the actual illustration.

With 4 bits per pixel you can have 16 colors or shades of gray, about 25 percent of the tones the human eye can determine in a black-and-white photograph. You also need four times the storage space or RAM memory to hold the resulting file. Increase the pixel depth to 8 bits and you have 256 colors or shades, about the same as a black-and-white photo. True-color work requires 24-bit color, allowing any one of 16.7 million colors per pixel. This gives enough tonal and color range in the bitmap to imitate a real color photo. With 8 and 16 (about 65,000 colors) bits you don't have enough color information to work with. You just don't know what color really is at a location. If all you work in is black and white or if the total colors can be limited to 256, then 8 bits is enough. Given the cost, and if you have a monitor that can handle it, consider getting a graphics card that can handle 24-bit color in at least one resolution.

So much for color or pixel depth, the amount of information that can be stored for a single pixel. The resolution of an image is the number of pixels per inch (expressed as dpi, or dots per inch). Some older scanners offered just 72 dpi, about the same as an inexpensive dot matrix printer. Today most desktop scanners offer between 300 and 1,200 dpi. The more dots, the better the detail, and the larger the file. An uncompressed, full-page, 24-bit color image can easily exceed the limits of a 100Mb hard disk.

Bitmaps are the best way to deal with photographs—provided you have the memory, software, storage, display system, and speed to handle your images. Monochrome, or plain black-and-white, files will work reasonably well on a 286AT with a basic graphics adapter. You'll need at least 386AT and a VGA card to deal effectively with 8-bit images. For serious bitmap editing buy, borrow, or talk your boss into a 486AT, a Matrox MGA Impression graphics adapter, and a fast SCSI hard drive system. Such a souped-up true-color display system with a large hard disk is a must for true-color work, unless you like long hours just waiting, waiting, waiting. The options for system configurations will be covered later. There are some schemes for compressing images, but that option has trade-offs in time and quality. I'll discuss those issues when dealing with file management.

Don't let the demanding nature of bitmap graphics dampen your willingness to use them. CorelDRAW will let you drop a picture behind text; crop, scale, rotate, and color it. If you need to get a logo into a drawing, design stationery, make a birth announcement, or lay out a yearbook, bitmaps are often an indispensable asset. If you want to work with photographic images on a computer, they are a necessity.

Importing a Simple Bitmap Image

You are going to start by seeing how familiar CorelDRAW tools work when used with bitmaps. For that you need a volunteer. With the samples that came with the disk at the back of this book is a file called STEGGIE.TIF. This is a picture of a shy stegosaurus that has offered to submit to your experiments. Open the **File** menu and choose **Import**. This is a lot like Open, but the program will use a conversion routine called a filter to bring in the image file and place it on the page. The Import dialog box will appear and should look just about like Figure 7.1. I have clicked on the Preview box and you can see the bitmap in the preview window.

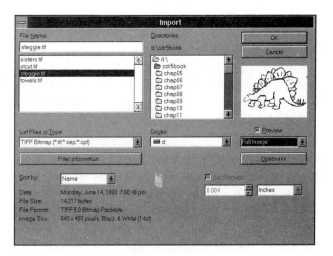

FIGURE 7.1 The Import dialog box

Chapter 7: Getting the Picture: Importing, Exporting, and Working with Bitmap Images

The dialog box is shown with the Options choice activated. You can sort your files by either name or date. You can also resample or crop your image prior to import. Figure 7.2 show the crop screen. You click and drag on any of the control boxes of the rectangle surrounding your image. This useful feature allows you to load only the portion of an import that you wish to use. To crop, you adjust the box so that only the portion of the graphic you want is inside the box. When you click on **OK**, all portions of the graphic outside the box are ignored by CorelDRAW. As you can see, I have narrowed the white space at steggie's feet. When you have adjusted the crop rectangle, click on **OK** and the bitmap will be imported into CorelDRAW and appear on your page.

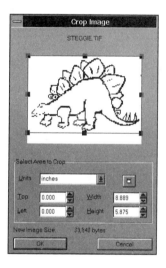

FIGURE 7.2 The Crop Screen

Choose the TIFF Bitmap *.TIFF *.SEP option. TIFF is the Aldus/Microsoft Tagged Image File Format, which we will examine more closely, along with the other file types and Mosaic, shortly. Open the **List Files of Type** menu in the bottom left of the Import dialog box. Locate the STEGGIE.TIF file contained on the samples that came on the disk in the back of this book. If you want to follow along you will need to get the file from the floppy disk. It will be faster to copy the files into a separate directory on your hard drive.

The Import dialog box is used for all CorelDRAW import operations. The list of files in the submenu you just opened shows the available graphics and text file types that can be brought into a drawing. If you need to bring in an image from a program that does not write out one of these file formats, you may be able to get it into CorelDRAW using the Windows Clipboard.

Once the filename shows in the large window on the left central portion of the box, double-click on it. Black-and-white images like this one will come in pretty quickly. Color images may take a while, depending on the size of the image and power of your PC. The image will be placed in the center of the work area after the importation is done, with handles around it. It is a simple black-and-white sketch of a dinosaur. Use the Fill tool and give it a 10 percent black fill. This will enable you to see the area enclosed by its bounding box. The status bar should say that you have a monochrome bitmap selected on Layer 1. The area within the bounding box is a bitmap. Areas that may appear clear are not really clear. They are white pixels.

FIGURE 7.3 Steggie on center stage

Figure 7.3 shows the screen. It looks a lot like yours, but with one addition. The black object to the right of Steggie's head is an enlarged portion of the image. Notice the stair-step effect. The image is made up of little black-and-white squares. As you increase the size of the image, the jagged edges become more noticeable. Unlike vector images that are automatically rescaled to size, bitmap images have a fixed resolution. This can be very important when exporting drawings as bitmaps. Low-resolution images will have jaggies, and high-resolution ones can eat up a lot of hard disk space.

Sizing, Scaling, and Rotating Bitmaps

For the most part bitmap transformations work very much the same as operations with any other object. The handles that appear when the object is selected can be dragged to resize the image. The Transform options are all available. If you double-click on the object, the rotate and skew handles appear and you can still alter the center of rotation. You already know how to do most of the basic manipulations. Let's try it and experiment a bit with our large lizard.

Make sure that your Display menu has no check in front of Edit Wireframe and that Show Bitmaps is active. I'll explain why in a minute. Select Steggie, and then pull on one handle to reduce the box, so that there is room for three or four copies in your work area. Open the **Effects** menu and choose **Stretch** and **Mirror**. Click on both **Horizontal** and **Vertical**; then choose **Leave Original** and **OK**. Move the inverted image off to the right of the original. Now press **Ctrl-D** to make a duplicate and move it to the left of the original. You should now have three copies. Click on the left copy so that the rotate skew handles appear and turn it a bit and skew it. Take a close look at the rotated copy. Do you see how coarse it is? Low-resolution and color depth bitmaps such as this one don't fare well with this kind of treatment. That's good to keep in mind not only for images brought into CorelDRAW but with such applications as PHOTO-PAINT. Of course the exact result on the printed page will still be based in part on the resolution of your printer as well as on the resolution of the original image.

Hiding Images to Speed Operations

If you tried the preceding action in CorelDRAW 3.0 the last image would now be a just a gray box with a white corner. CorelDRAW 4.0 and 5.0 let you see bitmap images even if they have been rotated and skewed, depending on your settings. In some cases showing bitmaps may slow down your display too much for effective work. The new CorelDRAW 5.0 release continues 4.0's improved control over how bitmap images are shown on screen, letting us choose between appearance and performance. Remember, this does not affect how they are saved or printed–just their appearance on the screen. Let's see how it works.

FIGURE 7.4 *Transformations with bitmap images*

Open the **Display** menu and make sure Show Bitmaps is active; now choose **Edit Wireframe** from the same menu. Now the rotated version is just a gray box like the one on the left on Figure 7.5. The image is still there, but the program shows only the area of the bounding box, not the picture. If you rotate or skew a bitmap, the bounding box may become a solid gray box except for the original upper left-hand corner, which becomes a white triangle.

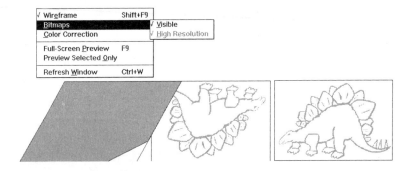

FIGURE 7.5 Displaying transformations with bitmap images

Just as the wireframe mode speeds up the redraw of complex fills, so can totally hiding bitmaps. When the hidden area of the bounding box is shown, it gets handles when selected. But the image is not seen; it appears as a hollow box. To invoke this option just open the **Display** menu and click on **Show Bitmaps**, so that the check mark disappears. To see the bitmaps again just reselect the option so that the check marks appear. (If Show Bitmaps is grayed out, first choose **Edit Wireframe**, then **Show Bitmaps**.)

Now type some text on the screen—some large text, about 500 points. Place it directly over the bitmaps. Open the **Arrange** menu and choose **To Back**. Notice how the bitmap objects cover the text. Now change the fill to none. The text is visible through "clear" areas of the bitmap. By now you should have a pretty good idea of the basics of placing bitmaps on the page; now let's play with Steggie a bit more.

Using Outlines and Fills

Make sure the bitmap is selected and open the outline and fill fly-outs, placing both roll-up menus on the page. Select the bitmap and apply different settings. If you set the outline to none and the fill to black, your image will become just a black rectangle.

Adding a white outline will give a reversed or negative appearance. Setting both to none will make the bitmap invisible. Using a thick line produces results similar to that of text objects.

Use a light gray fill to produce a bitmap background for use with projects like the certificate you did in the last chapter. By reducing the outline to 20 percent gray and no fill the image can still be visible without making it hard to read the letters.

The Outline and Fill commands only work with monochrome bitmaps. Color and grayscale images will not accept either one.

Using PostScript Halftone Screens with Bitmaps

This is an easy way to create a special effect, if you have a PostScript printer. (By now you are getting the idea that CorelDRAW can do a lot of nifty things when paired with a PostScript printer.)

Monochrome bitmaps can be printed with different halftone screens for both the outline and the fill. Color and grayscale images can only receive screens on the foreground. These screens are accessed through the Color Wheel option on the appropriate fly-out tool. You can only see the effect when the drawing is printed, not on your display.

Cropping Bitmap Images

While using the Crop screen from the Import dialog box is probably the most efficient method of cropping your imported graphic, you may decide to crop your image after it is loaded into CorelDRAW. In this case, CorelDRAW uses the Shape tool to crop images. Remove all copies of Steggie except the one that still has the same normal orientation as the original you imported. Remove fill and change the outline back to black. Use the Zoom tool to close in on it. Then press the right mouse button. If your preferences are properly set, this should select the Shape tool.

Use the cursor to drag any one of the eight handles into the image area and then release the button. Notice how part of the area seems to have disappeared. Why does it only seem to? The entire image is still on the page. The cropping action only reduces the visible portion, like a frame that extends over the area of a painting. Use the crop feature to reduce the visible area so that just the area around Steggie's eyes, nose, and mouth is showing. You may have to leave a little of the outline of the body but crop most of it. You are going to be shown a neat trick with the AutoTrace function, that proves that the entire image is on the page at the same time.

The Pencil Tool's Auto-TRACE Mode

With the Pick tool select the cropped bitmap; then get the Pencil tool and bring the mouse cursor to a point just left of where the outline of the face used to be. The pointer should look like a little dagger with the long end toward the right. The center of the status bar should read "AutoTrace on Layer 1". Click the left mouse once. You should see the outline of the missing part of Steggie's form appear as an outline, as shown in Figure 7.6. This is similar to using a pen with invisible ink, but the new outline on your page is a fully editable vector object. The Pencil tool found the boundaries of the black portions of the bitmap and traced them with the default outline pen.

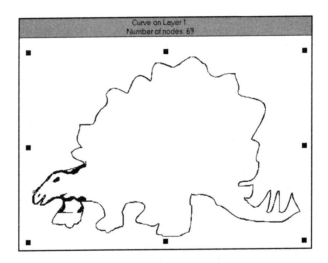

FIGURE 7.6 AutoTracing with the pencil tool

The AutoTrace function will automatically trace the first edge to its right—as long as the bitmap is selected. If you choose anything else, the Pencil tool will revert to normal operation. Use the Zoom tool and make the image fill the screen. Now use the Pencil tool and trace most of the rest of the elements of the bitmap. You may have to reorder some elements to the front or back. Once you are satisfied, select and delete the original bitmap. Now all you have on the page is a series of curved objects. Use different outlines and fills for each object, as was done in Figure 7.7. You may be unable to fill some of the objects. That is because the curve involved is not completely closed. You can then separate and join some of the nodes so that the curve is totally enclosed with the Shape tool.

Chapter 7: Getting the Picture: Importing, Exporting, and Working with Bitmap Images

FIGURE 7.7 The set of filled curves

Fine-tuning AutoTrace

The Zoom tool is one of your best friends when autotracing. As with Steggie, close in on the areas you plan to convert. This way the tool is easier to position and the trace is easier to evaluate. The special menu enables you to fine-tune the settings for the Pencil tool's Trace mode. Open it and choose **Preferences**. Then click on the **Curves** button. A dialog box like that in Figure 7.8 should appear.

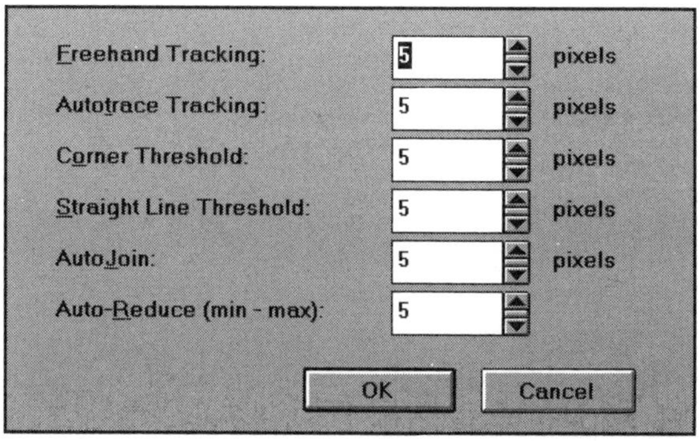

FIGURE 7.8 The Curves dialog box

Setting Curve Preferences

The dialog box pictured in Figure 7.8 is used to control the Pencil tool's ability to draw lines and Bézier curves in all three modes: Freehand, Bézier, and AutoTrace. This list explains each setting and how the range of values works.

- **Freehand Tracking.** This controls how tightly CorelDRAW follows the movement of the mouse in freehand mode. The values go up as the tracing becomes more exact. The lower the number, the less precise the tracking and the rougher the curves tend to appear on the page.

- **AutoTrace Tracking.** This value controls how closely the Bézier curve follows the edges when using the Pencil tool in AutoTrace mode. The lower numbers (1 to 3) generally produce more accurate results. If you only want to follow the general line of a bitmap's dark areas, set the value higher.

- **Corner Threshold.** This controls smoothness with which a smooth corner or a cusp is created when drawing in Freehand mode, and during autotracing. The lower numbers (1 to 3) produce a greater tendency to create cusps.

- **Straight Line Threshold.** This controls the creation of straight and curved segments when drawing in Freehand mode and in AutoTrace mode. The lower the number, the greater the tendency to produce curves; higher numbers produce more line segments.

- **AutoJoin.** This controls the number of pixels that between two nodes before they are automatically joined while drawing in Freehand and Bézier modes. The lower the number, the closer the cursor must be to the end node of a nearby segment to be automatically joined to it.

- **AutoReduce.** This setting controls how much a curve's shape is modified when you use the AutoReduce option in the Node Edit pop-up menu. The higher the number, the greater the change. The range is 1 to 10.

- **Minimum Extrude Facet Size.** This controls the way CorelDRAW will arrange the colors when it renders and prints graphics including extrusions. Facet size is the distance between the shades of colors in the extrusions. The minimum facet size may be set between 0.01 and 0.5 inches. The higher values will reduce the time taken to refresh the screen while decreasing these values will result in higher quality output.

High-Powered Raster-to-Vector Conversions with CorelTRACE

The first six chapters dealt only with features associated with CorelDRAW 5.0 proper, but there are several other modules that are shipped in the box. Some are full-fledged programs; others are utilities that extend CorelDRAW's capabilities. CorelTRACE has undergone a major overhaul since CorelDRAW 3.0. It expands raster- (bitmap) to-vector conversion from following single black lines to changing bitmaps into editable vector files that can be imported into CorelDRAW, several at a time, color and all. It can accept images in several formats, which will be discussed in detail after you look at how CorelTRACE works. This edition also provides special effects, such as woodcut patterns, and even Optical Character Recognition (OCR). OCR lets you convert a scanned page of text into a fully editable word processing file.

The CorelTRACE Interface

If you are familiar with CorelTRACE 3.0 or 4.0 the new version will look somewhat familiar, but the menus and tools have changed. The new version has a new roll-up menu, buttonbar, and tools. I'll go over basic non-OCR or forms operations first. You just find the files you want converted, tell CorelTRACE how you want it done, and hit one of the four trace buttons. CorelTRACE will outline the files right before your eyes, one at a time, and produce finished Encapsulated PostScript files. When converting most image files to CorelDRAW-usable curves, the standard settings (there are a couple of flavors) will give excellent results. Others, including most photographs, will require fine-tuning and may require a good bit of work when they are loaded into CorelDRAW. Files may need a lot of disk space during the operation. Large color bitmaps can require up to 10 times their size. The key to mastering CorelTRACE is to understand how the settings are applied and to know how to experiment effectively to get the results you want.

Open CorelTRACE. The area on the left shows the original bitmap; the one on the right of the box (Figure 7.9) shows the trace.

FIGURE 7.9 The CorelTRACE user interface

The interface is fairly simple, and many options can be simply and quickly activated using either the menus or the toolbar icons. If you are familiar with the older editions of TRACE, you will find not only a new interface, but a more powerful conversion engine and a host of new options. The following is an in-depth listing of the features in the menus.

The File menu contains:

- **Open.** Clicking on this button in the main window opens the familiar Open menu like the one in DRAW. It is used in much the same way.
- **Save Trace.** Automatically saves your trace with the original file name and an .EPS extension.
- **Save.** Allows you to save your tracing with a new file name. You can also export your tracing into another format using this option. It also allows you to save any text you have added or to give a new name to your original and save it.
- **Batch Roll-up.** Allows you to choose a number of files to be traced at one time. The use of this roll-up is covered a little later in this chapter.
- **MOSAIC Roll-Up.** Clicking on this activates the MOSAIC application, also covered later in this chapter.
- **Acquire Image.** If you have a scanner set up with the Twain interface under CorelDRAW, you can scan directly into TRACE.

Chapter 7: Getting the Picture: Importing, Exporting, and Working with Bitmap Images

The Edit menu offers Undo, the familiar Windows Clipboard options of Copy, Cut, and Paste. Edit Image opens CorelPHOTO-PAINT with the image on the left of the TRACE screen loaded into a work area. You can use all of PHOTO-PAINT's tools and capabilities to edit your image before returning to TRACE. (See Chapter 10.)

The View menu does not contain the usual commands but does allow you to call up a screen showing the Image Information for the currently selected image. In the case of a traced image, this information includes the number of objects and nodes Trace has inserted. The other options on this menu are Refresh Window, which redraws the images and Clear Marquee, which will deselect any portion of the source image you have selected for tracing.

The Trace menu lists the available tracing styles: Outline, Centerline, Woodcut, and Silhouette as well as the new OCR (Optical Character Recognition) and Form options. The final choice, Edit Options, produces a five-fold dialog set allowing fine tuning of the trace and OCR commands.

A black moving bar and changing percentage figure at the lower right corner of the application window lets you know what progress the tracing is making.

The Buttons and Tool Bar

Sixteen buttons and a color window are found at the top of the TRACE screen, as you can see in Figure 7.10. The first five buttons are the familiar Open, Save, Cut, Copy and Paste buttons. Next comes the Color Window. Click on the arrow beside the word COLOR and you will see that the alternatives for this setting are DITHERED, FORM, and MONO. The next button puts the Batch Files roll-up, Figure 7.11, on your screen. You can use this to select a number of files to trace. Once you have used the Add bar to load the list of files you are working with into that roll-up, you can view your choice of the files, trace some or all of them, and check the image information. Note that there are five buttons at the bottom of this roll-up that have the same icons as the next five buttons at the top of the screen.

FIGURE 7.10 The TRACE button bar

FIGURE 7.11 The Batch Files roll-up

The next two buttons look like a pencil sitting on a line. The first is touching a thin line; this selects the line tracing method. The button with the thick line traces the lines and edges of a monochrome image. The differences between these methods will be explained shortly.

The next button looks like a hatchet and selects the woodcut tracing method; the button after it selects the silhouette. The button with the A on it, which looks just like the text tool button in most of the other Corel applications, applies OCR (Optical Character Recognition) to scanned documents. The last button in this grouping looks like a page of text or maybe a form. It starts a Form method of tracing scanned documents and is used when the scanned document is a form that includes lines and boxes as well as text.

The next button is the Tracing Color box, which lets you choose colors for silhouettes or woodcuts. Next is a button showing a circle with an "i" in it; clicking on this shows the image information screen. Last is a button with a question mark and an arrow on it. Clicking on this changes your cursor to the icon on the button. Move the arrow to any of the buttons or tools and click; a help screen for that function will come up. Some operations are not available for a particular image; in these cases, the button will be faded out indicating that the option is not available.

Six tools are available on the toolbar for TRACE. They are shown in Figure 7.12. The first one is the familiar Pick tool, which allows you to place a marquee around the area of the image you wish traced. The third and fourth tools are the familiar Zoom tool, one with a + to magnify and one with a - to zoom back. The second and third tools are Magic Wands. With the + Wand, you can select all of an image that is the color you click the wand on. The - Wand deselects all the clicked color. The last tool is the eyedropper and allows you to select the trace color for silhouette and woodcut traces from the colors in your original image.

FIGURE 7.12 The Trace tool box

The Image Info Box

Image info under the Display menu can tell you useful information about an image and provide clues on how to process the conversion. In some cases you may even want to take a file into a bitmap editor and tune it up before running the trace. The data for different types of files vary, so the information produced by this command will not always be the same, even with files having the same extension.

Use the TIFF image shown in the Display window as an example. In Figure 7.13, the Information window shows the name of the file, the file type, known compression, the pixel depth (8 bits), the size in both inches and pixels, the resolution, and the color palette. If the selected graphic had been traced, the number of shapes and nodes TRACE had created would be given.

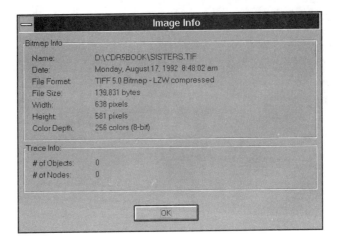

FIGURE 7.13 The bitmap information

As you can see, CorelTRACE gives you a lot of information about an image, but why do you need it? Because converting bitmaps is an art as well as a technology. There are so many variables. The resolution of the original, its colors, tones, contrast, file format, method of compression, quality of the artwork, and how it was created can all have an effect on the way an image converts.

Do a couple of simple conversions using the monochrome bitmaps provided with the CorelDRAW samples. That will give you a bit of hands-on experience with the program before getting very technical. Then we can examine the options in more detail and cover the finer points of using CorelTRACE.

Running CorelTRACE

Selecting Files

Make sure CorelTRACE is running and close all other applications. That will improve performance. If you have an older or underpowered system, this is always a good idea. If you are running a 486, it is not so important—but still helpful. (If you are working on an old 386 and use TRACE a lot, it will probably drive you to shop for a new system.) Move some of the bitmapped clipart files from your Corel CD or program disks. Then choose **Open** on the Files menu or **Add** in the Batch Files roll-up and open a file.

Checking the Image Information

I loaded SISTERS.TIF from the disk included with this book and then chose the **Information** button and got the box shown in Figure 7.13. Load a line art file such as HAUNTEDI.TIF from the CD or your disks and compare the information box to the one in Figure 7.13. Notice how the Bits Per Pixel under Color Depth is 1. That means that there is only 1 bit per pixel, so we have a monochrome image. For SISTERS the box also tells you that the file is compressed using the LZW method. There are a lot of different compression schemes. If CorelTRACE supports the format, the file will be expanded before conversion. If the method is not compatible, the trace will not work. Click **Exit** to return to the main window.

Performing the Trace

Once the file or group of files in the Batch Files roll-up is identified, click on the Outline option on the Trace menu or on the first of the four trace buttons. Try it. As the process progresses, the percentage completed will appear at the bottom of your screen. When a file has been converted and the new file created, the tracing will appear in your right-hand window. If you look in your default directory there will be two new EPS files. Now choose the **Lines** and **Shapes** trace option (the second of the trace buttons) and retrace HAUNTEDI.TIF just as you did before. When the program asks if you want to overwrite the existing file choose No and give it a new name.

To bring the traced drawings into CorelDRAW you must use the **Import** option under the Files menu. Open CorelDRAW and import the original TIFF and both EPS versions of the HAUNTED bitmap. You should use the CorelTRACE .EPS import filter for the traced files. Place all three copies side by side; then zoom in so that they fill the work area. The copies look almost exactly like the original. But there are some very important differences. Leave your samples on the page and let's examine them a bit.

A Closer Look at Methods

The Line method converts anything it identifies as an individual element of the image and then matches the color or fill. Use this method if the image has black backgrounds; lots of small, curved objects; and color or grayscale originals. Be aware that CorelTRACE does not "see" more than 256 colors or shades of gray.

The line and shapes method traces the lines in the image. A thin line is reproduced as a thin line in the trace, but it is a line, not an object, as with the Outline method. Some thicker lines are converted to objects. This is the way to go if the image has a lot of fine lines, such as a floor plan or technical drawing for a parts manual.

In Figure 7.14, three variations have been arranged as described earlier; then the fill was added to the copies. Look to the lower left of the labels on the bottom row. The number of nodes is almost the same, but there are about three times the number of objects in the centerline example. The right peak of the roof became an object using Outline but there was a break in the underlying element when traced with a Centerline setting so the object did not fill.

FIGURE 7.14 Comparing outline and centerline traces

In Figure 7.14 all the outlines and fills are the same for the objects in each row. Although the images look almost the same with a black outline and white fill, the lower

Chapter 7: Getting the Picture: Importing, Exporting, and Working with Bitmap Images

row shows the contrast between the two conversion methods. For images like this the Outline method has a definite advantage.

Putting in a Good Word for Line and Object Traces

If images like the one you just used were all you had to worry about, the basic outline settings could be used all the time. But many objects have a lot of fine lines with open interiors. That can lead to real problems unless you use the Centerline method. Find the file CTR_GEOM.TIF or a similar practice image on your CD or disks and put it in your TRACE sub-directory. Trace it using the Outline method; then change the Tracing option to Lines and Objects and retrace. Once again change the second traced file's name so it ends in c (the name, not the extension). Once all the tracing is completed, load the original and the two new files into CorelDRAW and line them up side by side. Give the two traces both black fills and a 0.21-point outline. The result should be about like that shown in Figure 7.15.

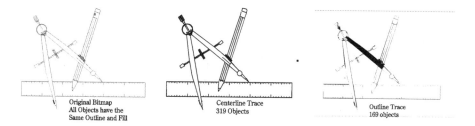

FIGURE 7.15 The advantages of the Line and Object method

As you can see in Figure 7.15, the differences in the filled traces are quite dramatic. One unneeded fill turned up in the one done by the Outline method traced image on the right. The one in the middle has almost one-third more objects. It is a very good copy of the original image. Remember that for the Line and Object method to work properly, the original must have black lines on a white background. Corel 4.0 greatly refined the outline trace mode, and the difference between these images done in 4.0 and 5.0 isn't as great as that between images done in 3.0. However, it is clear that there can be a difference, depending on the image you started with.

A Closer Look

Move all three objects so that the ends of the pencils are close together. Then use the Zoom tool to close in on them. Make it look like Figure 7.16. Notice how jagged the bitmap image on the left is compared to the line and object trace on the middle. Since the figure is a bitmap screen, the lines will not be as smooth as they are on your screen. One of the advantages of CorelTRACE is the ability to smooth out lines, since the vector graphic is not resolution dependent. Neither trace got all the fine details. The crimp marks on the barrel of the eraser were lost, and both left it as an open area. Look also at how the centerline example caught the difference in thicknesses on the long lines but missed them on the end of the eraser at the wood. The outlined trace on the right did not show any detail in either the pencil body or eraser.

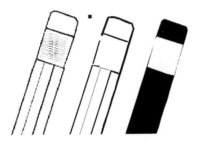

FIGURE 7.16 Comparisons draw some fine lines

Woodcut and Silhouette Tracing

Creating Woodcut Effects

In CorelDRAW 4.0 two new trace methods have been added and these are little changed in 5.0. The Woodcut trace delineates your image in the manner of a woodcut (or linoleum block). You can define the fineness or coarseness of your woodcut in the Settings menu. Load the STEGRAY.PCX file, which you should find on the disk that came with this book. This is the steggie bitmap with shades of gray in the fills added in PHOTO-PAINT. From the Trace menu, choose the **Edit** option and select the

Chapter 7: Getting the Picture: Importing, Exporting, and Working with Bitmap Images

Woodcut card from the dialog box set as shown in Figure 7.17. For your first tracing, leave the settings at default. Click the **Default** button and **OK**; then either click on the person-shaped icon on your button bar or select **Woodcut** from the Trace menu.

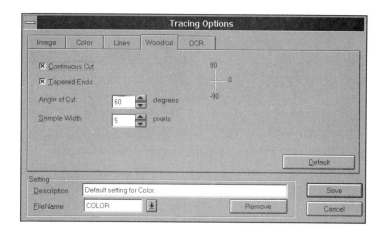

FIGURE 7.17 The Woodcut settings dialog box

You will notice that the default setting makes a very coarse image. Go back into the Settings menu and change the Sample Width from 20 pixels to 5 pixels. Check the **Continuous Cut** and **Tapered Ends** checkboxes. Then click on **OK** and make another woodcut tracing. In Figure 7.18 STEGRAY.PCX was traced as a woodcut with continuous lines, 20-sample pixel width, and 30-degree angle of cut. Figure 7.19 shows the same grayscale image traced using tapered ends, 5-pixel width, and 60-degree cut.

FIGURE 7.18 Grayscale version of Steggie and a Woodcut trace

FIGURE 7.19 Same grayscale image with different Woodcut settings

Silhouette

To try out the Silhouette mode, first load STEGGIE.TIF again. To use the silhouette, you must first select a suitable portion of the image. From the tool bar choose the magic wand tool and click inside Steggie's main body. Then click on the silhouette icon (which will have become very bright to indicate it can be activated). Steggie's body will appear as a solid black mass in the tracing window. Return to the original Steggie and click the magic wand on the white area inside one of his armor plates. Hold down the **Shift** key and click inside the rest of the plates on Steggie's spine. Then click again on the **Silhouette** button. The silhouettes of the plates will be added to the one of the body. Figure 7.20 shows a partial silhouette. It's a good idea to click the **Silhouette** button fairly frequently as you have selected the areas you want. It's easy to aim the pointer a little wrong and select more than you want.

FIGURE 7.20 Steggie in Silhouette trace

Custom Settings for Optimum Results

CorelTRACE uses some very detailed analysis to perform its conversions. You can alter many of the settings to meet your own special requirements. If you have a type of image that you trace on a regular basis, the custom settings can be named and saved for future use. All these settings have trade-offs. The simpler the trace, the easier to export and edit in CorelDRAW. You can remove the dithering in an image, added to improve the appearance of a bitmap, to increase the accuracy of your trace. Following curves tightly improves detail but adds complexity.

There are five dialog boxes in the Tracing Options dialog set. The definitions here give general guidelines on use, but remember that different systems and source files, as well as the final application for your traced file, will dictate the ideal values.

Each of these dialog boxes has a similar space at the bottom containing windows for file name and file description. Four files exist as defaults in CorelTRACE: the COLOR, DITHERED, FORM, and MONO, also seen in the window on the button bar. To create and save settings tailored to your own needs, you simply highlight the name in the file name window and type in a new name. Add a description and click on the Save button. At any time, you can click on the default button to return the dialog box to the application's default settings. To load any of the default settings, or any that you have created, click on the arrow beside either window and select the file you want to use.

The Image dialog box

The Image dialog box, shown in Figure 7.21, can change the appearance of your original graphic which will affect TRACE's handling of subsequent operations.

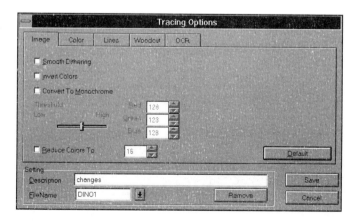

FIGURE 7.21 The Image dialog box

- **Smooth Dithering.** Takes out the scattering of pixels which many scanners or graphics programs add to give dot matrix a smoother look. This usually improves the trace produced from the image.
- **Invert Colors.** This option creates a negative image. In monochrome, they are white on black, Color Images will look like color negatives. Grayscale color orders are reversed and white background becomes black.
- **Convert to Monochrome.** Clicking on the Monochrome button changes the entire color map to 1-bit. When that option is checked, further fine controls are activated. These will enable you to set exactly how the colors in your original appear in the monochrome conversion.
- **Reduce Colors To.** Although CorelTRACE can read up to 256 colors, it can reduce the colors in the traced image to fewer than that in the original. You can also remove all colors to monochrome. Just pick the desired number of colors. The settings stay in effect until they are changed. (To convert an image to Gray scale, click on the Edit Image selection in the File menu and use the conversion function in PHOTO-PAINT. When you exit PHOTO-PAINT, your grayscale conversion will be loaded in the left-hand side of the TRACE workspace.)

You can try any of these filtering options on your image either when opening it, or when it is already on-screen. If the result isn't what you want, you can go back into the dialog boxes and modify the filter; TRACE then will update the image based on your most recent changes.

- **Edit Color Dialog Box.** This dialog box from the Edit Settings dialog set, shown in Figure 7.22, allows you to fine-tune the sensitivity and discrimination of the Magic Wand selection tool. This can be useful if you are attempting to produce a special image from a color photograph or other color image.

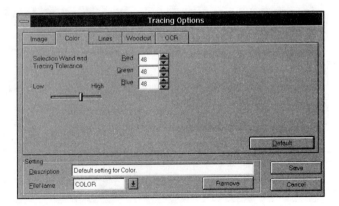

FIGURE 7.22 The Edit Color dialog box

Chapter 7: Getting the Picture: Importing, Exporting, and Working with Bitmap Images

- **Edit Line Dialog Box.** This dialog box, shown in Figure 7.23, controls the line width used to draw lines as the image is traced. Each of the controls in this dialog box can have a tremendous effect on the appearance of the final trace.

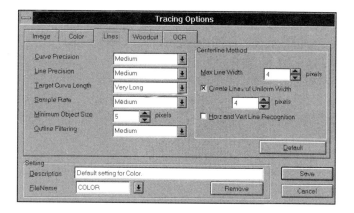

FIGURE 7.23 The Edit line dialog box

- **Curve Precision.** Setting this option to Very Good will force the trace to create more nodes as it follows the path of elements in the source file. This gives more detail but also creates a more complex file. For most work leave the setting in the middle at Medium.
- **Line Precision.** This control lets you decide how straight a line must be to be converted into a line instead of a curve.
- **Target Curve Length.** This controls the number of curves that can be placed in a trace. The shorter settings (toward the top of the drop-down list) increase the detail but add to the complexity of the drawing. This option must be coordinated with the Fit Curve and Sample Rate settings in the same box to make any real difference. Unless more detail is needed it is best to leave a value toward the bottom of the box.
- **Sampling Rate.** This setting controls how often the program will test to see if a node needs to be added. It is issued in conjunction with the Fit Curve and Curve Length settings. Once again, a more strict value (Fine) increases the resolution and adds complexity. Increase the value if you are working with a difficult or low-resolution image.
- **Outline Filtering.** This setting controls how smooth the outline TRACE uses will be. Selecting None means that all irregularities in the outlines perceived

by TRACE will be retained. Selecting Smooth Points will result in a simpler and smoother outline.

- **Minimum Line Width.** This allows you to choose how large or small a group of pixels in your original must be before it is traced. A low number increases the detail in a tracing; a high number will decrease it.

On the right-hand side of this dialog box appears a set of Centerline trace settings.

- **Create Lines of Uniform Width.** This checkbox allows you to specify that the tracing be done with lines of the same width. If Uniform Width is checked, you can specify how broad a line you want the finished tracing to have. Setting the Uniform Line option is not a good idea if you are tracing images with varying line weights or calligraphic effects.
- **Horz and Vert Line Recognition.** This checkbox allows you to correct an image that was scanned slightly off vertical. It will, in effect, straighten the lines in the image to true horizontal and vertical.
- **Woodcut Dialog Box.** This modification option was discussed earlier and the dialog box appears in Figure 7.17. Use this dialog box to define the size and shape of the "knife" used to make the "woodcut."
- **Continuous Cut.** This causes the lines to go from side to side without a break. Without this box checked, the lines break at the light areas.
- **Tapered Ends.** This gives a gradually thinning line toward the end of each cut.
- **Width.** This setting defines the size of the "knife" or "chisel" used to make the woodcut.
- **Angle of Cut.** This determines the angle the lines are made. The same image can look quite different from one line angle to another.

The OCR dialog box. Although OCR is outside the purview of this book, I put a file on the disk included with this book to help you test this function. It's the BACONOCR.TIF file. Load that file and click on the button with the A on it. A text file will appear in the right-hand window. Although the BACONOCR.TIF file is a graphics file, the file that TRACE produced can be brought into your word processor and edited.

General Guidelines for CorelTRACE

Here are some fundamental considerations when working with CorelTRACE. Feel free to experiment as needed, but as a rule start with the default Outline or Centerline methods first.

- Scan monochrome images at high dpi (300 and above). Go even higher if possible when working with fine lines.
- Scan grayscale and color images at lower resolutions, around 150 dpi.
- Remember that many monochrome images will convert very well with the basic settings but that more complex bitmaps may require fine-tuning.
- Full-color images and photographs will tend to look more like special effects, even with a lot of work.
- Don't forget that you can use CorelPHOTO-PAINT or another bitmap editor to clean up weak or broken lines and improve tone or reduce color before running a trace.
- The best image size is about 4 x 5 inches. There is a 3,000- x 3,000-pixel limit for CorelTRACE.
- Make sure when you are tracing several images at once that they are all the same resolution and will produce good results with the same settings.

CorelTRACE File Formats

To change images and illustrations created using CorelDRAW modules into applications like desktop publishing programs and word processors or to get graphics into CorelDRAW requires knowledge of file management, import and export functions. In this section, the file formats used by CorelDRAW and CorelTRACE will be discussed. There are some special considerations for some of the other modules that will be explained in the appropriate chapter.

Import Versus Export: What's All the Fuss?

In the last section you worked with tracing bitmap images in the TIFF and PCX formats and exporting EPS copies for use in other programs. Why do we have all these different extensions and why won't they work together? There are many types of file formats, each has its strengths and weaknesses. Some can handle color better than others, some produce smaller files, some are tailored to a specific printer.

When you wanted to import TIFF and EPS files into CorelDRAW a little while ago, you had to use an import filter, because those file types are not inherently compatible with CorelDRAW. CorelDRAW creates its own special file, the one with the .CDR extension. Those cannot be used directly by your favorite word processor or desktop publishing program, so you have to export them in a file format that the target application can read.

Some files are stored in bitmap format, others in vector. Some vector files have small bitmaps included in a header that enables a program to present an image to the user in a viewer before it is loaded. Look at the bitmap formats supported by CorelTRACE, then the filters for CorelDRAW, and finally the vector formats that can be used by CorelDRAW. It is a good idea to have a working knowledge of file formats and their limitations. It can come in handy when creating a file or importing it into a program. Using the Windows Clipboard also has its limitations, as will be discussed later in this chapter when working with CCapture.

CorelTRACE Import Formats

CorelTRACE can accept files in seven formats. If the image has more than 256 shades, only 256 colors or shades will be used. Each of the five is covered in alphabetic order in the following list.

- **BMP.** This is the native Microsoft Windows BitMap Picture format, and the one CorelTRACE uses internally during the conversion process. (This does not affect the original file.) CorelTRACE can use Windows 3.0 or 3.1 files, but not any earlier versions. You can include black and white or color; grayscale images are not supported. The Windows Paintbrush application is a BMP editor, and the Clipboard can cut and paste BMP images up to 64Kb in size. If an image is not already in BMP format, CorelTRACE will automatically make it into one during conversion.
- **GIF.** This is the common file format used to exchange graphics on the CompuServe Information Service (CIS). It can handle monochrome, gray scale, and 8-bit color at VGA resolutions. The letters stand for *Graphic Information File*. The Graphics Corner (GO CORNER) on CIS offers viewers hundreds of images free except for the cost of the connect time. Since graphic files can get large, the fees for these free pictures can add up.
- **PCX.** This format is the tried and true Z-Soft bitmap format, and since the original version of CorelPHOTO-PAINT included with CorelDRAW 3.0 was written by Z-Soft, it is a natural format for use with CorelTRACE. The images

can include up to 24-bit true color and gray scale. This was once the most popular PC graphic file format, but TIFF is overtaking it. Almost all scanning software can write a PCX file, but some offer only limited colors.

- **TGA.** The Targa Graphics Adapter (TGA) file format is a video capture format that is used by several screen grabber cards. If you have a Digital Vision Computer Eyes or Targa card, this can be an easy way to get images to trace right off a VCR or video screen. Although it is not really high-resolution, TGA is a well-known format that supports true-color and grayscale images.

- **TIFF.** The Tagged Image File Format (TIFF) is a standard developed jointly by engineers at Microsoft and Aldus. There are numerous variations that can support true color, gray scale, and monochrome. Be careful when working with TIFF files, since they can eat up a lot of disk space.

- **JPEG Format.** Some PC software and hardware allow users to reduce color and grayscale images using a new international standard developed by the same agency (Joint Photographics Experts Group) that developed the FAX standard.

- **Kodak Photo CD Format.** This is the new format used by Kodak to store digital images on writable CD-ROMs. The idea is that a user can take a roll of film into a lab and get the slides or negatives as well as a CD-ROM with them stored on it as well. Then the CD can be used to edit and print the images electronically—or even display them on a compatible home TV setup.

CorelDRAW Import Filters

CorelDRAW enables you to bring in a wide variety of vector and image files. Some can be edited; some can't. When planning to create or scan a file for use in a drawing, make sure you know if the features you need are supported. All CorelDRAW imports, except the Windows Clipboard and Object Linking and Embedding, are accessed via the Import option under the File menu. Select the file format type using the Import dialog box's drop-down menu; then locate the file and click **OK**. The older releases of CorelDRAW included a Technical Reference booklet that gave all the details, but that is a thing of the past. You can get a rundown under the Reference heading via the Help menu, but it was nice having a hard copy. Who wants to go to CorelDRAW's Help if you are using another program to create a file? The help is a great, technical support staff, but a hard copy comes in handy.

The following partial list is based on CorelDRAW 4.0. Many of these filters will work the same as with older versions of CorelDRAW, but not all. Entries are in alphabetical order by file abbreviation. In most cases the standard file name extension is the first three letters of the listing, followed by whether the format is bitmap or vector (if that is not a part of the format name). You can import monochrome, grayscale, and color bitmap files in most formats. What you see on the screen will depend on the type of display adapter and monitor you have.

- **BMP Windows (Bitmap).** These are BMP files conforming to the Windows BMP specification. They may be either color, gray scale, or black and white and will print accordingly, depending on your printer.
- **CMX.** This is a file format which contains all the information needed to represent a CorelDRAW image. However, CMX does not support any link information. For example, in CorelDRAW, the first and last object of a blend group are linked. When you export this blend group to CMX, the link information for these two objects is lost.
- **EPS Encapsulated PostScript (Vector).** This is a variation of the ASCII text file that is created when you send a file to a PostScript printer. It can include a header that contains a preview bitmap. There are several varieties of EPS files, some of which will not work with CorelDRAW. The variations are listed under Adobe Illustrator (EPS) and CorelTRACE (EPS).
- **Adobe Illustrator (EPS).** CorelDRAW can import Illustrator 88, AI 1.1 and 3.0 formats using this filter. It will work with some other varieties of EPS files created with other applications. Illustrator files are brought in as a single group of objects. You must use the Ungroup command located in the Arrange menu to manipulate individual objects. This filter does work with files that have been exported from CorelDRAW as AI EPS, but not as plain as EPS.
- **CGM Computer Graphics Metafile (Vector).** This is a widely used vector format in some technical and government applications that support color drawings. Several programs, such as Harvard Graphics, use CGM as a standard vector export option. When you load a CGM file, you may have to resize it because it will be bigger than the defined page. Although some programs can create CGM files with embedded bitmaps, CorelDRAW can't read them. If you are importing a file with text, make sure the fonts used are CGM compatible. Some character attributes or fonts may still be messed up after the file loads, but this usually isn't too hard to clean up.
- **CorelTRACE (EPS).** CorelTRACE files are brought in as a single group of objects. You must use the Ungroup command located in the Arrange menu to

manipulate individual objects. Files can include color data. This filter does not work with files that have been exported from CorelDRAW as EPS. CorelDRAW EPS files do not include an image header. To add an image header you can import the file into CorelDRAW and export it, but that is a one-way street.

- **DXF AutoCAD (Vector).** This is the export file format created with the AutoCAD DXFOUT utility while in that program. Save 3-D drawings with the view you want to import. Use polylines in your CAD work whenever possible to cut down on the drawing's complexity. This not only will reduce the import time but may help produce a copy that is closer to the original. The other way to get an AutoCAD file into CorelDRAW is to print it to disk as if the output device was a HP plotter and import it as a PLTfile. CAD drawings larger than 18 x 18 inches will be scaled to that size. The text used by AutoCAD is matched to the closest available CorelDRAW typeface. AutoCAD drawings can be very complex. Keep the file as simple as possible and refer to the CorelDRAW Import Help for detailed limitations.

- **GEM (Vector).** This is the format developed by Digital Research International, the folks that created CP/M and the GEM graphical user interface made popular by Xerox Ventura Publisher and GEM Artline. Although Windows has overtaken the graphical desktop interface, many people still use Artline and have collections of GEM files. CorelDRAW supports color imports, but GEM can handle only 16 colors. Many of the vector objects are editable once brought into CorelDRAW, but many may also load with different attributes. Some symbols, fills, and line ends will not import. Fonts will be mapped to a matching CorelDRAW typeface. You can spruce up an old GEM file and give it more colors and new life with a little work.

- **GIF CompuServe (Bitmap).** This is the common file format used to exchange graphics on the CompuServe Information Service (CIS). It can handle monochrome, gray scale, and 8-bit color at VGA resolutions. CorelDRAW can import files conforming to the 87A and 89A specifications. More information on this file format is available in the CIS On-line Graphics forum.

- **HPGL Hewlett Packard Plotter (Vector).** CorelDRAW can import and interpret a subset of the HPGL and HPGL/2 command language with a stepping factor of 1,016 plotter units to the inch. When you choose this Import option and select a file, you will get the HPGL Import dialog box. This is used to set the scale and define the colors of the pens in the drawing. The HP plotter does not support color as such but enables the user to use pens with colored inks to trace the image. If you need detailed information consult the manual for the software that created the file, your plotter manual, and the CorelDRAW Help command.

- **PCT Apple Macintosh PICT (Vector).** Objects in PICT format are handled differently from most other vector files. There will be two objects in one group. One object is the fill; the other is the outline. Text in the drawing can be edited once in CorelDRAW but may be messed up a bit during the transfer, and the fonts may not match. The older PICT format supported only monochrome, and the newer version can handle color. CorelDRAW supports both and can even manage to preserve the bitmap fills created on the Mac.
- **PIC Lotus (Vector).** Text will be editable in CorelDRAW, but colors are translated into no more than eight shades of gray.
- **PIF IBM Graphic Display Format (Vector).** CorelDRAW does not support GDF color mixing, so each object is placed on the drawing with its own defined color where they do not overlap. Type is imported as monospaced text or Toronto.
- **PCX Z-Soft/CorelPHOTO-PAINT (Bitmap).** CorelDRAW imports PCX files conforming to the following specifications: 2.5, 2.8, and 3.0. These files can contain one-, two-, or four-color planes. Files containing three-color planes cannot be imported.
- **TGA Targa Graphics Adapter.** This is the format used by Targa and other vendors for video capture files. CorelDRAW can handle both 16- and 24-bit color Targa files. It supports uncompressed color-mapped, uncompressed RGB, RLE compressed color-mapped images, and ATT-compatible RLE compressed images.
- **TIFF Tagged Image File.** Format The Tagged Image File Format (TIFF) is a standard developed jointly by engineers at Microsoft and Aldus. CorelDRAW supports black and white, color, and grayscale TIFF files conforming to the standard specification as well as many of those compressed using the CCITT, LZW, and Packbits 32773 compression formulas. Some compressed color TIFF files may not work. This includes some files using the international JPEG compression standard. With compression you will just have to experiment and see what works.
- **TXT ACSII Text Files.** CorelDRAW can handle plain ASCII text format. Use your word processor's export or nondocument mode to save the file. Text characteristics, such as bold or underlining, will be lost. Tabs and indents are converted to spaces, so it is best not to use them. There are character limits of no more than 4,000 characters, including spaces and carriage returns. Any material over that limit will be lost. You can add special characters from the upper ACSII set using the Alt key and the four-digit number shown in the

guide provided with the program. The numbers must be typed using the numeric keypad.

- **WMF Windows MetaFile (Vector).** This is the Windows vector format. Files created with non-CorelDRAW fonts will be changed to use the matching Corel typefaces.

A wide number of import filters for popular word processors, as well as Microsoft EXCEL are also provided.

CorelDRAW Export Filters

To get your finished drawing to a printer all you need to do is use the Print command. To get the same illustration to another program requires using the Export function. That's because CorelDRAW uses a special internal file structure that is unreadable to other applications. Not to worry. There are 21 different export filters that allow users to get drawings out in both vector and bitmap varieties.

If you are planning to move the graphic to a specific program check to see which import filters it supports. Then consider the complexity of the CorelDRAW file and if the image will be rescaled very much. Some fancy effects will not carry very well in vector format, and changing the size of a bitmap file can really reduce image quality. If you just want to extract the plain text see the section in Chapter 5 on Extract and Merge Back. The most robust and widely used export formats are TIFF and EPS, so use them whenever possible.

Export Basics

The basic procedure for handling exports is simple. Have the drawing you want to export open in CorelDRAW and go to the **File** menu. Choose **Export**; a File Selection dialog box will open. Use the drop-down menu in the lower left to choose the export filter, change to the destination directory and drive if needed, and give the file a name. When you click OK the new file will be created. If there is already a file by that name, you will be prompted to save it under a new name, cancel the operation, or overwrite the existing file. CorelDRAW will automatically add the extension that corresponds to the export format you selected. For some exports, such as EPS, another dialog box may appear. Select the desired options; then click **OK**.

You can export just a portion of a drawing. The only difference is that you must select the object or objects before opening the File menu and then click on the **Selected Only** box when the Export dialog box opens. The rest of the procedure is the same.

Exporting Bitmaps

There are a few general considerations when exporting CorelDRAW files to a bitmap format. After you make your choices in the Export dialog box and click **OK**, you will see the dialog box shown in Figure 7.24. You can use this box to set the number of colors, set the number of gray shades, and use a dithered color or grayscale palette. The number of colors and gray scales affects the size of the exported image. Using dithered shades is a good idea if you are reducing the number of colors or shades, but don't use them if there are fountain fills or color blends in the original without testing to see how they look after export. If you plan to edit the bitmap or resize it, don't use the dither option. You should dither only after editing.

You can also choose to compress the bitmap so that it takes up less space. Some formats are always compressed automatically. The Resolution options allow you to set the resolution in dots per inch for bitmaps exported full size. You can also set the size of the export using either a custom set of dimensions or one of the preset sizes. Remember that resolution and size will affect how large the file is.

The projected uncompressed file size shows the full size of the bitmap. Once compressed, the file will be smaller. Clicking on the **About** box opens a window showing the version of the currently selected export filter. Reset puts all the options back to their default values.

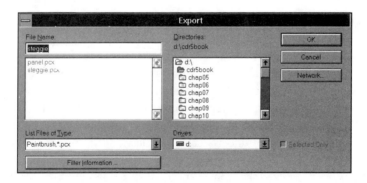

FIGURE 7.24 The Export dialog box

File Format Notes

File format notes are arranged alphabetically by file extension and give more information about exporting that file type. Bitmap formats are noted in the title. A brief rundown of the file type history was given under "Import." The discussion, which won't be repeated here, focuses on uses and limitations of some of the exported files.

- **BMP OS/2 (Bitmap).** Use this filter if you want to use a drawing as a simple bitmap in a program running under IBM's OS/2 operating system that does not support TIFF or PCX. For the best results scale the drawing or object to the exact size you want in the final image before exporting.

- **BMP Windows 3.0 (Bitmap).** This format does not allow grayscale information, but it does support color. It is the native Windows bitmap format used by Windows Paintbrush. For the best results scale the drawing or objects to the exact size you want in the final image before exporting.

- **CGM Computer Graphics Metafile (Vector).** This is a widely used vector format, but not as robust as Encapsulated PostScript. If you have bitmaps or PostScript textures, this is not a good choice. Many popular programs support this file format. Any fountain fills will be exported using the Preview Fountain Stripes setting in the Display dialog box accessed via the Preferences option of the Special menu.

- **DXF AutoCAD (Vector).** DXF exports are not for the novice. They can become very large and may not produce the results expected. You should have a good working knowledge of AutoCAD commands and features. Some CorelDRAW options are unsupported. There are no fills at all; bitmaps can't be moved; and calligraphic effects, dashed and dotted lines, and all line weights are converted to solid 0.003-inch-thick lines. Bézier objects are converted to polylines, and objects without an outline in CorelDRAW will be given an outline in the DXF export process. Fancy colors may not work, so limit the tints in CorelDRAW to primary colors for the best results and export using the 256 Color option. If you are exporting text, see the section in the Reference section of the CorelDRAW Help file for configuration information.

- **EPS Encapsulated PostScript (Vector).** This is probably the most robust of all the vector file formats, and it has some variations. One mentioned later is the Adobe Illustrator version that has a separate export filter. *CorelDRAW 5 does import its own EPS exports, however, this can be time consuming and occasionally difficult. So be very sure that you have saved a .CDR file if you ever want to edit this* *graphic in CorelDRAW in the future.* The EPS format can include an optional bitmap image header, so you can see what the image looks like in the target application. The actual file is really just a long list of PostScript codes that is shown on the page as a graphic. The dialog box shown in Figure 7.20 also enables you to control the resolution of the header. Higher resolutions look nicer but create a larger file. Unless you have a real need for a pretty preview, use a small size. Some applications can't show the header anyway, and some will not even load files with headers that are too large. Convert Color Bitmaps To Grayscale does just what it says. If you are using Pantone colors, they will be converted to CMYK values, since PostScript does not support Pantone. If you need an exact match use the TruMatch values. If you check the All Fonts Resident option, make sure that the fonts are really loaded into the final printer's memory, or you will not get the fonts you expect.

- **EPS Adobe Illustrator (Vector).** CorelDRAW can also produce EPS files in Illustrator 88, 3.0 AI version. This is an EPS subset that does not have all the features of the normal EPS filter, but unlike the other variety, the files can be brought back into CorelDRAW. Fountain fills and blends will not look as good, and PostScript textures won't be converted. Fit Text To Path does work, but each letter will become an individual object, as do any letters that have been modified using the Character Attributes command. Arrowheads are converted to separate curves. Bitmaps are not supported in this version of EPS. As a rule use the full EPS filter (above) whenever possible.

- **GEM (Vector).** This file format is best used if you have to get a simple drawing into a GEM-based program or one that does not support EPS imports. The complexity of all GEM graphics is limited. You can't have more than 16 colors, and bitmap objects are not allowed. Bézier curves will be converted to lines, and the corners may be broken. If you have to export to GEM, the filter works, but as a rule it is best to avoid it.

- **GIF CompuServe (Bitmap).** If you want to share your work with CompuServe (CIS) users as a bitmap or provide a free viewer, then GIF offers an easy way to do it. This is the file format sponsored by CIS. There are several variations, so not all programs that support GIF may be able to read your file. This is not a major bitmap format, so if you want the full potential of your raster image for later editing, export it as a TIFF or PCX file. The CorelDRAW filter exports using GIF version 89A with LZW compression.

- **PCT Apple Macintosh PICT (Vector).** Outlines on text will export only if you convert them to curves prior to exporting. Unconverted text will be brought into the Mac application using the default font. Bitmaps and two-color and

Chapter 7: Getting the Picture: Importing, Exporting, and Working with Bitmap Images

full-color fills in a drawing will not be converted at all, and PostScript textures will become gray fills. Filled objects with an outline export as a group of two objects; one contains the outline and the other the fill. Bands used to represent fountain fills in the exported file are determined by the Preview Fountain Stripes setting.

- **PCX CorelPHOTO-PAINT (Bitmap).** This is a well-known bitmap file format that can support color and gray scale. CorelDRAW exports PCX as version 3.0 using RLE compression.

- **PFB Adobe Type1 Font (Vector).** This filter is used to create a fully functional Adobe PostScript Type1 font that can be used with any program or printer supporting them. For more information see the section on designing custom fonts in the previous chapter. The export filters for fonts that were shipped with the first two versions of CorelDRAW 3.0 could not export Type1 fonts that had been created by modifying letters in an existing font. Corel Systems was working on the problem as this book was being written. If you are using CorelDRAW 3.0 Rev A or Rev B, make sure that you obtain the new filters before exporting. Failure to use the right filter could corrupt your font.

- **PIF IBM Graphics Display Format (Vector).** PIF files are limited to 16 colors, so choose your palette carefully when creating the original drawing and don't use a lot of fancy fountain fills and blends. PostScript textures, two-color and full-color pattern fills, and bitmap images are not supported. Text may not be spaced correctly in the export file.

- **PLT HP Plotter (Vector).** As with importing HP plotter files, export requires an understanding of the applications involved, the plotter setup, and how to match the CorelDRAW illustration to the limits of the target program or plotter. Be aware that all fills, bitmaps, and special pen effects will be lost, that curves are converted to line segments, and that colors will be matched to the nearest pen color defined in the CORELDRW.INI file. Any objects without outlines will be given an outline. Editable text can usually be edited after export.

- **SCODL Matrix/Imapro Slide Format (Bitmap).** Two-color and full-color fills, and PostScript textures are not supported. If you are using Agfa slide recorders, try using the Windows driver from Zenographics. This enables the unit to handle PostScript files. There is a slide page format that you can use to match the dimensions of a 35mm slide so that the final image is the right size.

- **TGA Targa (Bitmap).** This is not a widely used bitmap format, so make sure that your target application can use the file. CorelDRAW will compress the file as it is exported using a variation of Run Length Encoding (RLE).

- **TIFF 5.0 (Bitmap).** This is a very popular bitmap format that can come in a variety of flavors. The CorelDRAW filter is designed on the version 5.0 model and uses PackBits compression.
- **TTF TrueType Fonts (Vector).** This filter is used to create a fully functional TrueType font that can be used with any program supporting them. For more information see the section on designing custom fonts in the last chapter. The export filters for fonts that were shipped with the first two versions of CorelDRAW 3.0 could not export TrueType fonts that had been created by modifying letters in an existing font. Corel Systems was working on the problem as this book was being written. If you are still using CorelDRAW 3.0 Rev A or Rev B, make sure that you obtain the new filters before exporting. Failure to use the right filter could corrupt your font. A solution is to upgrade to version 4.0.
- **WMF Windows Metafile (Vector).** Any PostScript options, including PostScript textures, fills, and halftone screens, will not work, and bitmaps can't be included in WMF exports. These files can be very large and may fail to load in many popular programs, such as Ventura Publisher. The Fountain Stripes setting in the Special menu, Preferences option, and Display dialog box determine how many bands will be used to build radial and linear fills. Although you can include a header with WMF files, they may cause the file not to load.
- **WPG WordPerfect Graphic (Vector).** This can be a tricky export if you have text, fountain fills, or calligraphic outlines in your drawing. You should check the technical notes under Help and see the section under References about the settings of the CorelDRAW configuration files. Some of those settings can be adjusted to improve WPG exports. Bitmaps in a drawing will not export using this filter. Once you choose OK, a small dialog box will ask if you want to export using 16 or 256 colors. The latter may do a better job, but depending on your system, some colors may be reduced to shades of gray.

USING THE CLIPBOARD FOR IMPORT AND EXPORT

There is another way to get graphics in and out of CorelDRAW, the Windows Clipboard. This is handy. Just cut or copy in one program and then use the **Paste** command in the other. There are some limitations. Both programs must be able to use the Windows Clipboard and be running on the same system.

The Clipboard holds information, either text or graphics, in memory so that it can be moved between applications. When you use the **Cut** or **Copy** command in any application, the object is placed on the Clipboard. If there was anything in there at the time, it is overwritten. When you quit Windows, the Clipboard is discarded. If you are running in 386 Enhanced mode, you can copy the current screen onto the Clipboard with the **Alt-PrintScreen** combination. You can view and save the contents of the Clipboard by opening the Windows Clipboard Viewer application that is provided as part of the Microsoft Windows package. For more information on general Clipboard operations see your Windows user manual. The rest of this section is devoted to how the Clipboard works with CorelDRAW. Other applications may have different features.

Basic Clipboard Limitations with CorelDRAW

If an object to be cut or copied to the Clipboard is larger than 1,024Kb, there will be a warning that the object is too large to be put on the Clipboard. Click on **OK** to return to your drawing. In most circumstances (unless it is very complex), the object was copied in spite of the error report in the Window's Metafile Format (WMF). You can check on it using the Windows Clipboard Viewer. Some applications can accept WMF files larger than 64Kb, and some can't. Drawings containing the pattern fills, bitmaps, and PostScript textures are not supported.

Radial fountain fills can slow down a system when the object is being exported or copied to the Clipboard. Try using the blend techniques covered in Chapter 8 if it is too much of a problem. Blends are a kind of compound fountain fill.

Pasting the Clipboard into CorelDRAW

Text

Recall the limits on artistic text (250 characters) and paragraph text (4,000 characters). If you paste text from another program to the Clipboard and paste into CorelDRAW, the way the block is imported will depend on those same numbers. If you have less than the threshold for paragraph text, the object will come in as artistic. The font, outline, fill, and spacing will match those of the current default. If you need to bring in large blocks as artistic, separate them as you cut or copy.

Graphic Objects

Several WMF options are not supported by CorelDRAW. If your graphic does not come in as you want it, try exporting from the other application using a file format supported by CorelDRAW. One problem is with fills, since CorelDRAW will bring in all them as uniform fills no matter how they looked in the original.

Using the Clipboard Within CorelDRAW

With the Windows Clipboard you can copy an object inside CorelDRAW and then use the **Paste** command to drop a duplicate in another section of the program or a new drawing without using the .CDR import filter. When you copy directly to and from CorelDRAW using the Clipboard, all the object's attributes will be maintained.

OBTAINING IMAGES USING THE CCAPTURE MODULE

Among the modules shipped with CorelDRAW is the CCapture module. It is invisible while loaded, but if you press one of its hot-key combinations, the screen or a portion of it is copied to the Clipboard.

CCapture can produce a bitmap image of the full desktop, the active window, or just the contents of an active window. Although this is not as full-featured as programs like Image Pals, HiJaak, or Clip and Save, it is a handy tool for grabbing a quick screen shot. (Those other programs are all reviewed as third-party products later in the book.)

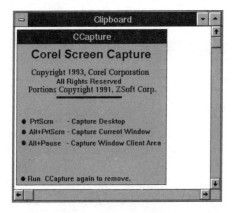

FIGURE 7.25 The CCapture Window

Let's run it now and capture the CCapture window itself. Double-click on the CCapture icon. It should be in the group with the rest of your Corel applications and should look like the CorelDRAW balloon with a net falling over it. A window will appear just like the one in Figure 7.26. It shows that the program loaded properly and explains the hot-key combinations. The **PrintScreen** key should capture the entire screen; the **Alt-PrintScreen**, the active window; and the **Alt-Pause** combination, just the contents of the active window. Press the **Alt-PrintScreen** combination.

Now open the Windows Clipboard viewer. That icon should be located in one of the standard Windows groups, depending on how your system is set up. It looks like a clipboard and will be located in the Main Group if you have not modified your group. Click on the CorelDRAW window so it becomes the desktop's active area and load a file or draw an object. Press the **Alt-Pause** combination and watch the viewer. The area inside the CorelDRAW window should appear in full color. The clipboard contains the last captured object. If you want to save the image you must either save it directly to a file or load it into another application.

FIGURE 7.26 The Clipboard with a Capture of the CCapture Window

Using and Removing CCapture

You may find that one or another of the hot-key combinations doesn't work on your system. It may be that the keyboard is configured differently or that another application is using those combinations. If your keyboard does not have a **Pause** key, try **Alt-Ctrl-Numlock**. Remember that since the program is using the Windows Clipboard, each new capture will overwrite the last one. To remove CCapture from memory, double-click on its icon a second time.

Chapter Summary

Bitmaps can greatly extend the use of CorelDRAW and give you the ability to add line art and photographs to your work. They can be manipulated almost like any other object, but some special rules do apply. Keep in mind that what you see on the screen may be more limited than what is actually in the image and that bitmaps can get quite large. Import and Export facts can be pretty dry. Refer to them as needed until you learn which file formats work best with the applications you use on a regular basis.

CHAPTER 8

Pushing the Envelope: Using CorelDRAW's Envelope, Blend, Perspective, and Extrude Special Effects

This chapter covers the following topics:

- Creating Special Effects
- Shaping Envelopes
- Working with Blends
- Creating Arrays
- Fitting One Object to Another's Path
- Giving Objects Perspective
- Using Mosaic for File Management

What Is So Special About the Effects Menu?

There is only one menu you haven't explored yet, Effects. Since CorelDRAW objects are really mathematical definitions of forms, outlines, and fills, you can change a formula to create the illusion of perspective, blend one object into another, and produce lighting and three-dimensional effects. Version 3.0 provided a whole new interface and souped-up capability that enabled you to see the result as you worked with the mouse. If you have used earlier versions of CorelDRAW, you have probably used some of these effects. Version 4.0 added Power Lines and Contouring to the special effects and gave you more controls for some of the options from earlier versions. CorelDRAW 5.0 widens your options still further and adds Lens effects and PowerClip. Effects commands can be combined and used with other program features to provide almost total control over the appearance of an object and its relationship to other elements of a design. Figure 8.1 shows you just a few of the special effects we'll be working with.

FIGURE 8.1 Special Effects

Getting Ready

Before you experiment with effects, you need to adjust your CorelDRAW setup. Since the roll-ups base the units of measure on the rulers, you need to set both to the same scale. Open the **Layout** menu and choose the **Grid Setup** option. Then set the Horizontal and Vertical Grid Frequencies to inches. Under the Display menu make sure that Rulers, Color Palette, and Edit Wireframe are off and that Status Line is on. Open a new drawing and set the page orientation to landscape. Now you're ready to have some fun. You'll go through the effects and then create a political button urging people to get out and vote that uses them all, along with the Fit Text To Path command.

The Effects Menu

Like the other menus, Effects is divided into categories by lines. Each area contains the commands or access to tools for one of the special effects. Here you will find some of the most dramatic controls offered by a draw program, and they can be combined together. Before you go on you'll look at the available commands, be introduced to a few new terms, and get an idea of what's in store. That will give you a chance to learn some new terms so that you can go exploring. Figure 8.2 shows the CorelDRAW Effects menu along with the Transform and Envelope roll ups. Contour, Powerline, Lens, and PowerClip will be covered in a later chapter, as will some of the more exotic options of the new CorelDRAW fills.

THE ENVELOPE, PLEASE

An envelope is a special kind of bounding box that enables you to shift the outline of an object or block of text. Four different kinds of envelopes are available, which are accessed via the Envelope roll-up, shown in Figure 8.2. Once an object has been enclosed in an envelope, you can pull and drag on handles and control points to pull the desired parts of the object into new shapes. Notice how the word Envelope has been contorted in Figure 8.1. It's sort of like a Bézier tool that works on the whole thing instead of just part of a line. You can use more than one envelope at the same time and copy it from one object to another. Clearing the envelope restores the object to its original shape.

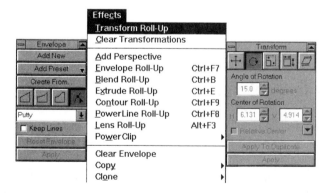

FIGURE 8.2 The Effects menu with Transform and Envelope roll-ups

Change Perspective

Perspective also uses a special kind of bounding box that is used to shape visual perspective. You can make the object seem to disappear into the distance or give the impression that the viewer is standing above it. In Figure 8.1 the word Perspective looks as if it is fading away on the right side. As with the Envelope effect, you can copy a perspective to another object and restore the setting to normal.

The Blend Effect

The Blend functions are controlled through an on-screen roll-up menu that gives you the ability to automatically create a series of objects that transform one shape into another. Look at the words on the right side of Figure 8.1. There are six steps starting at the top with the word Blend transforming into the word Objects as the effect progresses. Notice how both the letters and the fill are gradually converted. You can vary the number of steps, vary rotation, and even alter the path followed by the blend to match that of another object. Blended objects are dynamically linked, just like text fitted to a path. When you change the fill or shape of one of the blended objects, the entire effect is recalculated to adapt to the new settings.

Extruding Objects

Extruding objects is a very slick trick that gives shapes an appearance a bit like a three-dimensional sculpture. Extruding combined or blended objects allows you to produce complex three-dimensional effects in a fraction of the time it would take to create them from scratch.

Working with Envelopes

You've seen those big banners stretched across city streets announcing a fair or some other big event and watched it blow in the wind. Imagine that you could put a drawing on a banner and then shape it as the wind did. Visualize how the shape of the letters would change as the breeze bowed out the sign. Think of the effect if you twisted one end and pulled the other. (Your banner is made out of a material that stretches.) Make a sign that says Special Effects and try it. Choose the Text tool and type those words,

Chapter 8: Pushing the Envelope: Using CorelDRAW's Envelope, Blend, Perspective, and Extrude Special Effects

with the first letter in caps. Then press **Ctrl-T** and make the typeface Galleria 24-point normal. If you don't have that font, use another decorative serif typeface. Duplicate the text. Use the Zoom tool to make the second block of text fill the page and select it.

Open the Effects menu and click on the **Envelope** roll-up. A roll-up appears like the one shown in Figure 8.2. Make sure the first envelope shape is selected. It is the left-most button under Create From. Each one of the options provides a different kind of control, similar to the differences between types of nodes. The first one limits the action and form of the envelope to straight lines; the second, to an arc; and the third, to two curves. The last one is fully unconstrained with control point manipulations.

The eight boxes located in the middle and corners are the handles used to change shapes. The dashed lines show the boundaries of the envelope. Your cursor should change to the Shape tool. If not, click on the **Add New** button. Drag the top center handle up and the bottom center down about the same as the height of the text. Now drag the lower left handle down and the middle left handle in toward the center. Finally, pull the handle in the middle of the right side out toward the right and press **Apply**. The final result should look like Figure 8.3a. Now pull both of the sides in sharply toward the center, as in Figure 8.3b and press **Apply**. Notice how the letters on the ends are twisted out of shape. You can use an envelope to twist an object to a point where it can't be identified as the original.

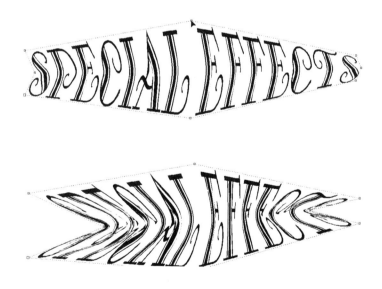

FIGURES 8.3a and 8.3b Using the straight line envelope

Canceling the Envelope Effect

The Clear Transformations, Undo, and Straighten Text commands can be used to return it to its normal shape, but each has limitations. The Clear Transformations command, under the Effects menu, will restore an object to the form it was in when you started. If you use more than one envelope, the Clear Transformations command will still return it to the appearance it had at the start of the last Envelope editing session. The Undo command will return the shape to that which it had just before the last movement, and the Straighten Text command only works with text objects.

Working with Arcs

Move the object you were working with off the page and duplicate the plain copy three times. Bring those into the center of the work area, align one on top of the other, and center them horizontally. Choose the top object, then select the second option on the roll-up, the Single Arc and press **Add New**. Now pull up on the box in the center of the top on the envelope. Notice how the text curves up to stay with the dashed line. Now drag the lower line up the same way. Then pull the lower corners down a little bit to increase the curved effect and press **Apply**. Figure 8.4 shows what all three objects will look like when you are done. Raise the location of the top object on the page and reposition the middle object so it is centered in the group. Use the upper and lower center handles to create the bowed-out appearance shown in Figure 8.4.

Reverse the editing of the envelope of the bottom object so that it is a mirror image of the top one. Pull the lower center handle down; then pull down the top center and adjust the top corner handles upward. The final set should look like Figure 8.4. Save the file as ENVELOPE.CDR before going on to the next step.

Using the Copy Envelope From Command

Duplicate the plain text again and select the copy. From the roll-up choose **Create From**. The cursor will change to a large arrow labeled From. Choose one of the objects with an edited envelope and click on it with the arrow. If you miss the object a dialog box will offer you a chance to try again. Once you click, the first block of text will be modified to look just like the other. If you repeat the command a second time using another object with a different envelope, the effects will be combined. That means that the target will not look just like the second object, but will be modified to reflect the changes from the shape of the first transformation. Try it; then overlay the two objects. Use different shades for the fills to make it easier to see what happened. This is very much like adding a second envelope. The first changes are made permanent and used as a starting point for any of the following effects. You'll get to that shortly. Open a new drawing without saving the file again.

FIGURE 8.4 Single arc envelopes

Throwing Some Curves

Let's get a little fancier with our objects. Type in the string Pushing The Envelope with the Text tool and pick a basic serif font. Now use the Ellipse tool to cover it with an oval. The oval should cover the text side to side but not extend very far above or below it. Give it a uniform light color fill. Use the **Shift-PageDown** key to place the oval behind the text; then combine the two objects using **Arrange**, **Combine**. Next, use the rectangle tool to draw a rectangle that covers the combined object and give it a dark fill. Use the **Shift-PageDown** key once again. You should have a masked oval object covering the rectangle with the background fill showing through the text in the mask. Duplicate them and move the copy out of the way; then zoom in on the original.

THE TWO CURVE ENVELOPE

The Two Curve or Double Curve Envelope is similar to a symmetrical node. Changes made by dragging a handle will be equal in their effect on both sides. Select the mask in your test object and Add New Envelope using the third envelope-double curve. Now drag the top center handle until it is resting near the bottom of the background box and apply the **Double Curve** Envelope. Take the lower line and pull it up to where the top was when you began. Notice how the line on either side of the handle moves in unison with the other side. The effect of moving both handles is a bit like twisting a towel. (See Figure 8.5a.) Pull out the upper right-hand corner and watch how the line changes. Press **Apply**. Look at the point where the twist occurs. Use the Zoom tool to close in on it as shown in Figure 8.5b.

FIGURE 8.5a Twisting a double curve

FIGURE 8.5b A closer look

The envelope is making the mask behave as if it were a three-dimensional object. There is a bit of a flaw. The two letters right at the break have been forced outside the bounds of the tortured ellipse. Notice how the masking effect is still there when the underlying fill is changed. Experiment with this envelope until you have a good feel for how it operates.

Chapter 8: Pushing the Envelope: Using CorelDRAW's
Envelope, Blend, Perspective, and Extrude Special Effects

The Unconstrained Envelope

Delete the twisted object; then use the Zoom tool to fill the page with the remaining copy. Remove the background rectangle. Select the masked object and choose the final Envelope option, **Unconstrained Envelope** and press **Add New**. An effect of this type is about the same as converting a rectangle to curves and positioning nodes at the handle locations. Experiment by moving the nodes around. The ones located in the center of each side have control handles that behave about like those found on smooth nodes, whereas the ones on corners act like cusps. Figure 8.6 shows the object as it was shaped using an unconstrained envelope.

FIGURE 8.6 Working with an unconstrained envelope

The Preset Envelopes

Corel has included a selection of preset envelopes to speed your work in the more common transformations. Type Preset Envelopes and from the Text roll-up select a type face like ShellyAllegro BT. Draw a circle and place the words on top of it. Fill the circle with a medium color, combine the text and circle, and make several duplicates. Select one of these combined sets and click on the Add Preset Bar. A Fly-out with a selection of preset shapes will appear like the one in the center of Figure 8.7. Apply one of these preset envelopes to your combined text and circle. You should get something like the examples in Figure 8.6a.

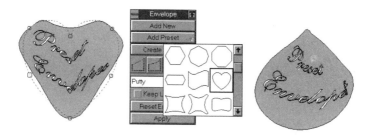

FIGURE 8.7 Applying preset envelopes

Once you have a good feel for how each envelope works, try changing the type of envelope and seeing how that changes things. Copy the current envelope to another object and use the **Clear Envelope** command. Envelopes can be used to do things like form text to fill the shape of other objects, something that would be very tedious to accomplish with just the Shape tool. You will be using that ability when you combine several effects at the same time later in the chapter.

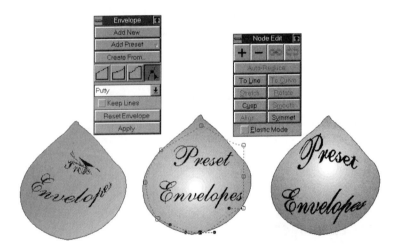

FIGURE 8.8 Fitting text to envelopes using the unconstrained mode

Working with Text in Envelopes

Some fonts will go into an envelope looking just the way you hoped they would; others, because of how they are constructed, won't have the appearance you wanted, as in the shape to the far left in Figure 8.8. As I've mentioned before, it's a good idea to make a copy or save the file before experimenting with effects. If a preset envelope doesn't work the way you wanted, start over, selecting the unconstrained option. You then can move the bounding boxes as well as refine the shape with the handles—just as you do in a regular node edit. The shape in the center of Figure 8.8 shows this process. If a node isn't in the mode that will give you the shape you want, double-clicking on the nodes will bring up the Node Edit roll-up and you can change node type and complete your editing. I added a fountain fill to the finished shapes in Figure 8.8. Paragraph text in a text frame can also easily be placed in a shape, most easily by using the **Create From** button.

A Few Rules

Envelopes are tools for defining the flow of a path, and thus the shape of an object. As with converting text to curves, they offer a lot of control. The effect of an envelope is like putting the object on a piece of clear plastic and then being able to twist it in any direction or shape. The exact way the object behaves is determined by the type of envelope placed around it. When working with this effect there are a few special considerations to keep in mind.

- Text in an envelope remains as text and you can still edit it as text without removing the envelope, but you cannot change individual character's attributes.
- You cannot edit nodes and curves within an envelope. To do that, clear the envelope first.
- The currently selected type of envelope is the default and will be used if you place an envelope around another object. This is true even if you close and reopen CorelDRAW.
- Working with envelopes is often an interactive process. It is not uncommon to use more than one envelope and then clean things up with the Shape tool. If you are doing a lot of complex editing, you might want to make duplicates of the object or group before making major modifications. That way you can see what the last change looked like as you work and have an easy way to compare different designs.

The envelope is a special way of defining the bounding box of an object and using the Shape tool to manipulate it. The better the understanding you have of paths, node editing, and control point operations, the better your control of the Shape tool will be.

Using the Control and Shift Keys for an Extra Twist

The **Control** and **Shift** keys can be used to change the way an envelope responds, so that moving one handle affects the opposing side. Draw a square, place a single letter in its center, and enlarge it to fill the square; then group them. Place a Straight Line Envelope (the one on top) around the group. Then use the **Shift** key, then the **Control** key and then both keys at the same time while pushing and pulling on one of the side handles.

Press **Alt-Bksp** (Undo) between experiments to return to your original rectangle. Figure 8.9 shows the results of using all three combinations of keys to push the previously described object in from the left using the left center handle. Holding the **Ctrl** key pushes both sides in the same direction by the same amount. The **Shift** key pulls both sides in or pushes out both sides depending on which way you pull or push the handle. Using both **Shift** and **Control** keys together pulls or pushes all four sides at the same time. This is a handy trick for producing symmetrical shapes. Try it with differently shaped objects and envelope combinations.

 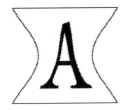 

FIGURE 8.9 The constraint controls

BLENDING IN

Blending is a powerful effect that enables you to shift the shape of one object into another's in a series of steps. The Blend command is easiest to describe after showing an example of it. Open a new drawing. Turn off the rulers but leave the status bar on and activate the **On-screen Process Color** Palette from the Display menu. Draw a large square; then place a tall, narrow ellipse in its center so the edges of the oval almost touch the top and bottom of your square. The oval should be no more than one-quarter of the square's width. It would be even better if it were thinner, but make sure you can see the open center of the round object. Give the two objects different-colored uniform fills. The final appearance should resemble the objects on the left side of Figure 8.10. Use the marquee method to select both objects.

Now open the **Effects** menu and choose the **Blend** roll-up option. An on-screen roll-up like the one in the center of Figure 8.10 should appear. Make sure the icon on the far left side is selected and that 20 is the value in the entry box under the word Steps. Click on the **Apply** button. The Blend operation will create a series of 20 objects gradually changing from a square into an ellipse like the example shown on the right side of Figure 8.10. The fills and outlines also change from one color to the other in a series of steps. In many ways, blending is much like Fitting Text To Path, but with a lot more control and with any kind of object.

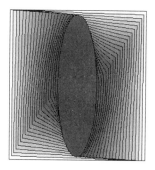

FIGURE 8.10 A simple blend

THEY'RE PRETTY, BUT WHAT ARE THEY GOOD FOR?

It looks impressive when blends are being built on the screen, but what are their practical applications? After all, how often do you need to make one word dissolve into another? Here are some practical applications:

- making highlights by blending fills that define the inner contours of an object
- creating word/picture-style special effects
- producing airbrush-style fills and tints
- creating a series of lines for forms by blending two identical lines with the required number of steps
- producing rainbow-colored backgrounds and fills
- easily increasing the three-dimensional appearance of a drawing

The following sections will provide a working understanding of how to create and manipulate blends. Later you will use blends in your advanced projects. Many of the most dramatic illustrations entered in the Corel System's annual art contest make extensive use of blends. Some of the winners explained their techniques, which are included in the interviews in Part Two.

How Blends Work and How to Define Them

To make a blend, you must have two objects selected. They cannot be a set of grouped objects. Once you give the command, a set number of intermediate objects is created, each one in turn shifting its shape so it looks more like the target object at the end of the string. All the parts are dynamically linked, so any change to the color, fill, or shape of an element will result in the entire blend being recalculated. A blended object is really a group of three elements: the two control objects drawn by the user at either end and a combined set of the program-generated shapes. If you are fitting the blend to the path of a third object, that object is a fourth element, a control curve.

All blend definitions are given using the on-screen roll-up menu, which has three primary modes: one for defining the number of steps and the degree of rotation, one for defining the color parameters of the fill, and one for fine controls of the nodes. The buttons at the bottom allow you to redefine the path of the blend and to apply the effect. There is another variation that will be discussed shortly. Figure 8.9 shows the normal versions of these nodes with labels.

 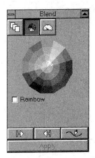 

FIGURE 8.11 The Blend roll-ups

The Primary Blend Roll-Up

The version of the menu on the left side of Figure 8.9 is the one that appears when you first place the menu on screen. Notice how the button with the three squares (Steps mode) in it seems to be pushed in. If you click on the button with the color wheel, the menu's top changes to look like the sample in the middle. In the Steps mode, the entry window is used to set the number of intermediate objects that will be generated. The Rotation button below the Steps window is used to set the total angle of rotation that will occur as the blend takes place.

The Color mode enables you to set the color parameters of the blend. Parameters are not the same as setting the fill or outline colors; instead they let you specify how the generated fill colors are handled by the program. The wheel in the top section of the menu is an HSB display. (HSB is discussed in the outline section in Chapter 1. You might want to review it.) A line maps the colors that the blend uses as the path progresses. If you click the Rainbow box, you can also choose which way the blend moves through the spectrum by pressing one of the buttons with an arrow on a circle just below it. For example, if you have an object at either end of a blend filled with red and orange, the rainbow will produce almost no change in one direction, since the colors are very close together on the wheel. You can go through almost the entire range of colors if you chose the other direction. The longer the line on the wheel, the wider the range of colors in the blend. The exact way a blend is filled depends on two factors: the fill of each of the two objects involved and the settings in this menu. Table 8.1 shows the results of different fill combinations.

Choosing Beginning and End Nodes and Mapping Nodes

The two buttons with the short arrows on the lower section of the roll-up are used to specify the start and end objects for a blend. You can also specify which node will start the run and which will end it. If you do not choose a specific node, then the center of rotation of the objects is used as a default.

Mapping to Another Path

The button to the right of the First and Last Node buttons is used to map the track of a blend along the path of another object. With this command you can create a series of objects that follow almost any shape. When this option is in use you specify the spacing of the objects in the blend rather than the number of steps. This is a handy tool for creating forms or filling an area with shapes. You'll use this to build part of a form and create a campaign button later.

Table 8.1 Fill variations with blends

Object A*	Object B*	Generated Blend Shapes
No fill	Fill	No fill
Fountain fill	Fountain fill (same type)	Matching fountain fill
Pattern fill	Any other fill	Object B's fill
Pattern fill	Pattern fill	Top object's fill
Radial fill	Linear fill	Radial fill
Radial fill	Uniform fill	Radial fill
Spot color	Different spot color	Process color
Spot color	Process color	Process color
Spot color	Same spot color	That spot color
Uniform fill	Fountain fill	Uniform blending to fountain
Uniform fill	Pattern fill	Uniform fill

*Except where noted it does not matter whether the control object is A or B.

The Node Controls

The Map Nodes button at the top of the roll-up (see the mode to the far right in Figure 8.11) allows you to select which node on each object is used to calculate the path of the blend. This can greatly change the final effect of a blend.

The Split button, second down on the roll-up, allows you to split one blend into two separate blends. Select a blend and click this button. A special cursor will appear over your work area and you can select any object in the blend except the first, the last, or the objects located next to the first and last in the blend. The object you select will become the last object in one blend and the first in a second blend. Draw a circle and fill it with red. Draw a square and fill it with green. Using the **Shift-Click**, select both objects and apply a blend. Then switch to the Node Controls roll-up and select the split bar. A crooked cursor will appear and you can select one of the intermediate objects in the blend. Move this object to the top of your screen and both halves of the blend will redraw, with the selected object making the turning point of the blends. After a blend has been split, you can hold down the **Ctrl** key while selecting an intermediate object in either of the blends. The Fuse Top or Fuse Bottom button will become active; by selecting one you will fuse your blend back into a single blend.

The effects available with the Split and Fuse options begin to get interesting when you do something like splitting a blend and using the object chosen for the split as the start and/or end objects for still other blends. By using the **Ctrl** key select combination and fusing back, lots of interesting—although not always easily predictable—effects may be obtained.

Dynamic Links and the Apply Button

As with all CorelDRAW roll-up menus, the **Apply** button must be pressed to make the changes set with the menu. If you do not like the effect, you can use the **Undo** command to return the drawing to the way it was before.

LEARNING ABOUT BLENDS

Simple Blends

The blend you just created was a simple blend, created using just two objects and the command. The resulting form is quite complex, but the computer does all the real work. Use your blend to explore how to manipulate this effect and see how the menu's basic commands are applied. Make a duplicate of the blend and place it directly underneath the first one. Now give the copy no fill and a thin outline. It should look like the leftmost set in Figure 8.12. The unfilled set is similar to a skeleton of the form. Select the top-filled object; then place it to the right of the first one. Resize the screen with the Zoom tool or resize the objects with the Pick tool to get a good work area.

Blends can eat up a lot of computer resources. To speed things up keep only the current set in the viewing area while working. If your computer is too slow for comfort with them all on the screen, delete the older copies as you make the next set. If you do, save a backup of the first set in case something happens (such as the power going off or a mistake). If you have a slow system and have to make do, don't forget the

Wireframe Edit mode under the Display menu. By not showing the fills, your blends will draw much faster. So once you have the color scheme figured out, you can speed things up. There are three things that really affect the performance of a computer working with these effects: CPU speed, the display adapter, and memory. Some options for dramatically improving performance will be discussed in the hardware section later in the book.

Dynamic Links

A simple blend has three dynamic elements, the two control objects and the generated blend group. Without any adjustments you can select and manipulate all three with the Pick tool. Use it to click on the edge of the filled copy on the right. Look at the status bar; it should read "control Rectangle on Layer 1" and should give the object's dimensions. Now click on one of the generated objects in the middle of the stack, the status bar will indicate that you have selected a Blend Group. Select **Wireframe Edit** from the Display menu. Click on a blank area to deselect all objects; then click on the outline of the ellipse. Note that the status bar indicates that the object is a control ellipse. Any object that can be used to alter the shape or path of a blend is a control object. CorelDRAW uses control objects to define the blend.

If you change the shape of any of the three elements, or any other attribute of a control object, the blend will be recalculated. Use the Pick tool to resize the ellipse to a circle about one-quarter the width of the rectangle and click **Apply**. (For every blend command from now on, remember to click **Apply** to execute it.) With the Align command center the ellipse in the rectangle. Make a copy, remove the fill, and place it under the version you just altered. The result should look like the second set in Figure 8.10. Notice how the dynamic link works. All the objects in the figure came from the original object, and the transformations were accomplished by editing the blend.

Make a third copy of the filled blend and place it to the right of the last set. Select it and reduce the size of the ellipse as small as you can. Use the **Blend** roll-up to increase the number of steps to 100. Click on **Apply**. Use the menu to set the fill to **Rainbow** and try both direction modes. Notice that the blend looks like a tunnel receding into the distance. Make an unfilled copy and place it below the one you just manipulated. Make sure the roll-up is set to **Steps**. Click on the different copies from left to right and look at the Blend roll-up settings as you do. Notice how the settings change to tell you how many steps the blend has.

Chapter 8: Pushing the Envelope: Using CorelDRAW's
Envelope, Blend, Perspective, and Extrude Special Effects

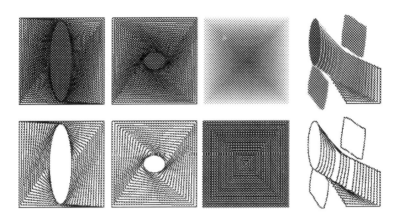

FIGURE 8.12 Editing a simple blend

Taking Blends Apart

There is one more experiment with simple blends. Create another copy and set the steps to 15. Notice the change take place as you press **Apply**. Resize the rectangle to about half its current size and make the circle the same size. The changes will occur as you release the mouse button. Now drag the ellipse up and outside the rectangle. The blend will follow, like a slinky toy climbing down a set of stairs. The objects are dynamically linked, but you can take them apart. Unlike other separations in CorelDRAW, this requires two steps, using the **Separate** and **Ungroup** commands located in the Arrange menu. All the elements will become single, unrelated objects. Try it. Make a copy and move it off to the side before continuing.

Select the copy of the blend and open the **Arrange** menu. Choose **Separate**. The status bar will note that three objects are selected. Click on the former control curves (the ellipse and the rectangle) and then on the blend-generated objects. It is a group with the same number of elements that was set in the Steps entry box. You will have to click on a blank area before selecting the group in the center. Now ungroup them. Use a marquee to select all the objects; there is a total of 17. You can move them without affecting any other element, since they are no longer linked.

FIGURE 8.13 *Manipulating a blend with special effects*

Mapping Nodes

All CorelDRAW objects have a path, and that path is defined as starting at the first node. That is not important to the user except when editing nodes or creating blends. The Map Nodes button enables you to specify which node in a control object is used as the beginning node when the intermediate objects are created. This can have a dramatic effect on the shape of the elements. Figure 8.13 shows two "identical" blends. The one on the left has been modified using the Map Nodes option. To use it you must have the blend selected and then press on the **Map Nodes** button. A cursor like the one in the figure appears. Use it to select the first node in the second control element. The cursor will be filled upside down, so that the hook is on the bottom. Click on the desired node in the other control element. Notice what happened to the intermediate shapes. No rotation is applied. The twist is due to the relationship between the first nodes.

Splitting Nodes

All blends have a beginning and end object. The Node Split option allows you to define one of the intermediate shapes as the end object for one blend and the beginning object for another, with both new blends making up the whole old blend. This allows you to do such things as bend a blend in the middle, as had been done in Figure 8.14, or move the objects making up the blend closer to each other on one end than on the other. The old beginning and end objects as well as the object selected as the split object may be used as first or last objects in new blends. The Fuse Start or Fuse End buttons usually undo work done since the blend was split.

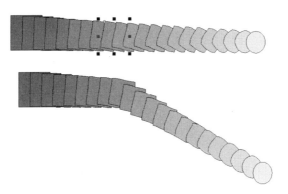

FIGURE 8.14 Splitting blends, moving individual elements, and performing transformations

Clear all the stuff out of the drawing except that last copy you made. (If it is not still a blend, make one that is.) Center it in the work area with the Zoom tool. Normal transformation controls and special effects can be used to manipulate a blend, but there are a few special considerations because of their nature. Select your blend, open the **Arrange** menu, and choose **Order, Reverse Order**. Notice how the control objects have been reversed from front to back. It is like fanning out a deck of cards in the opposite direction. You can use this command to put the front-most control behind the other one. You can move the group's position in relation to other objects, just like any other group.

Selecting Elements

Select the Pick tool and draw a marquee around the blend. If you are not in wireframe mode, press **Shift-F9** to change the display, since that mode is much easier when transforming blends. Not only does the screen redraw more quickly, but you can select individual elements with less fuss.

Keep an eye on the status bar as you select an element, since it's often hard to tell visually if the right one has handles. If you want all three objects at once, the marquee is the way to go. The control objects are special. They are both individual objects and are also part of the blend object. You can use almost any normal CorelDRAW command on a control object, including things like Place Duplicate and Node Edit. Any change that alters the position or appearance of the control will then be extended to the definition of the blend.

Transformations

Scale and rotate the blend by dragging on the handles. You will see that it behaves like any other CorelDRAW object. Now click on a clear part of the page to deselect the blend, then select the ellipse on the very end. The status bar should say that you have selected a control element. If not, try again. Drag on the handles and scale or rotate once more. As you make the changes, the shape of the blend is altered completely. If you transform a control object, the basic definition of the blend is altered. If you make a duplicate of a control object, the duplicate is not a part of the blend at all.

Rotations can be handled three different ways with blends, each producing its own effect. The Transformation menu and the rotate and skew handles work just as with any other object. The Blend roll-up menu enables you to set the angle of rotation for the objects within the blend group. That produces a corkscrew effect. If the number in the rotation window is positive, the twist will be clockwise. A negative number produces a counterclockwise turn. The third method uses the roll-up menu but gives an arc effect like that shown in Figure 8.15. First, the words for the outer arc are typed and selected; then the amount of rotation is entered. Next click so the rotate/skew handles are visible and move the center or rotation symbol (bull's-eye) up. The arc based on the angle of rotation will move through that symbol. The inner set of blended circles is done the same way and a rainbow fill is added.

Envelope Effects with Blends

You can combine effects, but using an envelope requires an extra step. Open a new drawing, create two objects (like a circle and a square), and blend them. Open the **Effects** menu with the blend selected. Select the **Envelope** roll-up. Press **Ctrl-G** to group the blend. Choose the **Unconstrained** option on the Envelope roll-up. Once the blend has been grouped you can apply envelope effects. To use the Blend roll-up you must use the **Ungroup** command. Figure 8.14 shows the results of editing a blend with an unconstrained envelope. The original is on the left with two uniform fills, and the edited copy is on the right with a radial fill. Notice how the envelope was pulled over the group and produced two twists. Ungrouping will turn the objects back into a blend. If you delete a control object, the blend group will disappear.

FIGURE 8.15 Mapping nodes

You can use envelope effects on an individual control object without grouping the blend. Any changes will only alter that control object. As you work, the entire blend will be recalculated to reflect the new shape of the control. The envelope will extend over the entire blend, so the visual reference may seem a bit strange. While in Wireframe mode, you can use the **F9** key to toggle between a full-screen preview and the work area.

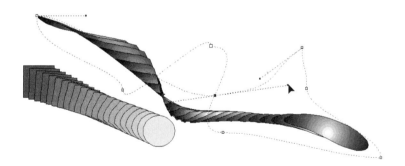

FIGURE 8.16 Editing a blend with an unconstrained envelope

Compound Blends

At one level, CorelDRAW sees the blend as a group; at another, it can treat it as a combined single object. You can use this sort of schizophrenic definition of an object to your advantage. You can also create or define additional control elements, both outside and within the blend. When a blend has more than two control objects it is called a compound blend. Although you can't blend two groups together, you can use the command to blend two control elements residing in different blends. You can also use multiple controls to redefine the path, fills, and intermediate shapes of a blend. Although this is a very powerful tool, it can be overdone and lead to very complex drawings.

A basic compound blend is created by adding one or more new controls within the blend group. The additional points are like nodes on a path. They can be used to alter the way the line moves through that location and give you the ability to redefine the fill in a section of the group. Open a new drawing and switch from a wireframe view to normal (if needed), so that you can see what happens with your fills. Draw a circle in the upper left and a square in the lower right of your work area; then fill them with two different uniform fills and blend using 15 steps.

Defining Additional Control Points

The ability to define additional control points is one of CorelDRAW's most powerful features, and DRAW 4.0 incorporated the Split options to make it easier to access. You can use any of the normal tools and transformations on any control point. The changes will then be used to define the blend's attributes. Click on **Split** in the Node Controls mode of the Blend roll-up. Select the fourth element from the top with the special cursor. Then give the object you selected a new fill and lift it up so that it is even with the topmost control object. Release the tool. Notice how the path and fill are altered. Select the blend and then select the eighth object the same way. Drag it down lower; then give it a new fill. Select and lift the fifth object from the bottom of the blend; then alter its position and fill. Figure 8.17 shows how the line was altered in the drawing. Use the Shape tool to node-edit the last object worked with. Take some time and experiment with different controls and combinations of compound blends.

Fitting a Blend to a Path

A blend can be fitted to the path of another object in a drawing, which forms an external control element of the blend. This kind of blend offers you the ability to use interval spacing instead of the number of steps to determine how a blend is drawn. Open a new drawing, set the Pencil tool to **Bézier** mode, and draw a set of curves that look like the slope of a hill going down from the upper left to the middle of the page. Put a couple of dips in it. Then give it a 2-point outline so it will be easy to see.

Chapter 8: Pushing the Envelope: Using CorelDRAW's Envelope, Blend, Perspective, and Extrude Special Effects

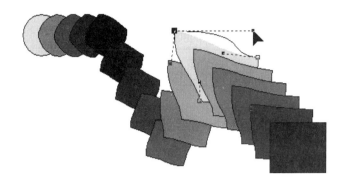

FIGURE 8.17 Working with split blends

Put the Text tool in Symbol mode and click on an area below the top of your line. Choose the Sports Figure collection and choose a figure like the skier (number 68) that is moving toward the right in an action pose and size it at 1.5 inches. Duplicate it and place the copy below the bottom of your "hill." Give each object a different-colored fill. Shift-click and select both symbols; then blend them with 20 steps. Now select the new blend and click on the **Fit To Path** button on the roll-up (the one that looks like an arrow pointing at a curved line). Choose **New Path**. The cursor will change to a wavy arrow pointed down. Place its tip on the curve you drew before placing the symbols. Don't set any other options; just click on the line and then on **Apply**. The before and after should look like Figure 8.18. The Blend roll-up will change, as shown in Figure 8.19, as you set the path.

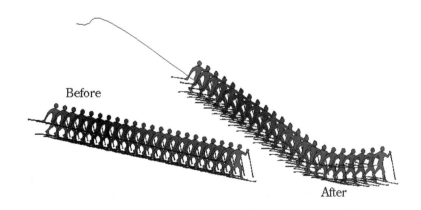

FIGURE 8.18 Fitting a blend to a path

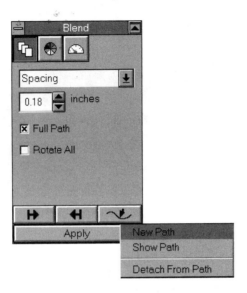

FIGURE 8.19 The Blend roll-up

There are three options on the Path drop-down menu accessed via the roll-up. The New Path option links the blend and the target object, the Show Path command places handles around the path object, and the Final option unlinks (detaches) the path and restores the simple blend.

Following the Path

Several special options are available when you set a blend on a path. Look at the top section of the roll-up in Figure 8.19. The drop-down menu has two options. Where it said Steps, it now also offers Spacing. You can use either method to set the interval of a blend. Instead of 20 figures on a path, you can tell CorelDRAW to place one every 2 inches. Look at Figure 8.18. Notice how the figures don't start at the top of the object. Click the **Full Path** option on and they will. The Rotate All box makes the blend objects follow the path and changes their angle to match changes in it. Select the compound blend you just made and shift the spacing to 0.5 inches; then check both option boxes just explained. The difference is shown in Figure 8.20.

Editing the Path

Choose the Shape tool and use it to alter the length of the control line. Now click on the **Path** button menu and select the **Show Path** option. Use the Pick tool to move the control objects on either end of the line. This command can be used like the Shape tool with Fit Text To Path to move objects interactively, but only control objects. Notice how the start location and spacing are altered as you work. You can use the Show Path command to redesign the fit of the path. To align the blend group to a new object, you must first select **Detach From Path** and then attach it to the new control path with the New Path command.

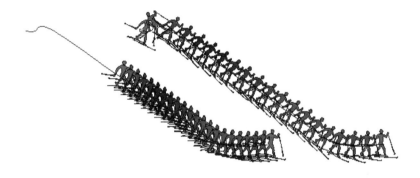

FIGURE 8.20 Using the Path options with a compound blend

Using Blends to Create Arrays

Some other draw programs offer an Array command. In computer-speak an array is a "collection of data items (objects or numbers) that can be treated as a single piece of data." This is similar to a blend. You are going to use a blend and a control path to create a checkbox with nine lines for a form. This is a lot quicker than placing duplicates. Open a new drawing and the **Blend** roll-up menu. Create a single straight horizontal line about as wide as the roll-up. Duplicate it and set them one on top of the other about as deep as the roll-up using **Ctrl** to place your duplicate directly in line with the first line. Now draw a vertical line that runs between them to the right. It should look like the objects on the far right of Figure 8.21.

Create a blend this way: Click on the two horizontal lines, open the Path button menu, and select **New Path**. Choose seven steps and no rotation, set the path to your vertical line, then click **Apply**. The menu will look like the one in Figure 8.21. The blend should create seven intermediate steps centered on the vertical line, a total of nine lines. Draw a rectangle around the entire group so that the top and bottom of the new box exactly cover the top and bottom and ends of the blend. Select the box and give it a light gray fill. Send it to the back and group all the objects. The final result will look like the object to the left of the dialog box in Figure 8.21.

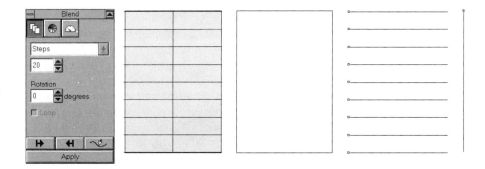

FIGURE 8.21 Using blends to create arrays

CREATING THE ILLUSION OF PERSPECTIVE

Between the involved discussions of Blend and Extrude you will now take a look at a simple effect, Perspective. There is no special roll-up menu, just interactive bounding boxes and x-shaped guides that represent the virtual vanishing points. Open a new drawing and type the word Perspective. Make sure it is selected; then select **Add Perspective** from the Effects menu. A dashed bounding box will appear around the text, and the Shape tool will be automatically selected. Use the magnifying glass tool with the "-" to jump back from the page. Move the bounding box until you can see both x's that will appear on the page. Then magnify it so you can see the word and the x marks, as I have done in Figure 8.22.

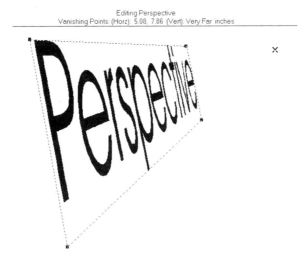

FIGURE 8.22 Editing perspective

The word is still a text object, and you can edit the contents even while it is in the Perspective Envelope. However, you can't edit individual character attributes. Figure 8.23 shows a word modified with the Perspective effect. Look at how the command can be used to change the visual viewing position. The first copy is normal; the second appears as if the viewer was almost underneath it. The third copy is receding down and to the right. Note the x on the far right. That is a vanishing point. It indicates where parallel lines in the object would disappear to. The fourth makes the viewers feel they are looking down on the word.

Use the Shape tool to drag the points on the corners of the bounding box. As you perform the edit, the cursor will change to cross hairs. The basic method is to move one of the control handles or a vanishing point. The vanishing points are only visible when the location they represent is within the viewing area. The **Ctrl** key works as a constraint, limiting movement to perfectly vertical or horizontal actions. Holding both the **Shift** and **Ctrl** keys will result in both sides being moved in or out by the same amount. Practice a bit with this effect and get a feel for how the controls work. Use both the envelope handles and the vanishing points.

FIGURE 8.23 The CorelDRAW perspective effect in action

You can add a perspective to an object and then select the Add Perspective command again. A new bounding box will appear and you can manipulate the perspective further, allowing some interesting twisted and bent appearances. Experiment with adding three or four layers of perspective changes. These changes can be discarded by clicking on the **Clear Perspective** command. You must click on it as many times as you used on the Add Perspective command to return your object to an unchanged line of text.

FIGURE 8.24 Effects of multiple Add Perspective commands

The Add New Perspective and Clear Perspective Commands

The Add New Perspective command places a new rectangular bounding box around an object without altering any current distortions. The Clear Perspective command returns the object to its original shape. Remember that if you have added perspective more than once, you must clear perspective as many times as you added it to return it to the original shape. If you want to do any Bézier editing on an object that is in a perspective bounding box, you should convert the object to curves and then select the Shape tool. If you clear the perspective, you will lose all changes made with the effect, and any other attempt to select the object with the Shape tool will return the effect's envelope, leaving you in Edit Perspective mode.

GIVING OBJECTS EXTRA BODY WITH THE EXTRUDE EFFECT

The Extrude roll-up offers a variety of commands for adding depth, a three-dimensional look that resembles old hot metal type or carved letters. It is also the easiest way to create boxes and produce lighting effects on objects with several sides. Figure 8.25 shows several samples and the Extrude roll-up in one of its four modes at the left of the figure, and at the right and left of the figure the two faces of this roll-up appear with the vanishing point defined numerically.

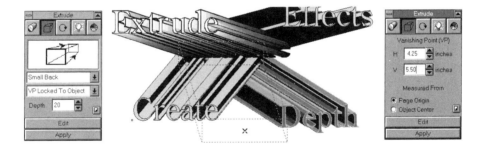

FIGURE 8.25 Extrude effects

Creating Extruded Objects

Start with a sample to see how this effect works. Open a new drawing and set the display to Wireframe. Draw a square and use the **Align** command to place it in the exact center of the page. Open the **Effects** menu and choose the **Extrude** roll-up or use the **Ctrl-E** shortcut. The roll-up menu will appear and your object will have an x and a dashed line inside of it, as shown above the A in Figure 8.26. The x is a vanishing point, like the one you just worked with in the Perspective command. The dashed lines that are the same shape as your object act as a wireframe extrusion. Change the Depth setting in the roll-up to 30. Now drag the vanishing point over to the right, as shown above the B in Figure 8.26. Notice how the wireframe follows the movement. It is showing the outline of the extruded object. Click on the **Apply** button. Give the object a light gray fill and a thick black outline. Then change the Display setting to exit the wireframe mode. The drawing should look like the example under C in Figure 8.26. The new object is much like the blends you worked with before. It contains a control object (the one you drew) and an extruded group that was generated by the program based on the settings entered in the Extrude roll-up menu. The resulting combined group is dynamically linked. The roll-up menu enables you to control the depth, rotation, lighting, and color of the object and its various surfaces.

If you use any other tools to select the object, the Extrude effect is stopped. To apply any other modifications with that effect you must select the object and click on either the **Edit** or **Apply** button in the Extrude roll-up if it is already on-screen.

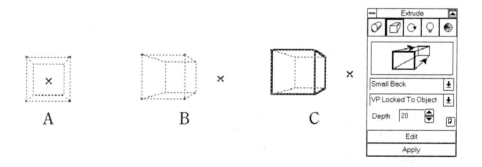

FIGURE 8.26 Working with the extrude effect

Understanding Extruded Components

Using extrusions effectively requires an understanding of how they are constructed. Look at Figure 8.27. The objects on the right are the same as the ones on the left. They are taken apart as an example. The square and the words Depth Control are the objects that were placed on the page. They are the control elements. The objects behind the controls are the extruded group that was generated by CorelDRAW. The exact number and shape of the objects in the group will vary as you adjust the settings in the roll-up menu. That is one reason it can take so long for the computer to update the effect. It must recalculate the entire object with each modification or movement.

Chapter 8: Pushing the Envelope: Using CorelDRAW's Envelope, Blend, Perspective, and Extrude Special Effects

The fill and outline of the Extrude group are taken from the ones applied to the control object. A closed shape with no fill will look like a wireframe and you will be able to see through the different parts. If you separate the control and then ungroup the generated parts, they can be individually filled as desired.

Look at the letters in the objects on the top. As with blends, you can select the control object commands (e.g., Place Duplicate) and only apply them to the control. But outlines and fills will be applied to the entire extruded group, unless you have specified other options via the Extrude roll-up. You can also give the group and the control object different fills or outlines by separating the control object from the extrusion and then selecting it for modification. That's what was done here, breaking the text away from the effect group and then adding a black fill. The text is still text and can be treated like any other text element. You probably want to make a duplicate before breaking them apart, in case you need to modify the original effect later. To use the Shape tool to node-edit the object you must also separate and ungroup it.

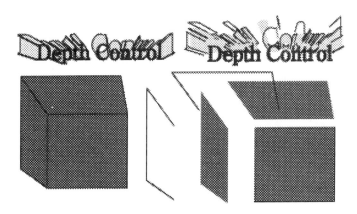

FIGURE 8.27 Exploded drawing of several extruded objects

Extrude is, like most of CorelDRAW's more advanced effects, a really intensive use of your computer's resources. All extruded objects are complex groups. A single five-letter word can contain more than 1,000 nodes and take 15 or 20 seconds to draw on a fast machine. When working with this command use the wireframe display whenever possible, until you need to see the object's outline and fill. Another good practice is to do any extrudes in a drawing first and then to move them off-screen until the drawing is almost complete. That way you have more memory available for the effect, and it is out of the way until you are ready to place it.

The Vanishing Point

The default location for the extrude vanishing point (VP) is the center of the page. If you move the VP manually to a different location, it becomes the default for any new uses of the Extrude command. The VP can be moved either by dragging it with the mouse or by using the H and V entry boxes located in the roll-up menu as described in this list.

The Depth setting controls the location of the vanishing point and its relation to the control object. This is what determines the length and orientation of the extrusion. Create an object or select the one already on your page and open the Extrude roll-up. Use it to follow along with this list and try the different settings as they are explained. If you have a slow computer, you may want to do this in wireframe mode.

- **Depth.** This setting alters the depth and direction of the effect by moving the vanishing point. The higher the number, the farther away the wireframe will be from the original object. For most people, using visual cues while dragging offers the best approach. As you make changes, the wireframe will move to show the outline of the new version. You can also enter numbers in the menu's Depth entry box, ranging from -99 to 99. The result will be shown on the status bar in inches. The way the numbers are calculated is a bit exotic. The infinity point is considered to be at 20,000 inches from the object, and the number you enter is used to determine the VP's location based on the following formula:

    20,000 inches - 20,000 x 100

    100 - The Depth Setting

- **Extrusion Types.** This controls the appearance of the effect in relation to the vanishing point. A number of options are available, each changing the way in which the object appears to be viewed. They include Small Back, Small Front, Back Parallel, and so on. The thumbnail window on the roll-up shows the general effect of each choice. In 3.0 you could choose between perspective on or off. This is now taken care of with the Extrusion Types. Choosing **Back** or **Front Parallel** gives you Orthogonal extrusions; all other choices give you a perspective extrusion.

CorelDRAW 5.0 has added some preset choices of vanishing point to the Extrude roll-up; these appear in a window below the Extrusion Types window. The default is to lock the vanishing point to the object. The second alternative is to lock the vanishing point to the page. You can also choose to copy the vanishing point from another object, clicking on this will produce a spiraled arrow letting you click to indicate the object from which Extrude is to copy. You can also share the vanishing point of another object by clicking on the last alternative and then on the object you wish it to share with.

- **H and V Entry Boxes.** These numerical boxes are located by clicking on the small page icon right above the Edit bar on the roll-up. These settings shift the vanishing point horizontally (H) and vertically (V) by that amount from the zero point if the Page Origin checkbox is selected. If the Object Center checkbox is selected, the vanishing point is measured by the distance of the center of the object selected.
- **Rotation.** If you click on the second vertical button on the left side of the menu, the Rotation settings are made available. The left side of Figure 8.28 shows the Interactive mode. Click on the arrows to rotate the object in the direction you want. To return the object to its original position click on the x in the center of the sphere. For exact control of the object's rotation, choose the numeric mode by clicking on the button on the lower right above the Edit button. The menu will change to look like the one at the right of Figure 8.28. Type or use the arrows to place values in the appropriate Entry box.

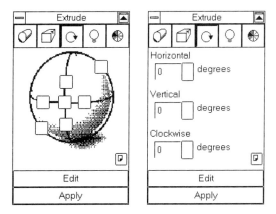

FIGURE 8.28 The Rotation controls

- **Lighting.** The third option down on the left set of buttons is the Lighting control, as shown in Figure 8.29. This enables you to adjust the intensity and direction of the light source. To activate the command you must click on the top of the switch just to the left of the wireframe box. The sphere inside the wireframe box represents your object, and the location of each of three possible light sources is indicated by circles with the number of the source in them. To move the light source, drag the appropriate circle to a point where lines on the wireframe box intersect. The Intensity control adjusts the shading of the object's fill, simulating a varying amount of light directed onto the object. If some surfaces are too dark, increase the intensity. Type the value you want to use or drag the slide control.

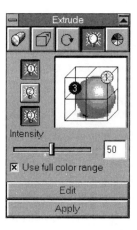

FIGURE 8.29 The light sources

- **Coloring.** If you click on the last of the left-hand-side buttons, you are given the Color controls for extruded surfaces shown in Figure 8.30. The Use Object Fill option will fill the extruded surfaces with the control object's color. Solid Fill offers a palette displayed by clicking on the button to its right; then you choose a color from the color swatch. The Shade option fills the extruded surfaces with a blend between two colors selected from the palettes displayed when you click on the From and To buttons.

Chapter 8: Pushing the Envelope: Using CorelDRAW's
Envelope, Blend, Perspective, and Extrude Special Effects

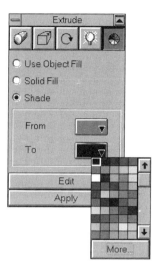

FIGURE 8.30 Color controls

- The last alternative for coloring in the Drape check box. Clicking this will cause CorelDRAW to treat the objects fill in quite a different way. Regular fill for an extrusion fills each surface of the object independently, as shown in the upper extruded box in Figure 8.31. If you click on the **Drape** box, the fill is continuous around the corners and on the surfaces of the extruded object as seen in the lower box in Figure 8.31.

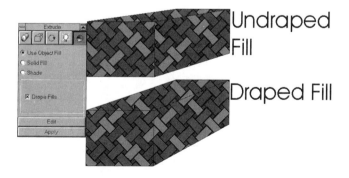

FIGURE 8.31 Effect of the Draped fill

- **The Edit and Apply Buttons.** Use these buttons to place a currently selected object into Extrude Edit mode. Although the wireframes may move to show the effects of any changes in position, the changes are not actually applied until the Apply button is used.

- **Extrude Presets.** The first button on the left-hand side accesses a large number of already developed extrusions with fills. If you choose a preset from the list box it will apply basic extrusions quickly and accurately. One of these is seen in Figure 8.32. These presets include such effects as Metallic Gold and ThreeD. A sample of the selected preset appears in the roll-up. The preset look is maintained regardless of the size of the object Is. If you have two objects, one larger than the other, and apply the same preset, the smaller object will not be as deep as the larger one. Vanishing points are not shared by objects sharing the same preset.

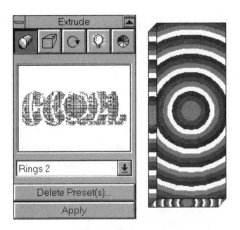

FIGURE 8.32 Using Preset extrusions

You can save your own extrusions by selecting your extrusion and clicking on the **Save As** button. You can add descriptions like those attached to the presets. Figure 8.33 shows the Save As Preset Extrusion dialog box.

FIGURE 8.33 Saving your extrusions

RIGHT ON THE BUTTON

After all this talk about special effects, it's finally time to put them to work. A group of concerned citizens has asked you to design a button that promotes the idea of people getting out and voting on election day. This project has been made a little more involved than such a task might normally be, so you can use as many effects as possible. Open a new drawing. Set the rulers off for now, but leave the status bar and on-screen palette on. Two flags from the clipart collection will be used. If they are not available you can just design a couple of filled rectangles to stand in for them.

While you work, keep in mind the balance of the final work, not the exact size. You can rescale the button when you are done. That way the object can be as large as possible without having to use the Zoom tool all the time. If you are producing work that will be printed using a laser printout as camera-ready copy, consider leaving the work a larger size. That way your printer can reduce it with the plate camera and get a better reproduction.

A Field of Stars

Draw a circle using the Ellipse tool while holding the **Ctrl** key and center it on the page. Make it large enough to work with easily. Select the Text tool in Symbol mode and place a copy of Stars 1 #52 on the page (if you have that symbol collection loaded). (The U.S. flag is used in this design. You can use another flag that has another symbol, such as a maple leaf for Canada.) Duplicate it and open the **Effects** menu; choose the **Blend** roll-up option. Blend the two stars to your circle and use the **Full Path** option to get a circle of stars. When the circle is the way you want it, give it a white fill and a thin outline; then delete the ellipse you used as a template. Draw two circles, one on either side of the stars. Place them in back. The inner circle should have a gray fill and a white outline. The outer one needs a blue fill and a red outline. These colors match the U.S. flag. If you want to use another one, choose a color scheme that fits your design. Group the objects when they are the way you want them. The basic design should look like Figure 8.34.

FIGURE 8.34 The circle of stars

Showing Your Colors

The clipart collection provides a host of flags. The U.S. and Tennessee flags were chosen for this button. You can use one or two flags. Place them one at a time in the central section of the design; then use the **Perspective** effect to arrange them so that they are receding toward the back of the inner circle, as shown in Figure 8.35. The flags were left somewhat small and scaled down in size toward the center vertically. Experiment with the visual effects of making larger or smaller flags and shifting the perspective. If you want the inner edges of the flags to match, use a guideline drawn down the center. Remember that a CorelDRAW design is only finished when you want it to be. If you or the client want changes later, all you have to do is reopen the file and make the revisions. (Of course, some are easier to do than others.)

Chapter 8: Pushing the Envelope: Using CorelDRAW's
Envelope, Blend, Perspective, and Extrude Special Effects

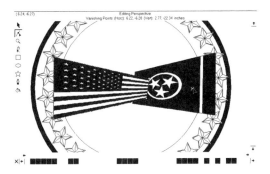

FIGURE 8.35 Altering the flags with the Perspective command

Making a Statement

It's time to place your message. The design calls for two sets of text curved around the top and bottom of the outer ellipse, and a third block fitted inside the center. With the normal Text tool type, If You Don't Vote and You Don't Have A Voice as separate blocks. Use any font. Place the first object above the button and the second below it. Adjust the size so they will each wrap about one-quarter of the way around the button. They can be the same size or slightly different. Which do you think looks best? Use the **Fit Text To Path** command to align them with the outer circle. Use the **Variable Offset** option to get the text slightly outside the outline (see Figure 8.36).

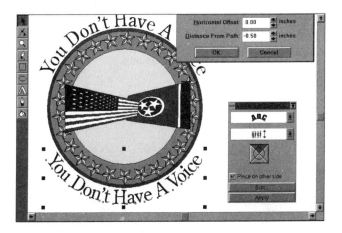

FIGURE 8.36 Fitting the outer text objects

One Final Effect

Create a block of text with just one word, VOTE, in the same font as the other text. Give it a black fill and a thick white outline. Set the outline to fit behind and be scaled with the object. Scale it with the Pick tool so that it fits side to side inside the inner circle. Open the **Effects** menu and choose the **Envelope** command. Then use the **Single Arc** option. Edit the envelope so that the word VOTE exactly fills the inner area. Figure 8.37 shows the editing in progress.

FIGURE 8.37 Editing the envelope

Fine-tuning the Design

Once you have the button looking right, save it and print a proof. Examine it for flaws, words that are not spelled correctly, and whether you like the overall appearance. Figure 8.38 shows the final design after the flags are reworked. Guidelines were pulled on the inner and outer edges, top and bottom. Then those lines were used to help get everything perfect. The larger flags give more depth and balance to the design.

Chapter 8: Pushing the Envelope: Using CorelDRAW's
Envelope, Blend, Perspective, and Extrude Special Effects

349

FIGURE 8.38 The final design

FILE MANAGEMENT USING MOSAIC

Mosaic is a program that acts as a visual comprehensive file management utility for CorelDRAW. The hard-copy documentation for Mosaic with CorelDRAW 5.0 is very terse. The last page in the CorelDRAW 5.0 user's manual (section on Mosaic pgs. 509-514) tells you that help is available by clicking on the Help item on the menu bar. Mosaic is not hard to use, and the help menus are adequate, but new users may not know how handy this utility can be. This section briefly explains some of the highlights. It assumes that Mosaic is loaded on your system; it is a part of the CorelDRAW package. You can use Mosaic as a stand-alone program by clicking on its icon. Use it whenever you search for a file. The Mosaic roll-up can be used in any Corel application and two roll-ups, each showing a different catalog can be on screen at a time. Mosaic supports Kodak's PhotoCD format and allows you to work with those files. You can open, view, and export those images.

Mosaic Basics

In order to use CorelMOSAIC with applications such as DRAW, TRACE, or PHOTO-PAINT, with the Mosaic rollup, a catalog containing the images you'll be using must already exist. To create a catalog you must open CorelMOSAIC. The interface is quite simple, as you can see in Figure 8.39, but using it can be tricky in places until you have tried it out. Start the Mosaic application and choose **Open** from the File Menu. Select a directory containing graphic files and, if you want to, choose the file extensions you wish to select from. When you have done this, click on **OK** and a window will appear containing thumbnails of your graphics. This is a temporary selection on graphics and you must open a catalog (allowing batch operations) or a library (which compresses the graphics) in order to make the particular collections of graphics more permanent.

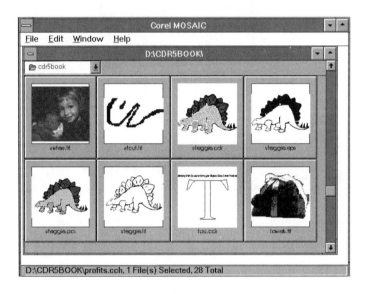

FIGURE 8.39 The MOSAIC Interface

Let's make a quick catalog just to see how; click on **New**, give your catalog a file name and click on **OK**. Also, in the File menu, click on **Open** and select a subdirectory containing graphic files. If it is a large directory, it will save time if you select a file type here also. Select a file from the temporary collection from the subdirectory and click-drag it into the window for your named Catalog. MOSAIC will ask confirmation that you wish to copy the graphic. You can select files for a Catalog by clicking them individually or by holding down **Control** when you click to select thumbnails from anywhere in the collection. To select a number of thumbnails in a row, click on the first one you want, move the mouse pointer to the last, and hold down the shift key while clicking on the final file. All the files between those two will be selected. Then just drag the pointer to the Collection and all those files will be made part of the Collection and will be easily available from inside other Corel applications.

Chapter 8: Pushing the Envelope: Using CorelDRAW's Envelope, Blend, Perspective, and Extrude Special Effects

There are five menu options that give access to all of Mosaic's features. In some cases choosing an option will automatically load CorelDRAW, such as the Export and Edit options.

Here is a breakdown of what each menu does.

- **File Menu.** These options all deal with basic file operations, including printing. New Catalog/Library and Open Catalog/Library offer ways to organize and store files. A Catalog will gather the names and locations of files, whereas a Library will make copies of specified files and compress them for efficient storage. Open Catalog either selects a directory and displays thumbnails of the files in it or opens a catalog or library you have already set up. Convert allows you to convert from one graphic format to another and also choose where the conversion should be stored. Print opens the CorelDRAW Print Dialog box and prints selected files. Print Thumbnails prints thumbnail images (reduced images of files) directly from Mosaic. Print Setup sets Printer options and allows you to choose preferences for titles when printing thumbnails. The Color Manager will help you fine tune Corel applications so that your monitor, printer and scanner will work together to give you the best possible color reproduction. The Color Correction command is less encompassing then the Color Manager and provides a choice between None, Fast, Accurate, Simulate Printer (in which case you should have found your particular color printer in the Color Manager clicked on it. Preferences enables you to change the size of thumbnail images in the Mosaic Display window as well as the spacing and other options, such as whether or not you want to enter confirmation for file deletion. Exit closes Mosaic and returns you to either Windows.

Only the file types you have selected will be shown in the Mosaic window. The thumbnail images are not available for all file types. If there is no thumbnail, a circle and diagonal line (like a No Parking sign) will appear in the thumbnail space over the filename. If the file type is unknown, a yellow diamond with an exclamation point will be displayed. Files from word processors, spreadsheets and so on may or may not be displayed with the icon of the application the files were produced in.

- **Edit Menu.** These options allow you to select and work with the files themselves. Select by Keyword enables you to use keywords to locate CorelDRAW files. The Select All option selects all thumbnails in the display for action with another command. Clear All deselects all files. Clicking on Update Catalog will cause MOSAIC to check the thumbnails against the originals in the listed directory. If you have deleted any of these files from your disk, they will now disappear from the Catalog. Expand Library Files does just as it says; it decompresses the files you have stored in the library. You'll probably need to check on disk space availability before applying this to more than a few files. Choosing Edit opens either CorelDRAW, CorelPHOTO-PAINT, or CorelSHOW (depending on the type of file selected) and loads the selected file. You can perform the same action by double-clicking on the thumbnail or filename. Import into DRAW opens CorelDRAW and places the selected graphic either into a new drawing or into an existing drawing. Delete takes the thumbnail out of the Catalog or Library but does not affect the file itself. The Extract text and Merge Back Text option transfers text to and from selected CorelDRAW files into ASCII text for editing. The Keywords option allows you to add or delete keywords that are associated with the file. Edit Description allows you to change the description saved with a Corel file. Get Info displays the file and the available information, including file size and date last saved.

Now let's try using MOSAIC from within CorelDRAW. Open the CorelDRAW **File** menu, and choose the **Mosaic** roll-up. The dialog box appearing in Figure 8.40 will appear showing whatever graphic files exist in the current directory. You can set the program to show all or only certain kinds of graphic files either by filename or as thumbnail pictures. Or you can open a catalog, such as the one you made above. To add a graphic from the MOSAIC roll-up to your drawing, simply click and drag it into the drawing. Click when your pointer is over the page to drop the graphic. CorelDRAW (or other Corel application) will place the graphic in the center of the page, importing it if necessary. So while it may seem a little troublesome learning how to set up Catalogs and Libraries, in the long run your trouble is more than paid back by the simplicity of this method.

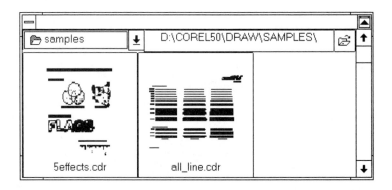

FIGURE 8.40 The Mosaic Rollup

Chapter 8: Pushing the Envelope: Using CorelDRAW's
Envelope, Blend, Perspective, and Extrude Special Effects

CHAPTER SUMMARY

The special effects offered by CorelDRAW give us the ability to add depth and detail to our drawings. In Section Two we will work with blends to create a complex drawing and see how award-winning artists use special effects to add life to their work.

"Huntress"—*G. Curry*

"Green Lizard"—*C. Purcell*

"Spirit"—J. Selman

"Neck"—*J. Vergil*

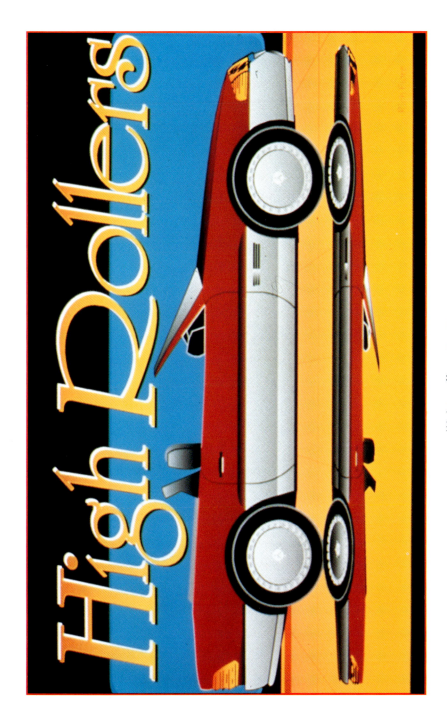

"Merc"—R. Fiore

"Divers" —D. Birckley

"Donut Shoppe" —*P. McCormick*

"Mesa"—*D. Miller*

CHAPTER 9

A Banquet of Possibilities: CorelDRAW's Advanced Drawing Tools

This chapter covers the following topics:

- Advanced Fill Techniques
- Conical, Custom, Rainbow Fills
- Working with Textured fills
- Using Contours and Powerlines
- Welding objects
- Using the Object Data Manager
- Dimensioning
- Using Layers
- Cloning Objects
- Exercise: Planning a Traditional Herb Garden

Introduction

In this chapter we explore some of CorelDRAW 5.0's most exciting features. This edition of the program not only enhances the way we can work with fills but expands our options dramatically. Textured fills offer an almost infinite variety of fractile-like designs, allowing us to use realistic random patterns for simulating such things as clouds and waves. Contours are similar to blends, but they can be created with only one object. Welding, on the other hand, allows us to combine several objects into a single path in a way that far exceeds that available with a simple Combine command.

The new cloning feature, along with improvements to layers, makes it much easier to create complex drawings that must be updated periodically like technical drawings. The Lens effect, new in 5.0, allows special effects to be applied to all or part of an object to magnify it, change the color effects, etc. PowerClip, also new in 5.0, allows you to combine objects in a truly remarkable way to create special effects with both artistic text and graphics.

In this chapter we will use those features along with the Object Data Manager to plan and represent a traditional English herb garden. This chapter also explains the dimensioning function that has been added to the Pencil tool. This feature is still limited in CorelDRAW 5.0 and does not provide the ability to update the label depicting the length of a line automatically as it is scaled. We can expect improved dimensioning capabilities in CorelDRAW 6.0.

To work through the material presented in this chapter you should be familiar with using Windows 3.1, have completed at least some of the earlier chapters, and have CorelDRAW properly installed and running on your system.

New Tricks with Fountain Fills

Fountain fills have always been one of the most fascinating features of CorelDRAW. It's fun to watch a radial or linear fill flood an area. CorelDRAW 5.0 extends the power of fountain fills with several new variations, and the new controls make it easier to define exactly how an object will look.

Chapter 9: A Banquet of Possibilities: CorelDRAW's Advanced Drawing Tools

One Way to Make a Mountain

Conical fills do a wonderful job of producing the appearance of three dimensions, particularly if you want something to appear to stand up off the screen or page. Let's draw a simple hill with a lake at its foot. There are three gradient fill buttons in the Fill roll-up–linear, radial, and conical. By holding the left mouse button at the current center; cross hairs appears. Move the "peak" as you move the mouse pointer. Figure 9.1 shows how it should look when you're finished. Experiment with moving the center of the fill for the lake to see if you can achieve more appearance of depth.

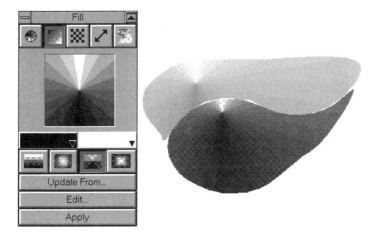

FIGURE 9.1 Making mountains conical fills

A new fill type has been added in 5.0; the Square fill. Like the other fills, a square fill can be moved off center in the object. The examples in Figure 9.2 has a frequency of 10, with finer fills, many different effects may be acheived.

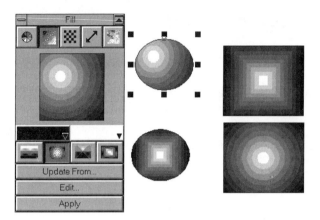

FIGURE 9.2 Square Pegs and holes

Conical fills can produce some interesting results when combined with other effects, as shown in the extruded cylinder in Figure 9.3. Experiment with various settings on the fills and the effect each has. Remember to include in your experiments some tries with draping or undraping the fill using the Extrude roll-up from the Colors face.

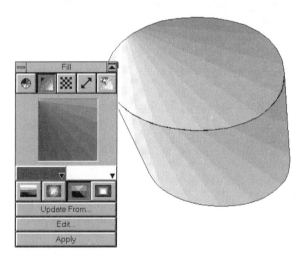

FIGURE 9.3 An extruded cylinder with a conical fill

For more ideas for using conical fills, see Chapter 20 and the examination of the illustration "Mesa4."

Chapter 9: A Banquet of Possibilities: CorelDRAW's Advanced Drawing Tools   **359**

More Fun with Rainbow Fills

In early versions, CorelDRAW users were limited to having only two color origin points for fountain fills. In other words, you could move from red to green with variations between, but you couldn't combine more than two colors or have a shift back and forth between colors. Now you can.

Let's see how these new features work by making a banner. Draw a long, narrow rectangle and use the envelope function to create a rippled effect. Open the **Fill** roll-up, choose **Linear Fill**, and **Edit**; click on **Custom**. The Edit Fills dialog box will look similar to that in Figure 9.4. Choose two different colors, such as magenta and green, and try each of the circular buttons in turn. These indicate the direction along the color wheel in which the fill will progress. The black line that will appear shows the range of colors that will be included in the fill.

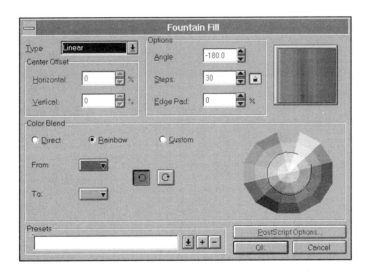

FIGURE 9.4 The Edit Fountain Fill dialog box

Now let's change the bands from horizontal to vertical. In the roll-up, hold the left mouse button anywhere in the preview window and move the pointer to the point at which you want the fill to originate. You will see a black line running from the center of the preview fill to the new location. Experiment with both rainbow directions on the banner.

FIGURE 9.5 Banner with rainbow fill

Even More Fun with Custom Fills

Going around in circles can get boring. There's a lot more that we can do with custom fountain fills. The Custom option allows us to create the effect of varying intensities, allowing us to set repeating highlights resembling those found on the kind of ribbon candy popular at Christmas. Let's try that. Select the banner and open the **Fountain Fill Color Options** dialog box if it isn't already on your screen. Choose **Custom** in the blend section. Notice the two squares in the top corners of the Preview window in the From-To section of the dialog box. Click on the leftmost square. See the little dart that appears to the right of it? Click on one of the colors on the palette in the dialog box. See how the color has been added to the preview of the fill. Click twice more on the square and drag the darts to different positions underneath the Preview window. Repeat the same process for the square on the other side, making sure you interpose markers from the two different sides between each other. This technique allows you to mix several or different intensities of colors within a single fountain fill. Figure 9.6 shows an example of this technique being used.

Chapter 9: A Banquet of Possibilities: CorelDRAW's Advanced Drawing Tools

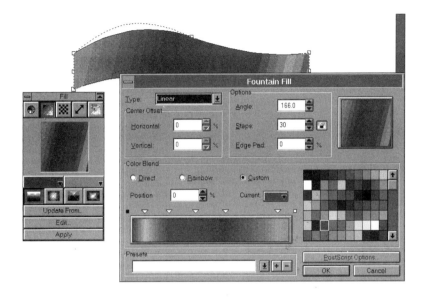

FIGURE 9.6 Custom fountain fills with the Edit Fills dialog box

Move your dialog box right under the banner and adjust the markers to create a varied custom fill. Practice with this technique until you get comfortable with it before moving on.

CorelDRAW 5.0 Texture Fills

One of the more interesting developments in computer graphics in the last few years has been the application of fractile designs to create patterns within illustrations. Fractile math can be used to simulate a variety of patterns and even produce lifelike landscapes. Part of the power of fractile design lies in its randomness. The new CorelDRAW Texture Fills use a random pattern generator to produce a similar effect.

Each texture has a series of options that can be set to control the appearance of the fill. There are no hard-and-fast rules that can be used when working with textured fills; there are too many variations. Some parameters will change the appearance much more radically than others. If you develop a texture that you really like, you can save it for future use as well as save it as a starting point for further experimentation.

CorelDRAW provides over 100 different bitmap textures, including gravel, clouds, paper textures, and common surfaces. By combining different attributes—such as color, softness, density, and brightness—and the random number generator you can create an almost infinite variety of patterns.

The best way to understand how the texture fills work is to experiment with them. Create a circle on your page and access the **Fill** roll-up from the tool bar. Click on the bitmap texture button, which is the fourth one down on the left-hand side of the roll-up. Although we could set our styles directly from here, let's use the more detailed dialog box accessed by clicking on the **Edit** button. Open up the samples texture library by accessing the first drop-down menu in the dialog box.

Click through several of the styles to get an idea of the variations, both in appearance and in the various controls. For instance, blocks allow you to control not only shade and light but the amount of eastern light, northern light, density, and softness. Cloudy nebula let you vary texture and brightness as well as control the color in each quadrant and two energy states. Notice that in the middle of the dialog box there is a headline indicating the style name. The samples are actually set values for different styles that can be accessed by going back to the texture library and choosing the styles. Draw a circle so it fills about half your page, click on **Edit** in the Fill roll-up, and choose **Banded Malachite**. Your dialog box should look like the one in Figure 9.7.

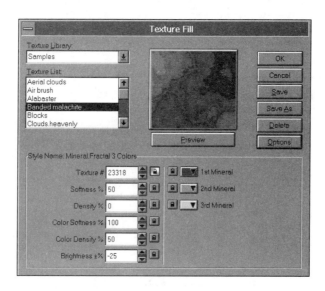

FIGURE 9.7 The Texture Fill dialog box

Notice the little padlock symbol alongside each of the options in the dialog box. This indicates the status of the random number selector. If the lock is open it indicates that the random number generator is selected. Each time you click on the **Preview** button, the values for all the unlocked fields will be changed randomly, giving you a different variation on the fill. If you wish to set the values specifically, you must make sure the number generator icon is locked. Adjust the value several times using the **Preview** button; once you have a pleasing result, click on **OK**. Since we used the roll-up, we will now have to click on **Apply** to set the fill.

Clicking the lower right-hand corner of the Preview window in the roll-up provides a fly-out with previews of the fills. You may change libraries by using the first of the drop-down menus under the preview or access a specific variation within that library by using the second. As with the other roll-ups, Update From will let you copy values from another object. The Edit button accesses the full dialog box and Apply is used to finalize your selection.

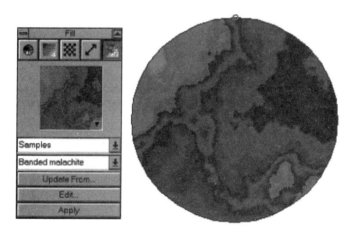

FIGURE 9.8 The Texture Fill roll-up

Keep in mind that bitmap images, especially color bitmap images, can consume a lot of your system's resources. If you get too ambitious working with texture fills, you may either slow your system down or run out of resources and be unable to complete an operation. If you find this happening often, you may want to check in Section Three of this book for tips on how to optimize your Windows installation and memory usage. Keeping that in mind, let's go on and experiment a bit with bitmap textures.

A Cloudy Day

In Chapter 2 we made a simple drawing of the sun setting over the ocean. Let's add some clouds to that, using one of the texture fills. Open that file (it should be called EXERCIS3.CDR) and select the rectangle that makes up the sky. Pick **Clouds, Heavenly** from the Samples library and then choose the **Texture Fill** dialog box, and click on the **Preview** bar until you find a variation you like. I used variation 9746 in the Texture # window, as shown Figure 9.9.

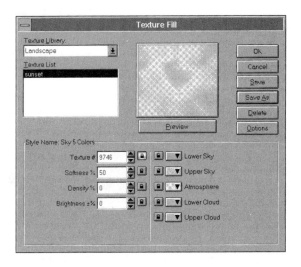

FIGURE 9.9 Choosing a Texture Fill from the dialog box

Click on the Preview bar until you are satisfied with the result. Now let's enter some custom colors as follows: Lower Sky: C=3, M=11, Y=0, and K=54; Upper Sky: C=1, M=17, Y=0, and K=29; Atmosphere: C=3, M=11, Y=0, and K=20; Lower Clouds: C=0, M=53, Y=91, and K=9; and Upper Clouds: C=0, M=42, Y=79, and K=14. Save your work if you wish by clicking on **Save As**. You must enter the name of a new library and the name of your texture. I called mine Sunset and just gave the library my first name.

Let's add texture to the water too. Swimming Pool 1 is a good starting point because the darker shades were already set to almost the same color that we had set the water to for the original fountain fill. All we have to do is to add a little orange to the high spots to represent the reflections from the sun on the waves. Set the colors for the waves as follows: Bottom: C=0, M=33, Y=64, K=5; Bottom Middle: C=0, M=34, Y=64, K=13; Middle: C=20, M=0, Y=0, K=52; Surface Middle: C=36, M=13, Y=0, K=52; and Surface: C=36, M=13, Y=0, K=33. These settings give the effect of the sun's light reflecting along a trough in the waves.

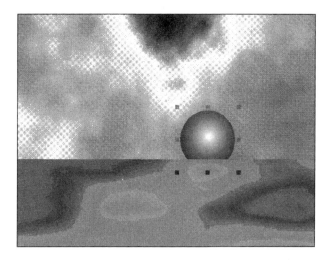

FIGURE 9.10 Sunset with texture fills

Corel's libraries of texture fills, while very extensive, are only the beginning. Each of the fills in the library may be endlessly varied using the Texture Fills dialog box. It is not possible in this book to cover all the the controls Corel gives you to work with texture fills. Figure 9.11 shows this dialog box with a complex fill in the priview window. Note the great variety of controls including the maximimim and maximum sizes of the bubbles, the directions and intensities of two light sources, the dark, medium, and light shades, and the brightness. Other texture fills provide other controls. In addition, click on the **Options** button in this dialog box and a further dialog box, like that shown in Figure 9.12 will appear. With this Texture Options dialog box, you can control the resolution of the bitmap and the size of the tile used to fill your graphic object. Remember that increasing the resolution of the bitmap and/or the size of the tile will tend to slow down the screen redraw.

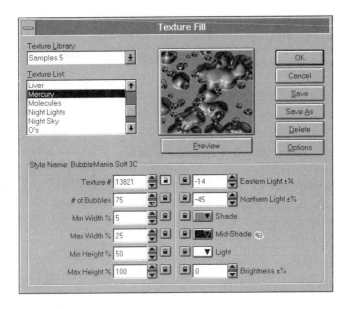

FIGURE 9.11 Texture Fill Controls

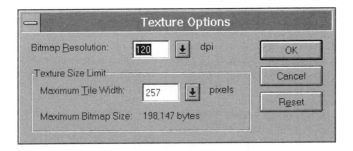

FIGURE 9.12 The Texture Options dialog box

Bitmap textures can run from the sublime to the surreal. Almost the only limitation to their variety is your own imagination. Since they can tax your system resources, it is probably a good idea to save a texture you like before you apply it and, if you are using several such textures, to save your drawing at each step along the way.

Chapter 9: A Banquet of Possibilities: CorelDRAW's Advanced Drawing Tools

USING POWERLINES

CorelDRAW's Powerline feature is similar to the pressure-sensitive and custom brush controls found in some of the new bitmap editing programs. We can use the Powerline controls to create custom tools mimicking the results obtained by various traditional artistic tools, such as dry brushes and calligraphy pens. The pressure controls can be used to adjust the effect as if you were using different amounts of pressure when drawing by hand. This can be especially effective with soft brushes and calligraphic effects.

Powerlines can be used as you work, or an effect can be tailored and applied to an existing object. Let's experiment a bit and see how they work. Open up the **Effects** menu and select the **Powerline** roll-up. The Powerline roll-up has a display window that shows the basic effect that will occur when using the form selected in the menu below it. Choose the Pencil tool and use it in connection with two or three different powerlines available from the drop down list to draw several lines on your page. Figure 9.13 shows several variations of the Powerline. Notice that you have to have the feature **Apply When Drawing Lines** selected to have the effect take place as you work.

FIGURE 9.13 Working with Powerline

Powerlines may be applied to many CorelDRAW objects, including text, as you can see in Figure 9.14. Twenty-four different presets are available from the Powerline roll-up. Using these as a starting point, you can adjust many of the factors affecting the line to customize the feature and then can save your version for the next time you want it.

FIGURE 9.14 Applying Powerlines to text

Select the Text tool and type the words **Fun With Powerlines** on the page. Scale this line so that it fills most of the page; then choose one of the powerline shapes and click **Apply**. Figure 9.14 shows one possible result. As you can see, Powerlines can be an effective tool for rapidly creating complex forms and exotic text. Keep in mind that the more complex lines become, the more memory and computer resources they consume. As with the other effects discussed in this chapter, powerlines can be very demanding. If you use them with large text strings or apply them to objects with many nodes, you may find yourself waiting for a while for the program to complete the work.

Adjusting the Nib

You'll notice that there are three buttons on the Powerline roll-up. The first one, which should have been active while you were playing originally, allows us to select Powerline preset shapes. Click on the second button, which looks like the nib of a pen. Surprise, it allows you to adjust the shape of the nib. This can be done in two ways. Notice the little page button down at the lower right-hand corner of the roll-up just above the Save As button. This toggles between the interactive or numeric control methods. Figure 9.15 shows some sample variations of different nibs with the interactive mode depicted on the left and the numeric model on the right.

To change the nib shape using the interactive method, place the cursor within the box and drag in different directions to change the shape and angle. Varying the intensity setting will vary the rate of calligraphic effect obtained.

Chapter 9: A Banquet of Possibilities: CorelDRAW's Advanced Drawing Tools **369**

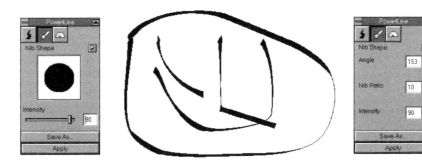

FIGURE 9.15 Adjusting nib settings

Adjusting the Speed, Spread, and Ink Flow Settings

Click on the final button, which is designed to look like a speedometer. Three possible settings can be controlled either by moving the slider bars beneath the entry or by entering a numeric value. The higher the speed setting, the more the line will seem to "skid" around corners as you draw. If speed is set to zero you will not be able to adjust the other values. The speed setting is more noticeable on sharp curves than on softer angles.

Think of the spread setting as a smoothness control. Higher values will produce smoother effects. If the speed control is set to zero you will not be able to adjust the spread control.

The ink flow determines how much "ink" is absorbed into your brush. The higher the value, the more virtual ink will be in your electronic brush. The Scale With Image button automatically adjusts the maximum width setting as a powerline is scaled. Keep in mind that this effect works only if you are using one o the corner handles of the bounding box to resize the object. Figure 9.16 shows the effect of modifying the speed controls on the powerlines shown in the preceding figure.

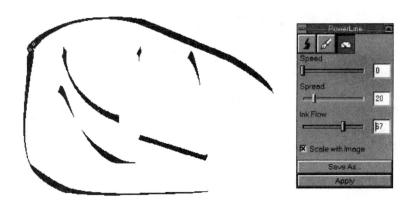

FIGURE 9.16 Adjusting the speed settings

The Shape tool can be used to edit Powerlines, just as with other curves inside CorelDRAW. There is an added function with this tool when working with powerlines—pressure edit, which is accessed via the Node Edit roll-up. This allows you to adjust the amount of spread in a powerline interactively with the shape tool. Figure 9.17 shows an example of this effect at work.

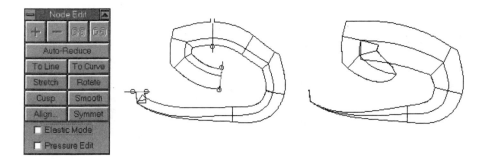

FIGURE 9.17 Editing powerlines with the Shape tool

The possible variations in line you can choose from using Powerline, although certainly not infinite, seem more than adequate for most people, however ambitious. Draw a line, duplicate it, and apply the Trumpet 1 preset Powerline to the first copy. Change the Pen and Speed, Spread, and Ink Flow options on the remainder. As you can see from Figure 9.11, a lot of quite different effects may be obtained.

Some Tips for Using Powerlines

It's usually easiest to use other tools to manipulate objects before applying Powerlines to them.

Choosing **None** from the Powerline roll-up menu will return the line to its original form.

Test an effect on a simple line before applying it to a complex object. Some of the effects will take precedence over others. The Nib, for example, will prevail over Speed settings.

If Ink Flow is below 100, you will run out of Powerline effect before the end of your line.

As with many actions in graphics, it's always a good idea to save frequently.

CONTOURS

Contours allow us to use one object to create an effect similar to a blend but using only one control object. Take a look at the snails shown in Figures 9.18 and 9.19. The one in the first figure was created using a traditional array of blends with two control objects; the second was produced using the Contour command. Blends offer more control, since you have two objects used to control the intermediate shapes, but contours can be quite effective for adding soft edges, shadows, or highlights in an illustration.

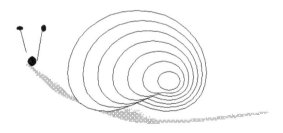

FIGURE 9.18 Snail and shell created using blends

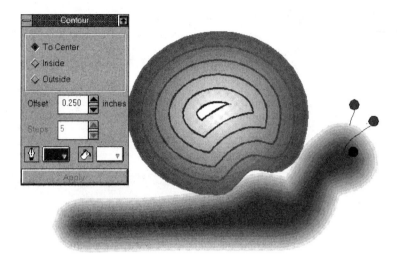

FIGURE 9.19 Snail and shell created using contours

Putting Contours to Work

So that you can get a better idea of how contours work and are applied, let's create another snail figure using this new effect. There are very few contour steps in the following screen shots to make them more obvious. You can smooth the effect, just as you can with blends by increasing the number of steps. Contours also offer three other controls based on the origin point of the contour. Keep in mind that the effect you see on your screen when working with contours and the effect that you get in your final printed version can vary, based on the different resolutions of the two devices.

Drawing the Snail Shell

We'll start our drawing of the shell by drawing a large ellipse and convert it to curves. Select the Shape tool, add a node to the bottom right of your ellipse, and form a slight depression at the bottom right, as shown in Figure 9.20. Fill it using a radial fountain fill that is darker toward the outside of the object, becoming lighter as it moves inward. Select the **Contours** roll-up from the **Effects** menu. Select **To Center** and enter 0.250

inches for the offset. Use the same fill color used for the dark fill color of your radial fill. Select 80 percent black for the line color. Adjust the width of the outline to 0.032 inches in the Outline Pen dialog box and **Apply** the settings. Your snail shell should look something like Figure 9.21.

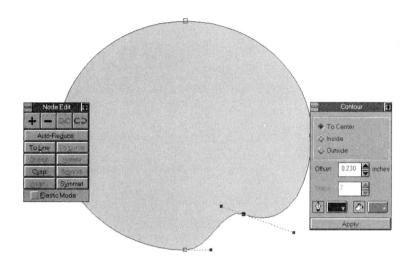

FIGURE 9.20 Shaping the snail's shell

FIGURE 9.21 Filled and contoured snail shell

As I mentioned earlier, there are three different ways to set contours. Notice the two snail shells in Figure 9.22. The one on the left was formed using To Center with an offset of 0.25 inches. If To Center is selected, the Steps option will be disabled, and the number of objects created will be determined, based on the value of the offset. The shell on the right shows the same object but with the contour set to Inside and an offset of 0.20 inches for five steps. As you can see, the narrower spacing for the second object resulted in a larger center object.

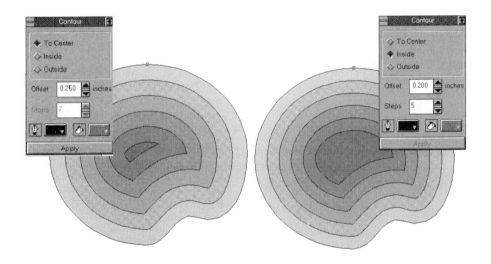

FIGURE 9.22 Comparing center contours with inside contours

Now let's form the snail's body. Draw a small ellipse (if you are feeling adventurous, try using a powerline to do it), and convert to curves. Select the Shape tool and adjust the object's path to resemble that shown in Figure 9.23. Make the body very slim, since we will be using an outside contour setting. Use the **Arrange** menu under Order to place the snail To Back. Press the space bar to activate the Pick tool and use the **Contour** roll-up to set Outside contour, a 0.050-inch Offset, and 10 Steps. Give the object no outline and a 60 percent black flat fill. Apply your settings. Your snail should look something like the one in Figure 9.13b.

Chapter 9: A Banquet of Possibilities: CorelDRAW's Advanced Drawing Tools

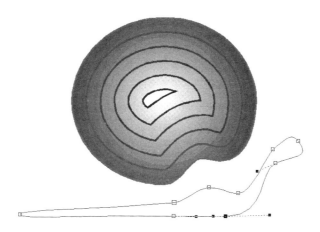

FIGURE 9.23 Shaping the snail's body

As mentioned at the beginning of this section, contours are in a sense an extension of the blend function of CorelDRAW.

THE WELDING WORKSHOP

Just as contour is a refinement of the blend function, welding is a variation of the Combine command. Combining is actually a grouping event, and when it's used CorelDRAW stores the selected objects as if they were a single object. The Weld function joins the outline paths at points of intersection and removes portions of an object's path that lie between intersecting points. Figure 9.24 points out the difference between using Combine and Weld commands. I drew three objects, a circle and two rectangles, and layered them in the appearance of a Celtic cross. I then duplicated them twice and combined one set and welded the other.

The results are shown in the center two objects in Figure 9.15. Although the pattern of the squares and triangles in the center of the combined object is interesting, it doesn't resemble the appearance of a Celtic cross very much. As you can see from the outline of the welded object on the far right of the illustration, the welded object only retained the outlined path of the three original elements.

Keep in mind that weld is a permanent transformation. Unlike grouping, in which you can use the Undo function, you cannot simply "un-weld" and pull the original elements out.

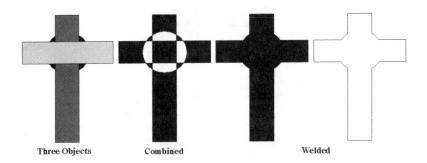

FIGURE 9.24 Results of welding shapes and lines

Welds can be a very quick way to create complex shapes and to simplify sections of a drawing. To use them effectively you must be able to visualize what your final object should look like. It is best to use a minimum number of objects as the basis of a weld, since it is easier to control the final result.

Order If You Please

You may have noticed that the welded object in Figure 9.24 assumed the black fill of the circle at the bottom of the stack of three objects used to create it. That's because CorelDRAW uses the attributes of the bottom-most object in the stack if you use a marquee select to define the objects in your weld. If you want to use a specific object to set the line and fill of your welded element, use another method to select the objects and choose one with the desired attributes last.

Let's try a simple experiment to see how this works. Objects to be welded must actually touch or overlap, unlike Combine, which allows you to "join" objects that are not physically connected. In CorelDRAW, touching is a relative term. You can actually weld objects that reside on different layers as long as those layers are active, so if you have four objects on two different layers, all overlapping one another visually, you can select and weld them into one object.

Draw a circle. Now draw a narrow triangle and place it so that it rests with one point away from the circle and the other two points within the circle's boundary. Use a blend, place duplicates, or use a similar technique to position additional triangles evenly around the boundary of your circle. Use the Pick tool and the palate at the bottom of the window to give each object a different-colored fill. Use the Pick tool to marquee-select all the shapes, and choose the Weld command from the Arrange menu. The result should look similar to that displayed in Figure 9.25.

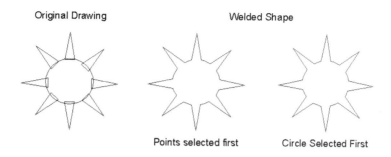

FIGURE 9.25 Welding irregular objects

Masking with Welds

Just as Combine can be used to make masks, so can welds, but the result will be a bit different. The U.S. flag that we made in an earlier chapter was very straightforward, involving one piece of clipart and some text. Welding with multiple objects and text is a bit more involved—at least in determining the results you will get. Use the Text tool to type the phrase "Welding Is a Handy Tool." Use the Rectangle tool to draw a box that covers your text; then draw two circles at either end. Select the box and two circles and send them to the back using the **Order** command in the **Arrange** menu. The results should look similar to the set of objects at the top of Figure 9.26. Marquee-select all the objects and weld them. The result should be similar to that shown in the figure's second group.

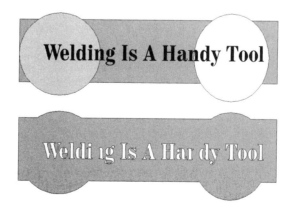

FIGURE 9.26 Creating masks with the Weld command

Take a close look at the text in our welded object in Figure 9.26. See how portions of the n in welding and the n in handy have been partially removed. This is because they touched the path of the circular objects. Notice that the portions of both ends that rested outside the circle remain after the intersections were removed. That's because the Weld function looked at the combined outlines of all elements within the selected objects. Welds offer much more control when making masks than combines, but they require more attention to detail and planning.

INTERSECTION AND TRIM EFFECTS

DRAW 5.0 has added two interesting tools to the Arrange menu, Intersection and Trim. These commands offer refinements on the Combine and Weld commands although in some cases the results may not appear any different. Lets go back to our Celtic Cross that we used to contrast Combine and Weld, shown in Figure 9.24, and see what happens when we use Intersention and Trim. As you can see from Figure 9.27, the Intersection command does not affect the original drawing at all, it creates a new element from the intersecting lines of the rectangles. You can see the newly created element moved to the side in Figure 9.27C. Since the circle was the last item created, the square takes its fill. If you select the elements separately, the new object will have the fill and other attributes of the last item selected.

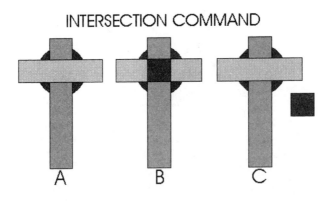

FIGURE 9.27 Effect of the Intersection Command

Chapter 9: A Banquet of Possibilities: CorelDRAW's Advanced Drawing Tools

The Trim command almost does the opposite of the Intersection command. Instead of creating a new object of the form it find in the intersections of the lines, it changes one or more of the selected objects so that they don't overlap. Figure 9.28, graphic A, shows the effect the Trim command had on the last object selected, in this case the circle. In B and C, you can see the different actions of this command depending upon the order in which the three elements were selected. The application of the inIntersection command causes the appearance of the selected objects to change as it superimposes a new object on them. When Trim is applied you rarely will be able to see the effects unless you separate the objects.

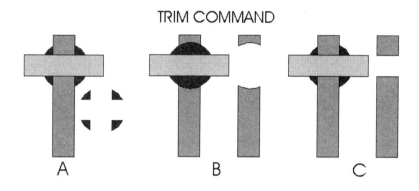

FIGURE 9.28 Effects of the Trim Command

Putting Intersection and Trim to Work

While you have probably already thought of a couple of uses for these commands, let's take a few minutes to experiment with these tools. Open the **Symbols** roll-up using the button with the star icon on the toolbar. From the Animals2 symbols, get the cat (#43) and place it on your page. Draw a circle somewhat bigger than the cat's head and place it so the lower left portion of the circle cuts neatly across the cat's neck, as I have done in Figure 9.29. Select both the cat and the circle, open the **Arrange** menu and click on the **Intersection** command. After a few moments, you will see control boxes around the cat's head. Drag the selected head to the side and you will have a cat, a circle, and a neatly decapitated head.

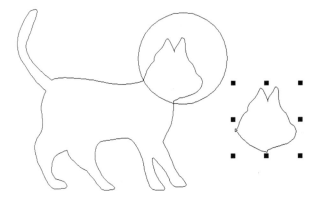

FIGURE 9.29 Using Intersection to create a new object

Now fill your circle with a color and place the separated head in the center of the circle. Select both objects and apply the **Trim** command. Figure 9.30 object created by Trim. The form of the cat's head has been neatly clipped out of the center of the circle. I have placed a fill and some text behind the trimmed circle to emphasize the effect.

FIGURE 9.30 Using Intersection and Trim to create a mask

TIP

The effects of Intersect, and particularly Trim, are initially less predictable when applied to multiple and/or complicated objects and some experimentation may be required to get exactly what you want. Remember that it is always a very good idea to make a duplicate of the graphics you are working on before applying these commands (as well as Weld and Combine). If you don't get what you want you won't have to attempt to reverse the effect, not always completely successful.

Trim and Intersection can also take a lot of time when applied to complicated forms. Work in wireframe view when using them and attempt to apply special effects and transformations to the finished object(s) rather than applying them before Trimming or Intersecting.

A Different Sort of Duplicate—the Clone Command

They are not exactly the same and it's important to know which one to use. The Clone commands make a duplicate of the selected object or objects. The original object becomes the Master object and when it is selected, you will see it so designated on the status line. (Notice the status line in Figure 9.31) However, the status line does not indicate it if you have selected a cloned object. However, if you click and hold the right mouse button on either, the Object menu will appear with a line at the bottom allowing you either to select the Master (if you've clicked on a clone) or select Clones (if you've clicked on a master object). Figure 9.31 shows the Object menu when a master or cloned object is selected.

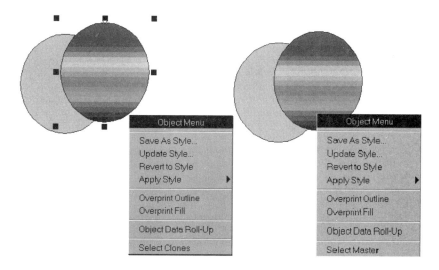

FIGURE 9.31 Selecting Master and Cloned Objects

The Master object and its clones are linked in a heirarchal manner. Any change you make in the master (subject to the command limitations detailed below) will also be made in all that master's clones. Changes in a clone will not take effect in the master or in any other of the clones. In fact, if you change an attribute in a clone, future changes made in the master, affecting that particular attribute, will not occur in that particular clone. For instance, if you change the fill of one clone, a change made later in the fill of the master will not affect that clone. It is important to remember this and to be sure that you have selected appropriately before making a change.

There are actually two Clone commands available in CorelDRAW 5.0; one in the Edit menu and one in the Effects menu. We'll start by examining the workings of the Clone command in the Edit menu. Using this command produces a duplicate of the select object(s) including all effects already applied to this object. Once the object is cloned, you can change certain of the attributes in the master object and effect identicle changes in its clones, This particular command will reproduce changes in Fill, Outline, Envelope and Perspective. Although you can use this command to clone objects to which any or all of the other effects (Extrude, Blend, etc.) have been applied, making changes in these effects in the master object will not affect the clones.

To understand these commands, let's try them out. Create an ellipse, fill it, and, with the circle selected, click on the **Clone** command in the Edit menu. You'll have a duplicate of the object placed where you have chosen in the Preferences dialog box (in the Special menu). Move the clone out beside the master object, and, with the master object selected, change the fill. The fill on the clone will change to match. Open the **Envelope** roll-up and apply an unconstrained envelope to the master object, now change that envelope and click on **Apply**. Your cloned object will change as mine has done in A in Figure 9.32. Rotate the master object and apply perspective as I have done in Figure 9.32C. The clone changes also.

Draw another ellipse and apply one of the effects in the Extrude menu. Figure 32C shows the Radial effect applied to the master object which I then cloned. The extrusion as well as the fill are seen in the clone. To duplicate the objects in Figure 9.32D, draw another ellipse, clone it and then apply the **Sunset** effect to the master object. You will see that the extrusion only takes place in the master object while the fill is duplicated in the clone. In fact, if you change the extrusion effect on the master object in Figure 9.32C, the extrusion will disappear from the cloned object although the fill will change to match any new fill you've placed on the master.

Chapter 9: A Banquet of Possibilities: CorelDRAW's Advanced Drawing Tools

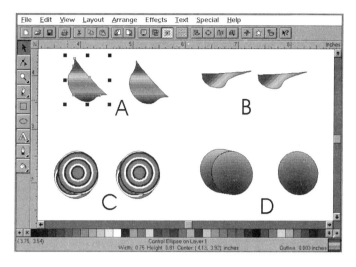

FIGURE 9.32 Changing clones with the Edit—Clone Command

The Second Clone

Think of the Clone command in the Effects menu as working backwards compared to the Clone command in the Edit menu. Let's experiment with this form of the command. Create several objects and apply effects to each as I have done in Figure 9.33. I have applied an extrusion effect to the text, taking care to set the vanishing point to the Locked to Page option. Remember that cloned objects will share a single vanishing point. If the point is locked to the object and then cloned, the results can be unsatisfactory. I applied a blend to the circle and rectangle. Now create a set of similar shapes.

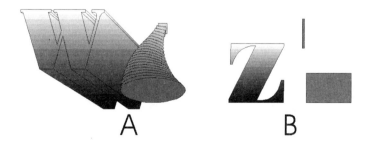

FIGURE 9.33 Setting up the exercise

Select a the two shapes to be cloned to the blend in A, and click on **Clone** in the Effects menu. A small fly-out, similar to the one in Figure 9.34 will appear. You'll probably note that some of the selections are available and some are not. In the figure, since I have selected two objects, Blend is the only appropriate clone available. When you have clicked on the appropriate alternative, your pointer will change to a heavy arrow. Click with this arrow on the object whose effects you wish to copy. The selected object will become a special clone of the master object you have clicked on and its effects will change in accordance with the effects applied to the selected master object. Figure 9.35 demonstrates this type of cloning.

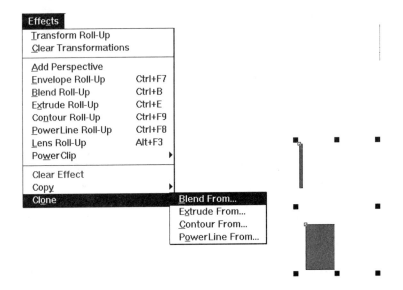

FIGURE 9.34 Applying the Effects menu Clone command

FIGURE 9.35 Results of applying the Effects menu Clone command

Chapter 9: A Banquet of Possibilities: CorelDRAW's Advanced Drawing Tools

Cloning Clones

Although you can't actually select a clone created with the Edit-Clone command, clones created under this command may then be clone linked in either direction with the Effects-Clone command. When you applied the Effects menu Clone command to your objects, you probably got extruded, blended etc. objects with the same old fills the original objects had. The Effects menu Clone command does not transmit fills, lines, perspective or envelopes. That's what the other clone command does. If the objects were originally created with the Edit-Clone command, you can change the fills, etc. of the whole group using those links, while working with the special Effects added through the Effects-Clone command.

Let's spend a few minutes on an exercise further exploring these two commands. With the Artistic Text tool type the letter "C" and, from the text roll-up set it in Britanic Bold or similar typeface. Apply the Trumpet 3 PowerLine to this letter and give it a fill. Draw a small rectangle next to the C and give it a fill also. Select both objects and clone them. After placing the cloned object in an appropriate place, select both master objects again and clone them again. Line up the master objects with the two clones extending to the right. Select the box of the second cloned set you created and give it a simple extrusion, being sure to choose the **Vanishing Point Locked to Page** option. Now select the master box, open the **Effects** menu, click on **Clone**, and on **Extrusion**. When the heavy arrow appears, choose the extruded box in the second clone. The master box will be extruded. With the master box still selected, apply a conical fill. All three boxes will receive this fill, but the box in the first clone set will not be extruded. Select the C in the first cloned set and change to a radial fill. Only this particular C will be affected by the command. You can check your results with mine in Figure 9.36. Now select the C in the master set and change it's fill to a verticle fountain fill. The radial fill you placed in the first clone will be changed as well as the fill in the second clone.

FIGURE 9.36 Using Both Clone Commands

Some things to remember when working with clones

- When you delete a master object, all its clones are deleted.
- Edit-Clone must be used if you want to make a copy of an object to which you have applied extrusions and certain other operations from the Effects menu. Duplicate may only make a copy of the original object.
- Extrusions Cloned from the Effects menu share vanishing points.
- You can't further clone an object that is itself a clone.
- When trying to select an object from which to Clone an effect, you have to select the original shape on which an extrude or other effect was based. This can sometimes be difficult to find.

FOCUSING THE LENS

CorelDRAW 5.0 has added two very powerful new tools, the Lens and the PowerClip. Both are found on the Effects menu. Let's learn about the Lens tool by putting it to use. First set your preferences and screen to match mine: Set place duplicate to 2 inches horizontal and 0 inches verticle. Remove the rulers and the pallette. Open the **Lens** roll-up from the Effects menu. Draw a few simple shapes, as I have done in Figure 9.37 and experiment with the various lens' Corel has provided.

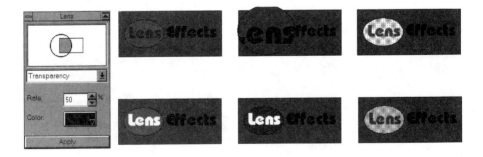

FIGURE 9.37 The Lens effects

Compared to some of Corel 5.0's tools and effects, the Lens is easy to use and understand, so lets put it to work.

Chapter 9: A Banquet of Possibilities: CorelDRAW's Advanced Drawing Tools

BEHIND THE 8-BALL—EXERCISE # 1

With the Ellipse tool, draw a perfect circle using the **Control** key to constrain it. Give it a radial fountain fill editing the fill to give it a 10% offset each way and an edge pad of 10. Your circle should look like mine over the A in Figure 9.38. I have used few steps in my fountain fill so it can be seen in the figure, you'll want to increase the steps.

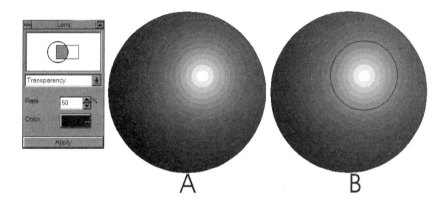

FIGURE 9.38 The filled circle and the circle of light

Picture this circle with a strong purple light shining on it. Let's use the lens tools to create this appearance. Draw a circle about the size of the patch of light that would hit the circle and place it over the lighter portion of the large circle. It should just about cover the lighter portion of the fountain fill like mine in the B portion of Figure 9.38. Select the small circle and apply the **Transparancy Lens** effect at a 50% rate and make the color purple, for the purple light. Choose **Apply** and a light circle will appear on your 8-ball. Adding the number is easy; using the Artistic Text tool, type an "8" in the smaller circle. Change to the select tool and size it appropriately and give it a purple fill. Click again on the 8 to get the rotation handles and rotate it until it looks right. While the 8 is still selected, duplicate it, give it a black fill and, using the Arrange menu, Order flyout, send it back one. Position it just behind the purple 8 to make a shadow. You can create a few reflection spots in white or grey and place them around the 8. I also drew a small black ellipse to make the shadow below the ball.

FIGURE 9.39 The Completed 8-Ball

Exercise # 2—Three Ways to Use the Power of PowerClip

The last new too`l found in version 5.0 is PowerClip, a seemingly simple command on the Effects menu. Let's start with the obvious to get our feet wet. Have you ever tried to place a line across a circle? The ends of the lines don't have the curvature of the circle. It's very difficult to do without the ease of powerclip. Let's do it now using the powerclip feature. Draw a circle. Draw in a few lines that go beyond the edges of the circle. Now group the lines. With the lines selected, open the Effects menu and click on PowerClip. A fly-out menu, shown in Figure 9.40 will appear. Choose Place inside container and, when the arrow appears, choose the circle. The lines will end precisely at the edges of the circle as shown in Figure 9.41.

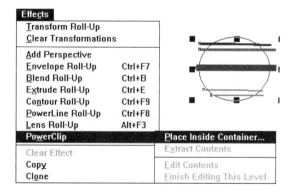

FIGURE 9.40 The PowerClip Fly-out

Chapter 9: A Banquet of Possibilities: CorelDRAW's Advanced Drawing Tools

FIGURE 9.41 Lines Power Clipped to the circle

Now that we've got the feel of it, let's do something a little bit more complicated. First draw an oval with the ellipse tool, open the fill roll-up and give it a radial fountain fill shading from black to white with the center offset far to the lower left. From the Symbols rollup, select a drawing, I used #59 from Aimals 2 Size it down appropriately and with the cat selected, open the Effects menu and click on PowerClip and then on Place inside container on the fly-out menu. The cat will appear inside the circle as you see in Figure 9.42.

FIGURE 9.42 Placing the Cat in the container.

So far it doesn't look like we've accomplished much. Let's continue by selecting the object made up of the cat and circle, click on the **Effects** menu, and on **PowerClip**. This time, click on the **Edit Contents** option as shown in Figure 9.43. The fill in the circle will disappear, the circle will become a light blue line, and the cat can be moved at will. Move the cat so that his rear legs and a little bit of his tail are outside the container. Then open the **Effects** menu again, click on **PowerClip**, and select the last option, **Finish Editing on This Level**. Your result should resemble mine seen in Figure 9.44 with the cat appearing to leap out of the circle. If we had made two circles, combined them to make a ring, extruded it, shaded it appropriately, our cat would appear to be jumping through a hoop.

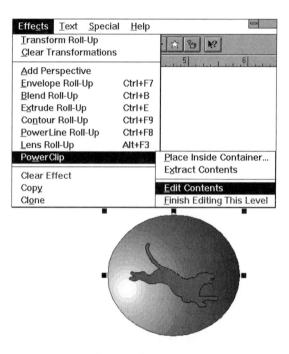

FIGURE 9.43 Editing the Contents of a Container

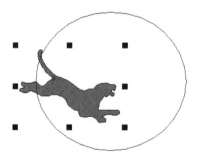

FIGURE 9.44 Changing the position of the object

Chapter 9: A Banquet of Possibilities: CorelDRAW's Advanced Drawing Tools

FIGURE 9.45 The Completed leaping cat

There are many other effects we can accomplish using PowerClip, in conjunction with the other tools and effects 5.0 gives us. To give you an idea of how far some artists have taken it, Figure 9.46 shows the results of work with this. A combination of trimming, PowerClip, welding, and other of CorelDRAW's facilities were used to create this drawing.

FIGURE 9.46 Where are we going...

Keeping Track with the Object Data Manager

At first glance it would seem that a graphics program, such as CorelDRAW, and a spreadsheet, such as Microsoft Excel or Lotus for Windows, would have little in common. However, some spreadsheet functions can be used to organize and track information about objects within a drawing. With the introduction of CorelDRAW 4.0, the developers includ an Object Data Manager. This submodule offers some of the number-crunching capability of a spreadsheet along with some of the information-tracking capabilities of a data base.

If all you ever create is single-page flyers or simple drawings, this feature may not seem very useful. If, on the other hand, you are a technical illustrator, someone producing catalogs, or anyone else involved in maintaining records related to the objects you draw, you may soon start to wonder how you ever got along without it. In fact, not only can you use the data manager to maintain remote information about objects (e.g., price, size, or weight), but you can use it as a tool for jotting down notes about how you created the object. The following paragraphs will familiarize you with how the Data Manager is used, and we will employ it in the following exercise. To use this feature effectively requires planning. You must have a clear idea of what information you wish to track and how it is to be organized. If you just create fields in a random order, you won't be able to summarize data meaningfully. A few simple guidelines can help you in planning your data base.

- Before you open up the Data Manager, list the objects you need to track. As you add new elements to a drawing you can modify this list. You might even want to create a data manager set containing this master list for easy reference.
- Next to each object on your list note the attributes concerning that object that you want to track. For example, you might want to list an object's weight, price, part number, and model number for a catalog. These are the fields for a given object.
- Once you have completed the preceding two steps, try to simplify your list by grouping categories of objects. In data base design there is a process called normalization. This is basically a series of steps designed to make sure your groups are neither too large nor too small. If you lump too many things into one category, it will be difficult to sort out individual information. If you make too many categories, it will become unwieldy.
- It's best to start small when working with data management to get a feel of how it will work best for you. Don't be afraid to modify as you go along. Although there may be certain things that are very easy to define that must be tracked, how they are organized is as much an art as a science.

Chapter 9: A Banquet of Possibilities: CorelDRAW's Advanced Drawing Tools

The Object Data Manager is accessed using a pop-up menu. If you have set your preferences so that the right mouse button controls the Object menu, all you have to do to open it is select an object and click the right mouse button. The menu will remain until you make a selection. If you use the right mouse button for another purpose, you can still use it to access the menu by holding the right mouse button until the menu appears.

When you click the right mouse button on an object in CorelDRAW, the Object menu will appear. You should already be familiar with it from our exercises in Chapter 6, when we worked with Styles. Select the **Data** roll-up from this menu; the window shown in Figure 9.47 should appear.

To get a better idea of how the Data Manager works let's use it to define an element. Either select an element from an existing drawing or draw a simple object and select it. Click or hold the right mouse button to get the Object menu and select the **Data** roll-up. The roll-up is an easy way to view information that has been entered about an object.

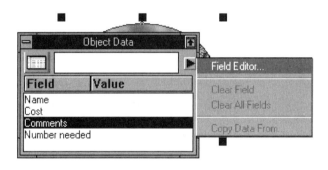

FIGURE 9.47 The Object Data roll-up

In the preceding illustration you will see listings in the lower window, such as Name, Cost, and Comments. Just like fields in a data base or column headings in a spreadsheet, a field indicates a class or attribute that we wish to track. The value is specific to the object you have selected. For instance, you might have a field titled Price. The value is specific to an individual object within the drawing. In a house plan you might have several different categories of lumber—2 x 4s, 2 x 6s, and so on—so you might have each category as a field with different prices for each one.

CorelDRAW! also lets us nest categories, so you might also organize your data as lumber for a major category and then the different sizes of wood that you work with. Arranging data in this way allows us to get a total price for a category based on the sum of individual prices and number of objects.

The Data Manager roll-up provides access to all the program's data-related functions and dialog boxes.

The icon button just below the title bar on the left opens the Object Data Manager. This is a spreadsheet-like interface for entering and working with several values at once or many different objects at the same time.

Next to that is the Edit Field window. This lets you quickly enter a value for the currently selected field related to the currently selected object. To enter a value, select the object, click on the desired field, click in the **Entry** box, and type. You can use the tab select method to shift quickly between objects in a drawing if there aren't too many of them.

You can increase the size of the list box as you would resize any window by dragging on a corner or side with the mouse.

The list box below that displays all fields for the drawing and their associated values for the currently selected object.

The arrow at the upper right of the object Data window opens a fly-out menu that offers several options, including the Field Editor, which is used to create new fields and edit their attributes. You can also clear a specific field or fields or copy data from one object's set to another.

Let's create some fields for our sample object. Open up the **Field Editor** shown on the left in Figure 9.48 Choose the **Create New Field** bar. You'll notice that Field0 has now appeared both in the text entry box and in the list of fields in the Field Editor. Let's call our first field Type. Just type the word and hit **Enter**. You'll notice that we had the option to add newly created fields to the list of default fields as well as all objects. Removing both means it will apply only to the currently selected object.

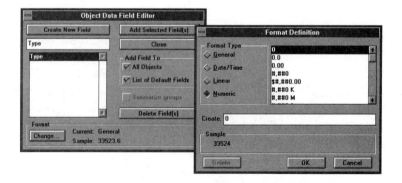

FIGURE 9.48 The Object Data field editor

Chapter 9: A Banquet of Possibilities: CorelDRAW's Advanced Drawing Tools

Click **Create New Field** again and add another one called Width. Now click on the **Change** button under Format at the bottom of the Field Editor. Another dialog box similar to the one on the right in Figure 9.48 will open.

Databases and spreadsheets do not handle all entries the same. Numbers, text, and dates can be manipulated in different ways, depending on the features of the program. For example, you can't add two text blocks together, but you might want to add, subtract, or average numeric fields. It could also be useful to calculate the time interval between two dates or limit some activity based on a date or time. Although CorelDRAW's Object Data Manager may not offer all the sophisticated functions, it does allow you to set formats and to perform some basic numeric and date functions. To do this we have to set the format of the field properly when it is created. If you don't plan to do any advanced functions on a field's values, it's fine just to leave it as general.

Let's set Width to points and picas. You'll notice that there are four different categories under format type; date, time, and numeric are just what they seem: calendar references and number formats. Linear lets us set a number of different units of measure: miles, kilometers, fractions of an inch. In this case, choose Linear and then choose points and picas from the selection window on the right of the bar.

The General format allows you to define your own variations. If you want more specific instructions on options under General format, check with CorelDRAW's on-line help for examples of the available options. Now add one more field, called Date, and give it a month/day/year format. Create three separate lines of artistic text: one saying "this is line one", one saying "this is line two," and one saying "this is line three". Make it about a half inch tall (or about a 40-point typeface). You'll notice that our three new fields have been entered in the list box in the roll-up. Select line one. The Type field should already be highlighted; if it isn't, select it with the mouse. Type line one. Click on Width and enter 45.1. Hit **Enter**.

You'll notice that the value in the list box now shows 3 picas, 9 points. The program automatically converted your points into the appropriate points and picas. Now enter a date value the same way—for instance, 3/2/93. Select line two. Give it "line two" for type; give it 44 for width; hit Enter; and give it a date of 3/7/81. Choose line three and open the fly-out by clicking on the arrow at the right of the Data Entry box. Choose **Copy Data From**. Your cursor will change to an arrow. Place it on the text on line one and click once. All the values will automatically be copied from the earlier object.

Clone line three using the command in the Edit menu. You'll notice that the values have once again been copied. Press **Ctrl-D**; a duplicate rather than a clone is created, and once again we can see that the data values have been copied. Marquee-select all five lines and click on the **Object Data Manager** button. Your screen should resemble that in Figure 19.49.

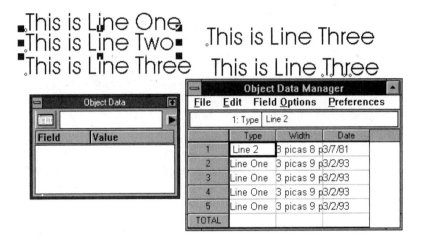

FIGURE 9.49 The Object Data Manager window

The new window that has opened on the screen shows all the objects. Had we only selected one or two, those would have been the only values that showed up. You'll notice that our field names appear on the bar at the top of each column and that the currently selected field and value appear in the boxes just above the column titles.

Adjusting the Appearance of the Data Manager

Look closely at the column value for width. You can see that part of the information is actually cut off. Place your cursor on the right edge of the width column header. The mouse pointer will change to a two-headed arrow. Drag it about half an inch to the right. When you release it the width of the column will be enlarged. You can reduce width by pulling in the opposite direction.

This interface is actually a mini-spreadsheet. You can copy data in and out from other Windows spreadsheets such as Excel or Lotus. Although the Data Manager may never become the weapon of choice for the nation's CPAs, it is a nice enhancement to CorelDRAW's tools for managing your drawings.

From the File menu you can print your document and control what will show up in the output. The Edit menu provides Cut, Copy, and Paste commands as well as Undo capabilities. Field options allow you to change the format of the currently selected value(s), summarize groups, show totals and hierarchies, and provide access to the Field

Editor. Preferences allow you to modify the levels of groups shown and customize what is displayed.

The bit of practice we have just had should enable you to navigate within the Data Manager. The following exercise will make you a little more familiar with it. It is beyond the scope of this book to cover all the different features or possible applications of the Data Manager, but you are probably now aware of how this new program feature can enhance your use of the program.

EXERCISE—PLANNING AN HERB GARDEN

If you flip through the pages of the Corel Art Show volumes, you'll see page after page of dramatic drawings and dynamic illustrations. You'll also see some technical work, exploded diagrams, and precise designs of instruments and machines. With its new features, CorelDRAW is becoming more capable in the technical illustration arena; the new features also make it more suitable for such projects as house plans and architectural sketches. Although some of these features are expected to be improved in version 5.0 (e.g., dimensioning), I decided to include in this edition an exercise to help you get more familiar with how these kinds of projects can be handled.

A traditional herb garden involves a good bit of planning, care, and maintenance. The planning comes in making sure that the right flowers, shrubs, and medicinal plants are arranged in a visually appealing manner that is also functional. During the course of the seasons and over the years different embers of the botanical community will be planted, harvested, and replaced.

CorelDRAW can be used not only to sketch out the design but to help plan the landscape, experiment with plant placement, and through the Data Manager calculate areas and costs as well as note planting and harvest times, note total areas for a given type of crop, and even calculate the yield. Although the following exercise may not be quite that thorough, it will serve to show you how to use the tools presented in this chapter.

Setting Up the Work Space

Before beginning, let's be sure we all have the same working environment. If you have anything on the screen, choose **New** from the File menu and set the page orientation to **Landscape**. In the Display menu turn the rulers on and set the right mouse button (in Preferences under the Special menu). Set the nudge to 0.01 inches and set the mouse right button to open the Object menu. In the Layout menu, open **Grid Scale** and **Setup**. Click on the **Use Drawing Scale** box, and open the drop-down menu showing Typical Scales and select the 1/2" to 1' scale. To make working with the rulers easier, change the world measure window from 24.0 inches to 2.0 feet. Your dialog box will look like Figure 9.50.

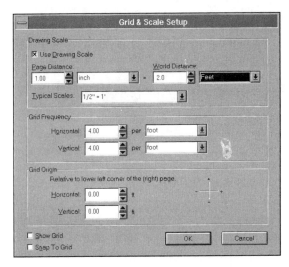

FIGURE 9.50 Setting the Scale

Welding the Paths

We are going to create a classic circle garden for this exercise. These have been popular in England for hundreds of years and have recently become fairly popular in this country. They not only provide a lovely addition to the landscape, but also give an almost constant supply of fresh flowers and useful herbs.

Let's start by pulling vertical and horizontal guidelines every two feet. These will be used to mark the edges and center of the herb garden.

Draw a circle about 12 feet in diameter. Use the Ctrl key and drag it out from the center of the guidelines. Now press **Ctrl-D** to duplicate this circle and move it off the page. We won't be using the first circle for a bit, but we will use it to set the basic pattern of the garden, and all the sizing must refer back to it.

Now make a 20-degree pie shape. This isn't too difficult if you remember to keep the left mouse key held down and watch the degree numbers in the status line while drawing. Remember that we make wedge shapes by electing the Node Edit tool, and moving the arrow inside the outline of the circle. Move the wedge to the vertical guideline marking the circle's center and rotate the wedge until it is centered over this line. Keep an eye on the center point for the rotation. Throughout your work with the wedges the rotation point must be kept at the center of your circle. Let's add dimension lines to this portion of our drawing. First we must change our Grid setup because the drawing scale selection, while changing the rulers to the scale we are using, thus saving us from doing conversions in our heads, does not provide measurement figures to the dimensioning tools. Deslect the Drawing scale check box, but leave the 1" to 2' filled in. Now select the horizontal scale tool from the Pencil flyout and move your pointer to the upper left corner of the pie shape. Click and hold the left mouse button and move the pointer to the upper right corner and double click. A line will appear from one corner to the other and there will be short verticle lines moving with your mouse. Move the pointer up above the rim of the pie shape and click. A dimension line like the one in Figure 9.51 will appear. Figure 19.52 shows the basic design toward which we are working. The wedges are going to be the paths through the four major divisions of our garden.

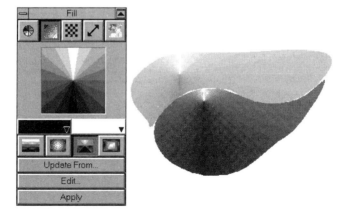

FIGURE 9.51 Adding dimensioning to our garden

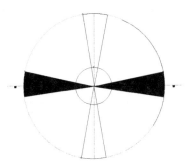

FIGURE 9.52 The four radial paths and the inner circle

Select the wedge and choose **Mirror** from the Effects menu. Pick **Mirror Vertical**, making sure the **Leave Original** box is checked. Click **OK**; a second wedge will appear in the lower half of the circle. Select the upper wedge again and rotate the wedge 90 degrees, again leaving the original. During this exercise feel free to use alternate methods to accomplish these tasks.

Select the Ellipse tool, placing the cross hairs over the guidelines at the center. Press the **Ctrl** and **Alt** keys and draw a small circle 3 inches in diameter. It should be directly in the center of the drawing and look like Figure 9.52. I've filled the wedges to make them show up a bit better in the figure.

Now for a little garden magic. Select your four wedges and the small inner circle and **Weld** them. Now we have a single cross-shaped object. These will be the walkways and centerpiece for our finished garden. It should now look similar to the example shown in Figure 9.53.

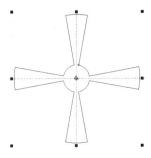

FIGURE 9.53 The garden paths and inner circle

Landscaping the Paths

Draw a small circle inside the object you just welded and fill it with a green. You can vary the season by choosing a lighter green or a darker one. This is where we can later put a sundial. Now fill the original circle, which will be the base for our herb garden green.

To complete our garden we need a circular path all the way around it. Duplicate the basic circle representing the herb garden and move this duplicated circle off the page. Duplicate it again and enlarge the duplicate to about half an inch larger all around. Use **Ctrl-A** and align the centers of both circles. **Weld** them and use **Align** again to place them at the center of the page.

Select the original circle. Order it to the back of your drawing. Select both the radiating paths and the ring-shaped outer path and make sure they have no outline. Use a Diorite Textured fill and give it a yellow and brown coloring similar to wood chips. The basic plan of your herb garden is complete and should look something like Figure 9.54.

FIGURE 9.54 The basic herb garden

Managing Our Crops

We're going to use CorelDRAW's Data Manager to keep track of the cost of our herb garden. Use the right mouse button to click on the radial and choose the **Data** roll-up from the Object menu. Click on the fly-out arrow and open the **Field Editor**. Click on the options to add fields to all objects and to turn the add to default list. Use the **Create New Field** button to add fields titled Name, Cost, Quantity, and Comments.

Highlight the field called Cost; change the format to numerical with a decimal point and close the dialog box.

Adding Values

Select the paths in your drawing and type bark in the Name field. Type $1.59 in the Cost field and 26 bags in the Quantity field. Be careful to press the **Enter** key after typing information in a field. If you fail to do that your entry may be lost. In the Comments field type, see about getting a truck-load.

Click on the spreadsheet icon in the upper left of the Object Data window. The Object Data Manager will open and you will see your entry placed in columns in this window. The Data Manager shows only those objects that have been selected in the drawing. We'll be returning to the Object Data functions as we add the sundial and plants to our garden.

Keeping Track of Time

What would a traditional herb garden be without a sundial? Start by drawing a circle; then place a wedge shape on it. An easy way to make the wedge is to draw a small rectangle, convert it to curves, and use the Shape tool to take out one node that will change it to a triangle. Place this triangle in your circle like the gnomon of a sundial, then duplicate it. Add a fountain fill to the duplicate and place it as the shadow. Group your sundial and place it in the center of your garden.

Planting Our Garden

Now that the basic garden is completed with paths, grass, and sundial, it's time to add some plants. We'll begin by adding about 12 Rose Geranium plants in the small circle around the sundial.

The Layers Roll-up

Layers provide a convenient way of separating the different plants that go into the herb garden, so let's place each type of plant on a different layer. This not only eases editing

Chapter 9: A Banquet of Possibilities: CorelDRAW's Advanced Drawing Tools   **403**

a complex drawing, but provides a convenient way to print or examine one particular portion of it. For example, we can print out just this layer with the geraniums on it to take with us when we do the planting.

Place the Text tool in Symbol mode and choose the Plants collection. Open the **Layers** roll-up from the Layout menu and click on the arrow at the top right to see the fly-out menu. Select **New** from that menu and accept all the defaults. Now all your Rose Geranium plants will be on Layer 2.

Planting Geraniums

Use the drag and drop method to bring in #86 (or other plant shape of your own choosing) and place it at the rim of the small inside circle. Click the right mouse button to bring up the Object menu and select the **Object Data** roll-up. Enter Rose Geranium in the name field, .89 in the Cost field, 12 in the Number field. Remember to hit the **Enter** key after the last entry.

With your first plant selected, use **Ctrl-D** to make a duplicate. Place the duplicate along the edge of the circle. Look at your **Data** roll-up. It has the name and price of the new plant already entered; the entry was duplicated with the image. Be aware that if you change the price or anything else in Object Data, your duplicated (or cloned) objects will not be updated. Each one will need to be updated separately. The center of your herb garden should look similar to the one shown in Figure 9.55.

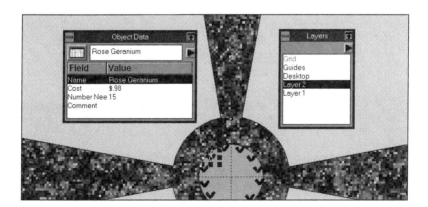

FIGURE 9.55 Plants and data for the herb garden

Continue duplicating the plants and place twelve of them evenly around the circle. When they are all placed, use **Shift**-click to select them all and to group them. Next, click on the spreadsheet icon in the Data roll-up. You should see all twelve of your plants entered on the spreadsheet with a subtotal showing the cost. If the subtotal doesn't show, click on **Summarize Groups** in the Field Options menu.

Now add the rest of the plants to your herb garden. Put each variety of plant on a separate layer. Be sure you enter data on the name and cost of each plant before duplicating. We used the following plants; feel free to use any that you wish. Add the following plants:

Name of Plant	Cost	Number Needed
Dusty miller	0.59	32
Chamomile	0.79	40
Sage	1.98	3
Bay tree	27.45	1
Rosemary	7.89	1
Lovage	4.98	1

If you want to use the same plants we did and use a fairly traditional design, complete the rest of the steps in this paragraph. Place the chamomile along the edges of the radial paths. They will grow low to the ground and edge the paths. The dusty miller has a pleasant, white-frosted look; use it to fill the corners on the inner edge of the four wedge-shaped beds and to edge the outside curves of these beds. The sage, rosemary, bay tree, and lovage are used to fill the smaller ends of the beds. Of course, to complete the herb garden a number of other plants, including parsley and thyme, will be needed. For this project I left the rest of the arrangement to you. My garden is shown in Figure 9.56.

A Comfortable Place in the Sun

Although there is a lot of work that can be done in an herb garden, it's also nice to just sit ad observe it. Start with a very simple bench (seen from above). Draw a rectangle and, using the Node tool, without converting the rectangle to curves, move one corner node

Chapter 9: A Banquet of Possibilities: CorelDRAW's Advanced Drawing Tools   **405**

slightly to round all four corners. Open the Envelope roll-up and curve the bench gently as you see in Figure 9.56. Now let's clone this bench so that if we decide to repaint, we can change all of them at the same time. Make four clones. Since we want to sit facing into our garden, place the master bench at the top of your garden then rotate each clone +90, 180, and -90 Degrees so each will be facing inwards. Select the master bench and giive it the wavy two-color fill that resembles wood grain and color it to suit yourself.

FIGURE 9.56 The completed herb garden

Chapter Summary

CorelDRAW lets us do a do a much better job than most of us could do with pencil and paper. Not only does it make it easier to create perfect circles and precise arcs, but it lets us interactively inventory and cost a project like this. As you can see from the preceding exercise and the features introduced in this chapter, CorelDRAW 5.0 is a much more robust graphic environment than its predecessors. Although it still has some quirks, we can expect to see additional enhancements to dimensioning and data management in the next release.

CHAPTER 10
VENTURA

- The CorelVENTURA Interface
- Exercise 1—Creating a simple publication
- Using Frames
- Tags, Styles, and Templates
- The Multi-File approach
- Publications, Chapters, Files, and Frames

THE DESKTOP REVOLUTION

Gone are the days when you would turn up at a print shop with a handful of manuscript, possibly typed, possibly not, and hand the entire newsletter, pamphlet, or book over to him. Desktop Publishing has given full control over the appearance of the end product to anyone with access to almost any sort of computer. Most of the printed material you see these days was produced on a PC or a MAC no more powerful than your own. A myriad of publishing programs are available from $15 shareware applications to those costing over $1,000 per copy. Ventura Publisher was early on the scene with outstanding capabilities and its own approach to organization. CorelVENTURA 5.0, fully updated and reorganized brings Corel's roll-up menu simplicity to the complexities of layout, indexing, cross-referencing, and all the other tasks a modern desktop publishing application must provide for the serious user.

WHAT IS A DESKTOP PUBLISHING APPLICATION?

Desktop Publishing, What and Why

To begin at the beginning, a desktop publishing program is an application tailored to receive text and graphics from word processors, paint, and draw applications and organize these elements into a finished printed page. While a DTP (DeskTop Publisher) is not a word processor, all but a few older or very inexpensive applications offer text entry and editing facilities, as well as spellers, search and replace, and thesaurus facilities. DTP's aren't graphics programs either, but most offer at least minimal drawing tools for the creation of boxes, lines, etc. A good DTP must be able to read text files from a large variety of word processors and graphics files in many formats. It must keep track of the files used to put together the finished publication, and it needs to be able to override any formatting the text has received before being imported, to conform with the overall look of the publication being produced.

Most important of all, a usable DTP must have good WYSIWYG (Anacronym of What You See Is What You Get). You must be able to see on the computer screen exactly what the printed page will show. And, with all these requirements, a good DTP application must manage all these things quickly, neatly, and without requiring a long learning time, or unreasonable concentration.

CorelVENTURA is organized to anticipate your needs. From the Quick Format roll-up to the Character Set roll-up, you can place those functions, and only those functions, that you will be needing right at your pointer-tip. Functions you don't expect to need won't clutter up your screen, but are quickly available when needed.

The VENTURA Desktop

Ventura provides many specialized tools and functions to aid in the production of long, complicated, and elaborate documents as well as providing basic typesetting for routine document production. It's impossible for me to go into all the possibilities of CorelVENTURA in this book, devoted primarily to DRAW. I will introduce the basic interface with brief descriptions of the various tools and menu items and then give you a couple exercises to help you begin to appreciate the scope of VENTURA's abilities.

The VENTURA 5.0 desktop, shown with a few of the roll-ups in Figure 10.1, is both like and unlike that of other Corel applications. The tool bar is very familiar although the text tool is clearly different. The text ribbon bar, below the menu bar and the button bar, shows other details than font, size, and style (or tag) although it works just like just about any other text ribbon. Let's check out the tools, buttons, ribbons, and menu's first to get oriented and then we'll put together a short publication to put our new knowledge to work.

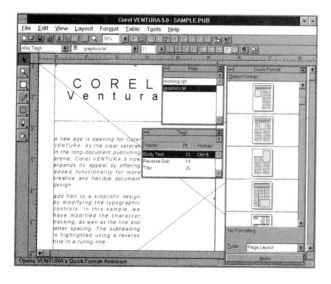

FIGURE 10.1 The CorelVENTURA Interface

At the top of the workspace appears the name of the application along with the name of the file currently open. At the bottom left, if you have selected something, will appear information abut the item selected and will indicate the presence of such things as frame anchors and cross references. At the right corner, you may see CAP, NUM, or SCRL indicating that you have the Caps-Lock, Num-Lock, or Scroll-Lock keys on. You will also see the number of the current page and an R or L indicating if it's a right-hand or left-hand page in a two-sided publication. Small arrows allow you to move backwards and forwards in the file.

The Toolbox

The VENTURA toolbox, Figure 10.2, will be very familiar to users of other Corel applications. The first tool, the Pick tool, is the familiar left-pointing arrow. It works just as expected as well as does the second tool, the magnifying glass. With this tool, with its fly-out, you can choose from a variety of preset views or use the glass with the "+" to define the area you wish to fill the screen. Click and hold on the arrow at the lower right corner of this button to see the options accessed on this tools flyout. New ones include one which sizes the page so that the area between the left edge and the right edge of the defined page both show on the screen. The last view on this fly-out will size the page so that it shows from top to bottom of the page.

FIGURE 10.2 The ToolBox

The next tool looks familiar if not quite the same as other Corel tools, however, this is the Frame tool and it's abilities are particularly important in desktop use. This tool allows you to add frames in which to place your text and graphics. On the Frame tool's fly-out you will find the Node tool we've used so much in DRAW. Fourth down on the Toolbar is the changed Text tool. This tool has two forms, accessed through its fly-out, one is the Freeform Text tool which allows you to make changes to individual words, characters, or paragraphs without affecting any others. The other face is the Tagged Text tool which allows you to add or edit text in a frame, or to format tagged paragraphs by overriding the tags. This formatting would be applied to all paragraphs bearing the changed tag.

The last three tools look and behave just like their counterparts in CorelDRAW. First is the Shape drawing tool, with a flyout that includes rectangle, rounded rectangle, ellipse, and line drawing tools. It also includes a new tool which creates a shadow box around the text you type into a frame. The Pen and Fill tools each have flyouts which are identicle to those of CorelDRAW. If you haven't practiced with the use of these tools in earlier chapters, please refer to those descriptions before continuing with this chapter. Like the tool bars in the other Corel applications, this can float or not and be visible or not. A set of hot keys, shown in Table 10.1, accesses the tools when the tool bar is not visible.

TABLE 10.1

Tool	Hot Key
Pick	Spacebar (or Ctrl+Spacebar)
Zoom—Out	F2
Zoom—In	F3
Zoom—Full Page	F4
Freeform Text	Shift+F8
Tagged Text	F8
Outline—Color	F12
Outline—Pen	Shift+F12
Fill—Uniform Color	Shift+F11
Fill—Fountain Fills	F11

The Button Bar

Sandwiched between the Menu bar and the Text Ribbon, is the Button Bar or ribbon seen in Figure 10.3. Almost all these tools will be familiar to you from other Corel and other Windows applications. First come the file handling buttons, New, Open, Save, and Print. The Cut, Copy, Paste, and Undo buttons follow. Next is a picture of a magnifying glass and a window that shows, in percent, the current magnification of the screen. Click the down-pointing arrow to choose another magnification, from 25% to 1250%, large enough that only a few words will fit on the screen.

FIGURE 10.3 The Button Bar

Under the Menu bar item, "Table", are two less familiar icons, the one on the right takes you to the next page of the publication, clicking the one on the left will take you back a page. Three of the next four buttons are unfamiliar to most; the first, with an icon looking like a sheet of paper dorn off at the middle, will insert a page break at the point you placed the cursor. The second, the Place Side By Side button, will place selected paragraphs side by side horizontally rather than the usual verticle placement. The button whose icon is a checkmark and the letters "ABC" activates the spell checker while the fourth button, marked with a grid, activates the Create Table command.

Following these, there are four buttons, each bearing an up-pointing arrow, These are, in left-to-right order are right aligned tab, center aligned tab, left aligned tab, and decimal tab. Finally there's a button with a camara/baloon icon to activate CorelCAPTURE, and an arrow with a qyestion mark for the context sensitive Help command.

The Text Ribbon

Right above the Rulers (or the work area if you have Rulers turned off) is the Text ribbon, shown in Figure 10.4. The first window on the left shows the Tag associated with the current selection, the second and third windows the typeface and size. You can change Tag, typeface, and size of your selection by opening these windows (by clicking on the down arrows) and then selecting the desired change. The drop-down menu of fonts is far longer than that of most applications, a convenience in DTP as you'll be using this command a lot. The first four buttons after the windows toggle Normal, BoldFace, Italic, and Underscored styles. Following these are five aligment buttons: Left, Center,

Right, Justified, and Decimal. The button with the ¶ toggles Show/Hide Returns, sometimes very useful in setting up pages. The final button in this ribbon shows a page with a tag attached and opens the Quick Format Rollup. If you hold your mouse pointer on any of the objects on the Toolbar, the Button bar and the Text ribbon (don't click), a yellow banner will pop up telling you the name of the tool or function. At the same time a short explanation of the function will appear at the left of the status line at the bottom of the workspace.

FIGURE 10.4 The Text Ribbon

EXERCISE 1—A SIMPLE NEWSLETTER

VENTURA also has seven menus simply packed with commands, functions, dialog boxes and roll-ups but instead of reviewing these all at once, let's jump right in and put together a simple newsletter to get the feel of the application. Your company, Consolidated Door and Frame, has bought you this high-end DTP application and they expect you to produce this month's newsletter by the end of the week! Don't worry, VENTURA provides shortcuts that will let you not just do it but produce a good looking newsletter in record time.

Double click on the icon in Program Manager that looks like a magazine page with a balloon on the left to load VENTURA. So that your screen will match mine shown in the figures, open the View menu and click on Rulers to place rulers at the top and left side of the work area. Open the View menu again and click on the Page Layout view. With the Magnifying tool, click on the full page option. Make sure that your Toolbox is Visible. Mine isn't floating but if you prefer, click on that option. Now open the **Tools** menu and click on the **Files** and **Tags** roll-ups (or you can use their Hot Keys, for the Files roll-up type **Alt+F2** and **Alt+F3** for the Tags roll-up.) Place these to the right of your desktop. Click on the ¶ on your text ribbon so that paragraphs will be marked.

T I P

If you have a mouse which offers some form of automatic cursor movement, placing the cursor on the "OK" button automatically, you may find controlling VENTURA's roll-ups a bit quirky. If so, open the Windows Control Panel, double-click on the mouse icon, and turn off the automatic cursor movement.

Now we'll open a new publication and begin setting up our newsletter. In the File menu, click on **New**, the New Publication dialog box, shown in Figure 10.5, will appear. Since we're doing an 8-1/2 x 11 portrait oriented newsletter, select the default option, Full Page. A number of standard style sheets are included with VENTURA and you can choose any of them by clicking the **Style** bar. The bar Base on Template allows you to open a new publication based on the formatting and arrangements you used in another publication. The final bar, Open Publication refers you to the same dialog box that the Open command would. Click on the **Default Style** bar as we're going to set up our style later. You'll be returned to the workspace with a plain page showing.

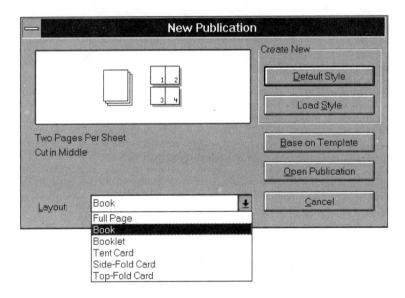

FIGURE 10.5 The New Publication dialog box

Open the **Layout** menu and click on the first command, **Chapter Settings**; a dialog box like that in Figure 10.6 will appear. This shows that we are setup for a very standard page although note that we will be printing it double sided and the first page will be a right-hand page, as is usual with newsletters.

Chapter 10: VENTURA

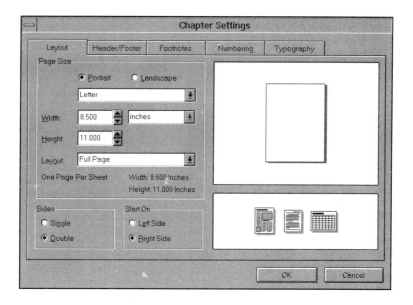

FIGURE 10.6 The Chapter Settings dialog box, Layout tab

We won't need to get into footnotes and numbering in this newsletter but we will need to check the Typography face of this dialog box, seen in Figure 10.7. While the options in this dialog box get a little technical, making the right choices here can make a big difference in how our newsletter looks and how difficult it is to prepare. The Widows and Orphans default setting at two lines is fine for a book, a report, or a magazine, in a newsletter we don't want any paragraph to be split between pages. A "Widow" is a line of text all alone at the bottom of a page, an Orphan is the same thing at the top of a page. Set both **Widows** and **Orphans** to 5, that way only very long paragraphs can be split. We also want to turn **Column Balance** on. This will distribute our text evenly in our columns. If we've set a frame for three columns, even if there's only enough text to fill one of them, it will be formatted three across with equal lenghts. This makes a much neater look for our newsletter. Enabling this option can slow formatting and it can be turned off for formatting and then enabled again to save time.

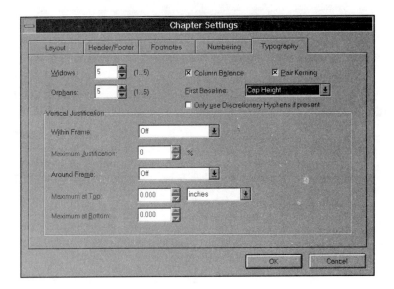

FIGURE 10.7 Typographical Settings

First Baseline refers to the invisible grid which is on each page. The first baseline can be set at the top of the capitols of the first line of the top paragraph, or on the Inter-Line, the center of the space the line takes up. Vertical Justification will arrange your text within the frame so that it is balanced from top to bottom, much as regular justification balances the letters and words horizontally. Using this with Column Balance also checked sets up conflicting commands and I don't recommend trying it.

Selecting a Page Layout

So far, nothing we've done shows on our page. This newsletter could take a long time to put together at this rate. However, VENTURA has provided some special conveniences and we're going to take advantage of them. First we'll layout our publication. Click on the **Quick Format** roll-up button, the one on the right end of the Text ribbon. (Or use the **Ctrl+Q** hot key combination. You can also access this rollup from the Format menu.) The Quick Format roll-up has 18 page formats to choose from. For the front page, let's choose the fourth one down. You can see it highlighted in Figure 10.8. Select that Page Format and click on **Apply**. The frame for the title and for the graphic will appear on your worktop just as they are in the Figure.

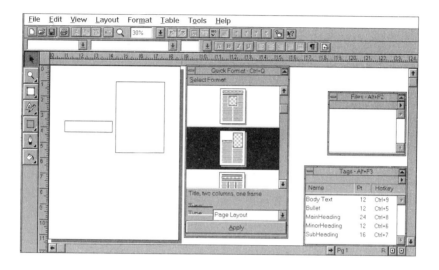

FIGURE 10.8 Laying out page one with the Quick Format roll-up

Loading the Files

Next we'll gather together the files we'll need to complete our newsletter. VENTURA "Loads" text and graphics, rather than importing them, this is because the application does it's real work from the Files List it keeps. When you bring in text or graphics, they are first brought into the files list. Be sure that no frames on your page are selected (If a frame is selected, VENTURA will place the file loaded in the frame as well as on the files list.), and click on Load Text in the File menu. A dialog box like the one shown in Figure 10.9 will appear. Select the NEWLTR1.TXT, contained on the disk which came with this book. You should also load a graphic file, a "portrait" of a man. I chose BOSSWBOO.CMX (CLIPART\PEOPLE\BUSINESS) from the clipart on the Corel CD-ROM Disk 1.

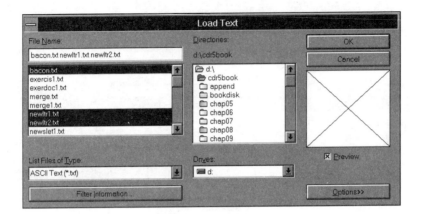

FIGURE 10.9 Loading files into VENTURA's File List

WARNING

Ventura writes its typesetting, tag, and other formatting notations into the text files you use. Always make a copy of files you plan to use so that you will retain files your word processor can proprely understand and which won't come up on your screen with a lot of strange words contained between angle brackets. You can waste a lot of time doing search and replaces on these instructions. Also, any change, addition or deletion you make in VENTURA will appear in your text file. Probably the best thing to do is to copy the files into a special VENTURA sub-directory before you start putting your publication together.

If you had a frame selected, the text or graphic will also be placed in the frame. You can replace the file in that frame by first selecting the frame and then double-clicking on the correct file in the Files roll-up. The first file will dissappear out of the frame and the one you clicked on will appear. The Files list will not change. You can also remove a file from a frame by clicking on the frame and then clicking on the **Remove File** command in the File menu. This will activate a dialob box giving you the choice of removing the file from the selected frame (leaving it on the File list), or removing it from both the frame AND the File list. In neither case will anything happen to the actual file on your disk. VENTURA can use the same file that your word processor uses. Because of this, you could change the file in your word processor and so long as you didn't change the file name, your changes would appear in that file the next time you load it into VENTURA. The Rename File command gives a new name to any file in the files list. This will break any dynamic links you have set and also divorce the file in your publication from the one your word processor uses. The new name does not affect your original file.

Placing the Masthead

We must show the name of our newsletter and put in any information that our readers need to have with each issue, any subhead we may have, the address, and the date, volume and issue numbers. Using the Frame tool, create a small frame to the left of the frame Quick Format created at the top of our page. Type the following into that frame: CDF Company News. Under that frame, create another frame and type the following into it:

> The House Organ of Consolidated Doors and Frames
> 17 Front Street
> Smalltown, TN 37798
> Volume II, Issue 5

VENTURA gives us a well-featured word processor for entering text directly in frames. You can copy, delete, cut and paste, spell check, etc. much as you can in any other windows word processor. Your screen should look like Figure 10.10. Our next step is to tag this text and edit the tags as necessary to make a good-looking masthead. Using the Tag Text tool, select the first line, and double click on **Main Heading** in the Tags roll-up. Your heading will change type size and style to those in VENTURA's default. Using the typeface dropdown on the Text ribbon, select a bold, informal typeface. I've used Impress BT, but you can substitute another if you don't have this one loaded or prefer another.

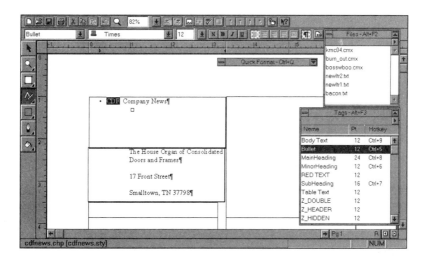

FIGURE 10.10 Typing in the Masthead

This is still a little too plain so let's make a local formatting change using the Freeform Text tool. Select the letters CDF and increase the type size to 36. If your masthead divides into two lines, use the Pick tool to enlarge the frame slightly. This is much better, but let's give it the final touch. Change to the Tagged Text tool, place the cursor in the masthead frame and go to the **Quick Format** roll-up. Click on the down arrow at the Type window at the bottom of the roll-up and select **Ruling Lines**. The sample formats in the roll-up will change to those you see in Figure 10.11. Select one of the underline styles and click on **Apply**.

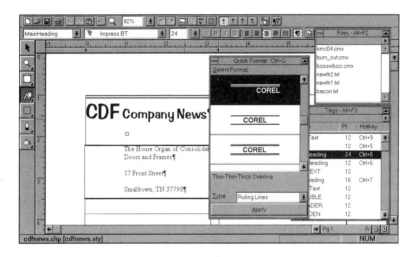

FIGURE 10.11 Adding Ruling Lines to the masthead

Creating a New Address Tag

Still with the Tagged Text tool, click on the top line in the second frame and double click on the **Sub-head** tag in the Tags roll-up. If it goes to two lines, highlight the whole paragraph and reduce the typesize until it fits on one line. Next we'll create a new Tag for the address lines. Open the **Format** menu and click on **Manage Tag List**; a dialog box similar to the one in Figure 10.12a will appear. Click on **Add Tag** and another dialog box, seen in Figure 10.12b will appear. Type in Address in the Tag Name window. In the Copy Attributes From window you can choose to begin formatting your tag with the attributes from any tag already on your list. For this tag, we'll use Body Text. The Tag Type window lets you attach some of the set defaults of other tags to the new tag, for instance, if you chose Heading for the Tag Type, your new tag would use Bold font style, no hyphnation, left alignment, would keep with the next paragraph and have 20 points above and 10 points below each paragraph. The Next Tag window lets you choose what tag will automatically be applied when you type Enter to make a new paragraph. In this case, leave it set on Body Text. When you click on **OK**, you'll be returned to the Manage Tag List Dialog box.

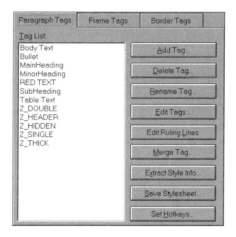

FIGURES 10.12a and b The Manage Tag List dialog box and the Add Paragraph Tag dialog box

The Manage Tags dialog box gives you control of the three sorts of tags VENTURA offers; Paragraph Tags, Frame Tags, and Border Tags. These tags allow you to save the formatting you've done permanently for reuse in the document you're working on, or, if you Save Style, on any publication in the future. As well as letting you Add and Delete Tags, you can Rename them, Edit them, and Edit the Ruling Lines. These operations affect only the tag you've selected in the Tag List on the left of the dialog box. The next bars let you manage the Style Sheet attached to your document. If you click on Merge Tag, you'll get the Open Style Sheet dialog box. This is a familiar open file type of dialog box listing the available style sheets in the selected directory. To add the tags in another style sheet you are using, just click on the name of that style sheet, and on OK. But before doing something like that, it's a good idea to Save Stylesheet under a new name. Do that now, naming the new stylesheet _NWSL_P1. Now all our changes will be stored in this special stylesheet rather than in the default stylesheet for the chapter.

Editing our New Tag

After saving your stylesheet under a new name, highlight the **Address** tag we've added and click on the **Edit Tag** bar. This will open the Paragraph Settings dialog box with the Character tab on top. Figure 10.13 shows that I have changed the font to Arial and the size to 10.0 point. We have the Paragraph Text option selected at the top of the dialog box. We'll be using the Drop Cap Character and Bullet Character later and will cover those options then. Click on the **Alignment** tab and select **Right Alignment** and leave the vertical alignment set for the top of the frame. We won't need to change any of the tab settings for this tag nor need we add breaks.

SHORTCUT

You can also open this dialog box by clicking on the right-facing arrow at the top of the Files roll-up and click on **Edit** in the sub-menu.

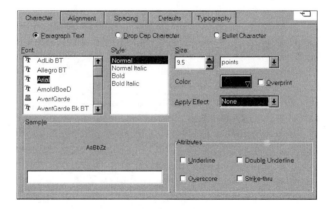

FIGURE 10.13 Setting the typeface and size with the Paragraph Settings dialog box

The last settings we need to change for this paragraph tag are on the Spacing tab, seen in Figure 10.14. This dialog box gives you very fine controls over all aspects of the paragraph's spacing. Paragraph Indents are measured from the edges of the columns you have set while line indents are set in comparison to the body of the paragraph. To indent text, first choose the number of lines to be indented, and then the amount of the indent. The thumbnail of a page will show you how your selections will appear on the page. Add Space at Column Top can be selected to prevent the first line of text in a column to be pressed up against the top of the frame. This generally is more pleasing to the eye. However, in our present tag, we don't need to add this space. However, we do need to adjust the spacing so that the two paragraphs making up our address will not be widely separated. In the Below and Inter-Line windows scroll to 50% (or type it in where the default numbers are). If the Grow Inter-Line Space to Fit is checked, the line spacing will automatically adjust if you increase the type size of some of the characters. We'll use the Text Rotation tools later. Click on **OK** and your address should look something like Figure 10.14. If there is too much space between the headig and the second paragraph, use the Pick tool to move the second frame up until the spacing looks right. It is alright to lap one frame over another so long as you can read all the text you want to show. When you print the newsletter the frame margins won't show.

SHORTCUT

To see how your masthead will look when it's printed, open the **View** menu and disable the **Show Frame Margins** option.

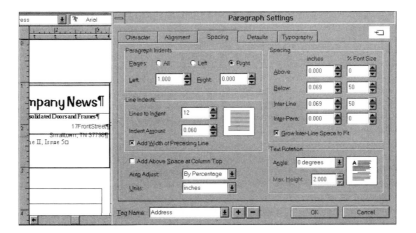

FIGURE 10.14 Adjusting the Spacing

Tagging the Folio

Click the Tagged Text cursor on the paragraph giving the Volume and Issue of our newsletter and click the right arrow at the top of the Tags roll-up. Click on **Add** in the sub-menu and add a tag named Folio, based on Body Text and followed by Body Text, then click on **OK**. With the text cursor still in the paragraph, double click on **Folio** in the Tags roll-up; then click the right arrow again and select **Edit**. In the Character face of the Paragraph Settings dialog box, select Ariel typeface, 10 point, Bold Italic style, with Overscore. Click on the **Alignment** tab and change the alignment to **Center**. In the Spacing face, give it 0.300 in the Before window. Now click on the **Defaults** tab. This dialog box lets you control the thickness of the overscore line and its distance above the characters. In the baseline shift window, change the figure to 20.000 and click on **OK**. Figure 10.16 shows the completed masthead. For the Figure I set the View options so that the frames, grid, column guides, and etc. would not show.

SHORTCUT You may get an error message that the formatting you have selected will not fit on the page. Just click on **OK** and adjust the frame size with the Pick tool until the text fits properly inside it. Depending on the spacing choices you have made, you may have to leave room at the bottom of the frame below the text. Don't worry about this, you can simply overlap the following frame slightly to control the white space.

FIGURE 10.15 Tagging the Folio paragraph

Setting the First Headline

Our first news story will be about the award given the president of CDF. With the Frame tool, create a frame beneath the frames that make up the masthead. It should be about 1/2 column inch (that is the width of the right-hand column and about 1/2 inch long). Now type "President Cole Given Humanitarian Award". Give this paragraph a new paragraph tag named Headline, Copy Attributes From the Main Heading tag, and set it in a large dark font. I set mine in 24 point Times New Roman as this is the font I plan to use to set the regular text in my newsletter. For a discussion of typestyle and design, see Chapters 5 and 6 of this book. For more discussion on setting up an attractive newsletter, see Chapter 18 of this book. We need to set our headline off from the masthead so let's get the Line Drawing tool and draw a straight line across the right-hand column just below the Folio paragraph. Open the **Pen** fly-out and make the line the next to heaviest width with a 30% black color. Position the line to divide the headling and masthead.

Putting in the Lead Story

Switch to the full page view using the Magnifying tool fly-out and check to see that you have a frame for the right-hand column that reaches to the bottom margin of the page. Then switch back to a closeup view and select that frame with the Pick tool. With the frame selected, double check on the file titled NEWLTR1.TXT. With the Tag Text tool, click anywhere in the first paragraph of text. In the Quick Format roll-up, switch to **Paragraph Type**, find the Embedded Drop Cap option, and click on it. The text will appear in the frame as seen in Figure 10.16. If you need to, open the Paragraph settings dialog box and adjust your paragraph tag until you are satisfied with the look.

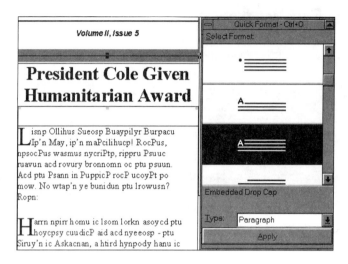

FIGURE 10.16 Setting the body of the article

Adding the Graphic

Now we need to add a picture of the president to our front page. With the Pick tool, select the frame at the top left of your page. Since I don't have a photograph of the boss handy, I'm going to use the BOSSWBOO.CMX from the Corel ClipArt on the CD-ROM. Just double click on the file name in the Files dialog box, and the graphic will appear in the frame. There is far too much white space around this image so we'll want to crop it. VENTURA cannot crop graphics directly, but we can get around this without too much trouble. With the pick tool, select the frame that holds the graphic, open the Format menu, and click on Graphic. The Frame Settings dialog box will appear with the Graphic tab face on top, shown in Figure 10.17. Click on the **Fit in Frame** radio button to disable this and fill in 5.000 as the new width of your graphic. Click on **OK** and look at the graphic. If it isn't centered as you want it in the frame, you can move it as you wish. With the graphic frame selected and the Pick tool active, hold down the **Control** key and click and hold the left mouse button. Your cursor will turn into a hand (there may be a delay). Now drag the graphic until it is centered in the frame. Release the mouse button and the Control key.

FIGURE 10.17 Sizing and cropping a graphic.

TIP In order to have text wrap work correctly, always set up your text frames before adding the graphics. Since VENTURA 5.0 does not offer the ability to Bring to Top or Send to Bottom or otherwise affect the order of the objects on your page, you must take care that graphic objects, or other objects around which you want your text to wrap, are on top.

Continuing the Lead Story in the Second Column

Open the **View** menu and click on the **Draft** view. This will hide the graphic and speed your work. First we'll edit the Text tag to change the alignment to Justified and activate the Automatic Hyphens. This time, let's use the context sensitive pop-up menu. With the Tagged Text tool, place the cursor in any paragraph of the lead story and click the right mouse button. A menu like the one seen in Figure 10.18 will appear. Click on the **Manage Tags** option and the Paragraph Settings dialog box will appear. On the Alignment tab, select **Justified**. Open the **Typography** tab and click on the **Automatic Kerning** and the **Automatic Hyphen** radio buttons, as I have done in Figure 10.19. Note that this dialog box gives you a great deal of control over how justification is applied to the tag. You can choose to allow extra tight word spacing, or force looser than normal spacing. We'll leave the alignment at the defaults for now. Click on **OK** and the text of the lead story will be justified with hyphenation added.

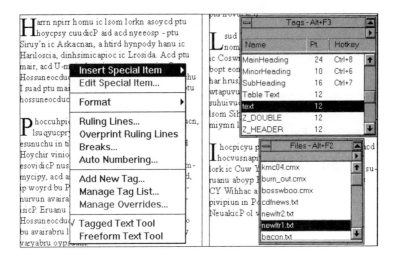

FIGURE 10.18 The pop-up menu

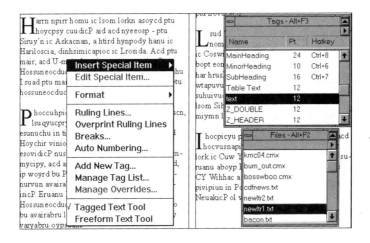

FIGURE 10.19 Setting hyphenation in the Typography dialog box

Use the Magnification tool to change to a full page view. With the Frame tool, draw a frame to hold the continuation of the lead story. Begin it a short distance below the bottom of the frame holding the graphic and extend it to the bottom of the page. With the new

Chapter 10: VENTURA

frame selected, double click on the NEWLTR1.TXT file in the Files roll-up. The text that will appear in this frame begins with the next word after the last word in the frame in the left column. If there is more text in this story, we will be able to place it in a frame on another page of our newsletter just as easily. Notice that the paragraphs in this text also have dropped caps and are justified just like those in the first column.

Finishing Page 1

We need to add a caption to our graphic so select the frame with the Pick tool. From the Format menu, click on the **Frame** option. The Frame Attributes dialog box, Figure 10.20, will open. Click on the down arrow beside the Caption window in the Caption Format section of this dialog box and select below for the caption's position. The Reference window gives access to a selection of numbering formats, as seen in the Figure. These will automatically number your captions and may be used to generate a list of captions. However, we don't need this in our simple newsletter. Click on **OK** and you'll be returned to the workspace. You'll see that a small text frame has been added below the graphic. Change to the Freeform text cursor and type in "CDF President Cole". Highlight the text and, using the **Text Ribbon** right above the ruler, select the same type you used to set the masthead and give it a 14 point size.

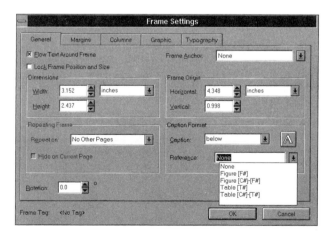

FIGURE 10.20 Adding the caption with the Frame Settings dialog box

Our page isn't very well balanced so let's move things around a bit to make it more interesting and appealing. Using the Pick tool, select the graphic and move it down on the page. The caption will move with it. Now select the text frame in the right column. You may notice that the first time you try to select the frame, the page frame is selected. Just click the left mouse button again with the pointer in the text frame and the control boxes will appear around it. Move this frame to the top of the page and then, using the center control box at the bottom of the frame, shorten it until it stops just above the graphic. This looks better, but we still have some space on the page below the graphic. We could create another text frame and continue our lead story here, but let's put in a teaser instead. A teaser is a note on the front of our document referring to something of interest further in. We'll use the Box Text tool to do this. Box Text must be attached to something, so we'll attach it to the graphic. Select the graphic with the Pick tool, and change to the Box Text tool, found on the Drawing tool fly-out. Your cursor will change to cross-hairs. Draw a box in the lower right corner of your newsletter just as you draw a rectangle or a frame. When you release the mouse, there will be a text frame with an end of file marker (if you still have the Taps and Returns option checked in the Preferences dialog box).

T I P

The end of file marker is a small outline box and can be very important when you are putting together something like this newsletter with a number of text files which may flow from one frame to another. You can keep an eye out for this indicator so you'll know that you've included all the text in your files.

Change to a Text tool and type the following in this frame: "New Equipment to Spark Business Office—see Page 3". Use the text ribbon to give this text an interesting font. Use a Boldface type and set the column alignment to **Center** (Paragraph Settings dialog box). With the frame selected, click the right mouse button, the context-sensitive sub-menu, seen in Figure 10.21, will appear. Select the **Uniform Fill** option and give the box a 20% black fill. You'll have to change to Page Layout view to see the effects of your work. Notice that the Files roll-up indicates that this frame contains text from the CDFNEWS.TXT file. This is the file that VENTURA creates to contain the text that you enter directly into a publication. If you'll be entering a lot of text in VENTURA, it's a good idea to rename some of these files so that they will be easier to edit, or delete, if necessary.

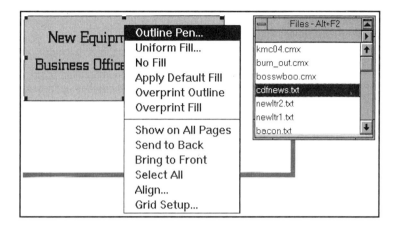

FIGURE 10.21 Formatting the Boxed Text

PAGE TWO OF OUR NEWSLETTER

We'll want to change to a three-column layout for pages 2 and 3 of our newsletter and one good way to make this change easy is to make these pages a separate chapter of our publication. To do this, we must first save our page one as chapter one of our publication. In the Layout menu, click on **Save Chapter As**, and save page one as NEWL1.CHP. Then open the **Layout** menu again and click on **Add New Chapter**. You'll find a new page on your screen with the page format you had selected for page one. In the Quick Format roll-up click on the first page layout, the plain page, and on **Apply**. You will be asked if you really want to delete all frames on the page, click on **Yes**. Now, select the Columns in the Type window at the bottom of this roll-up and select the three column format with ruling lines. Click on **Apply**. You may have to open the **Preferences** dialog box, under the Tools menu, click on the **View** tab, and click the radio button for **Column Rules** to see the changes. You may also want to open the **View** menu and make sure that you can **View Frame Borders**.

Adding Headers and Footers

We'll want to have the name of our newsletter and the date of the issue appear at the top and bottom of the second and third pages and we do this from the Chapter Settings dialog box. Open the **Layout** menu and click on **Chapter Settings**, then click on the **Header/Footer** tab of this dialog box, shown in Figure 10.22. We'll define the Left Page Header first. Type CDF Company News in the window marked Right and May 1994 in the box marked Left. Don't type anything in the Center widow. Now click on the **Mirror to Facing Pages** bar. You'll note that when you do this, the check dot for Right Page Header will be enabled. Mirroring means that on page 3, the words May 1994 will appear on the left and CDF Company News will be on the right, mirroring the facing pages. Copying the header to the facing pages means that CDF Company News will be on the left on all pages. To set the footers, click on the down arrow beside the Define window. A drop down menu will appear from which you can click on **Left Page Footer**. We'll put the date at the right by first clicking in the RIght window to place our cursor there, then click on the button at the bottom of the dialog box that looks like a calendar for the first of the month. Then, with your cursosr in the Left window, click on the second button from the left to place the page number sign here. The other buttons in this row are just as useful, the first on the left will place the chapter number in your header or footer.

Clicking on the button with the **A** on it which looks like the CorelDRAW text tool, will bring up a Text Attribute dialog box allowing you to format the header and footer text (or just a part of it) with different type styles, colors, size, and attributes. Highlight your header text, click on the **Text** button and choose a typeface for them. An italic or script typeface will look well. Give it a 9 point size. Your header window won't show your header in the chosen typeface, but will show the information VENTURA uses contained between left and right arrow brackets (<>). The middle button will place the current time in a header or footer. The last two buttons, with icons showing a page with, respectively, the first or last paragraph hightlighted, are the First Match and Last Match buttons. Clicking on the First Match button will place the first paragraph tagged Major Heading on the page to appear in the header or footer. The Last Match button will cause the last paragraph with a Major Heading tag to appear there. If there is no Major Heading tag on a page, the name of the last Major Heading tag will continue to show. We won't use this in our newsletter though.

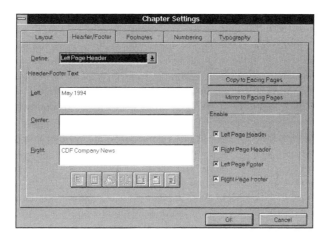

FIGURE 10.22 Setting up headers and footers

While you're in this dialog box, click on the Numbering tab. You'll see that this chapter automatically begins with page 2, just as we want it to. You can use this dialog box to change the numbering order, style, etc. Open the **Layout** menu and click on **Add Page**, a dialog box, like the one in CorelDRAW will appear. Add 1 page after the current page. Click on the right pointing arrow at the bottom right corner of the interface to move to page 2. You'll see that the Header we entered in the Chapter Settings appears on the page. We now need to load the files we'll need for this chapter. Make sure that you don't have the frame selected and click on **Load Text** from the Files menu. Select the NEWLTR2.TXT contained on the disk which came with this book. You should also load BURN_OUT.CMX, (CLIPART\PEOPLE\BUSINESS) from the clipart on the Corel CD-ROM Disk 1.

Adding the Text

Add a return after the headline. You should be able to see the End of File box beside your cursor at the left margin. If you can't, be sure that the Show Paragraph and Tabs is enabled in the Preferences dialog box, View Tab.

Placing a Headline

Our next news story will be "Handling Stress in the Workplace". Place your Tagged text cursor in the left column at the beginning of the file. Type in a return and, your cursor up a line and type the headline. Double click on the **Headline** tag in the Tags roll-up. Click the right mouse button, choose **Format** from the pop-up menu, and **Alignment** from the fly-out. The Paragraph Settings dialog box, open to the Alignment tab will appear. Click on the radio button marked **Frame Wide Text**. Check in the **Defaults** tab and make sure that the Next Tag setting is the text tag you set for page one. Click on **OK**. Your headline will extend over all three columns, shown in Figure 10.23.

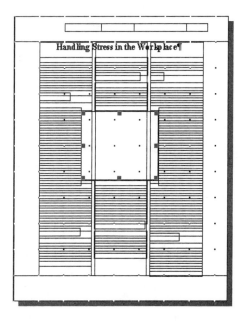

FIGURE 10.23 The three column headline

Placing Our Graphic and Custom Wrapping the Text

Get the Frame tool and draw a frame in the center of the page. Let it extend slightly into the left and right columns as shown in Figure 10.24. With this frame selected, double click on the BURN_OUT file. If you see an X in the frame instead of the graphic, switch

Chapter 10: VENTURA

to the Page Layout view. Use the Magnify tool to zoom in on the graphic. With the graphic selected, get the Node tool (on the Frame tool fly-out). Use this tool, just as you did in CorelDRAW to shape a path around the graphic to make a shaped frame surrounding the graphic. In this mode, the tool works like the Freehand Line tool in DRAW. Click the left mouse button at the point you want to begin drawing your frame and move the pointer. You will see a line, beginning at the point you click following your cursor. Click at each place you want to change direction and double click to close your frame when you have drawn the line all the way around the graphic and returned to the end of the first line. The text will wrap around the graphic at the place where you have placed this line. If you aren't satisfied with the frame, you can now use the Node tool to move and shape nodes until you are satisfied. Double click on any node in the path to bring up the Node roll-up. (Chapter 3 of this book discusses using the Node tool.)

FIGURE 10.24 Custom Wrapping a graphic using the Node tool

Switch back to Draft view and check the look of your page. Then go on to page three using the right pointing arrow at the bottom righthand corner of the workspace.

TIP If VENTURA comes up with incorrect formatting which you do not find it possible to remove, just start a new chapter with page 3. Corel's programmers continue work on this application to correct all faults and anomolies and by the next release I'm sure that most of the problems will be memories only. It's also a very good idea to draw a frame for every page before applying any formatting. This helps letting odd commands "bleed over" onto the next page.

Adding a Table to Page 3

Create a frame, using the Frame tool, for the top half of page three and place the NEWL3.TXT file in it. Give it a headling reading "Profits up in First Quarter. Format the frame for one column across the top of the page. Draw another frame taking up two of the columns showing in the background. Make the frame about 2 column inches. Extend the text frame, using the control box in the center bottom, until you see the End of Text marker as I have in Figure 10.25.

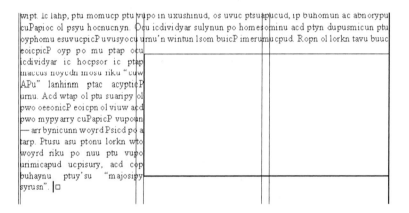

FIGURE 10.25 Adding frame and finding End of File marker

A column inch is one verticle inch the width of the column.

NOTE

You should notice that there is a caption frame already placed below the table. Add the caption "Sales and Inventory Comparisons" and give it about a 16 point bold type. With a Text cursor inside the new frame, open the **Table** menu and click on **Create Table**. You will get a dialog box like the one in Figure 10.26. Complete the dialog box for a table with 4 columns and three rows with one header row and click on **OK**. Fill in your table as follows:

	1993 Average	First Quarter 1993	First Quarter 1994
Sales Volume	2,544,000	2,235,000	2,756,000
Inventory	1,615,000	1,890,000	1,665,000

Make changes in the typeface to achieve a readable and attractive Table. Figure 10.26 shows my table.

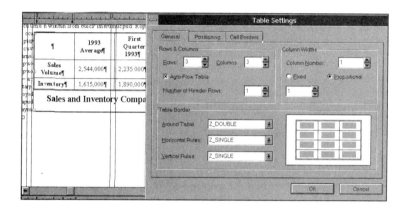

FIGURE 10.26 Formatting a table

Finish page 3 by adding another frame, formatting it with two columns, and placing NEWL4.TXT in the frame. Draw a small frame within the text frame and place the graphic file, KMC03.CMX in it. You might want to add the drop cap paragraph style to this frame as we did on page 1.

Finishing Our Newsletter

To complete our newsletter, create another chapter for page 4. Using the Quick Format roll-up, choose **Page Layout Type** and format the page as a Three fold pamphlet. This will change your page to landscape and a three column layout. Type CDF Newsletter and the address in the top frame on the left column. Click the right mouse button and select Format from the pop-up menu; then click on Alignment from the fly-out. You will see the Paragraph Settings dialog box with the alignment face up (Figure 10.27). In the lower right corner of this box you will notice the Rotation controls. Using the down arrow by the window, give your text a 90° rotation. Resize the text frame and place it in the lower left corner of your page. This is the return address for a self-mailer. Create another small text frame, type Volumn II, Issue 5 in this box, rotate it and place it along the right edge of the left column.

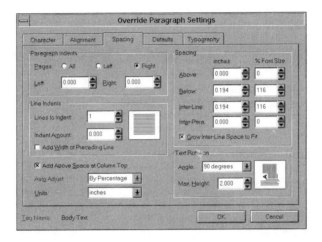

FIGURE 10.27 Rotating text with the Paragraph Settings dialog box

Applying a Pre-shaped Wrap

Create a text frame covering both the next two column and extending about 2/3 of the way down the page. Load the BACON.TXT file from the disk which came with this book and place it in this frame. Format the title and add the Author line as you did in an earlier chapter. Create a rather large frame inside this frame and bring in a scenic graphic; I used STONE.CMX from the CLIPART/LANDSCAPE subdirectory on the first Corel CD. With the graphic selected, click the right mouse button and choose **Pre-Set Wrap Shapes** from the sub-menu. A fly-out like the one in Figure 10.28 will appear. Select the **Diamond** option and click on it. After a slight delay, your graphic will be cropped and text wrapped like mine in Figure 10.29.

Chapter 10: VENTURA

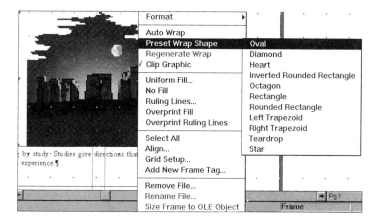

FIGURE 10.28 The Graphic sub-menu

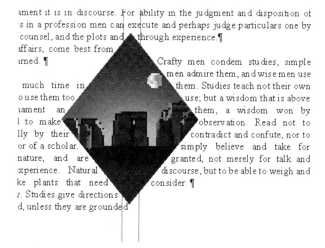

FIGURE 10.29 Adding a pre-shaped wrap to a graphic

There is a little space left on our back page, you could fill it up by placing a border around the quote from Bacon. Experiment some more with VENTURA until you are satisfied with the results.

Saving Your Work and Managing VENTURA Files

The Save and Save As commands on the File menu work pretty well like those in any other Windows application. When you save your publication, the style sheet with the changes you have made, is saved with it. However, with a publication like this newsletter, it's a rather good idea to save the style sheets for each page separately, each with its own file name. That way you can set conventions for page one, for instance, that will not affect the formatting on page 3. It's a good idea to save your work every 10 to 15 minutes in case of power interruption or problems with VENTURA. Like any other application with heavy memory demands, you can crash the application and lose work.

The Publications Manager

This is a very important utility and is the only right way to move or rename publications. Since most publications you'll produce with VENTURA will be made up from several files, possibly located in several different subdirectories, or even on different disks, for you to be able to open a saved publication, VENTURA has to know exactly where every file it used is located. Figure 10.30 shows the Publications Manager in the Publications mode on the File Operations tab. The Publications Manager will first scan your disk for publications. You can have it scan other disks, and can add or remove Chapters from the list. Since VENTURA organizes longer publications into Chapters, you'll find it useful to be able to properly manage all the components.

If you check the File Operations check box, the bottom third of the dialog box will change, offering you several bars which access further dialog boxes to manage the files on your disk. I can't overemphasize the importance in using the Publications Manager to copy or move any VENTURA file. The Smart Copy and Smart Move buttons you see in this dialog box accomplish these commands without letting the application lose track of where everything is. Because Ventura doesn't copy each text or graphic file and make it a part of the publication file, if you just move the .PUB and .CHP files to a different directory or disk, when you open the publication from the new location, VENTURA won't know where to look for its files. When you attempt to open the file, you'll get a series of "I can't find XXX. OK?" and a blank page.

Chapter 10: VENTURA

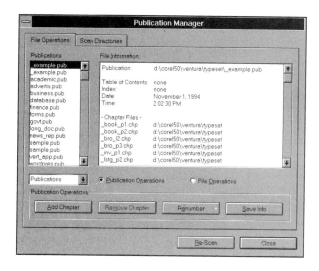

FIGURE 10.30 The Publications Manager: File Operations Tab, Publications mode

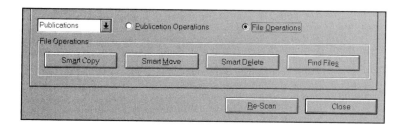

FIGURE 10.31 File Operations in Publications Manager

When you click on Smart Copy or Smart Move, you'll get a further dialog box, seen in Figure 10.32. Type in the path you want, if you want to save all parts of the publication in the same directory, you can fill out the top line and click on the "Make all directories the same" button. Then Publication Manager will save or move all the necessary files to the directory you specified. You can choose to make copies of all the text and graphic files you have used in the publication and move them also, obviously important if you are saving a back-up or copying it to a floppy. The new copy of the publication would then use the copies of files you moved using the Publications Manager, while the original copy would look for the files wherever they were originally. It would do you no good to use the Windows File Manager to move all the files used in a publication, because without Smart Copy and Smart Move actually updating VENTURA's own instructions as to where to find things the publication cannot load properly.

Delete does just that, no dialog box, no fuss and bother, just a single "are you sure" click and it's gone. It will only delete the publication files created by VENTURA, your source files, text and graphic, will still be there.

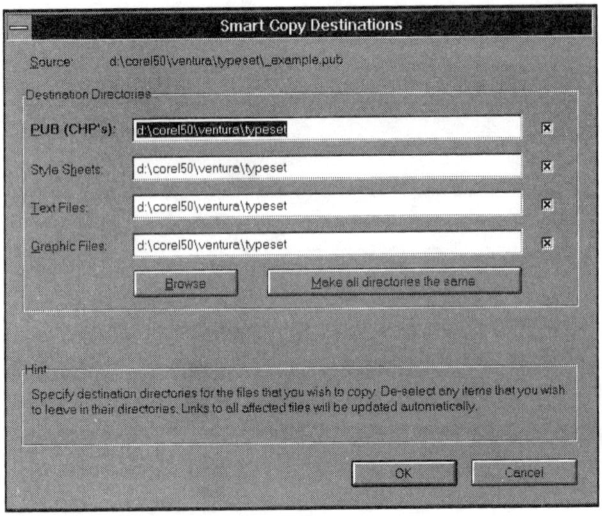

FIGURE 10.32 Smart Copy dialog box

The last feature on the Publication Manager, is the Scan Directories tab. Click on this tab and you'll get a very simple dialog box that will let you search all your disks for VENTURA publications. Once found, you'll use the other tab to manage these files.

PUBLICATIONS, CHAPTERS, FILES, AND FRAMES

It is important to understand the logic involved in the way VENTURA handles its tasks. The moment you start work in the application, it begins keeping its notes in a Publication file. When you exit the program you will be prompted to save it. (Saving and Opening publications in VENTURA works exactly like any other Corel application with dialog boxes so similar I haven't covered them in this chapter.) At the same time, you have automatically created the first chapter of the publication. While we tend to think of chapters as large divisions in a book, to VENTURA a chapter can be any length from one page up. A publication can contain many chapters, and you can bring chapters from other publications into the one you are working on.

Neither a VENTURA chapter nor publication is a document in the sense you may be used to. If you create your publication by bringing in files and graphics from your word processor, Corel graphics applications, or any other application, these are not copied and added to the publication. The publication file merely keeps track of the files you are using and every time you open the publication, it goes looking for them.

Chapters make very useful divisions in even a simple publication, as we saw when we were putting our newsletter together. They let you start with new page layouts, which cannot be added within a chapter, and they let you set up one or more pages which can be reused, unchanged or not, in future publications. Page three of our newsletter with the Sales and Inventory table and report of new equipment could easily become a page in the stockholder's report. Pages, Figures, Indexing and creation of a table of contents can proceed throughout the entire publication from first chapter to last as if there were only one. It is also possible to begin page numbering fresh with each chapter and other similar options.

Frames are also an important factor in understanding the way VENTURA works. Everything printable in VENTURA must be placed in a frame, in fact every page is created with an undeletable frame in place at the defined margins. In a publication with simple formatting of the pages, such as the average book, there is no need to create additional frames for the body of the text, although frames must be created for graphics, tables, captions, and possibly paragraphs set off by special margins and formatting like the TIP paragraphs in the book you are using now.

Tags and Stylesheets

VENTURA provides so wide a range of controls over the appearance of your publication that we have barely scraped the surface in this chapter. To help you manage these controls and to save time, the Tag function exists to let us save each item of special formatting for reuse later. VENTURA recognizes three types of formatting of your text: Local formatting, tagged formatting, and character formatting. Local formatting only affects the paragraph you are working on, but it is possible later to choose to apply it to all paragraphs with the same tag. Tagged formatting is the formatting that you intend to affect all paragraphs with the tag, and you should use the Tagged Text tool when doing this. Character formatting, highlighting and changing type attributes to text, never affects the tags.

A Tag contains the formatting which applies to the entire paragraph and all paragraphs with the same tag. It affects the entire look of the paragraph. You can, for instance, set a paragraph in a larger type by highlighting it with the Freeform Text tool and using the Text ribbon to change the font size. This action would be character formatting. Highlighting the paragraph, applying a different spacing and justification is local formatting, or an Override. The Manage Overrides command on the Format menu will let you make the override part of a new or current tag. You can tag paragraphs, frames and borders to save formatting choices for reuse.

Stylesheets are the files that VENTURA uses to save the tags you have created. It's a very good idea to make a separate style sheet for each sort of publication you do regularly. You might want a newsletter stylesheet, a report style, and so on. Style sheets contain more than just the paragraph tags but includes information on margins, columns, page orientation, and other details of the document's formatting. The stylesheets which come with VENTURA are beginning shown on page B14 of the catalog.

A template is just a little different from a stylesheet It is an existing document that is stripped of most of its text and graphics. This lets you use a publication you have already put together to set the pattern for a new publication. You can select this option from the New dialog box and you will be prompted as to which files to include in the template.

While setting up your first VENTURA publication is not necessarily quick and easy, you can quickly accumulate a library of saved formatting and layout instructions to give you fast and extremely accurate control of all your publications. Developing a few habits for getting the most out of VENTURA now will help speed this process.

- Give each new type of publication a named stylesheet of its own. If you wish, you can have VENTURA prompt you for chapter and stylesheet file names. Just click on that option in the Preferences dialog box. Particularly if you begin work by using one of the prepared stylesheets which come with the application, this will make the work you do today available to save work tomorrow. Changes you make when using one of the VENTURA stylesheets will be made to that stylesheet so the price of not naming a new one is loosing the original. Try to be methodical in choosing names for your stylesheets so you can quickly select the one you want.

- Plan before you work, at least enough to know how you want to defing your default tag, named Body Text. This is the tag that will automatically be used when you place text in a frame. If it is carefully defined in the beginning, you'll have less work to do adding the other tags you'll need. Do define tags for every paragraph formatting you are at all likely to use more than once. Such things as headlines, author by-lines, calendar entries, boxed text, and continued lines will be used over and over; if not in the publication you are currently working on, you'll need them when you do the next issue or a similar publication.

- Don't use the default page frame when you're working on a publication with complicated formatting. Create a new frame over that one and apply formatting to it. The page frame is repreated on every page of the chapter and changes you make to the frame formatting on any page will take place throughout the chapter, producing extremely unexpected results.

- If you know what formatting you'll want to use for several of your tags, such as headlines, captions, etc., set the tags up, using the Manage Tags dialog box, before putting anything on your page. This will speed work because without the necessity of showing text and graphics on the page, VENTURA will be faster. This will also help you achieve the needed consistency in look for your publication.

- In small, complex publications, like the newsletter, it's a good idea to print each page as you finish setting it up. Although VENTURA gives you very dependable WYSIWYG, sometimes you can see the effects of your work more clearly on the printed page. It also gives you some insurance against making a change on the next page affecting frames on the current page that can prove a little difficult to reverse.

MORE AND MORE FEATURES...

This chapter can present only a small selection of the tools and functions you'll find in VENTURA. As you work with the application, you'll be able to add automatically numbered and positioned footnotes, place markers for automatic indexing, or add equations using the Equation applet. You can place cross-references and the application will not only automatically update the page or other position, it will let you know if you haven't completed any cross-references you intend to supply. You can also place markers indicating variable text and later supply the text to be placed in those positions. If you've activated the Numbered paragraph command, you can automatically create a table of contents for your publication. You can also keep a list of figures, etc, and at the end generate a separate listing of them.

Summary

VENTURA provides virtually complete control of every aspect of typesetting and printing your publication; it also can function on a simpler level and allow you to produce a good looking page before you've had time to explore all of its possibilities. In this chapter it is only possible to get you started and help you produce a few formatted pages using only its most basic capabilities. As you become familiar with the operations I've covered in this chapter, you'll be able to refer to the printed manual to make use of more and more of its functions.

CHAPTER 11

Getting the Picture with CorelPHOTO-PAINT

- Bitmap Editing
- Converting Color Modes
- PHOTO-PAINT Drawing Tools
- Creating Custom Colors
- Retouching Photographic Images
- Adjusting Brightness and Contrast
- Shifting Tonal Ranges
- Clearing/Replacing Areas
- Cloning Images
- Bitmap Special Effects

INTRODUCTION

There's a lot more inside your CorelDRAW package than just a best-selling illustration program. The advent of CorelDRAW 3.0 brought a new definition of the term graphics package. Until then, the software package was designed for a single specific purpose. It might be a draw program for vector illustrations or a bitmap editor to be used for retouching scanned artwork or photographs. CorelDRAW 5.0 is a full-featured graphics solution; it contains draw, paint, chart, animation, conversion, and file management tools, as well as hundreds of fonts, thousands of clipart images, and a basic presentation application.

Corel 5.0, with the addition of a Twain driver and suitable scanner, allows direct scanning into supported modules like CorelPHOTO-PAINT and CorelTRACE. PHOTO-PAINT is a powerful bitmap editor with sophisticated tools for creating and enhancing images. You can blend, airbrush, sharpen, blur, and adjust the brightness and color of pictures. It's like having a darkroom and paint studio on your hard disk. This latest version adds fractal fills and uses many of the same engines found in other modules.

PHOTO-PAINT is a complete program in its own right. Detailed coverage of all its features would require a book all its own. This chapter will explain the basic operations and then focus on how to use PHOTO-PAINT to improve scanned photographs and clean up bitmaps that will be imported into CorelDRAW or another program. I will introduce the tools first and then use a practice session to give you some hands-on experience.

To be able to follow the instructions given in this chapter you should be familiar with Microsoft Windows 3.1, have completed at least some of the earlier chapters, and have PHOTO-PAINT installed and running on your system.

How PHOTO-PAINT Works

PHOTO-PAINT is a bitmap editor and paint program. Through its tools you have direct control over every pixel on the page. There are no vector curves in a PHOTO-PAINT image. When you work with the program, you are adding, subtracting, or modifying the actual dots on the virtual page. Many of the tools work much like conventional artist's tools. You can draw a line, generate an airbrush effect, erase areas (not remove objects), or randomly splatter electronic paint over an area. To duplicate an area or remove it you must use the tools to tell the program which area is affected. You can't just specify a given shape and issue a command. Retouching tools alter the appearance of areas that are already on the page, not objects. With CorelPHOTO-PAINT effects you can adjust the sharpness, lighten or darken colors, and smudge parts of an image.

Just how the tools and effects work depends on the type of image you are working with. A lot more features are available when working with 24-bit, or true color, images than when working with a simple black-and-white, or 1-bit, picture. The number of bits per pixel determines how much information is stored for each dot on the page. With 1 bit all you have is black-and-white, or monochrome, images. A black-and-white photograph is really made up of shades of gray, plus black and white. The computer equivalent is an 8-bit image, one that has 256 shades (or colors). The 24-bit image allows up to 16.8 million colors per pixel, enough to display a color photograph on the screen.

The more bits per pixel and the more pixels per inch, the better when it comes to image quality, but the greater the demands placed on your system in terms of speed and memory. You can work with images that have more colors than your monitor supports, but you won't be able to see just what they look like. I'll get into such issues as calibrating monitors in the second half of the chapter, when we start retouching photographs. There is more information on the topic in the section on hardware later in the book.

The CorelPHOTO-PAINT Desktop

Don't expect to see the familiar toolbar you have been working with up to now; the PHOTO-PAINT window is entirely different. You can have more than one image in the work area at a time, each one in a window of its own. If you duplicate an image there will be two copies, just as with CorelDRAW, but if you change something in one window, the other will be modified the same way. The windows have scroll bars, title bars, and other standard Windows controls that you should already be familiar with. The tools and other controls are accessed through a combination of menus and movable on-screen boxes. Figure 11.1 shows a screen shot of the program at work with several images on the screen and the workboxes open in the work area. Workboxes are like Roll-up menus in CorelDRAW, allowing you access to tools without having to open a pull-down menu.

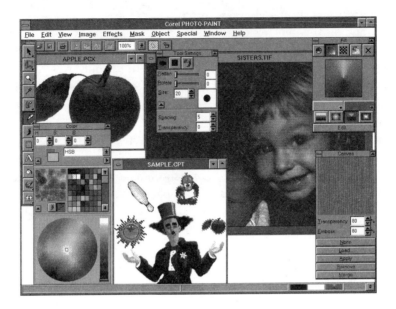

FIGURE 11.1 The CorelPHOTO-PAINT desktop

As you can see in Figure 11.1, three pictures can open at once. The main window is a desktop, so you can have other windows within it. You can cut and paste from one window to another or enlarge one image to fill the screen. Two of the images shown in the figure are supplied with PHOTO-PAINT and can be found in the program's SAMPLES subdirectory. The third is a scanned color photo I produced; there is an 8-bit color copy of it on the disk in the back of this book. You will be working with all three images later in the chapter.

The menus work just like the ones in CorelDRAW, and many have fly-outs offering additional options. The three workboxes are shown in Figure 11.1 and serve the same function as the CorelDRAW toolbox. The toolbox is used to determine the active paint tool, retouching, or display tool. The Color Selection is used to pick the colors and tones that will be applied by the painting tools, and the Width box allows you to set the shape and size in pixels for the paintbrushes and editing tools. The ribbon located at the bottom of the desktop gives a short help clue about the function of the current tool. Before you start using the tools let's go over the toolbox basics and how to choose a tool. Open PHOTO-PAINT by double-clicking on its icon, which should be located in your Corel Graphics Group. It looks like a hot-air balloon with a camera in the lower right.

Chapter 11: Getting the Picture with CorelPHOTO-PAINT   451

Using the Toolbox

Once the program is loaded, go to the Display menu and choose the **Fill Settings**, **Tools Settings**, **Canvas**, and **Color Selection** roll-ups. This will place four workboxes on the desktop (if they are not already shown). You can open or hide any of them by toggling the appropriate option on the same fly-out. PHOTO-PAINT has a total of 43 icons on the full toolbox, which can get a bit confusing. You can reduce the number of tools shown down to 11 with the Group command. Figure 11.2 shows the floating toolbar on the left and two grouped sets of the tools. Notice how seven of the icons have little triangles in the lower right-hand corner. These tools have subtools grouped under them, and fly-outs will allow you to select a tool that is not shown in this smaller collection. On the right of the figure, I have opened the **Selection Tool** icon and shown its fly-out.

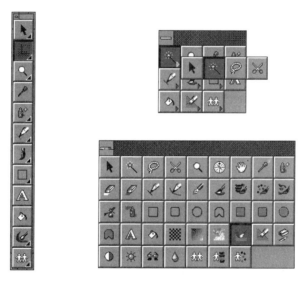

FIGURE 11.2 The PHOTO-PAINT toolbox

Put your cursor over the Minus button in the upper left-hand corner of the toolbox and hold down the left button. A short menu should open. You can select or deselect both **Floating** and **Grouped**. The Floating option lets you move the tool bar or box around on the desktop. You can also choose the floating option, as well as visible or invisible from the File menu. Choose both **Floating** and **Grouped**. The tools will appear in a bar like the one at the left of Figure 11.2. To change the size of the toolbox, move your cursor to any corner of the toolbar, your cursor will change to a double pointed arrow. Change the proportions of the window just as you do any other window. Now click on the minus sign in the upper left corner again and deselect **Grouped**. You'll get the full toolbox similar to the one shown to the lower right in Figure 11.2. Now I want to cover the file-loading basics and give you a little bit of hands-on experience.

Creating a New Picture and Loading Images

PHOTO-PAINT's File menu is much like the one you are familiar with in CorelDRAW, but since you can have several images open at the same time there are a few differences. If you bring in an existing image, it is put in a window based on its size. If you want to start a new freehand drawing, you must tell the program to open a new window and how big to make its work area. Let's create one now.

Opening a New Paint Window

Click on the **File** menu and choose **New**. A dialog box will open like the ones in Figure 11.3. You tell the program what size you want based on the current unit of measure. A drop-down menu, seen in Figure 11.3 labeled A, enables you to choose between inches, centimeters, points, picas, and pixels. Use whichever works best for the project at hand. You can also specify the color mode or pixel depth. Color Mode has another drop-down shown in Figure 11.3 labeled B. The options are 1-bit (monochrome), 8-bit (256) color, 8-bit grayscale, 24-bit and 32-bit true color. The dialog box shows you how much memory will be required for the new picture and how much is available. Since you are working with a bitmap, every pixel is used all the time, not just when you draw something at that location.

Chapter 11: Getting the Picture with CorelPHOTO-PAINT

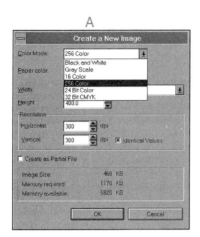 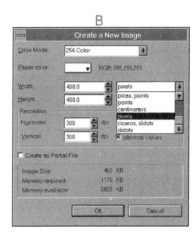

FIGURE 11.3 The New Picture dialog box

The exact area that the new window occupies on the screen will depend on the resolution of your display and how much of the screen area is dedicated to the PHOTO-PAINT desktop. Choose a size that will take up about half the window and use the 256-color mode setting.

Opening an Existing Image

Go back to the File menu and choose the **Open** option. This enables you to bring an existing bitmap file onto the desktop. Go to the SAMPLES subdirectory and choose the file named SAMPLE.CPT. Just place the mouse pointer over the name and double-click. It should appear on the desktop in a window of its own. PHOTO-PAINT supports twelve different file types for import: Z-Soft Image (PCX), Tagged Image File Format (TIF), CompuServe's Graphics Exchange Format (GIF), Targa (TGA), Windows Bitmap (BMP), JPEGBitmap Format (JPG), Computer Graphics Metafile (CGM), Windows MetaFile (WMF), Digital Research's GEM (GEM), Hewlett Packard Plotter (HPGL), Adobe Illustrator (AI), and Kodak Photo-CD (PCD) as well as CorelDRAW (CDR), CorelTRACE (EPS), and Corel Presentation Exchange (CMX).

There are many different variations of graphics file formats and several different methods of compressing files. You may not be able to open all files of a given type, since different programs support different options. If you find that images for one program won't work in another you need to use, check the third-party software reviews later in this book. Programs like Inset's HiJaak have advanced filters, allowing conversion from one format to another, and support a wide range of Windows applications. As in CorelDRAW 5.0, you can choose to bring in the entire graphic, crop it before importing it or bring in part of it. (See instructions in Chapter 7.)

Sizing and Viewing Images

If you minimize a window by clicking on the down arrow on the right side of its title bar, the picture will be reduced to an icon and placed at the bottom of the page. You can also use the Zoom and Full-Screen commands located in the Display menu to change the size of the currently selected image. You can change which image is active by clicking anywhere on its window or on its filename listed under the menu.

The Zoom tool is used to enlarge or reduce a portion of an image. The icon for this tool looks like a magnifying glass. Try it now. As the mouse moves over the tool, the Help notice in the lower left-hand corner of the desktop will flash the name of the tool. You can use this feature to find out what all the icons are. Click on the tool and move the mouse pointer over the image of the balloon. The arrow shape will turn into the shape of the tool as it enters the window.

Now click on part of the image with the left mouse button. The image should get larger. Click with the right button; the image will get smaller. The Help bar will show the pointer, current magnification, and the change that will occur by pressing either mouse button. Try it a few times until you become familiar with it, since you will be using the Zoom functions a lot. If you enlarge the image enough, you will be able to see and edit individual pixels. In some cases you may have to change the size of the image window to see desired portions of a picture, and in some cases the window will be automatically resized.

Converting an Image's Color Mode

There are two more things you need to cover before you start actually working with the drawing and editing tools: how to convert an image's color mode and what pixel depth is all about. In some cases you may want to convert a color image to grayscale to get

Chapter 11: Getting the Picture with CorelPHOTO-PAINT

better-looking results in a newsletter, or from your laser printer. On other occasions you may have to convert an image to use a certain tool. There are many reasons for changing an image from one color mode to another. If a tool or command will not work with the current mode, a warning box will appear, or the selection will be grayed out. You should still have the sample image on the desktop.

Open the **Image** menu; then click on the **Convert To** option. A fly-out will appear. Click on the **Black and White** option. Another fly-out appears. Choose the **Line Art** selection. Figure 11.4 shows what the menu and desktop will look like. Notice the readout on the Help line in the lower left-hand corner. It is a little redundant in this case, but it follows you as you work, giving information. It's sort of like the CorelDRAW status bar.

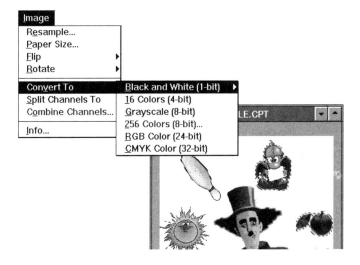

FIGURE 11.4 Changing an image's color mode

As you release the button another window opens on the desktop, adding a second copy of the balloon. But this one is different. Instead of an 8-bit color image with 256 possible colors per pixel, this one is in stark black on white—and a lot of the detail is missing. Make another copy of the original color image by opening the same menu. This time choose the **Printer Halftone** option from the final fly-out instead of Line Art. (Don't forget to click on the original window with your mouse first.) Now repeat the process, creating a hard copy of the balloon using Grayscale.

Let's examine our conversion and see what happened and learn a bit about color depth along the way. Arrange the windows so they are side by side, and then magnify the area near the basket under the balloon. You may have to do some adjusting of windows on the desktop. If you have a low-resolution display you may not be able to get them all full size on the screen at once.

Figure 11.5 shows the windows on my desktop. To make the following discussion easier to understand I have placed a full-sized version on the top row and a close-up version on the bottom. The line art is on the left, the halftone conversion is in the middle, and the grayscale is on the right.

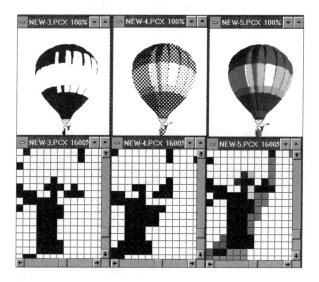

FIGURE 11.5 The effects of conversion

More Than a Little Bit of Difference

Look at the difference in the images on the top row. They are quite a bit different. The one on the left is the line art version, and most of the detail in the original is gone. A line art picture is a 1-bit image. That means that there is 1 bit of information for every pixel. Since the bit can be either on or off, you can have one of two colors, black or white. If the color or density is above a certain point, the pixel is converted to white. If it is lower than that, the pixel is copied into the new version as black. The bit is used to tell if that point in the picture is black or white. It is suited for line drawings, images without any intermediate shades or color. The only real editing you can do with them is to shift the pixel pattern. Notice that the palette shows only patterns of black-and-white dots.

DITHERING: A BETTER BLACK AND WHITE

The early PC's, scanners, and displays could not do much better than 1 bit; they didn't have the power. The human eye can discern about 64 shades of gray in an image, and the average photographic print contains about 256 shades of gray. That's why photographs seem realistic; the eye sees the picture as a set of continuous tones. If there are not enough shades in an image to make it look like one tone blends into another without a break, the image looks artificial.

Now look at the middle image. Notice the increase in detail, but a loss of sharpness. The middle shades seem to be there in the full-sized view, but it's still a 1-bit file. Look at the enlargement. Notice the irregular pattern in the bitmap compared to the same area shown on the left. This technique is called dithering. PHOTO-PAINT allows you to edit monochrome images with dithering patterns. Instead of just a straight pixel-by-pixel conversion, the program looks at the average values in the area and produces a pattern of pixels in a grid.

Let's say the grid pattern for an image is based on a four-pixel square. If the area is 50 percent gray then half the pixels in the grid are turned to black and half to white. If the area is 20 percent gray, it becomes totally white, and if 80 percent gray, then the entire grid is turned to black. Adding pixels to the grid increases the number of shades but reduces the sharpness. Viewed from a distance, or printed on a laser printer, the image looks more like a grayscale image, but it isn't.

Printers use a method similar to dithering known as half toning. An image is printed using a screen that breaks up the picture into dots. The darker the area, the more dots. Although dithering is not exactly the same, many programs use the terms interchangeably.

GRAYSCALE: THE BEST BLACK AND WHITE

The image on the right is an 8-bit grayscale. The extra data give you the ability to display any one of 256 shades of gray for any and every pixel in the image (2^8 gives 256 possible combinations). So an 8-bit image can record enough detail to rival a conventional black-and-white photograph. Look at the close-up. Notice the intermediate tones. PHOTO-PAINT has tools that let you shift the values of those tones: adjusting the appearance of brightness and contrast in areas of the image, adding sharpness or dulling areas, and manipulating them with special effects.

You can also use the 8 bits to represent 256 colors. The balloon you started with is an 8-bit color image. If you can choose just the right colors with just the right kind of image, you can get almost photographic results. But to get really good quality working with true color you need even more information per pixel, 24 to be exact (2^{24} gives 16,777,216 possible combinations). That's enough data to represent all the colors plus all the gradual shades and still be able to do editing. The human eye can notice very subtle differences in color. The number of bits per pixel is called color or pixel depth.

You Can Go Home Again—Sort of

With PHOTO-PAINT you can convert an image to 24-bit color, even if it has no color. You are not really changing the color. You are just determining how many bits are used to represent each pixel and how they operate. Understanding the principle of color depth and conversion is fundamental to success with PHOTO-PAINT. If some of the details are still a bit fuzzy, don't worry. As you work with the tools, everything should fall into place.

Exporting Your Work

The Save and Save As commands in the File menu work just like those in CorelDRAW, as do the Cut, Copy, and Paste options under the Edit menu. You can save pictures in the BMP, EPS, GIF, JPG, PCX, TGA, GEM, WMF, HPGL, AI, and TIFF formats. If you save your work as an EPS file you won't be able to reopen that copy in PHOTO-PAINT, so make a PCX copy as well. The EPS file will also be resolution-specific, so it won't offer any advantage over the bitmap formats.

Selecting and Defining Painting Tools

The PHOTO-PAINT tools can be grouped into several categories. Painting tools are used to place pixels in the picture. They let you draw lines, polygons, squares, and fill areas with color. Retouching tools are used to adjust the image, or part of an image, once it is already on the page. Selection tools are used to define the areas in a painting to be modified by a tool or command, and the Display tools change the area of the image seen in the active window. The following are the basic procedures common to all the tools:

- Have the toolbox on the desktop. Place the mouse cursor over the tool you want to use. As the pointer moves over a tool the name is shown on the Help line in the lower left-hand corner of the desktop.
- Click on the appropriate icon. If the toolbox is grouped, you may have to open a fly-out.
- Move the cursor to where you plan to work. As the pointer enters the image window it will turn into the shape of the tool.
- Click or hold the mouse button to begin work. With many drawing tools the left and right buttons will produce a different effect.
- The Undo command located in the Edit menu (or **Ctrl-Z**) will remove all actions since the tool was selected. If you move on to another function, the Undo ability for that use of the tool is lost. Once another tool is selected the effect becomes permanent. The tool that looks like it has a depressed button is active.

SELECTING AND USING PAINTING TOOLS

Create a blank window using **File, New**. With the mouse pointer click on the Fountain Pen icon in the toolbox (may be grouped under the Line tool). Bring the cursor onto the blank window that you created. As the pointer enters the active window it will change shape and look like the current tool's icon. The circle above the tip is the drawing point. Hold the left button down and draw a line. As you draw, the pixels under the pointer will change color.

Paint programs work very differently from CorelDRAW. There are three basic drawing functions. You can place pixels on the page, take them off, or change how they look. In the actual image there are no objects other than pixels. There is no inherent relationship between one pixel and the next. Draw another line next to the one you just drew and draw an x shape somewhere else in the work area. The term work area will be used in this chapter to refer to the current drawing window.

Erasing Your Work

Each time you select a painting tool PHOTO-PAINT opens up a temporary buffer and notes the changes made to the image. You can remove all the strokes made with just that tool, with the Undo command. Try it. Open the menu. The top line should read "Undo Pen." Select it. All the lines you drew are gone. When you change the active tool the buffer is reset, and you can no longer undo the modifications.

Sizing a Drawing Tool

The lines you just drew were placed in the work area at the default width. What if your line is too thick or too thin? The Tool Settings workbox controls how wide a row of pixels is changed when you drag a drawing tool over the work area. In some cases you can also control the angle of the stroke, similar to the calligraphic effect you can get with the Outline tool in CorelDRAW. You can change that setting at any time using the Tool Settings workbox. Figure 11.6 shows the Tool Settings dialog box as it appears when the Impressionism Brush is active. The top third allows you to choose the shape and, depending on the tool, the angle, as well as the width, or size, of the line. The middle third, which is available for some tools and not others, gives you a good deal of control over the effects the tool will produce. The bottom third of the Tool Settings dialog box is available for only a few tools but further customizes the tool's functions.

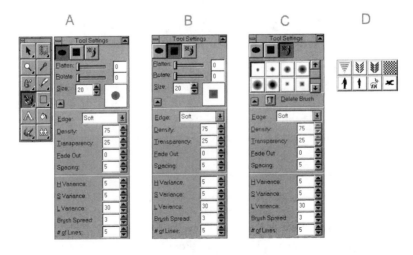

FIGURE 11.6 The three faces of the Tool Settings roll-up

Chapter 11: Getting the Picture with CorelPHOTO-PAINT

Move your mouse pointer just to the right of the number 20 in the Tool Settings workbox in Figure 11.6. You should see a cursor that looks like a pair of railroad tracks with arrows. This appears when the mouse pointer is between the two arrows and lets you drag to change the setting rapidly. You can also change the setting by typing in a new value or clicking on the arrows. The number value for a given line size will vary, based on the unit of measure. I generally leave it set at pixels, but you can also choose points, picas, centimeters, or inches.

Let's experiment. With the Pen tool selected use the mouse to adjust the size by either dragging the cursor or typing numbers. Double the number and draw a line. Cut the number and draw another. Now alter the brush style: move the flatten setting to about 50 and rotate to around 100 degrees giving a brush shape like the one shown in Figure 11.7. Draw another line, change the shape to one of the angle shapes, and then draw a circle.

 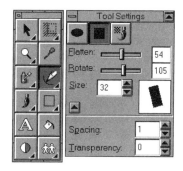

FIGURE 11.7 Changing the brush shape and angle

DRAWING WITH PHOTO-PAINT

With the technical details out of the way you can get to the fun part. Start by drawing a few simple shapes to make a cartoon face. Along the way you will draw, erase, cut, copy, and color an image with a variety of tools. The experience you have with CorelDRAW will speed things along.

Painting a Simple Face

Select the empty painting window you made a little while ago. Then choose the Hollow Box tool; click on its icon on the toolbar. Its icon looks just like that, a hollow box. That name will appear on the Help line as you place the cursor over it. In the Color Selection roll-up, select a white Background and fill and a black outline. Now bring the cursor back on the page and draw a box just as you would with the CorelDRAW Rectangle tool. Place the pointer at the starting point. (It will look like a set of cross hairs with a little square.) Then hold the left mouse button and drag it down and to the right. A thin line will follow as you move it. Make a square that fills most of the work area. When you release the button, that line will be replaced by a permanent box.

Now chose the Pen tool. Draw a face; add eyebrows, two eyes, a nose, and a mouth. The tool works like the CorelDRAW Pencil tool in Freehand mode. You don't have to be very artistic. Figure 11.8 shows how my screen looked as I finished the face.

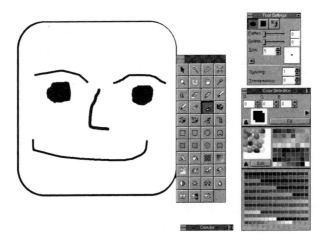

FIGURE 11.8 A simple face

Notice how the curved lines have jagged edges. The lines are not curves; they are just collections of pixels. It is similar to creating a mosaic. The artist uses black-and-white or colored tiles to form a picture. If you look too closely you can see where one tile joins another. Each pixel is like a tile. And there is a tile or pixel over every point on the painting. That is why bitmap images can take up so much file space on your disk.

Chapter 11: Getting the Picture with CorelPHOTO-PAINT   **463**

Improving the Design

I don't know about your image, but the eyes and mouth on mine could look a little better. Look at the tool icon that looks like a lasso. It is the third one to the right in Figure 11.9. If your toolbox is grouped, it may not be visible on your screen. Figure 11.9 shows the Tool Kit with the Lasso tool open. To open it, locate one of the four tools (Selections, Magic Wand, Lasso, or Scissors); then hold the mouse pointer over the little white triangle while pressing the left button. These are the PHOTO-PAINT selection tools. Whichever tool was used last will occupy that position in the toolbox. I have used one to draw a section box around the left eye in Figure 11.9. Just as in CorelDRAW, you must first select an area before issuing any commands.

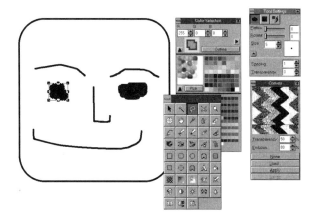

FIGURE 11.9 Using a Selection tool

Selecting Areas with the Lasso Tool

Bring the Lasso tool near the left eye; then drag it all around the eye. As you do this, a thin line will follow your movements. When you have returned to the starting point, release the mouse button. A box will appear around the eye. Press the **Delete** key. The pixels that represented the eye will be erased. Repeat the process for the other eye and the mouth. If you want, you can use the Selection tool to mark the areas to be removed. Choose it the same way; then use it like a free-form version of the CorelDRAW marquee selection.

You can't click on an entire object, like a circle or line, in PHOTO-PAINT. There are no defined objects, just collections of pixels. The Selection tools are designed to make it easy to tell the program which areas of an image are to be modified. You can also use the Selection tools to copy an area to the Windows Clipboard, and move it around on the page once it has been defined. But whatever is under the area when you place it in a new location will be lost. There is actually only one pixel in any given position at a time. PHOTO-PAINT can combine the values of two pixels in a location, allowing you to paint over something and create a transparent effect. The four Selection tools each serve a different purpose. The following list gives a summary of each one:

- The Rectangle Selection Tool icon is shaped like the selection tool selection in CorelDRAW and works the same way. The cursor is a cross-hairs shape with a box in the upper right.
- The Magic Wand icon is shaped like a wand with a star at the end. If you click on a spot, the wand will seek out the adjoining areas that have the same shade or color and select them.
- The Lasso icon is used to draw a freehand shape around an area. As mentioned, the icon resembles the loop of a lasso.
- The Polygon Selection tool (the scissors) is used to select polygon areas.

Once an area has been defined you can use commands, delete, move, cut, or copy the enclosed area. The four hollow boxes around the selection box are used to resize the image area, much like the ones you worked with the Pick tool. If you wish to make changes only in one special area of a picture, defining that area with one of these tools prevents your editing to stray outside the marquee.

Using the Palette to Choose Colors

Before replacing the erased parts of the drawing you should set the color values. In CorelDRAW you could set the outline and fill colors at any time, but not so with PHOTO-PAINT. Since it is placing the actual pixels as you work, you must specify the colors or shades ahead of time. (You can change one color to another later.) Make sure the Palette is open on the screen. Look at the far left side. There is a square there with an irregular outlined shape. The center of the shape shows the Fill color, the irregular line shows the outline color, and the area behind them shows the background color. In this context color includes shades of gray and dither patterns.

The outline color is the one that appears as you paint with a tool, and the Fill color fills any closed object. You can also paint with the fill color by using the right mouse button as you work instead of the left. The shades or colors available in a palette vary, based on the pixel depth. Figure 11.10, A and B, show the RGB color and grayscale palettes. The HSB palette can be folded up smaller by clicking on the little arrow buttons. HSB and CMYK as well as a standard palette are available. An exciting addition is the Image Palette, which analyzes the colors in the active image and makes all the hues and shades available. The numeric control dialog boxes at the top of the Color Selection roll-up allow fine-tuning of your color in any of the color processes.

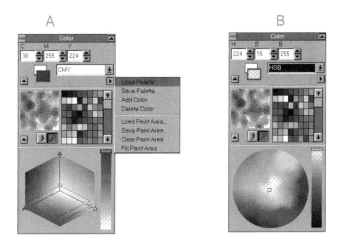

FIGURE 11.10 The CorelPHOTO-PAINT palettes

You can easily set your brush to any available color. Try it now. Click on the lower of the two boxes to the left of the window that shows the color model. Then point to a color in the Palette (the pointer will change to the medicine dropper) and click the left button. Or you can click on a color from your graphic with the right button and the fill color will be altered. Or select the tool that looks like an eyedropper from your tool box and click it on any color in your drawing. The outline color will change. To change the background color, click on the upper box in the Color Selection roll-up and then on a color. The background color is what the eraser uses to replace outlines or fills that you move the tool over with the left button held down. You can change line or background colors at any time. To change the fill color, activate the **Fills** roll-up and select a color. Remember that PHOTO-PAINT rollups differ from those in DRAW and you do not have to click Apply before the change takes place.

Working with the True-Color Palette

If you have a 24-bit window on the page, you don't see the full range of colors in the Palette, just a basic set similar to the 256-color version. With 16.8 million variations it would be a pretty big palette, and most users don't have true-color display systems anyway. Even the condensed image palette displayed when this option is selected can be confusing. So the program lets you pick colors directly from the image. Select the eyedropper tool and click on any color in the image with the left mouse button. The color at the point you clicked will become the outline color. Even if your system does not have a true-color adapter you can still work with 24-bit images. But you will not be able to see exactly what the final result will look like on screen.

Drawing Filled Circles and Copying Parts of an Image

Choose the ellipse drawing tool. If your toolbox is grouped, click and hold on the square icon and select the ellipse from the fly-out. These tools draw shapes that are outlined and filled with the colors chosen in the swatch. Open the fly-out by pressing the left mouse button with the pointer over the little white triangle in the lower right-hand corner of its icon. Select the icon that looks like a circle. Then add a pair of eyes following these steps:

- Use the left mouse button to draw a circle. If you make a mistake, you can erase it with the Undo command at the top of the Edit menu.
- Use the Selection tool to draw a box around the eye. Just get the eye, not any other black area. Don't move the box. If you do, the box will move, leaving a white hole in the image area.
- Open the **Edit** menu and choose **Copy**. This places a copy of the selected area on the Windows Clipboard.
- Choose **Paste** from the same menu. You will be given the choice of pasting it as a completely new image with its own window or as a selected item in the current window. Choose **As New Selection**. The copy, in its selection box, will appear in the upper left-hand corner of the current window. This copy can be moved without leaving a hole.
- Move the new copy into the location for the right eye. You can release the object to see if it is in the proper position and pick it up again without leaving a hole in the image.

- Once it is in the right place, click the left mouse button in an area outside the selection box. It will disappear, and the change will be permanent.

That was a bit more precise for getting a circle than drawing the eye with the Pen tool. The eyes should have a black outline and a red fill, because that is the way you set up the Palette. Now you are going to finish the restoration by adding a new, smoother-looking mouth.

THE CURVE TOOL, AND A LITTLE BIT OF BÉZIER

PHOTO-PAINT has the ability to define shapes with a tool that draws Bézier curves. You can adjust the lines somewhat as you do with the Shape tool in CorelDRAW, but when you are finished the curve is removed, and the pixels under it are filled with the primary color. After that you can no longer edit the line as a curve. If your toolbox is grouped, you may have to access the Curve tool by opening the Line tool fly-out. The icons look almost the same, like a pencil. The Line tool is shown drawing a straight line; the Curve tool appears to be drawing an arc. Open it now and drag a line straight across the area where the mouth should be, holding the left mouse button. Don't try to curve it; just make a straight line. Once you release the mouse a pair of nodes (hollow boxes) will appear at each end, and two control points (circles) can be seen along the path of the curve. Shape the mouth by dragging the circles down. Figure 11.11 shows my screen as I was editing the line. Once you have the curve the way you want it, click the mouse on an open area; the basic face will be complete.

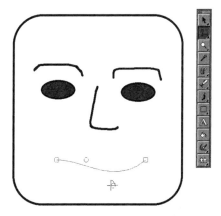

FIGURE 11.11 Editing a Bézier curve

Dressing Up the Image

A lot of neat effects can be produced with the PHOTO-PAINT tools. To get an idea of how they work, and a little practice with the interface, let's improve on the cartoon face. Figure 11.12 shows my picture as I was working with the SprayCan tool. This operates just like a can of spray paint. The longer you hold the button, the more paint lands on the target. If you just touch the button once or twice, a few drops are placed; if you leave it running, eventually the entire area will be painted solid. The width settings apply to this tool, so set them for a round shape and adjust the size to fit your own image. Figure 11.13 shows how I added hair with the Artists' Brush set on Oil7 in the Tool Settings dialog box. This gives a short, rough stroke. An impressionist brush and a pointillist brush as well as a softer paint brush are other possible choices.

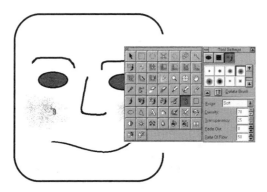

FIGURE 11.12 The SprayCan in action

FIGURE 11.13 Using the Artist's Brush tool

Chapter 11: Getting the Picture with CorelPHOTO-PAINT

You can get similar effects by following the steps outlined here. If you have difficulty with the instructions, review the material already presented in this chapter.

- Make sure that your face is 256 or 24-bit color.
- Select a reddish tone in the Palette for the outline color; then adjust it to one you want to use.
- Select the SprayCan tool. (See Figure 11.12 for reference.)
- Adjust the width, and use a round shape.
- Use the SprayCan tool to place red circles on the cheeks. Paint while holding down the right mouse button.
- Reset the color to a yellow or brown tone with the Palette.
- Select the Artists' Brush tool. (See Figure 11.13 for reference.)
- Work in strokes while dragging the tool over the upper portions of the square.

Our poor face has red-filled eyes with no irises. Let's give it blue eyes and take away the red. PHOTO-PAINT has a special tool that makes it a snap. First put in the blue eyes with the SprayCan tool. Change the foreground color and place a circle in the center of each eye that runs from the top to the bottom inner edge of each eye.

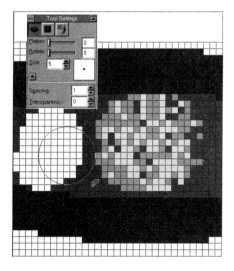

FIGURE 11.14 Adding a blue irise

In adding the blue, adjust the width of the tool to get just the right size. Use the Zoom tool to get a close-up area to work in. Don't forget that you can adjust the size of the image window on the desktop if needed. Figure 11.14 shows my screen as I worked on this part of the project. Do the same thing to both eyes.

GETTING THE RED OUT: THE WONDERFUL COLOR REPLACEMENT TOOL

Here's where life with PHOTO-PAINT gets interesting. In the early paint programs the only way to change pixels was to redraw them with a tool. Today you can tell the program to change just the pixels of a certain color with another as you drag the Color Replacer tool over the picture. That's how you are going to turn the red in the eye to a silver white.

Here's how it works. You set the color you want to remove as the outline color, and the replacement color as the background color. The easy way to do that is with the Eyedropper tool. Just select it from the graphic in the workbox and place it over the red in the eye; then click the left mouse button. You can select the secondary color the same way. Then select the Color Replacer tool and drag it over the area you want to modify.

Here are the steps for this part of our project. Just modify the right eye now. I'm saving something else for the left one. Use the screen shot in Figure 11.15 as a reference. The Color Replacer tool is selected.

- Set the primary color to the red in the eye with the Eyedropper tool.
- Set the secondary color to a silver-white custom color (the color you want the Color Replacer to use) the same way.
- Adjust the tool's width and shape. I used a Pen with a vertical shape that was wide enough to cover the entire eye.
- Drag over the areas to be changed.

Chapter 11: Getting the Picture with CorelPHOTO-PAINT

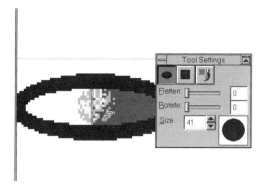

FIGURE 11.15 Working with the Color Replacer

Touching Up with the Eraser Tool

Unlike the Color Replacer tool, the Eraser tool removes anything underneath it when it is clicked or dragged. You are going to use it to clean up the other eye. The icon is the one to the left of the Color Replacer in Figure 11.14. As you can see, a white outline shows the pixels to be changed. Varying the width and shape of the brush will affect the area controlled by the Eraser. Select it and clear out the red pixels on the other eye. Then remove four adjoining pixels in the iris to create a highlight.

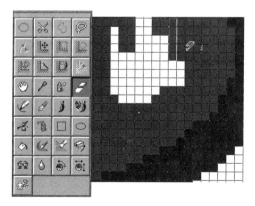

FIGURE 11.16 The Eraser tool

Adding Fills

Four area fill tools are available in CorelPHOTO-PAINT: Flood, Gradient, Texture, and Tile. If your workbox is grouped, only one of the icons will be visible. The final touch on your square face will be the addition of a fill. Figure 11.17 shows my painting after applying a radial fill. The color washes from the foreground to the background color based on the settings in the dialog box shown in the lower left-hand corner of the figure. Choose the Gradient Fill tool. Then open the dialog box by choosing the **Fill** roll-up in the Display menu. Set the Palette the same way you did to modify the eyes. There are three Gradient Fill variations: vertical, radial, and conical. The Balance setting works like the Pad option in CorelDRAW. Set up a fill with two skin-colored tones so that the radial fill will be lighter in the center. Place the tool anywhere in the clear part of the face and click the left mouse button. The fill will wash the area.

FIGURE 11.17 Applying a radial fill

Flood, Texture, and Tile Fills

If you want to experiment with the other fills just use the Undo command and use one of the other tools. The Flood will just cover the entire clear areas with the color. Setting a Tile fill is a little more involved. It is much like the Two-Color fill in CorelDRAW. It is composed of a pattern created by repeating a bitmap image over and over. Unlike CorelDRAW, you can use any supported bitmap, color, gray scale, or monochrome. I used one of the predefined patterns that are found in the \PHOTOPNT\TILES subdirectory to fill the background behind the square face. Your patterns may have been installed to a different location.

There are four steps in setting a Tile fill. Choose the Tile tool from the workbox; then open the **Options** menu and choose the **Tile Pattern** option. A dialog box like the one in Figure 11.18 will open. Locate the file and highlight it with the selection bar, or enter the name in the text entry box. If you know that it is the bitmap you want, click **OK**; then click the tool in the region you want filled. Remember that a bitmap image is a collection of pixels in rows and columns. The fill will cover the entire clear area when you set the starting point.

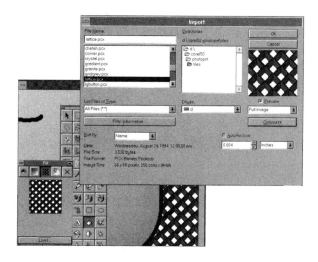

FIGURE 11.18 Setting tile fill

If you want to see what the fill will look like before loading, select the name and click on the **Preview** button. A thumbnail of the pattern will appear in the box. An Image Info box may also be opened like the one in Figure 11.18. It gives a complete rundown of the file contents.

A FEW MORE TOOLS

The preceding practice session covered most of the basics required to create bitmaps using PHOTO-PAINT. Before going on to the retouching features, I want to expand on how the program works a bit and introduce a few more tools. You can use the face as a test file to see how they work. Save your work, make a duplicate of the original (**Ctrl-D**), and make sure all the roll-ups are open.

The Locator Tool and Duplicate Command

There is a fundamental difference between the PHOTO-PAINT Duplicate command and the CorelDRAW Place Duplicate command. When you make a duplicate in CorelDRAW, the copy is independent of the original object. In CorelPHOTO-PAINT the copy is linked to the source. This lets you work on an area at one magnification in a window and see the effect at another. One very good reason for this approach becomes clear when modifying individual bits. The Locator tool places the same point at the same position in the windows for duplicates of an image.

Place both copies of the face side by side; then enlarge one copy until you can see the grid of the bitmap. Choose the Locator tool; the icon looks like a compass. In the full-view window click on the circle you drew on the left cheek. The magnified copy will jump to the same location. Now use a Drawing tool and fill in part of either picture with a color different from the current one. The change will be seen in both copies.

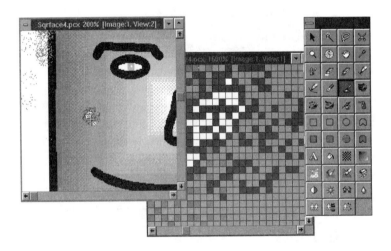

FIGURE 11.19 Using the Locator tool

Getting Information About a Picture

If you are not sure about the attributes of an image on the screen, PHOTO-PAINT can tell you. Open the Image menu and choose the Info option. A window will open giving current information about the image size, color depth, whether changes have been made, etc..

The Hand Tool

Choose the tool that looks like a hand. This is used to move an image around within a window. Place the pointer inside the window containing the magnified image and drag. The area centered in the window will move with the hand icon. This tool works just as if you were moving the object with your hand. When you have finished, close both copies of the file without saving and reopen the original version.

The Soft Tools

Another difference between draw and paint programs is the way the edge of an area is defined. Since draw programs use vector mathematics to set the shape of an element, the edge is just that, the edge. You can't have a gradual fall-off outside the path. There is an outline that is the actual boundary of a shape. Paint programs don't have objects. A shape is just a change in the topography of the bitmap. So you can feather the edges, because they are only visual edges, not attached to any specific element. In some cases the soft tools apply the primary color when the left mouse button is used. Some of the tools blur the existing colors, or copy/mix pixels from another portion of the image.

The Airbrush is an example of a soft tool, one that can be used to blur the distinction between one area and another. You can use the soft tools only with grayscale or 24-bit images, because you must have the ability to shade the tones as the effect progresses. Monochrome and 8-bit color (256 indexed colors) cannot be manipulated in gradations. Before experimenting with this tool you must convert the image to one of the appropriate types. Do that now. Once the changes are made the image cannot be changed back again. The Width and Palette workboxes operate just the same as with any other tools. I will cover some of these tools in more detail when discussing photo retouching.

Airbrush Effects

Select the Airbrush and set the **Width** and **Brush Shape** to a medium circle. Magnify an area of the face image so you can see the bitmap. Bring the tool over the image and paint by moving the pointer while holding the left mouse button. The effect should be similar to that shown in Figure 11.20. Notice how the pixels do not change color all at once but seem to be transparent.

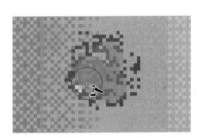 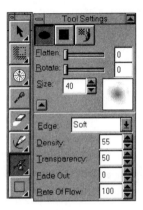

FIGURE 11.20 The Airbrush at work and the Settings dialog box

Choose the **Tool Settings** roll-up. If the lower half of the roll-up isn't open, click on the triangle on the bottom right. A dialog box like the one in Figure 11.20 will open. A number of the tools use this dialog box, but the options vary for each tool. I'll explain the ones that relate to all the soft tools first.

- **Edge.** This determines how hard or soft an edge the stroke will have as the paint is placed. The Hard setting gives a sharp line; a Soft setting gives a feathered appearance. Medium is between the two.
- **Density.** This option allows you to vary the overall softness of the stroke in fine increments, ranging from 100 (very soft) to 100 (hard). The lower numbers yield a finer stroke.
- **Transparency.** You can get a watercolor effect using this setting. The higher numbers make the paint seem more transparent. Settings range from 0 (opaque) to 100 (almost no buildup at all).

- **Fade Out.** This produces an effect like moving the airbrush from the surface or using less pressure with the brush. Once again the settings range from 0 to 100, with the higher numbers giving a smoother appearance.
- **Spacing.** This is not available for the Airbrush tool but is used to adjust the distance between the strokes as the tool is moved across the image. Settings range from 0 (closer together) to 100 (farther apart).
- **Rate of Flow.** This only applies to the Airbrush tool. It is like opening the amount of air flowing through the brush assembly. The higher the number, the greater the amount of paint delivered to the page for the same amount of time. The slowest setting is 0; 100 is the fastest.

The Paint Brush

The Paint Brush lets you draw in Freehand mode with the primary color using soft effects. Holding the **Control** key will limit the tool's effect to vertical/horizontal strokes. The **Spacebar** toggles the direction that is limited. The **Alt** key will allow it to make either vertical or horizontal strokes.

The Artist, Impressionist, and Pointillism Brushes

The Artist, Impressionist, and Pointillism brushes work basically alike. The Artist Brush lays down textured brush strokes of defined length and width, the Impressionist Brush lays down defined groups of strokes, and the Pointillism Brush lays down dots. Experiment with the effects obtained with these tools.

The Blend, Smear, and Smudge Tools

The Freehand Blend tool mixes two wet colors together, similar to working with finger-paints or watercolors before they dry. The Tool Settings roll-up has a slider to fine-tune the effect. The tool is used in Freehand mode, but the same result can be applied over large areas by selecting them and using the Blend filter. I'll explain the use of filters later in this chapter.

The Freehand Smear and Freehand Smudge tools are used to edge one color softly into another. They are used to smudge over small imperfections in an image, such as dust spots on a scanned photograph. Smear allows you to set the tool effects on the Tool Settings roll-up.

The Clone Tools

The clone tool is the final soft tool, similar to a freehand copy command. When using this tool two areas are active at once: a source and a target. As the mouse is moved the pixels from the source location replace those under the target location. You can copy backgrounds from one picture to another and clear out unwanted objects (e.g., telephone poles in front of a building). You can replace one object with another or use the Rubber Stamp option to repeat part of a picture over and over again. Here is how to use it.

- Click on the icon. It looks like two people holding hands.
- Change any settings required in the **Tool Settings** roll-up.
- Move the pointer over the area you want to copy from and click the right mouse button. A cross hair will appear. This is the center point of the area. If you want to move it at any time, just click at the new location with the right mouse button. It is best to have the entire area to be cloned visible if you can and to place the origin in the center of it.
- Move the tool to the insertion point. Drag the tool with the left mouse button. The transfer will be seen as you move the cursor.

The Impressionist and Pointillism Clone tools work much the same except that the cloned area will be duplicated in strokes or dots as defined by you in the Tool Settings roll-up.

THE MASK TOOLS

CorelPHOTO-PAINT 5.0 has added a set of Mask tools to the toolbox. These tools are used to define an area of a picture and then to either apply an effect to the area defined by the mask or to prevent an effect applied to the remainder of the picture to affect the masked area. This is extremely useful when a picture can be given emphasis by limiting the application of one of PHOTO-PAINT's special effects. The first of the mask tools, shown selected in Figure 11.21, is the Mask Picker, the next 6 tools are used to define masks and work exactly like their counterparts in the select tool box. The next tool is the mask brush and may be used to modify the mask, the last mask tool activates the node controls for the shape defining the mask allowing you to adjust the mask with great precision.

Chapter 11: Getting the Picture with CorelPHOTO-PAINT

FIGURE 11.21 The Mask Tools

Using Text

The PHOTO-PAINT Text tool functions like the artistic text function in CorelDRAW, except that the text must be entered into a dialog box. There is no direct on-image text placement. When you click OK, the block is placed at the point where you placed the tool. You are limited to entering about 10 lines of text in an image. Once it is placed the type becomes part of the bitmap and is no longer editable as characters. Given the powerful effects and scalable fonts in CorelDRAW, you probably won't use this tool except on rare occasion.

THE DRAWING TOOLS, A SUMMARY

Now that the basic drawing and viewing tools have been introduced and you have had a bit of experience, let's review the basic steps before moving on to retouching images.

- If you are planning to use a soft tool be sure the image is either grayscale or 24-bit color. Convert the picture if required.
- Select the tool by clicking on the icon.
- Set any color changes in the Palette.
- Adjust the tool's shape and width.
- Set any dialog box options that might apply.
- Apply the tool by placing it over the desired location and pressing or dragging the mouse button. Most tools offer different actions for the left and right mouse buttons.

Printing Images from PHOTO-PAINT

PHOTO-PAINT uses the Windows Print Manager and Control Panel to handle access to the printer. Open the **File** menu and choose the **Print** command. Please see the explanations of this dialog set in Chapter 5 of this book. The third selection in this box, the Options card, offers only Screen Frequency controls.

Retouching Scanned Images with PHOTO-PAINT

So far the discussion has been limited to using the tools to draw images. But CorelPHOTO-PAINT can also turn your computer into a digital darkroom. It has sophisticated editing commands for fine-tuning scanned images and creating special effects. You can use the retouching tools with drawn bitmap images, but the results are more obvious with photographs. In this section you are going to use PHOTO-PAINT to improve a color photo. Along the way the different issues involved with doing digital photography on a PC will be covered.

I've included a sample file called SISTERS.TIF on the disk that comes with the book. It started as a 24-bit image and was then converted to 256 color. You will convert it several times before finishing the chapter. You should copy it onto your hard drive and load PHOTO-PAINT before going on. If you have a scanner, you can use a photograph you have. Scan it in through your scanner program or through PHOTO-PAINT if you have installed that function. PHOTO-PAINT uses a TWAIN interface, so only TWAIN-compatible scanners will work within the CorelDRAW modulesùand you must have the proper drivers loaded in your start-up files. Other scanners can still be used and their files imported, but only via additional software.

A Little Bit More About Bitmaps

I have already talked about the basics of how bitmap images are formed and how much they can demand of your computer. Only recently has hardware been developed to give the PC the horsepower to handle 24-bit images. They demand a lot of resources. To do large-scale, true-color production properly you need a full-fledged graphics system. That includes a '486 with lots of RAM, a fast hard disk, a high-resolution monitor with a souped-up 24-bit adapter card, a good scanner, a dye-sublimation printer or film recorder for output, and a system for calibrating the scanner, monitor, and printer so they all agree that red is red and white is white.

But that doesn't mean that you can't get results on a VGA '386 with 4Mb of RAM, a basic Windows system. PHOTO-PAINT has some options that let you get the most from limited resources. If you only play with true-color images once in a while or only work with grayscale and 256-color formats, the basic Windows setup is all you need. Of course, the more, the better when it comes to PC power and graphics. If you need more information about possible system configurations and trade-offs, see the hardware section later in the book. Before working with the exercises, let's optimize the display for PHOTO-PAINT's operation.

Fine-tuning the Display System

Blue is blue and green is green, right? Sort of, but not quite. What color is the sky? Could you tell somebody else exactly what kind of blue you mean? Most of us have a pretty good idea of what sky blue is, but is that sky blue in the morning, in the late afternoon, or on a cloudy evening? When working with color images for reproduction you have to be able to match the monitor, scanner or other image source, and the final output device.

The same is true if you want accurate gray scales that give a pleasing image. It can be both frustrating and expensive to send off a file for slides and get green sky and purple grass. Most mismatches aren't that bad, but it gives you the idea of how important it can be to calibrate all the parts of the system. Before going on to actually working with scanned images you should adjust your monitor to the best display. PHOTO-PAINT offers extensive for adjusting the display to get more accurate results. Without an external reference, like a color probe, you can't really match all the variables, but using the available options will help quite a bit.

The Dithering Option

Open the View menu. Look at the Dithering option. If you are not in 24 bit color, you can choose between Error Diffusion and Ordered dithering. Error Diffusion looks best, but Ordered speeds screen re-draw. When the Error Diffusion feature is checked PHOTO-PAINT will improve the appearance of the screen if you have an adapter card that supports fewer colors than the image you are working with. It does not have any effect on the actual image or final output. It causes the program to halftone the images in the windows. This will slow down the system, so you may want to use it only for the final editing. If the display adapter already supports all the colors in the file, then this option has no effect at all.

Adjusting the Monitor's Color

The next command on the View menu controls the way colors will be seen on your monitor. You can choose between None, which will be very fast but will only approximate the colors in a complex color graphic; Fast, which approximates the colors; and Accurate, which will make every attempt to reproduce the colors accurately, but which will be rather slow, and if you are in 256 color mode, will still only approximate when dealing with a 24-bit image. The fourth option, Simulate Printer cannot be selected unless you have chosen a specific color printer. When selected, this option will produce on the screen the colors your printer will output.

Before making any adjustments you should make sure that the computer is being used under normal viewing conditions. If the monitor is not warmed up, if the lighting has been changed, or if the contrast and brightness settings are not in the usual position, the calibration won't be right. Any time you alter the viewing setup or monitor controls you should recalibrate.

Under the File menu, PHOTO-PAINT offers a Color Manager option. Click on this option and a dialog box like the one in Figure 11.22 will appear. This dialog box allows you to create a custom color profile exactly tailored to your system. If you click on the arrow beside the Monitor, Printer, or Scanner windows, a list of the more popular devices drops down. You can select your make and model from each of these lists, and choose between Automatch, Photographic and Illustration options. Corel advises using the Automatch unless your work requires even more precise controls. Give your profile a file name and click on **Generate**, keeping in mind the note at the bottom of the dialog box that the process could take time.

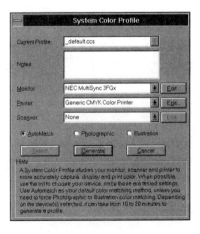

FIGURE 11.22 The Color Profile dialog box

If your needs are even more specialized, or your particular monitor (or printer, or scanner) are not on the list, you can choose the Edit option by clicking on the appropriate button to the right of each device. A dialog box like the one in Figure 11.23 appears. If you know the appropriate numbers, or have them in your devices manual, you should fill them in here. Otherwise you can select the Interactive button on the lower right and adjust the gamma and white point settings interactively. The Corel Manual has an in-depth discussion of color management in a separate small manual of that name beginning on page 479 of Volume 1.

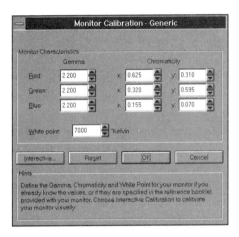

FIGURE 11.23 Defining a color profile

IMAGE ENHANCEMENT WITH FILTERS

Filters are commands that can be applied to images (or parts of images) to enhance their appearance or create special effects. Most can only be used with 24-bit or grayscale pictures. In this section we'll use the enhancement filters to tune up the SISTERS sample file. Not all images are created equal. Differences in scanning, exposure, and composition can produce less than ideal results. With PHOTO-PAINT you can spark up a dull image, remove unwanted portions, and balance the range of colors and tones.

Filters are more art than science for most users. You see what you want to with an image and then experiment with one or more filters until the picture looks the way you want it to. The job is done when the user is satisfied with the result.

I'll start with the global filters that work like standard printing controls in photography and will then move on to fine-tuning and special effects. Select and convert the picture of the two little girls to gray scale and leave both versions on the desktop. To get a better understanding of how the different enhancement tools operate, try them on both images. Open the **Effects** menu, choose **Color**, and the **Brightness and Contrast** option. Your screen should resemble Figure 11.24. If you move your cursor over the image in the preview window, the arrow will change to a hand and you can move around in the image to choose the portion you wish to observe. Clicking on the left mouse button will magnify the image, clicking on the right button will zoom out on it.

Manipulating Brightness and Contrast

Either the sliders or the text entry boxes can be used to shift the brightness, contrast, and intensity of an image. The scanned photo you are working with was taken using a flash, and the baby on the left is darker than the little girl who is holding her. Increase the contrast slightly by typing in a higher number. You may use the mouse on the arrow buttons instead. Test the effect by clicking on the **Screen Preview** button. Then shift the brightness. Shift the intensity. Keep working until the tones are pleasing. Try running the controls to extremes in various combinations to see how they work.

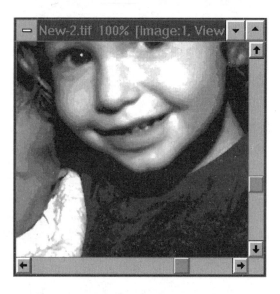

FIGURE 11.24 The original image in the Brightness-Contrast-Intensity dialog box

As the contrast is increased the middle tones disappear and the image shifts more toward a harsh black and white. Dropping the contrast level reduces the blacks and whites to grays, leaving the picture with a flat look. Moving the brightness controls shifts the light/dark ratio for the entire scale of tones. The intensity affects the brighter portions more than the rest of the image and can sometimes bring portions of an image out of the shadows. Once you have the picture the way you want it, click **OK**. You should be able to see detail in all but the darkest shadows, and the whites should be clean (free of gray tone). Then try the same controls on the 24-bit image and see how shifting values changes the appearance of the colors.

Experiment with the other changes you can make using this dialog box; Add contours, sharpen edge, etc. Only one of these parameters can be changed at a time. While you can observe the effect of each one on the image in the preview window, to experiment with using more than one of these filters, you must apply the first change to your image, select the dialog box again, and make the additional change.

Adjusting the Color/Gray Map

Adjusting the color/gray map is one of the most powerful but least understood tools for touching up an image. In traditional photography an image's range of tones can be plotted on a curve, showing the range of tones. PHOTO-PAINT plots a similar curve when you load the Color/Gray Map filter (under Tone in the Color fly-out in the Effects menu). By changing the shape of the curve you can adjust the range of tones or colors and their relationship to each other. Select the color image and select the **Filter** from the Edit menu. Figure 11.25 shows the Tone Map dialog box. Manipulating the shape of the curve alters the appearance of the picture. With a color image you can tune each channel individually.

The graph at the top of the box can be moved by dragging it with the mouse or through preset options. Open the preset drop-down menu and choose **Enhance Shadows**. Notice how the curve moves. Press **Screen Preview**. The dark areas of the picture are evened out and show more detail. Each of the preset enhancement options applies a standard curve adjustment that varies the response curve to favor a specific part of the image.

Now change the Channel setting from **All** to **Blue**. Now any modifications will only be applied to the blue component of the bitmap. Open the **Style** drop-down menu and select the **Curve** option. The active line in the graph will have five circles on it, like the one under the arrow in the figure. Drag on one of these and the curve will move with them. Make some adjustments and press **Screen Preview**. Notice how manipulating the curve can affect the image.

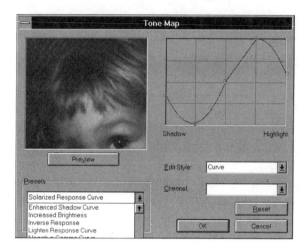

FIGURE 11.25 The Tone Map dialog box

Photographers refer to an image that lacks contrast as flat, meaning that its response curve is shallow. You can prove that by adjusting the curve. Select the grayscale version of the picture; then open the **Color/Gray Map** filter. Set Style to **Linear** and Channel to **All**. The line now has two circles at either end. Drag them so the line runs horizontally from one side to the other and press **Screen Preview**. The window is a flat gray. All the tones are reduced to one shade. Adjust the line so that the left side is at the top of the graph and the right side is at the bottom. Press **Screen Preview** again. The image has turned into a negative; all the values are reversed.

Select the **Freehand** option under Style. This is the third method of adjusting the curve. In this mode you can draw or pull any point on the line in any direction. Try it, with different shapes and color channels to see how it works. The Restore button returns the image to its original appearance.

You can save a curve to disk and use it later on similar images. Set up the pattern; then click on the **Save** button and give the setup a name when asked. To use the curve again click on the **Load** button and select the desired file.

Applying Equalization

A histogram is a very useful tool for analyzing and adjusting the range of tones in a picture. Figure 11.26 shows a typical sample. The bars represent the number of pixels in the image for a given tone. The darkest section is on the far left, and the lightest is on the right. The taller the bars, the more pixels in that category. Open the color version of your picture and choose the **Equalize** filter. This option generally makes whites whiter and black tones darker, while preserving the middle tones.

Look at the three pointers just below the graph area in the figure. Moving them will redistribute the shades and colors in the picture. The left one sets the floor for the shadows, the center one positions the mid-point of the response curve, and the right pointer controls the upper end of the highlights.

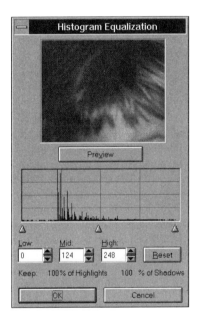

FIGURE 11.26 The histogram

When the filter is first selected a histogram will be plotted automatically. Press the Screen Preview button to see how well it improves the image. You can type in a value in the three boxes under the graph. It will shift the pointers to match that level. Try various combinations to see how the controls affect the image. Curve and equalization manipulation have less effect on images that have been underexposed. The sample image has some regions that are underexposed and some that are overexposed. Notice the difference in the amount of improvement between the two types of areas.

Touching Up with a Freehand Blend

Once a picture's tonal range and contrast are adjusted you may find that some of the areas have a banded look, as if there was a sharp break in tone along a line. The Freehand Blend tool is handy for touching up the image. Just gently smooth the pixels along the edge of the band. As you do, the area will soften. Use light strokes, so the effect is not as noticeable as the problem you were trying to fix. The Blend filter works just like the freehand version but covers an entire area or image automatically.

A Sharper Image

Sharpen is another handy filter. It examines the bitmap and reduces variations along tonal boundaries. The result is an apparent increase in image sharpness. Use the Lasso tool to select an area of the color image. When you shape an area you are sacrificing fine detail for the appearance of sharpness; it does not really improve the image quality.

Figure 11.27 shows a portion of the little girl's hair. I have sharpened the section above the dialog box by 37 percent with the Wide aperture setting turned on. Notice how the pixels have been altered. The selected area to the left of the dialog box has been modified using the settings shown in the screen shot. I used less than half the percentage and turned off the aperture option. If you sharpen a dark area of an image, you may get light-colored spots as the enhancement is applied.

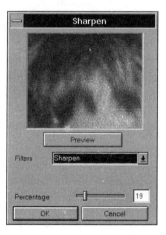

FIGURE 11.27 Using the Sharpen filter

Pay Attention to Details: Fine-tuning the Image

Once you have a picture looking pretty much as you want it, start working on the details. Examine the image by areas, noting imperfections. By now you have seen that using a filter often creates problems as well as fixes them. Look for places with spots, or where the tones don't blend quite right. Are some of the shadows too dense, or do some of the mid-tones look washed out? Cameras and scanners only work with the image and light available when the image was made. In most cases these will be the parts that need a little extra attention.

Most of PHOTO-PAINT's controls can be used over small areas and even individual pixels. The job is done when you feel it's done. The level of effort is not fixed. Some images will look fine with just a little contrast adjustment or equalization. But most could benefit from detailed corrections of minor flaws.

Touching Up with the Smear Tool

When I first started manually retouching photos one of the primary tools was a cotton swab with a bit of fine charcoal or dye on the tip. The PHOTO-PAINT Smear tool performs the same task. Find an area where the shift from one color or shade of darkness is not to your liking. Choose the Smudge tool. (It looks like a cotton swab.) Adjust the size and shape; then use it to smooth and mix the tones. Figure 11.28 shows how I worked on the highlights on the lower lip on the sample image.

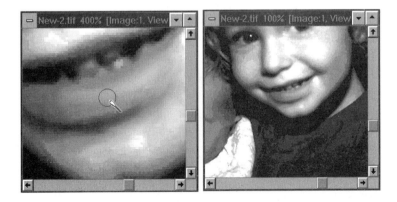

FIGURE 11.28 Retouching small areas with the Smudge tool

Managing Freehand Brightness and Contrast

What if a small area just doesn't have the right contrast or brightness? You could use the Lasso to select it, but there is a better way. Two tools enable you to get the exact degree of change you want freehand. The Freehand Brightness tool is shaped like a sunburst. When you choose it, the Tool Settings drop-down turns to a gray scale, even if you are working on a color image (except with monochrome files). Click with the tool on the brightness level you want; then paint with it. Figure 11.29a shows the Local Brightness tool at work. I have lightened the crease at the edge of the mouth and darkened the cheek. This is not an ideal retouching job, just an example of how the tool works.

The Freehand Contrast tool operates the same way. Choose it and the Tool Settings drop-down turns into a gradient bar. Choose the contrast adjustment by clicking with the tool; then paint with it. Figure 11.29b shows the contrasts on the cheek being modified. You can also enter a value in the box in the lower corner of the Palette for both tools.

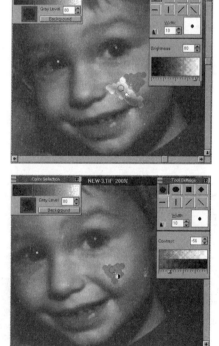

FIGURES 11.29a and b The Freehand Brightness and Contrast tools

Adding a Little Local Color

If you want to produce a rosy cheek, or add a little color to a highlight, the Freehand Tint tool is the answer. Try it. Select the color image and then the Freehand Tint tool. The icon looks like a pair of sunglasses. Now pick a color from the Palette. Paint an area smaller than the one you want to modify. Figure 11.30 shows the tool being used. I increased the covered area to make it stand out more. Then use the Smear or Blend tool to feather the edges and work the color into the area.

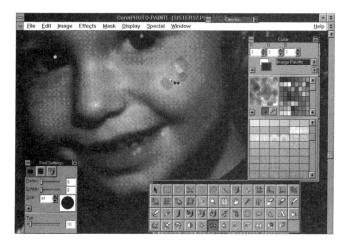

FIGURE 11.30 The Local Tint tool

Making Some Noise

One of the problems when electronically retouching scanned photos is that the results can be so smooth that an area looks artificial. The Noise filter, found in the Effects menu, simulates a grain effect, like that seen in traditional pictures. You can add or subtract noise or select from maximum to minimum noise. There are three settings in the Add Noise dialog box, as shown in Figure 11.31. The Variance can range from 0 to 255. The higher the number, the more pronounced the effect. You have the choice between Gaussian, Spike, and Uniform. Gaussian adds rather large pixels of noise, shown in the Figure, Spike much smaller ones in softer colors. Uniform just adds a grainy look.

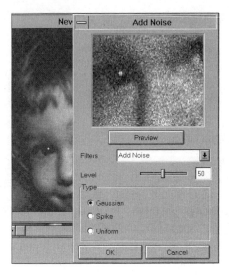

FIGURE 11.31 The Noise Filter dialog box

Putting It All Together

The preceding tools offer electronic retouching and enhancements once limited to skilled darkroom technicians. Think of the filters as part of the toolkit for refining your scanned images. Try a short exercise. Close in on an eye in the sample picture. Adjust the contrast for maximum detail; then rearrange the highlights, add a pupil, and sharpen the edges. If you want some more practice, place some eyelashes and change the color of the iris.

The Special Effects Filters

Beyond basic enhancement lies the realm of special effects. As with the other tools, you should convert a file to either gray scale or 24-bit before using them. CorelPHOTO-PAINT 5.0 has added a number of new special effects and space does not allow me to cover all of them. I'll go over the basics of a few basic filters, and show an example or two with the sample files. Use them as starting points for trying out each one. All these effects are located under the Effects menu.

Embossing Images

Embossing images is a neat filter that produces a three-dimensional effect that looks like the image has been redone as a bas-relief with grayscale and 24-bit images. Figure 11.32 shows two files that have been converted with the filter on either side of the dialog box. The arrow determines which direction the imaginary light source will come from to create the effect. In this case both images were filtered with the source from the upper left.

FIGURE 11.32 Using the Embossing tool

The Emboss Color options include three shades of gray (light, medium, and dark) and the three defined Palette colors (primary, secondary, and background). If you want to use a certain color, add it as one of the three before opening the dialog box. As you can see, most of the details of the image will be lost. If you are working with color, almost everything but the highlights will be converted to the embossing color.

The image on the left was converted to 24-bit color, embossed, and then converted to gray scale. The image on the right has been embossed; then the contrast and brightness were globally adjusted to emphasize the effect. You can tune up these images with the other filters and freehand controls just like any normal image. Combined with the granite tile fill as a background, the Emboss filter creates an appearance like carved stone.

Getting an Edge

The Edge filter is a bit like an auto-tracer. It locates the edges of either lines or pixels, depending on the level of sensitivity. A low number tends to ignore thinner lines; higher settings find almost all of them. The example on the left in Figure 11.33 was converted with Sensitivity setting at 1; the middle version was connected with the maximum sensitivity of 10.

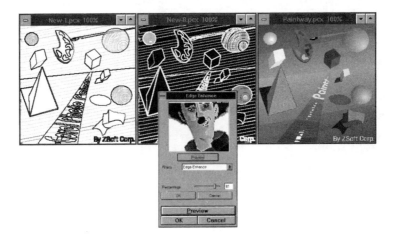

FIGURE 11.33 Edge filter effects

The Color option sets the color to be used for the areas left clear by the Edge filter. The example on the left was treated with white; the middle one was treated with a dark primary color. The Edge option lets you choose light- or dark-colored outlines. The Auto option lets the program adjust the outline.

Sharpening and Smoothing

The Image menu offers two general options, Sharpen and Smooth, which can be used to affect selected areas or the entire image. Each has a fly-out menu offering four options; each option has delicate controls to fine-tune your image. These options have effects similar to the Freehand Contrast and the Smudge tools, respectively, but are automated to cover large areas quickly.

Obscuring an Area with Pixelation

Open the SAMPLE file and convert it to 24-bit color. Then use the Selection Box tool to select the painter's palette in the upper center portion of the picture. Now choose the

Pixelate filter and apply it using the defaults. The results should look like the sample on the left in Figure 11.34, just like the hidden identity blocks on the evening news. I have increased the contrast to make it easier to see.

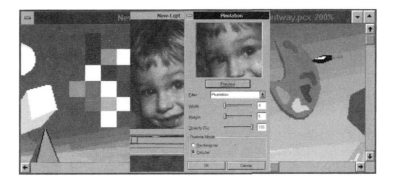

FIGURE 11.34 The pixelate effect

The pixelate effect is based on the underlying colors and is applied in the size specified in the Width and Height boxes. The range is from 1 to 16 pixels. If you click on the **Identical Values** radio boxes, the two values will be set to the same number.

The Motion Blur Filter

The Motion Blur filter is the quick and easy way to add the illusion of speed or motion to a picture. I opened the dialog box, chose the direction in which the apparent motion began, and set the speed for the filter. The results are shown in Figure 11.35. The range for the filter is from 1 to 50. It works best when the object has a flat background or by carefully selecting the region to be modified. The Smudge or Blend tools can be used to soften any unwanted streaking.

Several other useful effects are available, including Solarize, which gives a sun glare effect, and Psychedelic, which changes the colors to fluorescent shades. Artistic gives you the choice of changing all or part of the image to impressionist brush strokes or pointillist dots. The Jaggy Despeckle option blurs and softens all the edges, and Posterize removes color gradations, giving areas of pure color. Each of these options gives you the opportunity to produce an entirely new look from an image.

FIGURE 11.35 The appearance of motion

Transformations

In CorelDRAW, on-screen transformations are easy; just double-click and drag in the desired direction. Because PHOTO-PAINT's images are bitmaps, rotating and scaling images requires a lot more from the computer. As a result you must use the Image menu to order transformations of an entire image, or a selected area. All are executed as soon as you choose the option from the fly-out. You can apply the commands to an entire image, or to a portion, by first using one of the selection tools.

Resizing an Image with the Resample Dialog Box

You can adjust the size of a picture by choosing the Resample option on the Image menu. If you have checked the **Maintain Aspect** checkbox, the other side of the image will automatically be adjusted to match any number entered. You can specify the unit of measure using the **Preferences** option on the Special menu.

Percentage scaling is the most common way that traditional layout people size images. If you do a lot of resizing, consider buying a proportional scale from an art supply store. It is a circular calculator that is used to fit an image by scale into a specific area. Percentage scaling is most easily done through this menu also.

The Flip and Rotate Options

The Flip and Rotate options are simple. Just select the image or area to be transformed; then choose the option from the Image menu. To flip or rotate in increments (90, 180, or 270 degrees) just select the appropriate item from the fly-out menu found under the Flip or Rotate options in the Image menu. Figure 11.36 shows choices under the Rotate fly-out.

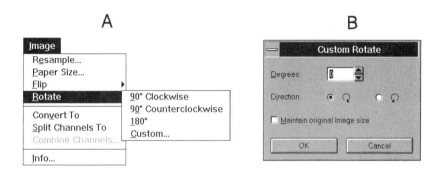

FIGURE 11.36 Rotation options and controls

Distorting Images

Selecting the Transformations option from the Effects menu gives you something like an Envelope in Draw. The image or selected area will be surrounded with a box with nodes or handles that you can pull around with the mouse. Three D Rotate does just that, with adequate controls to get the effect you wish. The Mesh Warp option works very much the way the Envelope does in DRAW and allows you to make very interesting warps in your graphic. The Perspective option is extremely memory demanding and requires a good bit of experimentation.

Inverting Images

You could create a negative image by adjusting the curve, but the Effects menu has a quicker way. Just select the area you want inverted, open the menu, and choose the **Invert** option under the Fancy command. In some cases the results may be a little different, especially if you are going to convert the color model after the inversion. Figure 11.37

shows the paintway image with an inverted copy on the left. Notice the banding and how differently the road in the center was handled in the negative.

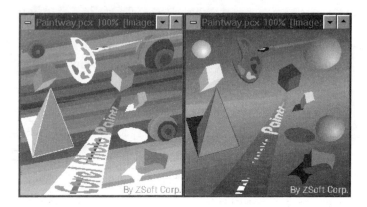

FIGURE 11.37 An inverted image

Producing Outlines

The Outline option is found with the Fancy filter (on the Effects menu), but without the controls. It automatically traces the image and converts it into an outline. The lines are the same color as the current edge of the area that formed the boundary of the shape. The background color is used to tint any area not outlined. Some radial fills may not look like they were outlined, because of the way the program interprets that area. Figure 11.38 shows the paintway picture after outlining. You can see how the radial fills were handled.

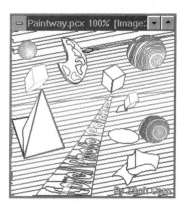

FIGURE 11.38 The paintway outline

Chapter 11: Getting the Picture with CorelPHOTO-PAINT

There are many exciting effects available in PHOTO-PAINT 5.0, far too many to go into in detail here. They are found under Fancy, Mapping, and Special in the Effects menu. Figure 11.39 shows you just five of those effects. The Preview windows 5.0 has added, along with the dialog boxes, most with controls, allow you both to asses the effects of applying one of these to your drawing, and to experiment with several before changing your graphic by fully applying one of them. You should always click on the **Checkpoint** command in the Edit menu before activating the Effects dialog boxes. That way, if after applying the effect you are unhappy with the results, clicking on **Restore to Checkpoint** will return your image to the point where you clicked on Checkpoint. Since memory tends to become a factor when working in PHOTO-PAINT, it isn't practical to make copies of your image each time you plan a change. However, saving different versions to file, each with its own file name, is very good insurance.

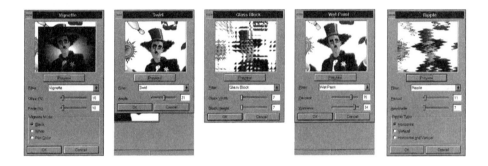

FIGURE 11.39 Some of PHOTO-PAINT's effects

PHOTO-PAINT has become such a full and flexible stand-alone program that it deserves a book all by itself. Unfortunately, time and space considerations do not allow me to fully explore the possibilities with you.

Masks

The new Mask tools make working with masks much easier and more effective. The tools work almost exactly like the regular selection and paint tools. Masking allows you to change part of an image, or protect part of an image from changes you are making to the rest of it. Again, the process of using masks is too involved to devote room to it in this book.

Chapter Summary

CorelPHOTO-PAINT gives you a variety of tools for creating and editing bitmap images for use in CorelDRAW or with other programs such as Ventura Publisher or PageMaker. Keep in mind the possible large file sizes and scaling problems when working with PHOTO-PAINT. The range of effects and possibilities for special effects make PHOTO-PAINT a very useful tool for the creation or artistic images as well as giving you the tools to retouch photographs or adapt images for your purposes.

CHAPTER 12

Making the Point with CorelCHART

This chapter covers the following topics:

- Setting Up Your System for Chart
- The CorelCHART Toolbar
- Using the Data Manager
- Creating Charts
- Working with 3-D Effects
- Annotating Charts
- Adjusting Data Presentation
- Exchanging Data with Other Applications
- The Fundamentals of Presentation Design
- Chart Types

Introduction

For most people a picture really is worth a thousand words when it comes to understanding numbers. CorelCHART can take a spreadsheet full of digits and produce images that explain what the numbers mean and help sort out their importance. The program offers 2 basic types of chart with about 50 variations, all of which can be enhanced with text, imported images, and special effects. You can use data prepared in other applications or use a spreadsheet-like Data Manager. This chapter covers the basic operation of CorelCHART, the method of choosing a chart type, and the fundamentals of presenting your data.

There's good news and bad news when it comes to working with CorelCHART. The good news is that the program operates very much like CorelDRAW and offers a wide range of chart types and features. The bad news is the limited import, export and customization capabilities, combined with a few quirky habits. If you have everything set up properly and work only within CorelCHART, everything should work well. The program is being enhanced, so improvements continue.

Before You Begin

The Windows environment has made it easier for software developers and hardware manufacturers to offer customers a graphical interface to use with their products. CorelCHART uses all the standard Windows features, offering drop-down menus, fly-out menus, scalable fonts, and the ability to open several windows at the same time. It also uses many system resources. Underpowered computers need to be configured carefully to run CorelCHART, and they need to have a working permanent swap file. For more information see the Windows User's Guide.

If you have a high-powered video adapter, you may need to reduce the resolution of the display and minimize how many applications are running with CorelCHART. Most of those cards and the program make heavy use of certain system resources. When the system level gets too low, CorelCHART may crash. You may notice that some of the screens in this chapter look a bit different, because I had to adjust my display system to make them. If you experience problems, unload any other applications and reduce any other system overhead you can.

Chapter 12: Making the Point with CorelCHART

The CorelCHART Interface

With all the warnings and file editing out of the way you can start to work with the program. Open your **Corel Graphics** Group and click on the **CHART** icon (it looks like a balloon with a bar chart next to it). After a short wait the initial screen should open. Only the File and Help menus will be available. Since you have already covered menus and toolbars in the preceding chapters, detailed instruction will be kept to a minimum. The basic tools work almost as they do in CorelDRAW. Many are exactly the same. The interface is shown in Figure 12.1.

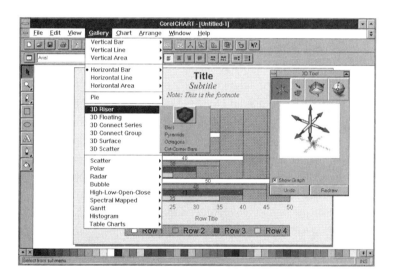

FIGURE 12.1 The CorelCHART interface

Opening an Existing Chart

Click on the File menu and choose the **Open** option. A dialog box like the one in Figure 12.1 will appear. Use it to go to the **Chart**, then the **3DSCAT** (Three-dimensional Scatter-Plot) subdirectory. Click once on the file named **3DSCAT04.CCH**. The .CCH extension indicates that this is a CHART file.

Notice the picture of the chart in the Preview window on the far right of the dialog box. Clicking the **Options** button shows an explanation of its type, design, and required data elements. In this case you would need three values (sets of data) to calculate the chart. Now **OK** the selection and you will take a closer look at the CHART interface.

The ChartView Editing Window

This screen should look fairly familiar. A Toolbar runs down the left side; it can be made movable like the one in DRAW! by an option off **Toolbox** on the View menu. Menus are arranged across the top. Beneath the menus is the Ribbon bar. Beneath it is the Text Ribbon bar, with options for adjusting text on the chart similar to the Edit Text dialog box in CorelDRAW. The center area holds the chart, and an on-screen palette is located at the bottom of the main window.

This is the interface that is used to dress up a chart after the type has been selected and the data have been entered or imported. If a tool or option is unavailable, the icon will be gray instead of black

The Data Manager

The Data Manager works much like a spreadsheet (to access the Data Manager, click on the icon which looks like a chart just above the pick tool). If you are familiar with Windows spreadsheet-style programs, such as Microsoft Excel or SPSS for Windows, you can probably start using most of the features with just a little bit of practice. The menus are different, because there is no direct manipulation of the chart from the Data Manager. Only data editing and tagging are performed here. The actual chart is only altered in the ChartView window. Both can be open at the same time. In fact, you can have more than one chart open at a time, but there is only one Data Manager. It shows the data for the currently active chart. These windows will be discussed after the tools are introduced.

The Basic CHART Tools and Controls

Many variations of charts are available, and the exact function of a tool and its availability will vary with the type being worked on. For example, if you create a a 3-D chart, the 3-D tools will be active. Choosing a different type of chart would make those tools unnecessary. As a specific type of tool is used, I will introduce it. Right now focus on the primary ChartView toolbar.

The Toolbar

There are two layers to each file. The lower one, called the Chart Layer, holds the actual chart and any text generated by the Data Manager. The upper layer, called the Annotation Layer, holds the objects created with the ChartView tools and menus. Objects created with the toolbar are always on top of the objects produced from the data.

There are 8 icons on the ChartView toolbar. Almost all functions are like their CorelDRAW counterparts. The actual draw functions are limited to the Annotation Layer. To use or activate a tool you click on the icon. In some cases you will be offered a fly-out menu. Dragging the mouse over the fly-out to the desired option and clicking selects it.

- **The Window Toggle Button.** The top icon is the **Data Manager** button. Clicking on it will change the active screen to the Data Manager. If the Data Manager is active, the icon will show a chart instead of the spreadsheet (clicking on that chart-type icon will return you to the ChartView window). Click on the spreadsheet icon now. Notice how the Data Manager appeared. The chart is still on the desktop. Open the Window menu and choose the **Cascade** option. Both windows will be arranged on the desktop. Clicking on the icon now will toggle one in front of the other.

- **The Pick Tool.** This is the same icon as for the CorelDRAW Pick tool, and it is used almost the same way for scaling, sizing, and selecting objects. Although CHART does use vector graphics for creating charts and text, you can't use this Pick tool for rotating and skewing. There is no Shape tool for direct Bezier-style manipulation of curves.

- **The Zoom Tool.** The Zoom tool is a fly-out menu with fixed magnification options based on the type of chart that is active. You don't drag over the area as you do with the CorelDRAW version. Open it now and use it to enlarge and shrink the chart.

- **The Pencil Tool.** This is another fly-out, with three options, as shown in Figure 12.7. Each one serves a different purpose. The one on the left is for creating straight lines; the second is for creating polygons. You use a single click to put a bend in the polygon and a double-click to end it. The third option draws freehand just like the Pencil tool in CorelDRAW.

- **The Rectangle and Ellipse Tools.** These both look and work just like the CorelDRAW versions, except that you can't use Transformations or edit the resulting objects as curves.

- **The Text Tool.** With this CorelDRAW look-alike on the Annotation Layer, you can enter and edit text directly on the screen. If you click on a title or footnote located on the Chart Layer, you can edit the object with this tool.
- **The Outline Tool.** Veteran Corel users will feel right at home with this tool. As in CorelDRAW, most objects have fills and outlines that can be defined by the user. The Outline tool fly-out menu is the same one used in CorelDRAW 5.0, but some of its dialog boxes are different. The top row starts with an icon that opens the outline Pen dialog box. The options include line width, corners, line caps and behind fill. Next coems the Pen roll-up. The rest of the top row options are preset line-width values. The bottom row holds the Color Selector icon and presents shades.
- **The Fill Tool.** This is almost like CorelDRAW's Fill tool, but not exactly. Fountain Fills, Two Color Fills, Full Color Fills, and Texture Fills are all available and offer the same selections as DRAW. The Pictograph roll-up, shown as the star at the end of the fly-out, allows you to use a graphic file for fill. The rest of the icons on the top row match the ones in CorelDRAW. The bottom row is similar, but the four icons on the right end produce preset patterns. The Color Selector dialog box offers the same color options as DRAW.

The Text Ribbon

The primary text controls are on the top of the window, under the menu bar. They are active when you are working in the Data Manager or if the Text tool is selected in the ChartView window. This Ribbon replaces the Edit Text dialog box in CorelDRAW and resembles ones used by many other Windows applications. The first two tools are drop-down menus for adjusting the typeface and font size. The first seven icons are all toggle switches. The first three, starting on the left, set Bold, Italic, and underlining to on or off. The next four adjust Justification to left, center, right, or full. The two just beyond them control letter spacing, and the last pair control line spacing. There is no way to specify numeric spacing.

CREATING A SIMPLE CHART

The best way to learn the fine details of CorelCHART is by working with graphs. I'll walk you through a simple bar chart to introduce the spreadsheet functions and basic data commands.

Opening a New File

To create a new chart you have to select an initial chart type and open the Data Manager. Select the **New** option from the File menu. The New dialog box, like the one in Figure 12.2, will open, providing access to the Chart Gallery and Sample Data. Make sure the highlight bar in the **Gallery** window is on the **Bar** option. It is the top one. Look at the sample chart types on the right side of the box. Click on the second one down on the right. Below the samples the information box should say you have selected the **Vertical Bars**; **Stacked Bars**. If not, click on the others until you find it. Make sure the **Use Sample Data** checkbox is blank; then click **OK**. When you build a chart from scratch, you might also want to set the paper size and margins. Those also work exactly as they do in CorelDRAW.

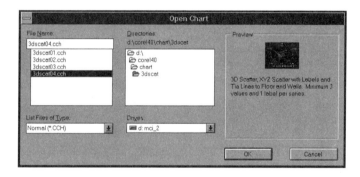

FIGURE 12.2 Selecting a chart type

Here's what you just did. The program uses a template to set up the basic format and to decide what tools should be available. By selecting a chart type, you gave it the information it needed. If you check the Sample Data option, the cells within the spreadsheet are filled with placeholders for the various parts of the chart. (A cell is a specific location in the spreadsheet grid, like A-1 or C-6.) This is a very handy feature, but right now you will be shown how to create a graph from scratch. That way you can see everything that has to be done.

WORKING WITH THE SPREADSHEET AND ENTERING DATA

The CHART Data Manager looks like a spreadsheet and even acts like a spreadsheet. That only speeds up the learning curve and data entry. In reality the spreadsheet is a fill-in-the-blank form for creating graphs. Once the data and text are entered, you tell CHART what to do with each cell or range of cells. The best way to see how it works is to do it.

The rows of the data entry area are lettered acrosse the top, starting with A, and the columns are numbered from 1, running down the page. Table 12.1 shows you what to enter in each cell. The table entry for column A, row 1 should be typed into the same location in the spreadsheet. Just place the cursor in the first location and type. A box shape will show which cell is active. After the data are in place you can use the mouse, arrow keys, or cursor to move the cursor to the next cell.

TABLE 12.1 Data for sample chart

	A	B	C	D	E
1	Ballistic Video Board Comparisons	Time in Seconds	Lower Numbers Are Better		
2	Windows Performance Tests	Display Adapter			
3	Shade Tree Benchmarks V. 2.1				
4					
5	Black Bart	The Marvel	Color	Red Queen	Rocket
6	Boot Windows	8	10	14	13
7	Redraw Bitmap	14	21	28	25
8	Corel Train	17	28	35	37
9	Green Lizard	90	121	187	168

The chart will show the time it took for four fictional video adapter cards to perform basic operations, such as loading Windows or displaying a drawing like Chris Purcell's *Green Lizard*, which is discussed in a later chapter.

Adjusting and Selecting Columns and Rows

As you type, the letters will appear on the row above the top of the spreadsheet area. When you press **Enter** or move to the next cell, the characters will be placed. You can replace data by re-entering the cell and typing something else. The default size of the columns will be too small for some of the entries listed in the preceding chart, and the letters won't all show on the screen. Don't worry; they're all there. Once you have all the data in place, move the mouse pointer to the gray header row on top. Set it right on the line between the A and B. Drag the mouse to the right. As you do the cursor will change and the entire column width will adjust with it. When the column is wide enough, release the mouse and continue the process until all the columns are the way you want them. Figure 12.3 shows how the window should look after everything is in place.

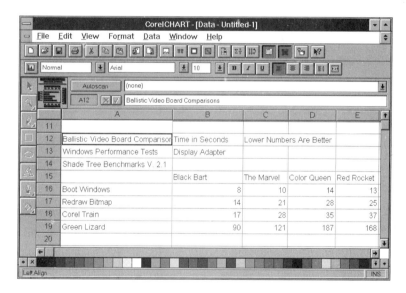

FIGURE 12.3 The completed spreadsheet

To select a cell just click on it with the mouse. As you move the pointer across the page it will look like a thick white cross. An I-beam cursor indicates a cell has been selected and that you can enter data. To select a row, just click on its number in the gray row to its left. Columns are selected the same way; click on the letter in the header row. You can select the entire sheet, even cells that are not visible, by clicking on the blank gray cell in the upper left-hand corner above the A and 1. Areas on the sheet can be selected by dragging over them with the mouse.

Tagging the Data

Now that all the data are in place you have to tag the cells so that the program will know what to do with the objects in the actual chart. There is a direct link between information in the Data Manager and the way it is displayed in the chart. So you must tell the program which cell holds a title, or a footnote, and which ones are to be used to make such calculations as those necessary for bars and pie slices. To do that each cell is assigned to one of several tags, which vary somewhat, based on the type of chart you are making. The tag contains the formatting information, so when you change to the ChartView window, the chart will look almost the way you want it.

The Autoscanner

If you typed the data in exactly as shown in the example, the Autoscan feature will do almost all the tagging automatically, based on the cell location. If you had checked the **Use Sample Data** box when you opened the new chart, there would have been labels and sample data in the appropriate cells for autotagging. Then you could have just replaced the sample with your information.

You don't have to select any cells to use the Autoscanner. The program is preset to look at certain cells. Click on the button located two rows under the View menu marked **Autoscan**. Once you have done that the majority of the cells should be tagged. I'll show you what I mean.

Viewing the Chart

Click on the button at the top of the toolbar that toggles between the Data Manager and the ChartView windows. From now on, you'll just be asked to change the view. At this point, go to the Gallery menu, select **Vertical Bar** and then select **Side-by-Side**. The chart in the center of the window should look like the one in Figure 12.4. The color scheme in the illustration has been modified to help it show up better in gray scale. Overall, it looks okay. But not all the information is there. That is because the Autoscan feature does not tag axis labels, such as the one that reads **Lower Numbers Are Better**.

Chapter 12: Making the Point with CorelCHART   **511**

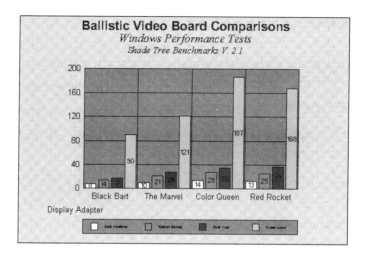

FIGURE 12.4 The basic chart

Let's go back to the Data Manager and tidy things up. Since you will be working back and forth a bit, being able to see both windows at once will make things a lot easier. Open the Window menu and choose the **Cascade** option. Then adjust the windows so that you can see the edges of both the chart and the spreadsheet. Now just click on the title bar; that window will be placed in front. If your display makes that arrangement difficult, fix your desktop the way you want it.

Tagging the Rest of the Chart

Look at the little diagram of your chart in the upper left-hand corner of the Data Manager window. It's called the **Preview**. It shows all the parts of the chart. One of its bars should be red, probably the one for the title at the top. The drop-down list to the right of the **Autoscan** button says Title. The name on this Tag Bar list can be changed to show any of the chart's tags. This drop-down list provides access to the list of available tags for this kind of chart. Select the cell containing **Time in Seconds**. Open the drop-down list and place the selection bar over the tag called **Y1 Title** and click the mouse button. The new name will replace **Title** in the menu header, and the drop-down list will close.

Using the Preview

Look at the **Preview**. Look at the horizontal red bar underneath the vertical bars. It shows the position controlled by the active tag.

Setting the Other Axis

Use the same technique: Select the cell and open the drop-down list, then choose the tag to experiment with tagging your chart.

Although the steps will actually tag the cells properly, the locations the Preview shows may not match the actual positions on the page. After you dress up the spreadsheet a bit (and uncover another quirk), we'll go over the ChartView and set things right.

Dressing Up the Spreadsheet

Before you start working in ChartView, let's format the cell display a little bit to get used to working with the Text Ribbon Bar at the top of the desktop. Click on the top or header of the **A column**. Notice how the column becomes black. Now press the **Center ALignment** button. It is the third button in from the right end. The text will jump to the center of the cell, in all the cells. Press the **B** (Bold) button and the highlighted text will be converted to Bold. In most cases when you select an area only the objects selected will be affected by a command. Of course the text display settings made here don't change the appearance of the chart in any way, so just format the spreadsheet the way that looks best on your monitor. I included this paragraph so that you wouldn't think something was wrong with your system.

Cleaning Up the Chart

Now it's time to see what the results of all this tagging produced. I'll warn you up front that you will have to do some cleanup, since the Preview does not fully reflect how the real chart looks. Change to **ChartView** and look for the words **Lower Numbers Are Better**. You can't find them? Well, that's another little quirk. A *template* is used to store specific instructions about how the chart is constructed. Using templates will be covered later in the chapter. In this case the axis titles are on the page, but they are turned off. Click the right mouse button in a clear area in the graph itself. The on-screen **Bar Chart Frame** pop-up menu will open. An example is shown in Figure 12.5a. Drag and choose the **Display Status** option. A dialog box like the one in Figure 12.5b will appear.

Chapter 12: Making the Point with CorelCHART

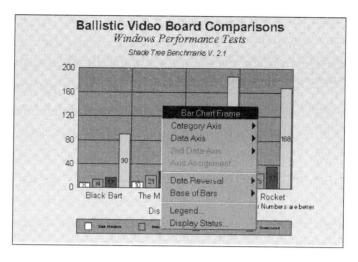

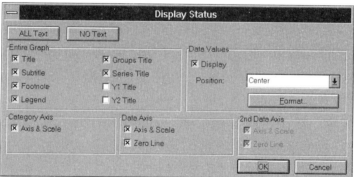

FIGURES 12.5a and b Setting the Display Status

This dialog box controls which of the tagged Chart Layer elements are actually shown or printed. Click on the **ALL Text** button. Most of the boxes will have checkmarks, and so they will be displayed in the chart. Click on the **NO Text** button; and the checkmarks go away. You can toggle them on and off with the mouse. You can use this box to customize the display quickly. Go ahead and make all the available boxes active. If some of the labels are still not visible they may be on-screen but colored the same as the background. In that case you need to change the colors using the **Pick** tool to select an object and the **Fill** tool to change its interior shade. The Pick, Fill, and Outline tools operate the same as the ones in CorelDRAW. The necessary details of their operation are contained in the first few chapters of this book if you need a review. If you still can't find **Lower Numbers are Better**, just click on the **Text** tool, click at the lower right corner of your graph, and type the words in. You can then format the text with the typeface and size you want. Text added to a chart from the Chart view behaves a little differently from text entered in the spreadsheet. Click on the words you typed in and use the handles to enlarge the size of the text frame. The type size will increase. Now select the words **Display Adapter** and resize that text frame; the font size doesn't change. To change this type, we must select a new point size from the drop-down list on the Text Ribbon.

Manipulating the Chart Layer On-Screen

When the Chart window is active you can format the titles, labels, and other objects located on the Chart Layer and even reformat the data into a different chart type. The first thing to do is to change the placement of the titles that are in the wrong place. Figure 12.7 shows the final edition of the bar chart. The title reading **Lower Numbers Are Better** is now in the lower right-hand corner. Use Figure 12.7 as a reference for relative size and position of the various objects you manipulate.

Rotating Title Test

The first step in adjusting the chart labels is to reset the text. Use the right mouse button and click on one of the letters in the words Time in Seconds. An on-screen menu will open like the one in Figure 12.6. If a checkmark is in front of an option, it is active. **Hotel text** runs vertically, like a sign in front of an old hotel. Click on it to toggle the checkmark on. The title will turn to portrait.

FIGURE 12.6 Rotating AxisText

Chapter 12: Making the Point with CorelCHART

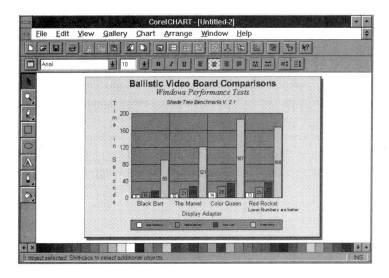

FIGURE 12.7 The Completed Chart

Repeating the process returns it to landscape. Use the same technique to rotate the other titles as appropriate. Don't worry about the size. That will be covered next.

Moving and Scaling Text

Look at the handles around the words **Display Adapter** in Figure 12.7. These are bounding boxes similar to the ones in CorelDRAW, but there are some differences. Place the pointer anywhere in the box except on one of the handles and drag it to a point under the names of the display cards. Don't worry about getting the block centered.

Now open the Arrange menu with the text still selected. Drag the point down to the **Align** command and then apply the **Center of Page** option and choose **Horizontal** from the menu. The block will be centered from left to right. The three options on the fly-out work very much like the **Align** command in CorelDRAW, with one exception. The center of the object is based on the center of the bounding box of the text. If one side of the box is larger than the other, the text won't seem to be centered on the page. To fix it you must either adjust the size of the box by dragging on the handles or manually position the object.

If the box is too small, part or all of the object will be hidden from view. To correct it you must resize the box. That does not change the size of the text inside a box, as it does in CorelDRAW. To scale text objects or change a typeface in the chart, you must select the letters and then use the Text Ribbon to enter new values. Use this method to reduce the **Time In Seconds** and **Lower Numbers Are Better** titles to fit neatly on the page. They should be vertical on the left and right sides of the graph, as shown in Figure 12.7. In order to accomplish this, we must delete the typed in words from the chart and return to the spreadsheet view. Select the cell with the **Lower Numbers** words in it, and tag it as the second **Y axis**. You can see by the red line in the Chart Layout window that it will now appear vertically on the right of the chart. Return to chart view and use the Point Size window to reduce the type size until it looks right. Use the **Pick** tool to balance them manually on the page. That completes the chart cleanup. Save the chart using the **File** menu. With the exception of the **Apply Template** and **Print** options, which you will use later, it works just like the one in CorelDRAW. You will be using this version of the file again, after you experiment with CorelCHART's 3-D effects.

Changing Chart Types and Using 3-D Effects

Right now you should have a reasonably complete but simple bar chart. In this section you are going to change it into a 3-D model and explore the Gallery menu. CHART offers 21 types of charts with over 50 predefined variations. That doesn't mean that you can use every type with any kind of data. The type of chart should be chosen based on the data involved and what you are trying to present. Chart selection and design will be covered later, after you have had a chance to work with the different controls. The review of software in Chapter 30 includes other third-party products that can help you produce professional charts and presentations.

The Gallery: Converting from One Chart Format to Another

In ChartView mode, use the mouse to open the Gallery menu. Each of the options is a category of charts that can be used to display your data. Select the one marked **3-D Riser** and open the fly-out. Then hold the cursor on the **Bars** option. Figure 12.8a shows how the menu should look. A sample of the chart will appear in the open area above the available choices. When you release the menu, the chart will have changed, resembling the one in Figure 12.8b. The colors have been modified to make it easier to see the print.

Chapter 12: Making the Point with CorelCHART

Some of the titles and labels have been moved and resized, based on the orientation of the new view. If you want to experiment with different charts, go ahead, but please don't modify anything else, and return to this same type of chart when you are finished.

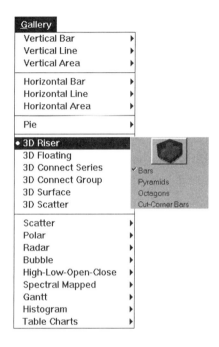

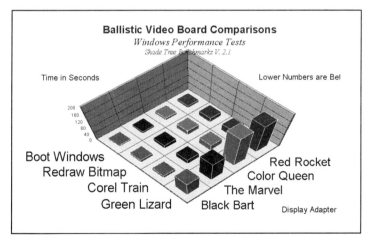

FIGURES 12.8a and b The Gallery menu and the 3D Riser chart

Adjusting the Chart Layer Text and Display

As you can see from Figure 12.8b, much of the text has changed size and location to fit the new angle of the display. Footnotes and titles do not automatically adjust as the chart is modified. Click on number **120** on the left side of the graph with the right mouse button. A Context menu will open, allowing you to set several options, as shown in Figure 12.9. This menu is always available for Chart Layer text objects. Some options will not operate if the commands are not suited to the current type of chart. For example, the 3-D option only works with 3-D views, and log scales can only be applied to data sets with all positive values.

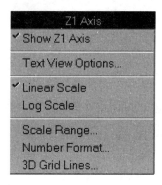

FIGURE 12.9 The Left Wall Axis context menu

With the same Context menu open, choose the **Text View Options** command. A dialog box will open like the one in Figure 12.10a. When you are working with 2-D charts, these settings let you determine if the text should automatically adjust to the bounding box, and if headers should change with a new perspective and remain the same size during transformations. If you experiment with them, undo your changes before continuing. Figure 12.10b shows the same dialog box in the 3-D text face, allowing you to have text conforming to the 3-D form.

Chapter 12: Making the Point with CorelCHART

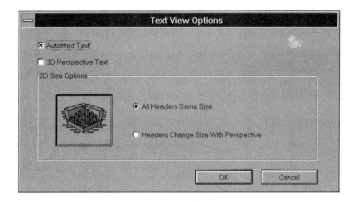

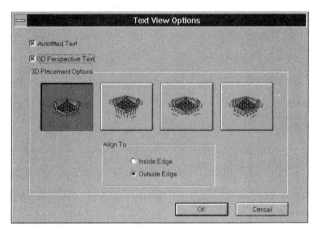

FIGURES 12.10a and b The 2-D amd 3-D Text View Options dialog boxes

Go back to the Context menu and open the **3-D Grid Lines** option. A dialog box will open like the one in Figure 12.11. This turns the grid lines on and off that can be placed along the walls, floor, and even the risers indicating the data. The Z-axis divisions can be made automatic, or can be set to a specific number using the **Text Entry** window in the lower right-hand corner of the box. Try turning all these lines on and off and see the effects they produce. The Z-axis options are only available with 3-D charts. The Context menu options shown in this section and in the last section are also available under the Chart menu on the main menu bar.

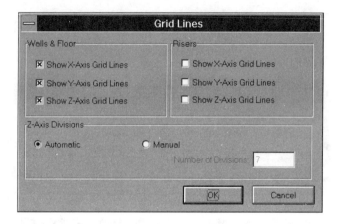

FIGURE 12.11 Setting the grid lines

ADJUSTING THE CHART WITH THE 3-D ROLL-UP

Many times when working with 3-D charts it is necessary to fine-tune the way the data are displayed. This is a fun part of working with CorelCHART. When you have a 3-D view on the screen, you can interactively adjust the angle, size, and relative positions using what is known as a Persistent tool. It is similar to the on-screen Perspective roll-up menu in CorelDRAW. I suggest that you save a version of your chart before you experiment with this tool.

The 3-D Tool, accessed from the View menu, has four modes. To change from one to another you press the icon at the top of the roll-up; the appearance of the central window then changes. Editing is done by holding a mouse button on one of the arrow controls. To give you an idea of what it can do, the **Rotation** mode (4th button) was used to shift the viewing angle of the graph as shown in Figure 12.12. The **Show Graph** box (3rd tool) allows you to work only with the wireframe and eliminates the possible confusing screen when the full graph is shown. As the mouse pointer is placed over an arrow and the left button is held down, the screen shows a wireframe with the new location. To make the actual change you have to press the **Redraw** button. The **Undo** button will return the graph to its original position *only* if you haven't given the **Redraw** command. These tools move the graph and the associated text, but not titles, footnotes, or anything on the Annotation Layer.

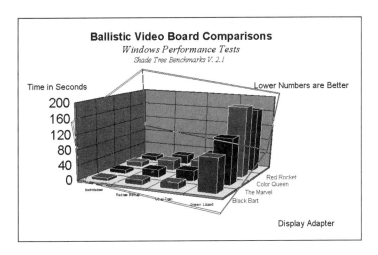

FIGURE 12.12 The 3-D View tool at work

The Movement Mode

The Movement mode is accessed through the leftmost button and shifts the position of the graph on the page. This is used to open up a large space for annotation text, such as an explanation of how the data were collected, or to add another graphic, such as a photograph or logo next to the graph. To use it, just hold down the arrow in the direction you want to move the chart. By combining directional controls you can place the graph anywhere on the page. The menu in this mode is shown in Figure 12.13a.

The Perspective Mode

The Perspective mode has three functions: Zoom, Perspective, and Two-Dimensional pan. It is the second icon from the left and is depicted in Figure 12.13b. Again you hold down the left mouse button on the appropriate arrow to make the graph shift on the page. The **3-D Zoom** changes the actual size of the graph, without changing its location on the page. This is the best way to resize 3-D charts. The **3-D Perspective** alters the appearance of depth of the walls of the graph. The **2-D** pan does not alter the size or shape of the graph but moves it either horizontally or vertically on the page.

FIGURES 12.13a and b The 3-D Movement mode and 3-D Perspective mode

3-D Box Proportion Mode

The 3-D Box Proportion mode is used to change the size of the different parts of the object in which the data are shown. Look at the arrows in Figure 12.14a. The arrows in front increase or decrease the thickness of the floor, and those on the top raise or lower the height of the walls. Move the ones where the wall and the floor meet and extend or shrink the width of that wall. The ones resting in the edges of the two walls adjust the wall thickness.

The 3-D Rotation Mode

The final icon sets the tool into Rotation mode and lets you turn the graph on all three axes without altering its size, shape, or center. It is shown in Figure 12.14b. When you are using the tools it is a good idea to leave the **Show Graph** option active, unless it slows down your system too much. The tools all serve one purpose: to orient the data displayed in the chart to the best angle for interpretation. To close the tool, click on the **minus** button in its upper left-hand corner. In general, you should use the 3-D Tool to adjust the view of the graph so that the information is easy for the viewer to see and understand.

 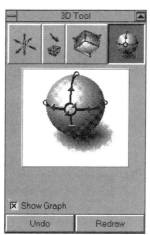

FIGURES 12.14a and b The Box Proportion mode and 3-D Rotation mode

THE CHART MENU OPTIONS

You have been working with various options that are found under the Chart menu, even though you have usually used the context-sensitive menus to apply them. The contents and options in the Chart menu vary, based on the type of graph and the data set in use. With all the variations available in CHART, it is beyond the scope of this chapter to explain every feature. It would also be excessive to detail the function and data requirements for every type of analysis involved. I focus on the bar and pie charts when showing you how to use the program, since they are the most commonly used forms for business presentations.

At the end of the chapter I have listed a couple of textbooks that cover some of the background material needed to understand how to apply the charts to research, statistics, and business procedures. I also cover basic reasons for using the more common chart forms and how to design graphs that can be easily used and understood. Many graphs fail to communicate because their creators don't follow a few basic rules.

This section gives a basic rundown of this version of the menu used for 3-D bar charts and shows another version for comparison. Full use of all the features offered by CHART requires a good understanding of statistical analysis. You do not need that level of training for many common chart applications. The **3-D Text** and **Grid Line** options and the **Vertical Axis** and **Display Status** options have already been explained.

The 3-D Bar Chart Options

Figure 12.15 shows the version of the Chart menu that applies to 3-D Riser charts like the one you have been working with. Figure 12.16 shows the hi-lo graph controls. As you can see, they are very different. Open the menu now and click open the first option, labeled **Preset Viewing Angles**. A fly-out like the one in Figure 12.15 will appear. Drag to one of the alternative views and click. Then release the mouse. The graph will be redrawn to the new specifications. This is a quick way to get a basic design in place on the page.

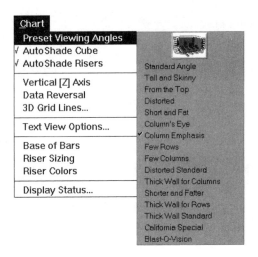

FIGURE 12.15 The 3-D Riser Variation of the Chart menu

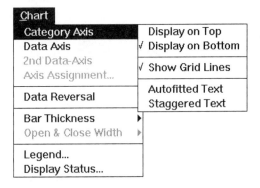

FIGURE 12.16 Hi-lo with open-close variation of the Chart menu

The Autoshade Functions and Setting Custom Fills

The same section of the menu toggles the **AutoShade Cube** and **Riser** commands on and off. Turn the **AutoShade Riser** option off and return to the **ChartView** window. Click on the tall riser to the far right of the chart. A riser is the vertical bar that represents the data. Now open the **Fill Tool** fly-out menu and drag to the **Two-Color Fill** icon just like the one in CorelDRAW, a checkerboard. Choose a different fill for each of the axes. Once you have made your selection, click on the **Apply** button. The new fill will be automatically repeated for all the risers in the row.

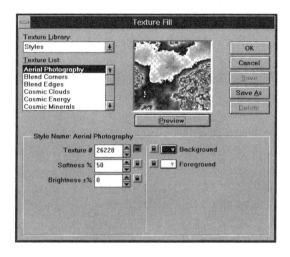

FIGURE 12.17 The Texture Fill dialog box

SHORTCUT

If you have a slow video display these fills can take a long time to redraw on the screen. Do this type of cosmetic design last. Size and place everything, check your tags and data, and then do the enhancement. You will save a lot of time.

Use the other options on the **Fill** fly-out to modify the other columns in the chart. I used a Fountain Fill, Aerial Photography Texture fill, a dotted two-color fill, and a basket full-color fill for my risers. You can apply the fills and patterns to any of the Chart Layer objects by following the same procedures you learned with CorelDRAW. As you can see in Figure 12.18, the wall behind the risers was also modified. Use the **Pick** tool to select the object, open the appropriate outline or fill function, set any dialog box options, and then **Apply** (**OK**) the selections. Just as with CorelDRAW, you can use the Undo command to return the object to its original state.

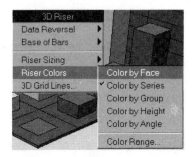

FIGURE 12.18 Setting custom fills on the chart layer

Riser Controls

The next-to-last option in the menu offers three controls over the appearance of the risers. Each one controls different aspects of how the risers are formed and appear in the graph. Figure 12.19 shows the results of making adjustments in riser size and data organization. These commands let you tailor the risers to fit specific needs. If you want to use different colors for parts of the risers, select the appropriate toggle from the Riser Colors option. Incidentally, this graph is rotated only to show you how the options affect the graph. You should never obscure smaller risers in the chart.

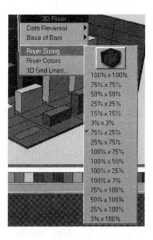

FIGURE 12.19 Adjusting the riser size

ANNOTATIONS AND THE ARRANGE MENU

In the beginning of this chapter I mentioned that every chart has two layers. The lower one holds what you placed in the Data Manager, and the upper one is for placing annotations, anything else you add to explain the graph to your viewers. It's easy to dress up an existing chart with arrows, notes, and other extras. But remember as you are designing layouts that objects on the Annotation Layer are always above objects on the Chart Layer.

Placing Annotation Text

Close your 3-D bar chart and **reopen** the 2-D version you saved before converting it. Then make sure you are in the **ChartView** window. Use the **Zoom** tool to make the chart fill the page. Now select the **Text** tool and click it within the chart page. Type the words **This Took Too Long!** As you type, the words will appear on the page. When you are done the letters may be too big or too small. Use the drop-down menus on the Text Ribbon Bar to change the point size to **12-point Arial** or a similar typeface. Now, if needed, use the **Pick** tool to adjust the size of the box so that it fits on one line. Adjust it so it is about in the same position as the example in Figure 12.20, which also shows how the text block looked before it was resized, as well as some of the steps that will be added next.

That's all there is to adding text notes on to the page. It's simple. A minor annoyance is that the text is not the same as the other blocks on the page. It is always on the top layer. You can not put it behind anything on the Chart Layer. In some systems resizing the view may alter the size of bounding boxes for some annotated text. The sample used here would be forced into two lines whenever you Zoom in to do other editing.

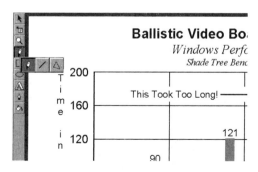

FIGURE 12.20 Adding an annotation

Adding a Pointer with the Pencil Tool

Open the **Pencil Tool** fly-out and choose the last icon in the row, the **Arrow**. Hold the **Ctrl** key down and draw a line from just after the end of the text toward the highest riser. The **Ctrl** key constrains the line to 90-degree angles, so your line will be perfectly straight. Use Figure 12.20 for a guide. The line is above the text on the Annotation Layer. Open the **Arrange** menu and pick **To Back** from the **Order** fly-out to put it back behind the letters. Like the text, the arrow is on the Annotation Layer. The Arrange menu function does not work with the Chart Layer objects. They are always on the bottom.

Adding an Ellipse and a Backdrop

Select the **Rectangle** tool and draw a rectangle. Select the **Ellipse** tool and draw a wide oval that just covers the annotation text block. Then use the **Pick** tool to drag it so that the lettering is half-covered. This will make it easier to work when the type is given a white fill. That's the next step. Use the **Fill** tool to make the oval black and the text white. Then remove the Outline from all three objects: the text, oval, and arrow.

Using the Pictograph Tool

The Pictograph roll-up is selected by choosing the star box at the far end of the **Fill** fly-out. You can load almost any graphics file into this tool and add the graphic to your chart. Because of the amount of system resources consumed by complex graphics, I suggest you use primarily simple line drawings in this option, or add more complex graphics only after all else is complete.

FIGURE 12.21 The Pictograph tool

Arranging Objects and Adding Backdrops

Place the text over the oval, select both objects with the **Shift-Click** method, and open the **Arrange** menu. Click the **Align** option to open the **Align** dialog box. Choose **Horizontal Center** and **Vertical Center**. The text should be centered on the oval. Now use the **Rectangle** tool to create a white box a little larger than the size of the annotation. Use the **To Back** command off the **Order** option to place it behind all the other objects.

The CorelCHART Arrange Menu

The Arrange menu in CHART is very similar to the one in CorelDRAW. Be aware that all these options can only be used with objects that are on the Annotation Layer. As with all other such commands, you must first select the object or objects to be arranged with the Pick tool before opening the menu. There is no marquee selection in CHART, so to choose multiple elements use the **Shift-Click** method. Since the commands in the top half of the menu are the same as the ones you already know from the first few chapters, they won't be repeated here. The new ones are listed later. Remember that the **Align** commands work on the bounding box, not the actual object. Since the size of the box is not fixed, it may affect the way the commands work.

- **Align.** This is the same as the Align dialog box in CorelDRAW. To use it choose the objects, then the command.
- **Make Same Size.** Use this to force one object to be the same size as another. Choose the object to copy from first, then the one to be modified.

ADJUSTING THE PRESENTATION OF YOUR DATA

There are several other things you can do with most types of charts to make your presentation easier to understand. In some cases the way the graph is organized makes it awkward to read; in other cases the way the data are ordered can hide important points. Assessing many of these factors requires some training in data analysis, but I will point out a few of the more common things to watch out for and show you how CHART can help.

Converting the Scale

Reopen the 2-D version of the bar chart you saved before you started working with the 3-D tool. Notice how the numbers for the fourth value are much taller than the others. In a simple chart like this it is not too important. The extra length just wastes space. Select any of the numbers on the scale to the left of the graph with the right mouse button. A context-sensitive menu such as the one in Figure 12.22 will open. Look at the checkmark in the second section. Check **Log Scale**. Then your bars should look like the ones in Figure 12.22. They have the same numbers, but the tallest bars are shorter. Look at the **Time In Seconds**. It is now based on a logarithmic scale. That keeps the proper ratio but lets you keep from having one set of bars so visually distant from the others. In this case that makes sense. You are comparing the height in each test, not the height between adjacent bars.

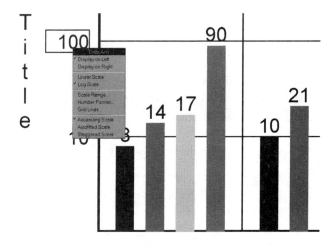

FIGURE 12.22 Changing to a log scale

Adjusting the Size and Order of the Risers

Now click the right button on one of the bars. A menu such as the one in Figure 12.23 will open. Choose **Bar Thickness**; the **Bar Riser** fly-out menu will appear. Select the **Maximum Thickness** option and your risers will be made thicker so that they fill their section of the grid. Now open the **Data Reversal** fly-out, which enables both options, as shown in Figure 12.23. Notice what happened to the order of the bars in the chart. They have been flipped right to left. This feature can be used to improve the appearance of the risers on the graph, or adjust the order of the variables being evaluated to make inspection easier.

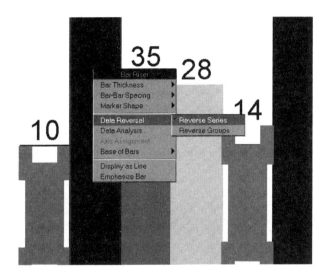

FIGURE 12.23 The Bar Riser menu

Performing Data Analysis

Open the **Bar Riser** menu again and choose the **Data Analysis** option. A dialog box will appear. If you choose one or more of its checkboxes, the appropriate values will be plotted as lines on top of the bars. The 16 available analyses include Means, Standard Deviations, and some Regressions.

Changing the Riser Text Format

Suppose you want to change the numbers that appear on the top of the risers. For example, you might not want to show decimal places or want dollar signs. Some information is better expressed as percentages or in scientific notation. If you click on one of the data numbers with the right mouse button, you will see the same dialog box as the one in Figure 12.24 called **Numeric**. You can alter the display of the data values and change their position in relation to the risers.

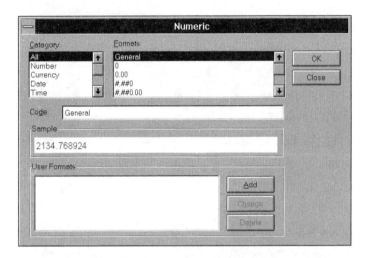

FIGURE 12.24 The Numeric dialog box

Pie Charts

Comparing what happens with the same data when it's used in both pie charts and bar charts is a good example of how different types of graphs are best suited to different purposes. It also gives me a chance to show the special controls CHART has for pie charts. **Close** the current file and open the earlier version you saved before you converted it from a 2-D model. Now go to the **Gallery** menu, open the **Pie** fly-out, and choose the first option, a basic pie chart. The menu and what your graph will look like are shown in Figure 12.25.

Chapter 12: Making the Point with CorelCHART

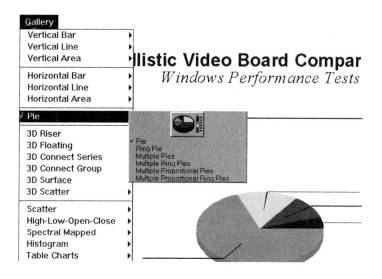

FIGURE 12.25 A Pie chart

Well, this isn't the most informative chart I've ever seen. The bar chart showed clearly the relative performance of each card. That's what bar charts are designed for, comparing relative results of several values of different items. They are excellent for things such as benchmarks and performance over time. Pie charts, on the other hand, show percentages of a whole. They are used to depict market share and other divisions of single primary values. As a result, the Data Manager tags did not really convert much of your data set. Only one of the adapter cards is shown, and the time values are missing.

Reopen the Gallery menu and choose the **Multiple Proportioned Pies** option. Now all four cards have individual pies, but the data are not available in a meaningful way. Each wedge shows what percentage of the total test time for that card was required to complete a given task. So it's obvious that a pie chart is not appropriate for graphing these data.

Let's look at some data that are suited to a pie chart. Copy the file **SALES.CCH** from the disk in the back of the book onto your hard disk; then open it in CHART.

Gaining Market Share

This chart details the market share of the Lolly Berry Candy Company. The copy of this chart in Figure 12.26 should be in full color. The pie chart serves as the template for two other charts that have been included on the disk in the back of the book. You can use them as samples for experimenting with different types of charts and working with templates. As you can see, the pie chart is already completed, depicting the current market share of a product compared to the competition.

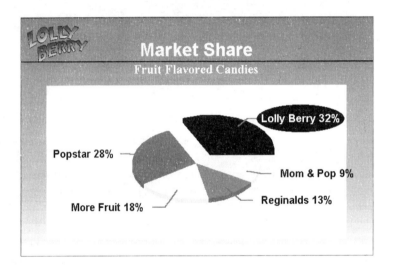

FIGURE 12.26 Comparing market share

The Data Manager

Use the button at the top of the toolbar and switch to the **Data Manager** window. It looks just about the same as the last one. Now open the list of tags in the drop-down menu to the right of the Tag Bar near the top of the window. As you can see, the available tags are a bit different. Not all the tags will be available with this type of pie chart. Each type of graph will have its own list, based on the way the data must be ordered. Open the **Data** menu. If you select a row or column first, you can use these options to reorder and sort the data and to change the numbering formats.

The Difference with Pie Charts

Return to the **ChartView** window and open the Chart menu. There are only three entries that are the same as the ones you used when working with the bar formats. Choose one of the pie slices and go back to the menu. Open the **Detach Slice** option and drag the mouse pointer slowly to the **Maximum** listing. The menu should look like the example in Figure 12.27.

FIGURE 12.27 The Pie Chart menu

Notice how the sample in the **Preview** moves farther out as you go down the list. This is how the sections of the pie are shifted in and out from each other. You can also change the size, thickness, rotation, and tilt with similar interactive menus. Try a few of them to get the hang of it on this chart. Then return things to normal by reopening your **Sales.CCH** file without saving your changes.

Adjusting the Slice Feelers

The data tagged as column headers in the bar chart were placed at the bottom of each group of the item's risers. In a pie chart the headers are placed at the end of a pointer called a slice feeler. To modify the feeler's length you use an interactive dialog box like that shown in Figure 12.28. It is accessed either through the Chart menu or by clicking on a pie wedge or feeler with the right mouse button and selecting the option from the context-sensitive menu. Then adjust the feeler by clicking and dragging on the little circles. This feature lets the header for a section of the chart be placed exactly as you want.

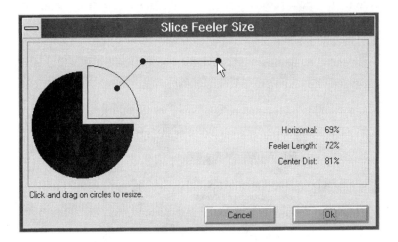

FIGURE 12.28 The Pie Slice Feeler dialog box

KEEP IT EASY TO SEE AND UNDERSTAND: PRESENTATION BASICS

By now you should understand the basics of the CorelCHART interface. Since there are so many variations it would be impossible to cover all the context-sensitive menus and explain each command. It is also beyond the scope of this chapter to teach statistics or data analysis. In this section the focus is on the principles needed to produce a chart that is visually appealing and easy to read. There is only one goal in creating slides to get your point across effectively. If the slide is difficult to understand or impossible to read, the message will be lost. CHART does not have the ability to produce title slides or any other graphic without data, but the guidelines below apply to other presentation materials as well. You can prepare title slides in CorelDRAW.

Keep It Simple

The most common problem with many presentations is the attempt to pack too many data into one chart. The average attentive viewing time of a chart is about 10 seconds. That's how long most of the people who see your work will try to figure it out. Keep each chart tightly focused on one fact or statement. A good rule of thumb is to try to explain the chart in one short sentence.

Make a List

The easiest way to make sure the chart is focused properly is by making a list of all the facts you want to highlight and then deciding what you need to show to prove those points. There should be at least one slide for each fact. The list will serve as a good planning tool for the talk as well, if there is one.

Break Up Large Collections of Data

If you have many different columns in your data set, consider breaking them up into several charts. Think of ways that the data can be grouped into subsets; then make a separate chart for each one. You can avoid the rather tedious practice of displaying several similar charts one after the other by adding other visuals, such as notes on how the information was collected.

Consider the Audience and Location

Who is going to see your charts? Some professionals will understand a certain type of chart because they use them all the time. To a stock trader the hi-lo chart can be understood in a glance. A sales manager should have no problem with a bar chart. With many charts, however, the viewer may not be experienced in looking at the data. The level of experience of the viewer is a good guide when you plan the complexity, titles, and types of graphics to use.

Another consideration is how the charts will be presented. If the presentation is in public, with 35mm slides, what kind of room will the presentation be made in? What is the illumination level? A dark room means that slides with dark backgrounds and white letters will be hard to see, and it will be even harder to take notes. How big is the room? For large rooms you should use bigger titles and legends so that the people in the back can see.

Plan the Colors

If your organization has a logo or company colors that are used in slides, make sure the colors in the background and the titles are compatible. Use distinct primary colors for bars, pie slices, and markers. There are people who have trouble discerning certain colors, and slides fade as they are used over time. To make sure the chart is understood, use different shapes and intensities, as well as colors, as markers for your data. CHART does not have the range of color palettes that CorelDRAW does. If you have a logo or other object that has to maintain certain shades, make it in CorelDRAW and import it. One trick in testing a design is to reduce the size of the chart on the screen and then to dim the monitor. See if you can make out the chart details and note the way the colors of the markers relate to the background. If one item is much brighter than the others under these viewing conditions, it is probably too bright.

Use Templates Whenever Possible

After you have considered the preceding factors, it's a good idea to design a master slide called a template. The basic colors and layout can be used in all the slides, with some variations for different chart types. This makes it easier for the viewer to identify the primary parts of the chart, such as titles, logos, footnotes, and legends. You can create the template in CorelCHART and use it as the background for all your slides. Not only will that give your presentation a more polished look, but it cuts down on the time it takes to make them. Using templates and imported data will be covered later in the chapter.

Don't Design Ransom Notes

Keep the typefaces down to no more than two, better yet, one. You can add emphasis with bold and italic variations. Use larger point sizes if the format of the slide allows it and if it looks balanced on the page. Of course, you don't want the words so big that the chart is hard to find. If you use clip art as a decoration or as a pictograph in the risers, be careful not to overdo it. Don't try to wow the viewer with the design. The point is to present the information. The best slides are ones that support the message.

Print All the Slides and Then Proofread Them!

Headlines are the most common places to find embarrassing typographical errors. It is harder to see large mistakes. Check the hard copy closely. You can run another set after everything is perfect and print them as handouts for the presentation.

A Chart Selection Primer

Choosing the right chart involves two things: knowing the result you want to see and understanding how your data can be organized. If you don't have the right kind of data, you can't use a chart properly. The chart types included with CorelCHART are each designed for a specific purpose, but all were designed with one thing in mind: to be a means of presenting data in a way that can help the viewer understand the information. In some cases the only viewer is the person who collected the data. A chart is a lot easier to make sense of than rows and rows of numbers. The following list gives a brief description of how the different types of charts are used. There are samples of each of these in the CHART Gallery if you want to see what they look like or to experiment with them.

- **Area Charts.** An area chart presents the data as a series of line segments, sort of like drawing a polygon in Freehand mode, with a point for each data item. The area underneath the line is filled; that's where it gets its name. This is a good chart for showing the amount of change over time. The volume of the area under a point shows the flow of change, like a waveform. This kind of chart is not suited for comparing values where the differences are large, or where there are many values in the series.
- **Bar Charts.** A bar chart is similar to an area chart, but it can compare the rate of change of several items at the same time. It is good at showing relative times or amounts for several items at once, such as the benchmark tests earlier in the chapter.
  1. **Basic vertical bar chart.** This is the simplest of the series, like the first one you worked with. Some people refer to vertical bars as column charts and reserve the term bar chart for graphs with horizontal bars.

2. **Stacked bar chart.** This is sort of a combination bar and pie chart. The bar is the total for a collection of items. For example, a series shows the sales of all the products made by a vendor, and inside the bars are totals for individual items. You can show what percentage of the market one company had over the others and which products were the most important for success.

3. **Horizontal bar chart.** This is similar to the vertical charts, but it should be limited to a single specific point in time or to one comparison. The orientation of the bars makes it difficult for most people to compare several different linked data sets at once.

4. **3-D bar charts.** These are technically the same as the 2-D versions, but the fancy layout is a bit more impressive. They are useful when you want to be able to shift the angle of view to highlight a particular range of figures.

- **Hi-Lo Value Charts.** This is the one to use for data that have to be depicted with the maximum and minimum values over a period of time. By looking at the chart it is easy to compare the highest value over time, the lowest, and the daily fluctuations. It is well suited to stocks, weather statistics, and similar applications.

- **Histograms.** You used histograms in the last chapter to see the amounts of each grayscale tone in an image. They are used to view the relative frequency of values in a series. School grades and test performances are often graphed by educators using histograms, to see if they produce a characteristic bell curve. If the peak of the curve is too far to one side or the other it may indicate that the testing procedure is too weak or too hard.

- **Line Charts.** This chart is also referred to as a series plot. It shows the change in a value over time. It is basically an area chart without the area, like drawing a line tracing the crest of a wave.

- **Pie Charts.** These charts are a good way to show percentages. They are good at showing how much one item in a series contributed to the group. The sales chart you looked at was a good example. It's easy to see which value gets (or contributes) a bigger piece of the pie.

  1. **3-D pie charts.** Like the 3-D bar chart, this is a more dramatic way to present the data and gives you a bit more to work with in making an appealing design.

  2. **Multiple pie charts.** These charts can compare changes in percentages over time or between two different data sets. If you try to use more than a couple of graphs in the same chart, the data get difficult to compare easily. In that case consider the data and choose another type of chart.

Chapter 12: Making the Point with CorelCHART

- **Scatter Plots.** This chart presents the items in a data set as dots placed on a chart. It is used to compare the values of two or more variables to detect a pattern of occurrence or frequency. It is a good way to show peaks in analog performance.
- **Spectral Map Charts.** The name implies one of the most common uses for this kind of chart. It plots relative populations or density within a data set. You must not only have the number, but a correlation to an identifier, such as an address or membership. If you wanted to know how many members of an organization lived in each state, this would be the chart to use.
- **Table Charts.** These charts are much like a dressed-up spreadsheet, a table with columns, rows, and headers. Textbooks and technical summaries use these charts to present the actual data set, so that it can be examined.

IMPORTING DATA, IMPORTING GRAPHICS, AND USING TEMPLATES

The CHART Data Manager is a handy tool for organizing and tagging the information to be used in a graph, but it leaves a lot to be desired as a spreadsheet. It wasn't designed to be one. Just as CorelDRAW and PHOTO-PAINT enable you to use files created in other applications, so can CHART. In many cases you may want to add a graphic to use as a logo, background, or other design element. Data and images are handled differently, but both can be imported and manipulated. You can, of course, use the Windows Clipboard to exchange things between programs. Since you have already covered the Cut, Copy, and Paste commands before, this section will focus on CHART's import filters.

Importing Data

To use an existing file from another application, you must have the program open and have the **Data Manager** window open. Then select the File menu's **Import Data** command. A file selection dialog box will open. Choose the type of file you wish to import, locate the filename, and double-click on it. The data will be placed in the Data Manager spreadsheet. Then arrange the data as needed and tag them. Once that is done you can move to the **ChartView** window and finish designing the chart.

Supported Files

CHART supports five basic types of spreadsheet and database file formats. Before creating a large amount of data make sure that the program can output a file that CHART can read. The best way to do this is to save a sample file in a supported format and try loading it into the Data Manager. Then check it. In some cases the file may not load and you will get an error message. Sometimes the filter may not be able to define all the data because of the source program's export method. Here are file types that CHART can recognize.

- **Comma Delimited Text.** This is a plain text ACSII file where each element in the data set is separated by a comma. The .CSV extension stands for Comma Separated File. This is a widely used format and generally works well as long as the source program does not add any extra commas. Most spreadsheets and databases can write this kind of file.

- **Lotus 1-2-3, .WKS.** Most standard Lotus spreadsheet files with this extension should load into the Data Manager spreadsheet. Lotus can also produce delimited files.

- **Microsoft Excel.** The Excel.XLS format is supported up to version 3.0. Later file formats can't be read. Excel has an extensive range of export filters and supports most of the ones on this list.

Not all files will work in all formats. Remember that you are mixing data handling from two programs. If you have a lot of information to import, try a small sample before exporting the bulk of the files.

Importing Graphics

You can use any of the file formats supported by CorelDRAW. Both programs use the same filters, so all the things that were said in the first few chapters about importing bitmaps into CorelDRAW apply to CHART. In Chart View, open the File menu and choose the **Import** command. Then choose the desired file from the dialog box, change directories if needed, and click **OK**. The file will be loaded in the ChartView window with handles. Then you can size and place it with the **Pick** tool. If the file size is too large, it will be resized smaller as it is being loaded.

What Good Is a Template?

Now that you have learned a bit about design and choosing a chart type, it's time to put the pieces together. If you are making only one chart, it's simple. Just collect the data, choose a chart type, and clean it up. If you are making a series of slides, especially if they include different chart types, it can be a bit more difficult. There are two approaches you can take, based on the type of chart and how you have embellished it. Every time a CHART file is created, a template is produced that stores the information used to produce it. That includes type of chart, color scheme, annotations, and other design elements that were used. You can transfer that formatting to a new or existing chart by using the **Apply Template** command, located in the File menu. Then (if everything works right) the chart on the screen will be modified to match the settings in the template.

You can use a template to store logos, copyright notices, and a standard color scheme. If you use the same template for all the charts in a series, all the elements will appear in exactly the same place in every one. That saves a lot of work and keeps things from jumping around on the screen as you move through your presentation. The steps for applying a template are listed later.

Using the Sample Slides as Templates

On the disk in the back of the book are three sample slides: the pie chart you already examined and two others, a line chart and a bar chart. They are saved in **.CCH** format. You can use them to experiment with switching between different template formats and copying a logo from one chart to another. There are also the three data sets from those files saved in **.CSV** format that can be imported and used to build charts. The file names are **SALES**, **PROFITS**, and **MARKET**. Samples are also provided with the program for each variety of graph. If you want to see how a template is applied to an existing chart, use the following steps, after loading all those files onto your hard drive. You may have to do some editing after using the samples to get things looking just right.

Applying a Template

- Open a new chart and the **Data Manager** window.
- Import data from a source or sample file.
- Tag the data as needed.
- Go to the ChartView window and open the File menu; then choose **Apply Template**.
- Locate and select the chart that has the format, images, and annotations you want to use in the new chart. Click **OK**.

The new chart should now have the same colors for chart objects as the one that was used as the template. In testing this feature I found that the assignment of colors worked very well and that annotations would be placed in exactly the same place as in the original chart. Data positions and bitmaps used as annotations were less reliable. In general, the feature works best when being applied to the same type of chart. Changing from one graph to another produced unpredictable results.

The Save As Option

If you are working with several chart types and need to keep the same design elements, you can get most of the benefits of a template with the Edit menu's **Save As** option. Open a chart and enter any fixed elements into the Data Manager; for example, titles, footnotes, and so on. Then add enough chart data to let the program build the graph. Unless there are some data to work with you can't open the ChartView window.

Now develop the color scheme, define the types and fills for the markers, and add any of the fixed annotations you want in all the charts. Save the file. Then reopen it and build the first of your real charts. Use the **Save As** command to save it with a new or existing name so that the master chart stays the same. Repeat the process for your other charts. After you get the first chart prepared, you can use it to see if the template feature will work with that file.

GETTING YOUR CHARTS OUT

So far you have focused on creating charts and getting data into them. Most people build charts to use them somewhere else. The **Print** functions are just about the same as those with CorelDRAW. Choose the **Print** command and your options; Windows does the rest (provided you have Windows set up properly for your printer). You can print to any Windows-supported device, including film recorders and typesetters. That's fine for hard copy, but what about getting charts out to other applications? There are two other ways to get your charts out: the OLE functions and the regular Windows Clipboard.

OLE, the Windows Magic Carpet Ride

A good way to move files between CHART and CorelDRAW is by using Windows' OLE (Object Linking and Embedding) function. To do that you must edit your **CORELDRW.INI** file. It is located in the same directory as the CorelDRAW program files. If you want more information about OLE, there is a full discussion of it in the next chapter.

Once you have made the change mentioned earlier you can use the **Copy** command in CHART's Edit menu to move the file out and the **Paste Special** or **Paste** command to place it in CorelDRAW. Once the file is in CorelDRAW, the intermediate metafile problem is not a factor, because the file is now just another object on the page and is in the proper format. If you do not make the change outlined earlier to your **CORELDRW.INI** file, the **Paste Special** command may not produce a complete file.

CHAPTER SUMMARY

CorelCHART offers a host of easy tools for quick presentations using predefined templates and sample data to get you up and running. The similarities to CorelDRAW and the context-sensitive menus make it easy to use. There are some quirks. Still, with all that is in the box, you can consider it an extra. To get the most out of the more advanced features does require some understanding of data analysis and statistics. *Statistics Today: A Comprehensive Introduction*, by Donald Byrkit, is a good reference that explains the concepts of statistics in a readable way (without much math training). Another good reference if you want to delve deeper is The *SPSS Guide to Data Analysis*, by Marija Norusis.

CHAPTER 13

CorelSHOW and Object Linking and Embedding

This chapter covers the following topics:

- Presentation Planning
- Object Linking
- Embedding Images
- Choosing a Background
- Designing Slides

Introduction

CorelSHOW uses drawings, images, and animations to produce electronic presentations and hard-copy slides or handouts. It does not create the objects, but uses Windows Object Linking and Embedding (OLE) functions to incorporate files made in other OLE-compatible applications. Since OLE is the key to using SHOW, it is also the key to understanding it. Before covering the way SHOW operates, I will explain the way OLE works. You must have Windows 3.1 installed for OLE operations or be using Windows 3.0 with the OLE extensions installed. If you are running the older version and are not sure your setup supports OLE, check your CorelDRAW and Microsoft Windows user manuals for more information. This chapter assumes that your system is able to use OLE options and that SHOW is properly installed.

Object Linking and Embedding

OLE is a feature of Windows that lets information be exchanged between applications as objects. A program that gives the data is called the server; the recipient is called a client. This sounds like cut and paste, but there is a difference. When you use OLE to put something into a document (call any file that receives OLE data a document), the client does not have to be able to recognize the data. The client program uses special interfaces in the Windows OLE code when it has to display an object or run the server to edit the information. If you want to edit the object, the original program that created the object is automatically loaded to do the work and closed after the changes are made.

Since SHOW is a client and CorelDRAW, CorelCHART, and CorelPHOTO-PAINT are servers, you can use anything created in those applications in a SHOW presentation. SHOW can use information created in any OLE server. It is *only* a client and cannot provide data to other programs. Some applications, such as CorelDRAW, can serve as both clients and servers.

OLE Terminology

There are special terms that are used when talking about OLE. For example, you can move data between programs using either linking or embedding. They are not the same thing. To really be able to understand OLE it helps to know what these terms mean.

Chapter 13: CorelSHOW and Object Linking and Embedding

The following list presents brief definitions followed by examples. After the list of terms, I'll walk you through a couple of OLE operations before moving on to SHOW. This should make the terms easier to understand.

- **Object.** This is anything that can be linked or embedded in a client document, like a drawing from CorelDRAW or a bitmap from PHOTO-PAINT.
- **Linking.** With linking, a separate source file is used to store data shared with other applications, and a pointer to that source file goes into the target file, not the actual data. When a link source file changes, all the linked files change as well. If you move or erase the source file, the link is broken and the information can no longer be updated. Links can be updated manually or automatically when a target file is opened.
- **Embedding.** This is similar to cutting, copying, and pasting between programs. The improvements are that the target program or client does not have to be able to understand the data, and that the server application is used to edit the object while it remains in the compound document.
- **Server or Source.** This is the program that was used to create the object to be linked or embedded into another application. The server (or source) applications may also be used to edit or display some types of OLE objects. CorelDRAW would be a server if you wanted to embed a .CDR file in a SHOW presentation.
- **Client or Container.** This is the receiver that stores or uses objects created by server applications. If you use CorelCHART to create a chart and use OLE to bring it into SHOW, SHOW would be the client (or container) application.
- **Compound Documents.** These are files containing data in different formats that were created in more than one program from more than one application. Compound documents can be assembled in an OLE client application, such as SHOW. Objects can be any linked or embedded object.
- **Packaging Objects.** You can use the Object Packager that came with your copy of Windows 3.1 to prepare data from a server so that a non-OLE client can receive the information.

USING OLE WITH CORELDRAW 5.0 APPLICATIONS

As with almost any data operation there are three primary steps in using OLE to move something from one program to another. You must identify the data to be used, tell the computer where it is to go, and tell how to get it there. The data used can be all or part of a file selected, just as you would to edit it in the program that created it. The exact steps are a little different, depending on whether you want to link or embed the data. Once an object has been placed, different procedures are used to edit the data, depending on which method you selected.

Embedding and Editing OLE Objects

There are two ways to embed an object. You can use the **Copy** and **Paste** commands located in the Edit menu or use the **Insert Object** command from the File menu. Let's try both with CorelDRAW and PHOTO-PAINT. You'll use the **Paste** method first; then I'll explain the **Insert Object** procedure.

- Open PHOTO-PAINT and load the face picture you saved.
- Choose the **Selection** tool from the **Toolbox**.
- Select all or part of the picture.
- Open the Edit menu and choose **Copy**.
- Close PHOTO-PAINT and return to CorelDRAW.
- Open CorelDRAW, go to the Edit menu, and choose **Paste**.

The copy will appear in the CorelDRAW workspace. This is the client application. Resize the image with the **Pick** tool; then open the Edit menu. Look at the bottom block. A new entry offers the ability to edit the PHOTO-PAINT picture, as shown in Figure 13.1.

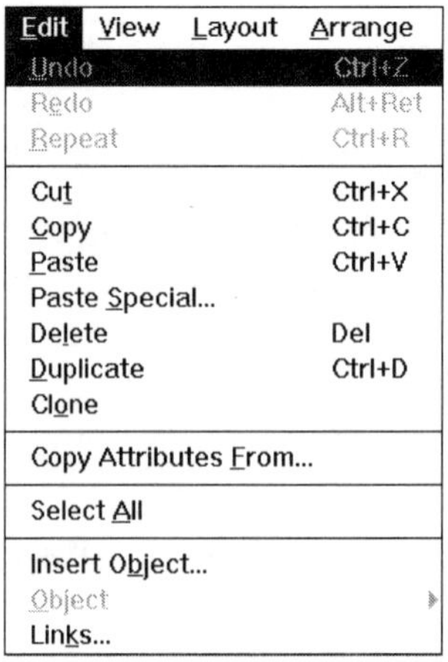

FIGURE 13.1 Editing OLE objects

Double-click on it. PHOTO-PAINT will reopen with a copy of the image in the workspace. Use the **Airbrush** or **Paintcan** tool to place some new color on the picture. The image you are editing is the one that is in CorelDRAW. Once you have finished modifying it, open the File menu. Another new line is present here. As the server, it was invoked to edit the object. By choosing the **Exit and Return** option as shown in Figure 13.2, the copy in CorelDRAW will be updated. Do that now. You could also choose to use any other PHOTO-PAINT command. Before closing PHOTO-PAINT, look at the dialog box in Figure 13.3. Choose **OK** to close the program, confirm the edits, and return to CorelDRAW. If you choose **No**, you will exit and return without making the changes. **Cancel** will return you to PHOTO-PAINT. The same procedure can be used with CorelSHOW and CorelCHART.

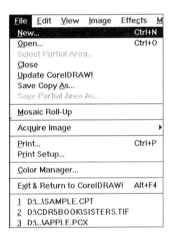

FIGURE 13.2 The PHOTO-PAINT File menu

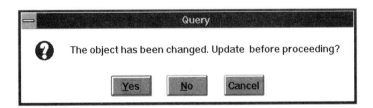

FIGURE 13.3 OLE Query dialog box

You can embed an object from the client application and copy it from the server, but it is more involved. The steps are as follows:

- Open a client application, such as SHOW, and choose **Insert Object** from the appropriate menu. In SHOW it will be on the Insert menu; in CorelDRAW, on the File menu.

- The **Insert Object** or **Object Type** dialog box will open. Select the name of the desired source application. If the name of the program you want to use is not on the list, it has not been properly defined during its installation as an OLE server. To use it you will have to follow the steps given in the appropriate user manual. The dialog box is shown in Figure 13.4.

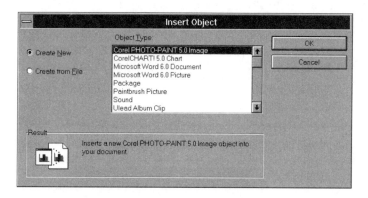

FIGURE 13.4 The Insert Object dialog box

- The source program will be loaded automatically. In some cases, as with PHOTO-PAINT, you may have to start an empty file. If so, the object will have to be loaded into that file to be used by the OLE function. Select the object you want to embed.

- Now open the File menu of the source application and choose **Exit** or **Exit and Return**. You may be offered a chance to update. If you say **Yes**, the OLE operation will be performed; say **No** and it will be canceled.

- You will be returned to the client program and the OLE object will be placed in it. The copy is just that, a copy. If you issue a command to edit the object, the source program will be loaded with the object in place. To update the edits, repeat the step outlined in the preceding paragraph.

Linking Objects

When you link an object, the actual information is still retained by the source program, and a linked copy is placed in the client file. You can link the same data in several programs, and when the information is updated all the copies are changed. Creating a link is easy. Open the source program and create or select the desired object. Use the **Copy** command and open or maximize the client application. Then use the **Paste Special** command to create the link and load the data. A dialog box like the one in Figure 13.5 will open, asking you to confirm the type of object and whether you want a normal **Paste** or **Paste Link**. If you choose a normal **Paste**, you will not be able to use the OLE features with that object.

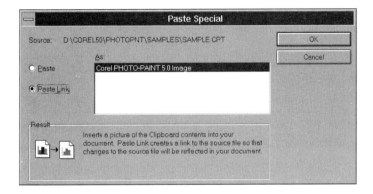

FIGURE 13.5 The Paste Special dialog box

Updating Existing Links

Once a link has been created, you can choose to have the information updated automatically any time a change is made to the source file or manually, so that you can choose if and when the update should take effect. The link functions are accessed from the **Link** dialog box shown in Figure 13.6.

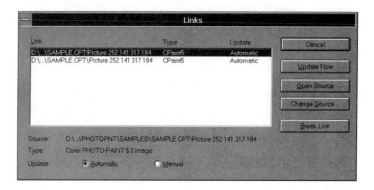

FIGURE 13.6 The Links dialog box

If you rename a linked file the link will be broken. You can re-establish it using the **Change Source** option in the dialog box. **Update Now** is used to update a link manually. You can use either the **Open Source** option in the box or the **Edit Object** command from the File menu to open the source program and link file for modification.

INTRODUCING CORELSHOW

CorelSHOW provides an environment for assembling, organizing, and viewing computer-generated presentations. You can display your results on a monitor or use the SHOW file to print hard copies or make slides. It is not a draw, paint, chart, or word-processing program. Almost all the elements used in its images are drawn from other applications. With the tools available in the rest of the programs included in the CorelDRAW 5.0 release, you should have no problem making professional-looking slides—if you know how to use them properly.

The CorelSHOW User Interface

The CorelSHOW interface uses drop-down menus and a Toolbar similar to those in CorelDRAW. Most of the File and Edit commands have already been presented, so they will not be repeated in this section.

Since you can't actually create full graphics, there are no drawing tools. Objects other than backgrounds are created in other applications and brought into SHOW using the OLE functions explained earlier.

SHOW's (or any program's) use of OLE can really put a dent in your system's resources. Be sure to close any unnecessary programs before starting the program. You should also make sure that your Windows configuration has been tuned for maximum performance. If the OLE functions do not seem to work properly, don't immediately blame it on SHOW. It is most likely something like a video driver (make sure you have the latest driver for your card). During the writing an earlier edition of this book, we had problems that required us to fix the video drivers used on our 24-bit adapters. Once that was cleared up everything worked fine.

The Viewing Modes

The program has four operating modes. The Slide View mode is used to assemble and edit slides, the Background View lets you construct the image's backdrop, Speaker's Notes allows you to prepare notes for each slide, and the Slide Sorter presents thumbnails of the slides in a given presentation. The SHOW desktop allows you to have more than one window open at a time, providing the ability to have two presentations open at the same time, so that you can compare slides or copy elements from one to another.

The CorelSHOW Desktop

The desktop is very similar to ones you have already learned about in the chapters on CorelDRAW and CorelCHART. The rulers, Pick tool, and menus work just like the ones in CorelDRAW. There are separate windows for each presentation, just as there are for each image in PHOTO-PAINT. Figure 13.7 shows the desktop with a slide loaded. This is the screen you will work with when actually preparing a slide in the Slide View mode. The appearance will be a bit different if you are using another view.

FIGURE 13.7 The CorelSHOW desktop—Slide View

The Menu bar is located on the top of the main window, just under the Title bar. There are seven menus, which are almost identical to the ones in CorelDRAW. There are fewer commands, and a few are unique. The Toolbar runs down the left side of the work area. The Pick tool is the only actual tool, and it is used to move, select, and size objects in a slide. The second icon is the Zoom tool, which works just as it does in DRAW. Next is the Text tool, which also works much like its counterpart in DRAW. The icon berneath it opens a library containing the available backgrounds. The next five tools activate SHOW's OLE capacities. The first opens an OLE connection to CorelDRAW; the second, to CorelCHART; and the third, to CorelPHOTO-PAINT. The next allows you to insert one of the 150 animation sequences and transitions included with SHOW, and last opens a fly-out with icons to create an OLE link to any other servers defined on your system.

In the center of the work area is the active slide. In Figure 13.7 the welcome message was created in CorelDRAW; the background is one of the standard ones found in the library. Across the bottom of the screen are Page (Slide) icons, and a pair of clocks. Clicking on one of the page numbers will put that slide in the active window. The clocks depict the amount of screen time when the current slide appears, and the total time for the entire presentation.

Across the top of the work area is the Ribbon bar. The first seven buttons are the familiar File, Print, and Cut and Paste commands. The button that looks like a movie camera activates the timer and runs the presentation. The next five change the view between the Slide, Background, Speaker's notes, Sorter, and Slide Numbering modes, respectively. The next icon sets the Timelines, governing how long each slide stays on the screen and the length allowed for transition effects, and the last lets you set a transition effect. At the far right, a window shows you how long the current slide will be displayed. Below the Ribbon bar is the Text ribbon, containing most of the familiar buttons and windows. At the right end of this ribbon is a button for creating a bullet list, the most frequently used style in presentations, and a button allowing you to change the color of the text.

USING CORELSHOW

The best way to learn CorelSHOW is to use it. I'll walk you through assembling a few slides and then cover a few other points. You should have CorelDRAW, SHOW, and PHOTO-PAINT properly installed on your system before proceeding. This chapter also assumes that you are familiar with both the operations of these other two programs and the Windows interface. If your system is not properly set up and if the applications are not properly defined for OLE operation, you will have problems running SHOW. Consult your documentation if something doesn't work.

Although not mandatory, it's a good idea to close any unneeded applications before running SHOW. Open the Corel Graphics Group and double-click on the icon that looks like a hot air balloon with a movie camera next to it. The SHOW desktop will appear. Click on the File menu and select the **New** command. A dialog box will appear. In it you can select the number of slides you want created. Don't worry if you don't know the exact count. It is easy to add or remove slides while you work. Figure 13.8 shows the dialog box.

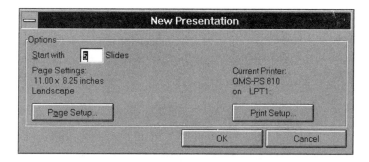

FIGURE 13.8 The CorelSHOW New Presentation dialog box

The dialog box also shows the currently selected printer, its port, the page dimensions, and the orientation (either portrait or landscape). To be able to lay out a design properly you must have the Page Setup properly configured. This is what determines the size of the page in the work area.

If the existing settings do not match your output device, change them before doing any work. Choose the **Page Setup** button in this dialog box; a new box will open. It is similar to the one in CorelDRAW. Check the appropriate box for the actual illustration size and page orientation, and whether you are using a custom setting define the page area. Then click **OK**.

Setting the Initial Background

Before you start making the first slide, you want to define the background. Each presentation has a background layer that is the same for all the slides. If you add something to the background for any slide, it will appear in all of them, no matter which slide it is placed.

Click on the icon just below the Text tool on the left side of the desktop. This opens the library of predefined backgrounds, as shown in Figure 13.9. You can use anything that can be imported into SHOW for a background. These have been added to a library just for use as backgrounds. If you want to change to another library you can do so by clicking on the **Change Library** button in the lower left-hand corner of the dialog box.

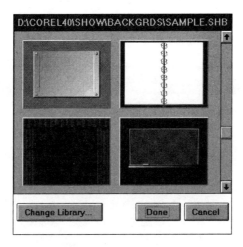

FIGURE 13.9 Selecting a background

The scroll bars on the right side of the box let you see additional backgrounds that did not fit in the window. Use them to locate the image that has a blue box with a white center space. Then click the **Done** button. If you exit without pressing Done, the background will not be loaded.

Creating the First Slide

You should now have a page with the same background as you just chose. In fact, all the slides have the same one. Press on the second number button in the lower left-hand corner. You will notice the same basic page. Now return to the first slide page by clicking on the first button. This is how to navigate between pages of a presentation.

Use the **Pick** tool and press on the **CorelDRAW balloon** icon in the Toolbar; then bring the cursor back on the page. The pointer will turn into a set of cross hairs. Drag the pointer to draw a box in the center of the page.

A Little OLE!

While SHOW 5.0 offers standard text functions, let's create our text in CorelDRAW both to practice a little with OLE, and so we can do some fancy things with it not available in SHOW. Assuming your system is set up properly, CorelDRAW should open with a blank page in the work area. Select the **Text** tool and type **Welcome To CorelSHOW** with a line break after the word **To**. Use the **Text** roll-up to set the type in 24-point Times Roman. If that is not available on your system, use another serifed typeface. Use a black fill and no outline. Now open the File menu and choose the **Exit and Return to CorelSHOW** option. You will be asked if you want to update; choose **Yes**. The SHOW desktop will reopen with the text placed on the page.

Doing Some Editing

There are a few improvements to be made with the type. First, use the **Pick** tool and resize the text so that it neatly fills the center of the page almost side to side. Now open the **Transition Effect** menu and choose the **Curtain Open** option for the opening and the **Curtain Close** option for the close. Then set the **Time On Screen** to 5 seconds. The slide should be similar to Figure 13.10. Press the **Run** button in the upper left-hand corner of the Ribbon bar, the one that looks like a movie camera. The screen will go to a full-sized view of the slide and run the special effects (note that it takes the program a few minutes to get the slide show ready to run). You can try some of the other options for transitions and vary the time. Since they are fairly self-explanatory, I won't go into detail about each one.

FIGURE 13.10 Editing the first slide

Returning to CorelDRAW

To edit the text you have to return to CorelDRAW. It's very simple. Just use the **Pick** tool and double-click on the text. CorelDRAW will be reloaded with the text already in the workspace. Let's change the fill to blue. Now exit with the same command you used last time. Click **OK** when asked if you want to update.

Improving the Background with PHOTO-PAINT

This slide show is going to contain three slides and an animation. Each of the slides will focus on CorelSHOW. The animation will be one of the samples included with the program. Our first slide looks a little plain, not much of an endorsement for the program. Click on the **Background View** icon in the Ribbon bar. It is the cross-hatched icon in the five that are grouped together. As you work, don't forget the **Undo** button if you hit the wrong command.

Chapter 13: CorelSHOW and Object Linking and Embedding   **561**

Choose the button in the toolbar which looks like a camera. Use the cross hairs just as you did for the CorelDRAW text. PHOTO-PAINT should open. Set up a new painting 1.25 inches high and 1 inch wide, with 256 colors. After the blank window appears, open the **File** menu, choose the **Paste From File** option, and select the **BALLOON.PCX** or another file included in the samples. If you want to, use any of the PHOTO-PAINT tools to make changes. Now save the new image and exit PHOTO-PAINT with the **Return to CorelSHOW** command. The balloon will appear on the page.

Setting Up a Grid and Rulers

Using guidelines and rulers is a good idea. The rulers can help you measure the size of objects and get exact placement. They work and are defined just like the ones in CorelDRAW, explained earlier in this book. So do the guidelines. I usually place a single guideline down the center of the page and then pull two more horizontal guides to break the area into thirds. Go ahead and do the same thing now. If the layout for a drawing or presentation calls for columns or other special elements, they can also be marked off with guidelines. Now return to the **Slide** View by clicking on the first View button in the gorup of five on the Ribbon bar. Figure 13.11 shows how my screen looked.

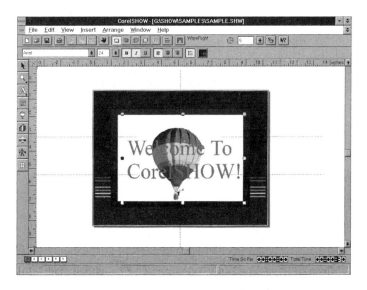

FIGURE 13.11 The first slide with grids and revised background

Making the Final Background

Well, that balloon sort of overpowers the rest of the page and makes it hard to read the type. In fact, I planned to use the balloon a lot differently. Change back to **Background** view with the Ribbon bar again. Now use the **Pick** tool to reduce the balloon to about 2 inches high. Then place it in the upper left-hand part of the slide, just inside the two lines.

Open the **Edit** menu and choose the **Copy** command. Resize the duplicate so it just covers the corner. Double-click on the copy and when PHOTO-PAINT loads, change the background color to black. **Copy** that object and place it in the upper right corner. Click on **Paste** again and move that copy to the lower left corner. You'll need to double-click and change the background color to blue. Then you can make a final copy, paste it, and place it in the lower right corner. Your screen should now look just like Figure 13.12.

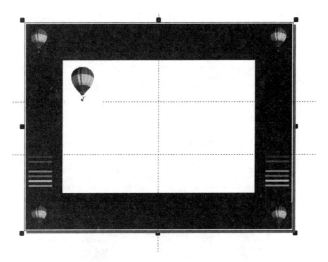

FIGURE 13.12 The final background

Adding the Second and Third Slides

Press the **2** button in the lower left of the desktop. A blank slide with the same background as the first should appear. Use the same method as before to add text to the page with CorelDRAW. Choose the icon from the toolbar, draw a box, and then add the following sentence with the **Text** tool in CorelDRAW: **It Can Use Images Created In Other**

Chapter 13: CorelSHOW and Object Linking and Embedding

Applications. Place **Returns** after **Images** and **Other**. Choose **Exit and Return**, choosing the **Update** option. The result is shown in Figure 13.13.

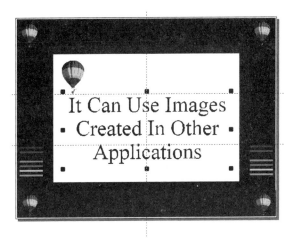

FIGURE 13.13 The second slide

Once the CorelSHOW desktop has reopened on the new slide, resize it and place it on the page so there is room for the large balloon above it. Click on slide number **3**; repeat the process. But this time enter, **That Way You Can Use All of Corel's Special Effects**. Place **Returns** after **Can** and **Corel's**. Now open the CorelDRAW **Effects** menu and use the unconstrained envelope to make the text look like the example in Figure 13.14. Once you have the object the way you want it, **Exit and Return** as before.

FIGURE 13.14 The third slide

Fitting Objects to the Page

There is one handy command in CorelSHOW's Arrange menu that is unique. By selecting **Fit Object To Slide**, the selected object will be expanded or reduced to the exact dimensions of the page. If the object's aspect ratio (height to width) is not equal to the slide's aspect ratio, it will be adjusted automatically.

Arranging Presentations in the Slide Sorter

If this presentation was being done with 35mm slides, you would use a light table to arrange them. Press on the fourth View button, and enter the **Slide Sorter**. This is like an electronic light box. You can use the **Pick** tool to drag slides into new arrangements. You can also renumber the images, change transition effects, and vary the time a slide will be assigned in the presentation. Experiment a bit with the mouse and change the way your show is defined. Run it to see what differences the changes make in the special effects and the ease with which you can view them. Figure 13.15 shows the current presentation in the Slide Sorter.

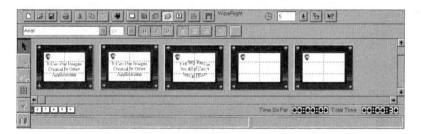

FIGURE 13.15 The CorelSHOW slide sorter

Inserting an Animation

You can also use animations within a presentation. They are inserted just like a slide. When the program reaches that point in the production, it will open the file and run it. Since I can't tell what kind of animation support your system has, you'll just use one of the samples that comes with CorelDRAW. Click in the fourth page icon; then open the Insert menu and choose the **Animation** option. The **Insert Animation** dialog box like the one in Figure 13.16, will open. Go to the **FILES** subdirectory and choose one of the four samples. The options in this box allow you to set the speed of the animation, repeat it a set number of times, run it in a continuous loop until the **Escape** key is pressed, or freeze the presentation after the animation is completed.

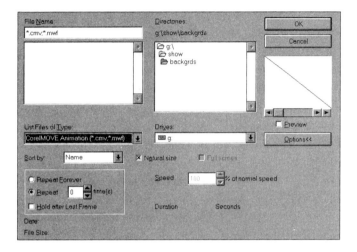

FIGURE 13.16 Inserting an animation

Timelines and Cues

SHOW 5.0 has added a Timelines window and controls and a Cue dialog box, allowing you to interactively set the duration of any slide in your show. By moving the lines to the right of this window, the time the slide will be shown is adjusted. Figure 13.17a shows six slides each with a 5 minute duration, while in Figure 13.17b, I have used my mouse to drag the times out for some of the slides. If you double-click on the icon of the **Clapper Board** to the ledt of a slide icon, the **Cue Information** dialog box (see Figure 13.18) will appear allowing you to change the way the slide show will progress. If you choose **Wait For** in the left-hand **Condition** window, and **Mouse Click** in the right-hand window, and **Continue** in the **Action** window below these, the slide selected will remain on the screen until you click your mouse. Experiment with the various controls you are given in this pair of dialog boxes; they allow you to customize a single presentation for multiple audiences—you can even have a short set of slides that won't be shown unless you take appropriate action—and increase the impact of your presentation.

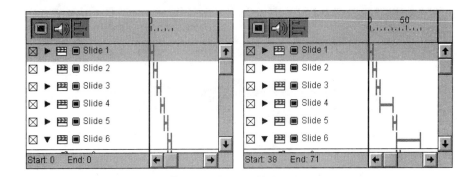

FIGURES 13.17a and b Using the Timelines window

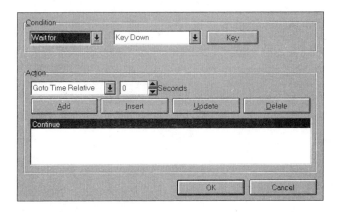

FIGURE 13.18 The Cue Information dialog box

Saving and Printing Your Work

Saving your work is accomplished just as in most other Windows applications. Open the File menu and choose either **Save** or **Save As**. You can also use the File menu to save a background and add it to a library for future use.

The **Print** command is a bit different from CorelDRAW's, since there can be several pages in a CorelSHOW document. Depending on the type of output device, you can set the range to include all or just some of the slides, set the print resolution, and the number of copies. You can also use this menu to print to file or collate copies.

Choosing Presentation Options

Of course you can also "print to the screen." Open the File menu and click on **Preferences**. A dialog set like the one in Figure 13.19 will appear. It allows you to set the slide advance to manual or automatic, run the show until the viewer presses **Escape**, display a pointer on screen during the show and use software decompression to reduce file size. The View tab of this dialog box, shown in Figure 13.20, lets you customize SHOW's interface, showing the Ribbon bar, etc.

The final option is to have the program generate the show in advance. I always leave this option on, because it makes the show run smoother.

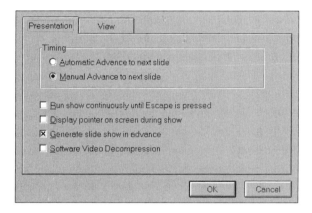

FIGURE 13.19 The Presentations Options dialog box

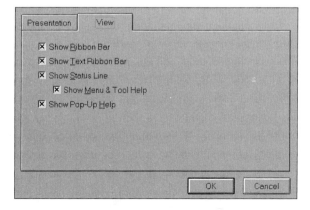

FIGURE 13.20 The View dialog box

Using the CorelSHOW Run-time Module and Designing Presentations

A run-time version is included with CorelSHOW. This program contains only the portions of the complete application needed to run a presentation. If you want to show a series of images produced in SHOW, then this module can be included to view them.

Using the module is simple. Just load it and the files on the system's hard disk; then open Windows, run the **CorelSHOW Runtime** application, and select the Presentation file. The interface looks just like the regular CorelSHOW window, without the production tools.

A Few Tips on Production

There are two basic rules to keep in mind when making slides or other presentation materials: Keep it simple, and make it readable. In general, a slide should not be on the screen for more than 10 seconds. That is the normal attention span of a viewer in the audience for a graphic. Each slide should emphasize one point, and illustrate it clearly. SHOW gives you the ability to use a consistent background and format for all your slides. By setting up a master slide for the entire show, you will avoid having elements that repeat and look like they are jumping around on the page.

Use a typeface and point size that are easy to read by someone standing in the back of the room. Pick one or two fonts for the entire production and use consistent point sizes and justification for each element. These include titles, subtitles, body text, and footnotes. There is an easy way to do that when creating title slides in CorelDRAW. Just place one letter for each element in the proper font on the edge of the page. Then duplicate it and use the **Edit Text** command to enter the text. You could also use the Copy Attributes From command to make the new object match the sample style of the reference character.

If your production is going to be viewed on a computer monitor, be sure to allow time in the script for the screen to redraw. Test it with the same type of display adapter that will be used for the final presentation.

Select colors that will blend well with the colors of the objects to be imported and still allow viewing the slide without eye strain. If the final product will be slides on film or overhead transparencies, use a medium-colored background for all the slides. Very light backgrounds can make it very hard to look at the screen in a dark room, and very dark colors will make the room dark.

Chapter Summary

CorelSHOW lets you create on-screen and slide presentations using objects created in other applications. To get the most from this program you must understand both Windows OLE functions and the basic skills of slide design.

CHAPTER 14

Saturday Morning Live: Fun with CorelMOVE

This chapter covers the following topics:

- Multimedia
- Animation Terms and Concepts
- The CorelMOVE Desktop
- Putting Together a Short Animation
- Working with Animation Actors and Props
- Creating Effective Presentations

The Computer-Multimedia Explosion

Saturday morning TV and the older Saturday afternoon cartoon matinees at the local theater, as well as such full-length animations as Walt Disney's *Beauty and the Beast*, are examples of what Hollywood can do with the magic of animation. CorelMOVE provides us with similar tools to create computer-generated animations for business presentations and just for fun. Traditionally, animations have been created by drawing individual elements onto sheets of acetate known as cels (the term *cel* developed because the original drawings were placed on sheets of clear celluloid and one could be placed over another, much as objects are stacked on top of each other in CorelDRAW).

A cel contains part of a frame. Groups of cels are assembled to form individual frames—a composite image making up one instant, if you will, in an animation. Each assembled group of cels is then photographed. An animation is a collection of frames. As it is projected, each frame is displayed in turn, showing a slightly changed view of the action. To make it easier to create the illusion of life in an animation, only the cels that require a new position for a given frame are updated. For example, a background may change very little from frame to frame, but a character running across the screen will require a change in the image for each new position of hands and arms, or change in facial expression.

CorelMOVE uses a similar method to produce animations. Each object or group of objects placed within a Corel animation exists as part of a collection of cels. A background, for example, which doesn't change at all may be fully drawn and rest on a single cel. A character or group of characters running across the foreground may actually take up 100 cels. Since many actions, such as running or walking, are repetitious, there may actually be only six or seven drawings that are used again and again to create the required series of steps.

CorelMOVE Makes It Easy

Traditional animation artists producing cartoons build collections of their characters performing certain activities, such as cats running away from dogs or kids climbing trees. In this way they build libraries of action sequences that can be reused as needed. CorelMOVE provides a ready library of elements on CD-ROM that can be combined to create ready-made presentations. You can use the tools within CorelMOVE and other modules such as CorelDRAW and CorelPHOTO-PAINT to produce original images.

Not Just Pictures

To use all CorelMOVE's features requires more than just a basic PC. To add sound so that you can hear your characters run across the page, hear the "splat" as something falls to the floor, or add music to your presentation, you will need a sound board, adequate disk storage space, and speakers. To use all the samples provided with CorelMOVE will require a CD-ROM drive, and you'll want a fast video card, a fast CPU, and enough memory that the program runs efficiently. Animation requires that images be drawn on the screen quickly enough to present the illusion of motion. If your machine operates too slowly, your movie will look more like a slide show. You will need a more powerful machine to create animations than to display them. Once the image is created, it can be saved into a self-contained display file.

A full discussion of how to create and produce animations would require its own book; this chapter explains the basics of CorelMOVE and animation techniques to help you get started. The best way to learn animation is to experiment with it. As we move through the exercise in this chapter, some of the terms and concepts may be unfamiliar. Don't worry; you'll get the hang of it as we move along.

Basic Principles of Animation

The movement in an animation is produced by presenting a series of still pictures. MOVE can present from one to 18 frames per second. Higher numbers of frames provide smoother motion but require more drawings and can consume enormous amounts of computer resources. Let's define just a few terms before we get started.

- **Path** is the movement across the screen that you set up for an actor to follow.
- **Cues** apply primarily to methods of interacting with an animation in a planned way. An animation may be paused until you click a mouse or give it some other signal, or it may be paused for a preset time period.
- **Cels** are almost the same as the separate pieces of paper that make up a classic animation. However, entrance and exit special effects take place within a single cell, although all actors' movements are synchronized.
- **Actors** move and change. Actors can follow paths you create. Each actor is actually a short, usually looped, animation sequence. Actors can be things as well as beings.

- **Props** may appear or disappear but are not active in the way actors are. A prop has only one form and one coloration. Entrance and exit special effects may be applied to props but not to actors.

THE CORELMOVE INTERFACE

Let's open CorelMOVE now. Click on its icon, the familiar balloon with a running man beneath it. When the program starts, only the File menu is enabled. Open the **Sample.CMV** from C:\COREL50\MOVE\SAMPLES. You should have a screen similar to the one in Figure 14.1.

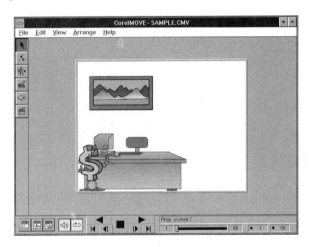

FIGURE 14.1 The CorelMOVE interface

The CorelMOVE Window

You should already be familiar with the basic elements of the Corel interface through your experience with CorelDRAW. The Menu bar, Title bar, and Toolbox all work the same as they do in CorelDRAW. In the center is the Animation window. The size of this window is fixed; if you reduce the size of CorelMOVE on your desktop, you may only see part of the animation window. To change the size of the window you must resize it using the **Animation Info** dialog box, located in the Edit menu. At the bottom of the area is the Control Panel, instead of the scroll bars that exist in CorelDRAW. Let's take a look at the function of each of these in turn.

Menus

CorelMOVE has five listings on the menu bar. The File menu is basically the same as other modules. **Export** has the added ability to save your animation in the **.AVI** format used by other Windows animation players. The **Preferences** option offers you a dialog set which includes a tab for **Playback Options**, **New Animation** parameters and **Imaging Options**, offering advanced control over the appearance of your animation. The **Playback** dialog box lets you set up the appearance of your screen for the animation playback as well as to halt it, set it to play over and over, and so on. We'll get into each of these options a little later.

The Edit menu also is much the same as other Corel applications. One variation is **Copy Frame**, which allows you to copy the current frame of the animation. The **Clone** option works just a little differently than Clone in DRAW; while any changes made to the master object will also be repeated in the clone, in MOVE, changes to the clone will appear also in the master and the other clones. **Animation Info** gives you a dialog box similar to Figure 14.2, showing how many actors, props, frames, and so on, you have placed in your animation. This dialog box allows you to change the total **Number of Frames** in your animation, set the **Speed** at which they are run, and choose which frame will appear in the **Thumbnail** in the **File Open** dialog box. If you have selected an actor or prop in the animation, the **Object Info** dialog box will appear.

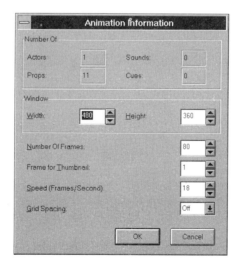

FIGURE 14.2 The Animation Information dialog box

The **View** menu offers the usual sort of options including whether or not you want one or all three of the roll-ups on screen, as well as the Toolbox and Control Panel. You can also toggle the information at the bottom of your screen by selecting **Control Panel**. This is the menu from which you can also run the animation. The **Arrange** menu offers the commands from DRAW allowing you to control which elements are on top or in the background. This is particularly important in an animation, as it controls the illusion of depth.

Three roll-up menus are available: **Timelines**, **Cel Sequencer**, and **Library**, which may be activated either from the **View** menu or from the Toolbar. These roll-ups will be discussed shortly.

The Tool Box

Although some of the tools in CorelMOVE may resemble those in other applications, they may take a little bit of getting used to. The **Pick** tool is still used for selecting objects. Keep a close eye on the bounding box that appears when you click on an object; it's easy to select the background prop instead of an actor or a foreground object. The second tool's icon resembles that of the CorelDRAW Shape tool. It is actually a **Path** tool and is used to select objects and define a path for them to move along. The third tool in the lineup is the **Actor** tool, with the icon of a gesturing man. It is used to create new actors. The three icons below them are the **Prop** tool, the **Sound** tool, and the **Cue** tool. These are also used to add new elements to an animation. Props and Sounds may be: added from files or libraries; created in CorelDRAW; or CorelPHOTO-PAINT and brought into CorelMOVE, or created directly in a CorelMOVE workspace called PAINT.

The Control Panel

The **Control Panel** has buttons that resemble those on a VCR or tape recorder and function in the same way. Pressing on the square in the center stops the action, pressing on the arrows to the left and right moves the animation forward or backward, and so on. To the left of the playback controls are three buttons. These are used to open up the **Timelines**, **Library**, and **Cel Sequencer** roll-ups. To the right of the playback control is the Status Line. This shows the currently selected object and the frame counter, and allows you to move forward or backward one frame at a time. The **Control Panel** is displayed in Figure 14.3.

FIGURE 14.3 The Control Panel

The **Status Line** indicates which object selected. If an **Actor** is selected, the **Status Line** will tell you how many cels are in the Actor's animation. A slider bar shows you graphically where in the animation you are presently located, and at the left end the number of the frame presently in the window appears. The number at the right end of the slider is the total number of frames in the animation.

On the far right are two arrows, one pointing up and one down. If an actor or a prop is selected, numbers will appear in these boxes indicating the first and last frames in which the object appears.

Putting Together a Simple Animation

Finding a Backdrop

Let's click on **New** in the File menu and give our animation a name. Your screen will show the CorelMOVE desktop with a blank window in the center. Open the **Library** roll-up from the View menu and click on the arrow near the top right of the roll-up to open the menu, as shown in Figure 14.4. Select the **Open Library** option and go to your CD-ROM. Find the **PROPS1.MLB** file under **Clipart\Move\Library** and double-click on the file name. If you have **Visual Mode** checked on your fly-out menu (as it is in Figure 14.4), you will see a thumbnail of a ringed planet setting over a potholed moon. Now click on the **Place** button at the bottom of the Library roll-up and the alien planet will become the backdrop for our animation. Notice that the backdrop for the animation is a Prop. If you do not have a CD-ROM, use **SAMPLIB.MLB** from \Corel50\Move\LIB. Note that I have deepened the color of the disabled options for the screen shots; your screen won't be identical to the Figure.

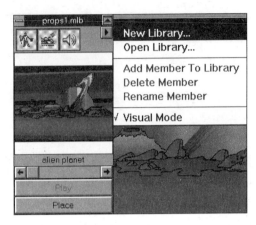

FIGURE 14.4 The Library roll-up

Double-click on the backdrop and the Prop Information dialog box will appear. Give it a name. I called mine **Backdrop**. You can see the settings I used in Figure 14.5. I have checked the box titled **Locked**; this is important in this case, as this option will hold the backdrop exactly where it is and I won't be able to move it by mistake.

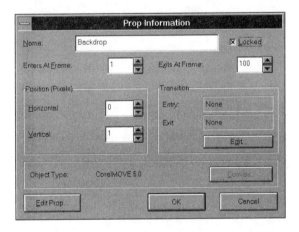

FIGURE 14.5 The Prop Information dialog box

Close this box and be sure the **Backdrop** prop is selected. Look down at the **Control Panel** and notice the numbers displayed at the right end. This shows that the planet appears in all the frames. Since this is a simple animation, we'll only use one backdrop for the entire production.

Adding a Text Title

Now we need to add a title to the animation. Click on the **Prop** tool (fourth one down on the Tool bar) and the **New Prop** dialog box will appear, looking like the one in Figure 14.6. Select the **Create New** checkbox and choose CorelDRAW 5.0 graphic as the **Object Type**; then click on **OK**. Once CorelDRAW has loaded, select the text tool and type a title for the animation. I called mine **The Battle of the Space Aliens for the Planet Corel**. Choose one of the less conservative type styles from those you have loaded. I used **Glacier**, which may not be available on your system. I used **magenta** for the fill and **purple** for the outline colors. Select ones that are pleasing to you. When the title is the way you want it, open the File menu in CorelDRAW and choose the **Exit and Return to CorelMOVE** option. Answer **Yes** when asked if you want the object updated.

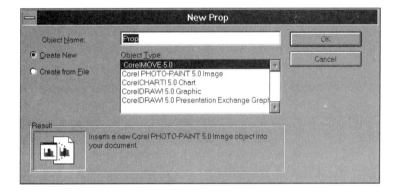

FIGURE 14.6 The New Prop dialog box

If the title isn't the right size, select it (be careful with the selection tool to be sure you get the object you want) and double-click. The **Prop Information** dialog box, like the one in Figure 14.5, will appear. While it is on screen, let's pep up our title. Let it enter at frame **2** and exit at frame **10**. Click on the **Edit** bar under the blanked out **Entry** and **Exit Transition** windows. The Transitions dialog box, like the one in Figure 14.7 will appear. You can preview the transition you have chosen by clicking on the **Preview** button. Unlike most Preview buttons in Corel applications, this one won't show the title in the preview, but will show it with a preloaded animation. Choose an **Entry and Exit Transition**. (These are described in the CorelMOVE manual (Vol. 1, p. 598), so I won't get into them here.)

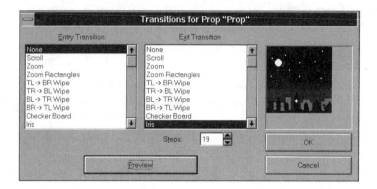

FIGURE 14.7 The Transitions dialog box

When you are finished, exit CorelDRAW normally. You will automatically be returned to CorelMOVE and your animation. The new title won't appear on your screen because it's set to appear in frame 2 and the animation is in frame 1. Space over to frame 2 to see it.

N O T E The automatic movement between two programs such as CorelMOVE and CorelDRAW is done using Window's *OLE* function (this stands for *Object Linking* and *Embedding*). When CorelDRAW 4.0 was written OLE was being revised by Microsoft and the Corel programmers had to use early code provided by Microsoft. You may have noticed that some clipboard and pasting functions within the Corel modules are very slow. With 5.0, some of the problems experienced earlier have been reduced. OLE still makes very heavy demands on your system. Make sure you sent your registration card for CorelDRAW 5.0 in, so that you can get information as new code may become available.

CorelMOVE has some text capabilities, although typefaces and styles are more limited than in CorelDRAW. For example, text entered in CorelMOVE cannot have one color for fill and another for outline. Adding text to animations can get tricky. If you add text to the backdrop, the text will be visible throughout the animation. On the other hand, if you make the text an actor, it will only be seen in the frame or frames you added it to. Usually, you will define text as a prop and indicate how many frames it is to appear in. This way you can apply the transition effects, as I did in our exercise. Occasionally it is desirable for text to move around and in this case, you would define the text as an actor. If you need more complicated text elements, you have to create them in CorelDRAW or another application and import them.

ADDING ACTION TO AN ANIMATION

Now that we have a backdrop and title, it's time to add some action. Open the **Library** roll-up, click the arrow on the upper right, and choose **Open Library** from the menu. Open the **ALIENS.MLB** library from the CD-ROM disk. This contains a collection of strange beings. These are actors, not props, and each of the files is a very short action sequence. Click on the **Play** button and the figures will go through the animation sequence in the thumbnail window.

NOTE: Since most of the animation files are only available on the CD-ROM, those readers without access to a CD-ROM reader will not be able to use some of the files mentioned in the rest of this chapter. If you don't have a CD-ROM, you will have to substitute your own files or possibly borrow copies from someone with a CD-ROM available. The SAMPLE library contains some quite usable dinosaurs and you can follow the steps of our exercise using these actors rather than the ones in the figures.

Open the **Alien and Pet** sequence in this library and click on the **Play** button to get an idea of what this actor can do. In your animation, go to Frame **8**, where we want the actor to make his entrance. From the **Library** roll-up, have the **Alien and Pet** actor in the **Preview** window and click on **Place**. When the actor is placed into the Frame, he will be larger than we want. Double-click on him and choose **Edit Actor** in the **Actor Information** dialog box. If you forgot to move to Frame **8** before placing your Actor, select the Actor and double-click to open the **Actor Information** dialog box again. Fill in the number 8 in the **Enters at Frame** box. Go and fill in **45** in the **Exits at Frame** box.

Editing Images in CorelMOVE

Since the actor is larger than planned for the final animation, we're going to edit our alian. Select the Actor and double-click. When the **Actor Info** box opens, click on the **Edit Actor** button in the lower left corner of this box. The small **PAINT** interface shown in Figure 14.8 will open. This applet is like a scaled down version of CorelPHOTO-PAINT and has fewer tools (you can use the advanced features and special effects that CorelPHOTO-PAINT offers by doing your work in PHOTO-PAINT and then copying your completed work into CorelMOVE).

FIGURE 14.8 The Paint Editor window

Click on the Edit menu and select **Scale All Cels** as I have done in Figure 14.9; type **50** in both the **horizontal** and **vertical** options in the **Scale By** dialog box and click on **OK**. All 8 cels in this animation will be resized. Changes selected in the **Options** menu apply to all the cels in the animation, which certainly saves a lot of time and trouble spacing from cel to cel and repeating commands. This global approach does have a drawback. Large animations may take a long time, especially on slower computers. When the actor is scaled down, open the File menu and click on **Apply** and then, again in the File menu, **Exit Paint**.

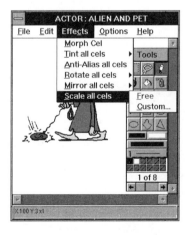

FIGURE 14.9 Scaling an actor

Chapter 14: Saturday Morning Live: Fun with CorelMOVE   583

SHORTCUT
There is no **Undo** command available in some MOVE commands and effects. Once something is done, it's done. Saving complicated manipulations several times while they are in process can save you a lot of time and trouble. You can also "save" cels in process with **Keep Paint**, off the Edit menu in the Paint Editor Window. Then you can later restore a cel to the "saved" appearance using **Revert Paint**.

Setting an Actor's Path

Next we need to draw a path for our Alien and his pet to take, otherwise he'll have to walk the pet standing in the same spot. Select the **Alien** with the selection tool, place the cursor over the **pet** (or over that portion of the actor reaching out the furthest to the left, and place him almost (not quite, more about that later) out of the animation window on the lower right. The next step is to set the **Registration Point**. This is the portion of the actor which actually will follow the path we'll create.

NOTE
The path process is just a little more complicated, because the this Registration Point also has a defined position in the animation—the point in the animation window where that portion of the actor presently is. We'll be placing the point on the actor's foot, and the point in the animation window where the actor's foot is when we do this will, for the moment, be the place where the path begins. Remembering this will help you understand better what is happening as you continue defining the actor's path.

Since we'll want our alien to walk along a path, we'll place the Registration Point at his leading foot. Click on the Edit menu in the **Paint** window. The last option on that menu, **Registration**, may or may not have a check mark beside it. Either way, select **Registration**. If it had a check, you have just removed the Registration Point given the actor when it was created. Open the menu again and again click on **Registration**. Now you have the opportunity to designate your own point, so click the cross-hair cursor that has appeared on the actor's foot. The cross-hair pointer will appear where you clicked and will be blinking. Open the File menu, click on **Apply**, and then **Exit**.

Now get the **Path** tool from the **Toolbar**; it's the one that looks like the **Shape** tool in CorelDRAW. The **Path Edit** roll-up will appear. Make sure that the **Allow Adding Points** box is checked. Click on the **Edit** button, a fly-out looking like the one in Figure 14.10 will appear. Look at the dotted-box outline, partially in and partially out of the Animation window; that's the actor, and the black dot just out of the Animation window on the lower right is the Registration Point. Click on the **Move Frame With Point** option. When this is checked, the path origin will remain attached to your actor, rather than to a point in the window, and the actor will move as you add to his path.

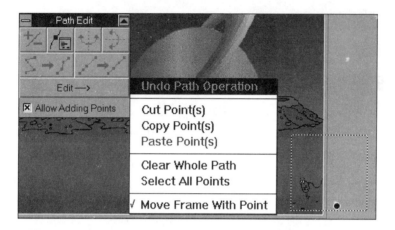

FIGURE 14.10 Beginning the actor's path

NOTE When we select the Move Frame With Point option, we detach the defined place in the animation where the registration originally fell and attach it only to the actor. Otherwise, moving the actor would add a section to the path causing unplanned movement in our animation.

Move your cursor a short distance in front of the Aalien and click, move an inch or so farther and click again. Continue drawing a path until you arrive at the far side of the screen. Figure 14.11 shows a path with one of the center nodes selected, and the actor's foot on the selected node. Click on the **Point Information** button on the Path Edit roll-up, and a dialog box like the one in Figure 14.11 will appear. The **Point Information** button is second from the left in the top row and looks like a node beside a menu. This dialog box shows exactly where the selected node lies within the Animation window. Click on the **Loop to Here** check box. When this box is checked,

AND there are more nodes in the path than there are cels in the actor, the actor will loop again and again through the path you have placed for him.

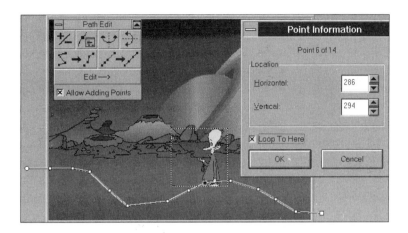

FIGURE 14.11 Setting an actor's path

Controlling an Actor's Speed

If an actor is moving too fast, adding points to the path is one way to slow him down. Select the **Actor**, and then select the **Path** tool. Open the **Edit** fly-out from the Path Edit roll-up, and click on **Select all Points**; now click on the **+/-** button in the **Path Edit** roll-up. The **Scale Path** dialog box, Figure 14.12 will appear. Increase or decrease the numbers in the boxes and it will add or subtract path nodes. If you want your actor to exit left and immediately enter right, use the **Shift+Click** method to select only the nodes on the curves of the path that indicate the actor's on-screen movement. Off-screen movement is indicated by the straight line from the end of the path to the node selected for the loop. Reducing the number of these nodes will speed the actor's reappearance in the animation, just as adding nodes to a portion or all of the path will slow the actor's movement. Now press the **F9** key to watch your animation. Your actor should wander across the foreground of the Aanimation Window to the left, then jerk quickly back to his starting point.

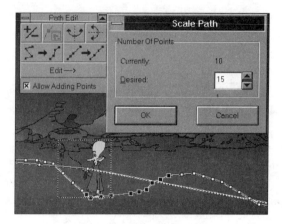

FIGURE 14.12 Adding nodes to slow movement

WARNING

It is quite possible to lose an actor by moving him out of the Animation Window, particularly while experimenting with paths. Run the entire animation to see if the path will bring the actor through any part of the window. If it does, find a frame in which the actor is visible, use the **Pick** tool to select him, and move him and/or adjust his path so that he is again placed where you want him. The **Edit** fly-out in the **Path Edit** roll-up has a **Clear Whole Path**, option and by using this you can begin again to define the path. If the actor has moved so far out of the animation window that it does not appear at all, a last resort is to open the **TimeLines** roll-up, select the name of the lost actor, and press the **Delete** key. You lose your actor but at least it isn't using up memory while being invisible.

Making the return trip invisible

As our path is now, the actor returns right across the center of our animation. We must construct his path so that the return trip will be invisible. With the **Node** tool, select the path node that is farthest from the lower edge of the animation window. If you have **Move Frame with Point** selected from the **Edit** fly-out, your actor will appear there. Switch to the **Pick** tool, select the actor and move him to the very top of the Animation Window. Using the **Pick** tool and selecting nodes at either end of the path, and from the straight-line return path, drag the return portion of the path down well under the Animation Window, as I have done in Figure 14.13. You can see the dotted box around the actor at the far right of the Animation Window. You'll probably see that the actor's head still appears in the animation, but when we bring him back down to the lower part of the window, his return trip will become invisible. Do this now and run your animation.

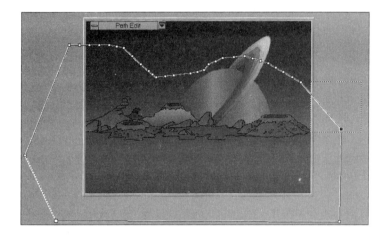

FIGURE 14.13 Setting a return path

There are other refinements of the path available in the **Path Edit** roll-up. The buttons with the semicircles let you rotate and mirror all or the selected nodes on the path. Below that, the left-hand button will smooth out the sharp corners in the path, and the right-hand button will even up the node spacing on the path.

Creating a New Prop

We can create new actors or props without leaving CorelMOVE. Let's add a sun to our animation. Our sun won't be moving around on the screen, so click on the **Prop** icon in the Toolbar. We will create our sun in the **Paint** workspace included in CorelMOVE. The New Prop dialog box will apear, along with the Paint Editor Toolbar and Palette. Use the **Spray Can** to make a fuzzy, red and orange **sun**. To select new colors for line and fill in the **Paint** module, click and hold on either of the two buttons right below the **Ellipse** and **Polygon** tools; a standard palette will flyout and, still holding down the left mouse button, move your cursor over the color you want. Release the cursor and the color selected will appear on the button bar. When you have finished painting a sun, click on **Apply** and then on **Exit**. Your sun will appear on the animation.

But we aren't in the right frame, so double-click on the sun to bring up the **Prop Information** dialog box. Put the number **52** in the **Starts at Frame** window and let it remain for the rest of the animation. Use the **Edit** button in the Prop Information dialgo box to produce the **Transitions for Prop "Sun"** dialog box, then choose **Zoom**. This will allow you to use the **Edit Zoom** dialog box. Give it a long zoom entrance so it rises slowly from the foreground to the sky. If you want to get fancy, you can make it set by setting a slow zoom exit.

Creating a New Actor

Creating a new actor is a little bit more involved. Since actors can change from cell to cell, frame to frame, and follow paths, we have to think of them differently. Theoretically, you must make a separate drawing for every frame of the actor's sequence. In practice, some fine options are built into CorelMOVE to make this job easy.

Click on the **Actor** tool in the CorelMOVE Toolbar. We will create our actor in CorelDRAW, using some of the symbols available in that application. When CorelDRAW is loaded, select the **Symbol** tool from the **Text** fly-out and place an **eagle** and a **dinosaur** on the page. Move the dinosaur over the eagle and use the **Node Edit** tool to **Delete** the nodes making up the eagle's tail feathers. Then **weld** the two together. After that, select the shape, change again to **Node Edit**, and click the **Auto-Reduce** button to simplify our actor. Figure 14.14 shows the result of the **Auto-Reduce**, as well as the special **Frame Select** roll-up which CorelDRAW has thoughtfully provided to help us. Our "**Dinofly**" is easier to work with in creating the illusion of movement when he has an outline the same color as the fill. That way there won't be any extraneous lumps or losses of outline as we use the **Node Edit** tool to move the wings, so give him a bright orange outline and fill.

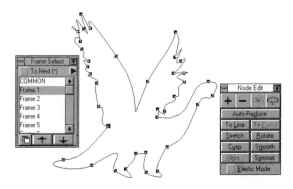

FIGURE 14.14 Auto-reducing nodes

Notice the new roll-up on the CorelDRAW workspace called **Frame Select**. This allows you to do all the work of animation in CorelDRAW and then to return with a completed sequence to CorelMOVE. You can choose to specify the total number of frames you expect to use at the beginning. If you check the **To Next** checkbox, you can place your image in its beginning state in Frame 1. When you edit that image, the changed image will appear in Frame 2, while the image in Frame 1 stays the same. You then continue by moving to Frame 2 and editing the image there for Frame 3. The process is a little confusing at first, but it makes adding the movement to your animation much easier. This function in CorelDRAW is only accessible when it is opened from CorelMOVE. Figure 14.15 shows several Frames in my animation.

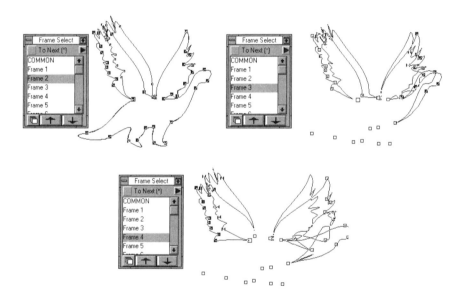

FIGURE 14.15 Creating an Actor and action sequence in CorelPAINT

In the beginning, you may find it easier to edit animations by adding Frames one at a time. Let's use that method now. **Copy** the **Dinofly** and add Frame **2**. Go to Frame 2 and Paste the **Dinofly**. Using the **Shape** tool's marquee, select the **nodes** making up one of the dinofly's wings and move the wing downward. Adjust as necessary and then, with the **Pick** tool, select the drawing and copy it. Repeat this process until you have enough frames to complete the movement. Do **Save** the sequence before exiting CorelDRAW in case of any problems.

You can also create a prop or actor for a CorelMOVE animation in CorelPHOTO-PAINT. Think of the possibilities of developing your actors from scanned photographs of friends. A good way to do this is to create the original image in CorelPHOTO-PAINT, and return to MOVE. When your image is placed in a cel and you double-click on it, the **Edit Actor** dialog box gives you the option of converting the object to CorelMOVE. Once it has been converted to CorelMOVE, however, you will not be able to edit it further in CorelPHOTO-PAINT. It's always a good idea to save images in the program in which they were created before taking them into another.

Let's create a second Dinofly. Click on the **Create Actor** button and choose to create it in CorelDRAW. Once you are in CorelDRAW, open your saved **Dinofly**. Don't add any Frames to this version; just return to CorelMOVE. Convert the object to a CorelMOVE file by double-clicking on the **Dinofly** and clicking the **Convert** button. Choose the **Edit Actor** button so we can animate it in the **Paint** window. Make a Copy of the Dinofly before proceeding. Click on **Insert Cells** in the **Edit** menu and Paste the copy in the second cel. Using the **Lasso** selection tool, select one of the **wings** as shown in Figure 14.16. If you click on the **Onion Skin** option in the **Options** menu, a pale copy of your original image will appear behind the image you are working on. This will help guide you in placing the wing. When the **Move** arrow appears, move the wing down, being careful to keep the lower end touching the body. Move the wings around until you are satisfied with the placement and angle.

FIGURE 14.16 Using the lasso selection tool to move portions of an Actor

When you are satisfied with this Frame, use the **marquee selection** tool to select and Copy the object, add cel **3**, and Paste it. Continue to change the wings in two more Frames, at which time you should bring them to the lowest point of their flying action. If you wish, get a little fancier and move the tail appropriately and even the head. Figure 14.17 shows five cels in this animation.

Cels **6**, **7**, and **8** merely reverse the motions in cels **2**, **3**, and **4**, so we don't need to redraw the objects. Copy cel **4**, add cell **6**, enter it, and Paste. Repeat this for cels **7** and **8**,

Pasting in cels **3** and **2**. Once you are finished, use the **Control Panel** to run and test your animation.

FIGURE 14.17 A simple animation sequence

Getting Things in Motion

It may seem that a movie is just a collection of still photographs with sound, and that an animation is just a sequence of pictures. However, it's more involved than that. In an animation we are trying to present the illusion of motion. To maintain the illusion, it must be believable. We've all seen movies or cartoons where an action or an object appeared out of place, or an actor walked in through the wrong door or appeared in a slightly different position, seeming to jump from one frame to the next. This discontinuity not only can destroy the illusion, but can also annoy the viewer. On a motion picture set, one of the most important details is continuity. In fact, a motion picture production company usually has at least one person whose total job is to make sure that continuity is maintained. So how can we maintain continuity in our CorelMOVE animation? By observing a few simple rules.

1. Make sure that all actors have logical entrances and exits.
2. Make sure that objects progress naturally from frame to frame. For example, if an actor is drinking from a glass of water, the water level needs to go down evenly. There can't be more water in the glass after a sip is taken than there was before the action was started.
3. If an actor exits to the right of the screen, he should re-enter from the right of the screen and vice versa. Although animations can take some liberty with this, it's still a good general practice to follow.

Professional animators make rough sketches of their scenes before beginning their detailed creations. This allows them to script not only what's in a frame, but also how it progresses from one frame to another. Even a set of rough notes or an outline can help with this process.

More Ways to Fine-tune Your Animation

The Cel Sequencer Roll-up

CorelMOVE has some sophisticated tools to help us perfect your animation. With the **Cel Sequencer** roll-up (accessed from its icon on the **Control Panel** or from the View menu; see Figures 14.18 and 14.19), you can completely control when and where an actor moves. It may be used to make an actor slowly change size as it moves about on the stage. Let's see how it works by making the second Dinofly jump into one of the craters in the background. Lay out a **Path** for this actor that ends in the mouth of one of the craters. Set the actor's Timeline so that it enters in Frame **56** and exits in Frame **81**. Apply **Scale Sequence** from frames **76** to **81** (click on Frame **76**, move pointer to Frame **81**, hold down **Shift** and click, and the range of frames is selected). Click on the upper right-pointing **arrow** at the right edge of the dialog box, and a fly-out menu like the one in Figure 14.18 will appear. Click on **Select All**, open the fly-out again and click on **Normal Cycle**. *Normal Cycle* means that the cels in the actor will play in numerical order. **Reverse** means they'll play from last to first, etc. Now click on the lower right-pointing **arrow** and set the scale action from **Large** to **Small**, as shown in Figure 14.19. Run your; animation, the Dinofly should disappear into the crater in a satisfactory way.

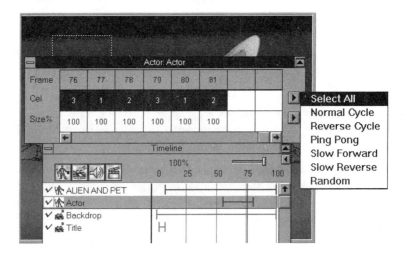

FIGURE 14.18 Setting up a disappearance with the Cel Sequencer

Chapter 14: Saturday Morning Live: Fun with CorelMOVE   **593**

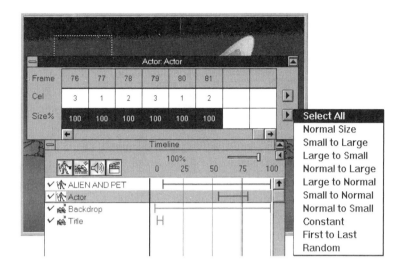

FIGURE 14.19 Making the Dinofly disappear with the Cel Sequencer

The Cel Sequencer may be used to delay an actor's actions by replaying one or more frames over and over until you are ready for the action to complete.

The Timelines Roll-up

Activate the **Timelines** roll-up by clicking the button on the **Control Panel** at the far left bottom corner of the workspace. Click on the **arrow** near the top right to extend the full fly-out. It represents graphically in colored lines the entrances and exits of your props and actors. Figure 14.20 shows the timelines for my animation. You can actually use the mouse to adjust entrances and exits by moving the beginning or end of a bar or you can move the whole bar to a different point in the animation. Double-clicking on any of the actors, props, or sounds listed in the timelines roll-up will access the **Object Information** dialog box.

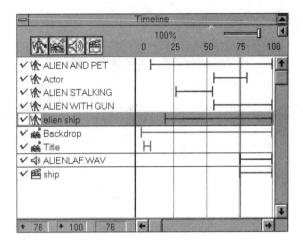

FIGURE 14.20 The Timelines roll-up

Cues

If animations are to be used as part of a presentation, you may want to have the action stop so that your audience will pay attention to something else. To do this, place a Cue where you want the animation to stop. Name the cue and select how you want the animation to resume. You can even set a cue to have the animation resume with a mouse click, unless a defined time period expires before the click. When the preset time has expired, the animation will resume. I have cued the space ship to pause until the sound is made in Figure 14.21.

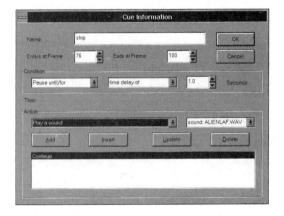

FIGURE 14.21 The Cue Dialog Box

Adding Sound to Animation

You can add and play sounds in your animation if you have a sound board in your computer. The libraries included on your second CD-ROM disk contain a variety of sound effects that can be used. You can also record sounds, save them, and add them to a library to be used in animation. CorelMOVE has tools that allow you to specify which frames have sound, to adjust the volume for each sound, and even to overlap sounds. Your sound system may have additional tools that can be used effectively with CorelMOVE. You can even edit sounds in a special window.

The Ultimate in Animation

When is a cat a hat? When you can apply *morphing* to the images. CorelMOVE 5.0 has added Morphing capacity and morphing will add excitement to your animations. While setting up a morphing of images is a little complicated, the results can be well worthwhile. Since some of the more popular morphing we've seen has been between people and animals, let's find some reasonably simple bitmaps to work with. Open CorelPAINT and load an image of an animal and one of a human face from your Corel disks or CD-ROM. I chose **ACTOR111** under **PEOPLE\ENTERTAINMENT** and **BLOODHOU** under **ANIMAL**. Here are the steps in creating your morphing image:

1. Load the beginning image into CorelPHOTO-PAINT (or DRAW). **Save** in the application's default format in the **MOVE** subdirectory.
2. Load the end image into either application, select **all**, and click on the **Copy** command in the Edit menu. This places the second image into the Window Clipboard.
3. **Exit** PHOTO-PAINT or DRAW and start or switch to MOVE. Click on the **Create Actor** button. In the **Create Actor** dialog box, choose the application you saved the beginning image in; then select the **Create From File** check box. Click on the **Browse** button, and find the beginning image you saved in the **MOVE** subdirectory. Highlight the **file name**, click on **OK**. MOVE will load the image as an actor.
4. Select the beginning image from the Animation Window and double-click on it to activate the **Actor Information** dialog box. Click on the **Convert...** button, and click on **YES** in the confirmation window.
5. Now click on the **Edit Actor** button, and the Paint applet will load.

6. Click on the Edit menu, and on the **Add Cells** option, In the small dialog box which will appear, select the **After Current Cel** option, and **Add** one cel to the actor.

7. Using the **slider** under the Toolbar, go to the slide you just created and open the **Edit** menu. Click on the **Paste** command. Your ending image will be pasted from the Windows Clipboard into the second cel of the actor. Size and position the image in cel **2** to match the one in cel 1.

8. Go back to cel 1 and open the **Effects** menu. Click on the **Morph** option; the dialog box seen in Figure 14.22 will appear. Decide how many steps you want to take between the two images. I chose **8**. Each cel in a morphed image resembles a single object in a blend created in DRAW. Remember that this is a memory- and time-consuming operation and pick the number of cels to insert carefully.

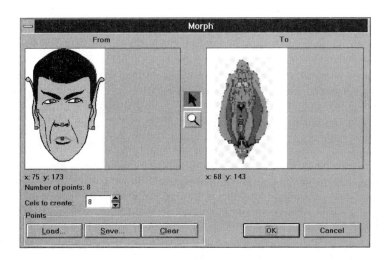

FIGURE 14.22 The Morph dialog box

Before we let MOVE beginning the morphing, we need to give it some guidance so that our actor will actually appear to be changing. This is done by adding paired **Control Points** to the images. Click on the nose of the **From** image; a green box will appear on that image's nose, and a red box will appear somewhere on the **To** image. Drag the red **Control Point** on the **To** image to its nose, or the place you want the nose in the **From** image to move towards. Choose several other features in the **From** image to link to the **To** image. The eyes, cheekbones, ears, chin, etc. will help the resulting morph to proceed keeping the metamorphasis recognizable.

Chapter 14: Saturday Morning Live: Fun with CorelMOVE

When your **Control Points** are set you can save them if you want, so that if you decide to morph the images again, that part of the work will be done. When you are satisfied, click on **OK**, and prepare to wait a few minutes.

When the morph effect is complete, click on the **Apply to Actor** button and then on **Exit**. Now run your animation to watch the process. Figure 14.23 showsn every other frame in my morph.

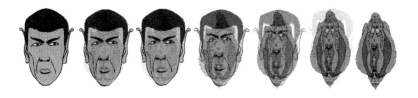

FIGURE 14.23 The completed morphed image

Chapter Summary

CorelMOVE lets us add a fourth dimension to our graphic toolkit by allowing us to animate our computer images. Although the tools are easy to use, mastery will take practice and use will require adequate computer resources. If you are seriously interested in developing your animation techniques with CorelMOVE, you might want to study the CorelMOVE manual in detail and to check out reference materials at your local library or art supply store.

In an Appendix called "Principles of Animation," the manual has a number of useful comments to make about developing successful animations. It reviews some of the principles that experience has shown to be important in successful presentations.

CHAPTER 15

Designing with Words and Symbols

LollyBerry logo

INTRODUCTION

There is a lot more to working with text than putting letters and words on a page. In this chapter we'll focus on using typography to convey a message and on how to handle type properly. The emphasis is on using type as part of a design. The exercises include designing a company logo with matching stationery and business cards. We'll also cover some basic principles of typography and tips on how to add a professional touch to text in drawings.

CorelDRAW's method of breaking text into two basic types, artistic and paragraph, is very similar to the way professionals divide typesetting jobs. Decorative type is used to capture the eye with few letters and lots of style. Logos and signs are a good example. The words are meant not to be read and studied but to present a simple message. The reader will only look at them for a few seconds, so the information or idea must be clear and concise. Text like "Gas Next Exit–Last Chance for Twenty Miles!" tells the motorist to stop now and buy here! If the text is too small or difficult to read or if the sign looks old and run-down, the message doesn't work. Such a sign is often the reader's introduction to a business, and first impressions are very important. Since artistic text is not meant to be used for long passages, there is more freedom when working with it. But remember that the goal of all typography is to convey a message. The final result must both be readable and have the desired content.

You have been reading most of your life, so you are an experienced user of typography. Although you may not be an expert on spacing, kerning, and all the technical details, your eye should be developed enough to know what you like and what you don't. One basic piece of advice: Keep it simple. The arrival of the laser printer and desktop publishing saw the advent of the ransom note school of design. Every font and special effect that could be used in a layout was used, just to prove that the user knew how to use (or misuse) them. Our arsenal of typographic controls is a toolkit. Like any set of tools, some are right for one task, some for another.

Choosing Typefaces

One example of fitting the right tool to the task is in choosing a typeface. Decorative text elements, including logos and symbols based on letters, are designed to set a mood or give a good impression. The design needs to give the right image to be effective. If a bank uses a logo that gives the impression the company is solid and responsible, that's effective. If the logo makes consumers think the bank is too trendy to trust, it may be giving out the wrong signal and hurt business. When organizations create a logo, they want a result that explains who and/or what they are about. A successful company relies on its logo to provide instant recognition of who it is and what it does. Consider how logos are used in advertising. Sometimes they are the only reference to who placed the ad. Look at what happens to a firm's public identity when it updates its logo; the result can (with the right ad campaign) change the company's image.

Logos don't exist in isolation. They have to work with ads, letterheads, business forms, cards, and annual reports. The appearance of the logo has to fit the image of the company and the type of business involved. Would you enter a hospital or clinic with a logo out front that looked like it was designed for a haunted house? CorelDRAW is a natural choice for designing logos. It offers a wide variety of typefaces and provides excellent controls for manipulating letters into new shapes. The first step in any design job is to define the scope of the project and identify what you are going to give to the client (even if it's yourself). The next step is to assemble the elements needed to complete the job.

If you have a project that involves text, the typeface is a critical component. It needs to fit with the overall design. In many cases the appearance of the font actually sets the tone for design. That statement may seem a bit extreme, but it is true. Usually when you start seeking out typefaces you choose a basic style of type and then look at variations of that type.

Measuring Up

Remember how type is sized? This topic was covered in Section One, and now it will be discussed in more detail. The point size for a given font is measured from the top of the ascenders to the bottom of the descenders. However, the point size is not the only thing to consider when fitting type for a job. Look at the difference in the length of the four lines of text shown in Figure 15.1. They are all the same point size, but the top line is almost a third longer than the one on the bottom. Now look closely at the difference in the relative height between the upper- and lowercase letters in the examples on the first and third lines. The Avante Garde sample is wider, and the lowercase letters are taller than the same text set in Lincoln. When you start looking for a typeface, don't forget to consider what space requirements are involved.

Art supply stores and vendors like Adobe Systems and BitStream have books with collections of typefaces. These are usually arranged by family or class of type. This makes it a lot easier to identify which ones might be suited to a specific task. There are no labels that say, "This is great for a small theater company," or, "Not suited for banks and other lending institutions." That is part of where the art comes in. The books usually contain blocks of print to show how the type looks when laid out. This can give you a good idea of how readable the font will be and will let you gauge the spacing.

Unfortunately, CorelDRAW does not have a grouped set of samples by type, so you have to work a bit harder to identify the typeface you want. There is a list in the user's manual with sample letters, and a large, folded sheet with full alphabets. The preview window in the Text Edit dialog box shows the first few letters of a font as you select it, but that is a tedious way to hunt for type.

Logos: Is a Word Worth a Thousand Pictures?

The essence of a logo is simplicity. The goal is to have the viewer immediately know whom the logo represents and to communicate a positive feeling. In some cases a logo is just a symbol, but most of the time it is a combination of letters and graphics or of the name worked into a symbol. The logo represents the company, much like a seal used to serve as a symbol for a ruler or guild in the past.

Our imaginary client for the exercises in this chapter, the LollyBerry Candy Company, offers a wide range of healthy fruit snacks. They want you to develop a logo and matching set of cards and stationery. The logo must be used in ads and on boxes, wrappers, and displays. It should be colorful and reflect the message that the products are made with healthy ingredients, all from natural fruit sources. This is a small start-up company with a small budget, and the owners don't want the materials to make them look like a big company with lots of glitz. The products will have to be easily seen amid the clutter of a checkout aisle in a supermarket, so the logo needs to be easy to read and colorful. They want to use it as the basis for the design of all their product packaging, so you have been asked to make the name stand out clearly.

Let's open CorelDRAW and set up the program for a little custom typography. The logo will be saved in CorelDRAW format, then imported to other drawings as needed. Set the page to Landscape, the right mouse button to Edit Text, and the display options to show the status bar, but turn off the rulers and color palette.

Casting Call

The first step is to narrow the typeface options. You want to be sure that the possible contenders will work with your design. Not all fonts contain all characters, so some typefaces may not have letters or symbols that will be needed later. Some may have letters

Chapter 15: Designing with Words and Symbols

shaped in ways that will not work with the other letters needed for the logo. It is a good idea to make a habit of setting up a sample block of text that includes letters that you know you will need, plus some others to see how the typeface behaves. Figure 15.1 shows a block constructed for the candy company. It has the firm's name, some numbers, punctuation, symbols, and some letter combinations to test kerning.

LollyBerry Candy Company
12769,©"[fi qQ%&*!vWAmp

**LollyBerry Candy Company
12769,©"[fi qQ%&*!vWAmp**

FIGURE 15.1 A sample type block

The text block is a very useful tool and serves several purposes. You can see if that typeface is suitable, both in style and in spacing, which helps clarify thinking about just what you want in the look of the font you finally choose. That is subjective. It also allows you to make sure that the font contains all the characters and symbols needed. You might place some difficult-to-kern letters in the block to see how well they are handled.

Not all typefaces contain a full set of characters, so you could finish a basic design and find yourself without an exclamation point. Make sure that any special letters you need, like trademark or copyright symbols, are included. You should include numbers because some fonts align numbers to the baseline and some do not. Take a look at the three samples in Figure 15.2. Notice the difference in the kerning between letters i and s. Note the overlap in the s and V as well as in the 7 and 9 for the Vivienne sample.

This is Palm Springs 135679

This is Vivienne 135679

This is Paradise 135679

FIGURE 15.2 Not all fonts are created equal

If you don't test how the letters you need will work together, you may have to reset the entire job. Sure, CorelDRAW enables you to create custom characters and manually kern letters. However, you can't do that if you are sending the job out to a service agency and want to use their PostScript fonts.

The Finals

Once the options have been narrowed to a few typefaces it is time to view them side by side. Looking at them together is the best way to see differences that aren't noticeable when studying them alone. Figure 15.3 shows nine possible contenders for our candy company project.

FIGURE 15.3 Choosing a typeface

Some variations are easy to spot. Notice the different ways the Y is shaped and the open spaces inside the letters B, O, and R. The words are run on two lines to make it easier to see the relative spacing. The sample in the center takes up more space than the others, but has very little white space. In most cases there is no absolute right or wrong selection with decorative type. Choose one that meets your technical needs and that you like. If you are modifying the logo with the Shape tool or Effects menu, the file will have to be exported, so having a matching font at the typesetter is not all that important. Choose Kabana Bold. If you do not have that font on your system, use another.

Curves Ahead

Select the Text tool and type **Lolly Berry** as a single block with one word on each line. Now open the **Arrange** menu and convert the block to curves, then from the same menu choose **Break Apart**. The converted text was combined, and you need to work with the individual letters. When you break the block the counters (open spaces) in the O, R, and B will look solid. Don't worry, it's just a little extra work. Use the Zoom tool to fill the page with the object. Open the **Fill** fly-out and place the **Fill** roll-up on the screen. Click on the **O** so that there are handles around it. Press the **Tab** key once. There should be handles around the center part of the letter. This is called the *counter*, which was turned into a separate object when you converted the block. Give it a white fill from the roll-up palette. Repeat the process until you have converted the fill in all the counters. Combine any letter with its counter(s) i.e., "o,b,r." When you are finished the text should look just like it did when we started, but the letters will be editable curves.

Shaping Letters With the Envelope

Next, we are going to manipulate the letters using Envelope effects, the Shape tool, and manual kerning. Then we'll add fills and some clipart to create a logo that looks like the example in Figure 15.4. Select the first **L**, open the **Effects** menu, and click on the **Envelope** roll-up. Select the **Straight Line** mode and the **Original Mapping** option; then choose **Add New**. Drag the upper corners out until the envelope outline looks about like the example in the figure; then click the **Apply** button. Try to do all the manipulations with the Envelope effect. Once you have the desired effect, use the **Create From** button to make the other **L**s identical. Do the same to the **O** in the top line; then adjust it the way you want it. The sample in Figure 15.5a is just a guide. Experiment and use your judgment. Don't forget the constraining effects of the **Ctrl** key. Repeat the process of editing and copying the envelope until all the letters are the way you want them. Ungroup and move the individual letters with the Pick tool as needed to get the right spacing; then regroup them. If some of the letters are too large or small once all the effects have been applied, resize them and adjust the relative positions. Leave the Envelope roll-up open; we'll need it again soon.

FIGURE 15.4 The LollyBerry logo

Adjusting the Words

Now that the letters are formed the way you want them it's time to get the curved form shown in Figure 15.5. Use a marquee to select each word in turn and group it with the **Ctrl-G** combination. Place a **Single Arc Envelope** (second fly-out option) around the entire top line. Work with the Shape tool until the envelope is about like the example in Figure 15.6. Then use the **Copy Envelope From** command to give the second line the same shape. Use the Pick tool to get the two lines positioned the way you want them. The basic design is almost done; all we need to do to the letters is add the fill and outline.

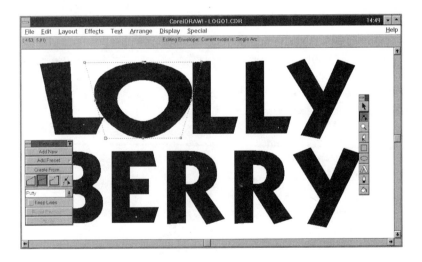

FIGURE 15.5 Editing the envelope

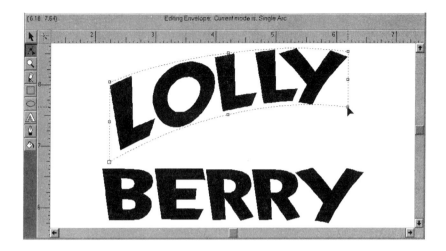

FIGURE 15.6 Shaping the line

Setting the Outline and Fill

Group both lines and open the **Outline Pen** dialog box. Choose a red color, a 0.75-point rule, 33 percent stretch, 26-degree angle, rounded corners, **Behind Fill**, and **Scale With Image**. Make any final adjustments for spacing that might have been affected by the new outline. Open the **Fill** fly-out and choose the on-screen roll-up. Use it to add a linear fill going from magenta to yellow, 15 edge pad, 110-degree angle. That completes the basic logo, which should look pretty much like the example in Figure 15.4. Save your work, but don't exit CorelDRAW. You will be using the logo as part of two other projects.

CREATING MATCHING STATIONERY

Use the **Copy** command to place a duplicate of your logo on the Windows Clipboard; then open a new document. Make sure the rulers are active, set the page to **Portrait**, and open the **Text** roll-up menu. Set **Snap to Guidelines** on under the Layout menu.

Set the view so you can see the entire page and the surrounding clear work area. Paste the logo, use the Pick tool to resize it to about two inches wide, and move it off to the left side of the page. Place the roll-up on the right side. You will be adding the logo to the design shortly, but first you need to set up a visual frame of reference and plan the job.

Planning the Design

Before you start working with the page, you should decide on some external considerations: paper and envelope sizes, paper stock, color, how the job will be printed, what kind of printer or typewriter it will be used with, and what kind of envelopes will be used for mailing. Look a little closer at these factors, since they are typical for many types of CorelDRAW jobs that are sent outside for production.

The best approach for the occasional designer is to get advice from a trustworthy printer. Take a printout of your design to a printer and ask about prices and problems involved in producing the office forms required. Do you want matching paper, envelopes, invoices, and cards? Ask about which type of printing will work best and whether you get a suitable color and weight of paper stock. What kind of ink is to be used? How should you provide a copy of your logo? Some shops can work with a CorelDRAW file (but you may have to work with them via mail); others can use an EPS file. Many will want hard copy. If you don't have a local print shop that can work with electronic files, you can get a typeset hard-copy master from an out-of-town service bureau; then take that to a nearby shop. All of this sounds complicated, but skilled printers know their equipment and what supplies work best with what papers. Ask to look at samples, and get a few sheets to take with you.

The type of paper and inks used will have a lot to do with the color fidelity and quality of the finished product. Letterheads should have a quality look, to give the reader a good impression. Invoices require a lot of information and generally have a more complicated layout. Printers often have preprinted forms they can customize by adding your logo and specific information. Business cards come in a wide variety of paper stocks and can be printed flat or with raised lettering. The way your logo is designed will have a lot to do with what will work best. Lots of fine fills and small details will make the job more difficult and hence more expensive. The envelopes to be used will have a bearing on how some forms are laid out. If you are using a window-type envelope that shows the mailing address (and maybe even the return address), you must make sure that the appropriate information lines up properly.

Chapter 15: Designing with Words and Symbols

Setting the Stage

The easiest way to may sure all the elements are in the right place is to set up guidelines for reference. It is suggested that you use a sequence with critical work that follows this basic checklist:

- Determine the usable margins of the page and set guidelines at those points. For this letterhead they are placed at one inch from the top and bottom and a half-inch from each side.
- Place a guideline at each crease point that would be used to fold a page into an envelope. Use these to get an idea of how the elements relate to the sections of the page. They can be removed as soon as you have all the elements identified.
- Draw a box with a light gray fill to scale for each mandatory element such as an address, stamp, and so on. Place them in their approximate position. As you work they will serve as placeholders to try different layouts.

The guidelines break the page into areas. In the case of a letter the central rectangle is the region normally used to type the message. The fold lines show how the page elements will fit together when the page is ready to go in the envelope. This can be handy for determining the placement of addresses when the final product will be used with window envelopes. A sample of a page with the guides and boxes in place is shown in Figure 15.7.

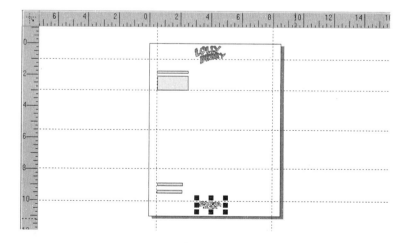

FIGURE 15.7 Using layout guides

Six basic positions are available on the page for laying out text on a letterhead or note card. You can place the logo and return address together at the top, separate them at the top, or split them top and bottom. If you have a list of directors or products to show, they can be placed along the side, in the margin. CorelDRAW makes it easy to test these layouts by moving and sizing the objects until you like the look. Remember, that's the whole idea of a layout. You want a good-looking design that gets your message across and is functional.

Filling in the Blanks

Now that we have played with the design it's time to make some decisions, replace blocks with text, and dress up the logo a bit. Put the company's return address in the bottom center and draw a thin rule above it. You can use the Align command to get it just right. Here are the steps.

- **Set the Type.** The address and phone number are 123 Strawberry Lane, Candytown, TN 33333, (615) 111-4444. Type the text in 10-point Kabana Book Normal, with center justification on three lines. This size is the same or a bit smaller than most body text. You don't want the address to detract from the correspondence. Use either a black or a dark gray fill.
- **Place It.** Use the **Align** command from the Arrange menu to center the block on the page. Then hold the **Ctrl** key and drag the block with the Pick tool to just below the guideline you placed at the bottom margin.
- **Draw the Rule.** Drag guidelines on either side of the text so that they touch the left edge of the C and the right edge of the last three letters on the right in the second row. Then use the Pencil tool to draw a narrow rule (line) between the two guidelines. Place it between the top of the text block and the margin guide.
- **Space and Kern the Text.** Use the Shape tool to adjust the line spacing so the descenders and ascenders have a reasonable amount of space. Then use the same tool to kern any letter pairs that are too close or too far apart. Figure 15.8a shows the line spacing, and Figure 15.8b shows kerning of the numbers in the address–the 1 and 2 are too close together. This is "try it and see what looks best" kind of fine-tuning. Remove the two guidelines when you are done. You can also copy the color fountain fill from the logo if you want to add a color accent to the bottom of the page. Most firms would not really want all this

color, but it gives you a chance to play with the tools. Try it and see how the fill washes as it moves down the lines of type. The effect is spread out because the original fill was applied one line at a time. You may need to adjust the angle of the fill to get things just right.

FIGURE 15.8a Adjusting line spacing

FIGURE 15.8b Kerning the address

A Professional Touch: En and Em Dashes

There is one thing wrong with the text block, typographically speaking–the dash between the numbers is a plain hyphen. Hyphens are not dashes. They are properly used to split a word between lines but not to break a string of numbers. Typesetters use a special dash called an en dash for that purpose.

So what's an en dash? Easy. It's a dash one-half the length of an em dash. Okay, so what's an em dash? It is a dash equal in length to the width of the capital M in the font being used. Ems are used the same way two hyphens are used by a typist. Needless to say, fussy typographers regard using the wrong dash as poor form and the mark of a novice. Before you change your telephone number here are the basic rules for using em and en dashes.

Em Dash

An em dash is used

- to function like a comma when a comma might confuse the reader–or when a sentence takes a rapid turn of thought.
- to set off divided quotations or to mark an unfinished sentence.
- to serve in place of a colon or set of parentheses.
- to set off a sports score or credit line.

In addition, two em dashes can be used together, without a space, to indicate a missing name or word. As a rule, em dashes have no space before or after them.

En Dash

En dashes are used

- to break strings of numbers, like a telephone listing.
- to separate two compound names that already contain a hyphen.
- to replace an occurrence of the words and or to in a sentence.

Placing Typographic Dashes

Choose the Text tool and select the hyphen. Now use the **Alt-0150** combination to replace it with an en dash. The **Alt-0151** combination will set an em dash. The typesetting trade uses spaces called em and en spaces, which have the same width as the dash of the same name. CorelDRAW does not support such spaces, so you have to make do with the program's interactive or dialog-based methods. Figure 15.9 shows a close-up of the address numbers with a hyphen used on top and an en dash underneath. On the bottom line em and en dashes have been labeled underneath their respective letters. As you can see, the CorelDRAW versions are not exactly the same size as the letters the measure is based on. The exact size of the program's dashes varies with the typeface.

(615) 111-3333
(615) 111–3333
Em M   En N

FIGURE 15.9 Comparing En dashes and hyphens

Dressing Up the Logo

Now let's turn our attention back to the logo. The basic design we did earlier was a generic form that could be used with the firm's packaging as well as for general logo purposes. Now we'll add some text, clipart, and symbols to underline the focus on fruit-based snacks.

Use the Zoom tool to focus on the logo. Use the Text tool to enter the words Candy Company. Set it in about 12-point Kabana Book Bold. Then use the Pick tool to scale it just a little narrower than the logo. Use the Envelope effect to curve it to the same basic shape. Don't give it an outline, but use a deep rose color. That's 60 magenta, 20 yellow, and 20 black.

Group the logo and the new text into one object. Size them to 2 inches wide, and place them so that the upper margin guideline runs through the middle of the word Berry. Use the **Align** command from the Arrange menu to center the logo over the return address. The result should look like Figure 15.10.

FIGURE 15.10 The final logo text

Adding the Clipart

Sometimes you may want to dress up a design with graphic elements or to include a professional symbol like a caudaceus. The CorelDRAW symbol library and clipart collections can save a lot of time and include a variety of fruit symbols. These can be imported or typed on the page, then reworked, sized, and filled. Experiment with some of them, and move the logo and address blocks around to see how these modifications change the tone of the design. The clipart offers a chance to experiment with using blends to shade and give depth to objects. Although the result may be a little bit of overkill for a single logo and letterhead design, the basic concepts presented in this section should give you a good idea of how to approach projects like this. Once you have everything the way you want it, save your work under a new name, and move on to the last part of the exercise.

Some Final Points on Letterhead Design

When you plan a letterhead make sure that the logo doesn't overwhelm the page. Get the size small enough to leave space for a normal-sized writing area. You took some liberties with your mythical candy company that would be out of place for a law firm or insurance agency.

Make sure that your type includes all the required information and check for accuracy several times. Leaving out the fax number, or confusing it with a voice extension, can lead to real problems–and don't forget the area code. List the proper mailing address if it is different from the street address. Some firms list both if they have a post office box.

If you have to list board members or officers, as many corporations and nonprofit organizations do, then consider using a fainter ink. A 60 percent gray is a lot less distracting when it is next to the body of a letter containing a financial summary. Many designers also divide the list with a thin vertical rule.

Creating a Matching Envelope

The envelope should present no problems once you have your letterhead finished. A new file can be created with the same page size as the finished product. Then just copy, resize, and place the logo and type into position. If you are using a window-style envelope, be sure to block out the area that will show the recipient so you don't overprint the clear area. It's a good idea to show your company's mailing address and telephone number on the envelope and leave space above the return address for the sender to list his or her name.

The Business Card

CorelDRAW does an excellent job of producing masters for business cards. You have already done most of the work for this one by designing the logo and setting the address. We can use the existing stationery file objects and rework them into a card. We'll also convert our process color objects into Pantone spot colors.

Before designing any business card you should check with your printer. Many different card styles, printing methods, and paper stocks are used with business cards. If you find a format you like, you can adjust your copy to match it. Ask if there is a particular size that would work best for your camera-ready copy. Sometimes giving a full-page version will improve the quality, making it look as good as one set by a typesetter. Another advantage of going to the printer first is to get ideas. The samples show the way other people have created cards. Some people plan the card in a traditional horizontal format; a few adopt a vertical layout. Check the size of the cut cards while you're at the printer so you will know how to set up your page in CorelDRAW.

In some towns only one or two printers do all the card printing for all the businesses in the area. Get prices for the number of cards you think you need, and for twice that many. Often the double run adds less than one-third of the cost of the first set to the total job. Once you have all the specifications, ink, card stock, number to be printed, and so on, check for the best price. Some shops mark up cards quite a bit; others offer discounts based on volume or even sometimes the day of the week. (The daily special is usually for a color or certain kind of job.)

Setting Up the Page

With the stationery file you just worked on saved to disk and opened in CorelDRAW, perform the following steps. Group the logo elements including the words Candy Company together. Resize them to about 1 inch wide. Then do the same with the address text and any of the clipart you want on the business card. Move the objects close together in the center of the page and marquee select them. Copy them to the clipboard and select **New** from the File menu. (This will enable you to bring the copied objects into the drawing at a reasonable size. Since you were working with a large page and are going to a much smaller one, the copied objects might be well out of the work area when pasted. Resizing and centering them will make it easier to position them in the new document.)

Setting the Paper Size

There are two ways to provide camera-ready copy to a printer: in exact scale and in a different size to be scaled as the printer makes the plate. As mentioned earlier, this is one of the items to check before starting work. Some printers like having both, one to scale and another as large as will fit on a regular page. By using a larger size you can increase the effective resolution of your printer. That gives you smoother lines and cleaner letters, especially on small paper sizes like a business card. If you enlarge the master to four times the size of the final copy on a 300-dpi laser, the effective resolution is 1,200 dpi, which is the same as a mid-range typesetter. An 800-dpi NewGen printer would provide an effective resolution of 3,200 dpi, more than the absolute resolution available with top-of-the-line imagesetters!

I do things the easy way when I can, and setting up for a business card is no exception. The standard business card is 3.5 inches wide and 2 inches tall. Use that as the working page size and turn the **Page Border** on in the Display option of the Page Setup dialog box in the Layout menu. That way you can see just what the final layout will look like without having to fuss with guidelines. To enlarge the artwork, just redefine the page to letter size, group the objects, and scale the entire design with the Pick tool. Go ahead and set your page to business card size, but don't close the Page Setup menu yet.

Adjusting the Paper Color

One of CorelDRAW's often overlooked features is the ability to set the color of the background paper. This allows you to see what a color scheme will look like when printed on your final paper stock. If you can get a Pantone, TruMatch, or CMYK value for the paper, you can get an exact match in the final print. Remember that you must use some form of calibration to get an exact correlation between the monitor and the paper. For more on calibration see the hardware section later in this book under "Display Adapters."

Open the **Layout** menu and choose **Page Setup**. Then click on the **Paper Color** button in the Page Setup dialog box. You will get the usual color section box; click on the **More** button at the bottom of the sample palette. Choose **Pantone Spot Colors** and then select **Names**. Click on color 169CV and use a 47 percent tint. The tint value is located in the middle of the dialog box. This is a warm color that will go nicely with your logo. Figure 15.11 shows the Page Setup and Paper Color dialog boxes. You can also enter the name of the color in the search window to select a shade.

Chapter 15: Designing with Words and Symbols

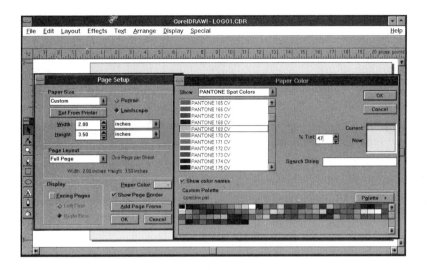

FIGURE 15.11 Setting up the page

After the page is set up, turn on the status bar and remove the rulers and on-screen palette if they are visible. As you work, you may want to shift between full-color and wireframe views. With a lot of blends, fountain fills, or text converted to curves your screen display may be slow. If so, just use wireframe views until you have to check the appearance or color of the outlines, fills, and paper color.

Placing the Logo

Use the Zoom tool to scale the screen so you can see the entire work area; then press Ctrl-V. The objects on the Windows Clipboard should appear on the page. Break them apart and place the logo in the upper right-hand corner. Move the other objects off the page and resize the logo to suit your own taste. Remember that it should be big enough to identify the company easily but not so large that it takes up too much space. Business cards often must contain lots of information, and you don't want your design to be too crowded. If it is, the card will be harder to read and the point size for items like phone numbers may be uncomfortably small. Figure 15.12 shows how the logo was sized and placed. Notice how you can place two pieces of clipart from the letterhead to balance the letters, but eliminate the rest of the fruit. The fruit was chosen in part because it would be easy to use the same fill as the one used for the letters.

FIGURE 15.12 Placing the logo

Replacing Process With Spot Colors

Four-color business cards would be quite expensive, especially if provided for everyone in the company. Even spot color can add significantly to the cost of cards. But if the printer can do a number of runs with the same color ink, he or she won't have to charge you for cleaning the press each time. Planning for color and working with your printer can save time and money. Using named spot colors is the easiest way to specify shades, so we'll convert the process tones to similar Pantone numbers. Figure 15.13 shows the Fountain Fill dialog box. Process CV Magenta and Process CV Yellow were used. The words Candy Company were converted the same way, using a uniform magenta fill with a 100 percent tint. The Copy Attributes From command was used and the same fill was used on the two fruit objects next to the characters. Unlike CorelDRAW 3.0 the names of the colors are not listed in the From and To sections asa reference.

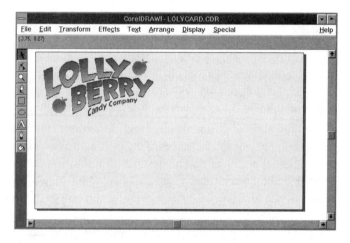

FIGURE 15.13 The Fountain Fill dialog boxes

Laying Out the Company Information

Now use the Zoom tool to adjust the view to see all the objects in the work area. Select the address information and open the Text Edit dialog box. Use the editing window to change the text to sit on two lines. The first line should contain the street address, city, state, and zip code. The second line is used for both the regular and fax telephone numbers. (Add a fax number (615) 222-4444.)

Once the edits have been made use the **Align** command to place them in the center of the page. Then hold the **Ctrl** key and drag the block to just above the bottom of the card. This is an easy way to get an object lined up with the center of the page. If you checked with your printer, he or she should have told you how much space was needed around the edges as a safety margin for cutting the cards. The plate holds several images of the design, the exact number based on the size of the paper to be used. Once the ink is dry the page is cut up. If the blade of the cutter is off a bit and there is no room for error, part of the job will have to be redone. When you pick up the final work it is always a good idea to inspect samples from various locations in the box. You are paying for the work, and it is your image that is reflected in the quality of the product. Figure 15.14 shows how the address block was placed. Some designs might look better if the text is set flush left and the information is broken up into several lines. This enables you to place the address on one side at the bottom and information about what your company does on the other. If you get a lot of E-mail or belong to CompuServe, you might want to add a line that holds your account number or ID. Set the type in Kabana Book Normal. The size should be balanced with the rest of the design but should not be so small that it is difficult to read. Then decide if the color should be a magenta or a solid black.

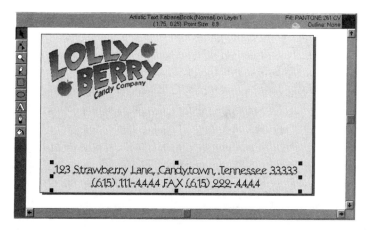

FIGURE 15.14 Placing the address block

Adding the Name

Almost done. All you need to do is add the name and title of the card's owner. Since the logo is the largest element on the page and takes up a lot of the upper left area, you will want to place the name so that it looks balanced. This is probably going to be a bit to the right of center. The same type as the one used for the address block was chosen when the title was set, and a larger point size of Kabana Book Bold was used for the user's name. Then the title was resized to fit just under the name. Finally, they were grouped and placed using the layout person's best friend, the human eye.

Batch Runs

Don't forget that CorelDRAW offers a batch mode for printing projects that have varying text but where most of the objects are the same. This was covered in Section One, as was the way in which it could be used for certificates. It is also a natural if you have to make a bunch of cards for different people in the same company. Just replace the name, title, and any other specific information in a merge file and print away. Figure 15.15 shows the final card with everything in place, ready to go to the printer. Printing concerns for both spot and process jobs will be covered later in this book. To get a full letter-sized version just set the page to letter; then group all the objects and enlarge them. If your printer would like a full page with all the cards at final size to shoot the plate directly from your master, use the **Place Duplicate** and **Clones** command and the grid to get things the way you want them. Not only have you saved the cost of typesetting by doing your own design, but you have taken control and learned more about CorelDRAW in the process.

FIGURE 15.15 The final card

Chapter Summary

Creating logos, stationery, and business cards is easy with CorelDRAW, but you need to follow some basic rules of design if you want professional results. Be sure to consult with a printer for tips on how to prepare your copy and on paper stocks and colors. Look at other companies' letterheads and cards for examples and ideas. Your local library may also be a good source of design books with samples that may spark your imagination.

CHAPTER 16
Creating Advertising Copy and Flyers

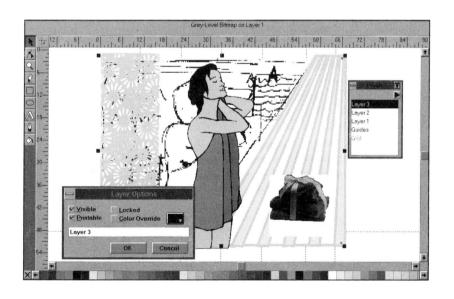

Display Ad

The Approach

CorelDRAW! is a great tool for one-page design projects containing both type and images, such as newspaper and other display advertising. The project is the creation of a half-page ad announcing a white sale for a department store. There are four files on the disk in the back of the book that you will need to import into CorelDRAW. They are named DISPLAY.TIF, DISPLAY.CDR, TOWELS.TIF, and PANEL.PCX. You might want to load them on your hard disk before starting the project.

Several things are missing from your project that would be in most ads. I'll cover them as you go along with a general discussion of advertising layout. If this were an actual ad we would need a copy of the company logo as well as any price information, trademarks, and the like. Of course this is more of a how-to session, rather than a full-fledged course in advertising design. We will concentrate on the basics and doing the artwork.

Setting Up CorelDRAW

Before getting into the drawing stage we need to set up the workspace. Make sure the rulers are showing. Go to the **Layout** menu and set the page to **Landscape** and **Letter Size**. Then choose **Grid Setup**. Set both of the Grid Frequency units of measure to picas. Open the **Layers** roll-up menu; we will be working with several layers. The sketch will be on Layer 1, graphics on Layer 2, and text on Layer 3. That way each part can be printed and proofed by itself. If you want to get fancy, name the layers as they are created.

The Grid System

A good way to work with these kinds of layouts is with a grid system. Drag guidelines into the page to separate them visually into areas: top and bottom, thirds, columns, and so on. These help in deciding where to place objects and in balancing the page. Keep this use of guides in mind as you work.

The Layout

In many cases a designer will work up a rough sketch of a drawing on paper to get an idea of how the different parts will work together and balance the page. This step has already been done for you. Import the file titled DISPLAY.TIF onto the page and size it to fill the printable area. The image is shown in Figure 16.1.

A sketch is just a rough outline of how the finished drawing will look. The idea is to place the elements and make sure all the principal design components are accounted for. The sample has the following parts:

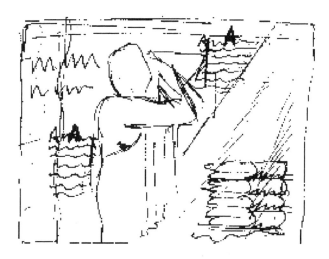

FIGURE 16.1 The rough-out drawing

- A line sketch of a woman wrapped in a towel and drying her hair is the central focus, and carries the theme of the white sale to the viewer.
- A stack of towels is placed in the lower right to show the product. In many ads several different products might be included.
- Three text blocks are on the page: a headline and two longer blocks. One long block is located behind the woman and the other is above the towels.

There are also two backgrounds: one on the left running vertical and another angling from the upper right to the lower center of the picture.

Setting Up the Page

The bitmap named DISPLAY.TIF will be the only object on Layer 1. Place it on the page using the **Import** option under the File menu. When you start drawing the ad use the **Layer** roll-up menu to make the sketch invisible and locked. You can turn it off and on as needed for reference. To access the dialog box click on the small arrow pointing to the right on the top of the roll-up menu and choose **Edit** from the fly-out. Figure 16.2 shows the ad with the graphic elements that will be on Layer 2 placed in front of the bitmap, as well as the roll-up menu and the Layer Options dialog box.

FIGURE 16.2 The graphic elements

Layers Roll-up Menu Functions

The main window shows the names of the layers that have been defined in the current drawing. Highlighting a layer with the mouse makes it active. Any new objects added to the current drawing will be placed on the active layer. The Grid Layer is an exception; it can never be the active layer. The **Ctrl-F3** combination opens the Layers roll-up window. The following list explains the different fly-out options.

- **New.** Opens the Layers Options dialog box, so you can name a new layer and specify its attributes.
- **Edit.** Displays the Options dialog box, so you can rename an existing layer or change its attributes.

Chapter 16: Creating Advertising Copy and Flyers

- **Delete.** Eliminates the selected layer and any objects on it. Be ready with the Undo command if you delete the wrong layer.
- **Move To.** Relocates any selected objects from their current layer to the active layer.
- **Copy To.** Places a copy of the selected object on the layer selected in the Layers list.
- **MultiLayer.** If this box is checked you can select and work with any object on any layer except those that are locked or invisible.

Drag guidelines to a point 3 picas in from each edge of the page and size the bitmap to be within them. This serves as the pad. In most cases you don't run an ad to the edge of the page sent to the printer. You will need areas to mark notes, print color information, and so on. In a real production setup you would have fixed dimensions for the printable area. In many cases ad copy is bled to the edge of the page; in other words, the area that will be printed goes right to the edge of the paper. You can still get a margin for notation by using a larger sheet than required for the actual picture area.

PLACING THE GRAPHICS

Add a second layer, which we will use for the graphics, from the Layers roll-up fly-out. This will hold everything on the page except the text and the rough-out. Cathy used another drawing made with marker pens to create the woman drying her hair. It was colored and scanned in 24-bit color. The file was cleaned up in PHOTO-PAINT and the bitmap was converted to vector using CorelTRACE. Since you may not have a scanner, the finished image is available in the file DISPLAY.CDR. Use Import to load it and place it in the center of the drawing. You can use the rulers in Figure 16.2 as a guide.

If you use this approach to create another drawing, keep the lines in the drawing connected and the rest of the page to be scanned as clean as possible. Breaks in lines will result in open paths, which won't take fills and maintain the original colors. You can scan in black and white, but TRACE can't map the colors to the new EPS file.

Working With Spot Colors

This exercise uses spot color. For each color in a drawing your printer will have to use different ink in a separate press run. That means more work, and it means more money every time you add a color. There is a trick that gives more tones to the picture without adding more inks. Select darker colors; then use tints to get lighter shades. Fill a small rectangle with the 100 percent tint of a color to be used and place it off the page. Then when you need a color, copy the tint from the rectangle and lower the tint as desired. All the tints can be handled with one ink. If you are only going to use a few tints of one color, you can also add those tones to the color palette at the bottom of the CorelDRAW window.

Placing the Woman

Import the file named DISPLAY.CDR. It contains the traced copy of the figure in the center of the ad. The skin tones are still there, but the towel the woman is using is plain white. There are several panels, some on the torso and some around the neck and hands. Create a rectangle and use the method described in the last paragraph with the Pantone Spot Color Palette to design a set of blue fills for the towel. Several panels make up the towel. Use a slightly different (varied by 10 percent) tint for each one over the torso. Use the same tint for the ones near the face and arms. Figure 16.3 shows the woman with a filled towel, the rectangles (moved in on the page just so you can see them), and the dialog box.

Creating the Striped Background

Select the Rectangle tool and create a long thin box the height of the page. Fill it with a 20 percent tint of a peach color. Add 20 percent green and a 0.8-point-wide outline. Duplicate and place the copy about 30 picas to the right of the original. Select both and open the **Blend** roll-up. Set the blend to four steps and click **Apply**. Draw a rectangle. Size it to cover the objects in your blend, and use the same outline as the stripes. Group the blend and rectangle together; then open the **Effects** menu. Select **Add Perspective**. Hold down **Ctrl** to constrain to horizontal while dragging the upper left corner half-way across the rectangle's area toward the right. The result should look like the object in Figure 16.4. I have added a rectangle to show the area covered before the envelope was applied and have darkened the outlines.

Chapter 16: Creating Advertising Copy and Flyers

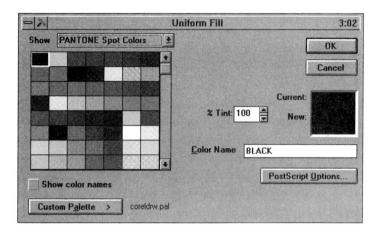

FIGURE 16.3 Filling the towels on the figure

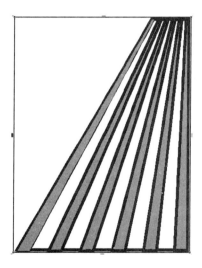

FIGURE 16.4 The background stripes

Adding the Towels

In the lower center of the striped background is a stack of towels. They are from a bitmap imported from the file TOWELS.TIF. The version on the disk in the back of the book has been reduced from 24-bit color to 4-bit (16 colors) to conserve storage space. Use the **Import** option from the File menu and load the file. Then place it with the Pick tool. Notice how there is a white area around it in the screen shot. The handles around the object are a clue. CorelDRAW gives everything a rectangular bounding box. Even though the image was cropped irregularly in PHOTO-PAINT, there is a dead space within that area. If the background was not a blend, you could use a mask and place the stripes in the foreground. Then you would not see the empty portion of the bounding box. Figure 16.5 shows the details with the figure of the woman for reference.

Creating the Left Panel

On the left of the ad is a blue panel. This started out as a bitmap and was converted to curves using CorelTRACE. The scanned file is on the disk that comes with this book, named PANEL.PCX. Open CorelTRACE and select the file. If you need to review the procedure, it is explained earlier in the book. Use the Outline method. On a 486/33 computer it took nine seconds to do the trace. Import the new EPS file into CorelDRAW, resize and ungroup it, and use the **Combine** command to merge the separate objects. Then give it a blue fill as shown in Figure 16.6. As with the rest of the exercise, use the finished sample as a reference.

PLACING THE TEXT

The last phase of the project is adding the copy that explains the purpose of the advertisement and tries to interest the reader enough to attend the sale. All the type will be placed on a separate layer. Use the **Layers** roll-up to create Layer 3 and make it active. Then close the **Layers** roll-up. Open the **Text** roll-up and select the Text tool. You are going to make four blocks of text: two in frames with drop shadows and two headline strings, one with a drop shadow.

Chapter 16: Creating Advertising Copy and Flyers

FIGURE 16.5 Adding the bitmapped towels

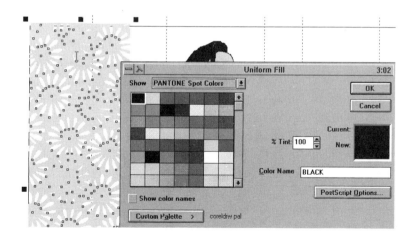

FIGURE 16.6 The left blue panel

A Point of Reference

Although the page for our ad does not have any columns in it, they would make placing text a lot easier. You can use guidelines to do the same thing, but you will have to make sure the text stays in line. The guides are just for reference. As a rule, text column widths should be based on the size of the type, the number of columns that must fit on the page, and the way the text is justified. If a column is too narrow the text won't fit properly. If the measure is too wide, the text will be harder to read (and less likely to be read). Set several guides as you work. The left body text should be on about a 10- to 12-pica column; the right one should be even wider. Experiment as you place the text and see what happens as you widen or narrow the measure. Try different justifications as well. I have not given exact spacing for the different text elements. Balancing a design is not an exact art, but a matter of training the eye. Feel free to edit the copy to get a better fit. The lines were left just a little off the perfect length for balance. Fine-tuning the text is one of the keys to successful layout.

The Main Headline

The main headline is the easiest. Click the Text tool over the blue panel on the left side of the ad about three-quarters of the way up. Type the words **White Sale** on two lines in 86-point Ottawa Bold. Duplicate it and fill the upper copy with black and the lower with 50% gray. Arrange the two blocks so that the gray one becomes a drop shadow located down and to the right. Figure 16.7 shows the result.

FIGURE 16.7 The headline drop shadow

The Second Headline

Place the Text tool in the lower right part of the page about 4 picas from the bottom margin. Type the phrase **100% Pure Cotton** in 30-point Ottawa Bold. Then use the Shape tool and drag the lower right marker to the right to increase the interletter spacing.

The Left Body Copy

Draw a text frame that straddles the vertical tile starting just below the level of the woman's shoulder. Click at the top of the frame with the Text tool and type in the text below. Use Ottawa 20-point normal. Adjust the frame as needed.

> Super Savings on luxurious, all-cotton linens, towels, and decorating accessories. Choose from a large assortment of designs and colors from the best brand names.

Add a Drop Shadow

Select the Shape tool and click on the lower-left-hand box of the first letter. Use the **Text** roll-up to set the Character Attributes to bold 48 point and click **Apply**. Copy the letter and fill the duplicate with gray. Use it for a drop shadow.

FIGURE 16.8 The left body copy drop shadow

The Right Body Copy

Use the same steps for the right block of text listed below. It should start just about even with the woman's nose. If the frame isn't deep or wide enough, use the Pick tool and drag down the bottom handle. Add a drop cap just as you did for the other framed text.

> All cotton. All towels. All sheets. All bathroom accessories. All on sale. All week. Styles include the classic French to the geometric modern. Colors are subtle to outrageous. Be early for the best selection.

Chapter Summary

Some general guidelines must be kept in mind when working with advertising-style layouts, and it is a good idea to be consistent with your design. People will notice the style and associate it with your business or organization. Here are a few of the more common conventions. A good bookstore or library can provide you with special texts covering this kind of work in greater detail.

- **Set Off the Ad.** Use a combination of white space and borders to set off the entire ad. Most newspapers use some variation of the inverted pyramid page layout. That means that copy is surrounded by ads stacked in a triangle or half-triangle based on varying sizes. You can open the local paper and see an example. Look at the ads. They are usually placed in a border. Try to avoid thick black rules. The industry calls them tombstone borders. White space helps separate your ad without the clutter.
- **Set Off the Logo.** The same thing applies to the company logo or trademark. You want people to be able to pick it out easily.
- **Proof, Proof, and Proof Again.** At least two people should proof the ad and check to make sure everything that is supposed to be there is. The location, phone, dates of a sale, prices, and anything else that should go in can be left out or entered with a mistake. Headlines are notorious for tripping up the proofreader.
- **Check the Size and Ratio.** Don't wait until the layout is complete–or worse yet, at the printer–before making sure that the size is right or that the percentage of enlargement or reduction by the plate camera is correct.

CHAPTER 17
Creating Complex Illustrations

LANDSCAPE INTRODUCTION

Beyond designing logos and letterheads, ads and announcements lies the realm of full-fledged illustration. This chapter explains how CorelDRAW is used to produce complicated designs and how to plan such drawings. To get a feeling for how such projects are carried out, I am going to walk you step by step through the creation of a landscape, complete with rolling hills, trees, a marsh, fields of flowers, birds, and the ocean in the background. Then as you read the following chapters explaining the procedures used to create award-winning art with CorelDRAW you will be better able to see how the artists used the program's tools in their own styles. As we work through this chapter keep in mind that there are many ways to approach any task in CorelDRAW. The one that is right is the one you feel most comfortable with and that suits the project at hand. While you follow the instructions, feel free to experiment; it's just an exercise. The goal here is to see how the tools are used to make something.

The Approach

Planning is a critical part of making a complex drawing like a landscape. You have to consider how lighting, perspective, and colors will work together to produce the desired visual effect. The final output also affects the approach. For example, what medium will you use to obtain a hard copy? This drawing will use a wide range of colors, and you must decide how the image will be reproduced. If you have access to a full-color computer printer like the Dye Diffusion Thermal Transfer (D2T2) units described in the advanced printing chapter, it's easy to get a single print. You can also use a film record or send the file to a service bureau to get a slide. Then that can be printed photographically. For press runs you must deal with four-color printing. There is more about that in the advanced printing chapter as well.

Cathy Cary, the artist who designed the LollyBerry logo and the display ad in the preceding chapters, also created the landscape used in this one. She started with a couple of photographs taken when she lived in California. From that she produced a rough sketch and decided on the basic design. It included a pair of wooded hills with a creek and flowers in the foreground. The foreground marsh and ocean background were added later. A second drawing was produced from the first by adding a border and enlarged flowers in front of the landscape.

Two important considerations in making the drawing were the angle of the lighting and a sense of depth. If the lighting was not consistent, the final image would appear unnatural to the viewer. To give the picture depth, the parts of the drawing farther back had to be reduced in scale, based on their apparent visual placement.

Setting Up

Artists working in oils keep their brushes and a palette to mix colors within easy reach. Draftsmen have a collection of tools needed for a project arranged nearby and ready. The clear areas of the CorelDRAW desktop can serve as a workspace, reducing the time needed to create a color or to add an object. As you work I'll point out shortcuts that can be used by placing objects just off the page.

Open a new drawing and set the page orientation to portrait. Make sure the status bar is turned on and the rulers are off. Just off the upper right-hand corner of the page draw a circle and give it a uniform yellow fill. This represents the light source. By referring to it you can gauge the angle and intensity of the shadows in the drawing.

CREATING THE HILLS

Our finished drawing will have a variety of objects resting on the slopes of several hills. So the first step is to draw the hills. The two hills in the foreground are duplicates that have been mirrored, and the front one was modified with a blend.

Forming the Basic Shapes

Open the Rectangle tool and draw a box that occupies the lower two-thirds of the page. Convert it to curves and drag the right corner down so that the object is lopsided. Select the Shape tool; then add nodes as needed and use the control points to give the outline a rounded shape. Fill the object with green.

Then duplicate and flip it using the **Mirror Horizontal** command from the Transform menu with the **Leave Original** box checked. Give the duplicate a linear fill, dark green to gold, with the Edge Pad set to 15 and angled toward the light source; then move it to the back. Figure 17.1 shows the first two objects in wireframe with the circle for the sun in position at the upper right.

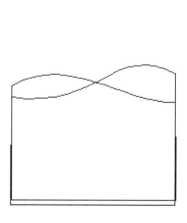

FIGURE 17.1 Forming the hills

Blending the Forward Hill

Now that the basic forms are in place you can create the shading effect in the foreground with a blend. The technique is to make two new control objects with no outline. The top one will have a golden fill, and the bottom one will match the hill in front. They will only occupy the top one-third of the hill. Blending in with the same color as the hill behind them will make it look as if the blend was part of the hill.

Select the hill in front with the Pick tool and then duplicate it. This will be the lower control object. Push the bottom of the duplicate up, reducing the top-to-bottom size to about one-third of the original. Make a duplicate of this shape and size it from the bottom until it is very thin; then adjust the shape of the curves. The final hill and the wireframes are shown in Figure 17.2. Above the wireframe are labeled copies of the two blend control objects for reference. Use the **Align** command from the Arrange menu (**Ctrl-A** shortcut) to align the tops of the three objects on top of each other. In other words, the original hill shape will be on the bottom, the medium-sized one above that, and the narrowest one on top. The tops of all three will be aligned at the same location.

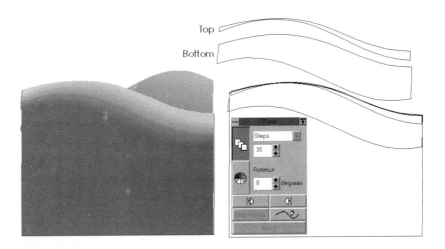

FIGURE 17.2 Creating the blend

The bottom and middle objects should have the same grass green uniform fill. The thin section on top should be given a golden yellow fill. Select the top two objects and blend in 30 steps with no rotation, as shown in the menu in Figure 17.2.

Making the Background Hills

From the upper left do a series of click and drag motions down and to the right with the Pencil tool in Bézier mode. Produce a curvier hill until the line is behind or below the top of the hill rising on the right side behind the blend. Finish the shape as a closed object. Fill it with linear fill, dark bluish green to a lighter shade, with a 15 Edge Pad setting that is angled toward your light source. Then use **Horizontal Mirror** and **Leave Original**. Arrange the two new hills behind the existing ones.

Modify the new hill and make it taller. Then fill it with lighter bluish-green linear fill. Arrange both objects to the back. The one that is highest on the right side of the drawing should be the rearmost object on the page. Figure 17.3 shows the outlines of the four hills. I have modified the thickness to make them easier to identify. Don't forget there is a copy in the full-color insert for reference.

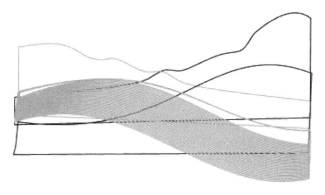

FIGURE 17.3 Outline of the hills

When you work with a complex fill that will be repeated or used again with slight modifications, draw a rectangle just off the page. Then use **Copy Attributes From** to map the fill to the box. When you need that fill again just copy the style to the new object.

ADDING THE OCEAN AND SKY

At this point in the project you should have four hills, covering the lower three-quarters of the page. If you have been consistent with the fills, the shading should look like the sun is shining down from off the upper right side of the page. It is time to occupy the clear space over the hills. You are going to add two elements—a body of water about even with the middle of the tallest hill and a blue sky above that.

Select the Rectangle tool and draw a box from side to side, just wide and tall enough to add the ocean in the background between the two rearmost hills. Give it a blue- or aquamarine-based linear fill. To show the color values of fills in this chapter, CMYK values will be used. So a listing of 82C, 40M, 0Y, and 15K will mean 82 Cyan, 40 Magenta, 0 Yellow, and 15 Black. That is what you used to start your linear ocean fill and went to 95C, 13M, 0Y, and 0K to finish it. There was a 52-degree angle and 0 Edge Pad.

Draw another rectangle from the top of the page to just under the lowest hill and all the way across from side to side. You used the same angle and pad with another linear fill. The colors went from 41C, 14M, 0Y, and 5K to 12C, 3M, 0Y, and 0K. Once you have finished, place the sky at the back and the ocean just in front of it with the Arrange command. Figure 17.4 shows the two new objects in place. I have reduced the right-hand hills to outlines and placed outlines around the sky and ocean to make them easier to see.

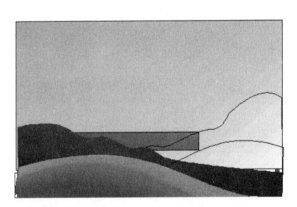

FIGURE 17.4 Placing the ocean and sky

ADDING THE FORESTS

Now that we have created the basic environment it's time to add the trees. One of the most daunting aspects of any drawing is the fine detail. Most viewers look at all the little things that add character to an illustration and think, "Oh boy, that looks like work.

Chapter 17: Creating Complex Illustrations

How long did that take?" In many cases they're right; it's lots of work. In the following chapters we will take close looks at several very complex drawings that took award-winners days and weeks of mousing around. But our landscape does not fall into that category. CorelDRAW will do most of the work for you.

There are three groups of trees in the background areas, and a large one on top of the closest hill. Each was formed from symbols placed with the Text tool, edited with the Shape tool and duplicated to make the groups. Figure 17.5a shows the trees contained in the Plants Symbol library. Figure 17.5b shows some of the possible forms. The tree on the left was reworked into the large tree and the group just behind it into the next valley. To its right is the model for the trees going up the right middle hill. The one next to it served as the starting point for the forest of pines running down the far right slope.

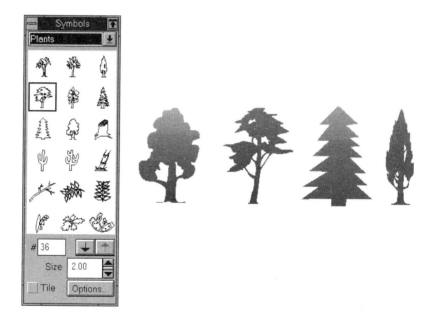

FIGURES 17.5a and b Selecting the trees

Open the Text tool, shift to **Symbol** mode, and place several different trees in the area just left of the page. These will serve as the templates for the different groups. Select one and zoom in so it fills the screen. Use the Pick and Shape tools to edit the object as needed. Then duplicate it. If you want to add other trees with different angles and heights, use the **Transformation** effects on some of the copies. Once you have a set, group and fill them. The trees in your drawing were filled with a linear fill, running from a green top to a brown trunk. It was easy to adjust the pad setting and get that result. That's simpler than breaking the objects into two and giving separate fills.

As you work use the Zoom tool and **Edit Wireframe** command to reduce the time it takes to redraw the screen. You can also use the fill patches mentioned in the last tip to hold fill objects, especially fountain and blend fills, until the drawing is nearly complete.

Putting Things in Perspective

Make several small groups of trees; then add and arrange them to produce larger groups. Figure 17.6 shows several variations. As you place them on the hills shift the size of each of the subgroups. This allows you to give the impression of depth, as the objects get smaller, the farther away they are from the viewer. Notice how the larger tree in the foreground of the completed drawing gives a sense of relative size and distance to the picture.

FIGURE 17.6 Grouping the forests

The Larger Tree and Its Shadow

Use one of the tree shapes and modify it so the image appears to be that of a large old tree with full foliage. Use another green-to-brown linear fill and no outline on it. Now duplicate it and rotate the copy to form the shadow. Remove nodes and edit to remove the trunk. Figure 17.7 shows the tree and shadow in both wireframe and filled versions. It also shows the detail of the eagle flying in the center of the drawing, discussed next.

FIGURE 17.7 The large tree and eagle

The Eagle, a Little License, and More Perspective

The eagle adds not only a visual element to fill the open center of the sky, but a sense of vertical perspective as well. It carries the eye of the viewer across the page. The shadow near the tree is smaller and back on the hill, accenting the bird and the shadow under the tree. There is a little bit of artistic license here, since the light should make the shadow fall in front of the bird. But that would not produce the same effect.

Figure 17.7 shows how the bird was created. One-half was drawn with the Pencil tool in Bézier mode, tweaked with the Shape tool, and duplicated; then the two parts were joined. The shadow is a copy that was filled just a little darker green than the hill under it. The gull flying to the left was added from the clipart collection, just to remind you to check there when looking for accents.

FORMING CLOUDS

What would a warm afternoon near the ocean be without some clouds in the sky? Blends make these objects easy to draw. Draw an irregular shape with the Pencil tool in Freehand mode, with many curves on the top and flattened somewhat on the bottom. Use **Ctrl-D** to make a copy. Fill the duplicate with a light sky blue color and squeeze it almost into a line with the Pick tool. Place it inside the first object near the bottom. Then fill the first cloud with an almost white tint and delete any outlines from both shapes. Select both and blend. To make the second cloud, just copy the first and then use the Pick and Shape tools to make the second cloud smaller. White tints on the bottom can suggest the reflection of the sea, whereas darker shades threaten storms. Figure 17.8 shows the two filled clouds next to one another in wireframe. If you are feeling adventurous, try one of the new two-color fills to fill the sky with a sunset sky full of glowing clouds.

FIGURE 17.8 The cloud formations

Adding the Creek, Marsh, and Flowers

Right now the drawing lacks depth. It needs something to pull the viewer's attention into the center from the foreground. S shapes and modifications of them have long been used by artists and photographers as key visual elements. The creek, marsh, and flowers in the finished drawing curve into the picture and bring the eye toward the curve of the hills. Let's add them now.

Creating the Creek

Draw a curved shape for the creek with the Pencil tool. Fill it with a dark to medium blue linear fill. Next draw an irregular shape at the bottom left as a small bank with a dark green fill. Press **Ctrl-D** to duplicate and fill the copy with a linear fill from dark green to a lighter green. Enlarge it a little and arrange it behind the small bank. Place both in the lower left-hand corner and group. Draw a larger, rounded shape for the bank behind the smaller shapes and along the creek. Fill it with a dark green and no outline. Duplicate the last object. You're going to do the same thing with this set of shapes as you did with the first hill. Fill the copy with a medium green. Resize one of them and blend. Arrange the resulting objects to the back of the other bank and group them together. Figure 17.9 shows how the creek and bank shapes look. I've added contrasting fills in the example on the left to make it easier to see, and wireframes on the right. You should have everything in that figure except the large gray element in the back.

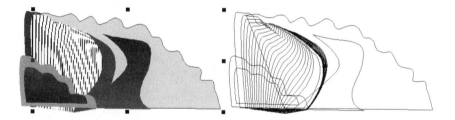

FIGURE 17.9 The creek, banks, and marsh

The Marsh

From the top of the last bank stagger a curving line with the Pencil tool in Bézier mode. It should angle down to the right as shown in Figure 17.9. Make it a closed path and fill with an angled linear fill, from dark bluish green to lighter bluish green. Arrange it behind the banks.

THE FLOWERS ALONG THE CREEK

Open the Text tool in **Symbol** mode and select the Plants collection again. Select flower shape number 33. Zoom in and fill the screen with it. You need to modify it a little for the fill you will use to work properly. With the Shape tool marquee select the bottom nodes of the stem and drag down until the stem is about the same length as the flowers. Figure 17.10 shows the single symbol in the center and wireframes in a group at the right. Once you have it the way you want, fill it with linear fill, starting with orange at the top, moving to green at the bottom. The green should be a little darker than the first hill drawn. Set the pad so that the flowers are mostly orange. Duplicate it about ten times and arrange it in a fairly tight group. Pay attention to the order they have, front to back, to give a sense of depth. Group them and duplicate. Resize different groups along the banks and hills to make them look closer or farther away. Run the flowers along the upper side of the creek from the right edge of the page to a point just under the large tree. Leave room to add marsh grass. Place a few flowers on the left side as well.

FIGURE 17.10 A flower arrangement

Adding the Marsh Grass

Our final touch is the marsh grass. It breaks up the sharper edges of the creek, banks, and marsh, as well as reinforcing the perspective. Draw a grassy-looking clump with the Pencil tool. Figure 17.11 shows how. Fill with a green different from the marsh, a little lighter, and use no outline. Duplicate three or four times; then group and duplicate them like the flowers. The right side of Figure 17.11 shows a full group ready to be placed. Make some groups lighter green. I put darker in front of lighter ones to add shading. Reduce the size of ones placed farther back to give perspective. You can add such details as animals, insects, or other flowers from clipart or the symbol library if you want.

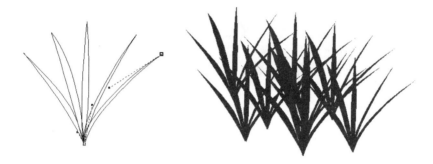

FIGURE 17.11 Grouping the marsh grass

Define the First Layer

Use **Select All** from the Edit menu and group everything in the drawing together with marquee select. Go to the **Layout** menu and select **Layers** roll-up, **Edit**. Check **Locked** and **Visible**; then select **New**. Layer 2 will appear, which you will use when drawing the frame and foreground flowers.

DRAWING THE FRAME AND FLOWERS

You may have noticed that you didn't worry much about getting objects near the edge of the page to line up exactly with the margins. That's because the frame you are about to place will cover any minor overlapping. Draw a rectangle just inside the edge of the drawing. Fill it with a gold color. This will be the inside edge. Draw another rectangle outside of that. The distance between the two will be the area of the frame. Fill the second box with the same gold color and arrange it to the back. Select both rectangles; then align them so they are centered on each other and combine. You should have a gold frame around the landscape.

Creating the Flowers

You could use objects from the clipart or the symbol library for the border flowers, but I decided to show you how it was done from scratch. Select the Pencil tool in Bézier mode. Draw a shape that looks a bit like a shoulder blade. Figure 17.12 shows the steps to take using the click-and-drag drawing technique.

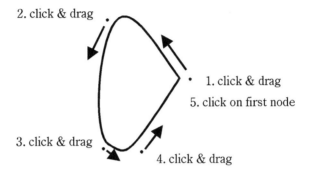

FIGURE 17.12 Drawing the first petal

The second petal is even easier. Use the **Mirror Horizontal** command from the Effects menu and select **Leave Duplicate**. Change it a little and duplicate it. Rotate the copy 90 degrees, and then select **Mirror Horizontal**. Make a smaller and narrower copy for the fourth petal with a couple of curves. Then use the Shape tool to adjust the curves to make them look natural.

Filling the Petals

All the petals are colored and changed into blends in the same way. Fill with a yellow or yellow-orange tint and no outline. Duplicate and change the fill in the copy to 0C, 45M, 97Y, 3K. Reduce the copy a little using the Pick tool and shift to constrain the transformation. Place inside the original so points are together. The copy on the right in Figure 17.13 shows one of the blends in wireframe. Hold **Shift** and squeeze the inside object a little. Select both objects and open the **Blend** roll-up, **Apply**, **GroupAll**, and repeat the process for the other petals.

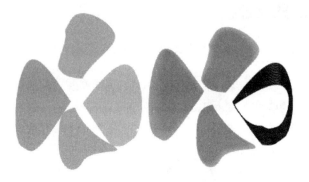

FIGURE 17.13 Forming and blending the petals

Place petals together at points. Arrange the two smaller petals in front of the larger petals. Draw some shadows on the left petal and arrange it behind. Select the large, top petal and shadow it. Then **Reverse Order** from the Arrange menu.

Drawing the Flower's Center

Now it's time to add detail to the flower. Draw an ellipse in the center and give it a radial fill going from darker orange on the outside to a red-orange center. Set the Edge Pad to 10. Draw several narrow ellipses, with a dark orange fill and medium yellow outline for pistil and stamens. Make eight to ten of them, rotate the group, and duplicate to get as many as you need. Then place them on top of the ellipse in the center of the petals. Figure 17.14 shows the details.

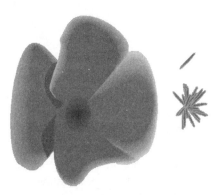

FIGURE 17.14 The final elements of the flower

Adding the Second Flower

Most of the work is done. To get the second flower duplicate the first and rotate the copy 90 degrees. Ungroup it and delete the shadow. Arrange the two side petals to the back, then select the bottom petal. Perform a **Vertical Mirror** and arrange it to the front. Use the **Edit Envelope—Not Constrained** to modify the bottom petal. Drag the corner node around until you get the effect you want. You may have to move the petals after you're done. This is not an exact science; it's art, and this program is just another tool. Figure 17.15 shows the completed flower.

Placing the Greenery Accent

The last step is adding the greenery behind the flowers. I used rosemary from the clipart collection, duplicated it, and modified the shapes. The product can be used as part of a greeting card project. Just group and reduce it; then adjust the page size to the area of the completed card. Use guidelines to show where the folds will go. Add text and flip the sections that will be printed inverted. Print and fold.

FIGURE 17.15 The second flower

CHAPTER SUMMARY

This project should give you a good idea of how complex illustrations are planned and created using CorelDRAW. The following chapters will provide additional insight as you meet with award winners and see how they use the program.

CHAPTER 18

Using Multipage and Frame Tools, Advanced Layout Concepts

- Planning Newsletters
- Designing for Multiple Pages
- Fundamentals of Newsletter Layout
- Working with Paragraph Text
- Working with Imported Text
- Wrapping Text Around Irregular Objects
- Preparing Camera-Ready Copy

Roll the Presses

One of the most common applications of desktop publishing is the newsletter. Thousands of newsletters are published in the United States every month. Churches, colleges, neighborhood clubs, political parties, businesses, and special interest groups all use newsletters to inform interested parties about activities, events, and items of mutual interest.

A newsletter is more like a miniature newspaper than a brochure or flyer; thus many of the techniques used by newspaper editors and production staffs can be scaled down and applied to their creation. This chapter will serve as an introduction to some of the fundamental skills required to produce effective newsletters.

The exercise on the following pages is designed not as a template for how to do a newsletter but as a way to demonstrate how to handle the different elements involved in preparing the pages for your printer. Before you type the first word or do the first picture you should have done some planning and have your copy and illustrations ready.

If you are just beginning to work with newsletters it might be wise to study existing newsletters whose look you like and adapt them to your own purposes. Before we actually start working with the newsletter, let me take a few minutes to explain some of the basics.

The Elements of a Newsletter

Planning

Generally, newsletters have to be completed by a specific time and within a given budget. The deadline is determined by when your newsletter must be in the hands of its readers. If one of the purposes of your newsletter is to advise readers of an upcoming meeting or an event, it won't do to have it arrive there after the meeting takes place. To accomplish this you must set realistic deadlines for writing the copy, editing it, completing the artwork, processing pictures, and having the print job done. Be sure to set realistic deadlines and keep in mind that editors tend to fret and hope that copy comes in early, whereas writers invariably procrastinate, planning to be finish at the stroke of the deadline. Having been both an editor and a writer, I can confirm that I do both, depending on my role. The easiest way to set deadlines is to start with the date that you want the newsletter in the hands of your reader and then work forward to set your deadlines from that date.

Distribution

Unless your readers come in and pick up their copies of your newsletter, you will have to distribute your publication. First-class mail will take two to five days (depending on distance) and cost about 30 cents for a four-page newsletter. Bulk mailing can take up to three weeks but costs about half as much as first class. If you need to get it there in a hurry, you will have to pay the surcharge for first-class mail. First-class mail involves another step too. Unlike bulk mail (where you can just print your permit number on the mailer), with first class you must use a stamp or other form of paid postage.

The Print Shop

You should check with your printer when doing your planning to find out how long he will need to complete the job. If you are planning on using more than one ink, it will take at least an extra day to allow the first ink to dry before the second press run can be made. Other things that may delay your job are special color inks, special papers, or complicated folding. If this is the first time you are doing your newsletter, you might want to mock up a sample and get quotes from different printers. If they do similar work and can fit your job in behind that press run, they may offer you a discount. Some printers also reserve one press in their shop each day to run jobs with a certain color ink. One newsletter I published for a local physician used blue ink. Every Wednesday a local printer handled blue print jobs without the extra press-cleaning charge colored ink normally carried.

You should also discuss page sizes and paper stock with your printer. Oversized pages can be folded to make four pages in one print pass. Different paper stocks and colors can help your work look more professional and give it a better "feel." Keep in mind that heavier papers will increase bulk and possibly postage costs.

THE DESIGN

Newspapers use a step called "dummying pages" to lay out their publications. When I was a young news editor I would use the services of two dummy editors who would take my stories and photographs and size them on the page, using styles of layout approved by our publisher. If you are your own publisher, editor, writer, and maybe photographer, you're probably going to be your own layout editor.

Start with a rough sketch and mark in the things that will stay the same from issue to issue. These will include your logo, masthead, mailing information, and probably the size and orientation of your columns. If you use a standard format from month to month, your readers will soon know where to find the calendar of events, the main story of the month, and other favorite items. Although you want your design to be interesting, there are advantages to keeping certain things the same. If you doubt this, think of what it would be like to not know where to find the classified ads or the funnies in the Sunday paper or how confusing it would be if the car ads were on page 1 and ads for white sales were found in the sports section.

A critical step in dummying pages is setting up your columns. In the following exercise we will show you several possible layouts. Some people like to use one big column that covers the entire page and mix some pictures in with it. This may get the information onto the paper, but it's boring and maybe not that easy to read. Some people divide their pages up into two or three columns and some mix one wide column with one narrow column on the page. This gives more flexibility.

Another consideration with column size is whether or not you will "jump" a story. In other words, if all the story doesn't fit in a column on one page, will you continue the story on another? Jumped stories are less likely to be read in full by your audience, and if you use them you will have to decide how you will indicate both where the story goes and where it came from on the appropriate pages. The alternative to jumping stories is editing them to fit. Would-be journalists are taught very early in their career to use the inverted pyramid style of writing. This is a simple technique of putting the most important elements of the story at the top of the article. No matter how long or short, any piece of journalism should always answer the following basic questions: Who? What? How? When? Where? and Why? A recent newsletter I received told me everything I needed to know about a meeting, except where and when it was to take place.

Once you have the rough design sketched out and have determined the size of your columns, you can get a fair idea of how much copy you can fit in a given number of pages. Newspapers and magazines base their total number of pages in part on how much news there is and in part (a fairly important part) on how many ads they've sold for that issue. You may or may not have advertising in your newsletter, but you probably do have a relatively fixed amount of money to spend on it. If all your news won't fit on four pages, you'll have to go to six pages (two sides, remember). That will increase the amount of work you have to do, the printing costs, and possibly the postage.

Be Flexible but Use a Consistent Style

As any newspaper editor will tell you, the planned copy is an ideal. Invariably, a picture won't be usable, an event will be canceled, a headline won't fit—there are all kinds of things, from minor to catastrophic, that will require a modification of your plans. Keep in mind that the goal in your newsletter is to communicate news and valuable information to your readers. Although you may have to move stories around to make them fit and change the wording of headlines so that they don't overrun into the next column, you need to keep a consistent look to your publication. Readers are easily confused when they can't tell where the story picks up after a column break or when headlines look like regular sentences. CorelDRAW 5.0 has styles and templates to help you keep consistency from issue to issue and make sure that all your headlines and paragraphs use the right font and point size.

In the following exercise we have chosen to be somewhat inconsistent from page to page so that we can fit several designs into a four-page newsletter. You may want to limit the variations from page to page.

CREATING A FOUR-PAGE NEWSLETTER

You have been elected to produce the monthly newsletter for an herbal society. This exercise gives us a chance to experiment with page layout and design and to work through the various steps in producing a typical newsletter. If you wish to go further into layout design, several excellent books are available at art stores, bookstores, and your public library. Keep in mind that design is a matter of taste. Within limits it is more an art than a science. It's a good idea to start simple and add flourishes as you go along.

To complete the steps in the following exercise, you should be reasonably familiar with Microsoft Windows and CorelDRAW. If you are comfortable with the materials already presented in this book, you should have no problems. Open CorelDRAW and set your page orientation to **Portrait**, turn on the rulers in the Status Bar if they are not already showing, and under Preferences set the right mouse button to **Text Edit**.

Designing the Masthead

The masthead is one of the most important design elements. Not only is it a primary design element on the front page, but it is in effect a logo for your publication. It should remain the same from issue to issue, so you should give great care to its design. If your company has a style manual that sets out specific fonts that should be used in publications, you will probably want to use that same font within your masthead and in the mailer. If appropriate, you may also want to use that for your general text font.

Masthead placement and size are far from fixed. In some cases the masthead is placed right at the top of the first page and runs all the way across from side to side. This is sometimes referred to as a banner style. The masthead may also be reduced and cover maybe half of one side. Some publications bring the masthead part of the way down the page, placing a story or teasers about articles within the publication above it. Another alternative is to turn the masthead sideways and place it in what would be the left-hand column. CorelDRAW makes it easy to experiment with these different techniques, so after our sample masthead is created, you might experiment with that to see how it looks.

NOTE It is often difficult to visualize design elements on a page when there are only one or two elements on a blank piece of paper. If you want really to see how an element like a masthead will look in a given orientation, you should dummy in some greek text and headlines and other elements so that your page has the appearance of a finished design. It would be hard to imagine how the color of a piece of clothing would look if you had no idea of the appearance of the person or the other clothes that they would wear with it. The same kind of consideration needs to be given to layout and design.

Page 1 and Designing the Masthead

Pull guidelines to make a 0.75-inch margin at the left and right (the right margin goes at 7.75 inches). Pull guidelines to set a 1-inch top margin and a 1.25-inch bottom margin (9.75 inches from the top of the page). Pull a guideline horizontally to 3 inches to mark the bottom of your masthead. Open the **Text** and the **Symbols** roll-ups.

Guides and guidelines can be very handy when working with layout and design for they allow you to place text and graphics more easily on the page. Some people have no trouble leaving them on all the time; some people find them a distraction. In this chapter I'll show the guides in the screen shots. Feel free to turn them on and off as it suits your need and your preference.

Type the word **erbletter** and set it in 54-point Lydian, Zapf Chancery, or a similar decorative type and size. Now click on the **Paragraph** button in the Text roll-up and increase the Character Percent of Space to 20 and press **Apply**. Now import NOUV_H from the clipart collection on the CorelDRAW 5.0 CD-ROM. If you don't have access to a CD-ROM reader, type a capital H as a separate artistic text object. Make it 70-point in the same typeface. To turn the H into a decorative capitol, we will take advantage of the plant library in the Symbols Roll-up. Select symbol 58 and change the size to 0.90 inch. Drag the symbol over to the left upright of the H and rotate it until the stem matches the H. Now drag a copy of Symbol 48 in the same size and rotate it to match the right upright of the H. Then reduce the size on the Symbol roll-up to 0.75 and drag a copy of #48 over to make the cross-piece as I have done in Figure 18.1. Then delete the text H and group the three symbols. Place it as the initial letter of the word Herbletter, the name of our newsletter.

FIGURE 18.1 Floral capital H created from the Symbols roll-up

Adding the Folio

Folio is the name applied to the volume and publication date information that is often placed adjacent to the masthead. If you are producing a regular publication, you may want to denote the volume and issue number. If you don't want to get that fancy, you can just center the month or period covered—Spring, Summer—in the center of the folio line. And of course there is no requirement that you have to have a folio at all. Of course, if you don't indicate when the publication was published, it makes it harder for someone to refer to it or to find it. The most common way to set off a folio is between a pair of rules. (A *rule*, remember, is the fancy name for a straight line in layout terminology.)

Let's put one on our sample issue. Select the Pencil tool and place it on the left-margin guideline just below the masthead. Click and move it over to the right-margin guideline while holding the **Ctrl** key. Click again to draw the line. Use the outline tool to give it the thickness you want. Very thick lines tend to disrupt the flow of the eye across the page, so, generally speaking, you want to stick to a thin line. A hairline or half-point rule will usually suffice to set off a folio. Press **Ctrl-D** to create a duplicate and place it about 1 pica below your first rule. Select the Text tool and type your folio. Just inside the left margin type Volume 3; Issue 4. Use the Pick tool, if necessary, to adjust it between the lines. Then return to the Text tool and type June 1995 and place it so that the 3 lines up with the right margin. Group the hairline rules and the folio text.

N O T E

You may want to save your masthead and folio as a Template.

Add the name and address as you see them in Figure 18.2 and get a decorative graphic of a plant either from the clipart collection or from the Symbols roll-up.

FIGURE 18.2 Newsletter masthead

Select all the objects making up the masthead, bring up the **Layers** roll-up from the Layout menu, and bring up the fly-out menu by clicking the arrowhead at the upper right. Create a new layer named Masthead. Select the masthead and get the fly-out again and click on **Move To**. Now click the black arrow cursor on Masthead on the Layers roll-up. The objects will be placed on that layer. Lock this layer to preserve your work.

The Page 1 Layout

The first page of a newsletter is very important. It needs to draw your readers' attention and hold their interest. Several elements can be used to heighten its appeal. Your most important story should be on the front page, or at least begin there. You can also use breakouts and teasers as text-based graphics to highlight important information.

Teasers are short lists, such as extracts from a calendar or a schedule of events. You may want to set them off in one corner of the page, separating them from the surrounding text with either a box rule or a gray background. A *breakout*, sometimes referred to as a *callout*, consists of a short quotation or key text from an article that has been enlarged and placed within the body of the text. The use of these elements is not limited to the first page. In our exercise we have placed a teaser on page 1 and breakouts on subsequent pages.

Page 1 of our newsletter includes not only the masthead but our lead story and a teaser in the form of a calendar of events. On this page we will use an unbalanced two-column format. The left column will be 2.125 inches wide. Place a guideline at 3 inches from the left-hand edge of the page. Then add two more 0.125 inch to either side. The space in between these guidelines is the gutter between the columns.

Placing the Teaser

Open a new layer and name it Calendar. Type the word **Calendar** in 24-point Century Old Style or a similar serif font. Then type as another artistic text object June 1995 and choose the same typeface as the word Calendar, 20 points. Center these words at the top of the left-hand column.

Import the HERBCAL1.CDR file you saved in Chapter 6 of this book. Size the text frame to fill the left-hand column. Using the Text tool, highlight the dates (e.g., June 6) and set them in 20-point boldface. Adjust the text formatting in this frame as necessary to fill the frame but not exceed it. Draw a rectangle around the calendar text and the headlines.

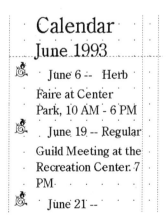

FIGURE 18.3 Front-page guidelines and the calendar column

If you wish, experiment with the teaser using decorative borders and different tints to set off the text. When you are satisfied with the result, move on to the next step.

Laying Out the Lead Story

Pull a new guideline horizontally to 4 inches from the top and one 0.125 inch above it, just underneath your folio rules. Open a new layer and call it Lead Story. Import the file found on the disk that came with this book, called HERBALS.RTF. Apply the No Margin Paragraph Style you saved earlier. Make sure that the type is set in a 12-point plain serif font similar to Century Old Style. Save it as a new style called Newsletter. This will be our body text, the text style used for all our paragraph text throughout the newsletter. Size the text frame from the 4-inch guideline to the guideline for the bottom margin.

Select the first line in this file and change the typeface to 26-point boldface. If you are using Century Old Style and have loaded most of the typefaces available, Century is a heavier companion to Century Old Style, which makes a very effective headline. Add a return at the end of the headline to give it more space before the body of the story. Select the whole first sentence of this story and increase the point size to 21 points. This variation in point size is one way to emphasize the importance of a story or to draw the reader's attention. You could also use a drop cap—making the first letter bigger—as another method of attracting the reader's eye. Feel free to experiment with variations. Your page should look similar to the one shown in Figure 18.4.

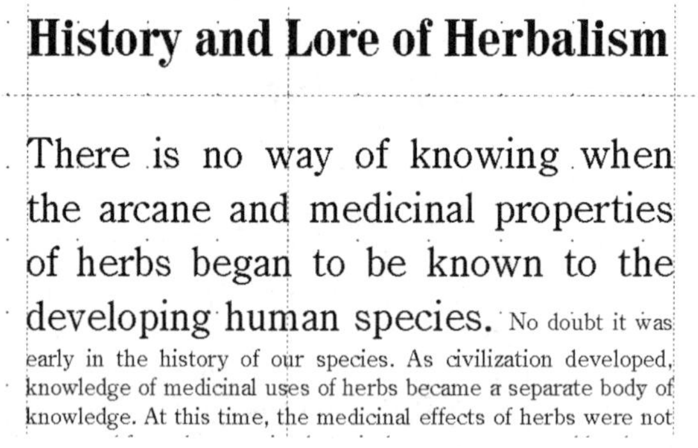

History and Lore of Herbalism

There is no way of knowing when the arcane and medicinal properties of herbs began to be known to the developing human species. No doubt it was early in the history of our species. As civilization developed, knowledge of medicinal uses of herbs became a separate body of knowledge. At this time, the medicinal effects of herbs were not

FIGURE 18.4 Lead story and headline on page 1

Now go to the bottom of the page and create a new, small text frame off to the side of the page. Type the words Continued on Page 2, setting them in 10-point italic. Place the

Chapter 18: Using Multipage and Frame Tools, Advanced Layout Concepts

frame flush right at the bottom of the lead story text frame, as shown in Figure 18.5.

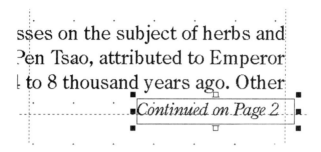

FIGURE 18.5 Placing the continuation line

You just placed a "jump". This tells the reader that the story has jumped to page 2. As I mentioned before, you need to let your reader know both where the story is going and where it came from. This makes it easier to locate the copy. In some cases you may wish to provide a repeat of or modify the headline for the story on the jump page. Your newsletter should look approximately like that in Figure 18.6.

FIGURE 18.6 The front page of our newsletter

The irregular page format is very useful for the first page of a newsletter. Short items of interest, calendars of events, lists of officers, meeting times, and so on, can all be run down the smaller column. The layout can be varied slightly from month to month, without distracting the reader, by switching the side on which the smaller column occurs.

One design element that is often not carefully considered is the justification of text. As a rule you should avoid full justification of text (i.e., making it flush left and right) in columns smaller than 3 or 4 inches across. This is because the number of spaces across a line will be too few to support proper justification. The result will be large areas of white space running between words as the program attempts to create enough space to get even margins. In general, you should use flush left in such cases. You might want to experiment with different justification settings for both columns on this page to see how this works.

Creating Page 2

Our second page will be a standard three-column format. This balanced approach offers more room for placing stories of mixed length and small graphics. It's also well suited to lists and classified advertising.

Let's start by adding a new page. Open the **Layout** menu and click on **Insert Page**; the Insert Page dialog box will appear. Click the **After** alternative and then **OK**. Remove the guidelines for the left-hand column we made on page 1.

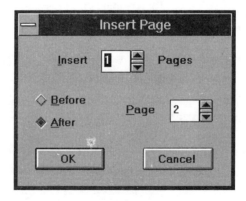

FIGURE 18.7 The Insert Page dialog box

Working with Master Layer

We are going to place a common header on the remaining pages, giving the name of the newsletter and the issue date. Open a new layer, name it Header, and then click on Master. Type the words June 1993, and set in 24-point Century Old Style or the typeface you are using. Place this text in the top right-hand corner of page 2 and pull a guideline to the bottom of the words. Copy or duplicate the word Herbletter from the masthead on page 1. Paste or place it in the upper left corner of page 2. Reduce the size until the letters fit between the guidelines, as shown in Figure 18.8.

FIGURE 18.8 The finished header

Draw a line under the words from margin to margin, placing it about 0.125 inch below the text. Go back to page 1 and double-click on Masthead in the Layers menu. When the Layer Options dialog box comes up, click **Set Options for All Pages** to off and click to take the checkmarks off **Visible** and **Printable**. This will keep the header from appearing on page 1 while it appears on all other pages.

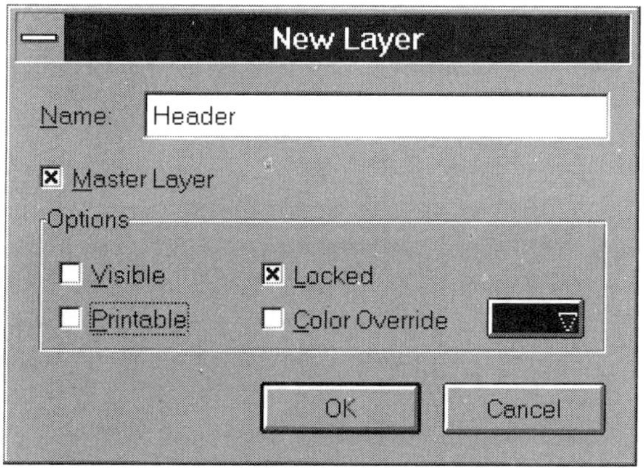

FIGURE 18.9 Preventing a master layer from printing or showing on a specific page

Now let's change to a three-column layout. In CorelDRAW 4.0, we had to figure out how much space we'll need for gutters and how much remaining space we will have for columns. In this new release, we can use the added frame capabilities to do this for us. We can forget all the math about gutters and column widths and quickly accomplish our three-column layout.

Import the file on the disk that came with this book called VIOLET.RTF and apply your saved newsletter style. Make sure that your text frame has 3/4 inch margins both left and right. Click on the **Frame** bar in the **Text** roll-up, the dialog box shown in Figure 8.10 will appear. Change the Number of Columns to 3 and check the **Equal Column Widths** box. Set the Width of column 1 to 2.2. The application will actually adjust this in order to make each column the same width, but approximating it in this box prevents your needing to resize the frame. Also set the Gutter to 0.20. Click on **OK** and your frame will be formatted with three columns. Place guidelines at each edge of the text in your columns to aid in later arranging of this page.

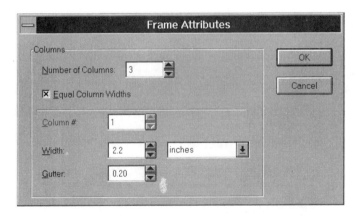

FIGURE 18.10 Setting up a three column layout using the Frame Attributes dialog box

Many times the exact amount of space you have will not work out exactly unless you use microns. The easiest way to fudge is to use a pica for your gutter throughout and adjust the margins to take up any slack.

Text and Graphic for Column 1

Make a new layer named Herbmon. Draw a text box at the top of the first column about 0.5 inch deep and type **Herb of the Month** as the headline. Set it in your serif font at 18-point Century Old Style boldface. Now import a floral drawing or bitmap from the clipart collection—or select any plant form from the symbol library and place and size the graphic to come to a guideline placed at 3.5 inches. The completed headline and title are shown in Figure 18.11.

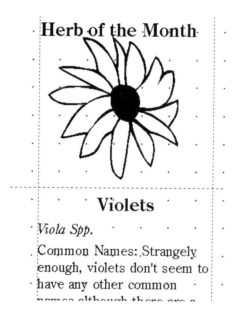

FIGURE 18.11 Completed herb-of-the-month column

Size the frame to fit inside the guidelines for column 1. Click on the **Paragraph** button in the Text roll-up, and in the Spacing aspect in the Before Paragraph box, change the percentage to 125 percent. Highlight the word Violets and change it to 16-point type with center alignment with the Text roll-up and click on **Apply**. Highlight Viola Spp. and change it to italic type. The completed headline and title may be seen in Figure 18.11.

Flowing Text from Frame to Frame

Next we need to continue the story that began on page 1. This is where we start to see that the desktop publishing skills of CorelDRAW 5.0 are better than those of its predecessors. In the past we would have had to cut and paste manually and go through all kinds of contortions to split a block of text. It was enough to make you go out and buy another program just for the purpose. CorelDRAW 4.0 made it automatic.

Go back to page 1 and click on the outline box at the bottom of the text frame containing the HERBAL.RTF text. Your cursor will change to the frame tool icon. Go to page 2 with the **PageDown** key and draw a text frame in the center column of the page. Apply the Newsletter style to the text and change the frame to 3 columns. On the first line in the frame type Continued from Page 1 and hit the **Enter** key. Highlight the line and change the type to italic. The top of your column will look like Figure 18.12

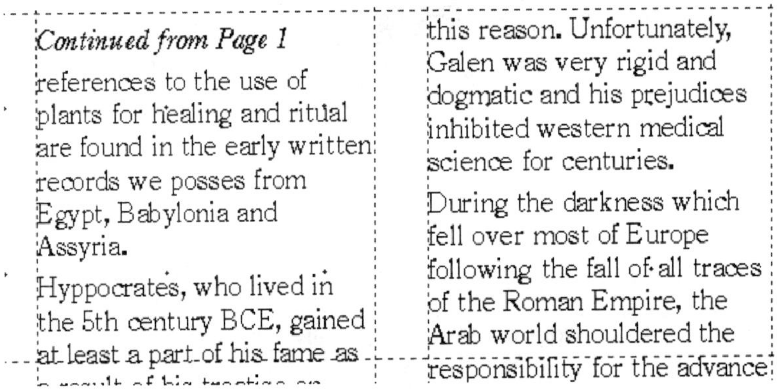
Continued from Page 1

references to the use of plants for healing and ritual are found in the early written records we posses from Egypt, Babylonia and Assyria.

Hyppocrates, who lived in the 5th century BCE, gained at least a part of his fame as

this reason. Unfortunately, Galen was very rigid and dogmatic and his prejudices inhibited western medical science for centuries.

During the darkness which fell over most of Europe following the fall of all traces of the Roman Empire, the Arab world shouldered the responsibility for the advance

FIGURE 18.12 Continuation of lead story

Click on the outline box at the bottom of this frame and draw a new text frame in the right-hand column. More of the text from this story will flow into this frame. At the beginning of the last line of text in this frame, type **Continued on Page 4**, change it to italic, and right-justify it, typing a return after the 4.

Adding the Breakout

At this point we'll add the breakout. The first thing we have to do is select the text that we wish to highlight. It should be selected for its ability to interest the reader of the article it was drawn from. In many cases this will be a dramatic quote or a principal statement made in the story. Just as with a thriller, you don't want to give away the whole thing in the breakout.

Locate the words "The first true 'English' herbal...." Using the Frame Text tool, highlight the whole sentence and copy it using the **Copy** command or the **Ctrl+C** hot keys. Now hit the **Enter** key 5 or 6 times to make about 1 inch of space between the paragraphs. We'll place our breakout in this space. Move your cursor outside the text frame, the arrow will change to cross-hairs. Draw a small text frame and **Paste** the sentence into it (**Ctrl+V**). Using the Text roll-up, change the font size to 14 point and the style to Bold. Adjust the frame as necessary. Using the Pick tool, move this small text frame into the space you made between paragraphs in your article. Size the text frame slightly narrower than the column; adjust the number of spaces in the original text as necessary to accomodate the breakout. Using the rectangle tool, draw a box around the breakout text and give it the second thickness available in the Outline fly-out as I have done in Figure 18.13.

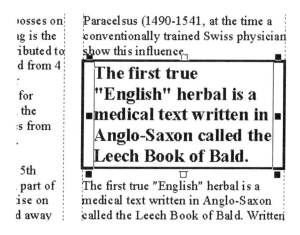

FIGURE 18.13 Adding the breakout

Note: If when you click on the outline box on page 1 the frame cursor winks off as soon as you move it, CorelDRAW has put the rest of the text on a page it added. Go to any pages after page 2 that you added and if you find a filled text frame, delete it. Then from page 1 or 2, delete any pages after page 2.

To finish up page 2 of our newsletter, place a small new text frame below the bottom margin centered in the middle column and type Page 2 in it. Give it the newsletter style and center it as you see in Figure 18.14.

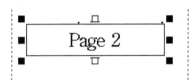

FIGURE 18.14 The page number

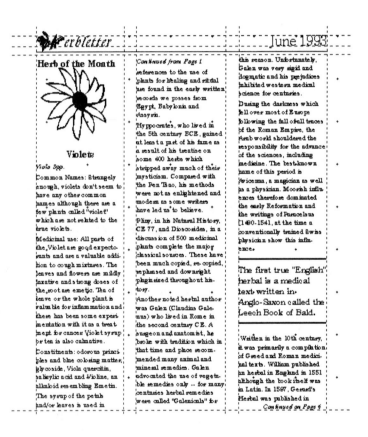

FIGURE 18.15 The completed second page

Page 3: Wrapping text around graphics

Now let's add another page either by using the **Insert Page** dialog box accessed from the Layout menu or by simply clicking the left mouse button on the plus sign at the

Chapter 18: Using Multipage and Frame Tools, Advanced Layout Concepts

bottom left corner of the interface. The Insert Page dialog box will appear. As you can see, the header appears on this page already because it is a master layer.

Open a new layer called Page 3 Grid. Import the file on the disk that came with this book named HERBAL.RTF. Don't worry that we have already used this story on pages 1 and 2. We are just going to use it to set our columns. Apply the newsletter style to this frame and carefully size it to the margins marked by the guidelines.

In the Text roll-up, click on the **Frame** button. Give your frame four columns with 0.25-inch gutter, click on **OK**, and **Apply**. Your text will appear in four columns, as it does in Figure 18.16. If your text isn't justified, click on that option in the Text roll-up and **Apply**. Now zoom in on about half the page and pull guidelines to each margin. When you have the guidelines set, delete the text file. You will have guidelines for a four-column format neatly on your page.

FIGURE 18.16 Formatting the text in four columns

The computer and desktop publishing software have reduced many complicated layout tasks to little more than a few mouse clicks. One of the most dramatic examples of this is wrapping text around a graphic. Using manual methods once involved physically arranging the type or cutting and pasting it around the object. In most cases this was limited to drawing a box around an object because of the difficulty of making irregular wraps around the object and properly spacing and kerning the text within the column. Although CorelDRAW 5.0 does not totally automate the process, it makes it easy enough for even a novice user to perform this feat quickly.

Wrapping Text Around a Graphic

Let's put a graphic on this page and practice fitting text around it. In the samples in your CorelDRAW\CLIPART\PLANTS\ subdirectory there should be a file named FLWR3.CDR. Import this file and size it approximately like the one shown Figure 18.17. Start a new layer named page 3.

Adding the Text

Place a guideline at the uppermost point of the flower. Import the file named BACK-REMD.RTF on the disk that came with this book. Apply the newsletter style (12-point Century Old Style) and size the text frame to fit the left column on page 3 with the top side of the text frame at the new guideline. Click on the outline box at the bottom of the text frame and flow the text into the second column.

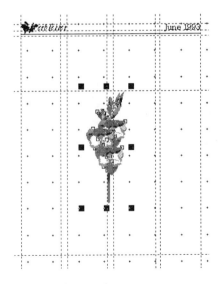

FIGURE 18.17 Graphic placed on page

Highlight the first sentence in the frame and click on **Copy** in the Edit menu. The Frame Tool cross-hair cursor will appear. Draw your text box across the top of the two columns between the header and the guideline you placed at 2 inches. The sentence will appear there. Cut the sentence in the story frame. Set the headline in a 15-point boldface.

Text Wrap Around the Graphic

Get the **Envelope** roll-up from the Effects menu; then select the text frame in column 2. Use the Shape tool to add three or four new nodes; then use them to shape the frame around the graphic, as I have done in Figure 18.18.

FIGURE 18.18 Using Envelopes to wrap text around graphics

Finishing Page 3

Import the EDITORIL.RTF file located on the disk that came with this book. Set it in 10-point serif type, justified, and place it within the third column of page 3. Use the word Editorial at the top of this file to make the headline using the cut and copy method we used for the first story. Now shape the text frame around the graphic and flow the rest of the text into the top section of the fourth column. Import the file named DISCLAIM.RTF and place it at the bottom of the second column. Set it in 10-point type, justified. Now highlight the word Notice and set it in boldface 12-point type centered. Draw a rectangle around it to make it more visible.

Import the file named WILLOW.RTF and place it at the bottom of the right-hand column. Type continued on page 4 and a return to replace the last line in the frame. Then change the words to italic and right-justify. Then make a small text frame centered at the bottom of the page in the margin and type Page 3 in it.

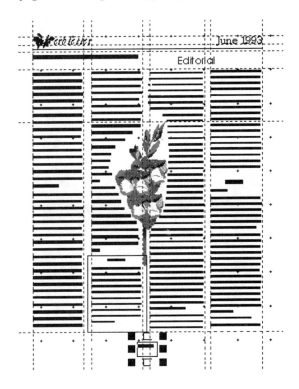

FIGURE 18.19 The finished page 3

Page 4 of Our Newsletter

NOTE Any time you find a text frame continuing the text flowing from a prior page, you can delete the frame without losing the text you'll later want to flow onto the page. The frames may be left until you are ready for them if they don't seem confusing.

Laying Out Page 4

On our last page we want to add a subscription blank, continue the stories that started on an earlier page, and place some more text and graphics as needed. Let's start by removing the four-column guidelines and leave only the guidelines for the margins and the header. Place a horizontal guideline at 7.5 inches to mark the top of the subscription blank we're going to design.

Start a new layer named Subscription. Draw a rectangle around the space at the bottom of the page and give it a border of the second narrowest line on the Outline Tool fly-out (0.028 inch). Duplicate the Herbletter logo in the header and place the duplicate at the top left-hand corner of the subscription blank. Finish the subscription blank to match the one in Figure 18.20.

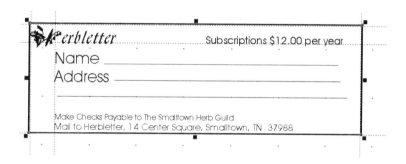

FIGURE 18.20 The subscription blank

Flow the rest of the lead story, HERBAL.RTF, into a frame at the top of page 4. Make sure the text frame extends the full width of the page between margins. Then click on the **Frame** button and force it three columns with a 0.25-inch gutter. Select out the sentence beginning the first full paragraph on the page and give it a book style box as you did on page 2.

Use the **Go To Page** dialog box from the Layout menu to jump to page 1 and find the calendar entry announcing the Herb Faire on June 6. Copy this using the **Copy** command in the File menu and jump back to page 4. Use the **Paste** command to set the headline. Open the Text Edit dialog box and add the word Remember at the beginning of the sentence and place returns to match those in Figure 18.21. Change the typeface to a 24-point font such as Zapf Calligraphic or Lydian. Select a frame from the Symbols roll-up, such as #72 from Borders2 used in the figure. Size the frame to accommodate the announcement. Add a 50 percent black fill to the frame.

FIGURE 18.21 Adding an announcement

The final step is to import the file named GRKTXT2.RTF located on the disk that came with this book. Size its frame so it fills the right-hand middle of the page and make sure the frame is wide enough to contain all the text with it set in a 10-point serif font. Set the headline 12-point bold and centered over the story.

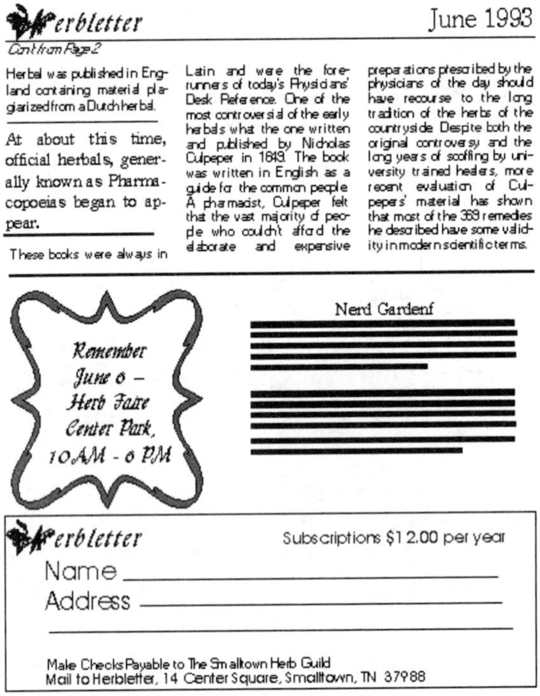

FIGURE 18.22 The completed page 4

Beyond Layout

The layout portion of your newsletter project is now completed. But it's not ready to go yet. There is still more paperwork. The next step is to print out a copy, or several, and go over them with a critical eye. Start by looking at it from a slight distance, say, 2 feet. Do the pages look balanced? Are they attractive? Now bring them to reading distance with a red pen in hand. Start with the headlines! This is where mistakes are most common and where they are most often overlooked by copy editors.

It's very easy to miss something that sounds right even if it is not really right. There's a big difference between their and they're. Getting it wrong can be a big embarrassment. You can't rely on a spell checker. If you put form where you should put from, it's still a properly spelled word and won't be caught. And you may have done a global search and replace and, oops, replaced the wrong word, so that Potomac becomes Potato.

Also make sure that all the illustrations are in the right place and that captions are underneath the right pictures. One of the few times I ever saw the presses stop when I was working on a daily newspaper was when I picked up a paper as it came off the machine and noticed that Senator Kennedy looked very much like Governor Jimmy Carter and vice versa. The publisher ordered the presses stopped until the names under the pictures had been put in their correct places.

Also make sure that you have the right margins and that the folds are in the proper places for any names or addresses. You don't want to come back from the printer and find that for some reason you cannot properly, or legally, mail your deathless prose to its eagerly waiting audience.

CHAPTER SUMMARY

There are many ways to lay out a newsletter, and there is no single right way. It's a matter of individual need and taste. This chapter has served as an introduction to both newsletter layout and the way in which CorelDRAW 5.0 can be used to produce effective publications. Corel executives have told me that they intend to improve and expand the desktop publishing and long-document-handling abilities of their product. In the next edition of this book, which will cover CorelDRAW 5.0, you can expect to find expanded discussion and enlarged exercises dealing with desktop publishing and document creation.

CHAPTER 19

A Quick Sketch of Peter McCormick

Venice by Peter McCormick

About the Artist

Peter McCormick retired from the insurance business, but *retired* is a relative term. What Pete has really done is change his focus from traditional business pursuits to the world of art and design. He moved to Maui and began making his living as an illustrator, later relocating to the desert southwest. He has no formal training in either art or graphic design, but his skill and careful eye are obvious in his work.

"I'm self-taught," Pete noted, "and have been working in the field for about twelve years." He started working in pencil, until he watched a PBS program on painting. "I bought the guy's book and some materials, saying to myself that I could do that," he added.

Today Pete uses CorelDRAW! extensively and also uses files from the program as the basis for other works as well. One favorite technique is to create a drawing and then to import and enhance it in Fractal Painter (a short review of that product is presented in Section Three of this book).

The View Along the Canal

Venice won the world grand prize in the Corel Third Annual Art Show contest for landscape and travel. And this drawing is not Pete's only contest winner. He is also very active with users groups and is always willing to help someone else become more proficient with CorelDRAW! and computer graphics.

In this chapter we will take a close look at how the *Venice* scene was created. Unlike some of the other illustrations in this section, *Venice* is not filled with fine detail and meticulous elaboration of a theme. Contrast *Venice* to Georgina Curry's *Huntress* or Chris Purcell's *Green Lizard*. The other two drawings use a variety of blends and many elements of fine detail to produce their effects. Pete McCormick's work is much more like a sketch or water color. It uses a balance of elements and simple forms combined with a judicious use of light and shadow to create its effect.

But the drawing was the product of much experimentation. "It is a composite of other work I have done," Pete said. The basic picture was sketched out quickly and then refined over several weeks. A lot of refinement was used to create the balance and interplay of light and shadow seen in the final result.

Something else is different in this example of Pete's work: people in motion. Six human figures are either walking, striding, or waiting along the canal. Simple fills are used for the majority of the objects on the page, and there are only three blends in the entire drawing. Pete has also used rectangles to frame his drawings, similar to that used traditionally to mat works that are to be framed, and has added a cursive, widely-kerned title at the bottom of his work.

Figure 19.1 shows the entire drawing in wireframe. This drawing is a busy scene that actually has several subelements in it. Each vignette is fleshed out with supporting elements, and the entire work is designed, as are virtually all the other illustrations in this section of the book, to carry the eye comfortably around the drawing.

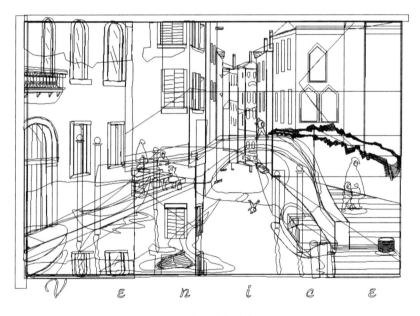

FIGURE 19.1 *Venice* in wireframe

If you refer to the copy of *Venice* located in the color insert, you will see that the sky and water in the canal are formed from two gradient fills. These two elements are given slightly different shades and lightened as they approach the horizontal center of the picture. Warm colors dominate the scene. The central colors are tans, a burnt orange, and muted reds. Accents are provided by the brilliant sky, the reflecting water, and the bright Italian sun.

A Collection of Miniatures

Figure 19.2 shows a close-up of part of the left edge of the scene. Three people are gathered by a gondola station. Pete has used CorelDRAW! implementations of traditional sketching techniques to shape his figures and made extensive use of two-color fills to produce his objects. Note how the figures of the people are outlined. The wall of the building, the tiles of the bridge, and the drapes in the window were all done using two-color fills. The globes on top of the poles are circular fountain fills that add highlights to the image. Reflections and movement in the water are done with quick, bold strokes.

FIGURE 19.2 Woman and child waiting for a gondola

The Man on the Bridge

At the center of the illustration is the view down the winding canal. To be effective the perspective must appear to diminish as you look down the canal. But that by itself would not be enough. There must be a flow in the way the canal moves through the page, and there must be a contrasting flow to provide a sense of perspective to the drawing. Figure 19.3 shows a man striding across the bridge.

FIGURE 19.3 The man on the bridge

Once again Pete has used bold shapes to create his sketch. The man contrasts against the background and creates a plane just behind the people waiting for the gondola. A series of solid and gradient fills is used to stucco the rail and underside of the bridge, and it curves down and to the right in a gentle S shape, leading the eye to the right of the picture. The man walking one way and the visual strength of the bridge going toward the right join the shadows on the buildings to keep the viewer's eye focused on the scene and centered within the sketch. Roughed-out boats in the background beneath the bridge, and a reflection formed from an irregularly-shaped object with a gradient fill, complete this portion of the scene.

The Man and the Boy

At the base of the bridge on the right-hand side of the drawing, a man is seen walking with a child. As throughout the rest of the picture, Peter McCormick has used simple, bold shapes to form his elements. This part of the drawing mirrors the woman with the little girl on the other side of the canal waiting for the gondola. The entire image presents a sense of balance, as seen in Figure 19.4.

FIGURE 19.4 A variation on the theme, man walking with a child

Several minor elements in this part of the drawing tend both to isolate it and to draw the eye back toward the center of the picture. The edge of the bridge and the plants, represented by a green blend just above the figures, is braced by the rectangles used to form the steps they are walking on. At the base of the bridge is another landing that leads back around to a boat pointed back up the canal.

A Little Accent

Although all the elements in the drawing are done in bold strokes, that doesn't imply that care wasn't given to how they appeared on the page or to the nuances of shading and light. If you look at Figure 19.5 you will see one of the boats tied up along the right side of the picture. On the left it has been taken apart into an expanded view—on the right, just as it was in the picture. Pete used several simple shapes to create this element very quickly, and four parts of it are used to provide shadow and depth. A gradient fill is used to form the inner curve of the bow with an irregular shape used underneath the box of cargo to provide the shadowing of the deck. An elongated teardrop is used to shadow the hull in the water.

Chapter 19: A Quick Sketch of Peter McCormick **683**

FIGURE 19.5 A closer look at the boat

The Long View

The upper half of the drawing is dominated by vertical structures formed by the buildings. Once again Pete has used simple shapes, but the way they are arranged not only gives them definition but adds to the sense of depth inherent in the composition. The fills were carefully selected to balance the tones and give the right feeling of morning light. The fills are a combination of gentle gradients and two-color fills. The details of the building are almost all simple rectangles or slightly-modified ellipses. The only complex fill is a stained glass window appearing in the right mid-ground, as seen in Figure 19.6.

FIGURE 19.6 The long view

Another accent adding a more realistic feel to the scene is the way in which objects were used to provide stark shadows along the sides of the building and along and underneath windowsills. These provide a separation between the foreground and the back of the drawing.

A View from the Balcony

In the left foreground is seen a portion of a balcony. It is a good example of how an artist can use simple shapes to provide the illusion of detail and a sense of perspective quickly. It shows the ability to see and portray the essential form of the elements in his work. Here several rectangles and a series of ellipses are used to form a balcony. Triangular supports and an irregular shadow are used to make it stand out from the pattern fill of the wall behind, as seen in Figure 19.7.

FIGURE 19.7 The balcony

A Final Perspective

Within the canal itself is a sinuously-shaped compound object representing ripples in the water. It compresses the open space within the canal and gives us a realistic sense of a reflection on the water as well as movement from a passing boat, as seen in Figure 19.8.

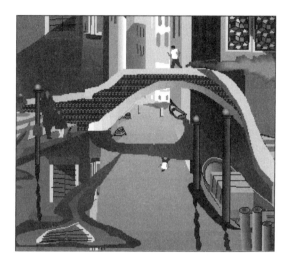

FIGURE 19.8 A reflection on the water

Chapter Summary

Venice is an excellent example of how a practiced eye can use simple shapes and obtain a dramatic and visually pleasing effect.

In *Venice*, Peter McCormick shows his mastery of both composition and CorelDRAW!

CHAPTER 20
The Pen and Ink Style of Deborah Miller

Castle

The word *plankowner* is a Navy term for a crew member who helped during the building of a ship. Deborah Miller has been involved with CorelDRAW from almost the beginning, as a beta tester and professional user. In a way she is a bit of a plankowner. A freelance artist working in Mesa, Arizona, her work shows a pen-and-ink style, reflecting her background in CAD and technical illustration. She has provided us with several of her works, including two of her winners in the CorelDRAW art contest. *Castle* is an example of how Deborah uses the program to imitate traditional pen-and-ink drawing. One of her later works, *Mesa*, is a montage of symbols that reflect both the part of the country in which she lives and the Native American portion of her heritage. The ball-valve illustration shows how she uses blends and layers for technical projects. The travel poster was designed to see how many complex elements the program could handle in a single file.

She has been working with computers since the early Tandy unit became available; then she went through a succession of systems: Commodore VIC 20, 64, and 128, and then on to a PC and CorelDRAW. "I've been doing graphics for twenty-six years," she said. "I started with blueprints and plans for RV's and trailers and then moved on to CAD work and advertising." She sees the computer as a major gain in productivity and enjoys playing with new software.

Building a Castle

The inspiration for the drawing in the opening figure is England's Bodiam Castle, built in 1386 by Richard III. There are two ways to draw a castle: quickly or slowly. This illustration is definitely of the latter variety. The drawing took a month to complete; every stone in the image is individually drawn. "To get a pen-and-ink rendition with CorelDRAW you have to work a lot with your fills," she noted. "I use a lot of custom fills to get the effects I want." This drawing won Second Place in January 1992 for landscapes in the CorelDRAW art contest. Like many of the artists interviewed for this book, Deborah often starts working from a sketch; but she does all her work on the PC, even the initial rough-out. In this case she used a photograph to aid her memory.

The Approach

Working from the sketch, Deborah first roughed out the walls and divided the project into sections. "I knew this was going to become a very involved file, so I had to work to simplify the drawing right from the start; otherwise the final file wouldn't even load," she said. Sections of the wall were done in five different files. After each one was completed, it was grouped and combined to reduce complexity. The final castle was assembled after all the portions had been created and simplified.

The foliage on the left was added to frame the castle and give a sense of scale. It makes the scene look as if the viewer were standing on a low hill across an open field in front of the structure. Blends added in the foreground add subtle S-shaped curves to lead the eye around the drawing's main elements.

"The original had water in front of the castle, and several parts of the wall had been damaged in the past. I took some liberties with the design and removed some of the parts I didn't want," the artist explained. Figure 20.1 shows the entire picture in wireframe mode, showing the elements used to give the appearance of a detailed pen-and-ink drawing.

FIGURE 20.1 The wireframe

Raising the Walls

Two rectangles were used to form a background wash with just enough difference in the gray tones to give a bit of contrast to the rest of the objects. The walls were drawn as panels or curves and filled with another gray fill. The slots in the ramparts are black-filled shapes laid on top of the panels. The smooth walls serve two purposes: to form the basic shape of the castle, and to set the primary color for the mortar that joins the stones. The stones were each fitted into place and cover almost the entire structure, using a combination of custom fills and percentages of a gray fill. Figure 20.2 shows the walls under construction.

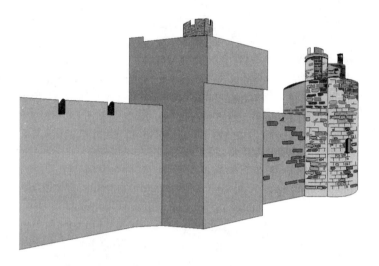

FIGURE 20.2 Constructing a wall panel

Tones play an important part in crafting a pen-and-ink effect. You have to vary the shades to create the texture of the drawing and give it dimension. With a draw program you can't use a little more ink to darken a tone. Planning the fills and alternating a random series require attention to the overall effect, not just the isolated area you are working on at a given time. The stones in each tower and turret had to be curved to fit the arc of that part of the structure. You can also see how Deborah used an overhang as the base for the battlement in the center of the Figure.

Detailing the Battlement

The main battlement tower on the right side of the drawing is the only place on the walls that uses a large number of blends, and it shows an interesting technique. Most of the complicated drawings in this book use blends to give an object shading and to define its contours. To heighten the pen-and-ink appearance, Deborah used a combination of blends and irregular objects to make the top of the tower look as if the ink had been built up more in one area than in another. Figures 20.3a and 20.3b show that portion of the drawing. You can see the underlying fills that were used to give the stonework a weathered look, as well as the blends that created the look of ink on ink.

FIGURE 20.3a The battlement

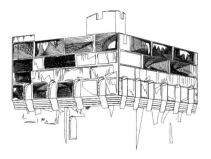

FIGURE 20.3b The battlement's wireframe

Adding the Minor Details

Once the walls had been drawn, the windows were placed over the stones. Several elements were used for each one to give the impression that the overlaid elements were drawn as an original part of the design with the stones. Figures 20.4a and 20.4b show a section of the central tower with a window made from three tablet-shaped forms. The first one was drawn and then duplicated and reduced two times. Each duplicate was given a different fill to make the window look like recessed stone with an opening in the middle.

FIGURES 20.4a and b The central tower window

Accenting the Effort

Look at the two stones to the left of the window in Figure 20.4a. Notice the dark-filled wedges that run down the wall. There's another one and a half stones to the left. They are a part of the series of accents that give the stonework a mottled and weathered look. They can be found frequently between the blocks of stone and uniform-filled wall panels.

Running around the base of the castle is a rim about the width of two rows of stones. Figure 20.5 shows a section of it filled, with the wireframe version below it. Lines and irregular triangles are used here as well to add accents that make the buildings look landscaped.

Blending the Foreground

Once the building was complete a foreground had to be added to draw the eye and maintain the tone of the rest of the picture. Figure 20.6 shows the two blends in filled and wireframe versions. The smaller blend on the right sits over the larger object. Both have been separated, pulled, and reblended to give them a washed appearance.

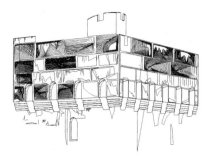

FIGURE 20.5 Using wireframe mode

FIGURE 20.6 The foreground

Framing the Image

The final step in executing the design was to frame the entire scene with a pair of trees, one on the left in front, and another behind on the viewer's right side. The trunk of the tree on the left has a custom two-color bitmap fill. "I keep a collection of fills made for just this kind of thing," Deborah said. A small rise in the earth is created by adding a couple of objects to the right of the tree and drawing some grass over them.

Figure 20.7 shows the two sets of objects in both filled and wireframe versions. The right rise in the hill is seen only in the filled section. The framing for the right side depicts some broken ground, and only parts of some branches are actually present in the viewing area.

FIGURE 20.7 The frame

Mesa, a Native Tapestry

The version of Figure 20.8 that appears in the color insert was drawn using CorelDRAW 3.0, and Deborah was kind enough to totally re-create the image using CorelDRAW 4.0 when that update of this book was done. This image began with the artist's fascination with the mountain range seen from her house and with one mountain in particular, the Lost Dutchman. It changes color during the day, "glowing orange and gold," she said, "and at night it sometimes takes on an eerie appearance." The mountain is considered sacred to all the local tribes, and it appears in the center portion of her drawing.

FIGURE 20.8 *Mesa*, Pushing the envelope with CorelDRAW

Deborah made extensive use of layers to make this image easier to manipulate, and extensive use of textured fills, as well as several blends and contours. Screen redraws of the fill image can take a long time. By isolating the visual portions of the image as needed she was able to simplify her work.

The base of the drawing (shown in Figure 20.9) is a hide, held tight with sticks in each corner. By using the textured fills (first introduced in version 4.0) and a fair bit of experimentation, Deborah was able to create a detailed and contoured appearance of treated leather or hide. The colors for the hide, as throughout the drawing, were kept to desert tones. During the last century some Western tribes used hides to draw tapestries depicting the events of the year. This drawing is filled with objects that Deborah wove into a picture expressing her feelings for the region she lives in. "I let it talk to me," she said, "and just kept working with the effect until it felt right."

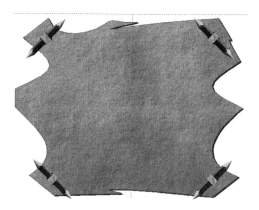

FIGURE 20.9 The background

Pulling the Hide Taut

The four wooden sticks that are used to pull the corners taut appear three-dimensional. The contouring on the shadow side was done using a blend. A small rectangle with textured fill was placed over the stick. The fill was varied somewhat to give it a different pattern, making it look as if the light were falling on it at a slightly different angle. As shown in Figures 20.10a and b, the four pieces of wood taken together reinforce the boundary of the illustration and add to the three-dimensional effect.

 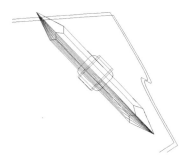

FIGURES 20.10a and b Detail of the sticks

Drawing the Mountains

The bleak landscape of the southwestern desert is full of sharp angles and earthen hues. Deborah has used such a landscape in a way that seems to give depth to the image while dividing it in the middle. The woman in the foreground seems to be gazing out over the mountains at the solar disk, adding perspective. Without this enhancement the work would probably appear to be a series of objects placed on a background, rather than a landscape. Figure 20.11a shows the filled mountain range, and Figure 20.11b shows the same portion of the drawing in wireframe. A basic outline was drawn, and a duplicate was flipped vertically and adjusted and filled to form the shadows at the base of the mountain. Overlying objects with slightly varying fills and a few blends were used to complete the range. The fills are done in a combination of indigo and rust-colored gradient fills, giving the landscape a gentle radiance.

FIGURES 20.11a and b The mountain range in fill and in wireframe

The woman in the right foreground (Figure 20.12) demonstrates two things, pen and ink style and two-tone color fills. As you can see from the wireframe, Deborah is still using somewhat of a pen-and-ink style in drawing her figures. By using a two-tone color fill, she was able to quickly produce the texture and color in the woman's clothing and on her face. A thick outline was used around the hair to help differentiate that portion of the woman from the mountains behind her.

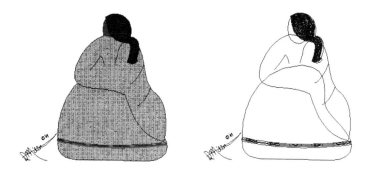

FIGURE 20.12 The woman in fill and in wireframe

The Pottery

The southwestern United States is a land of history and silent mystery. Within the canyons of the desert are the remains of ancient peoples. The ancient ones, or Anasazi, lived in this region before the arrival of the Navajo, the Hopi, and the Apache. In the lower left-hand corner of the drawing are three examples of Native American pottery (See Figure 20.13). Each is representative of a different heritage. In the foreground is a small vessel with vertical markings, typical of that found in the silent homes of the Anasazi. The largest pot is similar to that used by the Hopi, whereas the one to the right might be found among the Apache or the Navajo. In the original CorelDRAW 3.0 illustration, Deborah used a combination of drawing techniques and fills to create these pots. In the CorelDRAW 4.0 version, the program did much more of the work directly. As with the backdrop, the artist used a mix of two colors and textured fills along with blends to create the pots.

FIGURE 20.13 The three pots

Figure 20.14 shows the same collection of pots in an expanded wireframe. The pot on the left uses a series of blends that have been edited and enveloped to provide the complex design of the pottery. The Anasazi pot was originally drawn with blends and overlaid with a textured fill. The Apache/Navajo pot was a combination of blends that had been edited and enveloped over another object, which was then patterned with a textured fill. This shows how different forms of fills can be used in a single object to create effects that could not be done with a single fill alone. This is a fine example of the advanced features of CorelDRAW.

The Hopi pot in the background is the simplest of the three. The shape of one of the other pots was manipulated and recombined to form several objects that were then given a repeating pattern of textured fills.

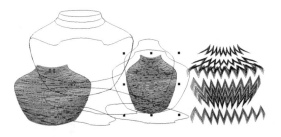

FIGURE 20.14 Examination of the pottery in wireframe

The Solar Disk

The sun is a constant presence in the desert's daytime sky and is the most sharply-featured major element in Mesa. Deborah used a series of blends, contours and conical fills, other gradient fills, and overlaying circles to create the effect of beaten gold. Figure 20.15 shows the filled version of this portion of the drawing.

FIGURE 20.15 The solar disk in fill and in wireframe

Looking at the same section of the drawing in wireframe shows the detail of how the solar rays are created, and also uncovers the conical fills on the nose, lips, and contours that were used to create the main elements of the face.

The final element in *Mesa* is the blanket in the upper right-hand corner. Although the direction of the blanket would seem to draw the eye out of the drawing, its flow actually brings your eye back down toward the mountain range and back toward the woman. She is looking toward the sun and draws your eyes along the curve of the pots, which brings you up to the sun, which is looking directly at you. The highlights on the sun slightly bring your eyes back toward the blanket, thus completing the circle.

GETTING TECHNICAL

Like many of the artists I interviewed for this book, Deborah often starts working from a sketch, but she does all her work on the PC, even the initial rough-out. Her illustration of the *Ball-valve* shows how CorelDRAW can be used for detailed technical projects, even though it lacks some of the features found in programs dedicated to the task, such as interactive dimensioning and arrays. Its combination of shaded and wireframe views was designed to show a new client her skills and was created from memory. "I have done enough of them in the past that I didn't need a model," she said.

NOTE Dimensioning can be a handy tool when making plans or diagrams. The unit of measure is based on the current grid or ruler setting. For example, if you are building a house, the unit could be set to feet–1 foot per inch. Draw an 8-inch line and the number printed above the line reads 8 feet. Since the number changes as you move, it is easy to draw to scale and you don't have to come back and add the numbers manually. You can also set the units to other kinds of intervals, such as hours or weeks. CorelDRAW 4.0 had limited dimensioning capabilities and the CorelDRAW 5.0 version of the dimensioning feature was not settled at the time of this writing, but should appear in a much improved form.

The Approach

The filled-in version of the *Ball-valve* is built around a frame, but Deborah remarked that even she would have trouble pulling out those elements. The primary tools for refining that part of the project were blends and the CorelDRAW Node Edit functions. For the wireframe she relied on the Pencil and Fill tools. Accuracy and proper scale are the watchwords for good technical drawing. To get the details just right Deborah put a 0.125-inch grid on the page, and did a finish session with working on 0.25-inch sections at a time. "I magnified the area with the Zoom tool and then went in and fine-tuned the shape," she remarked. The close inspection combined with the vector format of the final file resulted in a very clean drawing. Let's start our detailed examination with the wireframe.

Working Smart with Wireframes

At first glance the wireframe looks like a collection of lines that had to be painstakingly drawn, but that's not Deborah Miller's style. She commented that she didn't have the time for that approach and added that there was a better way. Figure 20.16 shows a filled and wireframe view of that part of her drawing. The cross-hatching is actually a custom fill. The objects are laid on top of each other to add detail or hide part of the fills.

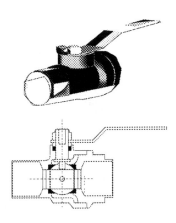

FIGURE 20.16 The filled ball-valve and wireframe

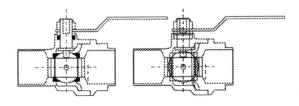

FIGURE 20.17 The ball-valve wireframes

In this area of the work you can see a combination of the pen-and-ink method combined with the object-oriented nature of CorelDRAW. She could have used a grid and drawn each line; the result would have been the same, but the effort much greater. "My time is worth money, and the faster I can get work out, the better," Deborah remarked. She started by drawing the outline of the basic form and then adding a two-color fill that gave it the pattern she needed. She also produced alternate fills that could be used to provide contrast for the objects that would overlay the first element.

Many new users don't consider just how much using the right fill can speed up a job, concentrating on getting the outline right first instead. All CorelDRAW objects have two parts, and if you think of how both will be used to form the element, the job goes a lot smoother. Figure 20.18 shows the CorelDRAW 3.0 Two-Color Pattern dialog box she used under view of the large shape and the entire wireframe. Setting the fill to white with black stripes makes the fill look like it is a series of lines. Adding additional elements with plain white, black, or alternate two-color fills will contrast with the underlying form and produce the line-drawing effect.

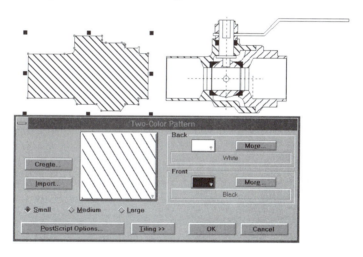

FIGURE 20.18 Using a custom two-color fill

Drawing the Main Body

The main portion of the assembly is composed of a series of objects that lie over the outline. Figure 20.19 shows an exploded diagram under the filled and unfilled assemblies.

You can see how the drawing was done by placing one shape on top of another. The somewhat c-shaped element between the two large filled ones lies underneath the white rectangle on the other side. The six vertical lines are used to delimit the ball chamber. "I grouped sets of objects frequently," the artist noted. "That was to keep from picking up a part of a structure I didn't want to move."

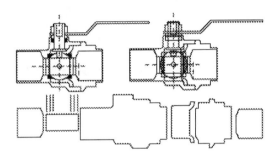

FIGURE 20.19 The main assembly structures

SHORTCUT

One thing I always do when working on this kind of project is to set the **CORELDRW.INI** file up so that an outline of an object moves with the mouse pointer. This makes it a lot easier to do two things: make sure of placement, and know exactly what you are moving around. The section later in the book on customizing CorelDRAW shows you how to set your system up the same way.

Getting precise placement takes a lot of attention to detail. Using the grids and rulers helps a lot. Another good habit is to pull in a guideline as a visual reference. You may not always want to turn the **Snap to Grid** feature on, but you can set the same option for the guidelines and then move it into place as you need it. That way, you control to which line the mark to object will align, not the spacing of the grid. I often duplicate an object or group before doing a lot of manipulation to it. That way if I make a mistake I can just replace it. You can save the file frequently as you work (always a good idea), but just duping the current element is a fast way to keep a basic backup.

Deborah Miller's work shows us a fundamental principle of good technical design: Keep it simple. The wireframe is a good example of how to construct a drawing that looks very complicated with a minimum of steps. But you must plan out your work in advance to really make use of the method. Here are some of the major points:

- Look at the structure and determine the primary shapes before doing anything.
- Design the drawing so the working boundary and the outline of the principal structure are the same.
- Use basic shapes when forming objects to reduce drawing time.
- Don't draw a line when the program can do it for you. That means using fills and **Place Duplicate** and **Copy** commands to cut down on the amount of mousing around you have to do.
- Group objects as a substructure to make it easier to place and size elements.
- Modify the magnification of the view to do fine-tuning at a relatively easy size.
- Use fills rather than open shapes. You can pick up a filled object at any point on its surface, but only the outline is active when you select a hollow object with the mouse.
- Use the Grid and Guidelines to speed up alignment; then fine-tune at a high magnification.
- Keep the effects of lighting in mind. Many artists draw a light source on the page and use it to help visualize the highlights and shadows as they work.

The Handle and Ball Assembly

As with the main body, the rest of the wireframe is composed of basic shapes that appear to be more than one object. Figure 20.20 shows the disassembled parts next to the full structure inside the main outline. The circle representing the ball is filled with stripes. The seating chamber looks like four wedges but is really just a single square. The entire section has only two irregular shapes, the handle and cap. The cap could have been made from two combined rectangles.

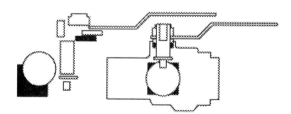

FIGURE 20.20 The handle and ball assembly

Once the figure was complete the reference lines and center point were added with the **Pencil** and **Ellipse** tools. If you have to include special symbols in a technical drawing, don't forget to check the Symbol Libraries. There are also clip art collections and special fonts that contain common drafting marks.

Creating the Filled Drawing

Like the wireframe, the filled model of the valve relies heavily on basic shapes for its structure. The shading requires the addition of more complex fills and blends to add detail. The angle and strength of the apparent light source are key to a realistic form. Before starting work on the objects, Deborah placed an object outside the viewing area to represent the position of the virtual light, and then drew arc lines to see how the shadows would be cast. She referred to these references when figuring out how to form blends and add darker sections to a set of elements. As with the other form, a basic outline was sketched before placing the objects. Figure 20.21 shows the filled model to the left of an unfilled rendition, over an exploded view.

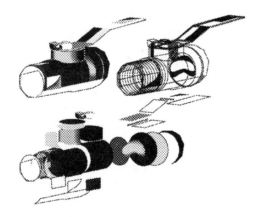

FIGURE 20.21 The filled and unfilled model, over an exploded view

There are several subgroups in this model: the handle, the cylinder, stop assembly, the threaded and angled front section, and the rear barrel (I am using descriptive words rather than plumbing terms). The handle is formed with extruded rectangles and a modified blend; the cylinder and stop comprise a collection of rectangles, circles, and a blend. The barrel required some node editing of one of its circles, several rectangles, and a few blends. The back of the model is mostly circles and blends.

Although this part of the drawing is a good bit more involved than the wireframe we just examined, the guidelines in the preceding bulleted list still apply. Deborah has stuck primarily to basic shapes, supplemented with fills. Since most of the primary objects are circles, she created a blend containing thirty of them so they didn't have to be created individually with the Ellipse tool. A few blends and a special effect or two add shading and make the job go faster. In the following paragraphs I have broken this section of the drawing into four groups and presented an illustration of each with a filled, wireframe, and exploded view.

Creating the Rear Barrel Section

This part of the model uses three circles, one blend and three irregular objects to produce a form that looks like a rounded form that is changing into a hexagonal shape. It is shown in Figure 20.22. The lighting effect for the entire subject is designed to look like it is coming from just slightly higher than the object and from the left. The light gray circle just in front of the rear-most object gives the appearance of a highlight on the rim of the barrel. It is almost entirely covered by another black circle the same size. This leaves just a sliver of gray showing.

FIGURE 20.22 The rear barrel area

A smaller gray circle sits forward of the group mentioned in the last paragraph. It is filled with the same color as the outside of the blend that is wedged between it and the body of the barrel. I left the lower irregular object out of the Figure so you could see the circles better.

The Forward Threads

The front of the assembly provides a good example of how preplanning can pay off when doing this kind of work. Somebody just trying to sketch the threads and collar with ellipses and individual fills would have spent a lot more time than needed to do the same job by combining basic shapes. That is the real difference between using a paint program and a draw program: in the latter you make the objects as easily as possible and let them do the work. One of the tricks to mastering CorelDRAW is *knowing how to analyze shapes that are not totally in view.*

Figure 20.23 shows the same combination of views that I am using in most of this section: a filled section, an exploded version, and a wireframe. The only elements that are not a basic shape are the hexagonal end and three of the highlights. Keeping it simple not only reduced drawing time, but also made the drawing easier to edit and speeded up the display. The circles that form the thread can be easily created by drawing one and then copying it into the new location with either the **Place Duplicate** or **Repeat** command.

FIGURE 20.23 The threads

The black-to-gray blend on the side of the drawing sits over, but does not completely cover, a gray rectangle. The two objects create the illusion of a shift in the shape of the barrel. The rectangles surrounding the circles are filled with different grays or blacks, matched to breaks in the hex-shaped neck.

The Top Cylinder

Just above the barrel is a cylindrical section that serves as the base for the handle assembly. This area points out how you can use blends, and control objects, to shade an illustration. The blend shown at the top right corner of the exploded drawing in Figure 20.24 feathers the tone, as if a shadow were building around the curve of the cylinder. The problem with a blend is that the shape should have a sharp contour toward the front. The gray irregular object in the lower left lies over the center of the blend grouping, giving it a clean edge. Once again Deborah has used two slightly overlapping ellipses with different fills to add a highlight on the top of the structure.

Chapter 20: The Pen and Ink Style of Deborah Miller

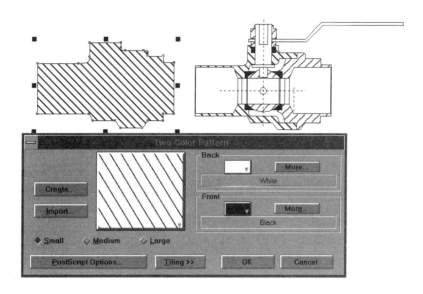

FIGURE 20.24 Forming the top cylinder

Making the Handle

The handle is one of those kinds of tasks that look pretty hard, but CorelDRAW will really do most of the work for you. The exploded and wireframe views in Figure 20.25 give away the secret: Instead of drawing all the nested rectangles by hand, use the **Extrude** special effect, break apart the combined object, and give each surface the appropriate fill or outline. Deborah added a finishing touch with two blends on the upper surfaces, one a highlight, the other creating a faint shadow.

Extrudes can be used to push out a curve into a ribbon, or a set of lines into a handle like the one in Figure 20.25. To do that requires being able to see how the final object can be pulled out of basic shapes. The best way to visualize an object is to look at the subject in two ways: as a basic wireframe and as a shaded object. Then draw the primary forms, open the **Effects** menu, and start work. These on-screen tools make these kinds of projects a lot easier than the dialog boxes found in older versions of the program.

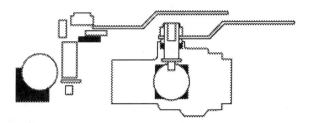

FIGURE 20.25 The extruded handle

Getting a Bit More Complicated

Above the handle is the hardware that holds it in place and limits its range. This part of the illustration requires a good bit of detail work. The small, many-faceted objects cast shadows and are made up of irregular shapes that need perspective. Figure 20.26 shows how it was done.

FIGURE 20.26 The handle hardware

Variations in fills take care of most of the shadow effects, but several objects had to be shaped to match the angle of the imaginary light source. The highlights on the edges were done with white lines. The **Perspective** effect is a handy tool when making something that has more than one visible surface.

A Few Other Possible Complications

Now that we have covered all the drawing aspects of this piece, it's time to point out a few things about technical drawing. Do you see the text below the wireframe in Figure 20.16? In most cases, these kinds of drawings have specifications for layout and how text is used. The type of font, size, and margins must meet the standard. If you are working on a project for a manual, it's a good idea to get a style sheet or sample to use as a guide.

Otherwise you may have to go back and redo all the text. This is especially true if your work includes warnings or other safety information.

JUST HOW FAR CAN YOU GO?

Deborah Miller's travel poster title, *Thailand*, was created to see how far she could push CorelDRAW on her system. "I just wanted to load up as much stuff as I could in my design and see what would happen," she said. The result is shown in the color section and below in Figure 20.27a. She won an award with her experiment, proving that fooling around can be productive. Although the file is not full of special effects, the rail fills and blends slow down systems except those with the fastest video cards.

 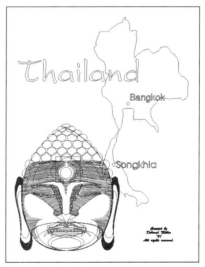

FIGURES 20.27a and b *Thailand*, in finished and wireframe form

The design is straightforward. A single rectangle forms a red backdrop to an ornately masked face. A map was added by modifying one in the clip art collection. A title in a slightly exotic typeface and a couple of place names were added to balance the layout. By now you should know enough about CorelDRAW's clip art and text functions to figure those elements out for yourself. The mask is the focus of the rest of this chapter.

The Approach

The artist mentioned during our interview that she likes to work a design from the bottom up, and this mask was done just that way, with one section resting on top of another–each adding a layer of complexity. "I generally like to draw the outline of the objects or make a sketch and work from that," she said. If we take away the fountain fills and reduce the blends to their fundamental lines, you can see just how much like a pen-and-ink drawing the mask really is. Figure 20.28 shows the final drawing of the mask filled on the left, and in wireframe on the right.

FIGURE 20.28 The finished mask

The base element is an egg shape that contains everything except the ears and the outer edges of the radial fills placed around the top (See Figure 20.29). The ears are made out of blends that have had the control object manipulated and filled separately from the rest of the blend group. Drawn on the base are two pairs of ovals that have been combined and filled. One forms the line of a chin. Over those are placed both the objects that form the mouth, and the creases at the edges of the lips. Notice how there is no real external source at this point. Deborah outlined this illustration much as she would if she were using traditional tools. Those parts of the drawing that are the same on both sides were drawn as halves and then duplicated and joined.

There are two other structures in the figure: the nose/eyes area and the shape that holds the fountain fill across the cheeks. The fill gives balance to the face. Without it, all the detail at the top would have turned the mask into a picture of somebody wearing a hat.

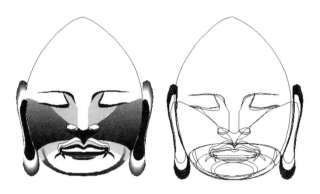

FIGURE 20.29 The foundation

The Fine Lines and Absolutes

Between the headdress and around the cheeks are a network of fine lines (see Figure 20.30). They are *not* done as a blend or using one of the program's repeat techniques. These were drawn by hand with the **Pencil** tool. First one side was created, and then duplicated, mirrored, and placed. Although most people use CorelDRAW with a mouse, Deborah uses a graphics tablet. It is a pad and a stylus combination. The action is a lot more like a pen or pencil. "Since I rough things out right on the screen, the mouse is just too coarse for me," she remarked, "and it doesn't feel natural."

FIGURE 20.30 Lining the face

Most tablets can be set in two different modes, relative or absolute. The normal Windows mouse works in relative mode. One inch of movement of the mouse is not equal to 1 inch on the CorelDRAW page. Most mice today have a ballistic feature. If you make small movements, the mouse pointer makes a small movement. When you move it fast, the rate of travel on the screen is much faster. Try signing your name with a mouse. Would your bank honor the check? If it looks good, either your mouse technique is very good or your handwriting is very bad. With the right driver a tablet offers absolute tracking. The motion of the stylus is exactly the same as the tracking on the page on the screen. The hardware section has more information about tablets, including the ones we used for some of the drawings done in this book.

The Headdress and a Bit About Style

The area above the eyes is the part of the drawing that can really slow down the computer, since it contains a large number of circles with radial fills. The lines in this section were drawn over another solid object, which adds substance to the space on either side of the gem in the center of the forehead. The edges of the circles holding the radial fills, like the solid shape outlining the jaw, keep the masked face from having a sharp, unnatural line around it. This illustration is also shown in the full color section. Look at it there and see how the combination of shapes and colors is used to balance the work. Consider how it would have looked if the background of the page was in a deep blue and the radial fills in a silver color. Imagine the face without either the cheek fill or the blends on the ears (see Figure 20.31).

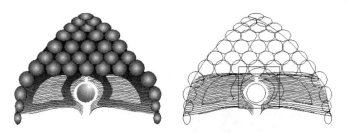

FIGURE 20.31 The headdress

There is no one "right" way to do most drawings. As an artist works, he or she develops tricks and a way of seeing, which over the years develop into a style.

A photography teacher I once had remarked that it took ten years of practice to have a style of your own. "The first decade is spent learning your tools and evaluating other people," he said. In a sense we never have a finished style, as long as we are willing to see the world around us and to learn.

CHAPTER 21
The Spirit of Jan Selman

ABOUT THE ARTIST

Although many graphic artists are adopting new computer-based tools with delight, acceptance by fine artists is still more the exception than the rule. One (successful) exception is Jan Selman. A resident of Cape Cod, she has been creating and selling work done on a PC. Although much of her art focuses on landscapes, she enjoys experimenting and working with new techniques, including creating vector and bitmap images.

Her work has appeared in several one-woman shows in her native New England and in London and is on display as part of permanent collections in two local museums. She trained on a National Scholastic Arts Scholarship at the School of the Museum of the Fine Arts in Boston and is affiliated with five galleries in the Northeast and Florida.

"I approach CorelDRAW! as a new box of tools," she said during our interview. "The key is to learn what the tools can do; it is another kind of media." She says that when ones creates art, you have to see the image first; then explore it with your tools. As she explores, a goal is to experiment with the tools in new ways. One of her favorite techniques with CorelDRAW! is to start a drawing in crayons and then to scan and manipulate the image before bringing it into CorelDRAW!. Although most users think of tiled bitmap fills, she sees them as an interesting and too often undervalued part of the program.

THE SPIRIT OF BEING AN ARTIST

Jan's poster shown in this chapter was prepared for an art exhibit at an area studio. It is a good example of how she uses tiled fills as the focus of a design. It is also an interesting blend of graphic elements and decorative type. Jan wanted to produce a poster that showed the artist as someone who is often hidden from public view. "The art speaks for the artist. We are generally separated from our audience as persons," she said, "We are viewed through our work.... So I wanted to create something that said, 'Here is the artist coming out and being seen.'"

The poster appears to be full of faces. Actually it is full of copies of one face, manipulated and duplicated several different ways. The variation and placement draw the viewer into the design.

The Approach

Since her poster would represent the display of fine art, Jan wanted it to have a fine-art quality. She wanted it to give the impression of the artists coming out into the open, being seen through the display of their creations. It had to appeal to the eye, yet the image could not outweigh the type–the message had to be read if people were to come to the show. To be a success, the design had to have a balance between the images and the text. Figure 21.1 shows the drawing slightly rearranged to make it easier to see the individual elements.

Chapter 21: The Spirit of Jan Selman   715

FIGURE 21.1 A closer look at the design

The Face

"I started with the face," Jan noted. "I drew it in crayon; then I scanned it, brought into a paint program, and changed the contrast to bring out the texture." The face is used in four of the five nontext elements found in the drawing. Figure 21.2 shows the large face that is located in the top center of the poster. This is the starting point for all but one of the nontext elements. It is a color bitmap.

FIGURE 21.2 The face

I increased the brightness and contrast a bit so it would be easier to see in a black-and-white reproduction. The dot pattern was created the same way by the artist. She manipulated the contrast to give the cheeks a patina like that of beaten metal. The color bitmap version of the face is used twice on the page, and they sit in the middle of the drawing from back to front. Both are partially hidden by the twisted object in front of them.

The Backdrop

To carry her idea of the artist emerging through the work, Jan used the face as the basis for the background by incorporating it into a two-color fill with large tiles. The deep ruby and black color combination almost obscures the face and provides a rich tone that highlights the golden face and compliments the rose color of the twisted form in the foreground. Figure 21.3a shows the complete tile. As you can see, it is not just a single face, but a pattern, shaped to fit the dimensions of the underlying page. Figure 21.3b is a screen shot of the CorelDRAW! 3.0 **Two-color Pattern** dialog box used to set up the tile. Rather than use the default **Small**, **Medium**, or **Large** options, she uses a custom size based on the dimensions of the bitmap.

 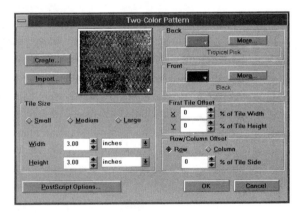

FIGURES 21.3a and b The background tiled bitmap and its dialog box

The Artist As Sculpture

In the beginning of this chapter I mentioned that Jan Selman likes to use tools in new ways. This serves three functions. If you can successfully push any tool beyond its normal limits, you learn a lot about how it works. In the case of artistic expression you can also find new techniques, and that can give your work a unique style.

The show the poster announced contained a collection of works in different media by several artists. Some of the pieces were sculpture; others included abstracts, computer-generated art, and portraits. Jan carried examples of them all into her design. The bitmap is a portrait that is worked into a computer-generated abstract. Creating sculpture is not a normal feature listed on the box that CorelDRAW! is shipped in, but that's where a little creative license with tools comes in handy. Figure 21.4 shows two views of the twisted form that runs down the center of the page.

FIGURE 21.4 The sculpture

The left side of Figure 21.4 shows the object as it looks in the poster, with its envelope visible. The face is another version of the bitmap, repeated using a different pattern and two-color fill. The basic shape was originally a rectangle that covered the entire page. Several different envelopes were used to twist the object into its current form. The design is that of an abstract sculpture, using the face of an artist as the material. Placed as it is, the faces in the color portraits are both partially hidden. The artist is hiding but is still seen in the work.

Adjusting the Tiles

The faces in the sculpture are more square than the others in the drawing and seem to have less detail. The face was modified again for this fill. The shape of the object itself is replacing the contours of the face as the representation of the artist. The increase in contrast makes the object a dominant focus of the poster. The shape is used to pull the eyes over the text of the show announcement.

Figure 21.5 is the dialog box that was used to specify the tile settings for the object (since the drawing was created in CorelDRAW! 3.0, we show an earlier form of this dialog box). Once again a custom fill is used. Compare these to the ones shown in Figure 21.3b. By adjusting the aspect ratio (the ratio between the vertical and horizontal measurements) the bitmap fill was adjusted to repeat with a smaller pattern that is a little taller than it is wide.

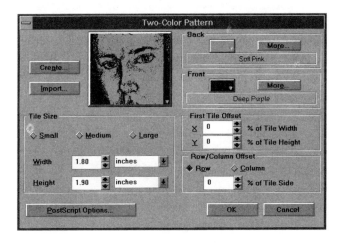

FIGURE 21.5 The sculpture's dialog box

Accenting the Announcement

The dark tones of the poster art would make it impossible to read black type placed in this illustration, so the white type is no surprise. But the mottled appearance of the background would distract the eye. Look at Figure 21.6. The white-outlined form with the black fill sits partially covered by the sculpture, which I have also outlined in white, but without a fill. This element gives extra definition to the start of the body text, making it easier to read and helping it to stand out from the rest of the objects on the page.

FIGURE 21.6 Adding a little definition

Setting the Type

Having a dramatic design gets the viewer's attention, but the type has to get the message across. Again, the font must match the message, and type has to be easy to read, The tone of the poster focuses on contemporary fine art, so the text must have a contemporary flair. All the text in the poster is set in Bahamas (Bauhaus ©ITC). The majority is Bahamas Normal, except for the Open House and Time listings. They were done in Bahamas Heavy.

Once a typeface was selected it had to be arranged on the page. A complicated poster such as this offers a layout challenge: The text has to fit the form of the design but still must make sense. In most cases the artist will decide in advance where the type will have to fit and then will adjust the design to fit. Magazines work this way: The artist or photographer is told that an image must be vertical and be able to be cropped in a certain way and that room must be left for the text elements. In this poster there are seven type elements in four groups. They are shown in Figure 21.7, with part of the body text omitted.

FIGURE 21.7 The type

The Headline

The title of the show serves as the main element, announcing the subject. The main headline needs to sum up the focus of the poster and to spark enough interest to make the viewers read further. If they say, "Oh, what a nice poster," and then move on, the message is wasted. Jan used a combination of design elements in setting this title. She created an outline font by using no fill for the text and gave it a two-point white outline to set it off from the underlying art. The letter spacing and leading are reduced, fitting the type into the curves between the cheek of the large face and the bow in the sculpture. The lines of those two objects draw the eye down the type.

The Announcement

On the right side of the page is the actual announcement, containing three elements: the headline; the body text, which tells about the show and artists; and the text giving the hours of the show. The headline is identical to the body text, except that it is larger. The first two elements are kerned just like the Title headline, continuing the modernistic look. Since there is more body text and it is smaller, the lines have more leading. As I mentioned earlier, a black form was used to help make the body text easier to see.

The Open House notice is set in Bahamas Heavy, and the kerning is more open. Using tight kerning with a heavy style of type would have been unattractive and more difficult to read. By using a more open style and placing the type by itself, the information stands out and is easy to find.

The Location

The last section of type contains the name and address of the studio. This block is really two objects and is normally spaced. Although the text runs a bit over the lower section of the sculpture fill, it is still readable. It might have needed a darker background if it was a longer block of text. By separating it from the rest of the type, Jan got around that problem. All the type was placed both to follow the flow of the design and to help reinforce it.

NOTE CorelDRAW! 2.0 files containing type may not load properly if artistic text strings approach the maximum size limit. Jan Selman's poster is a good example. The body text was created in two blocks in CorelDRAW! 2.0. The newer versions of the program have different text-handling code that supports TrueType. In some cases the TrueType font will be more complicated and not all the type will load. There are three options if you run into this problem: (1) You can use version 2.0 to edit the file. (2) You can copy and break the text into smaller blocks (all the text is still in the file; it just can't be displayed in one block). (3) You can set the **CORELDRW.INI** file to recognize the older WFN font. There is more information in the CorelDRAW! on-line help documents.

DESIGNING POSTERS

This chapter has focused on a poster that works—one that attracts a viewer, gets its message across, and pleases the eye with its appearance. Good posters always look simple, but as with a paper clip, it takes a mind with an idea to produce the invention. Some basic rules can help when working up a design. The following list summarizes them.

- **Communicate!** Above all else a poster has to get its message across. Anything that detracts from that premise reduces its value. When planning a design think of what you are trying to say and what your theme is. Jan Selman started with the knowledge of her subject and then developed the theme. That was the basis for her design. Your image must deal with the topic; don't let it wander.
- **Get Right to the Point.** Plan the words carefully. You don't have much time to get the message out. A long discussion will never be read, and if you wander, the viewer will stop paying attention. Keep the elements simple, clearly stating the concept.

- **Match the Image to the Message.** Jan Selman used art to give the message about the art show. Does your image communicate your point? What format will you be using? Large posters are seen from farther away than small ones. Is the image compatible with the size? In some cases a basic design may be used in different ways for different display formats.
- **Interest the Viewer.** Look at the design from the viewpoint of a passer-by. Would you give it a second look? Would you stop to read the text? It takes a combination of imagination and skill in implementing an idea to make a poster that works.
- **Keep It Clean.** Use a planned approach when laying out the design elements. Although some effects may make the poster more eye-catching, they may also make it harder to read or understand.

Keep It Simple

The basics of all good design involve a focused approach to the project. Just as with speaking, you have to know what you want to say before you say it. Posters are a popular form of communication and even decoration. The one we examined in this chapter was an Art Show winner because of a good design that used a theme that was well executed. When you start working on a poster (or any CorelDRAW! project), consider the work's purpose and the intended audience.

CHAPTER 22
Tim Moran: Getting Technical

A technical drawing

ABOUT THE ARTIST

Not every award winner in the Corel Art Contest is a trained professional artist. Tim Moran does illustration work, but he trained as an accountant. Today he splits his time between accounting and illustrating for a sporting goods firm. He uses CorelDRAW for a variety of tasks, including advertising, forms design, flyers, and catalogs.

"I have been using CorelDRAW for about three years," he noted during a recent interview. "It just sort of grew into part of my job because I took the time to learn the program. I really like using it. Doing my accounting on the computer gives me time to draw." Tim started doing computer graphics with the simple charts offered in the older DOS-based spreadsheets; then he migrated to paint programs. "I wanted to do screen printing for ads," he said. "We produce thirty-page catalogs, and CorelDRAW seemed a really great improvement."

THE APPROACH

With the installation of a new telephone system at work Tim was asked to produce a template that could be used to define how the various keys on the individual units would be allocated. Since there were a few tricks with CorelDRAW that he wanted to experiment with, Tim decided to create a technical illustration of the device rather than a simple schematic.

At first glance Tim's drawing of the telephone looks like it uses blends to achieve the smooth lines and detailed shading. In fact, the only blends in the entire illustration are the ones used for the cord. The project took about two and a half hours to complete, the shortest time for any of the works reviewed in this section of the book. Figure 22.1 shows the final drawing in a wireframe view.

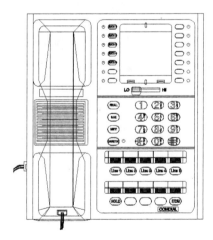

FIGURE 22.1 Wireframe view

In photographic illustration, like that used for catalogs, you want to be able see all the details without harsh shadows. To achieve this effect, photographers often use a tent. This is usually a fabric hood made of thin white material. Lighting is directed on the subject from outside the tent; then the picture is taken through a small hole. The result is very diffused lighting and faint shadows, like the kind found outdoors on an overcast day. Highlights are also subdued, so there are no glare spots, and colors are more saturated. This is a handy technique for making pictures of jewelry and glass objects. The same kind of light can be simulated with CorelDRAW to produce a realistic drawing that does not have dark shadows. That is the effect produced in this illustration. When you are trying to achieve the same result, look at pictures in catalogs or remember how things look on cloudy days as a model.

To get the exact scale, Tim used a ruler and measured the phone. "Then I set up a grid and drew the sections to the exact proportions," he remarked. While working he used the program's grid and rulers, changing the units of measure as the project progressed. The combination let him get a one-to-one reproduction. "In the beginning I used inches; then I moved down to smaller sizes. The final stage was at 1/20th of an inch. After everything was done I grouped and resized the final form to fit a standard page," he explained. That way the finished product was an exact scale model of the original.

The Telephone Base

Tim started by drawing three rectangles. The one on the bottom was drawn to the actual outer dimensions of the phone. Two more resting on either side of that object contain fountain fills that produce the impression of rounded edges. At this point the grid was in half-inch units, making it easy to size the outline. The status bar also showed the size of each object as it was scaled. The fills are based on gray scales, with slight variations in the fountain fills giving the illusion of depth. This is the method used throughout the project to give depth to the image.

The next step was to define the major components on the telephone's base. The handset receptacles, speaker, button pad, auto-dialer, and light bars were roughed-out with rounded rectangles and lines. This arrangement let Tim get the basic elements in place without cluttering up the page with detailed sections of the drawing.

The Buttons and Light Bar

Figures 22.2a and 22.2b are close-ups of the buttons and light bar on the bottom right half of the unit. The buttons were simple, made from rectangles that were rounded with the **Shape** tool and duplicated. Then they were each filled and the lower one was offset to produce a shadow. The grid was adjusted to a smaller size to make it easy to place the buttons in the right spot. The text on the buttons was a bit harder to place. Tim set the **Nudge** command at its lowest setting, 0.1 point. After placing the object on the button, he nudged it into place.

There are a lot of buttons, and a lot of letters. The most exacting part of the project, however, was the light bars. "The phone had lights that were made of plastic with a diamond pattern. I needed to make it look like they were raised and that light could shine through them," Tim said.

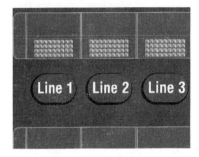 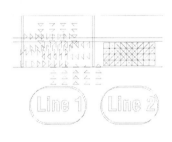

FIGURES 22.2a and b The light bar and buttons, filled and in wireframe

The buttons are made of rows of interlocking triangles that were drawn freehand. Four copies were made with the **Place Duplicate** command and then joined as a group. Once a set was made it was filled with one of four different uniform shades. The groups were assembled into the grid that makes up a light. Figure 22.2b shows the wireframe of one of the groups broken apart.

The Hi-Lo Slider

Above the touch-tone dialing buttons is a slider bar. It required designing a set of elements that would simulate a raised knob, the slot, and embossed letters. Figure 22.3 shows a filled view on top and a wireframe below. The slot was produced by using two rectangles. The upper one is narrow and filled with black to give depth to the side and add a shadow. The bottom one serves as the base of the slot and has a lighter fill, as if light was falling in on top of it.

The button itself is the first example of a technique used several times in the handset, the beveled edge. The top of the button has four rectangles. The one on top has been rounded with the **Shape** tool and given a very slight fountain fill that gets lighter as it proceeds toward the bottom of the page. The others were node-edited to slope into the top and are filled with black.

Two labels are attached to this group. The lower one has a lighter gray fill, making the set look like letters that are raised up from the surface.

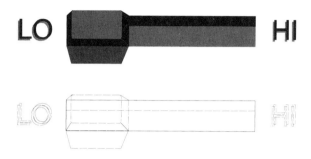

FIGURE 22.3 The volume slider

The LED Lights

Along the sides of several buttons are small red LED lights to indicate when a line is in use or an option is selected. This set of objects is hard to see in the black-and-white version of the drawing. Figure 22.4 shows the structure of one of the LEDs in wireframe under a filled version. Tim used a red radial fill inside a circle using the CMYK process model and reduced the black level slightly as the fill moved toward the center. A small white irregular shape was set near the center to add a highlight. The rim of the circle was given a thick black outline to set the LED off from the background.

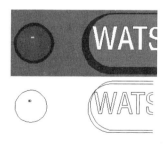

FIGURE 22.4 A LED assembly

The Speaker and Number Listing Cover

Underneath the handset is a speaker phone and a cover for labeling a phone number. The base of the speaker assembly is composed of two rounded rectangles. Both have been given a uniform fill and grouped. The lower one has a darker fill to give the impression that the speaker has been recessed into the body of the telephone.

Above that is a series of long narrow rectangles. In the real phone they are just depressions in the plastic cover. Inside some of them are slots for the combination microphone and speaker. In the drawing Tim has used two alternating series of objects to illustrate them. One series is a set of plain narrow rectangles, the second is an identical object with a black line inside it. A plain rectangle was drawn, filled, duplicated, and spaced the right distance from the other one. A line was drawn inside the lower one, and all three objects were grouped. The **Place Duplicate** and **Repeat** commands were used to create the rest of them. The finished assembly was grouped and placed in position. Then a simple rectangle was added above it to represent the clear plastic plate used to cover a label with the phone number. The **Align** command was used to center it over the speaker.

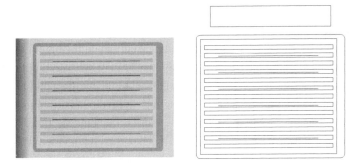

FIGURES 22.5a and b The speaker grill and number plate

The Handset

The other major component of the drawing is the handset on the left side of the telephone. In the real phone, a pair of recesses provides a resting place for the handset. Producing each one in the drawing required drawing four shapes: a rounded rectangle to enclose the entire group and three irregular shapes to mimic the curves and shading of the receptacle.

Chapter 22: Tim Moran: Getting Technical

Next, a long rectangle was created to serve as the back of the handset, and another rectangle drawn outside of it that would produce the outline of the finished group. Tim converted the second rectangle to curves; then he edited it with the Shape tool. The object was bent in at two points in the middle on each side to form the final shape.

To get the shading, additional objects were drawn, converted to curves, and fitted to the outline of the handset. Lighter tones give the final product the illusion of roundness. The final touches were adding the jacks and a bit of cord to both the base and the handset. For each one two small boxes were made, filled, and placed together. Then two freehand lines were blended to form the cord. Figures 22.6a and 22.6b show the handset assembly.

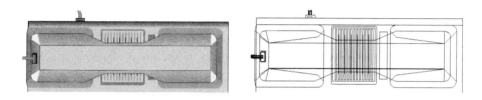

FIGURES 22.6a and b The handset

Chapter Summary

Although CorelDRAW does not offer all the fancy tools of CAD-type programs, it can be used for technical drawing. The easier interface reduces the time required to learn it. CorelDRAW 4.0 and 5.0 added several enhancements that would have made Tim's project a lot easier. Even though he did not use dimension lines, they could have been placed on the page as references. The Layers function is handy for grouping like objects and producing uniform fills. Tim Moran's work shows us how fountain fills and attention to detail can be used to produce lifelike illustrations.

CHAPTER 23

The Detailed World of Chris Purcell

THE ANATOMY OF A DRAWING

The incredible detail of Chris Purcell's *Green Lizard* grabs your attention. Within this one drawing are enough elements for several illustrations, many hours of painstaking placement, and many little tricks hidden among the lines and curves. Chris was kind enough to send four samples of his work for inclusion in this book, including the *Green Lizard* (Second Place, Plants and Animals, 1992), *Butterflies* (Award of Merit, 1991), and *Systems* (First Place, Logos, March 1992).

About the Artist

Chris Purcell has been working with CorelDRAW for three and a half years and with computer graphics for about four years. An artist at Compaq Computer, he had tried several packages before settling down with CorelDRAW. Chris noted that the other programs were either too slow or lacked the sophistication he demanded.

He earned a four-year college degree in scientific and technical illustration in his native England and has been working in the field since graduating in 1980. To improve his skills with CorelDRAW he often creates large personal projects that push the program to its limits. The *Green Lizard* is an example. He estimates the illustration took over 70 hours to complete. It was done before the release of Version 3.0, so the blends were created without dynamically-linked groups. Thus he not only worked without the contour and powerlines of later versions, but even lacked access to the Layers features or Roll-up menus. But the *Green Lizard* would have been a significant project even in the latest release.

"I try to keep working on things like that," he noted during an interview. "That's the only way to really learn. You have to set something up and then figure out how to do it." Although the casual viewer might assume that many of the smaller parts of the lizard's body were done using automatic functions, most elements were either done individually, were copied and modified, or used special-purpose blends. "I used lots of blends," Chris said, "I had to plan them very carefully, and then get them into just the right shape. If I goofed I had to start the blend all over again. The design would have been a lot easier with the new blend controls and layers," he added.

Planning the Lizard

One of the goals was to make the final product as accurate as possible, so Chris started by creating a hand-drawn master to work from and then imported the image as a bitmap into CorelDRAW. It was not used as part of the actual work or Auto-traced; it was used simply as a template and later removed. A master curve is set along the reptile's back and provides a reference for joining the two sections, the skeleton and the filled body. Figure 23.1 shows the major sections of the drawing. Since the file contains a large number of objects and curves, he had to make sure to reduce the complexity of the illustration by combining groups as he worked. The final CDR file is larger than 410K.

Chapter 23: The Detailed World of Chris Purcell

FIGURE 23.1 The basic forms

Converting the file to an EPS format for the chapter's opening drawing took so long that the Windows Program Manager thought the CorelDRAW filter had crashed. It took a little over three minutes before any translation activity began. Printing to a fast PostScript printer took over twenty-five minutes. Completely detailing all the objects in such a complex illustration would be too involved, so we will concentrate on the design features and how Chris used his electronic tools. To save on space, the body of the lizard will be rotated on the page in many of the following figures.

The Primary Lines

This drawing has a number of interesting design elements. To get the full effect you should take a look at the full-color plate printed in this book. The way the tail wraps around the left side of the body and points back toward the head, combined with the lizard's S-shaped posture, serves two functions: The body takes up less space, since it is curved; and the outline is a pleasing shape that draws the eye back into the form. The S-shape is a classic design in composition. The shadows are positioned as if there was a light source above and to the left of the body. This not only adds a feeling of depth, but also accentuates the folds in the skin and torso.

The Shadows

The shadows underneath the body emphasize the lines of the main drawing. They are contained in two groups, which were made late in the creation of the drawing. Figure 23.2 shows both, with the skeletal portion reduced for better viewing. Look at the foreleg claws and notice how they have been edited to mimic the effects of real lighting. This has also been done with the folds of the skin, since the angle of the lighting would not cast a perfect copy of the animal. Other shading objects were placed on the ribs, skull, and bones to provide definition. Once the individual elements in a section were completed, they were combined for greater simplicity.

Drawing the Head

Most animals have two sides that are basically the same. One side can be formed, copied, and modified to create the other half. Chris added more challenge with his combination view, since each side is unique. Each twist and turn in the torso requires different handling. On one side of the lizard the shapes and fills deal with bones; on the other, with scales and folds.

Figure 23.3 is a composite view of the lizard's head, created to show how it was produced. The center shows the combined objects as they are in the final drawing. To the outside of that are the wireframes and then a set of partially exploded views. The fills vary in color from start to finish, giving very subtle shifts in shading. The left side of the head is formed by placing a series of fountain-filled objects over the outline of the skull. The eye is formed the same way. The right side is composed mainly of blends fitted together like a puzzle.

FIGURE 23.2 Casting a shadow

Chapter 23: The Detailed World of Chris Purcell 735

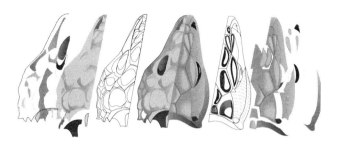

FIGURE 23.3 Exploded view of the head

Defining the Skeletal Structures

The bony structures on the left side of the body are a complex collection of shapes. The drawing on the left in Figure 23..4 shows how the lower leg looks; an exploded view is shown on the right. Chris often uses one shape for the form and another to give the shading. Some objects are blends that give the appearance of curves, or sloping surfaces. The ribs at the top of the figure and the joints in the toes are good examples. Unfilled shapes and open paths add sharp edges or breaks in the contours of a bone. Again he combined objects as he worked to reduce the complexity.

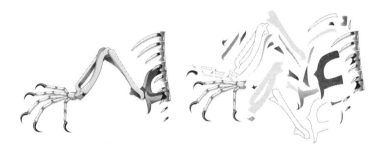

FIGURE 23.4 The bony structures

Creating the Filled Body

The platform for the right side of the body is a solid shape filled with green that runs from the base of the neck to the start of the tail. On top of that is a combination of blends and freehand lines that create the muscles and scales. Over that, another set of shapes gives the lizard his stripes and spots. If you look just below the bend of the knee there is an open space where the only fill is the underlying green of the outline object.

As the blends on the right lower leg are taken apart we see how real the muscles look. A broad series of lines along the torso and within the leg are contoured just like actual muscle. Chris admitted that his training in scientific drawing might have had something to do with this. "I wanted to make it as accurate as possible," he said. The fills vary in tone to shade the figure, and one blend placed just above the fill object produces a shadow on the lower part of the leg.

Blends and some freehand lines are used above the muscles to texture the scales. Figure 23.5 shows the lower right leg and the structures just mentioned. The bitmap cannot compete with the color plate for detail. A series of light-green filled shapes is used along the curve of the leg to add markings; another group runs on the lower edge of the torso to define the scales of the underbelly.

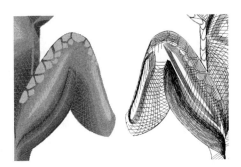

FIGURE 23.5 Shaping the body with blends

One of the most difficult objects to draw with traditional tools is the hand. A close look at how the lizard's claws are formed on the right side shows how Chris approached a very similar task. Remember that each leg and foot of this drawing is different. He could not simply copy one and flip it to get the objects for the other side. This step took a lot of time.

Figure 23.6 shows exploded views of the right foot. The top one is filled; the other shows just the outlines. On the left is a bitmap screen capture of the same area. The lowest level is the base color and shape. Over that the artist has placed a series of three objects to give the area the right look: first, filled shapes, to shade the sides; then short lines drawn with the Pencil tool to break up the toes; and finally, curves to give shape.

As with the other claws there are two objects: one for the base shape and another for the highlight. Now look at the area above the foot as it joins to the leg. A set of objects has been created to form a transition. Some illustrators would have just placed a line at this joint, but in this drawing a blend produces a gradual shift from the dun-colored foot to the green of the leg. Laid over that is a grid of lines under another filled shape. A similar approach was used for the upper right foot.

FIGURE 23.6 The right foot in detail

Forming the Tail

The final stop on our tour of this drawing is the design of the tail structures. There are two sets, one for the spine and another for the external segments. Here was a section where some automation came with the use of the Repeat command. The objects are simple closed shapes with fountain fills. The outline width is reduced as the lines progress and the elements get smaller. In Figure 23.7 the tail has been moved, rotated, and ungrouped so that we can see how the work was done. Some of the segments have been taken apart and unfilled to provide detail. To get them to fit, the spine was also resized.

Summary

The *Green Lizard* is an excellent example of how CorelDRAW can be used to produce very complex and detailed drawings. It also points out that you have to plan a drawing for two reasons: to get the look you want, and to get it printed. The CDR file goes through the laser printer without a problem, but the exported EPS is another matter. If Chris had not used these planned techniques as he worked to reduce complexity, he might not have been able to get a hard copy.

Another complex consideration is screen performance. The *Green Lizard* is a beautiful illustration, full of color and varied tones. The blends and fountain fills used to portray the subject use a lot of resources. If you want to do this kind of work and get home at a reasonable hour, make sure your computer and display adapter are top of the line–just like Chris Purcell's artwork.

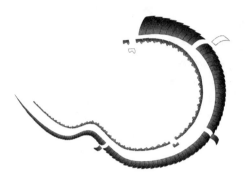

FIGURE 23.7 The tail segments

BUTTERFLIES

Compared to the drawing you just looked at, Butterflies is rather simple but elegantly designed. It contains a principal figure that has been duplicated several times and some converted text. Just as with his Green Lizard, there is a lot to learn from this artist. Figure 23.8 shows the finished work that won an Award of Merit in the first Corel art contest. It is included on the Corel Artshow CD-ROM disc and was Chris Purcell's first major CorelDRAW project.

The Approach

The body of the butterfly is the same on both sides. Consequently, only one side had to be drawn; then a mirror image was duped and placed on the other side. Fountain fills were used to get the colors. A simpler copy of the main figure was used for the four smaller butterflies fluttering behind the text. A basic roman-style serif font was used as the basis for the banner at the top.

Chapter 23: The Detailed World of Chris Purcell

FIGURE 23.8 Butterflies

If you look at the picture closely, you'll notice there are no shadows under the wings of the miniatures, just the central object. This serves to lift its wings off the page and adds depth to the picture. Look even closer and you can see that the shadow of the big butterfly is under the banner text. The wedge shape of the active drawing area, the angles of the smaller insects, and the lines of the type keep the eyes focused on the page, rather than leading them out.

True Design Is a Work in Progress

Talk to Chris Purcell; he will tell you that the flow of the drawing was not planned. He kept working with it until it looked the way he wanted. The best tool for any artist is the human eye. The essence of a design comes as the person works with the image, not out of the original thought. Chris started by just drawing a butterfly. "That was okay, but it needed something else," he said. Then he added the type, but that element needed some balance. "So I put in the smaller butterflies," he added. "That is the neat thing about CorelDRAW. You can keep working with it. If you are using traditional tools it's much harder to experiment. You don't produce more work; you produce better work."

The Foundation Elements

Underneath the colorful wings of the large butterfly are two filled shapes: one is the drop shadow, and the other is a dark backdrop for the wings. Figure 23.9 shows these two structures, but it can't show the black-to-royal-blue linear fill in the colored original. Fine details and gentle changes like that add to the appeal of the picture. The two shapes are basically the same curve, but the full outline has about twenty more nodes than the fifty-four in the dark outline of the wings.

FIGURE 23.9 The foundation

Adding the First Wings

The next step was to create one of the top wings. It was copied and flipped to make the other side. As with the *Green Lizard*, the drawing was simplified by combining and grouping objects as the work progressed. The primary colored elements of the wing are a combination of lines and shapes filled with a series of linear fountain fills. Chris noted that if he was working on this project today, he might have used blends for some of the objects. However, he was just starting to experiment with CorelDRAW. The lower section of one was completed next and then copied.

Figure 23.10 shows a filled version of the right wing on the left. On the right, the left wing is shown. The broad line with the calligraphic effect at the top is a highlight on the upper curve of the wing. It and the thin colored lines that vein the panels break up the large fills.

The linear fills in the main panels are individually set, with different angles and colors that almost look like the entire set of wings had been given one radial fill. But a radial fill could not have duplicated the feathered appearance. The T-shaped lines that run between the panels have a combination of linear fountain fills on the top and a solid fill on the bottom set.

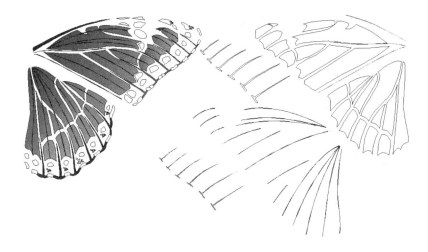

FIGURE 23.10 Drawing the wings

The White Markings

The darkly-filled outline serves as a backdrop for the white markings of the butterflies. Figure 23.11 shows the corner of the lower left wing. As you can see, each varies just a bit from the others. There are three combined groups of markings: the lower edge, the small dots, and the large inner ovals. The basic shape for each was created and then copied and modified in place.

FIGURE 23.11 The white markings on the left lower wing

The Layers feature that was introduced with CorelDRAW 3.0 would have been a handy tool for this task. A grid could have been used by using a special layer for each group, so that moving them out of the way or combining them would have been much easier. Naming layers is an easy way to keep track of sections of a drawing.

Drawing the Head, Thorax, and Abdomen

The central portion of the butterfly is not seated on the outline form, and is slightly larger than the space left for it between the wings. Once again the objects are single elements created using uniform and fountain fills. Figure 23.12 shows the entire structure on the left and an exploded view on the right. The eyes have three elements—the main orb and two highlights. As in Chris's drawing of the lizard, a basic form is overlaid with highlights to provide depth and to reinforce the outlines.

The two large dark-reddish objects, which are the outermost elements of the exploded view, make up the bulk of the abdomen. They are the base for the more detailed objects placed over them. The fill shows through as a series of bands down the body–saving several steps.

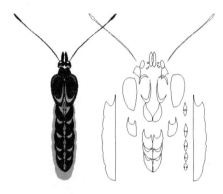

FIGURE 23.12 The body

Text—The Real Complication

The most mathematically demanding part of the entire drawing is the block of text that has been converted to curves. The modification of the letters adds a lot to the design and is not hard to accomplish. But the conversions to curves adds a lot of nodes to the final file. You'll return to that after you look at the letters.

The characters are set in Unicorn, Corel's variation of University Roman, a decorative typeface resembling an ornate Times Roman font. Figure 23.13 shows three samples of type: The top is unaltered Unicorn, the second shows the converted letters from the drawing, and the third is plain New Times Roman. The three blocks have been sized so that they are the same width. The top two lines are also the same height. You can see that the third line is smaller. If it had been made just as high as the ones above, it would have been 50 percent longer than the rest.

Chris changed the slope of some of the serifs and extended the R underneath the following letter. Then he gave the block a fountain fill that highlighted the tones in the butterflies. Finally, he kerned some of the characters and stretched it until the block was just a little wider than the outstretched wings of the big butterfly and he placed it under the antennae.

FIGURE 23.13 The converted text with samples

Is There a Problem?

The text looks pleasing and adds a lot more to the design than the same letters would if they had not been converted. The problem comes only when you export the design or send it to the printer. If your output device or target program does not have the resources to read the file, it will fail to load or print. The CorelDRAW.INI file has a setting that can help get the file printed–but a good bit more slowly. I ran into that problem with a high-quality PostScript device that has a dedicated processor and 12 megabytes of RAM. Once I adjusted the setting, things went fine, but the drawing printed very, very slowly. Complicated files can cause delays on a network. Another solution to the problem of printing complicated files is to turn on the **Auto Increase Flatness** option located in the **Print** dialog box. This will keep reducing the complexity of curves in a file until it prints. If you have a lot of cusps in your drawing, this setting may degrade quality. It works better with some files than with others, so you have to experiment.

In most cases your files will print just fine. Make sure that Windows, CorelDRAW, and your hardware are set up properly! See the sections on installation and configuration later in this book. CorelDRAW is a very powerful application. It uses a lot of resources. The wrong setting can eat up memory or drag out file operations. A few minutes of study can save hours of frustration.

Sometimes it's your hardware, not the program or Windows. Many older PostScript printers don't have enough memory or programming to handle the more complex features available in CorelDRAW. If you have a lot of trouble with output, contact your printer dealer. You might need to upgrade the printer's ROM to a newer version.

Butterflies in the Background

The last design element is the placement of four small copies of the butterfly behind the text. Chris told me he added the letters because the drawing needed something besides just one insect. Once the letters had been altered, he felt there was something missing. Placing the new objects added a sense of balance and improved the ability of the illustration to hold the viewer's eye. When they reached their decision, the judges probably took into account the attention given to the overall effect of the picture. Figure 23.14 shows the placement behind the outline of the letters.

FIGURE 23.14 The final touch

BUILDING A GOOD FOUNDATION

Most award-winning CorelDRAW artists display a sense of depth and understand the appearance of good lighting in their work. Chris Purcell won a monthly First Place award in the Logos category with his design entitled *Systems*. It uses a combination of drop shadows (somewhat of a trademark of his) along with fills that resemble glowing coals inside extruded objects, to give the work the appearance of rising off the page. A modernistic tile backdrop adds to the effect.

The image was created for Compaq Systems' Software Engineering Conference. "I wanted to design something that was more than just a pretty logo," Chris said. "The hands represent the synergy of the engineers working together." The base is a CPU chip, and the tiled design stands for the circuitry. "The idea is that one empowers the other. The circle in the center of the hands is the software, a disk if you will," he said.

FIGURE 23.15 Systems: The complete drawing

The Backdrop

The base of the graphic is composed of seven objects. Four are rectangles of the same size, the basic shapes easily made with the *Place Duplicate* command. Setting them in two sets, 45 degrees off from each other, was just as simple with the *Rotate* transformation.

After they were arranged the tile design was drawn with the Pencil tool, duplicated and rotated with the *Repeat* command, and placed on top of the second rectangle. Figure 23.16 shows the completed backdrop. One of the tile shapes was extracted, enlarged, and rotated into the center of the outlines on the right side.

FIGURE 23.16 The backdrop

There are subtle differences in the outlines of the shapes in this drawing. Chris used a series of different calligraphic settings in the elements to create minor variations in the appearance of the object. Once again there is the attention to fine detail. Figure 23.17 shows the settings in the *Outline Pen* dialog box that were used with the tiles. The pen settings for the hands were also tailored, producing different highlights in their edges.

The outline of one hand was drawn and then copied, flipped, and mirrored. Once the pair was fitted together it was duplicated three times and arranged in the pattern on the top. The cool blue fill was used to contrast with both the muted red of the circles outline and their bright red fill.

The extrusion of the hands is outlined to give it added depth and is filled with a radial fill resembling the glow of a fire, to symbolize the creative energy needed to create new computer systems. The linking of the hands and the interweaving of the different elements represent the way that all the elements–the human, hardware, and software components–must interrelate to produce a successful design.

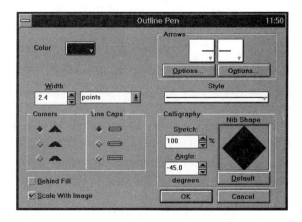

FIGURE 23.17 The pen settings for the hands

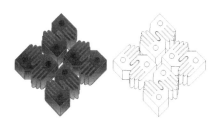

FIGURE 23.18 The hands

Fitting the Text

The type in the drawing is a design challenge faced by many illustrators working on corporate projects. Firms often define what fonts are to be used for all official publications, including annual reports, posters, packaging, advertising, and logos. The typeface is chosen to fit the company's image and gives a consistent appearance that aids in identifying the product as being from that organization. This can limit an artist's flexibility when using typography as part of a drawing. You can't use any font you want, so you must fit the type to the drawing. That's just what Chris did: He used the corporate typeface to spell out the name of the meeting. In fact, he went one step further: He used several design elements to balance the composition.

The title was divided into three lines. If the letters had been normally spaced, the words would have formed an hourglass shape, drawing the eye away from the illustration and out of the page. Manual letter and word spacing with the *Shape* tool were used to pull the text into a rectangular form. The lines add the appearance of type as an artistic element. The angled breaks in the lines carry the pointed end of the upper square down the page. The diamonds between the letters on the last line both reinforce the theme and break up the extra white space. Figure 23.19 shows the final text.

FIGURE 23.19 The text

Chapter Summary

The ability to take ideas of how something should look and turn them into something others can see and understand is important in creating good illustrations. CorelDRAW enables the artist to apply this ability by allowing one to change a shape or color without disturbing the rest of the design. A design is an ongoing process–adding here, changing there, as the image comes to life. Attention to the small details of that process is a part of Chris Purcell's work, and part of the reason for its success.

CHAPTER 24
The Worlds of Gary David Bouton

Astrotext by Gary Bouton

About the Artist

Gary David Bouton is a scribbler–not the kind that doodles on napkins, but a dedicated scribbler. "I like to sit down and just play with an idea, to see where it goes," he said. When clients come to his advertising firm, Exclamations, in Liverpool, NY, they often find one of Gary's experiments worked into their final design. His favorite tools are dry markers and pencils that he uses to create cartoons and caricatures. Many of those end up in the regional PC users' group newsletter he helps produce.

Gary holds a bachelor's degree in advertising design. After graduation he worked for an agency in Manhattan before moving back to his home town and opening his own business. He began experimenting with CorelDRAW! in early 1991, about six weeks before producing his first major project with the program, *Astrotext*. That drawing started out as a cover for a book and ended up winning a prize in the annual art contest.

Astrotext

CorelDRAW! is a two-dimensional medium, but *Astrotext* comes close to giving the view a three-dimensional experience. The idea is simple. A chrome globe floats over a scroll of parchment and reflects a bright sky and the letters on the scroll. The concept may have been simple, but it took a lot of work. "The globe was the easy part," Gary noted, "I have been working with chrome effects for years." The hard part was the text. The letters inside the ball have been converted to curves and individually placed by hand. Figure 24.1 shows the drawing as revised in CorelDRAW! 3.0. Although the text-handling features in later versions would make producing the script on the scroll much easier, the way the artist created the reflections, depth, and balance in this drawing make it worthy of our study. To see the full effect you should look at the copy in the full-color section.

Chapter 24: The Worlds of Gary David Bouton

FIGURE 24.1 *Astrotext* as revised in CorelDRAW! 3.0

The Approach

Gary began by drawing a rough sketch on paper. "I had to figure out just how the components would come together," he said. "I knew that this was going to be a very dense page with many elements." Because of the complexity, it was created in six sections to reduce the load on the computer while he worked. Only after the sections were done was the final image constructed. The final image can take several minutes to load on a '386.

"The hard part was going to be fitting the various text elements, so I had to figure out where they would sit on the page," Gary said. This involved creating the parchment and setting the type. To get the sweep of the scroll looking right, it had to widen as it moved toward the bottom, and the letters had to move with it. Then the ball was created with chrome highlights, and a mirror image of the text was fitted inside it. Finally, a bitmap background was fitted in behind the scroll. The first version he produced was in black and white, and the file totaled 110Kb. A color version came second with a 228Kb file size. Gary created a newer version in CorelDRAW! 3.0 with some extra effects to be used in a previous edition of this book. The changes between the two versions of the program, and differences in the drawing, resulted in a file totaling 903Kb.

Although new features in later CorelDRAW! versions would make the project a bit easier, the basic steps would still be the same. The only real changes would be in the creation of the background and using the text in a single block. I'll explain why the TrueType fonts increased the complexity so dramatically as you take a detailed look at the new version. Although the actual artwork started with the creation of the scroll, I'll begin with stars in the backdrop.

The Star Field Background

The original drawing used a two-color bitmap fill behind the scroll. A few colored dots on a black fill were tiled to produce a pattern to represent the night sky filled with stars. A few circles were drawn individually in the upper left-hand corner near the folded corner of the parchment.

In the new version, Gary decided to replace the bitmap fill with a random set of curves. Drawing all the shapes in the background would have taken a long time, so he used a shortcut. He splattered a piece of paper with ink placed on a toothbrush. This produced an irregular pattern and different-sized dots. The page was then scanned and AutoTraced. The resulting EPS file was imported into the file with the empty scroll. Gary then deleted the objects that were underneath it. A feathered effect was obtained by adding a blend at the bottom that changed from black to white.

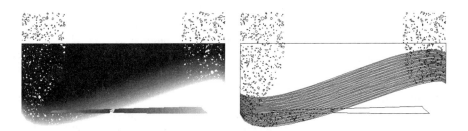

FIGURE 24.2 The new backdrop

A Dramatic Change

The new backdrop was the major factor increasing the complexity of the CorelDRAW! 3.0 version of *Astrotext*. Containing over 2,600 curves, the background slows even a faster system to a crawl and adds more than 500Kb to the CDR file. This would create the same problem in later versions of CorelDRAW! Common wisdom holds that bitmaps always take up more room on a disk than vector files. The fact is that complex vector drawings can require a lot of disk space, much more than a simple bitmap. Add to that the time it takes the computer to read the file, calculate the image, and create the display and you have a lot of overhead. But consider how long it would have taken to draw the 2,600 ellipses. Choosing which technique to use is a combination of judgment and personal preference.

Creating the Scroll

The real background for the drawing is the parchment scroll that looks like it is rolling out toward the viewer. Figure 24.3a shows an unfilled version. The basic shape is easy to produce: Create a rectangle; then pull out the bottom with an envelope. The sweeping effect adds a sense of dimension to the drawing, pulling the eye toward the center. The warm color of the scroll adds a contrast to the dark of the star field and the highlights on the chrome ball.

FIGURES 24.3a and b The scroll

To add detail to the plain design of the page, Gary placed a bit of shading and a cut in the edge at the bottom. The wedge produces the change in color, and a small break was added by breaking the line and adding nodes with the Shape tool. A little more work was required to produce the curled corner at the upper left, as shown in Figure 24.3b.

The Shape tool was used to alter the outline of the top of the scroll; then triangles were drawn to put in the curve. Radial fills give the shading across the top, and a darker fill adds the shadow on the page itself.

Setting the Type

It's easy to see that the type on the scroll has been altered and that it exceeds the 250-character limit imposed by CorelDRAW! on artistic text. To get everything done in version 3.0 required five blocks of text. The majority of the words on the upper portion were imported as paragraph text and placed in a frame. That was the easy part. Figure 24.4 shows the area where things get a bit trickier. To bring out the text as the scroll widened, Gary used four blocks of artistic text. The first word was placed on the same baseline as the last partial line of the paragraph text. First the type was set in a single straight line; then it was manipulated with envelopes to create the fanned-out look. Getting the effect to look just right required a lot of juggling.

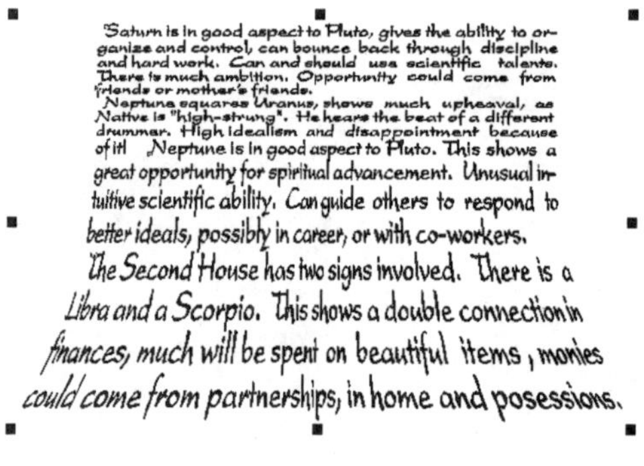

FIGURE 24.4 Adjusting the type on the scroll

A Problem with Numbers

The text on the scroll is one area where Gary could have really used the improved text features found in later versions with Paragraph and Frame modes. The older CorelDRAW! 3.0 user's manual notes that you can "have up to about 250 characters." The operative word is *about*. Because of the way CorelDRAW! handles artistic text, the actual

Chapter 24: The Worlds of Gary David Bouton

number will vary based on the complexity of the letters being used. That means that some fonts will allow more letters than others in a single element. In fact, the exact number can vary even in the same font if one block has more complex characters than another.

For the first version of the image, completed in CorelDRAW! 2.0, Gary used four blocks set in 12-point President (Present). This is a fairly complex typeface, so he was pushing the limit in the first three. Some trial-and-error work was required to fit everything in. When I tried to open the file into CorelDRAW! 3.0, each of the four artistic text objects was missing letters, and I was shown four error messages as the drawing loaded. The reason was that the older version used WFN-type fonts, which are not as complex as the TrueType editions used in 3.0 and later. The type on the scroll in the new rendition has all been converted to curves. Once the text is converted, the limit no longer applies, because you are no longer dealing with text.

Creating the Globe

The most striking element in the design is a chrome globe that floats over the page, reflecting the sky and earth. Of course the scene has a bit of artistic license, since there is only a black sky to reflect. Gary Bouton considers chrome effects a bit of a specialty. "I've been doing them for years with pen and paper, and I wanted to see if CorelDRAW! could match traditional tools," he remarked during our interview. Figure 24.5 shows the entire globe assembly and the radial fill that forms the shadow on the parchment in both filled and wireframe versions. Producing the mirrored effect was done in several stages, which are detailed later.

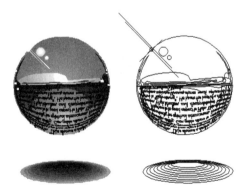

FIGURE 24.5 The complete globe

The Chrome Look

According to Gary, the most important factor in imitating chrome reflections with CorelDRAW! is understanding how actual bright metal reflections work. "Chrome has no color or surface character of its own," he noted. "There are generally three elements in the reflection: the sky, the ground, and a line at the horizon. The trick with chrome effects is to imitate the ground-horizon-sky formula. That's what I did with the globe."

Figure 24.6 shows an expanded view of the chrome effect portions of the globe, flanked by the filled assembly and the wireframe versions. It's a good bit easier to see how it works with the text out of the way. The upper and lower hemispheres are semicircles that have been given radial fills. The center of the fill was adjusted in each case to add a highlight at a specific location.

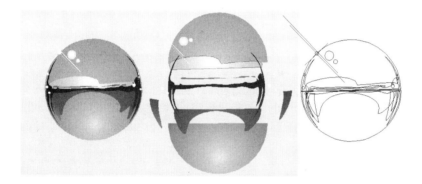

FIGURE 24.6 The details of the globe

Within the globe are several dark objects used to produce curved reflections on the object, one of which uses a very slight linear fill. The darkest element is an irregular line that denotes the horizon. These elements take care of the basic three elements of Gary's formula. The cloud bank is composed of a freehand shape with a light radial fill and a dark line to break up the shape.

The final touch was to place highlights on the surface. Most were just small silver-white radial fills. The one on the edge at the 10 o'clock position is a white circle with a cross running through it, made of three dashed lines.

The Reflected Text

The chrome was the easy part, according to Bouton. The mirrored text was another matter, not so much difficult as exacting. "I had to determine just where the ball would go in relation to the parchment and then figure out what words would be seen in the reflection on the underside of the ball," he said. "There are some unusual properties to chrome reflections; it's not the same as what you get in a regular mirror." Figure 24.7 shows the type as it was fitted over the ball objects on the left and a reversed and mirrored copy on the right.

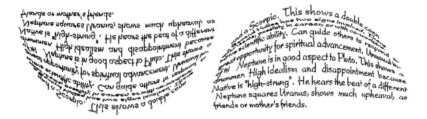

FIGURE 24.7 Fitting the text inside the globe

Normally, CorelDRAW! text is a combined object that can be transformed like any other object. In most cases the normal commands will meet all an artist's needs. The text inside the globe falls well outside the bounds of normal. To imitate the appearance of words on the parchment being mirrored off the ball, it was first duplicated and then flipped horizontally and mirrored. That was the first step.

The real work was in positioning each letter. It required converting the blocks to curves, uncombining the characters, and then arranging them to match the virtual reflection. Once everything was in place they were grouped together and manipulated with an envelope.

The Finishing Touches

Once all the primary sections were finished, the drawing was assembled; then the shadow was placed under the globe. To get more control of the shading than a radial fountain fill allowed, Gary applied a blend. "I used the stock colors of the parchment and placed it between the text and the scroll," he said. "That made it look as if the shadow was obscuring some of text." Once all the pieces were in place he fine-tuned some outlines and fills to produce a consistent appearance.

Quick Chrome

A few fills, some accents, and an understanding of the ground-sky-horizon formula can be used to create chrome text effects quickly. By varying the colors in the blends and ignoring the horizon, the same approach can be used to produce neon lettering. Gary sent an example of how he does it. It is shown in Figure 24.8, and the details of how it was done are explained in the following list.

FIGURE 24.8 Making quick chrome

- The first step is to create a mask with the letters in the center. Type the words and enclose them in another object such as a rectangle or ellipse; then combine them. The letters will become hollow. Give this object no outline, and fill it with the same color as the background of the area where you will place the chrome.
- Now create a shape behind the lower half of the mask. In the sample the original shape was a rectangle. Use the Shape tool to create an irregular upper surface.
- Add nodes and adjust them as needed. This is the template for the ground portion of the effect.
- Duplicate the new object and resize it vertically so it can be blended. Arrange the two elements on top of each other. Figure 24.9 shows the blend used for the ground. The upper and lower control elements have been pulled out to make them easier to see. The purpose of this blend is to create a gradual fill that darkens toward the top. The reflection on the chrome blacks up and

darkens as it moves toward the center. The idea is to simulate the same appearance. Use colors that will match the ones of the supposed "real world" such as green for a field of grass.

- Now repeat the same process for the sky. Draw a rectangle, duplicate it, adjust the size of the second copy, and blend and fill. Be sure to pick a color or shade that will contrast with the one you used for the lower blend. Place the new blend behind the first one. You can set the **Place Duplicates** and **Clones** to 0,0 and the new copy will be created right over the original, or align them with the **Arrange** command.

FIGURE 24.9 The ground blend

- The primary reflection is done, but the letters are still a little flat. In real chrome there would be highlights where the sun produces a bright spot on the surface of the metal. Look at the upper curve of the **S** and the ascender on the **k** in the back of Figure 24.8. Place some white or silver-white lines around the letters. You can also enhance the effect with selective dark areas to break up the tones. In nature there would be very few perfectly even reflections.

MAKING LETTERS REALLY STAND OUT

Embossing has long been a tool for adding a dramatic or elegant touch to printed materials and has required special handling at press time, and also extra expense. Although you can't actually emboss images inside CorelDRAW!, some techniques simulate the effect. Here are a couple of samples from Gary's collection.

The Logo

In keeping with his electronic image, Gray used CorelDRAW! and a paint program to create his logo. The idea was to produce a very simple image that would be easily recognized, indicate graphic design, and even be used as a signature if needed. Figure 24.10 shows the logo on the left, an expanded view in the middle, and a wireframe on the right.

The background for the letter was created in a paint program with a few freehand scribbles and then imported into CorelDRAW! The bitmap was converted with the Pencil tool in AutoTrace mode and then removed. The resulting object has a slight linear fountain fill.

FIGURE 24.10 A close look at a logo

The stylized letter **g** was produced by tracing over different geometric shapes, much like the traditional way of working with French curves to make angles and curved lines. Once the object was just the way he wanted it, Gary duplicated it three times. The slight offset of each one provides the basic embossed effect. The counter (hole) in the g is another set of objects that have been offset as well. Look at the way the fills are angled. The letter is lighter to the upper right, and the dark background shifts to the lower left. Arranging opposing fills is an excellent way to add highlights and increase an embossed effect. Notice how part of the letter seems to be protruding toward the viewer and the other side is receding into the background.

Creating a Cover

A different kind of embossed effect was the goal for the cover art of a musician's cassette recordings. The actual work was done in shades of blue and silver. Although the figures don't show the way color was used in the design, you can see how the photograph and text were used to create the illustration. Figure 24.11 shows the final product.

Chapter 24: The Worlds of Gary David Bouton   **761**

The starting point was the photograph. Rather than use it as a halftone, Gary scanned it and retouched the image in CorelPHOTO-PAINT. "I did a good bit of cleaning up, because I was going to convert it," he said, "Then after I got the EPS file I brought it into CorelDRAW! and edited it some more." He had a lot of rough edges to smooth out, and many of the lines would not fill properly without editing. He removed or combined about 300 of the 1,100 objects that were created during the conversion.

FIGURE 24.11 The cassette cover

Embossing the Text

The effect in this illustration is a bit different from the one in the logo you just examined. There the idea was to make the letter stand out boldly. Here the idea is to highlight the singer's first name and make the last name appear as if it was rising up off the paper. Figure 24.12 shows the letters with and without the background and in an expanded version to make it easier to see the different elements.

FIGURE 24.12 The raised type

One of the easiest ways to get one object offset from another by a specific small amount is with the **Nudge** command. In the **Preferences** option under the Special menu, the **Place Duplicate** command sets the amount an object is moved away from the original when duplicated. That is one way to get a duplicate in a specific location, but you have to set it each time to get the right amount of movement, and if the increment is small it's hard to select the new copy with the mouse. In the same dialog box is the setting for the **Nudge** command. Each time you select an object and press an arrow key, the object is shifted in that direction by this specified amount. I usually leave this set at a small value, such as one or two points, and the **Place Duplicates** and **Clones** at a larger one, such as a half inch. Then when I want to make an offset copy or shift an object just a little bit, I use the **Nudge** command.

Gary used the **Nudge** command to make three slightly offset copies on the words *Tamara* and *Anderson*, as shown on the left in Figure 24.12. In color the effect is more noticeable. The black-lettered word stands out from the page and is easy to read. All that was done to it was to add a slight, white-colored offset behind it. The last name is filled with the same color as the background and has both a white and a dark gray pair of offsets. The result is type that looks like it is rising off the page.

CARTOONING WITH CorelDRAW!

Before learning CorelDRAW! Gary used to sketch a lot of cartoons. He still does. Every month he produces several for greeting cards, users group newsletters, clients, and just for fun. The images still start out as hand-drawn figures, but then they are scanned, imported into CorelDRAW!, and traced for coloring, adding type, and exporting to a desktop publishing program.

How Stupid Can You Get?

This drawing was created for a column focusing on silly things people have done with computers that seemed like a good idea at the time. The image of the hand and the light socket was roughed out with pen and paper, and scanned with a hand scanner. The imported bitmap was selectively traced with the Pencil tool and filled. The inner control object on the blend in the background was pulled into shape with the Shape tool. The blend was given a red fill, and there is a rectangle behind it with a softer pink color. The idea was to produce a parody of an electrical shock. Figure 24.13 shows the drawing on the left and the blend in the outline on the right. Today Gary can use the Contour feature to get the same effect as blend with less work.

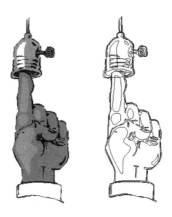

FIGURE 24.13 It seemed like a good idea at the time

Gary noted that he did not know how to use a real airbrush but that CorelDRAW! let him get much the same effect with blends and fills. The text was set in several blocks, and some of the letters were converted to curves so that they could be reshaped. The resulting image looks a bit like it was created in a paint program. So does the next example.

Bitmap Wizard

The little wizard was another illustration for a newsletter article. The production was much like the one described earlier. Once again a hand-sketched pen-and-ink drawing was scanned, AutoTraced, and dressed up with fills. Figure 24.14 shows the complete drawing to the left of a wireframe view. The thin lines in the original did not connect, so new outlines had to be added and lines joined to create fill areas. When cleaning up a trace Gary keeps cleanup to a minimum, to leave the freehand-drawing look to the cartoon.

The blend in the background is really two blends joined by a common object. This technique can give a seamless effect where they meet, since one blend begins as the other tapers off. Here's how it works. A blend is really two control objects, plus the series of shapes that CorelDRAW! generates when the command is given. The controls are still elements that can be treated separately from the rest of the blend. So Gary used one control object to act as one anchor for both of the blends (you can do the same with other parts of the blend if they are broken apart).

FIGURE 24.14 The Wizard

The fountain fills in the hat and apple are designed to add not only shading, but contrasting fill patterns. They raise the apple from the surrounding background, and the variations in tone simulate color. When working in black and white the artist does not have the luxury of color for emphasis or contrast. If you are working for a realistic effect in grayscale drawings, they will look more natural if you use shading and contrast that resemble a black-and-white photograph.

Chapter Summary

Gary David Bouton uses both computer-based and traditional methods to create his drawings, without a lot of fancy extras on his system. Like many users with professional training and expertise, he sees CorelDRAW! as another tool, a powerful one, for expressing his ideas.

CHAPTER 25
Rich Fiore: Bright Colors and Neon Lights

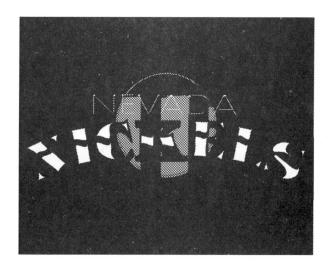

Nevada Nickels by Rich Fiore

About the Artist

The odds are good if you visit the casinos of Las Vegas or Atlantic City that you'll see some of Rich Fiore's CorelDRAW! images. He is the creative director at the Idea Center, which sits close to the action on Las Vegas's strip. It specializes in producing eye-catching designs that draw attention despite all the bright lights and noise in a gambling hall.

The *Nevada Nickels* logo was his first real project produced using CorelDRAW! He had been working with the program for about two weeks. "I'd do some things differently if I were working on that design today," he noted. "I hadn't experimented with blends yet, or some of the other effects that would have made things a lot easier." Today artists in his studio rely on CorelDRAW! for much of their work. "We have both Macs and PCs, but the program is so fast and easy to use on a PC that it has become a real favorite," Rich said.

The bright colors of the designs are often placed directly on transparent material using a special in-house procedure with Iris printers. These are very-high-end (and expensive) full-color ink output devices made in Germany that can read EPS files. Each print costs about $8, counting materials and ink. The Idea Center has two of the printers, about $125,000 worth of hardware and software. The maximum page size is 20 by 20 inches, and the print files can run as large as 100 megabytes. The final print can be backlit and used in a sign.

Nevada Nickels

Nevada Nickels was designed for the Nevada State Lottery, and won First Prize in the Logo category in the Corel Art Contest. The design looks simple, but there are a lot of steps involved. Figure 25.1 shows the wireframe view. Rich Fiore could have used blends to make both the neon and chrome letters. Instead the effects are a combination of hand-drawn lines and fountain fills. The coin that serves as a backdrop is a collection of nested circles.

The Approach

The logo was designed for the state of Nevada, and Rich wanted to make the design look like it really represented that state. "I went out to the state line and looked at the sign that welcomes people as they enter. It had a picture of a miner on it. I didn't copy the design, but it gave me an idea," Rich explained. The illustration has six parts: the neon text spelling out the name of the state, the chrome word **Nickels**, a bright metal coin, a view of the mountains with the sun in back, and two rectangles from the background.

FIGURE 25.1 *Nevada Nickels* in wireframe

The dark blue, copper, red, gold, and silver colors increase the visual strength of the illustration. Since the final work will often be viewed as a transparency, the colors were also chosen for a deep luster when backlit. Iris camera output is based on spot colors. They include process cyan, magenta, yellow, and black; so the process model could be used when specifying fills and outlines.

Casting the Nickels

The chrome letters were the most exacting part of the drawing. The typeface selected was Timpani (Tiffany ©ITC), a bold-looking, sharply serifed face that would extrude very cleanly. The letters were arranged, extruded, converted to curves, then broken apart. After that a collection of lines and fills was used to give the characters a metal sheen.

Adding the Neon Lights

Unlike the chrome lettering, the word **Nevada** is plain artistic text. The typeface is Vogue Normal, which has been duplicated and offset to create a drop shadow. There are several tricks that were used to produce the neon effect without using blends. A very slight shift in color using a linear fill was used in the letters in the foreground. It runs from Hot Pink to Neon Red. Hot Pink is composed of 80 magenta and 40 yellow, compared to Neon Red's 100 magenta and 60 yellow. The result is a fill with a bright reddish cast that stands out from the background color and alters color just a little as it moves down the page. On top of the characters is a series of white lines and small ellipses that are placed along the centerlines of the letters. When they are combined with the fill and surrounding colors, this gives the text a liquid quality. Figure 25.2 shows the two blocks of type in both wireframe and filled versions, plus an expanded view of one letter in the center.

FIGURE 25.2 The neon type

Creating the Coin and Lighting Effect

The Ellipse tool and Repeat commands sped up the creation of the colored coin that repeats the theme of the design, provides a backdrop for the landscape, and accentuates the lettering. There are five nested circles, resting on a rounded rectangle, all with specific fills that give a three-dimensional stamped look to the finished product.

The three inner circles serve as the face of the coin and its stamped bezel. The top circle has a radial fill that starts on top with bright yellow and changes to brick red toward the bottom. The middle object has a uniform orange fill that makes it look like the coin is higher in the center and tapers toward the rim. The middle circle is black on top and light orange on the bottom, providing extra contrast to both the rounded rectangle behind it and the landscape just below its upper curve.

One of the outer two circles was outlined and combined with a triangle that was rotated with the Repeat command. It was duplicated to create the second one. Both are the same size, but with different fills, and are slightly rotated in relation to each other. This gives the objects the appearance of the edge of a coin. Linear fills are used to increase the three-dimensional effect. The bottom one is a 40 percent gray at the top ranging to 50 percent at the bottom. The inner one is filled with walnut at the bottom and black at the top. If you look at the color plate of the coin, you can see that the apparent illumination is coming from above and to the left. Figure 25.3 shows the assembled group on top and an expanded version below.

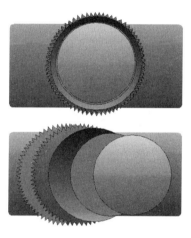

FIGURE 25.3 The construction of the coin

The Background

Nevada Nickels has two background elements. The inner rounded rectangle has a linear fill that goes from black to dark blue. This is designed to highlight the coin and lettering in front of it. It is shown in Figure 25.3. A large black rectangle serves as the main background. When the drawing is printed on an Iris camera and the copy is backlit, the black provides an opaque area, making the rest of the drawing and its colors stand out more clearly.

The Landscape

The design so far has been nicely balanced; the lighting effects, neon, chrome, and colors add lots of visual appeal. But if Rich had left out the mountains and sun, the illustration would not have been as attractive. The landscape gives a focal point to the drawing and brings the viewer in for a closer look. When the image is backlit the sun, neon highlight, and chrome complement each other very well. Look at the color plate and notice how the colors in the landscape repeat primary fills in the rest of the drawing. Figure 25.4 shows how this section was formed.

FIGURE 25.4 The landscape

The basic shapes are simple: a semicircle background, a radial-filled circle for the sun, six edited triangles, and a short line segment for a bit of a visual break. The landscape's sky goes from purple to neon red, repeating a color from the neon **Nevada**. The sun goes from autumn red to yellow, picking up a color from the coin. The mountains are a combination of walnut and light orange, using colors from the edge of the coin. Close examination shows that the word **Nickels** and the backdrop rectangle also share a shade of blue. This illustration has several themes, and a lot of attention is given to detail to execute them. The way the coins, colors, letters, and landscape work together is what makes this illustration so pleasing to look at.

ATTRACTING HIGH ROLLERS

The *High Rollers* design won a Fourth Place CorelDRAW! Art Contest award for technical illustration. Like *Nevada Nickels*, it uses a carefully planned color scheme. There are no blends used to shape the objects, just well-placed fills. Figure 25.5 shows the finished drawing. There is a copy in the full-color section of the book.

Chapter 25: Rich Fiore: Bright Colors and Neon Lights   771

FIGURE 25.5 *High Rollers* by Rich Fiore

The Approach

High Rollers is composed of five major elements: the car, its reflection, the text, and the tiled area on the bottom. The car took a bit of research, since Rich wanted to get the right proportions when drawing it. That involved a quick trip to a dealer's showroom and tracing the outline. The highlights in the picture are all produced with fountain fills—a large number of fountain fills. This is one of those jobs best done in wireframe. The file size is not that large, but screen redraws and print times are fairly long.

Creating the Car and Reflection

The basic form of the car was produced as a straight outline. The detail is all produced with a combination of fountain fills. Contrasting silver linear fills define the bottom half, and several variations of red and black ones are used on top. Black and gray form the shapes of the seats and windshield; orange and yellow give a glow to the lights. Figure 25.6 shows the car in both filled and wireframe views, with the reflected copy in between.

Once the car was completed, it was duplicated and scaled into place. You don't have to flip an object; just drag one of the top handles down past the bottom ones. That was not the end of the task. The fills were redefined to mute their intensity, and several highlights were eliminated completely. Just flipping the car would have reduced the realism considerably.

FIGURE 25.6 The car and its mirrored image

The Tires Were the Hard Part

The most complicated part of the drawing was making the first tire. Figure 25.7 shows filled and expanded views of the final group. Two circles, one gray and one black, were used for the rubber portion of the tire. The gray circle under the black one adds a highlight to the rim. Two more circles, with different silver linear fills, serve as the base of the hubcaps. The bottom one can be seen around the rim. It is blacker on top and lighter on the bottom than the one above it. The combined effect is similar to the coins described in *Nickels*.

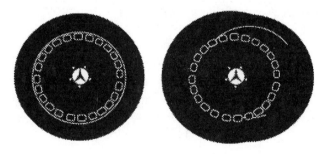

FIGURE 25.7 Making the tires

The really tedious part was placing the twenty-five indentations in the hubcap. Another gray circle was drawn outside the inner ring of the hubcap; then a rounded rectangle was created and placed on top of it. That was duplicated and each one was given a custom fountain fill matching the desired lighting angle.

The *High Rollers* headline is set in Unicorn, CorelDRAW!'s rendition of University Roman. To get the embossed effect Rich used three layers: the fountain fill on top, a white layer in the middle, and a black base. The fill on top picks up the colors of the car and the tile underneath it. To set the type and get the capital letters just right, the text was placed as four blocks, one for each of the lowercase portions of the words and one for each uppercase letter. The result is shown in Figure 25.9, with the **R** pulled apart, the white layer outlined, and the headline sitting on a light gray background. The **H** and the **R** may look a bit different from the standard Unicorn letters, but they haven't been converted to curves. The three copies of each letter were grouped and then pulled a bit with the Pick tool. The **H** was skewed toward the right on top, pulling the viewer's eye along the headline. The other letters, except for the **R**, were also pulled, but more slightly, to the right. The **R** was stretched in the same direction but left upright. The shape of the letters has been set over the windshield of the car, accenting the line and pulling the eye down into the center of the picture.

FIGURE 25.8 The headline

The Backdrop

Behind the length of the car is a blue backdrop. At first glance it looks like a simple round rectangle with a linear fill. Figure 25.9 shows the details. The large blue panel has two blue rectangles, with opposing fountain fills. The one in the back is slightly larger than the one in front. The visual effect is a panel that lightens as it moves up and that has a highlight around the lower rim. The panel sits on a large black rectangle that has two more thin ones at its base. These act as a transition between the backdrop and the tiles below. Figure 25.9 gives an expanded view of the backdrop.

FIGURE 25.9 The backdrop

The Mosaic Floor

The final element in the design is the tiled floor, containing twenty-four squares. One panel of eight was drawn and filled with an orange-to-red linear fill. On top of these was placed a series of random lines; then everything was grouped and duplicated twice. The Perspective tool was used to make the panel look as if it was receding toward the back. The lighter edges of the tile repeat the horizontal line of the car; the colors were chosen to accent the effect. The reflecting copy of the car has a fill that carries the same glow where it covers the tiles.

As in the other drawing the full-color scheme is an important part of the design, with minor variations of color and fill and adding to the overall balance of the picture. The linear fills have been created with very small shifts in color, and the tints in the car are used again in the tiles. The dark area at the top makes the letters stand out when the image is lit from behind.

Keeping It Light

The two examples of Rich Fiore's work that we examined were both created for backlit displays. Light and color are his basic tools, and his style shows a deep understanding of their interplay. The saturated colors were carefully chosen not only to draw attention, but to produce a luminous glow. Although most of us will not use CorelDRAW! to create images that must stand out among the distractions of a casino, we can all learn something about design from these two drawings.

CHAPTER 26
The Vision of Wil Dawson

ABOUT THE ARTIST

Until recently Wil Dawson of Tulsa, Oklahoma, was a desktop publishing specialist for IBM. He started using CorelDRAW! 1.0 at work in 1990, after having used several paint programs on the job. "The effects stunned me," he noted during an interview for this book. "The effects were great." He added that he could see a lot more potential in the new graphics package than just making signs for his employer. He is currently working for a small software company doing documentation and uses his knowledge of CorelDRAW! extensively.

Along with computer art Wil enjoys creating images with acrylic paints and photography. He also admits that he enjoys working with clay. His personal art often takes on a life of its own, and Wil follows inspiration as it leads him to the finished form. He noted that the effect was much like a novel he once wrote. "The characters took on a life, and I just watched as the story developed," he said.

Moonlit Flight was his first winner in the CorelDRAW! Art Contest, with a design based on a photograph he took of his daughter as she stepped out of their swimming pool. He said, "I turned the picture a bit and got the idea and then experimented to see if I could get the effect I wanted. Once I saw it could be done, I just kept experimenting."

The border effect is designed to have the same effect as matting does for a framed piece of artwork, setting off the area and creating an area of color that will add to the overall appearance. The face of the woman appears as if it were being softly lit by the moon as the motion of the wind draws back her hair.

Moonlit Flight

Moonlit Flight combines several elements designed to balance and draw attention to the face and form of its subject. Figure 26.1 shows both the complete work on the left and a wireframe view on the right. At first glance this looks like a very simple drawing, with a couple of rectangles, a few lines, some blends, and a little text. Closer examination reveals both complexity and some interesting tricks.

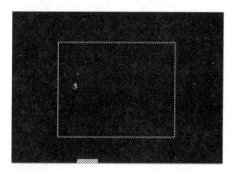 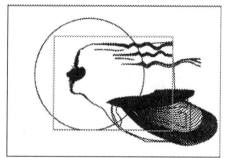

FIGURE 26.1 *Moonlit Flight and its wireframe*

Framing the Image

Although Wil started working with the shape of the face, we'll start with the background, frame, and border. Figure 26.2 shows filled and wireframe views side by side of the four rectangles and one radial fill used to provide both a border and depth to this drawing.

Chapter 26: The Vision of Wil Dawson

 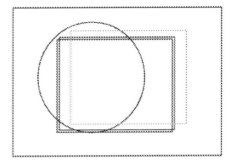

FIGURE 26.2 *The background, frame, and border*

- **Background Rectangle.** The bottom black rectangle serves as a dark backdrop for this low-key portrait. In photography a low-key effect is obtained by adjusting the exposure so that the contrast is raised to accentuate highlights in a field of shadow.
- **Radial Light Source.** The blue radial fill accentuates the outline of the face and acts as the apparent light source that is producing the bright areas in the drawing. The proper use of lighting in a drawing is one of the secrets to creating realistic illustrations with CorelDRAW! Notice how the brightest point in the fill is placed behind the strongest rim on the neck and forehead.
- **Beveled Mat Rectangle.** Galleries and frame shops often use two or three mats when framing a picture, cutting the boards so that their beveled edges and exposed surfaces add accent colors to display the art to its best advantage. Wil has used the gray rectangle to get the same effect.
- **Mat Board Rectangle.** The large rectangle around the central area serves two purposes: It imitates a conventional mat board, and it hides portions of the objects extending underneath it.

The Title Text

The technique used for placing the title text was very simple. Just enter the string, add a couple of extra spaces between the words, and use the Shape tool to get the interaction between the words and the letters just right. Using the wrong style of typeface could easily detract from the overall appearance of the drawing. A heavy font, or one that was too ornate, would have limited the free-flowing feeling of movement that the woman's face and streaming hair provide. Wil used Penguin Light, the Corel version of Linotype's Peignot Light typeface. The thin, clean lines and open counters of this font add to the overall design, and the fill places a color highlight that works well with the blue tones of the subject. Figure 26.3 shows the text and the settings in the **Edit Text** and **Text Spacing** dialog boxes.

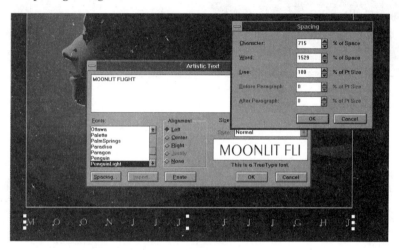

FIGURE 26.3 The text characteristics

Type Weight

So what is this "light" type? Light beer and light candy bars have the same basic ingredients as their regular counterparts, but they are less filling. Unlike such foods, however, light type has a full flavor of its own. Such adjectives as light, heavy, narrow, and condensed–when applied to a typeface–denote a change in weight. When type was cast in hot metal, the font boxes would be lighter or heavier, but the real meaning behind the extra word still lies in the way the letters look on the page.

A light typeface has characters that have been mathematically compressed so that more letters can be placed on the page in the same amount of line space. This form of type is very popular for forms and some types of documentation. In *Moonlit Flight* the narrow face has been chosen for its open look. A light face also reduces the amount of black type on the page, making it look lighter. Designers (and amateur typesetters) can use a given font for any of several reasons. Don't confuse light, heavy, and condensed with bold and italic. There are bold and italic forms of most light and heavy fonts.

Outlining the Face and Hair

The outline of the face was the first thing Wil drew; then he fit the rest of the design around this principal element. Figure 26.4 shows the primary line and facial features. Notice how the large block follows the general outline but leaves the such detail areas as the cheeks, base of the eyes, lips, and chin to be defined by other elements. I have left some of the secondary lines and parts of the blends in the figure to make it easier for you to understand how the shapes relate to each other. Wil seems to build up the face much like a sculptor adds sections of clay to a frame and uses the subject's anatomy as a reference to both form and structure.

One of the real secrets to mastering CorelDRAW! is the ability to see shapes as elements of an image and to understand and then form objects that match those elements on your page. Another major component of creating a visual representation of the real world is to make effective use of the apparent light falling on your subject.

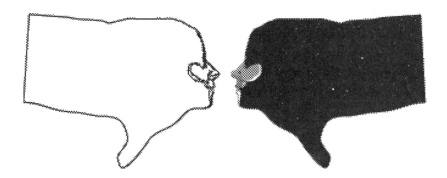

FIGURE 26.4 The basic outline

Beginning photographers, whose work centers on the use of light to create an image, are shown how light falling from different angles changes the appearance of the subject and can even alter the mood of the final print. Have you ever noticed how the old horror movies often had a light aimed up at the monster's face? That's the reverse of normal illumination from above. It gave the impression of a ghoulish countenance. Side-lighting, where the light is brighter on one side, can make a person seem thinner, since the other half of the face will be in shadow. Portrait photographers usually use several lights. Two in front illuminate the face and give modeling with slight shadows. Another light above the subject highlights the hair, and one behind the subject gives depth to the background.

Look at the extra objects that have been added along the forehead and length of the neck in the wireframe on the left in Figure 26.5. These have been given a light fill and placed partially behind the main outline. This allows the highlight to keep a smooth and even line. Notice how the triangle in the middle of the nose area and the other two objects were created to form shadows. The radial fill also helps separate the face from its surroundings, and the two eyebrows provide a point of reference in the area around the top of the nose.

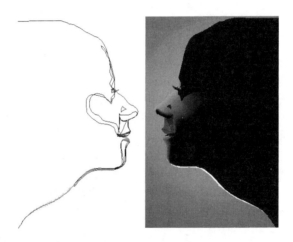

FIGURE 26.5 Using highlights to separate and define shapes

Blending in the Facial Features

Almost every art contest winner talks about blends and how important they are. Almost every one of them uses blends in their work with an individual flair. Wil Dawson is no exception. Although he claimed to have no particular style, some differences can be seen that are worth noting. A few paragraphs back I noted that he seemed to define subjects a bit like a sculptor would form a sculpture with clay. This is also how he uses blends–like contouring the surface of a statue. This image was created in CorelDRAW! 2.0. Today we can use the Contour function the way Wil used these blends.

When they are used to shape an object, CorelDRAW!'s blends are a lot like the lines on a topographic map: The closer the lines, the faster the rate of change. If you compare two blends on the same objects over the same distance and one has twice as many objects in the group, that one will look smoother to the eye; the changes will be more subtle. Figure 26.6 shows the blends used to form the shapes on the woman's face. Notice how dark and close the lines are on the chin and on the ridge of the cheekbone in the wireframe view on the left. The breaks between the close and more distant lines give the feeling of a shift in the contour of the face. Imagine a thumb moving clay and watching the form change as the finger shapes the surface. Notice the break along the cheek and how the lines look as if they were pushed into place. With the Contour feature now available in CorelDRAW!, it is even easier to use this concept to mold objects into a specific form.

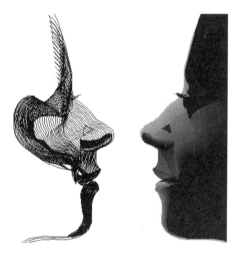

FIGURE 26.6 Forming the face with blends

The Shoulder and Flowing Garment

The drawing has the outlines of a shoulder and flowing cloth in the lower right-hand area. This portion of the design is a combination of individual objects and blends. The darker objects placed on top of the blends give the groups their shape. It's like a masking technique where two objects are combined so that the center area is hollow. Figure 26.7 shows a close-up of the objects in both wireframe and filled views.

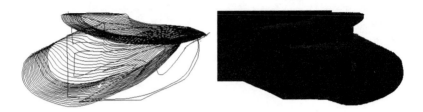

FIGURE 26.7 The shoulder area

Forming the Hair

If there is one thing you learn as you work with CorelDRAW! it is that there are a lot of different ways to do a task or solve a problem. Some users might have drawn lines or used blends to create the hair flowing back on the woman's head. But Wil Dawson created rectangles that he converted to curves and node-edited to get just the look he wanted (see Figure 26.8). The strands add a highlight in the dark upper corner and impart a sense of motion that gives a vital feeling to the illustration.

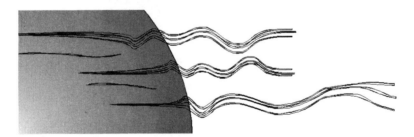

FIGURE 26.8 The final touch

A Word About Colors

The color plate *Moonlit Flight* in the four-color insert shows the subtle blue shades that the artist used. Since really only two colors are used, besides black, prints of this illustration could be produced using spot color. Picking the lightest matching Pantone color would allow the printer to add more black to get the intermediate shades. The only other press run needed would be one to add the gold-colored print. The night feeling is enhanced by dark blues. Movie producers have used blue filters over their cameras for years to enable them to shoot nightlike scenes in daylight.

My thanks to Wil Dawson for agreeing to share his work with us and for taking the time to explain it to me.

CHAPTER 27
The Elaborate Designs of Georgina Curry

Huntress

About the Artist

Some people have the mistaken notion that programs like CorelDRAW can't handle such traditional artistic tasks as portraits. Fortunately, Georgina Curry never believed it. Her contest entry, *Huntress*, is a stylized study of Clara Bow dressed in a Native American motif. It won the Best of Show award at the 1993 CorelDRAW Art Contest. I had the pleasure of being a judge at the awards and watching her and her partner Gary Moss accept the trophy, plus two bars of gold. Now we all have the enjoyment of viewing her work.

Georgina is the artistic partner at The Electronic Easel located in Phoenix, Arizona. She creates package designs, logos, and other commercial productions using CorelDRAW and Quark Express. "I really like working with CorelDRAW. Its only real limitation for me is its printing. Some of my work either takes a long time to print or won't output without modifications," she noted. "So I find myself using both products, with about 80 percent of my projects being done in Corel." She has been avidly working with art since childhood and holds a B.F.A. degree from Edinboro University in Pennsylvania. "Most of my work focuses on people; I just don't seem to get around to landscapes," she notes.

Her business manager, Gary Moss, is an accountant who left the fast track of the financial industry to explore the world of computer art. He centers his efforts on marketing and keeping the firm's computer inventory on-line. The firm handles a wide range of graphic design and illustration for clients and was one of the first design firms in the area to adopt the PC, rather than a Macintosh.

Huntress: The Birth of a Winner

Huntress is one of the most complicated and largest (non-bitmap-related) CorelDRAW files I have ever worked with, taking up over 2.2Mb on my hard drive. With a souped-up system, *Huntress* takes just under 11 minutes to load. I use it on a regular basis to give products brought into the lab for testing a real-world workout. A color print hangs on the wall in my office for its aesthetic value, for it shows good use of light and color, accent and balance, in its design.

Chapter 27: The Elaborate Designs of Georgina Curry

FIGURE 27.1 *Huntress* in gray scale and wireframe

As with many of the other pieces of work in this section of the book, Georgina Curry started out to see how far she could push CorelDRAW, resulting in the creation of a winner—in this case, the grand prize winner for the CorelDRAW art show in 1993. "I really wanted to challenge both myself and the program," Georgina noted. "I saw the lizard that won last year and became fascinated with the potential of the program. I do a lot of figure work and was looking through some old movie photos." Georgina told me that she had no clear-cut idea of how she wanted the drawing to look; she just kept working with the interplay of black and white and color. As you can see by looking at the drawing (you might want to refer to the full-color image in the color insert), the face (except for the red lips), the coronal feathers, and the breastplate of the drawing are all in gray scale; the beadwork, feathers, jewelry, and scarf are in vivid colors. The face took about a day and a half to create, and Georgina worked on the rest of the image over the next three months. The headdress actually started out as a necklace.

The starting point for this drawing was a black-and-white photograph of silent film star Clara Bow. Georgina scanned the image to use as a reference and then began drawing a face using CorelDRAW. There is no remaining bitmap in any portion of the final drawing.

Interplay of Color and Tone

When you look at *Huntress* you see an interplay of color and tone that are used both to draw the eye and to add drama. The face is a stark, high-key portrait similar to the fashion work of Richard Avidon in the 1950s. If you look at the center third of the drawing from top to bottom, you see it start out in black and white, move into color, go back into black and white, and then change into mixed black and white and color as you move from the feathers to beadwork to the face on to the breastplate.

The arrangement of colored feathers on either side of the face draws you into the most dramatic portion of the drawing, the eyes, which is where Georgina started her work. We'll start our detailed examination with the face.

FIGURE 27.2 The face of a huntress

Figure 27.2 shows detail of the face except for the highlights in the lips. As you can see, Georgina has used a combination of blends under the eyes and in the eyebrow, along with highlights within the eyes, to make that the most arresting portion of the drawing. The appearance of high-key side lighting was created with the use of several objects. Notice how the edge of the face on the right is outlined with a light gray fill, whereas a series of objects was used on the left side (as you look at the drawing) to give definition to the shadows.

Figure 27.3 shows an exploded view of the face, giving a better view of the complex arrangement of objects used to create the shadows. I mentioned in the beginning of the chapter that many people don't think of draw programs as suitable for handling portraiture. One reason for this is the difficulty in creating appropriate shadow detail. Georgina does an excellent job of showing us how this is accomplished. As you can see, it takes a very careful eye to determine the boundaries of shadow and the interplay of light and darkness.

FIGURE 27.3 The objects of the face: An expanded view

Huntress was a work that progressed slowly. In Figure 27.4 we see the face with the accents added on the lips and the lower portion of the headdress with the earrings. Although the shadows on the face and eyes required a careful eye, the jewelry required meticulous attention to detail. The first row of beads fringing the face and the large silver medallions used over the forehead and ears serve as a boundary, along with the turquoise choker between the black-and-white portions of the center and the rim of color around it.

The beadwork in *Huntress* required painstaking effort. Georgina could have simply created a group of beads using blends and then given them fills. But that would have created a mechanical-looking row of circles. To avoid this she placed each element individually. You can see in Figure 27.4 how well this innermost section of jewelry highlights the face and provides a border.

FIGURE 27.4 The face bordered by the inner row of jewelry

The Medallion

The medallion is a collection of radial fills. This technique of obtaining a three-dimensional appearance is one we will see several times in Section Two. The base of the medallion itself is a series of nested circles with offset radial fills. (See Figure 27.5.) The interplay of angles gives a sheen that resembles light striking raised surfaces. The raised balls on the surface of the medallion employ a slightly different technique. Each one is composed of two radial fills. One is black or dark gray and serves as a shadow; the second is an offset radial fill that serves the raised silver object itself. If you employ this technique be very careful to make sure that the angle of your lighting is consistent with the way it would appear in reality. Georgina used the same medallion but rotated and shifted perspective to create the earrings.

Grayscale beads were used along with large gems to serve as a border between the colored beadwork and the face. A close-up of one section is shown in Figure 27.6. Once again you can see how much attention had to be paid to the direction of the highlights. See how the angle of the gradient fills in the beads is also portrayed in the spectral highlights in the emerald gem. If you look at the color insert, you'll see that this is a subtle effect but necessary to provide not only realism but also proper balance to the drawing.

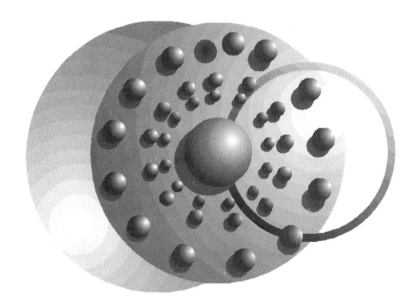

FIGURE 27.5 Expanded view of the medallion

FIGURE 27.6 The framing beadwork

The Beaded Headband

Figure 27.7 shows two things: the careful attention paid to the highlights when creating the drawing and the intricate placement of each bead. Notice the large emerald pieces in the lower portion of the figure. The highlights have been slightly modified to indicate specific light sources and match the overall illumination of the drawing. Highlights are also seen just to the right of the central diamond of beads matching the highlights in the jewelry. Radial fills by themselves would not give the right quality to the beaded headdress.

Colors had to be carefully selected and matched and variations custom-designed to give the right shades, interact with each other, and provide the right feeling. This portion of the drawing uses very muted colors and the kind of sheen that is seen on Native American river reed baskets similar to those made by the eastern band of the Cherokee nation. This subtle color provides a chromatic border and tie-in to the brighter colors of the large beads above it and the vivid colors of the feathers below it. All three bands of beads provide a half-moon shape pointing down at both the feathers and the face matching the flow of grayscale feathers that surround them. This effect helps draw the eye back into the drawing and the direct gaze of the Huntress' eyes.

FIGURE 27.7 The headband

The Upper Headdress

The uppermost portion of Huntress consists of two elements: a ring of grayscale feathers rising up out of a crown of colored beads. The colored beads are just a series of ellipses given offset radial fills, but each offset had to be adjusted to maintain the appearance of the angle of illumination. The other thing that Georgina did to give a three-dimensional appearance was to vary the color. The upper area on the viewer's left has a slightly muted color compared to the ones on the right. The ellipses on the right also have larger highlights than the ones on the left.

FIGURE 27.8 The upper headdress

All the feathers, both gray scale and color, were produced from one master feather. This original feather, as shown in Figure 27.9, was produced from four master objects. Georgina first created the body of one feather by drawing its outline as a closed object and placing several other irregular objects within it that were edited with the **Shape** tool. This series was then combined and a duplicate was mirrored 190 degrees. The second object was then modified slightly. The same technique was used to create the object that became the tip of the feather. The resulting four objects were aligned, grouped, duplicated, and placed in position. Figure 27.9 shows one of the feathers as a group on the top and an exploded view on the bottom. Each object was given its own radial fill.

FIGURE 27.9 Creating the feathers

Huntress would have a very unbalanced look with the wide corona of the upper headdress without the collection of feathers on either side of the face. As I have mentioned, all the feathers in the drawing were created using one master feather. To get the collection of feathers shown in Figure 27.10, Georgina placed one feather off to the side, ungrouped it, and then repeatedly duplicated it, giving each feather individually colored gradient fills, making extensive use of the **Fill** roll-up. By ungrouping she was able to color the long body of the feather while leaving the tip black. Each feather was then regrouped, placed, and adjusted using the **Envelope** and **Perspective** commands. When she had completed one side, she made a duplicate, mirrored it, moved it to the other side, and then made minor adjustments in tint and feather placement.

Chapter 27: The Elaborate Designs of Georgina Curry   795

FIGURE 27.10 An abundance of feathers

The Choker and Breastplate

Georgina repeated the flow of the gray scale in the breastplate below the face. You may have noticed as we worked through the illustrations in this chapter so far that she used black base objects for the beaded area and the choker on the neck. This helped the objects within these elements stand out on the page and gave them a more vibrant tone. She used irregular rectangular shapes with offset linear fills to form the turquoise tiles in the choker and within the necklace. Radial fills were used for the beads, and the silver medallion was reduced and repeated several times to complete the necklace. The triangle was drawn and modified by the **Shape** tool as the basis of the breastplate and then a series of irregular objects with varying gray fills was used to provide shadow detail for the necklace, feathers, and hair. Once again this required a meticulous eye to visualize the shape of the shadow from the original object and the angle of illumination.

FIGURE 27.11 The breastplate, choker, and necklace

The Braids of the Huntress

There are three major accents on the breastplate: the necklace, which we have discovered; the woman's hair hanging down in braids; and her scarf. We'll deal with the braids now. Figure 27.12 shows the complete structure of one of the braids and shows just how much detailed work went into creating this portion of the drawing. First Georgina had to produce the hair itself and then produce irregular objects and place them as highlights, as shown in Figure 27.12b. A series of decorative retainers for the hair and feathers and beaded tassels for the end of the braids were also added. To make the hair stand out appropriately, Georgina also created objects beneath the braids to show shadows on the breastplate. As a final touch she placed individual strands as if they had worked free from the braided hair.

Chapter 27: The Elaborate Designs of Georgina Curry 797

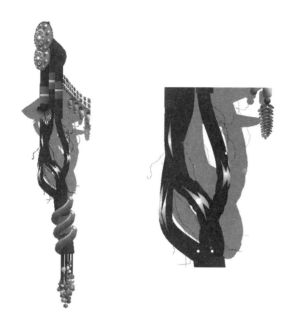

FIGURE 27.12a and b The braided hair

The braids of hair involved more than just drawing the plaits themselves. At the top of the strand are wraps that were used, and a variation of these is used at the bottom to hold the beaded tassels. Figure 27.13 shows details of each of these elements. As you can see, the tubes were created using a series of rectangular shapes with varying fills laid over each other to produce a cylindrical and banded appearance. The modified S shapes in the right of the figure that were used for the tassels were augmented with elongated crescent shapes that were given complementary linear fills to produce highlights.

The final artistic element in this drawing is the elaborate scarf that is draped over the woman's left shoulder. To get the appearance of folds, Georgina used several objects, and once again used background objects to provide a black backdrop. An irregular pattern was created and laid over the scarf by drawing a triangular shape, adding several objects over it, and then modifying it to place along the length of each panel. By carefully adjusting the shape of each of these objects, she gave a rounded appearance similar to that found in Scottish kilts that have been sewn using piper's pleats. This makes the cloth lie as if it were rolled into tubes, even though it really is a simple pleat. This design element is repeated along the base of the object in a golden tone. To produce this effect Georgina had to draw another series of objects that were highlighted using a series of blends. Some of the panels of the scarf were formed from blends that are very carefully nested over each other to emphasize the draping effect (see Figure 27.14).

FIGURE 27.13 Details of the decoration of the braids

FIGURE 27.14 The scarf filled and in wireframe

Chapter 27: The Elaborate Designs of Georgina Curry

PORTRAIT OF A WINNER

As you can see from the preceding discussion, *Huntress* is not a simple work of art but a complex collection of interwoven elements. Although Georgina did not start out with the entire design in her mind's eye, she carefully crafted each element to fit within and balance the whole. The result was not only personal satisfaction but success in the premier contest of computer graphics, or as Corel calls its annual contest, "The Academy Awards of Computer Graphics." It was a pleasure to be able to examine this piece of art and talk with its creator, and to be able to share it with you.

CHAPTER 28

Hardware Issues: Caring for and Improving Your System

In This Chapter...

- Choosing Hardware
- Updating Your System
- Improving Performance
- Basic System Maintenance
- Memory Management

What This Chapter Is About

How much time do you spend at your computer? If you're like most graphics users, a good bit of your day is spent staring at a display screen, moving a mouse, and pressing keys. If that computer is not running right, or not configured for the kind of work you do, you are probably spending more time than necessary in front of it. If that computer is involved with how you make money (or how your employer does), having a well-tuned system can make a difference.

This chapter focuses on two areas. The first is preventive maintenance that will keep your system running better and with fewer problems. A regular routine to make sure your hard disk is running right and that important files are safe will save you time in the long run. The second is the optimization of your system for maximum performance. In some cases that means adjusting the two start-up files, CONFIG.SYS and AUTOEXEC.BAT, or cleaning up your hard disk. In other cases it might mean adding additional hardware or software to your system. By naming a package I am not endorsing it over a competitor; it's just that I know and have used that product. Individual purchasing decisions should be made based on your system, needs, and budget. There are so many possible ways to configure a system that it is not feasible to cover all the options and devices that might be added to it. I have focused on the areas that will optimize your electronic graphics workplace.

Making the Most of Memory

There will always be faster CPUs. As with the 486 and the 386, the Pentium's day in the spotlight will be limited. The 486 was supposed to have been used as a network server, costing $20,000. As I write this you can buy full 486 systems for under $1,200, and Pentiums for about $3,000 with a good hard drive and fast graphics adapter. Of course you can add all kinds of bells and whistles to a PC and drive up the price, but that is not the point. The CPUs get faster. If you are willing to pay for a faster one, you will benefit from increased performance. But a new computer is not the only way to boost performance, and thereby speed up your work. There are other things you can do to boost the power on your desktop.

Get Every Bit of Conventional (and Unconventional) Memory

The most obvious thing you can do is make the most of your system's resources. There are things Windows must have on a system, and things that Windows *likes* to have on a system. RAM falls into both categories. If you have less than 8Mb of memory in your PC, seriously consider adding more. If you have 8, consider adding more memory. Four MB work better than 2, 8 work better than 4, 16 work—well, you get the idea. If you are using CorelDRAW! for serious work, your PC should have at least 8Mb of RAM.

Use Your Memory Better (and Maybe Get a Newer Operating System)

If you run Windows 3.x there is a high memory manager on your PC. For most people it is the HIMEM.SYS that can be used with either DOS or Windows. If you opted for the basic configuration, you probably also have SMARTDRV.SYS loaded into memory to cache your hard disk and there is some kind of swap file to provide virtual memory. To check, you can look at your CONFIG.SYS file, and the 386 Enhanced option in the Windows Control Panel. These drivers and setups are basic. They are designed to work on the broadest range of PC configurations possible. But every PC is different, and many can control system resources better than the vanilla setup created during program installation.

If you have not upgraded to DOS 6.2 or are not already using a high-memory manager with DOS 5.0, consider doing so. There are many things in the new software box from Redmond that will help CorelDRAW! run better. First on the list is improved memory management and recovery of high-memory areas—the space between the 640K ceiling of conventional memory and the end of the first 1,024K. The MemMaker utility automatically examines your system and reworks your AUTOEXEC.BAT and CONFIG.SYS files to allow as many of your drivers and TSRs to be moved into that upper 384K as possible. That leaves more room for memory-intensive software like Windows and CorelDRAW!

Of course, as you have also probably noticed, CorelDRAW! likes a lot of hard disk space as well as RAM. DOS 6 shipped with DBLspace. This is an on-the-fly compression routine that packs those files tightly on your disk and then opens them back up as needed by a program. If you want compression without DOS 6, consider a program like Stac Electronics' Stacker. Don't expect as much compression on program files. You can even use Stacker on a network drive. Remember, though, that this is a software solution, and not as fast or as reliable as a larger hard drive. Use it only if you need it. And back up all your important files first.

That brings us to DOS 6's new Windows-based Backup and Restore programs. Although they are nicer than the old character-mode DOS programs, I still prefer a tape unit from Colorado Memory Systems. I seem to be in a minority. A recent *PC Magazine* study found only about one in seven users made regular backups with a tape unit. If you make your living with a computer and don't have real backups, not just an occasional floppy save, you are asking for trouble. More about that later.

Microsoft has included some other new goodies that should be on any serious system: an antivirus snooper and a utility that lets you interrupt the CONFIG.SYS routine if it locks up. I used to keep a third-party shareware program on my system that did the same thing under DOS 4.2, but it wouldn't work with DOS 5.0. Now I get the same features for free (well, almost free).

If you have a high-memory manager and don't need (or desire) DOS 6.0's hard disk compression software, the older edition may be all you need or want. After all, if it isn't broken—don't fix it.

Third-Party Memory Managers

Several firms are making software that will recover more area in high memory than DOS 5.0 or even DOS 6, and the same firms offer enhancements for the newer operating system. One such program is 386MAX from Qualitas. They make separate versions for regular PCs and PS/2s. Without Max or HIMEM.SYS my system would have only 460K of memory after loading all the device drivers needed to keep everything running. With HIMEM.SYS I get 503K, but with Max the total is 590K. If I drop the driver for the optical drives, the total increases to 623K. Not bad. The setup is very easy. You are walked through all the steps with on-screen help, and backups of the files to be modified are made by Max before they are changed.

Qualitas also includes a disk cache that replaces SMARTDRV, but you can use either one. Make sure you use one of them. And you should experiment with the virtual memory options. Some systems work better with a permanent disk cache, others with temporary files, and still others with none at all (if you have enough RAM).

Reducing Overhead

Take a look at your CONFIG.SYS file. Does it have lines calling drivers that you've never heard of, installed by programs you rarely use? Is your AUTOEXEC.BAT file littered

Chapter 28: Hardware Issues: Caring for and Improving Your System

with programs that you previously ran with DOS, but seldom use now? Place a semicolon in front of suspect lines in the CONFIG.SYS and a REM statement in front of the ones in AUTOEXEC.BAT. If everything still works fine you've gained memory and reduced the confusion in your setup.

Another option is to disable any occasionally-used drivers when they are not needed. A neat software package called Dynamic Memory Control lets you load and unload device drivers without having to reboot your computer. In fact, you can set up batch files to reconfigure the machine while it's running. If you have a lot of drivers—say, from various SCSI devices—this can be a very useful addition to your library. Most of the programs I mention can be easily found in any mail-order ad or at your local computer store. This one is a little more obscure, so I'm including the address: Adlerspaerre & Associates, 501-1803 Douglas St., Victoria, BC, Canada V8T 5C3.

Hard Disks: Keeping Things Running Smoothly

Hard disks are wonderful things. They store lots of files, speed up file operations, and do not require food or water. They do require that the owner spend some quality time with them. Failure to perform a little routine maintenance will slow your system down and can lead to disaster. This section points out a few things every CorelDRAW! user should do on a regular basis to keep things in good working order. There are four basic steps to take if you want to have an efficient hard disk system (beyond going out and buying faster hardware): make sure that your disk's file system is in good working order; remove unnecessary files; reduce fragmentation; and periodically test the components. I'll go over basic care and backup and will discuss the options for upgrading PC storage systems.

Not a Matter of If, but When...

Eventually it happens to everyone. You spend time looking for a file that is no longer there, or instead of a C:\ prompt the computer presents the dread message: "No boot device present, insert disk in drive A:", or Windows refuses to load properly. There can be several reasons for such problems, and it is beyond the scope of this book to teach everything about caring for your system. But there are a few things that can make these kinds of problems easier to resolve. Here are some of the things I do to avoid catastrophe (for more on this subject, as well as PCs in general, see my book *Upgrade & Maintain your PC*).

The Dark and Stormy Night Disk

Problems are always easier to fix if you have the right tools, and in many cases the right tool for correcting a hard disk problem is another disk. The Dark and Stormy Night Disk (DSND) is often all you need to get a system up and running, or at least to find out what is wrong. The name is one I jokingly came up with once when teaching a computer science class. I use it to refer to a disk with all the primary files used to normally boot a system and utilities needed to inspect the hard disk. There are many potential uses for this tool, and I update mine whenever I make a major revision to my system setup, or install new software.

To create a DSND, first format a disk that matches the type used in your A drive and put the system files on it (**Format** it with the **/s** option). Then **Copy** your **CONFIG.SYS** and **AUTOEXEC.BAT** files to it. Then add any device drivers—the ones for your mouse, video card, CD-ROM drive, scanner—called for by these files. Finally, **Copy** the DOS programs: **Debug**, **Fdisk**, **Chkdsk**, and **Format**. If you have room, add any other disk repair programs, such as Norton Disk Doctor and a text editor. The disk can be used to aid with a variety of problems, from the simple to the totally disastrous. Here is a partial list of tasks this disk should be able to do:

- Replace device drivers overwritten by a new program's setup routine. I have used this several times when a new program installed a custom version of my scanner driver and nothing else would use it.

- Boot the system if the hard drive fails, and have the tools needed to assess what is wrong and, if needed, restore the drive.

- Replace **COMMAND.COM** if the wrong version is accidentally copied into the root directory from another, older disk.

- Restore the **AUTOEXEC.BAT** and **CONFIG.SYS** files if the system won't boot or is behaving strangely after installing either new hardware or software that modified them.

- Keep handy all the routines needed to install a new hard disk on the system.

- Even if you have a tape backup or other external copy, you should maintain a current DSND. If the configuration files are wiped out, the system may not boot, or the special driver for your tape unit may go down. It's a lot easier to just pop in the disk than fuss around trying to find a boot disk and read the files with **Edlin** or even DOS **Edit**.

Back Up Your Software Configurations

These days most Windows software has its own configuration file, modifies Windows files, or does both. Because of that you should make backups of the **WIN.INI** (Windows installation), **SYSTEM.INI** (system installation), and other special start-up files. Corel applications usually keep their .INI files in the same directory as the actual program file. I have started adding those to my DSND. On several occasions I have had to go to the disk and retrieve one or another start-up file after some new piece of software figured it knew how to set up my system better than I did. Many save the old file with an .OLD or .BAK extension, but that's not much help if you can't locate the offending command.

It's also a good idea to back up your Windows System directory and related drivers and DLLs. Many of them are placed there by third-party products, such as CorelDRAW!, your communications program, or a treasured utility. If you have to reinstall Windows, those extra files may be gone, and having a backup copy can save having to reinstall the entire package.

The Basics of Backup

In the days of smaller storage systems you could manually back up to floppy disks without much problem. Today's larger drives make the backup task one that requires a more automated approach. The best method for a given user will depend on the amount of data, the speed requirements, and the money available for a backup system.

With prices of less than $300, quarter-inch tape or DC2000 units are an inexpensive way to handle backups. Cartridges run about $30 each and can hold over 250Mb of compressed data. Maynard and Colorado Memory Systems are among the better-known manufacturers. The drives can usually be attached to the computer's floppy drive controller and will run automatically at preset times with the bundled software. External cases and special controller cards are available, offering improved performance and the ability to use one drive for several systems. These are ideal.

The drawbacks with quarter-inch tape are speed and limited space. DC2000 units will top out at a 700Mb drive in late 1993. These are the slowest of the dedicated backup units and are not well suited to backing up gigabyte drives in a reasonable amount of time (using several tapes) on a busy network.

The Next Step Up

My latest backup addition is a PowerTape unit from those same folks at Colorado Memory Systems. They come in both 2-gigabyte (Gb) and 4Gb units for under $2,000 list price. The 2Gb is about $1,100 through mail-order vendors. It includes a SCSI adapter and the usual CMS software. They offer reliable operation and large capacity, with speeds three times or more than those of the older QIC-80 versions.

Another option is 4mm digital audio tape (DAT). Units that use this method are faster than DC2000 drives and have helical scan heads much like those use in VCRs. DAT units can handle up to 2Gb on a single tape and come in both internal and external models. There are also 8mm helical scan drives designed to store 5Gb per tape. They are only available in external models. Right now all helical units are pretty expensive and are more suited to demanding network applications. Expect to pay from $1,500 to more than $3,500 for the 4mm variety, and $2,400 to more than $4,500 for the 8mm units. For busy networks and machines that are almost always busy (like dial-in units at service bureaus), helical units offer reliable operation with minimal downtime.

The most important thing about backup is finding a method that is effective for you. You must not only purchase it, but *use* it. Important files should be backed up regularly, with one copy stored off-site in case of fire or other disaster. Think about how much time it would take to re-create the data (if that's even a possibility). Consider the reaction of unhappy customers, or IRS auditors, when you have to say the job or financial data are lost.

Not all backup solutions are based on fancy hardware. Programs such as FastBack and Norton Backup are fine for keeping extra copies if your demands are not too large. You can select which files should be saved to disk and have the program do the work at specified times. These programs are just like the ones that come with tape units, without the drive.

Keep It Clean

The best way to reduce hard disk problems is to keep your files nice and neat. Since you can't see them, that may sound a bit strange. But one of the most common reasons for poor computer performance is a messy hard disk. DOS is not a good housekeeper. Instead of placing all the parts of a file in one location, it puts pieces of the data anywhere there is room. This increases the time it takes to save, delete, or read a file into a program. It also makes your hard disk work a lot harder. If you exit a program improperly, or Windows locks up and you have to hit the reset button, you may end up with parts of files left on the disk. New programs often add unnecessary files that take up space. All these things degrade performance. Let's examine some of the things you can do to tidy things up.

Clear Out Unwanted Files and Subdirectories

Over time all hard disks pick up a collection of files that never get used. Many applications load the entire contents of the installation disks when they are installed, or make backup copies of setup files like AUTOEXEC.BAT or WIN.INI. Many users make extra copies of files and leave them in several directories, later forgetting all about them. These extra files take up hard disk space and make it harder to locate the ones you need or to back up the system.

Periodically culling old files is a good habit to develop. The Windows and CorelDRAW! manuals have lists explaining what each file is used for and if it can be removed. Keeping files in subdirectories based on type or project is a good way to organize a disk. Then when the information needs to be archived, it's easy to do. If you have enabled the auto-backup option on programs like CorelDRAW! or Word for Windows, you may be producing a lot of files unintentionally. They generally use the extension .BAK. I check and remove old backup copies about once a week.

Using CHKDSK

Included with your copy of DOS is a program called CHKDSK.COM, which stands for "check disk." This is one of the most valuable programs in the box, and one many users never run. This program checks the integrity of your disk's file system and can fix problems you didn't even know you had. If you have exited a program improperly or if Windows locks up your system, there may be fragments of lost or temporary files on your disk. They take up space and slow things down. CHKDSK can recover the data and clear up the wasted space. You should run CHKDSK on a regular basis. Some people even place the command in the AUTOEXEC.BAT file, so it runs every time the computer is restarted. It's a good habit to run it every few days, or any time the computer or a program locks up.

Exit Windows *before* running **CHKDSK** with the **/f** option. Failure to exit Windows can result in loss of data. You can run it without the switch, but it's safer to always exit Windows first.

If you are unfamiliar with running CHKDSK here are the basics; just follow along. You must either have the file's directory in your path statement, or be in the directory where CHKDSK.COM is located. Then type **CHKDSK** followed by the letter of the drive you are checking, and a colon. To check drive C type **CHKDSK**. The **/f** switch means that you want the program to recover any lost clusters (parts of files). If you leave it off the computer merely reports problems without fixing them. Now press **Enter**. The computer will pause for a few seconds and then issue a report that looks something like this:

```
Volume MAX_1 created 05-02-1992 10:57p
Volume Serial Number is 4037-1E00

2 lost allocation units found in 2 chains
Convert lost chains to files (Y/N)?y

261869568 bytes total disk space
    77824 bytes in 2 hidden files
   823296 bytes in 189 directories
176181248 bytes in 4152 user files
     8192 bytes in 2 recovered files
    49152 bytes in bad sectors
 84729856 bytes available on disk

 4096 bytes in each allocation unit
63933 total allocation units on disk
20686 available allocation units on disk

655360 total bytes memory
366832 bytes free
```

Reading the Chkdsk Report

The first line tells which drive was checked and the date it was formatted. My report also shows two lost chains; these are fragments of files that were produced once when Windows locked up. I set the /f option when I ran the program, so the program collects and stores the data in files with names like FILE0000.CHK, FILE0001.CHK, and so on. If the data are text, you can look at and recover them with a word processor. If they are program files, there's not much hope for recovery.

The program also reports if it found any problems with your directory or file structure, along with the total and available levels of disk and system memory. If Chkdsk indicates cross-linked files, you may have a more serious problem, such as a controller or hard disk starting to fail. If that is the case, be sure to back up critical data and consider using some of the more advanced hard-disk utilities mentioned later in the chapter.

Reduce Fragmentation

One of the most common culprits in poor hard disk performance is DOS's habit of breaking up files as they are saved. Although it is normal for DOS, it's not good for you or the hard drive. The longer it takes to load or remove a file, the longer and harder the drive has to work. Large CorelDRAW! files or bitmaps can take much longer to load when they are fragmented. That slows you down and shortens the life expectancy of your disk. And if you ever accidentally erase a file and want to use a program such as PC Tools or Norton Utilities to recover it, the odds for success are better if the file is unfragmented. You can check for fragmented files with Chkdsk. Type **CHKDSK *.*** then press **Enter**. If the program finds any fragmented files it will add a list at the end of the report like this:

```
C:\LOGFILE.TXT Contains 9 non-contiguous blocks
C:\COLLAGE.EXE Contains 4 non-contiguous blocks
C:\386MAX.PRO Contains 2 non-contiguous blocks
```

DOS 6.0 offers a program for unfragmenting files called Defrag, which was developed by Symantec—the people who produce the Norton Utilities. If you have an older version, such as DOS 5.0 or 4.2, there are a number of very good programs around from other vendors. Norton Utilities, Mace Utilities, and PC Tools Deluxe are very popular. I use Norton's Speed Disk about once a week, after running Chkdsk. If you work with large image files a lot, you might even want to run it more often than that. Defragmenting can take from a few minutes to over an hour. I generally run it while I'm off at lunch or dinner. Most of these programs also check out the drive to make sure it is running properly and offer summaries of disk usage. Figure 28.1 shows Norton Speed Disk in operation. The white areas have been closed up and defragmented. The **X**s are either unmovable files or the Windows permanent swap file, and the **B**s show areas on the disk that are marked as unusable (Bad).

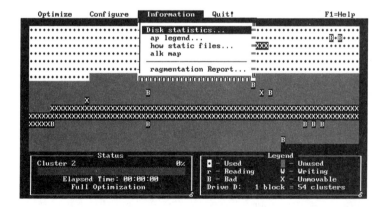

FIGURE 28.1 Using Norton Speed Disk

Never turn off your computer while a program such as Speed Disk is running, and don't use it during storms or other times when the power might fail. If the program crashes, you can lose data and cross-link files. Unload any TSR (Terminate and Stay Resident) programs before defragmenting. If you have an unusual drive configuration, make doubly sure everything important is backed up before trying the program the first time. If you have a normal configuration, you should still make sure you have a good backup. The benefits well outweigh the work, and you should keep backups anyway. More about that later.

Testing Your Drive

Over time the mechanical parts of the drive lose alignment with the magnetic low-level format. As this progresses the heads have a harder time locating and reading the data. A Read command makes up to 10 tries before reporting an error. If the problem occurs very often, you may be risking all the data on the drive.

You may be able to use a program such as Spinrite II from Gibson Research or Calibrate from Symantec to low-level-reformat your drive without having to lose the data. But many larger, modern drives and controllers don't let the system manipulate the low-level format, so such programs will not operate.

VIRUSES

The last software subject to be discussed is viruses. There are warped people in the world who want to prove that they are clever—if not wise, moral, or very smart. Even shrink-wrapped and CD-ROM-based programs are not immune to viruses, but generally they are much safer. If you want to be sure that someone is not launching a joke at your expense, invest in an antivirus program and use it after loading new software or downloading files from another system. Be sure to update the program when new versions are released to make sure it can identify new strains.

The basic rule in hard disk care is **Pay Attention!** Know your system. If things don't seem quite right, there is probably something wrong. Keep good backups and perform regular maintenance and diagnostics. You will save yourself a lot of time, and—sooner or later—your data.

Chapter 28: Hardware Issues: Caring for and Improving Your System   **813**

WHAT ABOUT HARDWARE?

The only constant in the PC industry is rapid change. Every 18 months or so a new processor takes over as the standard, offering about twice the performance of the one before it. I wrote the first edition of this book using two machines: a 486/33 and a 386/33. Since then I have had several 486/66's, and currently have several Pentium-based (the fancy name for the 586) PCs. I also changed from 650Mb and 350Mb ESDI-based hard drives (I'll explain about drives and drive types in a bit) to 545Mb and higher SCSI-2 disks. Why? In a word, performance. The faster machines, drives, and video cards speed up loading an image, snapping a screen shot, and making a print. That means I get the book done faster, and maybe even have time to play with my daughters as the work progresses.

You don't have to go out and buy a whole new system to take advantage of new hardware. A PC is made up of parts, and parts are parts—almost. I upgrade by swapping old components for new ones. A new motherboard and processor can perk up your day, and a faster hard drive or display system can get a project out more quickly. There is a difference in quality between a cheap card or drive and a top-of-the-line model. And some great ideas don't stand the pressures of the real world, so it pays to shop carefully.

The key is to stay in touch with trends in the PC marketplace and to know what and when to buy. The first rule is simple—don't buy the latest craze. Those products are on the "bleeding edge" of technology. The early runs of a new gadget will be improved within four to six months, and the later versions will cost 10 to 30 percent less. Remember the first Texas Instruments digital calcuators? I bought one of them in 1970. For only $129 it performed all four basic math functions and showed the answers on a red LED display. Today a $40-unit (not adjusted for inflation) runs rings around it, performing functions I'd have to go back to school to understand. Of course, I get paid for testing beta software and writing about new products. Part of my fees cover the hours of frustration when my computer won't boot or the display wobbles and weaves. For the average user it's better to wait until the pain level drops down, and you can cope by reading the user manuals.

Hold off buying decisions for a few weeks until the reviews of the newly-shipping product come out; don't run out and buy when the first reports come in from the front. Then ask yourself if a new product or system really offers performance or features that will make your life or workplace better. If the answer is yes, consider adding just the parts you need to make it work. That costs less than a whole new system and allows you to spend more on the parts that really make a difference. If the cost is too steep, wait.

The prices will drop as competition and new developments advance. Let's take a look at some possible areas of improvement, and a few current trends.

Getting on the Right Bus

Before discussing add-on cards and souping up PCs, I'd like to mention expansion buses and SCSI adapters. If you are like most PC owners, the computer on your desk (or alongside it) has an ISA (Industry Standard Architecture) bus. That means it contains basic 16-bit expansion card slots modeled on the original IBM AT style machine. The PC's bus is a data channel used to communicate between the computer's Central Processing Unit (CPU—such as a 486) and such devices as your display adapter, disk controller, or mouse. The other two common types of buses for attaching peripherals are the 32-bit technologies: MCA (Micro Channel), developed by IBM for the PS/2 series computers, and EISA (Extended ISA), developed by several other vendors to compete with MCA.

Both EISA and MCA were designed to offer faster data transfer and (allegedly) easier installation of new cards, but neither have gained much acceptance. There are two reasons for this: higher cost, and a lack of products that use them. Older 16-bit cards will work in EISA machines, but without any improvement in performance. MCA slots accept only MCA cards. Not that many devices have been converted to EISA or MCA models. The result is that most of us still have ISA machines. Someone at Intel remarked, "The war between EISA and Micro Channel is over, and ISA won." But such things as your Windows screen display, graphics applications, networks, and larger hard drives are all hampered by the poor data throughput of the ISA bus. There is an alternative.

The Local Bus Is an Express

One of the latest trends in expansion bus technology is VESA Local bus, or VL for short; VESA stands for "Video Equipment Standards Association," the folks who defined Super VGA. VL uses a special controller chip that can manage up to three cards at up to 130Mb per second (sustained, not burst). It also allows communication directly between CPU, memory, and expansion cards. The slots look like regular slots with an extension in the front. You can still use regular ISA cards in them. The cost of a VL card is about $20 to $40 more than a regular one, and the additional cost of a VL motherboard is less than $100. The improvement in video, hard disk, and SCSI performance is stunning, so VL is a real choice for anyone using a PC for graphics—such as

CorelDRAW! owners. You don't have to buy a whole new system to get a local bus. Lots of vendors are marketing VL-bus cards. I use one for video and another for running my SCSI peripherals. I'd never go back to ISA for those functions—I get at least twice the performance of my old configuration.

If you have an existing ISA 486 machine, consider swapping the motherboard. Some VL boards are available for about $150 wholesale. The hard drive, floppies, memory, and other parts can be kept, and the conversion should only take about an hour. If you don't know how to replace a motherboard, check with a local user's group for help or get a quote from a computer shop. Such periodicals as *PC Magazine* and *Computer Shopper* carry ads for companies that sell parts. I rely on Micronics for my systems and added two VL-based motherboards just before I started writing the previous edition of this book. One was an ISA motherboard with two VL slots, the other an EISA/VL combo.

The VL bus is not the end of the story. Intel is pushing an alternative called PCI (Peripheral Component Interconnect). It allows up to 10 devices (including the CPU) to use the local bus for data transfer. This design is finding favor with Pentium-based systems, which are now near the $1500 price point for entry-level systems, and they may be $500 cheaper by the summer of 1995 if the past is much of a guide. In response, VESA is releasing an upgraded version of the VL bus, and on it goes.

SCSI: A Bus Within a Bus

If you use CorelDRAW! consider getting a CD-ROM if you don't already own one (I'll get to that topic soon). If you get a CD-ROM you will most likely end up with a SCSI (Small Computer System Interface) card in your system. SCSI is the way power users add new components to their PCs. Speed, simplicity, and free expansion slots are SCSI's siren song. The concept is simple. One card connects up to seven devices to your computer and promises data throughput rates of up to 40Mb per second (with Fast-Wide SCSI-2). You can mix hard disks, CD-ROM drives, tape backup units, printers, scanners—almost anything. Adding a new device is allegedly as simple as plugging it in on the end of the chain. SCSI adapters come in ISA, EISA, and local bus varieties. I use an UltraStor U34F VL bus SCSI host adapter in one system, with a Conner FAST SCSI hard drive. The performance is about four times as fast as that with an ISA-based system with a popular IDE drive.

Several trends make SCSI's promise of high-performance and slot-saving abilities very desirable. SCSI is a natural for networks and for multitasking, multithreading operating systems, such as OS/2, UNIX, and Windows NT. These environments can take advantage of SCSI's ability to manage large storage devices and grant access to several devices at the same time. SCSI's ability to chain several devices to one card makes a lot of sense for device-intensive multimedia applications, which can require an extensive array of peripherals from CD-ROM drives to large hard disks and even rewritable optical drives.

And only SCSI hard disks are capable of attaining the capacities that you will need for serious multimedia use: Even one-sixteenth of a screen of compressed, adequate-quality, 60-second motion video can take up about 15Mb of disk space, and a stereo 16-bit, 44.1kHz .WAV sound file consumes over 10Mb for every minute of sound. Hard disks conforming to the SCSI-2 draft specification are typically available in sizes of up to 3Gb. Compare that to IDE disks, which have just begun to arrive in 1Gb capacities, and with ESDI disks, a nearly defunct technology that also topped out at a little over 1Gb in most instances. SCSI's high throughput also makes SCSI hard disks the recommended choice for all DVI (Digital Video Interactive) capture boards.

SCSI demands understanding for both its fascinations and its faults, in large part because it is not like other PC interfaces. For one thing, no PC operating system currently provides seamless support for SCSI, as DOS and OS/2 do for IDE and ESDI disks, so that capability has to be added by loading drivers. But SCSI goes beyond interfaces like these because it is more than just another way to hook up a hard disk. Rather, it is a full-fledged, bidirectional, intelligent I/O subsystem.

The SCSI expansion card, or host adapter, actually runs a self-contained expansion bus. Data is transferred directly among all units on the SCSI chain, including the host adapter, which handles all communications with the host computer. Each device is intelligent, with its own internal controller that sends, receives, and executes SCSI commands through the host adapter. A device can handle data internally almost any way it wants—as long as it communicates to the adapter using SCSI commands and formats. This gives SCSI its flexibility (though there is some slight overhead in handling the instructions). A new device or transfer method that was not even dreamed of when the SCSI standard was written can be incorporated, as long as the host adapter can control it with legal SCSI commands.

On minis, Macs, and many UNIX workstations, SCSI support is built directly into the operating system kernel and hardware (either on the motherboard or on a preinstalled backplane), so integration is not much of a problem. Third-party products' drivers have to conform not only to the SCSI standard, but to that computer's system requirements.

But the PC is different. In the past, a specific SCSI peripheral would often be designed to work with one or perhaps even a few specific host adapters, but was not likely to work with any other adapters, chiefly because no one—not the device manufacturer or the host adapter vendor, and certainly not DOS—supplied the appropriate drivers (In some cases, that is still true today, but it is getting better).

Unlike bad movies, SCSI's sequels get better. The SCSI-2 standard, which has been on the books for around seven years and should be finalized by the time you read this, fixes a lot of the compatibility problems by tightening up the SCSI hardware specs. In SCSI-2, a tighter command language leaves less room for host adapter approaches that support only vendor-specific devices. The authors of the standard also added new command extensions that leave the door open for new devices in the future: for instance, standardizing some commands that are common to a type of device—such as "retension tape" for a tape drive—so that the commands can be written in firmware (put onto a chip) instead of implemented in specific drivers.

And the SCSI-2 standard authors didn't forget speed. SCSI-2's Fast and Wide specifications can provide outstanding performance. Fast SCSI runs twice as fast as the original specification, with a maximum transfer rate of up to 10Mb per second over an 8- or 16-bit data path (in practice, achieving the maximum transfer rate is more likely over a 16-bit path). Wide SCSI extends the SCSI data path to either 16 or 32 bits and can be coupled with Fast SCSI; Wide SCSI allows throughputs of 20Mb per second over a 16- or 32-bit path, whereas Fast-Wide SCSI provides 40Mb per second transfer over a 32-bit path or 20Mb over a 16-bit path. Of course, you'll need the right hardware to support Fast, Wide, and Fast-Wide SCSI before you see the performance gains. For instance, to access the full 32-bit expanded bandwidth available through Wide and Fast-Wide SCSI, you'll need either an EISA, MCA, or Local Bus PC.

SCSI is beginning to see dramatic changes in the way the host adapter is integrated with the PC operating system and the devices are installed. For example, for some host adapter cards there are all but automatic installations.

Not all adapters are created equal, however. Take, for instance, the ASPI-based Adaptec 1542C and the ASPI-based UltraStor U34F VL-bus adapter. The Adaptec 1542C has one of the best firmware setups going; there are no jumpers and only one bank of DIP switches to control its ID and memory address. Holding the Ctrl-A combination during bootup accesses the adapter's firmware, with easy-to-use menus for setting up the card, termination, accessing advanced support options, and formatting hard disks. The Fast SCSI UltraStor U34F, on the other hand, still has jumpers and switches to set.

ASPI (Advanced SCSI Programming Language) is currently the most popular universal driver approach, with a huge library of device modules available. The A in ASPI used to stand for Adaptec, the company that introduced it; other SCSI device vendors have licensed the right to use ASPI with their products. Although DOS does not support ASPI, a base level of ASPI support is written into OS/2 2.1 and SCO UNIX ODT 2.0

and is being written into Windows NT. Operating system support of ASPI eliminates the need for a separate ASPI universal driver, though device modules are still necessary.

Corel Corporation, which makes your favorite drawing program, is the General Store on the SCSI frontier. It has given ASPI a real boost in the marketplace by designing ASPI device module drivers for almost every conceivable brand-name SCSI device and testing them for compatibility. Its CorelSCSI toolkit includes a wide range of DOS, Windows, OS/2, and Novell NetWare device drivers for CD-ROM, optical drives, jukeboxes, and other products. CorelSCSI provides automated installation routines that work very well for adding supported devices. CorelSCSI also comes with handy SCSI bus scanning utilities that provide information about components on ASPI chains and their attributes. It also includes basic tape backup programs for DOS and Windows and a slick CD-ROM audio player that works under Windows and maintains a database of your titles and tracks. The package is also bundled as an extra-cost option with most major host adapters.

If you are thinking about a new system or hard drive, consider SCSI. You will find it offers better performance, easier configuration, and more free slots. And think about using a local bus host adapter; you will thank yourself every time you load a complex file and don't have to wait for the hourglass as long as you used to. Now that we have covered how to connect devices to your PC, let's look at what to add to that bus.

Choosing a Storage Subsystem

What a difference a decade makes. Ten years ago a power user's desktop computer sported two floppy disk drives. The original Macintosh came with one floppy drive built in, and the basic IBM PC offered a floppy drive and cassette tape port. Of course that was also a time when word processors required about 60K of disk space and most personal computers had 128K of RAM. Today's storage requirements are much more demanding, and your options are much more confusing. A current state-of-the-art system may include a variety of storage media, including magnetic and optical devices, backup hardware, and compression software.

Graphic applications have always constituted one of the most intensive uses for a microcomputer. With today's scanners, color graphics, soft fonts, clip art, sound, and large programs like CorelDRAW!, an 80Mb, or even a 200Mb hard disk just isn't enough. In short, desktop publishers need to be power users when it comes to understanding storage. This requires cutting through the confusion about storage systems and developing a mass storage plan.

Chapter 28: Hardware Issues: Caring for and Improving Your System

Divide and Conquer

One way to develop a mass storage plan is to divide storage into levels based on data access requirements and to outline long-term goals. First-level or primary devices are ones that store frequently used information (major programs, current projects, and the like) and allow you to retrieve it quickly. Hard disks and RAM drives are the major products in this category. Secondary storage products are designed to hold data that are not used as often or that require very high capacity (items such as clip art, multimedia, large databases, and less-frequently used programs). This group includes floppy disks and CD-ROM and other optical devices. They are not as fast as primary units, but they offer lower cost per megabyte stored. Third-level products are those that are used for archival storage and system backups. Tape units are the most common form of products for third-level storage.

There are four primary goals to keep in mind when planning a storage system: user productivity, data security, cost, and future expansion. The best way to ensure day-to-day productivity is to have a storage system that provides fast and ready access to currently needed files and programs. The primary storage device should be large enough to hold all of them and should operate fast enough that the user does not spend a lot of time waiting for the computer. As the system grows, less-frequently used files can be stored on a secondary device to free up room on the main drive. Smaller systems can use backup software and floppy disks or an inexpensive tape unit to maintain archive copies of valuable files. As the system keeps growing, the owner can add the appropriate hardware: another hard disk, an optical drive, or a more sophisticated backup unit.

Generally speaking, the lower the storage level, the cheaper the cost per megabyte. Hard drives run about $.75 per megabyte, with the faster units costing more. CD-ROM averages about 20 cents a megabyte. Tape is even cheaper, only a half cent or less each megabyte. Rewrite-capable 1Gb magnetic/optical (MO) or phase change (P-C) and 400Mb WORM (write once–read many) optical storage cartridges cost around $200 each. The most cost-effective solution will vary. There is a trade-off between time and money.

There are a large number of variations on the design theme. Some firms like to use removable drives or cartridges, allowing sensitive data to be secured in a safe when not in use. Some have duplicate removable drives at workstations and typesetters, providing an easy way to move files from one system to the another. You can have one high-capacity backup unit shared on a network or moved from unit to unit. The real key is to have a clear picture of your needs and the options available. It is false economy to save a few dollars on a hard drive that costs hours in wasted time waiting for a publication to load. It can be a disaster to scrimp on backup and lose valuable files.

I have two primary workstations that serve as good examples. The first holds a single large hard drive as the primary unit, a combination P-C/WORM optical unit for secondary storage and backup, and a CD-ROM drive. This unit can handle large scanning jobs and store the resulting files on the optical drive. The backup software writes all new and revised files to the P-C cartridge every morning at 3 AM. The second has a very large hard drive and a tape backup unit. This unit is not used for large jobs, so secondary files are stored on tapes, just like the backups. The combination drive costs about $4,000, more than 12 times the cost of the tape unit.

The Venerable Hard Drive Offers More Choices Than Ever

A magnetic hard disk is the principal mass storage format for most computer users. A hard disk subsystem is composed of two pieces of hardware—the drive and its controller interface. The Mac is centered on the Small Computer System Interface (SCSI) as the means of letting the drive and computer communicate. The only real selection issues are drive speed, disk capacity, and cost. Mac owners are more limited when it comes to hard disk options. PC users are not limited to SCSI drives; there are several other competing interfaces.

The Integrated Drive Electronics (IDE) drive offers a low-cost solution. In most cases an IDE drive is at least 20 percent cheaper than a SCSI drive of the same size. IDE interface cards (called paddle boards) are a fraction of the cost of a SCSI host adapter card. As with SCSI, most of the controller functions are placed on the drive itself, and performance is comparable. SCSI wins hands down if you want to hook a bunch of drives to a network server or if you need a very large disk. And SCSI is the most common interface for optical drives. That means you may (allowing for possible compatibility problems) use the same host adapter to add up to seven devices to the computer—while using only one expansion slot. In general, use IDE if that is the only drive you plan to use with the system, you are on a budget, and it's under 400Mb; otherwise choose SCSI.

Other PC hard drive interfaces include the Enhanced Small Device Interface (ESDI), Run Length Encoded (RLE), and the aged Seagate MFM. ESDI drives are being phased out, and the others have all but disappeared, with the increasing popularity of IDE drives. You might find a deal on one of these, but the shelf life is limited.

Measuring Hard Drive Performance

There are all kinds of indexes used to measure drive performance. The best overall guide to I/O speed is the average access time. For DTP applications you want the lowest number you can afford. The slowest you should consider is about 13 milliseconds. The other really important number is the external transfer rate. This is the amount of data in megabytes the unit can get to the host computer per second. The actual amount will be limited by the controller and the capability of the host to accept data. The key here is to match the speed to your system's upper limit.

The internal transfer rate is the speed with which the drive can move data from the disk to its own buffer. This is limited by the rate at which the drive spins and is the number that tells the unit's actual throughput. The buffer size denotes the amount of RAM in the drive or controller cache. This RAM is used to store the most recently used data, saving the system the trouble (and time) needed to get it from the disk. Don't spend a lot of money on hardware cache; you can do the same thing with software for a fraction of the cost.

Optical Offers an Advantage

One form of storage any CorelDRAW! owner should consider is a CD-ROM drive. Using the CD-ROM that came with in the Corel package will add to the value of your software investment and make life easier at the same time. The number of available fonts on the Corel CD is greater than for the floppy distribution. It is faster to install via CD-ROM, and the clip art and symbols are more accessible. The CD-ROM can hold up to 650Mb of read-only data on a single removable disk. Drives vary in cost and performance. NEC makes a model that spins four times as fast the original model, and costs about four times more than basic mail-order types. If you don't have a CD-ROM drive now, check out *PC Magazine* or some other major publication for recent reviews and articles on the state of the art and the best buy.

Databases, such as Ziff-Davis Computer Select, and standard reference works, such as the Oxford English Dictionary, are available on CD-ROM. The number of available commercial disc titles is increasing dramatically, and the cost of producing a CD-ROM disc makes it a cost-effective option for many applications. In volume it costs less than $10 a disc to produce a CD-ROM title. The external drives are more expensive than internal models. CD-ROM is slower than hard drives, and many older units are slower than floppy drives. CD-ROM lets you have access to complete libraries on-line. One CD-ROM disc I have holds the complete text of a stack of manuals more than 12 feet high. The medium is a natural method for distributing photographs and clipart.

Maxtor, long a leader in hard drives, has moved into the rewritable optical drive market with its Maxoptix subsidiary. Its Tahiti 5.25-inch drives offer 1Gb (500Mb per side) cartridges with 25ms to 43ms access times. That may not be running as fast as a traditional hard drive, but the gap is closing. Micronet Technology is another strong contender, with a wide range of 3.5-inch high-performance rewritable optical systems.

For archival records WORM (Write Once–Read Many) optical drives are ideal. They allow data to be recorded but never erased. Software makes the unit appear like a read/write device, but you can look at the historical copies of revised files. Once the cartridge is full, you can no longer add files.

Some vendors offer complete combination drive kits that can accept both WORM and rewritable optical cartridges with drivers and SCSI interface. The Corel Kurata drive has both a WORM and Phase Change (P-C) capability. Phase Change drives allow writing with one pass, compared to two passes for the slower Magnetic/Optical (MO) drives. This improves speed but shortens media life expectancy compared to MO units. A P-C cartridge has about 100,000 read/write cycles compared to a million or more for MO platters. Corel has been a major developer of PC SCSI drivers for several years.

There are many factors to consider when purchasing any storage device. The first is compatibility with existing (and planned) system components and software, followed by size and affordability, and then overall performance. The new drive should be easy to integrate with existing components. Mixing two different drive types takes up an extra expansion slot. If you are planning to add optical units, think SCSI. Look at the type of files you work with, how much space they consume, and what can be off-loaded to secondary storage. Planning can save money, make it easier to do backups, and allow easy management of important files. Leaving any factor out of the equation is asking for trouble. Get a unit with a good warranty, a reasonable return policy, and first-class technical support. A well-tuned storage system saves you time and gives you peace of mind.

The Display System and the Need for Speed

If you want to increase CorelDRAW!'s performance by a factor of 10 on your existing PC, throw away your old VGA card. That's right. If you do a lot of desktop publishing or graphics on a PC, you use Windows and probably spend a lot of time waiting for your screen display. Installing a souped-up video card can really improve the speed with which your display works, making Windows seem five to 10 times faster. You may get more colors, better WYSIWYG, and higher resolution at the same time.

Windows has changed the way we look at our computers, literally. Instead of moving characters around on our monitors, we have started moving pixels, lots of pixels. The graphics interface is a bitmap picture, and as resolution and colors go up, the demands on the computer go up even faster. If all things were equal in terms of performance, a true-color Windows system would grind to a halt.

Chapter 28: Hardware Issues: Caring for and Improving Your System

Older-style display cards (such as VGA, EGA, and CGA) are known as dumb-frame adapters. They rely on the host computer to handle processing, which is acceptable if you don't have to move too many pixels or show too many colors. A screen display of 1,024 x 768 with 256 colors is about the upper limit for dumb-frame Super VGA cards. Obtaining that resolution requires about 800K of video RAM and a good bit of processing. With most new publishing programs running under resource-hungry Windows, that's about as far as a dumb-frame adapter can go. Newer, more powerful adapter cards are sounding the death knell for the VGA standard.

1992 saw a frenzy of development by video card vendors as the Windows market expanded. The combination of new chips and local bus technology offers us the opportunity to choose from a wide range of new products. During late 1992 and the first half of 1993 a new video card was announced at the rate of about one a day! Prices for high-performance cards during that same period fell to about one-third of what they were in December 1991. But beware of fancy ads and claims of fast benchmark scores. During testing I have found vendors developing drivers that cheated during benchmark testing. With the publicity and new tests, that problem should be a thing of the past when this book is on the shelves, but with so much market share at stake, the temptation will still be there for some less scrupulous developers. The real test is not in a single number, but in how the card works under your own real-world conditions. I have seen cards that ran the *PC Magazine* benchmarks five and six times faster than a competitor, but that could only load a file twice as fast. That still saves a lot of time spent looking at the hourglass, but it is not as great as the test would suggest.

Just keep in mind that there is no simple test that really compares the differences between adapters. Some vendors have legitimately optimized software drivers or board designs for certain tasks, offering impressive results, only to fall short in other areas. Some cut costs but offer poor performance. The best test is to use the card with the real-world applications you use. Don't just rely on benchmarks or claims that a board is faster than the competition.

High-performance adapters (let's call them smart cards) fall into one of two major categories: accelerators or coprocessors. An accelerator, or fixed-function processor, such as the S3 Inc. 86C928 (S3), can take part of the load for handling display processing from the host computer. A coprocessor such as Texas Instrument's TI 34020 is an actual CPU that can be programmed to handle almost all video operations. The advantage of a coprocessor is its flexibility, but it increases the card's price.

There are other cost-performance issues. More resolution requires more memory. A 1,024 x 768 x 24-bit card needs about 4Mb of RAM. To get the most speed it should be VRAM instead of the slower (and cheaper) DRAM used in some budget cards.

To change the board's digital data into the analog signal your monitor can use requires a digital-to-analog converter (RAMDAC). A RAMDAC can cost a vendor from about $25 to over $300. A top-of-the-line card is almost an add-on computer dedicated to handling display functions. As with a PC the hardware is only part of the system. Smart display systems need smart software. The video driver can make or break a Windows system. If you are going to spend the time and money to soup up your display, take the time to investigate the players. Be sure you buy a brand that comes from a company that supports its products and has solid drivers. If the company says the driver you need is on the way, either wait or look elsewhere.

A Bright New World

Buying a new display system is a bit like ordering for a group of people in a Chinese restaurant. There are a lot of options to consider. There are a wide range of designs and prices in each category. You need to identify how much resolution you require (or can afford). The next step is to decide how many colors you have to display and then to shop for the best price/performance trade-off. Serious publishing requires at least 1,024 x 768 resolution. The more resolution, the easier it is to draw a line or to lay out a page. The 640 x 480 and 800 x 600 resolutions don't allow viewing a readable full page. The higher resolutions, 1,024 x 768 and above, do. The more resolution, the more power you need, so that the video response is not the slowest part of your system. A 386 with a fast display may seem faster than a 486 with a slow one.

For prepress, color presentations and critical color design or retouching, 24-bit true color (16.7 million shades) is becoming a necessity. For users with less demanding needs, a 16-bit "high-color" card may suffice, but expect to see posterization in gradient fills and less than photographic-quality color bitmaps. With the prices on 24-bit cards dropping, high color is not a good choice (it isn't even an issue unless you are on a very tight budget). If your work involves only monochrome or spot color applications, the high-resolution 8-bit (256-color) smart card may be the best buy. Since this is a period without defined standards, know your vendor. Will they be able to offer new drivers as Windows is upgraded? Do they have good technical support and are they known for the quality of their products? Let's look at some of the major competitors in each category and some of the things to watch when making a purchase.

True color is pretty and photo-realistic. Once you get used to a fast 24-bit card, everything else seems too pale. You can also spend a lot of time waiting for a slow 24-bit card. The major things to watch for in this category are the quality of the driver (it sounds like I've said this several times, but it can't be overstated), speed, monitor requirements, and the way in which it handles VGA. DOS does not directly support 24-bit color adapters, so you need VGA capability on the card, or you must have an additional VGA card installed in your system.

The performance of a true color card is dependent on a number of factors: the interface bus, the type and amount of video memory (VRAM is faster and more expensive than DRAM), the quality and resolution of the Windows driver, and the type of RAMDAC and accelerator or coprocessor. Slower but less expensive cards such as those mentioned earlier are good choices for users who need only true color some of the time.

Fasten Your Seat Belts, Please

While this chapter was being written I was given an early copy of a new board design to evaluate. It is the first of the next generation of hot video cards and promises to bring true workstation performance to the PC. Initial testing (remember that this board was not yet in production but will be on sale when you read this) showed dramatic performance gains. The new chip has been developed by Matrox, a company known for its high-end true-color display adapters, such as the TI TMS34020-based Impression AT-S. The new MGA (Multimedia Graphics Architecture) series of boards based on a proprietary chip set shipped in volume in mid-1993. The company also has a new 64-bit chip available.

Like the ATI Mach 32, the Avance ALG2201, and the S3 family, the Matrox chip accelerates common graphics functions such as BitBits and pattern, polygon, and rectangle fills. But in many ways the Matrox design goes beyond current accelerator offerings. For instance, it also accelerates advanced CAD functions, such as 3-D Gouraud shading, z-buffering, and character drawing.

These and other features of the chip set hint that Matrox is positioning its MGA products as low-cost PC alternatives to dedicated graphics workstations. The Matrox chip is optimized for 486-based and Pentium systems, and with enhancements for Intel's PCI (Personal Computer Interconnect) local-bus specification in mind. It has a 128-bit-wide bus, with 64 bits for graphics and 64 bits for video output. The 64-bit graphics bus is twice as wide as most existing adapters. Boards based on the Matrox chip will take full advantage of the 64-bit block-write capability of VRAM and sport a 32-bit multiplexed bus/host interface. Although it handles 64-bit instructions internally, the Mach 32 chip cannot handle 64-bit block writes.

An MGA prototype board was provided as I wrote this chapter. The Matrox chip set's wider internal bus and 64-bit block-write capability could translate into performance that is as much as 12 times as fast as most existing Windows accelerators.

Other additions and innovations for this chip include a direct interface to a laser printer to accelerate printing, a mouse port, video windowing capabilities, animation acceleration, and 32-bit-per-pixel support.

All versions of the MGA will have VGA on-board, and all will support 24-bit true color. The boards offer ISA, MCA, VL-bus, or PCI connections. EISA, and S-bus (Sun SPARC workstations) products are under development. There are or will be drivers for Windows 3.1 and Windows NT (including Open GL), OS/2 2.x, DynaView ADI/AutoCAD, and SunSoft Solaris 2.0. Also bundled with the cards will be a JPEG compression utility for Windows, a ClearType antialiasing utility, and mode-switching software.

Options planned for the MGA series take advantage of the design's high throughput. VideoPro is a daughtercard NSTC/PAL encoder that can provide desktop- or broadcast-quality TV video output. All versions of the MGA chip will be compatible with the Matrox Marvel video-in-a-window board.

If You Just Want Speed and Need Less Color

Some cards offer "high-color." These are adapters with 15- or 16-bit capability. But 32,768 or 65,536 colors offered by high-color displays are not enough for critical work. With high color you will still see posterization and not be able to manipulate each pixel exactly. So if you want more than 256 on-screen shades, consider spending extra for a true-color board.

The more colors, the more processing, memory, and disk activity when reading files. If you don't need extra color, you can opt for more speed and lower cost. Accelerated boards at 1,280 x 1,024 or 1,024 x 768 with 256 (8-bit) colors will do very nicely for a lot of users. The S3 and other accelerators offer a real boost to Windows performance, without taking a big bite out of your wallet. Since this segment of the market is getting crowded, vendors are working on improving value to increase sales.

The ATI Ultra is a good example of a well-designed accelerator card. It packs a lot of features into a single slot, if all you need is 8-bit operation. Capable of up to 1,280 x 1,024, resolution it has a built-in mouse port, full 8514 compatibility, Super VGA support, and the ATI Mach-8 accelerator that really makes Windows fly. The card is also equipped with ATI's Crystal Font technology to improve text performance and clarity for Windows applications.

As with the high-priced true-color cards, you should take some time when shopping. There is a wide range of price and performance, and more money does not always mean better engineering or support.

Getting the Picture

The popularity of Windows has changed the monitor market too. In the magazine *Personal Publishing*'s original display issue six and a half years ago, I recommended the original NEC MultiSync as a good choice. Three of them are still in service in my lab, one with a 24-bit adapter. But the newer MultiSync 5FG ($1,000 street price) is the one I'm using to write this chapter. Paired with a Matrox MGA I get not only a fast 1,024 x 768 true-color display, but also flicker-free operation, 17-inch flat screen, color calibration controls, and an edge-to-edge picture without annoying image jumps when I move from VGA to true-color modes.

NEC has done an outstanding job in producing the FG series with Windows users in mind, and once again it is the standard to measure others with. The high-contrast glass is polished, offering sharper images, the unit meets the Swedish radiation and magnetic emissions requirements, and the antistatic screen seems never to need cleaning. It comes with connections for both Mac and PC adapters. There are several good monitor makers, and we can expect to see competition drive them to offer a host of good products for Windows users upgrading their systems. In choosing a monitor for a new display adapter make sure that the two are well matched. Slow screen-refresh rates (below 70Hz) and interlaced operation can cause eye strain and are not suitable for demanding applications such as graphics design or publishing.

Have It Both Ways

Radius has a solution for those users who can't decide between a landscape or full-page portrait monitor. The Radius Pivot (when coupled with the companion SVGA Multiview card) can be turned between horizontal and vertical while operating. An internal switch detects the change and rotates the image. In both portrait and landscape modes you can view a full page 1,024 x 768 with 256 colors. At 640 x 480 the combination can deliver a 32,768 high-color palette.

The Pivot is a handy tool for users who have to switch between full-page and normal portrait operation, but there are some drawbacks. The monitor's switch works only with the special SVGA multiview card. When using other cards, the Pivot functions only in landscape mode.

Using the Pivot is very handy for users who want a full-page monitor without the hassle of special drivers and the ability to have a landscape display for all the normal applications that don't call for a portrait view. But be advised that the monitor only works its magic with special display cards.

The Wave of the Future

Forget arguments about what will be the next PC graphics display standard. It's here and its name is Microsoft Windows. For most desktop publishers there are only a few real questions when choosing a display system. Does it have the resolution and color depth needed? Is it fast enough? And does it work well under Windows? If it does not, look elsewhere. If it does, look at the price tag and decide if the price is right for you.

POINTING IN THE RIGHT DIRECTION WITH GRAPHICS TABLETS

Most Windows users own a mouse. The little beast is used to point, click, and draw. With CorelDRAW! you can do a very good job with a mouse. But there are better options if the little rodent is not all you desire. After all, you learned to write with pencils. You use graphics tablets with a stylus, which feels and works just like a pen, to draw, point, and click. In other words, the mouse is designed to point and the tablet to draw.

Two major differences account for that. Mice do not normally offer an absolute position; instead they offer relative movement. If you move the mouse 1 inch on the pad, the mouse might move 1 inch on the screen. Move it 1 inch a little faster and the pointer might speed all the way across the screen. The degree of movement of the pointer is relative to movement. Tablets generally can set position in two ways, relative and absolute. If you move the stylus 1 inch on the tablet, the position of the pointer will move exactly 1 inch on the virtual page. This means you can draw or trace with precision on the pad.

There are several varieties of tablets. Most have a firm surface, either raised at an angle or lying flat. Numonics offers a flexible grid that is very thin, reducing the clutter next to your PC. There are also several types of pointing devices. Stylus handles may have click devices built into the side or activated by pressing the tip down quickly. The problem with using the latter type with CorelDRAW! is that you may draw or move an object when you click on the page. There are also pucks, which look like a four-button mouse with a set of cross hairs in a clear plastic plate in front. The drawing point sits at the center of the cross hairs. This type is a favorite of CAD users.

The really big difference between tablets is sensitivity. Some, such as the Wacom units used while writing this book, can change function based on how hard you press on the tablet surface with the stylus. Programs such as Fractal Painter (see the next chapter) change the thickness of a line or the way paint is placed on the page, based on the amount of pressure applied. CorelDRAW! may support pressure-sensitive devices in the future. Although the company has not made any announcements, it is a possible enhancement.

The two Wacom tablets are well-designed. Both units sport cordless styluses and pucks. So when they are used, they feel just like regular drawing. The smaller one has a drawing area about the size of a regular mouse pad, 6 x 9 inches, and sits flat on the desk. The larger one is 12 x 12 inches. It can be equipped with an electrostatic surface. Press a switch and a paper placed on top will stick to the pad. Another nice feature shared by both is that you can have a mouse and the tablet active under Windows at the same time. Just use whichever one works best for a task.

Chapter Summary

To get the most out of your CorelDRAW! investment, you must know how to get the most out of your system. One of the real advantages of the PC's open design is the ability to tailor a configuration to your specific needs. The PC market is constantly changing, so you have to study and shop carefully.

CHAPTER 29
Third-Party Software and Miscellaneous Products

In This Chapter...

- File Conversion and Screen Capture
- Image Management
- Desktop Publishing
- Statistics
- Special Effects

What this Chapter is About

CorelDRAW is a wonderful package, but adding other programs to your electronic desktop can enhance your work and make both Windows and CorelDRAW work better. This chapter is a grab bag of software products that have come to my attention and that I use frequently. They are usually not the only products in a category, just the ones I have come to appreciate. Some were used extensively in writing this book. This chapter has been included to offer readers ideas for possible additions to their libraries. Since several of these products could fall into different categories, I have not tried to put them in rigid groups. The headline titles give clues to what the programs are designed to do. I have included system requirements and contact information for the companies but left out price and version numbers, since those may change while this book is in print.

The opinions are my own, and unsolicited. The industry is constantly churning out new goodies, so next time this chapter will hold short reviews of other applications, and the icons on my desktop will not all be the same.

When you go shopping I hope you'll find new and nifty treasures to share with others too. If you find a good one, let me know. My CompuServe ID is 74035,705.

Squeegee Makes Windows Manageable

If you use several programs at once and have a large hard disk, you need Squeegee. If you only use one or two programs, you may not need it but would still find it useful. It is an invisible desktop organizer that includes the best replacement for the Windows File Manager I've seen yet. The idea is simple. Click anywhere on the open desktop and get a list of your most-used programs, groups, and several Squeegee utilities. Click on one and the program is loaded.

That's fine, but what is even better is its ability to set up a listing like a batch file. Open the menu with a click and several programs open, each loading with the files you want, ready to go. While writing the book I used this program constantly. I could load CorelDRAW with the current exercise, Word for Windows with the current chapter, and Image Pals set up for screen captures. One click did it all. Figure 29.1 shows the Squeegee menu and the Quick Filer on my desktop.

Chapter 29: Third-Party Software and Miscellaneous Products

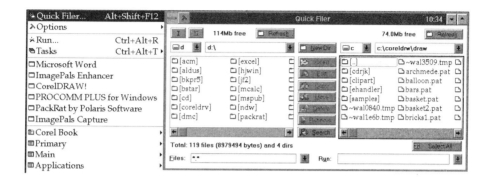

FIGURE 29.1 Using Squeegee

The Quick Filer is similar to my favorite DOS-based file utility, Norton Commander, and features a strong search engine to locate misplaced files, copy, move, delete, and so on. The program can also be launched from the icon you see on the left of the Quick Filer title bar. It pops up on the active window if you have enabled the option, just like the clock on the right side of the bar.

Squeegee lets you link a file type to several different applications, define default directories for programs, and arrange Windows the way you want to work. It runs on any system that can run Windows 3.0 or later. The only problem I found was when writing the chapter on CorelCHART for this book. Then I had to unload Squeegee because CHART wanted the room. Otherwise it is a constant companion. You can get more information from ICOM Simulations, 648 South Wheeling Rd., Wheeling, IL 60090; tel.: (708) 520-4440.

IMAGE PALS CAPTURES WINDOWS

Image Pals 2 is well worth considering if you need to manage graphics and multimedia files, make screen captures, or scan and edit bitmap images. It's the program I used to capture, clean up, and manage almost all the figures for this book. It's produced by U-Lead Systems, the same company that created Aldus PhotoStyler, and supports every monitor type, from monochrome to 24-bit true color. It contains three primary modules. Album is a combination file manager and operating shell. Editor handles scanning, photo retouching, and bitmap editing. SCapture is a very sophisticated screen-shot utility.

The SCapture module is outstanding, but limited to the Windows environment. You can define almost any hot-key combination and screen region and then send the captures to the Clipboard, a file, the Capture window, an Album file, or the printer. A really slick feature is the ability to define the type of cursor that will be included in the shot. You can choose one of four standard Windows cursor shapes, choose any special pointer used by an application, or omit the cursor entirely. The selected shape will be captured, no matter what pointer is on the screen. It even worked when I used a display card with a hardware cursor.

As the image is captured the program can: automatically crop; change color depth; adjust the background color; modify the resolution; and add frames, keylines, or drop shadows. I snapped 15 images at one time into the capture window without any problems, except slowing the system a bit. Figure 29.2 shows the Image Pals 2 **Capture** window.

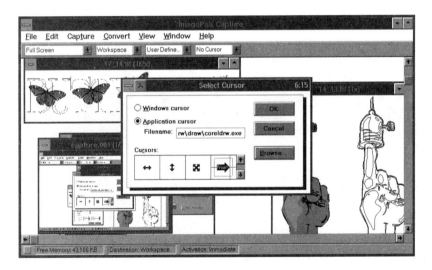

FIGURE 29.2 Image Pals 2 in Action

Album is an electronic light table and library. Images are collected into groups called Albums. You can specify files individually, or automatically include any files in a given directory. The program then generates a master file that contains thumbnail images of the files along with the file type, name, size, compression method, date stamp, and an optional description. The thumbnails are shown in a window, like slides laid out for viewing, with the collected information in the selected file displayed below. You can view, sort, print, compress, rename, delete, move, copy, and convert images individually or in batches using menu commands and dialog boxes. It supports a wide variety of file types including TIFF (both PC and Mac), PCX, Targa, BMP, GIF, JPEG, and EPS. The EPS format is for export only. The rest can be imported, exported, and displayed. Compression options vary with file type and platform.

I created albums containing more than 40 images several times while working on this book. The images displayed well, and I could show the thumbnails at several resolutions. Creating an album can take several minutes, and the master file can eat up a megabyte or more of disk space. The program will prompt you with a request to proceed with the operation after calculating and displaying the final file size. The drawback is the lack of real support for working with EPS images from any other program.

There are a variety of print options. I used the batch commands to print both thumbnails and full-size hard copies of all the screen shots in this book. You can specify the size, page setup, and information for the prints; then let Image Pals do the work while you go on to another task. The import, export, and print options are the same for all three modules. Album has a toolbar that can be customized with icons for up to eight other programs. You can load one with a selected file by dragging and dropping the thumbnail onto the desired application's icon.

Editor is a sophisticated image editor with some paint program capabilities. Image adjustment controls include: brightness and contrast; hue and saturation; gamma, highlight, shadow, and midtone manipulations; a magic wand tool for area selection; and filters to sharpen, average, blur, emboss, and create a mosaic effect. Images can be scanned in or imported from other applications. The program includes drivers for the most popular scanners. It can also stitch multiple scans into one file, a handy feature for users with hand scanners. Paint tools are not as extensive as in dedicated programs, but Enhancer offers an airbrush, text tool, paintbrush, on-screen color palette, and line tool. It runs on any Windows 3.x PC. For more information contact U-Lead Systems, Inc.; 970 West 190th Street, Suite 520; Torrance, CA 90502; tel.: (310) 523-9393.

HIJAAK IS A MASTER TRANSLATOR

HiJaak for Windows is one of those programs that should be a part of the software library of any Windows user needing to get files moved from one program or system to another. You can view and enhance 23 bitmap and 15 vector-graphic file formats, ranging from Amiga's IFF to WordPerfect's WPG. Image manipulations include rotation, resizing, and color reduction, as well as contrast and brightness adjustments. Monitor support ranges from monochrome to 24-bit true color. If your display system is limited to 256 colors, HiJaak lets you view images using either a fixed or dynamic palette. You can view several files at once, but the screen redraws are a bit slow. Figure 29.3 shows the HiJaak desktop.

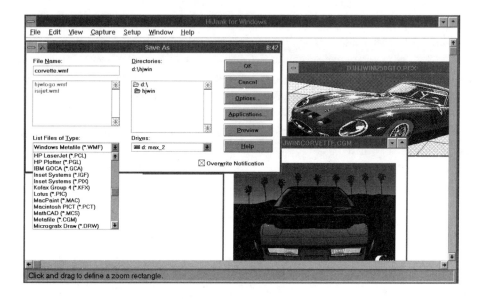

FIGURE 29.3 The HiJaak Desktop

Windows screen captures are straightforward. Just load the program, set up the capture screen, hit the designated hot-keys, and name the file. A drawback is that the key combinations all involve either the **Ctrl** or **Alt** keys, making it impossible to capture some Fly-out and drop-down menus. The program is produced by Inset Systems [71 Commerce Drive, Brookfield, CT 06804-3406; tel.: (203) 740-2400] and requires a Windows 3.x-capable PC with 5.5Mb of hard disk space minimum (more for bitmap conversions).

SPSS FOR WINDOWS

If you need to include statistical data in a presentation, consider SPSS for Windows. You can export the results to CorelDRAW and use its fancy layouts to display your findings. The SPSS brochures bill this program as capable of providing "real stats, real easy." Although some people may never think of statistics as easy, SPSS for Windows offers a solid engine with easy access to professional tools for those who need to use them.

This is an exceptional Windows version of a classic statistics package. Although all the modules available in the mainframe versions are not yet available under Windows, they are on the way. Like the mainframe versions, SPSS for Windows is broken up into several modules that can be bought separately. Only two modules were available in the summer of 1992, with six others due to be ready in several months. When it is complete, the Windows release will offer all analysis tools provided with the mainframe versions.

The older versions of SPSS on larger systems like the VAX are powerful, but the program's interface is primitive at best. The Windows version provides the same engine, but what a difference its GUI interface makes! Each primary function—data entry, charting, and so on—is given its own window and menu. Instead of having to use a proprietary command language, all commands can be executed using dialog boxes with context-sensitive help and an on-line glossary. The option buttons are designed to keep all features no more than two layers from the menu or window level.

Data entry is done using the same kind of spreadsheet approach as Chart. The ribbon spaces on the top of the column are used to define variables. Just double-click on one and a dialog box opens offering all the tools needed for definition. You can display either labels or values in the cells, and both can be entered or modified at any time. A nested dialog box offers complete information on a variable and any annotations. SPSS can import Excel XLS, Lotus WKS, dBase, Oracle, SQL Server, SLYK, and ASCII data directly into a data window. Templates can be used to automatically define variables to be used with a new or imported data set. Figure 29.4 shows SPSS for Windows at work.

The Basic module is needed to run the rest of the modules and performs summary and means comparisons, frequencies, cross-tabs (the last two features include multiple response), t-tests, one-way ANOVAs, and linear regressions. The Professional module adds cluster, multidimensional scaling, proximity and reliability, plus factor and discriminate analysis. Planned additions include Advanced Statistics, Tables, Trends, Categories, CHAID, and Lisrel (linear structure) modules. New features are automatically added to the existing basic menus during installation, so there is no need to shift from one program to another. This program likes a lot of resources. If you need serious statistics, run it on more than the basic system requirements. It runs all right on a 386 for small data sets, but for heavy number crunching get a 486. For more information, contact SPSS, Inc.; 444 North Michigan Ave.; Chicago, IL 60611-3962; tel.: (312) 329-2400.

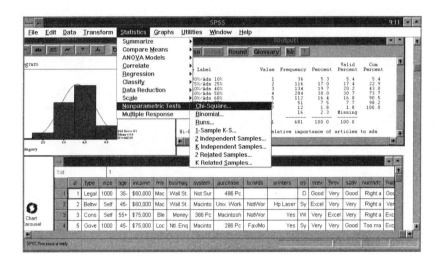

FIGURE 29.4 SPSS for Windows

FRACTAL PAINTER: AN ART STORE ON DISK

Fractal Painter is fun, a collection of virtual tools that mimic traditional art supplies. There are the usual airbrushes, pens, and fills you expect in a paint program, but that's just the beginning. There are dirty markers, Japanese brushes, water colors, and all kinds of goodies. The program's brushes work just like the real thing, with bristles that can be adjusted to almost any shape.

As you create a drawing the pigments, chalks, and inks build up as they would on paper. And there are all kinds of papers: smooth papers, rough papers, and special effects textures. To create a painting you open a window by specifying the size based on pixels, and choose a paper type. Then select a tool, color, and any special effects, and draw. You can mix media and apply friskets to mask areas. Painter also supports pressure-sensitive tablets such as the Wacom, mentioned in hardware chapter. The program is simple to use, but likes a lot of power. You'll need a 486 with at least 6Mb of RAM, but a Pentium is better. To get the full benefit, a 24-bit display adapter and matching monitor are recommended. The program offers the graphics power to go with them. The latest version added text support, improved cloning features, and the best pressure-sensitive tablet support going.

The folks at Fractal Design also produce a grayscale version of the program called Sketcher. They can be reached at 101 Madeline Drive, Suite 204; Aptos, CA 95003; tel.: (408) 688-8800.

MICROSOFT PUBLISHER: DESKTOP WIZARD

Microsoft Publisher is an easy-to-use desktop publishing package aimed at entry-level users producing short documents. Of course, now that CorelDRAW 5.0 includes Ventura Publisher, I don't really need Microsoft Publisher any more; but if you have Version 4.0 or earlier, and aren't going to upgrade for a while, Publisher may be of help. It has a feature called Page Wizard works like the Auto-Format feature in Word, and automatically builds generic newsletters, brochures, and other standard publications. A series of menus walks you through the available options. Once the selections are made, you can watch the publication take shape as a learning exercise. New users will find Wizards are a quick way to create a polished design. More experienced users can still use the feature to reduce the work required to add things like calendars or advertising to a document. Publisher also offers a variety of templates for common types of publications and forms, or you can build a document from scratch.

Every element on the page, text or graphic, sits in a frame. Select a tool from the ribbon bar and drag a frame into place. Then just type text, import a graphic, or use a Wizard. Resizing is handled by dragging the edge of a frame. This approach is very intuitive and is well-suited for occasional users. Although text frames can be linked together, there are no style sheets or ways to make global formatting changes. Publisher is not designed to handle long documents. These qualites, of course, are the forte of Ventura Publisher.

The rulers located at the top and left side of the work area can be moved to any position on the page. It's like having a T-square inside the screen. I wish other graphics applications would copy the idea. There is no automatic text-wrap around an image. The way around this is to draw frames, forcing the text into an irregular pattern. Background pages can be used to place items that repeat on every page. The program will run with any Windows 3.x-compatible computer. Call Microsoft at (800) 426-9400.

Figure 29.5 shows the MS Publisher rulers in action. The calendar was created to show the dates of my wife's family reunion. The layout, dates, and artwork were all generated by a Wizard.

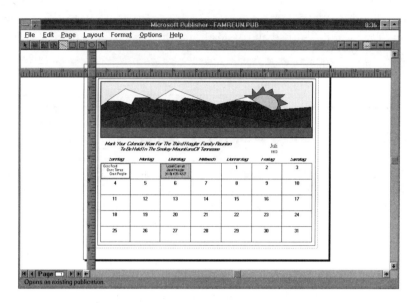

FIGURE 29.5 Microsoft Publisher's Rulers in Action

FRAMEMAKER IS VERY TECHNICAL

Framemaker is an industrial-strength publishing program. Like SPSS, FrameMaker has been around on other systems for a while but just recently moved to Windows. A tag-based formatting system and templates let you quickly build complex layouts and apply them to text created in other word processors. This version offers all the features found in the UNIX and Mac editions: footnotes, equations, cross-references, and a fancy tables generator. It also comes with a built-in word processor and drawing module and allows you to work with more than one document at a time. With Version 5.0 of CorelDRAW, which includes the well-known and very powerful Ventura Publisher, I expect to use it more and Framemaker less.

The program is geared more toward long documents, such as books and technical manuals, than it is to short and design-intensive projects, which are the province of CorelDRAW or such programs as Microsoft Publisher. You can easily move documents between versions on different platforms, including Mac, NeXt, Sun, SCO, UNIX, and Windows.

A special feature is the ability to show and hide portions of the text or graphics based on special conditional tags. This is a very powerful option for publishers who have to produce several variations of the same document. You can import files from CorelDRAW through the OLE and Clipboard functions or by exporting them in a supported file format.

If you need an integrated publishing solution for long documents, you might want to get more information. Contact Frame Technology, 1010 Rincon Circle, San Jose, CA 95131; tel.: (408) 433-3311.

A Gallery of Special Effects

Gallery Effects is a collection of filters that apply 16 different special effects to bitmap images. These resemble such artistic techniques as dry-brush strokes, mosaic, smudge stick, and fresco. Using the program is simple. Just load the image, then choose the effect from a menu. A dialog box lets you sample the effect on part of the image in a preview window. Different effects offer different controls. When the adjustments are the way you want, click **OK**. If the final result is not to your liking, use the **Undo** command and try again.

Gallery Effects supports TIFF, Targa, and Windows BMP formats. If a program supports PhotoStyler plug-in modules, you can use the effects directly within it. Fractal Painter, reviewed earlier, is one such program. If you like playing with bitmap images, this is a neat utility. This program requires at least a basic Windows 3.x system. Contact Aldus Corp., 411 First Ave. South, Seattle, WA 98104; tel.: (206) 628-2320.

INDEX

A

absolute positioning, 62-63
active layer, 250
actors (in animations), 573, 581-587
    creating new, 588-591
    editing, 581-583
    invisible return path, creating, 586-587
    path of, setting, 583-585
    speed of, controlling, 585-586
Add New Perspective command, 336
advertising layouts, creating, 624-634
    columns, using, 632
    CorelDRAW setup for, 624
    drop shadow, adding, 633
    graphics, placing, 627-630
        background, creating, 628, 629
        spot colors, using, 627-628
    grid system, using, 624
    headlines, 632-633
    layout design, 624-627
    text, placing, 630, 633, 634
Airbrush tool (PHOTO-PAINT), 475-477
aligning nodes, 118
Alignment dialog box, 18, 19
Alt-E, 132
Alt-Enter, 132
Angle of Cut option (Edit Line dialog box), 290
animation, 572-574
    action sequences, adding, 581-591
        continuity, maintaining, 591
        editing images, 581-583
        new actors, creating, 588-591
        new props, creating, 587-588
        path of actor, setting, 583-585
        return path, creating invisible, 586-587
        speed of actor, controlling, 585-586
    backdrops for, 577-578
    fine-tuning, 592-597
        with Cel Sequencer roll-up, 592-593
        cues, 594
        with Timelines roll-up, 593-594
    inserting, with CorelSHOW, 564-565
    morphing, 595-597
    sound, adding, 595
    text titles, adding, 579-580
Animation Information dialog box, 574, 575
annotations (CorelCHART), 527-528
Apply button, with blends, 323
arcs
    creating, 51, 52
    with envelopes, 312, 313
area charts, 539
Arrange menu, 93-97
    CorelCHART, 529
arrays, creating, with blends, 333-334
Arrowhead Editor, 32
Arrows Options (Outline Pen dialog box), 31-32
Artist brush (PHOTO-PAINT), 477
artistic text, 600
    embossing, 759-762
    entering, 143-144
    in envelopes, 316
    exercises using, 154-155, 164-168
    paragraph text vs., 142

ascender, 153
ASPI, 817-818
Astrotext (Gary Bouton), 749-758
AUTOEXEC.BAT, 802-805
AutoJoin setting (Curves dialog box), 274
automatic hyphenation, 194
AutoReduce setting (Curves dialog box), 274
auto-reducing nodes, 119
Autoscanner (CorelCHART), 510
Autoshade function (CorelCHART), 525-526
AutoTrace mode, 272-274
Autotrace Tracking setting (Curves dialog box), 274

B

backups, hard drive, 807-808
BACONOCR.TIF, 290
Ball-valve (Deborah Miller), 699-709
bar charts, 539-540
baseline, 153
   aligning text to, 160
   fitting text to flexible, 174-175, 177
   with paragraph text, 199
batch runs, for business cards, 620
Behind Fill check box, 34-35
beveled nib, 34
Bézier, Pierre, 64
Bézier curves, 102-106
   and control points, 105
   example using, 102-104
   and nodes, 105
   and paths, 104
   and segments, 105
   and subpaths, 105
Bézier mode, 64, 106-108
birds, drawing, 643
bitmap images, 2, 3, 263-306. *See also* PHOTO-PAINT
   Auto Trace function with, 272-274
   CCapture, obtaining images using, 304-306
   converting to vector images, with CorelTRACE, 275-293
      Centerline method, 283
      checking image information, 281
      custom settings, 287-290
      file formats, 291-293
      guidelines, 290-291
      Image Info box, 279-280
      interface, 275-279
      Line method, 281-282
      Outline method, 282-283
      selecting files, 280
      silhouette tracing, 286
      smoothing out lines, 284
      woodcut tracing, 284-286
   cropping, 271
   export filters with, 297-302
   fills, using as, 82
   hidden images, 269-270
   import filters with, 293-297
   importing, 266-268
   monochrome, 265, 271
   outlines and fills with, 270-271
   PostScript halftone screens with, 271
   resolution of, 268
   rotating, 269
   scaling, 269
   sizing, 269
   system requirements for handling, 480-481
   transformations of, 268-270
   Windows Clipboard for importing and exporting, 302-304
Bitmap Size radio buttons (Two-Color Pattern Editor), 80
Blend filter (PHOTO-PAINT), 488
Blend roll-ups, 318-321
blends, 310, 318-334
   additional control points, defining, 330
   Apply button, using, 323
   arrays, creating, 333-334
   beginning and end nodes, choosing, 321
   Color mode, 321
   compound, 329-330
   defining, 320
   dynamic elements of, 324-325
   envelope effects with, 328-329
   example using, 318-319
   fill combinations, results of, 322
   fitting to path, 330-333
   landscape, hills in, 638
   mapping nodes with, 326
   mapping to another path, 321
   node controls, 322-323, 327
   primary roll-up for, 320-321
   selecting elements, 327-328
   simple, 323-324
   speeding up work with, 323-324
   splitting nodes with, 326-327
   Steps mode, 321

Index

taking apart, 325-326
transformations with, 328-334
    additional control points, defining, 329-330
    arrays, creating, 333-334
    compound blends, 329-330
    envelope effects, 328-329
    fitting to path, 330-333
uses of, 319
vs. contours, 371
blocks, text, 142, 603
BMP files, importing, 292
BMP OS/2 files, exporting to, 299
BMP Windows files
    exporting to, 299
    import filters with, 294
borders, creating, 225-226
bounding boxes, 51
Bouton, Gary David, 749-764
Box Text tool (VENTURA), 430
Break Apart command, 172
breaking apart nodes, 118
breakout, adding, to newsletter, 666-668
brightness, adjusting (PHOTO-PAINT), 484-485, 490
brochure, three-fold (exercise), 251-260
Bullet dialog box, 195, 196
bullets, adding, 244-246
buses, 814-815
business cards, 615-620
    batch runs, 620
    company information, layout of, 619
    logo, placing, 617-618
    name and title, adding, 620
    page, setting up, 615, 617
    paper color, adjusting, 616, 617
    paper size, setting, 616
    spot colors, using, 618
Butterflies (Chris Purcell), 738-744

C

CALENDAR.RTF, 244
Calibration Bar option, 215
Calligraphy setting (Outline Pen dialog box), 33-34
callout's, 64
Cancel button, 11
cap height, 153
cartooning, 762-764

Cary, Cathy, 636
Castle (Deborah Miller), 687-693
CCapture module, 304-306
CCH files, 503
CD-ROM
    CorelDRAW on, 7
    fonts on, 138
    as storage subsystem, 821-822
cels, 572, 573
Cel Sequencer roll-up, 592-593
centering text, 18
center justification, 148
Centerline method (CorelTRACE), 283
center of rotation, 6
Center option, 216
certificate, designing and printing (exercise), 225-230
CGM files
    exporting to, 299
    import filters with, 294
Chapter Settings dialog box (VENTURA), 414-415
chapters (VENTURA), 442-443
character angle, adjusting, 163
    with fitted text, 183
Character Attributes dialog box, 19, 35, 146, 147, 151, 152, 160-161, 199
Character dialog box, 191, 192
Chart Layer (CorelCHART), 512-516
    moving and scaling text, 515-516
    rotating title test, 514-515
    text and display, adjusting, 518-520
Chart menu (CorelCHART), 523-526
check boxes, 11
checkmarks, 13
CHKDSK, 809-811
chrome effects, creating, 758-759
circle(s)
    Ellipse tool, drawing with, 51
    power clipping lines to, 388-389
Clear Perspective command, 336-337
Clear Transformations command, 312
click-and-drag drawing
    dual-pull, 122-123
    single-pull, 120-121
client (container), 549
Clone Frame option, 216
clones, 381-386
    cloning, 385
    Edit menu Clone command, 382-383

Effects menu Clone command, 383-384
   guidelines for working with, 386
Clone tool (PHOTO-PAINT), 478
closed paths, 68
   drawing, 123-124
clouds, drawing, 364-366, 643
CMX files, import filters with, 294
CMYK color model, 41
Collate Copies check box, 212
Color bar, 11
Color button (Outline Pen dialog box), 28-29
color/gray map, adjusting (PHOTO-PAINT), 485-486
Coloring setting (Extrude roll-up), 342-343
Color Manager command, 22
Color mode (blends), 320
color models, 38, 40-43
   CMYK, 41
   HSB, 42
   RGB, 41
Color Override button, 250-251
Color Profile dialog box (PHOTO-PAINT), 482
Color Replacer tool (PHOTO-PAINT), 470-471
color(s)
   in charts, 538
   converting, 44
   describing, 37-38
   process, 38
   spot, 37-38, 43
   and system speed, 826
columns
   adjusting and selecting spreadsheet, 509
   in brochure, 253
   and dummying, 654
   in newsletter, 664-665
   paragraph text, adding to, 243-244
combining, 96-97
   welding vs., 375
comma delimited text, 542
Command buttons, 11
complex drawings, 635-649
   landscape example, 636-649
      bird, adding, 642-643
      clouds, forming, 643
      creek, adding, 644
      flowers, adding, 645-649
      forests, adding, 640-642
      hills, creating, 637-639
      marsh, adding, 644-645
      ocean and sky, adding, 639-640

   setup, 636
   planning, importance of, 636
compound blends, 329-330
compound documents, 549
CompuServe, 292, 300
CONFIG.SYS, 802-805
conical fills, 70, 357, 358
conical fountain fills, 86
constraints, with envelopes, 317-318
container (client), 549
Continuous Cut option (Edit Line dialog box), 290
contours, 371-375
   blends vs., 371
   example using, 372-375
contrast, adjusting (PHOTO-PAINT), 484-485, 490
Control Panel
   CorelMOVE, 576-577
   Microsoft Windows, 221
control points, 105
   defining additional, 330
   using, 111
Convert Spot Color To CMYK option, 217
Convert to Monochrome option (Image dialog box), 288
Convert True Type to Type 1 option (Separations Tab), 218
Copy Attributes From... command, 134-135
Copy Attributes From dialog box, 135
Copy command, 133, 200
copying objects, 58-59
CorelCHART, 5, 501-545
   annotations, adding, 527-528
   Arrange menu, 529
   Chart Layer, manipulating, 514-516
   Chart menu, 523-526
      autoshade functions, 525
      custom fills, setting, 525-526
      riser controls, 526
      3-D bar chart options, 524
   creating simple chart with, 506-507
   format, converting chart, 516-520
   importing into, 541-542
      data, 541-542
      graphics, 542
   interface, 503-506
   and OLE, 544-545
   presentation guidelines, 536-541
   presentation of data, adjusting, 529-536

Index

data analysis, performing, 531
pie charts, 532-536
risers, adjusting size and order of, 530-531
riser text format, changing, 531-532
scale, converting, 530
slice feelers, 535-536
spreadsheet, working with, 507-514
cleaning up chart, 512-514
columns and rows, adjusting and selecting, 509
tagging data, 510-512
templates with, 542-544
3-D tool, 520-523
viewing charts, 510-511
CorelDRAW
quitting, 22
version 5.0, features of, 4-5
CorelMOVE, 6, 572-597
action sequences, adding, 581-591
continuity, maintaining, 591
editing images, 581-583
new actors, creating, 588-591
new props, creating, 587-588
path of actor, setting, 583-585
return path, creating invisible, 586-587
speed of actor, controlling, 585-586
backdrops, 577-578
fine-tuning animations, 592-597
with Cel Sequencer roll-up, 592-593
cues, 594
with Timelines roll-up, 593-594
hardware requirements for, 573
interface, 574-577
Control Panel, 576-577
menus, 575-576
tool box, 576
window, 574
morphing, 595-597
sound, adding, 595
text titles, adding, 579-580
CorelPHOTO-PAINT. *See* PHOTO-PAINT
CorelSHOW, 6, 554-569
additional slides, adding, 562-563
animations, inserting, 564-565
backgrounds
final background, 562
initial background, 558-559
creating slides, 559
cues, 565, 566

editing with, 559-560
fitting objects to slide, 564
grid and rulers, setting up, 561
guidelines for production with, 568
interface, 554-557
desktop, 555-557
viewing modes, 555
PHOTO-PAINT, improving background with, 560-561
presentation options with, 567
printing, 566
Runtime application with, 568
saving work, 566
Slide Sorter, 564
timelines, 565-566
CorelTRACE, 5-6
button bar, 277-278
menus with, 276-277
raster-to-vector conversions with, 275-293
Centerline method, 283
checking image information, 281
custom settings, 287-290
file formats, 291-293
guidelines, 290-291
Image Info box, 279-280
interface, 275-279
Line method, 281-282
Outline method, 282-283
selecting files, 280
silhouette tracing, 286
smoothing out lines, 284
woodcut tracing, 284-286
tools, 278-279
CorelVENTURA. *See* VENTURA
Corners options (Outline Pen dialog box), 30
Corner Threshold setting (Curves dialog box), 274
counters, 153, 605
CPUs, 802
Create From command (Envelope roll-up), 312-313
Create Lines of Uniform Width option (Edit Line dialog box), 290
Create Pattern option (Special menu), 85
creek, drawing, 644
Crop Marks option, 215
cropping bitmap images, 271
CSV files, 542
Ctrl key
as Constrain key, 24

with envelopes, 317-318
Ctrl-D, 134
Ctrl-Insert, 133
Ctrl-N, 25
Ctrl-O, 21
Ctrl-P, 22, 211
Ctrl-Q, 108
Ctrl-Shift-T, 146
Ctrl-T, 146
Ctrl-Y, 92
Ctrl-Z, 63, 132
cubic polynomial curve segments, 104
Cue dialog box, 594
cues
    with animations, 573
    CorelSHOW, 565, 566
Curry, Georgina, 785-799
Curve Precision option (Edit Line dialog box), 289
curves
    converting text to, 170-173
    drawing, in Bézier mode, 106-111
        paths, 109-111
    drawing, with Pencil Tool, 120-124
        closed paths, 123-124
        dual-pull click-and-drag drawing, 122-123
        single-pull click-and-drag drawing, 120-121
    vs. lines, 105
Curves dialog box, 273-274
Curve tool (PHOTO-PAINT), 467-470
cusp nodes, 113-114
    changing node to, 118
custom fills, creating, 79-88, 360-361
    fountain fills, 86-88
    full-color pattern fills, 82-85
Custom Palette Button menu (Outline Color dialog box), 39-40
custom typefaces, designing, 230-231
Cut command, 133, 200

D

dashed lines, options for, in Outline Pen dialog box, 30
dashes, en vs. em, 611-613
Data Manager (CorelCHART), 504
Data Manager roll-up, 393-394
DAT (digital audio tape), 808

Dawson, Wil, 775-783
decorative typefaces, 141
default fills, setting, 71
default outline, 44-45
default settings, 190
Delete command, 134
Delete key, 134
deleting
    nodes, 117
    objects, 30
Densitometer Scale option, 215
Density setting (Airbrush tool), 476
Depth setting (Extrude roll-up), 340
descender, 153-154
descender lines, 153
design
    for advertising layout, 624-627
    of brochure, 252-253
    for four-page newsletter, 653-655
    of logo, 602
    of posters, 721-722
    of stationery, 608, 614
    type as factor in, 140, 600-602
desktop, 7-9
    CorelSHOW, 555-557
    PHOTO-PAINT, 449-450
    VENTURA, 409-410
Desktop Layer, 95, 249
desktop publishing, 408-409
dialog boxes, 10-12
dictionary, 184-185
digital audio tape (DAT), 808
digitizing tablets, 64-65
display
    fine-tuning, with PHOTO-PAINT, 481-483
    and system speed, 822-828
display boxes, 11
Display Status dialog box (CorelCHART), 512-513
display typefaces, 141
dithering, 457
    with PHOTO-PAINT, 481
DOS 6.0, 803-804, 811
double curve envelopes, 313-314
Download Type 1 Fonts option (Separations Tab), 218
dragging, 56
Drape check box (Extrude roll-up), 343
Drawings List, 22
draw programs, 2-3

drop shadows, 633
DSND disk, 806-807
dual-pull click-and-drag drawing, 122-123
dummying, 653-654
Duplicate command, 134
duplicating objects, 58-59
DXF files
    exporting to, 299
    import filters with, 295
Dynamic Memory Control, 805

E

Edge filter (PHOTO-PAINT), 493-494
Edge Pad, 87
Edge setting (Airbrush tool), 476
Edit Color dialog box, 28
Edit Fills dialog box, 359-361
Edit Layer dialog box, 250-251
Edit Line dialog box, 289
Edit menu, 131-135
    Clone command, 382-383
    Copy Attributes From... command, 134-135
    Copy command, 133
    CorelTRACE, 277
    Cut command, 133
    Delete command, 134
    Duplicate command, 134
    Edit Object command, 135
    with Mosaic, 351-352
    opening, 132
    Paste command, 133
    Paste Special command, 133-134
    Redo command, 132
    Repeat command, 132
    Select All command, 135
    Undo command, 132
Edit Object command, 135
Edit Text dialog box, 146-147
effects. *See* special effects
Effects menu, 61, 309
    Clone command on, 383-384
8-ball exercise, 387-388
EISA bus, 814
Elastic mode, 119
ellipses
    drawing, 50-51
    placing text on, 178
Ellipse tool, 50-52

arcs, creating, 51, 52
circles, drawing, 51
CorelCHART, 505
with envelopes, 313
icon for, 15
oblongs, drawing, 50-51
wedges, creating, 51, 52
embedding, 549-552
embossing text, 759-762
Embossing tool (PHOTO-PAINT), 493
em dashes, 611-613
Emulsion check box, 215
en dashes, 611-613
entry boxes, 12
Envelope roll-up, 309
envelopes, 309-318
    arcs with, 312, 313
    with blends, 328-329
    canceling effect, 312
    with Clear Transformations command, 312
    with Straighten Text command, 312
    with Undo command, 312
    constraint controls, 317-318
    Create From command with, 312-313
    curves, adding, 313
    example, 310-311
    guidelines for working with, 317
    preset, 315-316
    text in, 316
    two curve, 313-314
    unconstrained, 315
envelopes (stationery), 614
EPS files, 291-292
    exporting to, 299-300
    import filters with, 294-295
Eraser tool (PHOTO-PAINT), 471
erasing, with Pencil tool, 66
E-scale, 152
exercises. *See also* newsletter (four-page); newsletter (simple)
    certificate, 225-230
    cloudy day, 364-366
    8-ball, 387-388
    herb garden, 397-405
    sign, 16-19
    simple face, 462-477
    snail shell, 372-375
    snowman, 124-131
    sunset, 97-100

three-fold brochure, 251-260
Export dialog box, 298
export filters, 297-302
exporting, 20
    bitmap images, 297-304
        file formats, 299-302
            Windows Clipboard, using, 302-304
    from PHOTO-PAINT, 458
Export... option (File menu), 21
extended character sets, 186
Extract command, 207, 223
Extract Text dialog box, 208
Extrude roll-up, 12, 337
extruding objects, 310, 337-345
    construction of extruded components, 338-339
    example, 337-338
    preset, 344
    saving, 344-345
    and vanishing point, 340-344
Extrusion Types setting (Extrude roll-up), 340

F

F2 key, 36
F5 key, 107
F8 key, 154
F9 key, 37
F11, 86
face exercise, 462-477
Fade Out setting (Airbrush tool), 477
fast open, 22
file formats
    with CorelCHART, 541-542
    with PHOTO-PAINT, 453-454
File Information option, 214
File Info Within Page option, 213-214
File menu, 20-22
    CorelCHART, 503-504
    CorelMOVE, 575
    with Mosaic, 351
    PHOTO-PAINT, 452-453
File menu (CorelTRACE), 276
files
    bitmap, 2
    managing, with Mosaic, 349-352
    new, 20
    organizing, on hard drive, 808-812
fills, 69, 356-366
    with bitmap images, 270-271

with blends, 322
conical, 357, 358
custom, 360-361
custom, creating, 79-88
    fountain fills, 86-88
    full-color pattern fills, 82-85
default, setting, 71
fountain, 356
halftones with, using, 73-75
with paragraph text, 198-199
pattern, 79, 80
PHOTO-PAINT, adding in, 472-473
rainbow, 359-360
roll-up menus, setting with, 72-73
square, 357-358
texture, 76, 361-366
two-color, 76-79
uniform, setting, 71-72
using bitmap images as, 82
Fill tool, 69-71
    components of, 69-71
    CorelCHART, 506
    fly-out menu for, 69
    icon for, 15
filters
    export, 297-302
    import, 293-297
    with PHOTO-PAINT, 483-488
        brightness and contrast, manipulating, 484-485
        color/gray map, adjusting, 485-486
        equalization, applying, 486-487
        freehand blend, touching up with, 488
        Sharpen filter, 488
Fiore, Rich, 765-774
First Baseline setting (VENTURA), 416
first node, selecting, 111-112
Fit Text To Path command, 174-175
Fit Text To Path Offsets dialog box, 178-179
fitting blends to path, 330-333
    editing path, 333
    special options, 332
fitting objects to slide (CorelSHOW), 564
fitting text to path, 173-184
    baseline, 174-175, 177
    distance from path, 177
    Edit commands, using, 178-179
    ellipses, 178
    fine-tuning, 180-183
    flipping text, 177-178

Index

horizontal placement, 175
    rectangles, 178
    techniques for, 184
    vertical orientation, 176
Fit To Page option, 215
flatness, controlling, 218
flipping images (PHOTO-PAINT), 497
Floating option (PHOTO-PAINT), 451-452
flood fills, 472
flowers, drawing, 645-649
    centers, 648
    greenery, 649
    petals, filling, 647-648
flowing text between frames, 239-240, 665-666
fly-out menus, 8
folio, adding, to newsletter, 657-658
font(s), 138-139
    in brochure, 252
    changing, 146
    definition, 140
    scalable, 149
    styles of, 148-149
font size, 153, 154
footers, 432-433
forest, drawing, 640-642
For Mac option, 212
formatting
    paragraph text, 235-237
    saving, 237
Fountain Fill dialog box, 86-87
fountain fills, 70, 86-88, 356
    creating, 86-87
    edge padding, adjusting, 87
    fill angle, adjusting, 87
    number of stripes, setting, 87
setting (Separations Tab), 218
Fountain Stripes option, 87
Fractal Painter, 838-839
fragmentation, reducing disk, 810-812
Frame Attributes dialog box, 193, 243, 244
Framemaker, 840-841
frames
    attributes of, 193
    entering text directly into, 191-193
    flowing text between, 239-240
    with imported text, 234
    interactively adjusting size of, 196-197
    with paragraph text, 234-235
    in VENTURA, 443

Frame Settings dialog box, 429
Frame tool (VENTURA), 411
Freehand Blend tool (PHOTO-PAINT), 477
Freehand Brightness tool (PHOTO-PAINT), 490
Freehand Contrast tool (PHOTO-PAINT), 490
Freehand mode, 64-65
Freehand Smear tool (PHOTO-PAINT), 477-478
Freehand Smudge tool (PHOTO-PAINT), 477-478
Freehand Tracking setting (Curves dialog box), 274
full-color fills, 70
Full-Color Pattern Fill dialog box, 83
full-color pattern fills, 82-85
full justification, 148
Full Path option (Blend roll-up), 332
Full-Screen Preview (View menu), 37
Fuse Bottom button (Blend roll-up), 323
Fuse Top button (Blend roll-up), 323

G

Gallery Effects, 841
Gallery menu (CorelCHART), 516-517
GEM files
    exporting to, 300
    import filters with, 295
Geometric Shapes layer, 254
GIF files
    exporting to, 300
    import filters with, 295
    importing, 292
graphics
    adding, to newsletter, 426-427, 434-435
    advertising layout, placing in, 627-630
        background, creating, 628, 629
        spot colors, using, 627-628
    importing
        into CorelCHART, 542
        with Windows Clipboard, 304
    paragraph text, adding to, 241-243
    wrapping text around, 668-671
graphics programs, 2
graphics tablets, 828-829
gray, 253
grayscale images, 457-458
greek, 235
GREEKTX1.RTF, 235
GREEKTX2.RTF, 241

Green Lizard (Chris Purcell), 731-738
Grid Frequency, 89, 90, 92
Grid layer, 94
grid origin, 92
grids, 91-93
    with advertising layouts, 624
    CorelSHOW, 561
Grid Setup dialog box, 196
Grid Setup option, 308
Grouped option (PHOTO-PAINT), 451-452
Grouping objects, 96-97
guidelines, 90-91
Guides layer, 94
gutter width, 196, 216

H

halftones, 73-75, 457
    with bitmaps, 271
handles, 8
Hand tool (PHOTO-PAINT), 475
hanging indent, 244
hard drive, 805-812
    backups of, 807-808
    emergencies, DSND disk for, 806-807
    organizing files on, 808-812
    as storage subsystem, 820-821
    tape backups, 807-808
    testing, 812
    using CHKDSK with, 809-811
hardware, 802-829
    buses, 814-815
    CorelMOVE, requirements for, 573
    display system, 822-828
    graphics tablets, 828-829
    hard disks, 805-812
    keeping up with changes in, 813-814
    memory, 7, 802-805
    SCSI card, 815-818
    storage subsystems, 818-822
        CD-ROM drives, 821-822
        dividing data storage, 819-820
        hard drives, 820-821
    VESA local bus, 814-815
    and viruses, 812
headers, 432-433
headlines
    adding, to newsletter, 434
    advertising layout, adding to, 632-633
    newsletter, adding to, 425

    in poster, 720
herb garden exercise, 397-405
hiding bitmap images, 269-270
high memory manager, 7
High Rollers (Rich Fiore), 770-774
Hijaak for Windows, 835-836
hills, drawing, 637-639
    background hills, 639
    basic shapes, forming, 637
    blending, 638
hi-lo value charts, 540
HIMEM.SYS, 80
histograms, 486-487, 540
Horizontal Placement menu, 175
horizontal skew, 176
Horz and Vert Line Recognition option (Edit Line dialog box), 290
hot-keys, 10, 13, 20
hot zone, hyphenation, 194, 247
HPGL files, 295
HSB color model, 42
Huntress (Georgina Curry), 785-799
hyphenation
    automatic, 194
    paragraph text, setting for, 246-247

I

IDE hard drives, 820
illustrations, complex. *See* complex drawings
Image dialog box, 287-288
Image Info (Display menu), 279
Image Pals, 833-835
Import dialog box, 266-267
import filters, 293-297
importing, 20
    bitmap images, 266-268, 291-292
    into CorelCHART, 541-542
        data, 541-542
        graphics, 542
    text, 203-207
        exercise, 205-207
        and frames, 234
        modification of imported text, 207-210
        performing import, 204-205
        preparation, 204
Import... option (File menu), 21
Import Text dialog box, 204, 205
Impressionist brush (PHOTO-PAINT), 477
indents, setting, 248

Index

Indents dialog box, 195
ink flow, adjusting powerline, 369
insertion point, 180-181
interface, 7-9
    CorelCHART, 503-506
    CorelMOVE, 574-577
    CorelSHOW, 554-557
    PHOTO-PAINT, 449-452
    VENTURA, 409-413
internal edit functions, 131
interparagraph spacing, adjusting, 201
Intersection command, 378-381
interword spacing, 151
Invert Colors option (Image dialog box), 288
inverting, in PHOTO-PAINT, 497
invisible layers, 250
ISA bus, 814
italic, oblique vs., 148

J

joining nodes, 118
JPEG format, 293
jumps, 654, 661
justification, 147-148
    in brochure, 253
    and kerning, 159

K

kerned pairs, 159
kerning, 159-163
    aligning to baseline, 160
    controlling, with Character Attribute dialog box, 160-161
    definition, 159
    fitted text, adjusting with, 181-182
    and justification, 159
    manual, 159-160
    with Shape tool, 159-160
    with stationery design, 610-611
keyboard shortcuts, 9, 20
Kodak Photo CD format
    importing, 293
    with Mosaic, 349

L

landscape example, 636-649
    bird, adding, 642-643
    clouds, forming, 643
    creek, adding, 644
    flowers, adding, 645-649
    forests, adding, 640-642
    hills, creating, 637-639
    marsh, adding, 644-645
    ocean and sky, adding, 639-640
    setup, 636
Lasso tool (PHOTO-PAINT), 463
Layer One, 95
layers
    in brochure, 253-254
    with paragraph text, 248-250
        active layer, 250
        color override, 250-251
        invisible layers, 250
        locking option, 250
        master layers, 248-249
        multilayer option, 250
        printability, 250
    working with, 93-95
Layers roll-up window, 626-627
layouts. *See* advertising layouts, creating; newsletters
Layout Style drop-down menu, 216
Layout Tab (Print Options dialog box), 215-216
leading, 150, 151, 153, 157
left justification, 147-148
Lens tool, 386-388
letterhead design. *See* stationery, creating
ligatures, 159
Lighting setting (Extrude roll-up), 341-342
linear fountain fills, 86
Line cap settings (Outline Pen dialog box), 30-31
line charts, 540
Line method (CorelTRACE), 281-282
Line Precision option (Edit Line dialog box), 289
lines
    curves vs., 105
    drawing, 107
    power clipping, to circle, 388-389
    setting width of, with Outline tool, 26, 29
    smoothing out bitmap, 284
    straight, 66-67
linking, 553
    definition, 549
    updating links, 553-554
Local Tint tool (PHOTO-PAINT), 491
Locator tool (PHOTO-PAINT), 474
Locking option, 250

logos, 602-607, 760-762. *See also* business cards; stationery, creating
   adjusting words, 606-607
   curves, adding, 605
   enhancing, 613
   outline and fill, setting, 607
   placing, on business card, 617-618
   shaping letters, 605-606
   typeface, choosing, 602-604

M

Map Nodes button (Blend roll-up), 322, 326
markers, 39
   merge, 223-225
marquee, 36
Marquee Select, 199
marsh, drawing, 644-645
masks
   with PHOTO-PAINT, 478-479, 499
   with welds, 377-378
master layers, 248-249
   with newsletter, 663-664
Master object (clones), 381-382
mastheads, creating, 419-420, 655-657
MCA bus, 814
McCormick, Peter, 677-685
measurement tools, 93
MemMaker utility, 803
memory, 802-805
   program requirements, 7
   third-party managers, 804
Menu Bar, 8
menus
   CorelMOVE, 575-576
   drop-down, 9-10
   fly-out, 10
   roll-up, 12
Merge Back command, 207, 209-210, 223
Mesa (Deborah Miller), 694-699
MGA boards, 825-826
Microsoft Publisher, 839-840
Microsoft Windows, 7
   Control Panel of, 221
   working with, 221
Miller, Deborah, 687-712
Minimum Extrude Facet Size setting (Curves dialog box), 274
Minimum Line Width option (Edit Line dialog box), 290

mirror images of objects, creating, 58
miter nib, 34
monitors. *See* display
monochrome bitmap images, 265, 271
monospaced type, 139
Moonlit Flight (Wil Dawson), 776-783
Moran, Tim, 723-729
morphing, 595-597
Mosaic, 6
   file management with, 349-352
Mosaic roll-up, 352
Moss, Gary, 786
Motion Blur filter (PHOTO-PAINT), 495-496
mountains, drawing, 696-697
mouse
   drawing lines with, 66-67
   opening menus with, 13
   with VENTURA, 413
moving objects, 55-56
Multilayer option, 250

N

Named Color palette selector, 44
NEC, 827
negatives, printing, 215
Nevada Nickels (Rich Fiore), 765-770
New command (File menu), 25
new files, 20
New From Template... option (File menu), 21
New Layer dialog box, 249
New option (File Menu), 21
New Picture dialog box (PHOTO-PAINT), 452-453
New Presentation dialog box (CorelSHOW), 557-558
New Prop dialog box, 579
New Publication dialog box (VENTURA), 414
newsletter (four-page), 652-675
   assessment of, 675
   design for, 653-655
   distribution of, 653
   first page
      layout of, 658-659
      and masthead, 656-657
   folio, adding, 657-658
   fourth page, 672-674
   master layer, working with, 663-664
   masthead, creating, 655-657
   planning, 652-653

printing, 653
second page, 662
teaser, placing, 659-660
text, 660-662
    breakout, adding, 666-668
    flowing, 665-666
    with graphic, 664-665
    wrapping, around graphics, 668-671
third page, 668-672
newsletter (simple), 413-439
    balancing page, 430
    caption, adding, 429
    custom wrapping text, 435
    folio, tagging, 424
    graphics, adding, 426-427, 434-435
    headers and footers, adding, 432-433
    headlines, adding, 425, 434
    lead story, entering, 425-429
    loading files, 417-418
    masthead, placing, 419-420
    new address tag, creating, 420-422
    new address tag, editing, 422-423
    page layout, selecting, 416-417
    pre-shaped wrap, applying, 438-439
    table, adding, 436-437
nibs, 33-34, 368-369
Node Align dialog box, 119-120
Node Edit menu, 116-117
nodes, 51, 105
    with blends, 321-323
    editing, with Shape tool, 116-120
        adding nodes, 117
        aligning nodes, 119
        auto-reducing nodes, 119
        breaking apart, 118
        changing type of node, 118
        To Curve option, 117
        deleting nodes, 117
        Elastic mode, 119
        joining, 118
        To Line option, 117
        rotating nodes, 119
        scaling nodes, 119
        sketching nodes, 119
    first, 111-112
    limiting number of, 113
    moving, with Shape tool, 131
    placing, with Shape tool, 131
    reducing number of, 119
    second and third, 112

selected vs. non-selected, 105
selecting, 111-113
    first node, 111-112
    second and third nodes, 112
types of, 113-116
    cusp nodes, 113-114
    smooth nodes, 115-116
    symmetrical nodes, 114-115
NODES.CDR, 113
Node Split option (Blend roll-up), 326-327
Noise filter (PHOTO-PAINT), 491-492

O

Object Data Manager, 392-397
    accessing, 393
    adjusting appearance of, 396-397
Object Data roll-up, 393
Object Handles, 8
object linking and embedding (OLE), 548-554. *See also* CorelSHOW
    and CorelCHART, 544-545
    and CorelMOVE, 580
    embedding and editing OLE objects, 550-552
    linking objects, 553
    terminology, 548-549
    updating links, 553-554
Object menu, 237
object-oriented programs, 3
objects, 15. *See also* transformations
    center of rotation of, 60
    combining, 96-97
    deleting, 30
    duplicating, 58-59
    grouping, 96-97
    mirror images of, 58
    moving, 55-56
    in OLE, 549
    out from center, drawing, 58
    precise placement and alignment of, 88-97
        Arrange menu, using, 93-97
        grid, using, 91-93
        guidelines, using, 90-91
        rulers, using, 88-90
    rotating, 59-60
    scaling, 56-57
    skewing, 60
    stretching, 57-58
    text, 141-142

curves, converting to, 170-173
modifying, 158-159
oblique, italic vs., 148
oblong shapes, drawing, 50
ocean, drawing, 639-640
OCR dialog box, 290
OK button, 11
OLE. *See* object linking and embedding
1:1 option (Zoom tool), 36
On-Screen Palette, 9
opening, 20, 21
Open... option (File menu), 21
open paths, 68
optical drives, 821-822
option bars, 11
Options bar, 11
Orphans setting (VENTURA), 415
outdents, 244
out from center, drawing objects, 58
Outline Color dialog box, 28-29, 38-40
Outline Filtering option (Edit Line dialog box), 289-290
Outline method (CorelTRACE), 282-283
Outline Pen dialog box, 27-28
Outline (Pen) tool, 16-17, 25-35
   arrows, 31
   becoming skilled with, 27-28
   Behind Fill check box, 34-35
   calligraphy with, 33-34
   colors with, 28-29
   CorelCHART, 506
   corners, 30
   fly-out menu for, 26
   icon for, 15
   line cap settings, 30-31
   predefined line width, setting, 26-27
   roll-up menu for, 45-46
   Scale With Image check box, 34-35
   styles, using, 33
   using, 25-26
   width, setting, 29
outlines
   with bitmap images, 270-271
   with paragraph text, 198-199
   paths vs., 68
   PHOTO-PAINT, 497

P

packaging objects, 549

Page, 8
Page Counter, 9
Page Setup dialog box, 9-10, 206
Paint Brush tool (PHOTO-PAINT), 477
paint programs, 2, 3
palettes, 43-44
   PHOTO-PAINT, 464-466
Pantone Matching System (PMS), 43
PANTONE.PAL file, 43
paper color
   adjusting, for business cards, 616, 617
   selecting, 206
Paragraph dialog box, 193-194, 235-236
paragraph text, 142, 191-201, 234-251, 600
   adding graphic to, 241-243
   bullets, adding, 244-246
   columns, adding, 243-244
   cutting, copying and pasting, 200
   entering text into frame, 191-192
   in envelopes, 316
   flowing text between frames, 239-240, 665-666
   formatting, 235-237
   and frame attributes, 193
   frame size, adjusting, 196-197
   hyphenation with, 246-247
   indents, setting, 248
   interparagraph spacing of, 201
   layers with, 248-250
      active layer, 250
      color override, 250-251
      invisible layers, 250
      locking option, 250
      master layers, 248-249
      multilayer option, 250
      printability, 250
   and paragraph attributes, 194-196
   tab settings with, 247-248
   text styles, applying and saving, 237-239
   transforming, 197-200
      baselines, 199
      character attributes, 199
      outlines and fills, 198-199
      straightening text, 199
   wrapping, 241-243
Paste command, 133, 200
Paste Special command, 133-134
Paste Special dialog box, 133-134
paths, 68-69, 104. *See also* fitting text to path
   in animations, 573

Index

blends along, 321
closing, 123-124
in CorelSHOW, 583-587
defining, 109-111
fitting blends to, 330-333
    editing path, 333
    special options, 332
pattern fills, 79
PCI, 815
PCT files
    exporting to, 300-301
    import filters with, 296
PCX files
    exporting to, 301
    import filters with, 296
    importing, 292-293
Pencil tool, 64-67
    AutoTrace mode with, 272-274
    Bézier mode, 106
        exercise, 106-108
        vs. Freelance mode, 120
    CorelCHART, 505, 528
    drawing curves with, 120-124
        closed paths, 123-124
        dual-pull click-and-drag, 122-123
        single-pull click-and-drag, 120-121
    erasing, 66
    Freehand mode with, 64-65
    icon for, 15
    straight lines, drawing, 66-67
Pen Size option (Two-Color Pattern Editor), 80
Pen tool. *See* Outline tool
perspective, 310, 334-337, 642
PFB files, 301
photographic images, 264-266
PHOTO-PAINT, 5, 70, 80, 448-500
    color mode of image, converting, 454-456
    dithering, 457
    drawing with, 461-467
        Airbrush, 475-477
        Color Replacer tool, 470-471
        Curve tool, 467-470
        Eraser tool, 471
        Hand tool, 475
        Lasso tool, 463-464
        Locator tool, 474
        Mask tools, 478-479
        Paint Brush, 477-478
        palette, choosing colors with, 464-466
        soft tools, 475
    erasing work, 460
    existing image, opening, 453-454
    exporting work, 258
    file formats supported by, 453-454
    fills, adding, 472-473
    grayscale images, 457-458
    image enhancement, 483-488
        brightness and contrast, manipulating, 484-485
        color/gray map, adjusting, 485-486
        equalization, applying, 486-487
        freehand blend, touching up with, 488
        freehand brightness and contrast, managing, 490
        local tint, adding, 491
        Noise filter, 491-492
        Sharpen filter, 488
        Smear tool, 489
    improving CorelSHOW backgrounds with, 560-561
    Info option with, 475
    interface, 449-452
        desktop, 449-450
        toolbox, 451-452
    masks with, 499
    new picture, creating, 452-453
    painting tools with, 458-461
    printing images from, 480-483
        display system, fine-tuning, 481
        dithering option, 481
        monitor's color, adjusting, 482-483
        scanned images, retouching, 480
    sizing images, 454
    special effects with, 492-496
        Edge filter, 493-494
        Embossing tool, 493
        Motion Blur filter, 495-496
        Pixelate filter, 494-495
        Sharpen option, 494
        Smooth option, 494
    transformations with, 496-499
        distorting images, 497
        flip and rotate options, 497
        inverting images, 497-498
        outlining, 498-499
        resizing, 496
    viewing images, 454
picas, 29, 149, 196
    setting, with Object Data Manager, 395
PIC files, 296

Pick tool, 52-63, 107
   CorelCHART, 505
   icon for, 15
   selecting objects with, 53-55
      marquee, using, 54
      Shift-Click method, 54
      space bar, using, 55
      tab select, 55
   with text, 144-145
   transformations with, 55-60
      center, drawing objects out from, 58
      duplicates, 58-59
      mirror images, 58-59
      moving objects, 55-56
      rotating objects, 59-60
      scaling objects, 56-57
      skewing objects, 60
      stretching objects, 57-58
Pictograph tool (CorelCHART), 528
pie charts, 532-536, 540
PIF files
   exporting to, 301
   import filters with, 296
Pixelate filter (PHOTO-PAINT), 494-495
pixel depth, 265
pixels, 2, 265
Place Duplicate command, 474
Place On Other Side command, 177-178
planning
   complex illustrations, 636
   newsletters, 652-653
PLT files, 301
Plus key, 58
PMS (Pantone Matching System), 43
Pointillism brush (PHOTO-PAINT), 477
points, 26, 149, 151, 196
   setting, with Object Data Manager, 395
point sizes, 156-157
ports, printer, 221
posters
   guidelines for designing, 721-722
   by Jan Selman, 713-721
   Thailand (Deborah Miller), 709-712
PostScript, 138
   bitmaps, using halftone screens with, 271
   halftones, 73-75
   textures, 70, 76
PostScript Options (Outline Color dialog box), 40
PowerClip tool, 388-391

Powerline roll-up, 367
powerlines, 367-371
   guidelines for using, 371
   ink flow, adjusting, 369
   nib settings, adjusting, 368-369
   Shape tool, editing with, 370
   speed, adjusting, 369
   spread setting, adjusting, 369, 370
PowerTape, 808
predefined bitmap fills, using, 77-78
preferences, 13-14
Preferences dialog box, 49
presentation guidelines
   CorelCHART, 536-541
   CorelSHOW, 568
preset envelopes, 315-316
preset extrusions, 344
Preview Fountain Stripes option, 87
Preview Image option, 213
Printable option, 250
Print command, 210
Print dialog box, 211-212
printer
   and brochure design, 252
   configuring, 222
   troubleshooting, 220-221
Printer Color Profile check box, 212
printing, 210-225
   CorelSHOW, 566
   merging, 222-225
   newsletters, 653
   outside program, printing CorelDRAW files, 220-222
   from PHOTO-PAINT, 480-483
      display system, fine-tuning, 481
      dithering option, 481
      monitor's color, adjusting, 482-483
      scanned images, retouching, 480
   Reference toolbar, using, 214-219
Print Manager, 221-222
Print Merge, 22, 223-225
   target drawing, 223
   text source file, 223-224
Print option (File menu), 22
Print Options dialog box, 213-214
Print Range option, 212
Print Separations option, 217
Print Setup option (File menu), 22
Print Tiled Pages option, 216
process color, 38, 40-43

proofreading, 253, 539
property sheets, 12
Prop Information dialog box, 578
proportionally spaced type, 139
props (in animations), 573, 587-588
Publication file (VENTURA), 442
Publications Manager utility (VENTURA), 440-442
Purcell, Chris, 731-748

Q

Quick Format roll-up (VENTURA), 416-417
quitting CorelDRAW, 22

R

radial fills, 70
radial fountain fills, 86
radio buttons, 11
Radius Pivot monitor, 827
rainbow fills, 359-360
RAMDACs, 824
raster images, 265
Rate of Flow setting (Airbrush tool), 477
rectangles, placing text on, 178
Rectangle tool, 23-25
    CorelCHART, 505, 528
    with envelopes, 313
    icon for, 15
Redo command, 132
Reduce Colors To option (Image dialog box), 288
Reference toolbar, 214-219
Registration Marks option, 215
Relocation settings (Extrude roll-up), 341
Repeat command, 132
resizing, in PHOTO-PAINT, 497
resolution of bitmap images, 268
RGB color model, 41
right justification, 148
riser controls (CorelCHART), 526, 530-532
roll-up menus, 12
    setting fills with, 72-73
rotating
    bitmap images, 269
    nodes, 119
    objects, 59-60
    in PHOTO-PAINT, 497
    text, 176
rounded nib, 34

rows, adjusting and selecting spreadsheet, 509
Rulers, 8
rulers, 88-90, 93
    CorelSHOW, 561
rules, 26, 152
Runtime module (CorelSHOW), 568

S

Sampling Rate option (Edit Line dialog box), 289
sans serif, 140
Save As... option, 21
    CorelCHART, 544
Save option (File menu), 21
Save Style As dialog box, 237-238
saving files, 20
    CorelSHOW, 566
    formatting attributes, 237
    VENTURA, 440, 442
scalable fonts, 140, 149
scale conversion (CorelCHART), 530
Scale With Image check box, 34-35
scaling
    bitmap images, 269
    nodes, 119
    objects, 56-57
scanned images, retouching, with PHOTO-PAINT, 480
scanners, 264, 265
scatter plots, 541
SCODL files, 301
Screen Frequency control (Separations Tab), 218
scroll bars, 9
SCSI cards, 815-818, 820
second and third nodes, selecting, 112
segments, 105. *See also* curves; lines
Select All command, 135
selecting
    with blends, 327-328
    nodes, 105
    symbols, 170
    tools, 15
selection windows, 11
Selman, Jan, 713-721
Separate command (Arrange menu), 325
Separations Tab (Print Options dialog box), 216-219
serif, 140, 153, 154
server (source), 549

Set Flatness To option (Separations Tab), 218
Shape tool, 24, 51, 107-108, 111
   adjusting spacing with, 150
   control points, using, 111
   editing nodes with, 116-120
      adding nodes, 117
      aligning nodes, 119
      auto-reducing nodes, 119
      breaking apart, 118
      changing type of node, 118
      To Curve option, 117
      deleting nodes, 117
      in Elastic mode, 119
      joining, 118
      To Line option, 117
      rotating nodes, 119
      scaling nodes, 119
      sketching nodes, 119
   editing powerlines with, 370
   with envelopes, 317
   icon for, 15
   manual kerning with, 159-160
   moving nodes with, 131
   placing nodes with, 131
   selecting nodes with, 111-113
      first node, 111-112
      second and third nodes, 112
Sharpen filter (PHOTO-PAINT), 488
Sharpen option (PHOTO-PAINT), 494
Shift key
   with envelopes, 317-318
   with Rectangle tool, 24
Shift-Delete, 133
Shift-Insert, 133
shift, controlling, 161-162
   with fitted text, 183
shortcuts, keyboard, 9
Show Grid option, 92
Show menu (Outline Color dialog box), 39
Show Path option (Blend roll-up), 333
signs, drawing, 16-19, 164-168
silhouette tracing, 286
simple blends, 323-324
single-pull click-and-drag drawing, 120-121
sizing bitmap images, 269
sketching nodes, 119
skewing
   objects, 60
   text, 176
sky, drawing, 639-640

slice feelers (CorelCHART), 535-536
slide sorter (CorelSHOW), 564
small capitals, 152
SMARTDRV.SYS, 803
Smear tool (PHOTO-PAINT), 489
Smooth Dithering option (Image dialog box), 288
smooth nodes, 115-116
   changing node to, 118
Smooth option (PHOTO-PAINT), 494
snail shell exercise, 372-375
snap points, 92-93
Snap To Grid option, 92
Snap To Guidelines option (Layout menu), 90
snowman exercise, 124-131
sound, adding, to animations, 595
source (server), 549
spacing
   adjusting, 150-151
      with fitted text, 181-182
   interparagraph, 201
Spacing setting (Airbrush tool), 477
special effects, 308-349
   blends, 310, 318-334
      additional control points, defining, 330
      Apply button, using, 323
      arrays, creating, 333-334
      beginning and end nodes, choosing, 321
      Color mode, 321
      compound, 329-330
      defining, 320
      dynamic elements of, 324-325
      envelope effects with, 328-329
      example using, 318-319
      fill combinations, results of, 322
      fitting to path, 330-333
      mapping nodes with, 326
      mapping to another path, 321
      node controls, 322-323, 327
      primary roll-up for, 320-321
      selecting elements, 327-328
      simple, 323-324
      speeding up work, 323-324
      splitting nodes with, 326-327
      Steps mode, 321
      taking apart, 325-326
      transformations, 328-334
      uses of, 319
      vs. contours, 371
   envelopes, 309-318

Index

arcs with, 312, 313
  with blends, 328-329
  canceling effect, 312
  constraint controls, 317-318
  Create From command with, 312-313
  curves, adding, 313
  example, 310-311
  guidelines for working with, 317
  preset, 315-316
  text in, 316
  two curve, 313-314
  unconstrained, 315
example using, 345-349
extrude, 310, 337-345
  and construction of extruded components, 338-339
  example, 337-338
  preset extrusions, 344
  saving extrusions, 344-345
  vanishing point, 340-344
perspective, 310, 334-337
with PHOTO-PAINT, 492-496
  Edge filter, 493-494
  Embossing tool, 493
  Motion Blur filter, 495-496
  Pixelate filter, 494-495
  Sharpen option, 494
  Smooth option, 494
spectral map charts, 541
speed, adjusting powerline, 369-370
Speed Disk, 811-812
spell-checking, 184-185
Split button (Blend roll-up), 322-323
spot colors, 37-38, 43
  with advertising layouts, 627-628
  on business cards, 618
Spot Fill dialog box, 73-74
SprayCan tool (PHOTO-PAINT), 468-469
spread, adjusting powerline, 369
spreadsheets (CorelCHART), 507-514
  columns and rows, adjusting and selecting, 509
  tagging data, 510-512
SPSS for Windows, 836-838
square fills, 357-358
Squeegee, 832-833
standard tints, 70
stationery, creating, 607-614
  clipart, adding, 614
  design considerations, 608, 614

en and em dashes, 611-613
envelopes, 614
  logo, enhancing, 613
  return address, aligning, 610-611
  setting up guidelines, 609-610
Status Bar, 24-25, 93
Status Line, 8
STEGGIE.TIF, 266
stems, 153
storage subsystems, 818-822
  CD-ROM drives, 821-822
  dividing data storage, 819-820
  hard drives, 820-821
straightening text, 199
Straighten Text command, 163
  with envelopes, 312
straight lines, drawing, 66-67
Straight Line Threshold setting (Curves dialog box), 274
stretching objects, 57-58
stripes, setting number of, 87
styles, 148-149, 238-239
stylesheets (VENTURA), 444
Styles menu (Outline Pen dialog box), 33
subpaths, 105
sunset exercise, 97-100
symbols, 142, 168-170
  as bullets, 244
  libraries, accessing, 169
  manipulating, 170
  placing, 168
  selecting, 170
symbol typefaces, 141
symmetrical nodes, 114-115
  changing node to, 118
SYSTEM.INI, 807
Systems (Chris Purcell), 744-747

T

tabbed property sheets, 12
table charts, 541
tables, adding, to newsletter, 436-437
tabs, setting, 194, 195, 247-248
Tag function (VENTURA), 420-424, 443-444
tagging data (CorelCHART), 510-512
tape backups, 807-808
Tapered Ends option (Edit Line dialog box), 290
Target Curve Length option (Edit Line dialog box), 289

TAU.CDR, 179
teasers, 659-660
technical drawings
    Ball-valve (Deborah Miller), 699-709
    by Tim Moran, 723-729
telephone, illustration of, 723-729
templates (CorelCHART), 512, 538, 542-544
text, 141-142. *See also* artistic text; paragraph text; text objects
    advertising layout, placing in, 630, 633, 634
    centering, 18
    with CorelMOVE, 580
    editing existing, 146-147
    embossing, 759-762
    entering, 141
    in envelopes, 316, 317
    importing, 203-207
        exercise, 205-207
        and frames, 234
        modification of imported text, 207-210
        performing import, 204-205
        preparation, 204
        with Windows Clipboard, 303
    justifying, 147-148
    outlined, 34-35
    path, fitting to, 173-184
        baseline, 174-175, 177
        distance from path, 177
        Edit commands, using, 178-179
        ellipses, 178
        fine-tuning, 180-183
        flipping text, 177-178
        horizontal placement, 175
        rectangles, 178
        techniques for, 184
        vertical orientation, 176
    Pick tool with, 144-145
    spacing of, adjusting, 150-151
text blocks, 142, 603
Text Editing dialog box, 146-149
    changing typefaces, 146
    existing text, editing, 146-147
    justification, 147-148
    styles, changing, 148-149
text objects, 141-142
    curves, converting to, 170-173
    modifying, 158-159
text ribbon
    CorelCHART, 506
    VENTURA, 412-413

Text roll-up menu, 201-203
Text tool, 143-144
    CorelCHART, 506
    icon for, 15
Texture Fill dialog box, 364-366, 525
texture fills, 70, 361-366
Texture Options dialog box, 365-366
textures, PostScript, 76
TGA files
    exporting to, 301
    import filters with, 296
    importing, 293
Thailand (Deborah Miller), 709-712
Thesaurus, 185
third-party memory managers, 804
3-D tool (CorelCHART), 520-523
    Movement mode, 521
    Perspective mode, 521
    3-D Box Proportion mode, 521, 522
    3-D Rotation mode, 521-522
three-fold brochure, creating (exercise), 251-260
TIF files, 291-293
    exporting to, 302
    import filters with, 296
tile fills, 472-473
Tiling button, 79
timelines (CorelSHOW), 565-566
Timelines roll-up, 593-594
Title Bar, 8
To Curve option, 117
toggles, 13
To Line option, 117
Tone Map dialog box, 485, 486
toolbar (CorelCHART), 505-506
toolbox, 8
    CorelMOVE, 576
    PHOTO-PAINT, 451-452
    using, 14-15
    VENTURA, 410-411
tools. *See also* specific tools
    selecting, 15
    uses of, 14-15
Tool Settings dialog box (PHOTO-PAINT), 460-461
Trace menu (CorelTRACE), 277
transformations
    absolute positioning, 62-63
    of bitmap images, 268-270
    with blends, 328-334
        additional control points, defining,

Index

329-330
  arrays, creating, 333-334
  compound blends, 329-330
  envelope effects, 328-329
  fitting to path, 330-333
clearing, 61
menus, using, 61-62
of paragraph text, 197-200
  baselines, 199
  character attributes, 199
  outlines and fills, 198-199
  straightening text, 199
with PHOTO-PAINT, 496-499
  distorting images, 497
  flip and rotate options, 497
  inverting images, 497-498
  outlining, 498-499
  resizing, 496
with Pick Tool, 55-60
  center, drawing objects out from, 58
  duplicates, 58-59
  mirror images, 58
  rotating objects, 59-60
  scaling objects, 56-57
  skewing objects, 60
  stretching objects, 57-58
Transform roll-up menu, 61-62
Transitions dialog box, 579-580
Transparency Lens effect, 387
triangles, creating, 67
Trim command, 378-381
troubleshooting printer, 220-221
TrueType fonts, 138
Two-Color Fill dialog box, 80-82
two-color fills, 76-79
Two-Color Pattern Fill dialog box, 77-79
two color pattern fills, 70
two curve envelopes, 313-314
TXT files, 296-297
type. *See also* kerning
  angles of individual letters, altering, 163
  character angle of, controlling, 161
  choosing, 156
  as design tool, 140
  effects of, 156
  and leading, 157
  measuring, 151-156, 601-602
  monospaced, 139
  proportionally spaced, 139
  scalable, 140

shift of, controlling, 161-162
size of, 156-157
spacing of, adjusting, 150-151
straightening letters, 163
styles of, 148-149
vertical shift of, setting, 161-162
typefaces. *See also* fonts
  categories of, 140-141
  choosing, 600-601
    for logo, 602-604
  custom, 230-231
  definition, 140
  need for restraint in use of, 141, 156, 538-539
  serif vs. sans serif, 140
type families, 140
typesetting, 139
typography, 138-141
  and design, 140, 600-602
  development of, 139
  measurements, 149
  terminology, 140-141

U

Unconstrained Envelope option, 242-243
unconstrained envelopes, 315
Undo command, 51, 63, 132
  PHOTO-PAINT, 460
Ungroup command (Arrange menu), 325
uniform fills, setting, 71-72
Upright Letters option, 176
Use Custom Halftone option, 217
user interface, 7-9

V

vanishing point
  definition, 335
  with extrusions, 340-344
vector graphic files, 292
vector type, 3
Venice (Peter McCormick), 677-685
VENTURA, 408-446
  backing up, 418
  chapters in, 442-443
  file management with, 440
  frames in, 443
  guidelines for using, 444-445
  interface, 409-413

button bar, 412
desktop, 409-410
text ribbon, 412-413
toolbox, 410-411
mouse with, 413
Publication file of, 442
Publications Manager utility with, 440-442
saving work, 440, 442
simple newsletter (exercise), 413-439
   balancing page, 430
   caption, adding, 429
   custom wrapping text, 435
   folio, tagging, 424
   graphics, adding, 426-427, 434-435
   headers and footers, adding, 432-433
   headlines, adding, 425, 434
   lead story, entering, 425-429
   loading files, 417-418
   masthead, placing, 419-420
   new address tag, creating, 420-422
   new address tag, editing, 422-423
   page layout, selecting, 416-417
   pre-shaped wrap, applying, 438-439
   table, adding, 436-437
stylesheets with, 444
Tag function with, 420-424, 443-444
vertical offset, adjusting, 177
vertical orientation of text, 176
vertical shift, 161-162
   adjusting, with fitted text, 183
vertical skew, 176
VESA local bus, 814-815
View menu, 13-14, 49
   CorelMOVE, 576
   CorelTRACE, 277
viruses, 812
Visible option, 250
Visual Selector (Outline Color dialog box), 39

W

wedges, creating, 51, 52
welding, 375-378
   combining vs., 375
   in herb garden exercise, 398-400
   masking, 377-378
   order with, 376
   permanence of, 375
   ws setting (VENTURA), 415
   ption

Edit Line dialog box, 290
Outline Pen dialog box, 29
Windows. See Microsoft Windows
Windows Clipboard, 142
   import and export, using for, 302-304
      limitations, 303
      pasting Clipboard into CorelDRAW, 303-304
   using, within CorelDRAW, 304
Windows Notepad, extracting and editing text using, 208-209
Windows Scroll Bar, 9
WIN.INI, 807
Wireframe Edit mode (blends), 324
wireframe mode, 37
wireframes, with technical drawings, 700-703
WKS files, 542
WMF files
   exporting to, 302
   import filters with, 297
Woodcut Dialog Box option (Edit Line dialog box), 290
Woodcut Settings dialog box, 285
woodcut tracing, 284-286
Work Area, 8
WORM optical drives, 822
WPG files, 302
wrapping text, 241-243
WYSIWYG, 408

X

X-height, 153, 154
X-line, 153, 154
XLS files, 542

Z

Zoom tool, 15, 35-37
   with autotracing, 273
   CorelCHART, 505
   fly-out menu for, 35-36
   icon for, 15
Zoom tool (PHOTO-PAINT), 454
Z-shaped folds, 266

About the CD

Installing the files located on the CD that came with this book is quite simple.

The Corel Magazine CD Sampler

Corel Magazine has generously donated a demonstration of their CD sampler files to this book. Some of the material mentioned in the program is not available, but the tutorial files are a treasure trove of information in themselves. Specifically, the .DRW files are not on this CD. For more information, the Sampler program will direct you how to contact Corel Magazine for a full version of the their program.

To install the Sampler program, change to the **CORELMAG** directory on the CD and type **SETUP**. A Windows Setup program will launch and install the Sampler files for you. If the program encounters files existing in your Windows directory, it will give you an error message. Just select the **Ignore** button and the program will still install correctly, it just will adjust itself to the files missing on your computer. If it encounters fonts you already have on your system it will not install over them. Select **OK** for each font your computer encounters.

The Tutorial Files

All the tutorial files are compressed in the file named EXAMPLES.EXE. Create a directory on your hard drive, possibly in the main Corel directory. Then type **Examples** at the DOS prompt or use the File Manager **RUN** command. The files will automatically be extracted for you.

SetDRAW

SetDRAW is a high quality Windows Shareware program that will help you tuen the performance of CorelDRAW. Users can now easily and safely adjust the settings found in the DRAW.INI file called CORELDRAW.INI. Registration is very easy, and at $25, also very affordable. Enclosed on this disk in the SetDRAW directory are five files:

1. SETDRAW4.EXE—The SetDRAW 4.0 program files.
2. VBRUN200.EXE—The Dynamic Link Library that SetDRAW requires.
3. UNPACK.BAT—Unpacks the SetDRAW program on your hard disk.
4. INSTALL.TXT—This file.
5. WHATMEM.COM—Displays available memory and disk space.

To install SetDRAW, follow the following instructions:

1. Type **UNPACK C**: to unpack SetDRAW onto your C: drive.
2. To unpack SetDRAW on another drive, substitute another drive designation for C.
3. Follow the instructions the computer gives you.

Installing MemWatch

MemWatch is a simple utility, written in Microsoft Visual Basic, that displays abailable system memory as well as real-time changes in memory use. It also includes a graphical display of System, GDI, and User resource demand, as well as a count of the number of tasks running. MemWatch will stay on top of all your other windows, so you can see at all times what changes are taking place.

David Warren originally wrote MemWatch as an application prototyping tool so I could see, in real-time, the demands applications make on system memory and to gauge the effects of any optimizing modifications. It is also very useful for non-programmers who just want to see how Windows applications (and Windows itself) make use of system memory.

To use MemWatch, just copy MEMWATCH.EXE from its directory on the CD to your hard disk. It doesn't need to be in any particular directory, although most users install it in their Windows or Windows/System directory.

Just add MemWatch to any Program Manager group, or select RUN from the file menu, type MEMWATCH and click OK. Be sure to include the full path if you installed MEMWATCH.EXE someplace other than your Windows directory. When MemWatch appears, you can move it to any convenient place n your desktop. It will remember its new location and return there every time you start it. If you run out of desktop, run MemWatch n icon. The MemWatch icon title will display the changing amount of memory.